ESSENTIAL OILS

INTEGRATIVE MEDICAL GUIDE

Building Immunity, Increasing Longevity, and Enhancing Mental Performance with Therapeutic-Grade Essential Oils

By

D. Gary Young, ND

Fourth Printing November 2013

www.LifeSciencePublishers.com

ISBN 0-943685-34-6

Printed in the United States of America 10 9 8 7 6 5 4

The information contained in this book is for educational purposes only. It is not provided to diagnose, prescribe, or treat any condition of the body. Theinformation in this book should not be used as a substitute for medical counseling with a health professional. Neither the author nor publisher accepts responsibility for such use. In cases where inflammation may be present, exercise extreme caution in the application of essential oils to the skin.

ESSENTIAL OILS
INTEGRATIVE MEDICAL GUIDE

Building Immunity, Increasing Longevity, and Enhancing Mental Performance with Therapeutic-Grade Essential Oils

By

D. Gary Young, ND

Life Science Publishing
www.lifesciencepublishers.com

Section I
Background / Chemistry / Safety

Section II
Single Oils / Hydrosols (Floral Waters)

Section III
Blends

Section IV
Vita Flex / Raindrop / Auricular
Emotional Response / Longevity

Section V
Application Methods / Reference Guide

Section VI
References / Appendices / Index

Table of Contents

Section I

Section II

Section III

Section IV

Section V

Section VI

Acknowledgments

No significant medical endeavor can be pursued without the support of many people, and this book is no exception. There are thousands of colleagues and patients, who over the years and in countless ways, have given me the understanding and the strength to pursue a new and fascinating field of healing, the foundation of which is contained within this book.

There are a few whose direct commitment to this project has been so exceptional that they must be mentioned here.

My wife, Mary, and her mother, LaRue, who have stood by me through the years without complaint, making sure that our family and home remained strong, organized and healthy, even when my schedule often became almost unbearable.

Marc Schreuder, my personal researcher and assistant writer, whose determined study, enthusiastic support, and photographic mind have helped consolidate an enormous amount of information into a useable text. His contribution to this work is invaluable.

Karen Boren, my editor at Essential Science Publishing, who deserves very special recognition for three years of expertly sifting through an endless volume of medical and biochemical research, and then crafting it into easily-understood information.

Brian Manwaring, president of Essential Science Publishing, and his wife and partner, Helen, who have been the driving force in pushing me to complete this challenging project in spite of my very busy schedule.

Jean Noël Landel, my partner in France, and his family, for their unwavering support for the last 12 years.

To all the patients and staff members of my clinics in Mexico, I owe a special debt of gratitude, because that is where I began my first studies in healing with essential oils.

More recently, I am especially appreciative of the staff at the Young Life Research Clinic in Springville, Utah, and their tireless efforts to help me find new and more effective ways to heal with essential oils.

I will be forever indebted to the following, who have trained me in many, many ways to more fully understand essential oils and how they work.

Marcel Espieu and the late Henri Viaud, my early teachers in essential oil distillation, for the countless hours they spent tutoring me. I am fortunate to be able to continue to work with Marcel as he assists me in a consulting capacity with a recently acquired lavender farm in France.

Hervé Casabianca, for his outstanding education and training in GC analysis and essential oils quality control.

K. Husnu Baser, PhD, chairman of the biochemistry dept at Anadolu University in Eskisehir, Turkey, for his intensive training in using gas chromatography and mass spectrometry for proper quality analysis of essential oils.

Pierre Franchomme, for his example of thoroughness in the medical biochemistry of essential oils.

Pioneering French physicians, Jean-Claude LaPraz, MD, Paul Duraffourd, MD, and Daniel Pénoël, MD, for their expertise and training in the medical/clinical application of essential oils.

Radwan Farag, PhD, one of the foremost publishers of essential oil research, at the Biochemistry Dept of Cairo University, for many hours of study and discussion on the medical benefits and possibilities of essential oils.

Preface

Essential oils are some of the oldest and most powerful therapeutic agents known. Most people today are unaware that they have an impressive, multimillennium-long history of use in healing and anointing throughout the ancient world. Dozens of essential oils are cited repeatedly in Judeo-Christian religious texts and records show they were used to cure virtually every ailment known to man at that time. Frankincense, myrrh, lotus, cedarwood, and sandalwood oils were widely used in ancient Egyptian purification and embalming rituals. Other oils, like cinnamon, clove and lemon, were highly valued as antiseptics hundreds of years before the development of today's synthetic medicines.

With the advance of antibiotics and prescription drugs during the last century, natural therapeutic agents, especially essential oils, have been largely overlooked. Only during the last decade have essential oils begun a resurgence in popularity in the United States, as their broad-spectrum antibacterial and therapeutic action is rediscovered by many researchers and health-care professionals. No doubt part of the reason essential oils have been slow to emerge—especially in the United States—is because they were heavily extended and adulterated for commercial use, destroying their therapeutic biochemistry and making them useful only as air-freshening or flavoring compounds.

In their pure state, essential oils are some of the most concentrated natural extracts known, exhibiting significant and immediate antiviral, anti-inflammatory, antibacterial, hormone-balancing effects. In clinical practice, they have been shown to have a profound influence on the central nervous system, helping to reduce or eliminate pain, release muscle tension and provide strong emotional uplift.

The chemical structure of an essential oil is such that it can rapidly penetrate cell membranes, travel throughout the blood and tissues, and enhance cellular function. As I have worked with essential oils on patients, it has become very clear that there is a powerful life force inherent in many essential oils, which gives them an unmatched ability to communicate and interact with cells in the human body.

After using them in clinical applications for two decades now, there is no doubt in my mind that essential oils are ordained as medicines for mankind and will provide critical medical solutions in the future. I truly believe they are the missing link of modern health care, bringing allopathic and holistic practice together for optimal health in the 21st century.

My interest in these amazing natural essences began as I worked intensely with natural herbs in my clinic in Mexico. Not coincidentally, almost every therapeutic herb can be distilled into an essential oil. The key difference is that the herb's essential oil can be from 100 to 10,0000 times more concentrated—and therefore more potent—than the herb itself.

In the beginning, I was stunned by two fundamental observations. First, I began to see that essential oils were very potent, in some cases more potent than prescription drugs. Second, despite their concentration and strength, unlike prescription drugs, the essential oils generated no negative side effects. The implications of these two simple facts are profound. For me it was a mobilizing wake-up call that started me on a life-changing research odyssey that has taken me to universities, museums and distilleries around the world. I sought out and studied with some of the finest experts in essential oils in France, Egypt, and Turkey. I traveled the ancient Frankincense Trail through Oman and Saudi Arabia ending in Petra, Jordan. I tracked down and photographed the world's oldest known distiller at the Taxila Museum in Pakistan, as well as the recently discovered balsam distillery found west of the Dead Sea at Ein Gedi, high in the hills near the Judean desert in Israel. Dr. Hervé Casabianca, one of the authors of the AFNOR standards used to certify therapeutic-grade essential oils, taught me a great deal about gas chromatography and mass spectrometry, helping me discern how to produce the finest possible essential oils.

With training from Marcel Espeiu, the late Henri Viaud and many others, I designed and fabricated my own distilleries (five at this writing, with a combined total of 21 distilling chambers) so I could control the distillation process using very low heat and very low pressure. Today I operate four substantial herb farms totaling over 2,000 acres dedicated to the production of essential oils. My study of essential oils has become a consuming life's work that continues to expand every year.

The driving force behind it all is very simple. I've seen essential oils solve health problems that other doctors had labeled "unsolvable." I've seen illnesses and infections disappear that had long resisted prescription drugs. I've witnessed essential oils provide powerful relief with no side effects. Sometimes the effects of administering essential oils were so dramatic that the patients themselves called it "miraculous." And while no one fully understands yet 'why' or 'how' essential oils provide such significant benefits, the fact is that they do. With pure essential oils, millions of people can find relief from disease, from infections, from pain, and even from mental difficulties. Their therapeutic potential is enormous and is only just beginning to be tapped. I acknowledge with gratitude the direction of a Divine Hand in creating and helping us now re-discover the health possibilities inherent in these natural substances. It is a pleasure to share with you, through this book, my great love and appreciation for essential oils and their amazing benefits.

Dedication

In August of 2000, the most significant event in my life took place with the birth of my son, Jacob. What made this event so miraculous was that through careful and diligent applications of essential oils, his mother went through the pregnancy and delivery normally, without serious complications, even though she was in her 50s.

Within minutes after his birth, Jacob was introduced to essential oils and now daily asks for and receives essential oil applications. The bond that has been established between this little boy, his mother, and myself, sealed with essential oils, is something more powerful than anything I have ever before experienced.

I dedicate this book, with eternal gratitude, to my dear wife, Mary, my special son, Jacob, and to the medical future of essential oils.

Foreword

In July 2002, U.S. Secretary of Health and Human Services Tommy G. Thompson told an American Medical Association gathering, "We are dealing with a system of healthcare delivery that is, at its root, dysfunctional." U.S. healthcare expenditures for 2002 are projected to reach $1.5 trillion dollars, yet a survey of the health status of people from 175 nations placed the United States 17th in the rankings. It is an expensive lesson for us to learn, but spending money does not guarantee health.

In the midst of this gloomy outlook is one bright ray of hope. D. Gary Young, ND, has opened a new door to better health using a long-forgotten natural medicine: therapeutic-grade essential oils.

Health and well-being are precious to someone who has spent any time confined to a wheelchair as Gary Young has. By learning how to heal himself after conventional medicine gave up on him, he is creating a clear path for others to follow. By focusing on promoting wellness, he reintroduces lessons taught by healers of old.

Not satisfied to search for quality essential oils to purchase, Gary devoted years to learning how to grow plants, and then harvest and distill them himself to capture every healing molecule found within. If the design of a distiller was imperfect, he went to the metals shop and fabricated a better one. He demanded virgin land, pure water, and no chemicals as the components of his own herb farms.

A growing number of healthcare professionals from MDs to chiropractors to naturopaths are finding their way to essential oils. Not only is there a long history of usage of these oils, but a growing body of new medical research is confirming their powers. And at the forefront of this trend in the United States stands D. Gary Young, conducting essential oil research and scouring the world for the purest oils available.

In further groundbreaking work, Gary discovered how to combine the benefits of essential oils with high quality nutritional supplements, creating some of the finest nutritional products available today.

I am pleased to recommend this essential oil book to all health-minded people, be they medical professionals or simply consumers seeking a more natural means of healthcare.

—Ronald M. Lawrence, MD, PhD

CHAPTER 1

Essential Oils: The Missing Link in Modern Medicine

Yesterday's Wisdom, Tomorrow's Destiny

Plants not only play a vital role in the ecological balance of our planet, but they have also been intimately linked to the physical, emotional, and spiritual well-being of people since the beginning of time.

The plant kingdom continues to be the subject of an enormous amount of research and discovery. At least 30 percent of prescription drugs in the United States are based on naturally occurring compounds from plants. Each year, millions of dollars are allocated to universities searching for new therapeutic agents that lie undiscovered in the bark, roots, flowers, seeds, and foliage of jungle canopies, river bottoms, forests, hillsides, and vast wilderness regions throughout the world.

As the most powerful part of the plant, essential oils and plant extracts have been woven into history since time immemorial. Essential oils have been used medicinally to kill bacteria, fungi, and viruses. They provide exquisite fragrances to balance mood, lift spirits, dispel negative emotions, and create a romantic atmosphere. They can stimulate the regeneration of tissue or stimulate nerves. They can even carry nutrients to, and oxygenate the cells.

What Is an Essential Oil?

Essential oils are aromatic volatile liquids distilled from shrubs, flowers, trees, roots, bushes, and seeds.

The chemistry of essential oils is very complex: each one may consist of hundreds of different and unique chemical compounds. Moreover, essential oils are highly concentrated and far more potent than dried herbs. The distillation process is what makes essential oils so concentrated. It often requires an entire plant or more to produce a single drop of distilled essential oil.

In this photo Gary Young demonstrates how bark is cut on a frankincense tree in Oman so that "tears" of liquid exude, which then harden into resin.

Essential oils are also different from vegetable oils such as corn oil, peanut oil, and olive oil. They are not greasy and do not clog the pores like many vegetable oils can.

Vegetable oils can become oxidized and rancid over time and are not antibacterial. Most essential oils, on the other hand, cannot go rancid and are powerful antimicrobials. Pressed oils and oils high in plant waxes such as patchouli, if not distilled properly, could go rancid after time, particularly if exposed to heat for extended periods of time.

Essential oils are substances that definitely deserve the respect of proper education. Users need to be fully versed in the chemistry and safety of the oils. However, this knowledge is not being taught at universities in the United States. There is a disturbing lack of institutional information, knowledge, and training on essential oils and the science commonly known as aromatherapy. Only in the Middle East, the Orient, and Europe, with their far longer history of using natural products and botanical extracts, can one obtain adequate instruction on the chemistry and therapy of essential oils.

The European communities have a tight framework of controls and standards concerning botanical extracts and who may administer them. Only practitioners with proper training and certification can practice aromatherapy. However, in the United States, the regulatory agencies have not recognized these disciplines or mandated the type and degree of training required to distribute and apply essential oils. This means that in the U.S. individuals can bill themselves as "aromatherapists" after a brief class in essential oils, and apply oils to people—even though they may not have the experience or training to properly understand and administer them. This may not only undermine and damage the credibility of the entire discipline of aromatherapy, but it can be dangerous to patients.

Essential oils are not simple substances. They are mosaics of hundreds—or even thousands—of different chemicals. Any given essential oil may contain anywhere from 80 to 300 or more different chemical constituents. An essential oil like lavender is very complex with many of its constituents occurring in minute quantities—but all contributing to the oil's therapeutic effects to some degree. To understand these constituents and their functions requires years of study.

Even though an essential oil may be labeled as "basil" and have the botanical name *Ocimum basilicum*, it can have widely different therapeutic actions, depending on its chemistry. For example, basil high in linalool or fenchol is primarily used for its antiseptic properties. However, basil high in methyl chavicol is more anti-inflammatory than antiseptic. A third type, basil high in eugenol, has both anti-inflammatory and antiseptic effects.

Additionally, essential oils can be distilled or extracted in different ways that have dramatic effects on their chemistry and medicinal action. Oils derived from a second or third distillation of the same plant material are obviously not going to be as potent as oils extracted during the first distillation. Also, oils that are subjected to high heat and pressure have a distinctly simpler (and inferior) profile of chemical constituents, since excessive heat and temperature fractures and breaks down many of the delicate aromatic compounds within the oil—some of which are responsible for its therapeutic action. In addition, oils that are steam distilled are far different from those that are solvent extracted.

Of greatest concern is the fact that some oils are adulterated, engineered, or "extended" with the use of synthetic chemicals. For example, pure frankincense is often extended with colorless, odorless solvents such as diethylphthalate or dipropylene glycol. The only way to distinguish the "authentic" from the "adulterated" is to subject the essential oil to rigorous analytical testing using state-of-the-art gas chromatography, mass spectroscopy, and NMR (nuclear magnetic resonance).

However, even gas chromatography doesn't identify a natural chemical from a synthetic one. That is why it is very easy to engineer oils or extend poor quality oils to make them smell and look good.

Unfortunately, a large percentage of essential oils marketed in the United States fall in this adulterated category. When you understand the world of synthetic oils as well as low-grade oils cut with synthetic chemicals, you realize why unsuspecting people with their untrained noses don't know the difference.

Different Schools of Application

Therapeutic treatment using essential oils follows three different models or frameworks: French, German, and English.

The English model advocates diluting a small amount of essential oil in a vegetable oil and massaging the body for the purpose of relaxation and relieving stress.

The French model prescribes the ingestion and neat (undiluted) topical application of therapeutic-grade essential oils. A common form of internal use is to add a few drops of an essential oil to honey, a piece of bread, or a small amount of vegetable oil. Many French practitioners have found that taking the oils internally yields excellent benefits.

The German model focuses on inhalation of essential oils. Research has shown that the effect of fragrance and aromatic compounds on the sense of smell can exert strong effects on the brain—especially on the hypothalamus (the hormone command center of the body) and limbic system (the seat of emotions). Some essential oils high in sesquiterpenes, such as myrrh, sandalwood, cedarwood, vetiver, melissa, and frankincense, can dramatically increase oxygenation and activity in the brain. This may directly improve the function of many systems of the body.

Together, these three models show how versatile and powerful essential oils can be. By integrating all three models with Vita Flex, auricular technique, touch therapy, spinal touch, lymphatic massage, and Raindrop Technique, the best possible results may be obtained.

In some cases, inhalation of essential oils might be preferred over topical application, if the goal is to increase growth hormone secretion, induce weight loss, or balance mood and emotions. Sandalwood, peppermint, vetiver, lavender, and white fir oils are effective for inhalation.

In other cases, however, topical application of essential oils would produce better results, particularly in the case of spinal or muscle injuries or defects.

Topically applied, marjoram is excellent for muscles, lemongrass for ligaments, and wintergreen or birch for bones. For indigestion, a drop or two of peppermint oil taken orally may be very effective. However, this does not mean that peppermint cannot produce the same results when massaged on the stomach. In some cases, all three methods of application (topical, inhalation, and ingestion) are interchangeable and may produce similar benefits.

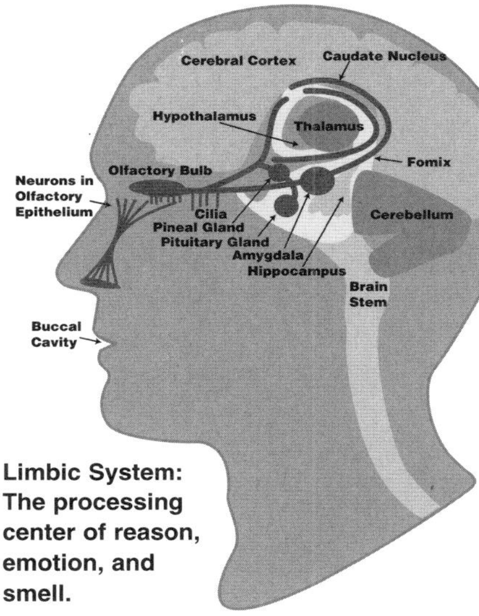

Limbic System: The processing center of reason, emotion, and smell.

The ability of essential oils to act on both the mind and the body is what makes them truly unique among natural therapeutic agents. The fragrance of an essential oil can be very stimulating—both psychologically and physically. The fragrance of other essential oils may be calming and sedating, helping to overcome anxiety or hyperactivity. On a physiological level, essential oils may stimulate immune function and regenerate damaged tissue. Essential oils may also combat infectious disease by killing viruses, bacteria, and other pathogens.

Probably the two most common methods of essential oil application are cold-air diffusing and neat (undiluted) topical application. Other modes of application include incorporating essential oils into the disciplines of reflexology, Vita Flex, and acupressure. Combining these disciplines with essential oils enhances the healing response and often produces amazing results that can not be achieved by acupuncture or reflexology alone. Just 1–3 drops of an essential oil applied to an acupuncture meridian or Vita Flex point on the hand or foot can produce results within seconds to 1–2 minutes.

Several years ago at a university in Europe, a professor well known in the field of aromatherapy commented that anyone who claims to cure diseases using essential oils is a quack. However, there are many people who are living proof that essential oils can be used to engineer recoveries from serious illness. Essential oils have been pivotal in helping many people live pain-free after years of intense pain. Patients have also witnessed firsthand how essential oils have corrected scoliosis and even restored hearing in those who were born deaf.

For example, a woman from Palisades Park, California, developed scoliosis after surviving polio as a teenager, which was further complicated by a serious fall and a dislocated shoulder. Suffering pain and immobility for 22 years, she had traveled extensively in a fruitless search to locate a practitioner who could permanently reset her shoulder. Upon learning about essential oils, she topically applied the oils of helichrysum and birch, among others, to the shoulder. Within a short time she became pain free as the shoulder relocated. She was able to raise her arm over her head for the first time in 22 years.

When one sees such dramatic recoveries, it is difficult to discredit the value and the power of essential oils and the potential they hold.

Mankind's First Medicine

For many centuries essential oils and other aromatics were used for religious rituals, the treatment of illness, and other physical and spiritual needs.

Records dating back to 4500 BC describe the use of balsamic substances with aromatic properties for religious rituals and medical applications. Ancient writings tell of scented barks, resins, spices, and aromatic vinegars, wines, and beers that were used in rituals, temples, astrology, embalming, and medicine. The evidence suggests that the people of ancient times had a greater understanding of essential oils than we have today.

The Egyptians were masters in using essential oils and other aromatics in the embalming process. Historical records describe how one of the founders of "pharaonic" medicine was the architect Imhotep, who was the Grand Vizier of King Djoser (2780 - 2720 BC). Imhotep is often given credit for ushering in the use of oils, herbs, and aromatic plants for medicinal purposes.

While touring the Temple of Isis on the island of Philae several years ago, I was pulled aside by an Egyptian guide who told me to follow him. He said, "I will show you what you came to Egypt to find." Intrigued, I followed him and was taken to a room not shown to tourists. He told me the hieroglypics on the wall depicted a ritual called "Cleansing the Flesh and Blood of Evil Deities." The guide told me that essential oils were used in this three-day purification ritual which would prepare the person for the afterlife and one day returning to their embalmed body. I snapped a quick photo (see page 8) and left with much to ponder.

Later, Dr. Radwan Farag, a leading essential oil researcher and colleague at the University of Cairo, told me his Egyptologist friends confirmed that this was a sacred room and expressed surprise that I had been allowed to see it. In the Egyptian culture "evil deities" represented negative emotions and neuroses. I couldn't help but reflect that just as today we work to remove negative emotions from our lives, the ancient Egyptians tried to free themselves from what they perceived as harmful influences.

Gary Young at the Temple of Isis where ancient Egyptians depicted their use of precious essential oils.

Many other hieroglyphics on the walls of Egyptian temples depict the blending of oils and describe hundreds of oil recipes.

An ancient papyrus found in the Temple of Edfu contained medicinal formulae and perfume recipes used by alchemists and high priests in blending aromatic substances for rituals.

The Egyptians may have been the first to discover the potential of fragrance. They created various aromatic blends for both personal use and for ceremonies performed in the temples and pyramids.

Well before the time of Christ, the ancient Egyptians collected essential oils and placed them in alabaster vessels. These vessels were specially carved and shaped for housing scented oils. In 1922, when King Tut's tomb was opened, some 50 alabaster jars designed to hold 350 liters of oils were discovered. Tomb robbers had stolen nearly all of the precious oils leaving the heavy jars behind. Some of them still contained oil traces. The robbers chose oils over a literal king's ransom in gold, showing how valuable the fragrant essential oils were to this ancient civilization.

Two Egyptian priests stand at the head and foot of the person undergoing the three-day cleansing ritual that included use of essential oils. This hieroglyphic is found in the Temple of Isis in a room rarely shown to tourists.

Gary is standing in the doorway of the room at the Temple of Isis on the island of Philae where he learned about a long-lost ritual also known through Egyptian oral traditions.

In 1817 the Ebers Papyrus, a medical scroll over 870 feet long, was discovered. Dating back to 1500 BC, the scroll included over 800 different herbal prescriptions and remedies. Other scrolls described a high success rate in treating 81 different diseases. Many of the remedies contained myrrh and honey. Myrrh is still recognized for its ability to help with infections of the skin and throat and to regenerate skin tissue. Because of its effectiveness in preventing bacterial growth, myrrh was used for embalming.

The physicians of Ionia, Attia, and Crete (ancient civilizations based in the Mediterranean Sea) came to the cities of the Nile to increase their knowledge. At this time, the school of Cos was founded and was attended by Hippocrates (460-377 BC), whom the Greeks, with perhaps some exaggeration, named the "Father of Medicine."

The Romans purified their temples and political buildings by diffusing essential oils. They also used aromatics in their steam baths to both invigorate the flesh and ward off disease.

Early History of Essential Oil Extraction

Ancient cultures found that aromatic essences or oils could be extracted from the plant by a variety of methods. One of the oldest and crudest forms of extraction was known as enfleurage. Raw plant material (usually stems, foliage, bark, or roots) was crushed and mixed with olive oil or animal fat. Other vegetable oils were also used. In the case of cedar, for example, the bark was stripped from the trunk and branches, ground into a powder, soaked with olive oil, and placed in a wool cloth. The cloth was then heated. The heat pulled the essential oil out of the bark particles into the olive oil, and the wool was pressed to extract the essential oil. Sandalwood oil was also extracted in this fashion.

Enfleurage was also used to extract essential oils from flower petals. In fact, the French word *enfleurage* means literally "to saturate with the perfume of flowers." For example, petals from roses or jasmine were placed in goose or goat fat. The essential oil molecules were pulled from the petals into the fat, which was then processed to separate the essential oils from the fat. This ancient technique was among the most primitive forms of essential oil extraction.

Other extraction techniques were also used. Some of these included:

- Soaking plant parts in boiling water
- Cold-pressing
- Soaking in alcohol
- Steam distillation by passing steam through the plant material and condensing the steam to separate the oil from the plant

Many ancient cosmetic formulas were created from a base of goat fat. Ancient Egyptians formulated eyeliners, eyeshadows, and other cosmetics this way. They also stained their hair and nails with a variety of ointments and perfumes. They probably used the same aromatic oils that were used in the temples. Such temple oils were commonly poured into evaporation dishes for fragrancing the chambers associated with sacred rituals and religious rites.

Fragrance "cones" made of wax and fragrant essential oils were worn by aristocratic Egyptian women who enjoyed the oils' rich scents as the cones melted with the heat of the day.

Ancient Arabians were another early culture that developed and refined a process of distillation. They perfected the extraction of rose oils and rose water, which were popular in the Middle East during the Byzantine Empire (330 AD - 1400 AD).

Other Historical References

Throughout world history, fragrant oils and spices have played a prominent role in everyday life.

Napoleon is reported to have enjoyed a cologne water made of neroli and other ingredients so much that he ordered 162 bottles of it. After conquering Jerusalem, one of the things the Crusaders brought back to Europe was solidified essence of roses.

The 12th century mystic, Hildegard of Bingen, used herbs and oils extensively in healing. This Benedictine nun founded her own convent and was the author of numerous works. Her book, *Physica*, has more than 200 chapters on plants and their uses for healing.

Biblical and Ancient References to Essential Oils

There are over 200 references to aromatics, incense, and ointments throughout the Old and New Testaments of the Bible. Aromatics such as frankincense, myrrh, galbanum, cinnamon, cassia, rosemary, hyssop, and spikenard were used for anointing and healing the sick. In Exodus, the Lord gave the following recipe to Moses for a holy anointing oil:

Myrrh	"five hundred shekels" (about 1 gallon)
Cinnamon	"two hundred and fifty shekels"
Calamus	"two hundred and fifty shekels"
Cassia	"five hundred shekels"
Olive Oil	"an hin" (about 1 1/3 gallons)

Psalms 133:2 speaks of the sweetness of brethren dwelling together in unity: "It is like the precious ointment upon the head, that ran down the beard, even Aaron's beard: that went down to the skirts of his garments." Another scripture that refers to anointing and the overflowing abundance of precious oils is Ecclesiastes 9:8: "Let thy garments be always white; and let thy head lack no ointment."

The Bible also lists an incident where an incense offering by Aaron stopped a plague. Numbers 16:46-50 records that Moses instructed Aaron to take a censer, add burning coals and incense, and to "go quickly into the congregation to make an atonement for them: for there is a wrath gone out from the Lord; the plague is begun." The Bible records that Aaron stood between the dead and the living and the plague was stayed. It is significant that according to the biblical and Talmudic recipes for incense, three varieties of cinnamon were involved. Cinnamon is known to be highly antimicrobial, anti-infectious, and antibacterial. The incense ingredient listed as "stacte" is believed to be a sweet, myrrh-related spice, which would make it anti-infectious and antiviral as well.

The New Testament records that wise men presented the Christ child with frankincense and myrrh. There is another precious aromatic, spikenard, described in the anointing of Jesus:

> And being in Bethany in the house of Simon the leper, as he sat at meat, there came a woman having an alabaster box of ointment of spikenard very precious; and she brake the box, and poured it on his head. Mark 14:3.

The anointing of Jesus is also referred to in John 12:3:

> Then took Mary a pound of ointment of spikenard, very costly, and anointed the feet of Jesus, and wiped his feet with her hair: and the house was filled with the odour of the ointment.

My Search for Ancient Essential Oil Traditions

While studying at the University of Cairo, I was told about Egyptian traditions regarding the time Christ spent in Egypt. These stories tell how the Christ child was hidden in caves along the river banks and given refuge by the priestesses of the Temple of Dendara. Further legends tell how Christ was taught by the priests of the temple of Edfu and was given five alabaster jars of essential oils. The Egyptians believe that Christ took those oils back to his homeland as he began his ministry.

As I traveled the ancient Frankincense Trail I heard legends of how merchants brought frankincense and myrrh to city Ubar, mentioned in the Quran as Iram, the "city of towers." This fabled city was a center of commerce for 3,000 years. The city is 150 kilometers inland from Arabian Sea, north of the town of Salalah, Oman. It was discovered in 1992 by tracing ancient desert roads that showed up on satellite imagery. I was there shortly after the excavation of the city from beneath 12 meters of sand, and took pictures by ruins where I believe frankincense and other oils were distilled.

Traditions name the king of the Lost City of Ubar as King Ad (also known as King Shaddad ibn 'Ad), a grandson of Noah who was reputed to have gold, frankincense, and myrrh passed down from Adam and Eve.

Merchants came to Ubar from Sri Lanka, China, and India bringing their spices and silks to trade for resins and precious oils. Camel merchants would take these goods and travel across the Empty Quarter to the red rock city of Petra. There other merchants from Athens, Alexandria, and Damascus would trade for the silks, linens, spices, and resins and load their camel caravans and travel to their various countries.

In Egypt, Queen Hatshepsut sent an expedition to the land of Pwenet (called Punt in the Bible and now known as Eritrea) to bring back precious aromatics and incense, and this was recorded on the walls of her temple near Thebes. "I have reached the incense terraces," she proclaimed.[1] She created a botanical garden along the rampways to her temple with the plants brought back from Punt. Her royal navy brought the lotus plant from India, which through culturing and crossbreeding resulted in the treasured blue lotus.

I visited another archaeological find west of the Dead Sea in Israel. Long believed to be a military outpost, the ruins at Ein Gedi were discovered to be the site of an ancient balsam distillery after excavations began in 1995.[2] The tower was part of fortifications needed to protect the site which manufactured the rare and costly balsam oil, which, according to the Talmud, was used to anoint the kings of Israel.[3] In addition to the tower, the site was protected from robbers by a steep incline and a large wheel-like stone that could be rolled across the doorway.

1. Edwin T. Morris, *Fragrance: The Story of Perfume from Cleopatra to Chanel,* Charles Schribner, New York, 1984, page 59.
2. The Balm of Gilead: Is Ein Gedi's Long Lost "Secret" Revealed in a Newly Excavated Tower? *Biblical Archaeology Review,* Sept./Oct. 1996, pages 18-19, 24.
3. Ker. 5b, TJ, Sot. 8:1, 22c

Members of the Young family at the rock-carved building called "The Treasury," in Petra, Jordan. This was a major trading stop along the Frankincense Trail.

I am standing in the balsam oil vat to show its depth at the Ein Gedi distillery, where the costly oil was produced in a carefully guarded complex.

In the photo above, you can see the 7-foot-long rectangular vat where the balsam essence was collected through a pipe leading from the forecourt where balsam plants were cooked. Hebrew University archaeologist Yizhar Hirschfeld also found a tiny perfume bottle in the 25 stone cubicles found above Ein Gedi where balsam factory workers probably lived.

The Rediscovery

The reintroduction of essential oils into modern medicine first began during the late 19th and early 20th centuries.

During World War I, the use of aromatic essences in civilian and military hospitals became widespread. One physician in France, Dr. Moncière, used essential oils extensively for their antibacterial and wound-healing properties, and developed several kinds of aromatic ointments.

René-Maurice Gattefossé, PhD, a French cosmetic chemist, is widely regarded as the father of aromatherapy. He and a group of scientists began studying essential oils in 1907.

In his 1937 book, *Aromatherapy*, Dr. Gattefossé told the real story of his now-famous use of lavender essential oil to heal a serious burn. The tale has assumed mythic proportions in essential oil literature. His own words about this accident are even more powerful than what has been told over the years.

Dr. Gattefossé was literally aflame—covered in burning substances—following a laboratory explosion in July, 1910. After he extinguished the flames by rolling on a grassy lawn, he wrote that "both my hands were covered with rapidly developing gas gangrene." He further reported that, "just one rinse with lavender essence stopped the gasification of the tissue. This treatment was followed by profuse sweating and healing which began the next day."

Robert B. Tisserand, editor of *The International Journal of Aromatherapy,* searched for Dr. Gattefossé's book for 20 years. A copy was located and Tisserand edited the 1995 reprint. Tisserand noted that Dr. Gattefossé's burns "must have been severe to lead to gas gangrene, a very serious infection."

Dr. Gattefossé shared his studies with his colleague and friend, Jean Valnet, a medical doctor practicing in Paris. Exhausting his supply of antibiotics as a physician in Tonkin, China, during World War II, Dr. Valnet began using therapeutic-grade essential oils on patients suffering battlefield injuries. To his surprise, they exerted a powerful effect in combating and counteracting infection. He was able to save the lives of many soldiers who might otherwise have died.

Two of Dr. Valnet's students, Dr. Paul Belaiche and Dr. Jean-Claude Lapraz, expanded his work. They clinically investigated the antiviral, antibacterial, antifungal, and antiseptic properties in essential oils.

Because of the work of these doctors and scientists, the healing power of essential oils is again gaining prominence.

Today, it has become evident that we have not yet found permanent solutions for dreaded diseases such as the Ebola virus, hantavirus, AIDS, HIV, and new strains of tuberculosis and influenza. Essential oils may assume an increasingly important role in combating new mutations of bacteria, viruses, and fungi. More and more researchers are undertaking serious clinical studies on the use of essential oils to combat these types of diseases.

The research that I conducted at Weber State University, as well as other documented research, indicates that most viruses, fungi, and bacteria cannot live in the presence of many essential oils, especially those high in phenols, carvacrol, thymol, and terpenes. This, perhaps, offers a modern explanation why the Old Testament prophet Moses used aromatic substances to protect the Israelites from the plagues that decimated ancient Egypt. It may also help us

This terra-cotta distiller is displayed in the Taxila Museum in Pakistan and is the oldest known distillery in existence. It has been dated to approximately 400 B.C.

understand why a notorious group of thieves, reputed to be spice traders and perfumers, was protected from the Black Plague as they robbed the bodies of the dead during the 15th century.

A vast body of anecdotal evidence (testimonials) suggests that those who use essential oils are less likely to contract infectious diseases. Moreover, oil users who do contract an infectious illness tend to recover faster than those using antibiotics.

CHAPTER 2

How Do Essential Oils Work?

Therapeutic-Grade Essential Oils

One of the factors that determines the purity of an oil is its chemical constituents. These constituents can be affected by a vast number of variables, including: the part(s) of the plant from which the oil was produced, soil condition, fertilizer (organic or chemical), geographical region, climate, altitude, harvesting methods, and distillation processes. For example, common thyme *(Thymus vulgaris)* produces several different chemotypes (biochemically unique variants within one species) depending on the conditions of its growth, climate, and altitude. One chemotype of thyme will yield an essential oil with high levels of thymol, depending on the time of year it is distilled. The later it is distilled in the growing season (ie., mid-summer or fall), the more thymol the oil will contain.

Proper cultivation assures that more specific chemotypes like *Thymus vulgaris* will maintain a good strain of thymol, where as with wildcrafting, you may produce linalol and eugenol thyme on the same mountainside.

An example of this was shown in studies at the University of Ege botany department in Izmir, Turkey where it was found that among *Oreganum compactum* plants within a 100 square foot radius, one plant would be very high in carvacrol and another would be high in another compound. Wildcrafting plants cannot guarantee the same chemotype even on the same hillside.

The key to producing a therapeutic-grade essential oil is to preserve as many of the delicate aromatic compounds within the essential oil as possible. Fragile aromatic chemicals are easily destroyed by high temperature and pressure, as well as contact with chemically reactive metals such as copper or aluminum. This is why all therapeutic-grade essential oils should be distilled in stainless steel cooking chambers at low pressure and low temperature.

The plant material should also be free of herbicides and other agrichemicals. These can react with the essential oil during distillation to produce toxic compounds. Because many pesticides are oil-soluble, they can also mix into the essential oil.

As we begin to understand the power of essential oils in the realm of personal, holistic healthcare, we will appreciate the necessity for obtaining the purest essential oils possible. No matter how costly pure essential oils may be, there can be no substitutes.

Although chemists have successfully recreated the main constituents and fragrances of some essential oils in the laboratory, these synthetic oils lack therapeutic benefits and may even carry risks. Why? Because essential oils contain hundreds of different chemical compounds, which, in combination, lend important therapeutic properties to the oil. Also, many essential oils contain molecules and isomers that are impossible to manufacture in the laboratory.

Anyone venturing into the world of therapy using essential oils must use the purest quality oils available. Inferior quality or adulterated oils most likely will not produce therapeutic results and could possibly be toxic. In Europe, a set of standards has been established that specifies the types and amounts of principal constituents that a quality essential oil should have. Known as AFNOR (Association Francaise de Normalisation) and ISO (International Standards Organization) standards, these guidelines help buyers differentiate between a high quality essential oil and a lower grade oil with a similar chemical makeup and fragrance. The therapeutic effects of the essential oils in this book are based on oils that meet or exceed AFNOR standards.

Science and Application

Essential oils and human blood share several common properties: They fight infection, contain hormone-like compounds, and initiate regeneration. Working as the chemical defense mechanism of the plant, essential oils possess potent antibacterial, antifungal, and antiviral properties. They also ward off attacks by insects and animals. The ability of some essential oils to work as hormones helps them bring balance to many physiological systems of the human body. Oils like clary sage and sage that contain sclerol, for example, have an estrogenic action. Essential oils also play a role in initiating the regeneration process for the plant, the same way the blood does in the human body.

This similarity goes even deeper. Essential oils have a chemical structure that is similar to that found in human cells and tissues. This makes essential oils compatible with human protein and enables them to be readily identified and accepted by the body.

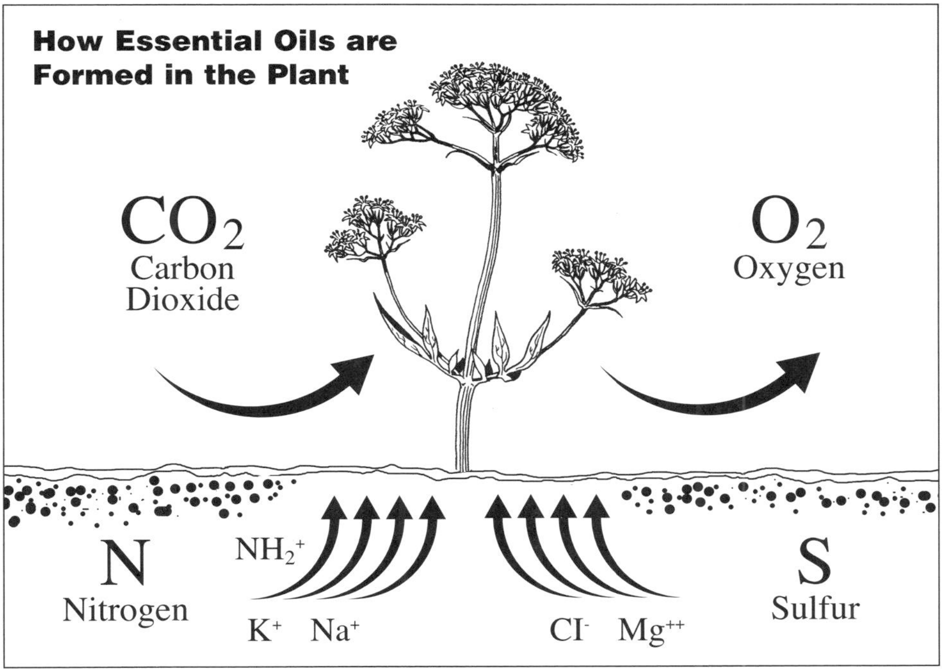

Minerals and carbons are combined with nitrogen in the soil to form amino acids in the plant. These amino acids form proteins that contribute to essential oil formation. Essential oils and amino acids like phenylalanine share a similar aromatic structure.

Essential oils have a unique ability to penetrate cell membranes and diffuse throughout the blood and tissues. The unique, lipid-soluble structure of essential oils is very similar to the makeup of our cell membranes. The molecules of essential oils are also relatively small, which enhances their ability to penetrate into the cells. When topically applied to the feet or elsewhere, essential oils can travel throughout the body in a matter of minutes.

The ability of some essential oils, like clove, to decrease the viscosity or thickness of the blood can also enhance circulation and immune function. Adequate circulation is vital to good health, since it affects the function of every cell and organ, including the brain.

Research indicates that when essential oils are diffused, they can increase atmospheric oxygen and provide negative ions, which in turn inhibits bacterial growth. This suggests that essential oils could play an important role in air purification and neutralizing odors. Because of their ionizing action, essential oils have the ability to break down potentially harmful chemicals and render them nontoxic.

In the human body, essential oils stimulate the secretion of antibodies, neurotransmitters, endorphins, hormones, and enzymes. Oils containing limonene have been shown to prevent and slow the progression of cancer. Other oils, like lavender, have been shown to promote the growth of hair and increase the rate of wound healing. They increase the uptake of oxygen and ATP (adenosine triphosphate), the fuel for individual cells.

European scientists have studied the ability of essential oils to work as natural chelators, binding with heavy metals and petrochemicals and ferrying them out of the body.

Today approximately 300 essential oils are distilled or extracted, with several thousand chemical constituents and aromatic molecules identified and registered. The quantity, quality, and type of these aromatic compounds will vary depending on climate, temperature, and distillation factors. Ninety-eight percent of essential oils produced today are used in the perfume and cosmetic industry. Only about 2 percent are produced for therapeutic and medicinal applications.

Because essential oils are composites of hundreds of different chemicals, they can exert many different effects on the body. For example, clove oil can be simultaneously antiseptic and anaesthetic when applied topically. It can also be antitumoral. Lavender oil has been used for burns, insect bites, headaches, PMS, insomnia, stress, and hair growth.

Importantly, because of their complexity, essential oils do not disturb the body's natural balance or homeostasis: if one constituent exerts too strong an effect, another constituent may block or counteract it. Synthetic chemicals, in contrast, usually have only one action and often disrupt the body's homeostasis.

Using European AFNOR/ISO Standards to Identify Quality Essential Oils

One of the most reliable indicators of essential oil quality is the AFNOR (Association Francaise de Normalisation) or ISO certification (ISO is the International Standards Organization which has set standards for essential oils, adopted from AFNOR). This standard is more stringent and differentiates top quality essential oils from similar oils with inferior chemistry (For examples of AFNOR specifications, see Appendix A).

As Research Engineer at Centre National de la Recherche Scientifique (CNRS), Dr. Hervé Casabianca—who holds a doctors degree in organic chemistry—worked with many of the finest European scientists and doctors in helping to create the AFNOR standards, and was a voting member of AFNOR at the time of the standards' adoption.

He shared these standards in North American when he collaborated with me at Young Living Essential Oils in 2000. During that collaboration, the Young Living chemistry laboratory and GSI chromatograph were calibrated to recognized European standards.

Dr. Casabianca explained that the primary constitutents within an essential oil had to occur in certain percentages in order for the oil to meet the AFNOR standards. Using these standards, many oils such as frankincense or lavender can be checked to see if they do indeed have the proper balance of chemical constituents. If some constituents are too high or too low, the oils cannot be certified.

For example, the AFNOR standard for *Lavandula angustifolia* (true lavender) dictates that the level of linalool should range from 25 to 38 percent and the level of linalyl acetate should range between 25 and 34 percent. As long as the oil's marker compounds are within the specified ranges, it can be certified as meeting AFNOR standards.

As a general rule, if two or more marker compounds in an essential oil fall outside the prescribed percentages, the oil does not meet the AFNOR standard. A lavender oil produced in one region of France might have a slightly different chemistry than that grown in another region and as a result may not meet the standard. It may have excessive camphor levels (1.0 instead of 0.5), a condition that might be caused by distilling lavender that was too green. Or the levels of lavandulol may be too low due to certain weather conditions at the time of harvest.

By comparing the gas chromatograph chemistry profile of a lavender essential oil with the AFNOR standard, one may also distinguish true lavender from various species of lavandin (hybrid lavender). Usually lavandin has high camphor levels, almost no lavandulol, and is easily identified. However, Tasmania produces a lavandin that yields an essential oil with naturally low camphor levels that mimics the chemistry of true lavender. Only by analyzing the chemical fingerprint of this Tasmanian lavandin using high resolution gas chromatography and comparing it with the AFNOR standard for genuine lavender can this hybrid lavender be identified.

Currently, there is no government agency responsible for certifying the quality of essential oils. The only recognized indication for quality in an essential oil is if it meets AFNOR or ISO standards.

To my knowledge, Young Living is one of the few essential oil producers in North America that has been collaborating with recognized analytical chemists in Europe to ensure that their essential oils meet AFNOR standards.

In the United States, few companies use the proper analytical equipment and methods to properly analyze essential oils. Most labs use equipment best suited for synthetic chemicals—not for natural essential oils analysis. Young Living Essential Oils uses the proper machinery and has made serious efforts to adopt European testing standards, widely regarded as the "gold standard" for testing essential oils. In addition to operating its analytical equipment on the same standards as European laboratories, Young Living is continually expanding its analytical chemical library in order to perform more thorough chemical analyses.

Properly analyzing an essential oil by gas chromatography is a complex undertaking. The injection mixture, column diameter and length, and oven temperature must fall within certain parameters. Unless someone has gone to France and Turkey as I have and been trained in the analytical procedures of a gas chromatograph, they will not understand how to accurately test essential oils.

The column length should be at least 50 or 60 meters. However, almost all labs in the United States use a 30-meter column that is not long enough to achieve proper separation of all the essential oil constituents. While 30-meter columns are adequate for analyzing synthetic chemicals and marker compounds in vitamins, minerals, and herbal extracts, they are far too short to properly analyze the complex mosaic of natural chemicals found in an essential oil.

A longer column also enables double-phased ramping, which makes it possible to identify constituents that occur in very small percentages by increasing the separation of compounds. Without a longer column, it would be extremely difficult to identify these molecules, especially if they are chemically similar to each other or a marker compound.

While gas chromatography (GC) is an excellent tool for dissecting the anatomy of an essential oil, it does have limitations. Dr. Brian Lawrence, one of the foremost experts on essential oil chemistry, has commented that sometimes it can be difficult to distinguish between natural and synthetic compounds using GC analysis. If synthetic linalyl acetate is added to pure lavender, a GC analysis cannot really tell whether that compound is synthetic or natural, only that it is linalyl acetate. Adding a chiral column can help, however, in distinguishing between synthetic and natural oils. This addition allows the chemist to identify structural varieties of the same compound.

This is why oils must be analyzed by a chemist specially trained on the interpretation of a gas chromatograph chart. The chemist examines the entire chemical fingerprint of the oil to determine its purity and potency, measuring how various compounds in the oil occur in relation to each other. If some chemicals occur in higher quantities than others, these provide important clues to determine if the oil is adulterated or pure.

I have demanded the highest quality oils, insisting that each batch coming into Young Living be tested by highly trained chemists at independent European laboratories which utilize AFNOR standards.

Adulteration of essential oils will become more and more common as the supply of top-quality essential oils dwindles and demand explodes. These adulterated essential oils will jeopardize the integrity of aromatherapy in the United States and may put many people at risk.

Adulterated Oils and Their Dangers

Today much of the lavender oil sold in America is the hybrid called lavandin, grown and distilled in China, Russia, France, and Tasmania. It is brought into France and cut with synthetic linalyl acetate to improve the fragrance. Then propylene glycol, DEP, or DOP (solvents that have no smell and increase the volume) are added and it is sold in the United States as lavender oil.

Often lavandin is heated to evaporate the camphor and then is adulterated with synthetic linalyl acetate. Most consumers don't know the difference, and are happy to buy it for $7 to $10 per half ounce in health food stores, beauty salons, grocery and department stores, and through mail order. This is one of the reasons why it is important to know about the integrity of the company or vendor from which you purchase your essential oils.

Frankincense is another example of a commonly adulterated oil. The frankincense resin that is sold in Somalia costs between $30,000 and $35,000 per ton. A great deal of time, 12 hours or more, is required to properly steam-distill this essential oil from the resin, making the oil very expensive.

Frankincense oil that sells for $25 per ounce or less is cheaply distilled with gum resins, alcohol, or other solvents, leaving the essential oil laden with harmful chemicals. Sadly, when these cut, synthetic, and adulterated oils cause rashes, burns, or other irritations, people wonder why they do not get the benefit they expected and conclude that essential oils do not have much value.

Some statistics show that one company uses twice as much essential oil as is produced *in the entire world*. Where are these "phantom" essential oils coming from?

In France, production of true lavender oil *(Lavandula angustifolia)* dropped from 87 tons in 1967 to only 12 tons in 1998. During this same period the demand for lavender oil grew over 100 percent. So where did essential oil marketers obtain enough lavender to meet the demand? They probably used a combination of synthetic and adulterated oils. There are huge chemical companies on the east coast of the U.S. that specialize in creating synthetic chemicals that mimic every common essential oil. For every kilogram of pure essential oil that is produced, it is estimated there are between 10 and 100 kilograms of synthetic oil created.

Adulterated and mislabeled essential oils present dangers for consumers. One woman who had heard of the ability of lavender oil to heal burns used "lavender oil" purchased from a local health food store when she spilled boiling water on her arm. But the pain intensified and the burn worsened, so she later complained that lavender oil was worthless for healing burns. When her "lavender" oil was analyzed, it was found to be lavandin, the hybrid lavender that is chemically very different from pure *Lavandula angustifolia*. Lavandin contains high levels of camphor (12-18 percent) and can itself burn the skin. In contrast, true lavender contains virtually no camphor and has burn-healing agents not found in lavandin.

Adulterated oils that are cut with synthetic extenders can be very detrimental, causing rashes, burning, and skin irritations. Petrochemical solvents, such dipropylene glycol and diethylphthalate, can all cause allergic reactions, besides being devoid of any therapeutic effects.

Some people assume that because an essential oil is "100 percent pure," it will not burn their skin. This is not true. Pure essential oils may cause skin irritation if applied undiluted. If you apply straight oregano oil to the skin of some people, it may cause severe reddening. Citrus and spice oils, like orange and cinnamon, may also produce rashes. Even the terpenes in conifer oils, like pine, may cause skin irritation on sensitive people.

Some writers have claimed that a few compounds, when isolated from the essential oil and tested in the lab, can exert toxic effects. Even some "nature-identical" essential oils (a structured essential oil that has been chemically duplicated using 5 to 15 of the essential oil's chemical compounds in synthetic form) can produce unwanted side effects or toxicities. Isolated compounds may be toxic; however pure essential oils, in most cases, are not. This is because natural essential oils contain hundreds of different compounds, some of which balance and counteract each other's effects.

Many tourists in Egypt are eager to buy local essential oils, especially lotus oil. Vendors convince the tourists that the oils are 100 percent pure, going so far as to touch a lighted match to the neck of the oil container to show that the oil is not diluted with alcohol or other petrochemical solvents. However, this test provides no reliable indicator of purity. Many synthetic compounds can be added to an essential oil that are not flammable, including propylene glycol. Or, flammable solvents can be added to a vegetable oil base that *will* cause it to catch fire. Some natural essential oils high in terpenes can be flammable.

Fact or Fiction: Myths and Misinformation

Much of the published information available on essential oils should be regarded with caution. Many aromatherapy books are merely compilations of two or three other books. The content is similar, only phrased and worded differently. Because the information has been copied from sources that have never been documented, the same misinformation repeatedly surfaces.

Many aromatherapy books claim that essential oils, such as clary sage, fennel, sage, and bergamot, can trigger an abortion. Several years ago, a rumor circulated about a laboratory research project in which the uterus of a rat was turned inside out and a cold drop of clary sage oil was applied to the exposed uterine wall. When this caused a contraction of the muscle, clary sage was labeled as abortion-causing. One must ask, what would have happened if cold water had been dropped on the exposed uterus? The uterine wall would likely have contracted in response. Following this reasoning, water could be labeled as abortion-causing as well.

The truth is that to our knowledge, there has never been a single documented case that clary sage, lemon, sage, or bergamot essential oils have caused an abortion. Sclareol, a compound in clary sage, is not an estrogen, although it can mimic estrogen if there is an estrogen deficiency. If there is not an estrogen deficiency, sclareol will not create more estrogen in the body. As a rule, essential oils bring balance to the human body.

The belief that pure essential oils will not leave a stain when poured on a tissue is also unfounded. Any essential oil high in waxes will leave stains. Oils like frankincense, cedarwood, clove, ylang ylang, blue cypress, or German chamomile may also leave a noticeable residue. However, an essential oil spiked with synthetic diluents or solvent may or may not leave a stain.

The Powerful Influence of Aromas on Both Mind and Body

The fragrance of an essential oil can directly affect everything from your emotional state to your lifespan.

When a fragrance is inhaled, the odor molecules travel up the nose where they are trapped by olfactory membranes that are well protected by the lining inside the nose. Each odor molecule fits like a little puzzle piece into specific receptor cell sites that line a membrane known as the olfactory epithelium. Each one of these hundreds of millions of nerve cells is replaced every 28 days. When stimulated by odor molecules, this lining of nerve cells triggers electrical impulses to the olfactory bulb in the brain. The olfactory bulb then transmits the impulses to the gustatory center (where the sensation of taste is perceived), the amygdala (where emotional memories are stored), and other parts of the limbic system of the brain. Because the limbic system is directly connected to those parts of the brain that control heart rate, blood pressure, breathing, memory, stress levels, and hormone balance, essential oils can have profound physiological and psychological effects.

The sense of smell is the only one of the five senses directly linked to the limbic lobe of the brain, the emotional control center. Anxiety, depression, fear, anger, and joy all emanate from this region. The scent of a special fragrance can evoke memories and emotions before we are even consciously aware of it. When smells are concerned, we react first and think later. All other senses (touch, taste, hearing, and sight) are routed through the thalamus, which acts as the switchboard for the brain, passing stimuli onto the cerebral cortex (the conscious thought center) and other parts of the brain.

The limbic lobe (a group of brain structures that includes the hippocampus and amygdala located below the cerebral cortex) can also directly activate the hypothalamus. The hypothalamus is one of the most important parts of the brain, acting as our hormonal control center. It releases chemical messengers that can affect everything from sex drive to energy levels. The production of growth hormones, sex hormones, thyroid hormones, and neurotransmitters such as serotonin, are all governed by the hypothalamus. Thus, the hypothalamus is referred to as the "master gland."

Essential oils—through their fragrance and unique molecular structure—can directly stimulate the limbic lobe and the hypothalamus. Not only can the inhalation of essential oils be used to combat stress and emotional trauma, but it can also stimulate the production of hormones from the hypothalamus. This results in increased thyroid hormones (our energy hormone) and growth hormones (our youth and longevity hormone).

Essential oils may also be used to reduce appetite and produce significant reductions in weight because of their ability to stimulate the ventromedial nucleus of the hypothalamus, a section of the brain that governs our feeling of satiety or fullness following meals. In a large clinical study,[1] Alan Hirsch, MD, used fragrances, including peppermint, to trigger significant weight losses in a large group of patients who had previously been unsuccessful in any type of weight-management program. During the course of the six-month study involving over 3,000 people, the average weight loss exceeded 30 pounds. According to Dr. Hirsch, some patients actually had to be dropped from the study to avoid becoming underweight.

Another double-blind, randomized study by Hirsch[2] documents the ability of aroma to enhance libido and sexual arousal. When 31 male volunteers were subjected to the aromas of 30 different essential oils, each one exhibited a marked increase in arousal, based on measurements of brachial penile index and the measurement of both penile and brachial blood pressures. Among the scents that produced the most sexual excitement, was a combination of lavender and pumpkin fragrances. This study shows that fragrances enhance sexual desire by stimulating the amygdala, the emotional center of the brain.

In 1989, Dr. Joseph Ledoux at New York Medical University discovered that the amygdala plays a major role in storing and releasing emotional trauma.[3] From the studies of Dr. Hirsch and Dr. Ledoux the conclusion can be drawn that aromas may exert a profound effect in triggering a response from this almond-shaped neuro-structure.

In studies conducted at Vienna and Berlin Universities, researchers found that sesquiterpenes, found in essential oils such as vetiver, patchouli, cedarwood, sandalwood and frankincense, can increase levels of oxygen in the brain by up to 28 percent (Nasel, 1992). Such an increase in brain oxygen may lead to a heightened level of activity in the hypothalamus and limbic systems of the brain, which can have dramatic effects on not only emotions, learning, and

1. Hirsch, AR, Inhalation of Odorants for Weight Reduction, *Int J Obes,* 1994, page 306
2. Alan R. Hirsch, MD, FACP, *Dr. Hirsch's Guide to Scentsational Sex*, Harper Collins, 1998 1993 Dec. 20;58(1-2):69-79
3. LeDoux, JE, Rationalizing Thoughtless Emotions, *Insight,* Sept. 1989

attitude, but also many physical processes of the body, such as immune function, hormone balance, and energy levels. High levels of sesquiterpenes also occur in melissa, myrrh, cedarwood, and clove oil.

People who have undergone nose surgery or suffer olfactory impairment may find it difficult or impossible to detect a complete odor. The same is true of people who use makeup, perfume, cologne, hair sprays, hair coloring, perms, or other products containing synthetic odors. These people may not derive the full physiological and emotional benefits of essential oils and their fragrances.

Proper stimulation of the olfactory nerves may offer a powerful and entirely new form of therapy that could be used as an adjunct against many forms of illness. Essential oils, through inhalation, may occupy a key position in this relatively unexplored frontier in medicine.

Chemical Sensitivities and Allergies

Occasionally, individuals beginning to use essential oils will suffer rashes or allergic reactions. This may be due to using an undiluted spice, conifer, or citrus oil, or it may be caused by an interaction of the oil with residues of synthetic, petroleum-based personal care products that have leached into the skin.

When using essential oils on a daily basis, it is imperative to avoid personal care products containing ammonium or hydrocarbon-based chemicals. These include quaternary compounds such as quaternariums and polyquaternariums. These compounds are commonly found in a variety of hand creams, mouthwashes, shampoos, antiperspirants, after-shave lotions, and hair-care products. In small concentrations they can be toxic and present the possibility of reacting with essential oils and producing chemical byproducts of unknown toxicity. These chemicals can be fatal if ingested, especially benzalkonium chloride, which unfortunately is used in many personal care products on the market.

Other compounds that present concerns are sodium lauryl sulfate, propylene glycol—extremely common in everything from toothpaste to shampoo—and aluminum salts found in many deodorants.

Of particular concern are the potentially hazardous preservatives and synthetic fragrances that abound in virtually all modern personal-care products. Some of these include methylene chloride, methyl isobutyl ketone, and methyl ethyl ketone. These are not only toxic, but they can also react with some compounds in natural essential oils. The result can be a severe case of dermatitis or even septicemia (blood poisoning).

A classic case of a synthetic fragrance causing widespread damage occurred in the 1970s. AETT (acetylethyltetramethyltetralin) appeared in numerous brands of personal care products throughout the United States. Even after a series of animal studies revealed that it caused significant brain and spinal cord damage, the FDA refused to ban the chemical. Finally, the cosmetic industry voluntarily withdrew AFTT after allowing it to be distributed for years. How many other toxins masquerading as preservatives or fragrances are currently being used in personal care products?

Many chemicals are easily absorbed through the skin due to its permeability. One study found that 13 percent of BHT (butylated hydroxytoluene) and 49 percent of DDT (a carcinogenic pesticide) can be absorbed into the skin upon topical contact (Steinman, 1997). Once absorbed, they can become trapped in the fatty subdermal layers of skin where they can leach into the blood stream. These chemicals can remain trapped in fatty tissues underneath the skin for several months or years, where they harbor the potential of reacting with essential oils that may be topically applied later. The user may mistakenly assume that the threat of an interaction between oils and synthetic cosmetics used months before is small. However, a case of dermatitis is a possibility.

Gary Young is standing on the ruins of the city of Ubar. Centered around a desert oasis, Ubar became a major center for the frankincense trade. As the trade increased, the city was walled and towers were built to offer protection from thieves who knew frankincense was more costly than gold. Long covered by desert sands, the Lost City of Ubar was discovered in 1992 by tracing ancient camel trails that showed up on satellite images.

This twisted, scrubby frankincense tree is just outside Salalah, Oman, in a rocky desolate area. From cuts made in the bark of these rather homely trees exudes the precious resin tfrom which comes the richly fragrant frankincense essential oil, treasured worldwide.

CHAPTER 3

The Chemistry of Essential Oils

Unlike synthetic chemicals, essential oil chemicals are diverse in their effects. No two oils are alike. Some constituents, such as aldehydes found in lavender and chamomile, are antimicrobial and calming. Eugenol, found in cinnamon and clove, is antiseptic and stimulating. Ketones, found in lavender, hyssop, and patchouli, stimulate cell regeneration and liquefy mucous. Phenols, found in oregano and thyme oil, are highly antimicrobial. Sesquiterpenes, predominant in vetiver, cedarwood, and sandalwood, are soothing to inflamed tissue and can also produce profound effects on emotions and hormonal balance.

The complex chemistry of essential oils makes them ideal for killing and preventing the spread of bacteria, since microorganisms have a difficult time mutating in the presence of so many different antiseptic compounds. At the March 2000 International Symposium in Grasse, France, Dr. Bérangere Arnal-Schnebelen presented a paper showing the antibacterial properties of essential oils against several infectious agents. Spanish oregano and cinnamon essential oils tested at above 95 percent efficiency against *Candida albicans, E. coli,* and a *Streptococcus* strain. This is significant as we face life-threatening, drug-resistant viruses and bacteria.

Key Chemical Constituents in Essential Oils and Their Effects

Constituent	Representative Oil	Effect
Ketones	Sage	mucolytic
Aldehydes	Lemongrass	calming
Esters	Lavender	balancing
Ethers	Tarragon	balancing
Alcohols	Ravensara	toning
Phenols	Savory	stimulant
Terpenes	Pine	stimulant

The essential oils of ravensara, melissa, oregano, mountain savory, clove, cumin, cistus, hyssop, and frankincense are highly antibacterial and contain immune supportive properties that have been documented by many researchers, such as Daniel Pénoël, MD and Pierre Franchomme. These oils are found in varying amounts in the immune support and antimicrobial essential blends presented later in this book (see Chapter 9).

Understanding Essential Oil Chemistry

Basic Chemical Structure

The aromatic constituents of essential oils (i.e. terpenes, monoterpenes, phenols, aldehydes, etc.) are constructed from long chains of carbon and hydrogen atoms, which have a predominantly ring-like chemical structure. Links of carbon atoms form the backbone of these chains, with oxygen, hydrogen, nitrogen, sulfur, and other carbon atoms attached at various points of the chain.

Essential oils are chemically different from fatty oils (also known as fatty acids). In contrast to the simple linear carbon-hydrogen structure of fatty oils, essential oils have a far more complex ring structure and contain sulfur and nitrogen atoms that fatty oils do not have.

The terpenoids found in many essential oils are actually constructed out of the same basic building block—a five-carbon molecule known as isoprene.

When two isoprene units link together, they create a monoterpene; when three join, they create a sesquiterpene; and so on. Some of the largest molecules found in essential oils are triterpenoids, which consist of 30 carbon atoms or six

Vegetable Oil
Long Chain Carbon Structure
LAURIC ACID

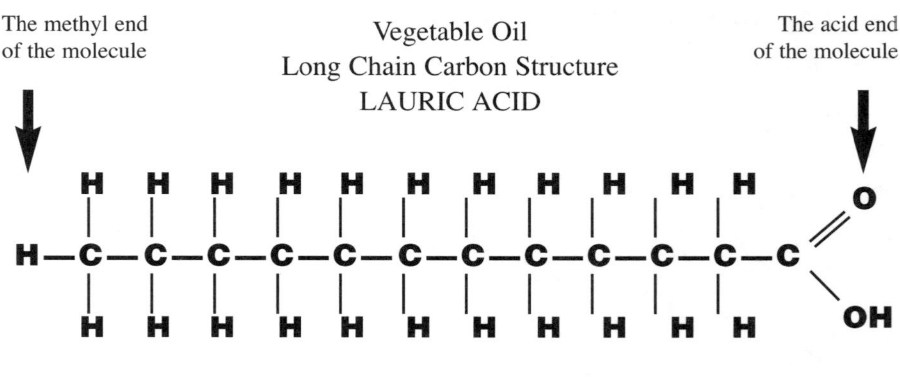

isoprene units linked together. Carotenoids, which consist of 40 carbons or eight isoprene units, only occur in essential oils in tiny quantities because they are too heavy to be extracted via steam distillation.

Different molecules in an essential oil can exert different effects. For example, German chamomile *(Matricaria recutita)* contains azulene, a dark blue compound that has powerful anti-inflammatory compounds. German chamomile also contains bisobolol, a compound studied for its sedative and mood-balancing properties. There are other compounds in German chamomile that perform different functions, such as speeding up the regeneration process of tissue.

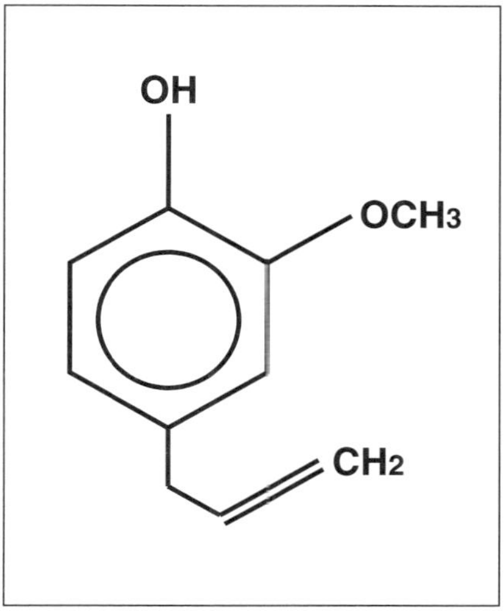

Eugenol—An aromatic molecule found in several essential oils including clove. Clove oil has been used as an antiseptic for many years.

Chemotypes

A single species of plant can have several different chemotypes based on chemical composition. This means that basil (*Ocimum basilicum*) grown in one area might produce an essential oil with a completely different chemistry than a basil grown in another location. The plant's growing environment, such as soil pH and mineral content, can dramatically affect the plant's ultimate chemistry as well. Different chemotypes of basil are listed below:

Ocimum basilicum CT linalol fenchol (Germany)
— **antiseptic**

Ocimum basilicum CT methyl chavicol (Reunion, Comoro, or Egypt)
— **anti-inflammatory**

Ocimum basilicum CT eugenol (Madagascar)
— **anti-inflammatory, pain-relieving**

Another species of plant that occurs in a variety of different chemotypes is rosemary (*Rosmarinus officinalis).*

Rosmarinus officinalis CT camphor is obviously high in camphor. Camphor serves best as a general stimulant and works synergistically with other oils, such as pepper (*Piper nigrum*), and can be a powerful energy stimulant.

Photo taken just after my presentation at the Third UNIDO Workshop on Essential Oils and Aroma Chemicals Industries, October 8, 1995, held at Anadolu University in Eskisehir, Turkey. From left to right: Dr. K.Tuley De Silva, from the Industrial Development Organization of the United Nations (UNIDO); Dr. W.S. Brud, President, Pollena Aroma, Warsaw, Poland; myself; Dr. K. Husnu Baser, Director of the Medicinal and Aromatic Plant and Drug Research Center at Anadolu University, Eskisehir, Turkey.

Rosmarinus officinalis CT cineol is rich in 1,8 cineol, which is used in other countries for pulmonary congestion and to help with the elimination of toxins from the liver and kidneys.

Rosmarinus officinalis CT verbenon is high in verbenon and is the most gentle of the rosemary chemotypes. It offers powerful regenerative properties and has outstanding benefits for skin care.

Thyme (*Thymus vulgaris)* also has several different chemotypes. Some of these are:

Thymus vulgaris CT thymol is germicidal and anti-inflammatory.

Thymus vulgaris CT linalool is anti-infectious.

FLORA RESEARCH CERTIFICATE OF ANALYSIS

We are the specialists in the quality control of essential oils.

A full service analytical laboratory to handle all of your testing needs.

Data File Information

Data File:	c:\star\module16\kger006.run
Channel:	A = DB1 RESULTS
Sample ID:	981201005
Operator (Inj):	jk
Injection Date:	12/01/98 11:17:57 PM
Injection Method:	c:\star\gerkato.mth

Injection Notes: YLEO geranium YL# 10481

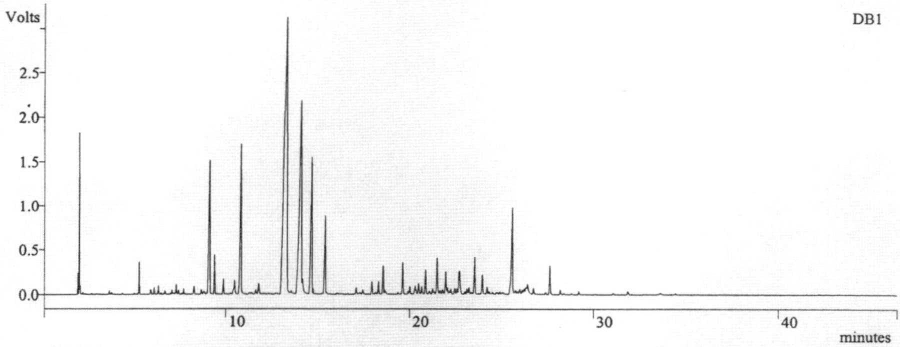

#	Peak Name	Percent of Total	Ret. Time (min)	Area (counts)
1	methane	0.3169	1.873	37276
2	a-pinene	0.6488	5.238	76307
3	myrcene	0.1782	5.865	20957
4	d-limo./cis-B-ocimene	0.2629	7.273	30923
5	linalool oxide 1	0.2405	8.269	28283
6	linalool oxide 2	0.1413	8.670	16615
7	linalool	5.8887	9.130	692622
8	cis-rose oxide	0.9901	9.398	116452
9	trans-rose oxide	0.4185	9.876	49226
10	menthone	0.6640	10.479	78105
11	isomenthone	6.3667	10.833	748848
12	a-terpineol	0.1421	11.622	16715
13	citronellol	30.2439	13.305	3557271
14	citral	0.0619	13.538	7282
15	geraniol	14.9584	14.075	1759402
16	cityl. formate	6.2222	14.649	731857
17	gnyl. formate	2.8178	15.395	331428
18	gryl. acetate	0.1971	17.075	23183
19	peak	1.1656	19.627	137094
20	6,9-Guaiadiene	0.4073	20.301	47905
21	g-epi-eudesmol	5.0657	25.598	595823
22	cityl. tiglate	0.6101	26.426	71765
23	gnyl. tiglate	0.9855	27.632	115919
	Totals	**78.9942**		**9291258**

Status Codes:
R - Reference Peak

The results of this analysis show that the sample is pure and free from common adulterants. No evidence of adulteration was detected at this level of testing.

Report prepared by:

James P. Kababick, Director

Date of report: December 4, 1998

Document not official unless bearing the Flora Research flask and flower seal.

Sample of a gas chromatograph chemical profile.

Gary meets with Turkish scientists at Andalou University in Eskisehir. Subjects he studied here were essential oil chemistry, absolute extraction, and gas chromatography.

CHAPTER 4

How to Safely Use Essential Oils

There are important guidelines to follow when using essential oils, especially if you are unfamiliar with the oils and their benefits. Many guidelines are listed below and are elaborated further throughout the chapter. However, no list of do's and don'ts can ever replace common sense. It is foolish to dive headlong into a pond when you don't know the depth of the water. The same is true when using essential oils. Start gradually, and patiently find what works best for you and your family members.

Basic Guidelines for Safe Use

1. Always keep a bottle of a pure vegetable oil handy when using essential oils. Vegetable oils dilute essential oils if they cause discomfort or skin irritation.
2. Keep bottles of essential oils tightly closed and store them in a cool location away from light. If stored properly, essential oils will maintain their potency for many years.
3. Keep essential oils out of reach of children. Treat them as you would any product for therapeutic use.
4. Essential oils rich in menthol (such as peppermint) should not be used on the throat or neck area of children under 30 months of age.
5. Angelica, bergamot, grapefruit, lemon, orange, tangerine, and other citrus oils are photosensitive and may cause a rash or dark pigmentation on skin exposed to direct sunlight or UV rays within 3-4 days after application.
6. Keep essential oils well away from the eye area and never put them directly into ears. Do not handle contact lenses or rub eyes with essential oils on your fingers. Even in minute amounts, oils with high phenol content, such as oregano, cinnamon, thyme, clove, lemongrass, and bergamot, may damage contacts and will irritate eyes.

7. Pregnant women should always consult a health care professional when starting any type of health program.
8. Epileptics and those with high blood pressure should consult their health care professional before using essential oils. Use caution with hyssop, fennel, basil, wintergreen/birch, nutmeg, rosemary, peppermint, sage, tarragon, and tansy oils.
9. People with high blood pressure should avoid using sage and rosemary.
10. People with allergies should test a small amount of oil on an area of sensitive skin, such as the inside of the upper arm, for 30 minutes, before applying the oil on other areas.

    The bottom of the feet is one of the safest, most effective places to use essential oils.
11. Before taking GRAS (Generally Regarded As Safe, listed in Appendix B) essential oils internally, test your reactions by diluting one drop of essential oil in one teaspoon of an oil-soluble liquid like agave, olive oil, or soy or rice milk. Never consume more than a few drops of diluted essential oil per day without the advice of a physician.
12. Do not add undiluted essential oils directly to bath water. Using Epsom salt or a bath gel base for all oils applied to your bath is an excellent way to disperse the oils into the bath water.

    When essential oils are put directly into bath water without a dispersing agent, they can cause serious discomfort on sensitive skin because the essential oils float, undiluted, on top of the water.
13. Keep essential oils away from open flames, sparks, or electricity. Some essential oils, including orange, fir, pine, and peppermint are potentially flammable (See Appendix J).

CAUTION: Essential oils may sting if applied in or around the eyes. Some oils may be painful on mucous membranes unless diluted properly. Immediate dilution is strongly recommended if skin becomes painfully irritated or if oil accidentally gets into eyes. Flushing the area with a vegetable oil should minimize discomfort almost immediately. DO NOT flush with water! Essential oils are oil-soluble, not water-soluble. Water will only spread the oils over a larger surface, possibly worsening the problem.

Before You Start

Always skin test an essential oil before using it. Each person's body is different, so apply oils to a small area first. Apply one oil or blend at a time. When layering oils that are new to you, allow enough time (3-5 minutes) for the body to respond before applying a second oil.

Exercise caution when applying essential oils to skin that has been exposed to cosmetics, personal care products, soaps, and cleansers containing synthetic chemicals. Some of them—especially petroleum-based chemicals—can penetrate and remain in the skin and fatty tissues for days or even weeks after use. Essential oils may react with such chemicals and cause skin irritation, nausea, headaches, or other uncomfortable effects.

Essential oils can also react with toxins built up in the body from chemicals in food, water, and work environment. If you experience a reaction to essential oils, it may be wise to temporarily discontinue their use and start an internal cleansing program before resuming regular use of essential oils. In addition, double your water intake while using essential oils.

You may also want to try the following alternatives to a detoxification program to determine the cause of the problem:

- Dilute 1-3 drops of essential oil to 1/2 tsp. of massage oil, vegetable mixing oil, or any pure vegetable oil, such as almond or olive. More dilution may be needed, as necessary.
- Reduce the number of oils used at any time.
- Use single oils or oil blends, one at a time.
- Reduce the amount of oil used.
- Reduce the frequency of application.
- Drink more purified or distilled water.
- Ask your health care professional to monitor detoxification.
- Skin-test the diluted essential oil on a small patch of skin for 30 minutes. If any redness or irritation results, dilute the area immediately with a pure vegetable or massage oil. Then cleanse with soap and water.
- If skin irritation or other uncomfortable side effects persist, discontinue using the oil on that location and apply the oils on the bottoms of the feet.

You may also want to avoid using products that contain the following ingredients to eliminate potential problems:

- Cosmetics, deodorants, and skin care products containing aluminum, petrochemicals, or other synthetic ingredients.
- Perms, hair colors or dyes, and hair sprays or gels containing synthetic chemicals. Avoid shampoos, toothpaste, mouthwash, and soaps containing synthetic chemicals such as sodium laurel sulfate, propylene glycol, or lead acetate.
- Garden sprays, paints, detergents, and cleansers containing toxic chemicals and solvents.

You can use many essential oils anywhere on the body except on the eyes and in the ears. Other oils may irritate certain sensitive tissues. See recommended dilution rates in Appendix F.

Keep all essential oils out of reach of children and only apply to children under skilled supervision. If a child or infant swallows an essential oil:

- Administer a mixture of milk, cream, yogurt, or another safe, oil-soluble liquid.
- Call a Poison Control Center or seek immediate emergency medical attention if necessary.

NOTE: If your body pH is low (meaning that your system is very acidic), you also could have a negative reaction to the oils.

Topical Application

Many oils are safe to apply directly to the skin. Lavender is safe to use on children without dilution. However, you must be sure what you are using is not lavandin labeled as lavender or genetically-altered lavender. When applying most other essential oils on children, dilute them with a carrier oil. For dilution, add 15–30 drops of essential oil to 1 oz. of a quality carrier oil as mentioned previously.

Carrier oils, such as a vegetable mixing oil, extend essential oils and provide more efficient use. When massaging, the vegetable oil helps lubricate the skin. Some excellent carrier oils include cold-pressed grapeseed, olive, wheat germ, and sweet almond oils, or a blend of any of these.

When starting an essential oil application, always apply the oil first to the bottom of the feet. This allows the body to become acclimated to the oil, minimizing the chance of a reaction. The Vita Flex foot charts (see Chapter 10) identify areas for best application. Start by applying 3–6 drops of a single or blended oil, spreading it over the bottom of each foot.

When applying essential oils to yourself, use 1–2 drops of oil on 2–3 locations twice a day. Increase to four times a day if needed. Apply the oil and allow it to absorb for 2–3 minutes before applying another oil or getting dressed (to avoid staining clothing).

As a general rule, when applying oils to yourself or another person for the first time, do not apply more than two single oils or blends at one time.

When mixing essential oil blends or diluting essential oils in a carrier oil, it is best to use containers made of glass or earthenware, rather than plastic. Plastic particles can leach into the oil and then into the skin once it is applied.

Before applying oils, wash hands thoroughly with soap and water.

Massage

Start by applying 2 drops of a single oil or blend on the skin and massaging it in. If you are working on a large area, such as the back, mix 1–3 drops of the selected essential oil into 1 tsp. of pure carrier oil (such as a vegetable mixing oil or a massage oil base).

Keep in mind that many massage oils such as olive, almond, or wheat germ oil may stain some fabrics.

Acupuncture

Licensed acupuncturists can dramatically increase the effectiveness of acupuncture by using essential oils. To start, place several drops of essential oil into the palm of your hand. Dip the acupuncture needle tip into the oil before inserting it. You can pre-mix several oils in your hand if you wish to use more than one oil.

Acupressure

When performing acupressure treatment, apply 1–3 drops of essential oil to the acupressure point with a finger. Using an auricular probe with a slender point to dispense oil can enhance the application. Start by pressing firmly and then releasing. Avoid applying pressure to any particular pressure point too long. You may continue along the acupressure points and meridians or use the reflexology or Vita Flex points as well. Once you have completed small point stimulation, massage the general area with the oil.

Warm Packs

For deeper penetration of an essential oil, use warm packs after applying oils. Dip a cloth in comfortably warm water. Wring the cloth out and place it on the location. Then cover the cloth loosely with a dry towel or blanket to seal in the heat. Allow the cloth to stand for 15–30 minutes. Remove the cloth immediately if there is any discomfort.

Cold Packs

Apply essential oils on the location, followed by cold water or ice packs when treating inflamed or swollen tissues. Frozen packages of peas or corn make excellent ice packs that will mold to the contours of the body part and will not leak. Keep the cold pack on until the swelling diminishes. For neurological problems, always use cold packs, never hot ones.

Layering

This technique consists of applying multiple oils one at a time. For example, place marjoram over a sore muscle, massage it into the tissue gently until the area is dry, and then apply a second oil, such as peppermint, until the oil is absorbed and the skin is dry. Then layer on the third oil, such as basil, and continue massaging.

Creating a Compress

- Rub 1–3 drops on the location, diluted or neat, depending on the oil used and the skin sensitivity at that location.
- Cover the location with a hot, damp towel.
- Cover the moist towel with a dry towel for 10–30 minutes, depending on individual need.

As the oil penetrates the skin, you may experience a warming or even a burning sensation, especially in areas where the greatest benefits occur. If burning becomes uncomfortable, apply a massage oil, vegetable mixing oil, or any pure vegetable oil such as olive or almond, to the location.

A second type of application is very mild and is suitable for children, or those with sensitive skin.

- Place 5–15 drops of essential oil into a basin filled with warm water.
- Water temperature should be approximately 100ºF. (38ºC.), unless the patient suffers neurological conditions; in this case, use cool water.
- Vigorously agitate the water and let it stand for 1 minute.
- Place a dry face cloth on top of the water to soak up oils that have floated to the surface.
- Wring out the water and apply the cloth on the location. To seal in the warmth, cover the location with a thick towel for 15–30 minutes.

Bath

Adding essential oils to bath water is challenging because oil does not mix with water. For even dispersion, mix 5–10 drops of essential oil in 1/4 cup of Epsom salts or bath gel base and then add this mixture under a running faucet. This method will help the oils disperse in the bath evenly and prevent stronger oils from stinging sensitive areas.

You can also use premixed bath gels and shampoos containing essential oils as a liquid soap in the shower or bath. Lather down with the bath gel, let it soak in, and then rinse. To maximize benefits, leave the soap or shampoo on the skin or scalp for several minutes to allow the essential oils to penetrate. You can create your own aromatic bath gels by placing 5–15 drops of essential oil in 1/2 oz. of an unscented bath gel base and then add to the bath water as described above.

Shower

Essential oils can be added to Epsom salts and used in the shower. There are special shower heads containing an attached receptacle that is filled with the essential oil/salts mixture. This allows essential oils to not only make contact with the skin, but also diffuses the fragrance of the oils into the air. The shower head receptacle can hold approximately 1/4 to 1/2 cup of bath salts.

Start by adding 5–10 drops of essential oil to 1/4 cup of bath salt. Fill the shower head receptacle with the oil/salt mixture. Make sure neither oils nor salts come in contact with the plastic seal on top of the receptacle. This should provide enough salt material for about 2–3 showers. Some shower heads have a bypass feature that allows the user to switch from aromatic salt water to regular tap water.

How to Enhance the Benefits of Topical Application

The longer essential oils stay in contact with the skin, the more likely they are to be absorbed. A high-quality lotion may be layered on top of the essential oils to reduce evaporation of the oils and enhance penetration. This may also help seal and protect cuts and wounds. Do not use ointments on burns until they are at least three days old.

Diffusing

Cold-air diffuser

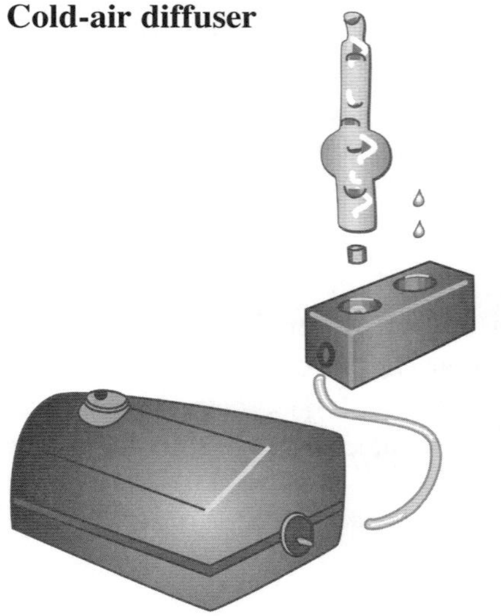

Diffused oils alter the structure of molecules that create odors, rather than just masking them. They also increase oxygen availability, produce negative ions, and release natural ozone. Many essential oils such as lemongrass, orange, grapefruit, *Eucalyptus globulus*, *Melaleuca alternifolia*, lavender, frankincense, and lemon, along with essential oil blends (Antibacterial Blend and Antimicrobial Blend), are extremely effective for eliminating and destroying airborne germs and bacteria.

A cold-air diffuser is designed to atomize a microfine mist of essential oils into the air, where they can remain suspended for several hours. Unlike aroma lamps or candles, a diffuser disperses essential oils without heating or burning, which can render the oil therapeutically less beneficial and even create toxic compounds. Burned oils may become carcinogenic. Research shows that cold air diffusing certain oils may:

- Reduce bacteria, fungus, mold, and unpleasant odors.
- Relax the body, relieve tension, and clear the mind.
- Help with weight management.
- Improve concentration, alertness, and mental clarity.
- Stimulate neurotransmitters.
- Stimulate secretion of endorphins.
- Stimulate growth hormone production and receptivity.
- Improve the secretion of IgA antibodies that fight candida.
- Improve digestive function.
- Improve hormonal balance.
- Relieve headaches.

Start by diffusing oils for 15–30 minutes a day. As you become accustomed to the oils and recognize their effects, you may increase the diffusing time to 1–2 hours per day.

Place the diffuser high in the room so that the oil mist falls through the air and removes the odor-causing substances.

By connecting your diffuser to a timer, you can gain better control over the length and duration of diffusing. For some respiratory conditions, you may diffuse the oils the entire night.

Do not use more than one blend at a time in a diffuser as this may alter the smell and the therapeutic benefit. However, a single oil may be added to a blend when diffusing.

Always wash the diffuser before using a different oil blend. Use natural soap and warm or hot water.

If you don't have a diffuser, you may add several drops of essential oil to a spray bottle, add 1 cup purified water, and shake. You can use this to mist your entire house, workplace, or car.

To freshen the air, use the following essential oil blend:

- 20 drops lavender
- 10 drops lemon
- 6 drops bergamot
- 5 drops lime
- 5 drops grapefruit

Diffuse neat, or mix with 1 cup of distilled water in a spray bottle; shake well before spraying.

Other Ways to Diffuse Oils

- Add essential oils to cedar chips to make your own potpourri.
- Put scented cedar chips in closets or drawers to deodorize them.
- Place any conifer essential oil such as spruce, fir (all varieties), cedar, or pine onto each log in the fireplace. As they burn, they will disperse an evergreen smell. This method has no therapeutic benefit, however.
- Put essential oil on cotton balls and place in your car or home air vents.
- Place a bowl of water with a few drops of oil on a wood stove.
- Dampen a cloth, apply essential oils to it, and place it near the intake duct of your heating and cooling system.

Humidifier and Vaporizer

Essential oils such as peppermint, lemon, *Eucalyptus radiata*, *Melaleuca alternifolia*, and frankincense make ideal additions to humidifiers or vaporizers.*

* NOTE: Test the oil in the vaporizer or humidifier first, some essential oils may damge the plastic parts of vaporizers.

Other Uses

Inhalation

Direct

- Place 2 or more drops into the palm of your left hand, and rub clockwise with the flat palm of your right hand. Cup your hands together over the nose and mouth and inhale deeply. (Do not touch your eyes!)
- Add several drops of an essential oil to a bowl of hot (not boiling) water. Inhale the steaming vapors that rise from the bowl. To increase the intensity of the oil vapors inhaled, drape a towel over your head and bowl before inhaling.
- Apply oils to a cotton ball, tissue, or handkerchief (do not use synthetic fibers or fabric) and place it in the air vent of your car.
- Inhale directly.

Indirect or Subtle Inhalation (wearing as a perfume or cologne)

- Rub 2 or more drops of oil on your chest, neck, upper sternum, wrists, or under the nose and ears. Breathe in the fragrance throughout the day.

Vaginal Retention

For systemic health problems such as candida or vaginitis, vaginal retention is one of the best ways for the body to absorb essential oils.

- Mix 20–30 drops of essential oil in 2 tablespoons of carrier oil.
- Apply this mixture to a tampon (for internal infection) or sanitary pad (for external lesions). Insert and retain for 8 hours or overnight. Use tampons or sanitary pads made with organic cotton.

Rectal Retention

Retention enemas are the most efficient way to deliver essential oils to the urinary tract and reproductive organs. Always use a sterile syringe.

- Mix 15–20 drops of essential oil in a tablespoon of carrier oil.
- Place the mixture in a small syringe and inject into the rectum.
- Retain the mixture through the night (or longer for best results).
- Clean and disinfect the applicator after each use.

Water Distillers and Filters

You can apply oils like peppermint, lemon, clove, and cinnamon to the post-filter side of your water purifier. This will help purify the water.

Dishwashing Soap

To add fragrance or improve the antiseptic action of your liquid soap, add several drops of essential oils such as lavender, *Melaleuca alternifolia*, fir, spruce, pine, lemon, bergamot, and orange.

Cleaning and Disinfecting

A few drops of oil may be added to the dishwasher to help disinfect and purify. Some popular oils are pine, orange, tangerine, lemon, and peppermint, although any antibacterial oil would work well.

Painting

When painting, add 1 teaspoon of your favorite essential oil to one gallon of paint. Mix well. The oil will counteract the unpleasant smell of paint. Because essential oils are not fatty oils, they will not leave oil spots on the walls.

Laundry

Essential oils may be used to enhance the cleanliness and fragrance of your laundry. As unpleasant as it seems, dust mites live in your bedding, feeding from the dead skin cells you constantly shed. Recent research has shown that eucalyptus oil kills dust mites. To achieve effective dust mite control, add 25 drops of eucalyptus to each load, or approximately 1 tablespoon to a bottle of liquid laundry detergent.

You may also add several drops of essential oils to the rinse cycle, such as fir, spruce, juniper, lavender, cedarwood, wintergreen/birch, or rosewood.

Instead of using toxic and irritating softening agents in the dryer, place a washcloth dampened with 10 drops of lavender, lemon, melaleuca, bergamot, or other essential oils. While the oils will not reduce static cling, they will impart a distinctive fragrance to the clothes.

Surface Cleansers: Counters, Furniture, etc.

Instead of purchasing standard household cleaners for surfaces, you can create your own natural, safe version by filling a plastic spray bottle with water and a squirt of dishwashing soap. Add 3 to 5 drops each of lavender, lemon, and pine essential oils. Shake the spray bottle well, and your homemade cleaner is ready to spray. This simple solution is extremely economical, yet it cleans and disinfects as well as any commercial cleaner.

Please keep in mind that some of the oils, if used directly, may stain some surfaces, such as linoleum.

Additional antibacterial and antiviral oils that are excellent for cleaning include cinnamon, clove, *Eucalyptus globulus,* thyme, juniper, *Melaleuca alternifolia,* spruce, lemongrass, and grapefruit.

Floors and Carpet

By combining essential oils with common household products, you can create your own nontoxic aromatic floor and carpet cleaners.

To clean non-carpeted floors, add 1/4 cup of white vinegar to a bucket of water. Then add 5–10 drops of lemon, pine, spruce, *Melaleuca alternifolia*, Antibacterial Blend, or another suitable oil. If the floor is especially dirty, add several drops of dishwashing soap. This will clean even the dirtiest floor.

To make a carpet freshener, add 16–20 drops of essential oils to a cup of baking soda or borax powder. Mix well and place in a covered container overnight so that the oil can be absorbed. Sprinkle over your carpet the next day and then vacuum the powder up.

You may also saturate a disposable cloth or tissue with several drops of essential oil and place it into the collecting bag of your vacuum. This will diffuse a pleasant odor as you clean. If your vacuum collects dirt into water, simply add a few drops into the water reservoir before cleaning. This refreshes both the carpet and the room.

Insecticide and Repellent: Dust Mites, Fleas, Ticks, Ants, Spiders, etc.

Many of us use synthetic chemicals to deal with insects. Single oils such as lavender, lemon, peppermint, lemongrass, cypress, *Eucalyptus globulus,* cinnamon, thyme, basil, citronella, and the Antimicrobial and Antibacterial blends (see Chapter 9), effectively repel many types of insects including mites, lice, and fleas. Peppermint placed on entryways prevents ants from entering.

If you need moth repellents for your linens and woolens, avoid toxic commercial mothballs made of naphthalene. Natural essential oils like citronella, lavender, lemongrass, Western red cedar, or rosemary can just as effectively repel moths and other insects. You can make a sachet by placing several drops of essential oil on a cotton ball. Wrap and tie this in a small handkerchief or square of cotton. Hang this cloth in storage areas or add it to your chest of linens. Refresh as often as necessary.

You can put this sachet in your bureau drawers to keep your clothes freshly scented. Lavender and rose are classic scents. For children's sleepwear, Roman chamomile is especially fragrant and relaxing. To scent stationery, stretch out an oil-scented cotton ball and place it in an envelope.

Hot Tubs and Saunas

Hot tubs, jacuzzis, and saunas act as reservoirs for germs, especially if used frequently. Lavender, cinnamon, clove, *Eucalyptus globulus*, thyme, lemon, or grapefruit can be used to disinfect and fragrance the water. Use 3 drops per person. For saunas, add several drops of rosemary, thyme, pine, or lavender to a spray bottle with water and then spray down the surfaces. Scented water can also be used to splash on hot sauna stones.

CAUTION: Some essential oils may damage plastic sauna/spa filters or hoses.

Deodorizing: Kitchens, Bathrooms, etc.

The kitchen and bathroom are often a source of odors and bacteria. Use the following mixtures to freshen, deodorize, and disinfect the air, work areas, cupboards, bathroom fixtures, sinks, tiles, woodwork, carpets, etc. These blends are safe for the family and the environment.

Since essential oils separate easily from water, always shake well and keep on shaking the bottle as you use these mixtures. They will deodorize and clean the air, instead of covering the odors.

Single oils:

- Rosemary CT cineol with lemon, *Eucalyptus globulus,* and lavender

Blends:

- Lavender with Antibacterial Blend

Recipe #1
Mix:
- 2 drops rosemary CT cineol
- 4 drops lemon
- 3 drops *Eucalyptus globulus*
- 4 drops lavender with 1 quart water
- 1 cup water

Shake the mixture well and put it in a spray bottle.

Recipe #2
Mix:
- 3–4 drops lavender
- 5–6 drops Antibacterial Blend
- 1 cup water

Shake the mixture well and put it in a spray bottle.

Recipe #3
Mix:
- Pine with chamomile, *Melaleuca alternifolia*, lemongrass, or clove

Toothpick Application:

Dip end of wood toothpick into oil and apply to mixtures when one drop of oil is too much.

Cooking Tips:

- Ginger, cinnamon, clove, or nutmeg can be added to spice up gingersnap cookies. Use the toothpick application method.
- Lemon, orange, mandarin, or tangerine oil can be added to a regular sponge or bundt cake recipe.
- Peppermint or spearmint oil can be added to chocolate cake, brownie, or frosting recipes.
- Nutmeg, cinnamon, clove, or ginger oil can be used in pumpkin pie or spice cake recipes.
- Oregano, marjoram, thyme, or basil can be put in tomato sauces for spaghetti, pizza, ravioli, and lasagna recipes. Use the toothpick method of application.
- Lemon, clove, orange, mandarin, or peppermint oil can be added to enhance the flavor of puddings and fruit pies. Add 1–2 drops for 4–8 servings.
- Lavender, Roman chamomile, orange, tangerine, lemon, peppermint, wintergreen, and melissa can be used to make herbal teas. Mix 2 drops essential oil with 1 tsp. of agave syrup and stir into a cup of warm water.
- Lemon, orange, mandarin, tangerine, or peppermint can be mixed into a cool refreshing drink. Mix several drops of essential oil with 1 tsp. of agave syrup and add to a pitcher of cold water.
- Cinnamon, clove, lavender, basil, German or Roman chamomile, or lemon can be used to flavor agave syrup. Warm the agave until it becomes a thin liquid, then stir in your favorite oil.

Cooking

Many essential oils make excellent food flavorings. They are so concentrated that only 1–2 drops of an essential oil is equivalent to a full bottle (1–2 oz. size) of dried herbs.

As a general rule, spice oils impart a far stronger flavor than citrus oils do. For strong spice oils (such as oregano, nutmeg, cinnamon, marjoram, tarragon, wintergreen, thyme, or basil), you can dip a toothpick into the oils and stir food (after cooking) with the toothpick. This controls the amount of essential oil that is put into the food.

Some oils that can be used as spices are: basil, cinnamon, clove, fennel, ginger, lemon, marjoram, nutmeg, oregano, peppermint, rosemary CT cineol, sage, spearmint, tarragon, coriander, grapefruit, mandarin, orange, wintergreen or birch, black pepper, and thyme.

For a recipe that serves 6–10 people, add 1–2 drops of an oil and stir in after cooking and just before serving, so the oil does not evaporate.

Internal and Oral Use as a Dietary Supplement

All essential oils that are Generally Regarded As Safe (GRAS) or certified as Food Additives (FA) by the FDA may be safely taken internally as dietary supplements (See GRAS and FA lists in Appendix B). But ingesting essential oils should only be done under the direction of a knowledgeable health professional.

In fact, many oils are actually more effective when taken orally in very small amounts. Essential oils should always be diluted in vegetable oil, agave syrup or rice milk prior to ingestion. More or less dilution may be required, depending on how strong the oil is. More potent oils, such as cinnamon, oregano, lemongrass, and thyme, will require far more dilution than relatively mild oils, and very mild oils like lavender or lemon may not need any dilution at all.

As a general rule, dilute 1 drop of essential oil in 1 tsp. of agave syrup or in at least 4 ounces of a beverage.

Usually no more than 2 or 3 drops should be ingested at one time (during any 4–8 hour period). Because essential oils are so concentrated, 1–2 drops are often sufficient to achieve significant benefits.

Essential oils should not be given as dietary supplements to children under six years of age. Parents should exercise caution before orally administering essential oils to any child, and again, oils should always be diluted prior to ingestion.

Essential oils are extremely concentrated, so they should be kept out of reach of infants and children. If a large quantity of oil is ingested at one time (more than 5 drops), contact your health care physician and a Poison Control Center immediately.

CHAPTER 5

Cleansing

The Risks of Internal Pollution

As the human body ages, there is a risk of greater and greater buildup of chemical contamination in our tissues. As toxins accumulate, the body is more likely to suffer the energy-robbing effects of poor health and degenerative diseases.

This is why cleansing the body is so important. When the body is purged of heavy metal contamination, undigested foods, and internal pollution, it relieves enormous stress on the organs and tissues. Immune function is enhanced and stress on the liver, in particular, is reduced.

Cleansing becomes especially important whenever animal products are consumed, such as meats and dairy products. These foods are loaded with naturally occurring, disease-related microbes. According to Robert O. Young,[1] PhD, DSc, meats contain an average of 300,000–3 million microorganisms per gram, or roughly 336 million per serving. Cheese contains from 300,000–1 million microorganisms per gram; milk, 20,000 microorganisms. These animal products can be a major source of internal pollution. Clean plant food, on the other hand, contains only 10 microbes per gram.

Humans were built to be primarily plant-eaters, not meat-eaters. Our long intestinal tracts are similar to many plant-eating species and are specifically designed by nature to digest a high-fiber, high-roughage, plant-based diet. Its long length allows enzymes a chance to unlock the nutrient value of the food. This contrasts markedly with the short intestines of flesh-eating animals, which are designed to quickly digest and pass through meats, without allowing them to putrefy, feed fungi, and create illness.

What happens when meats and dairy products are consumed by humans? Lacking fiber, these proteins move through our lengthy intestines very slowly and easily become trapped in the intestine's many nooks and crannies. Acting

1. Robert O. Young, Ph.D., Shelley Redford Young (contributor) *Sick and Tired?: Reclaim Your Inner Terrain,* Woodland Publishing, 2000.

like toxic time bombs, putrefying pockets of undigested food gradually release their payload of heavy metals, chemicals, hormones, and toxins directly into the blood and tissues. Even worse, this undigested debris is fermented by our body's naturally occurring yeast and fungi, polluting us with toxic byproducts called mycotoxins. These mycotoxins have been linked to many diseases.

Who Needs Cleansing?

Everyone needs cleansing. All of us are stressed, to a lesser or greater degree, by an ever-mounting buildup of toxins, chemicals, bacteria, and parasites. A distinguished medical researcher, Kenneth Bock, MD, states that humans are "walking toxic dumps." Why? Because of the industrial wastes, herbicides, pesticides, additives, and heavy metals we unknowingly absorb from our food, cosmetics, air, and water—even the mercury fillings in our teeth. Moreover, humans are at the top of the food chain meaning we are subjected to concentrated doses of potentially harmful chemicals from the meats and dairy products we consume.

According to a large 1990 survey by the Environmental Protection Agency, every single person tested showed some evidence of petrochemical pollution in their tissues and fats. Some of the chemicals found included styrene (used in plastics), xylene (a solvent in paint and gasoline), benzene (a chemical found in gasoline), and toluene (another carcinogenic solvent).

Cleansing allows the body to work towards fighting off the disease and not be encumbered or overloaded with the accumulation of toxins, mucous, and parasites that have built up over the years.

Understanding a Complete Cleansing

The ideal cleansing program should combine high water consumption with high-potency herbs, digestive enzymes, and therapeutic-grade essential oils. Essential oils have a special lipid-soluble makeup, which gives them a remarkable ability to penetrate cell membranes, break up undigested food, and oppose toxins. Essential oils also deliver oxygen, which has an unparalleled ability to inhibit the growth of many types of microbes. In fact, many essential oils have been studied for their unique antimicrobial, antifungal, and antiparasitic properties. Some oils, like rosemary, have demonstrated significant antiseptic activity, with documented research appearing in many scientific journals.

A cleansing program should target many different parts of the body (colon, intestine, stomach, liver, and pancreas) and cover many different types of internal pollution, including waste buildup, heavy metals, parasites, fungi, and yeast.

When Should You Cleanse?

Cleansing your system should not be done once or twice a year. It should be continuous.

Cleansing is especially important for anyone over 40. With age comes a greater buildup of debris in our bodies caused by decreased production of the stomach acids and enzymes. Without proper enzyme production, we lack the ability to properly break down undigested proteins and other fermenting debris that obstruct our digestive system and impede the assimilation of nutrients.

To get the most out of any cleansing regimen, one must drink plenty of distilled or purified water (never chlorinated tap water) throughout the day. A good rule of thumb is to divide your body weight (in pounds) by half, then drink that number of ounces of water. For example, a 150 pound person should drink 75 ounces (about 7–8 glasses) of water daily.

The Stanley Burroughs Master Cleanse[2]

The Master Cleanse is not a fast, but a cleansing program. A true fast consists only of water, while the Master Cleanse incorporates a mixture of lemon juice, maple syrup, and cayenne pepper that is consumed throughout the day and is a source of calories, vitamins, and minerals.

The Master Cleanse is ideal for anyone who is not diabetic and can safely cleanse for at least 3–7 days. The ideal duration of a cleanse is 1–3 weeks. As with any program of caloric restriction, however, it is strongly recommended that you consult with your health care professional before undertaking any extended fast or cleanse.

Program:

Take the juice of 1/2 fresh lemon (preferably organic).
Mix the juice with 8 oz. of distilled water.
Add 1–2 tablespoons of grade B maple syrup.
Add up to 1/10th tsp. of cayenne pepper (red).

Start with a pinch or two of cayenne and gradually increase to 1/10 tsp. Do *not* put the cayenne pepper (capsicum) into capsules and take separately from the lemonade drink. It changes the action of the formula, and if sent directly to the stomach it can cause inflammation and excessive mucous secretion. This may lead to sinusitis or to bowel mucous, and can even contribute to inflammatory bowel syndrome.

2. Stanley Burroughs, *Healing for the age of Enlightenment,* Burroughs Books, 1976, pp. 12-37.

Drink as many 10 oz. glasses per day as required according to your body weight. If you weigh 100 pounds, then you should drink half your weight in ounces which would be 50 ounces or 5 glasses.

Grade B maple syrup is one of the most balanced of all sugars, containing a balance of positive and negative ions. Grade B does not enter the bloodstream as rapidly as honey or sugar which is better for people who react adversely to sugar, (becoming restless, sleepless, and energetic after consuming sugar), or may be borderline or pre-diabetic. (Diabetics should substitute blackstrap molasses for the maple syrup, using up to 1/4 tablespoon.)

Contrary to popular belief, lemon is not acidic in the body. It turns alkaline in the mouth. If an acid-like reaction is observed when using lemon with water, it is because of the minerals in the water. Distilled water will not react in this manner.

Cayenne pepper is a blood vessel dilator, a thermal warmer, and provides vitamin A. People who have type O blood tend to have poor circulation. As a result, their body temperature may drop during a cleanse. Because cayenne is an herb known for its ability to warm and restore circulation, it may be taken internally and used topically (especially on the feet, but in small amounts).

Cayenne pepper is also thermogenic. When used in a dietary program, it can facilitate an increase in the body's ability to burn fat.

For the deepest cleanse, it is recommended that you cleanse for at least two weeks. (Again, consult with your health care provider before embarking on any calorie-restricting program.) Exercise enhances the cleansing action of the program.

During the middle and later phases of the cleanse, the body chemistry changes, and energy levels may begin to increase. One may experience minor discomforts such as headaches, upset stomach, or low energy as toxins and parasites are released from the body. These symptoms will be short-lived.

It is important to have a positive attitude during cleansing or fasting. If you are unaccustomed to the process, you can prepare yourself by fasting one day a week. Sunday, or your Sabbath day, is a wonderful day for this purpose. The biggest obstacle to successful cleansing is fear of failure and not knowing what to expect.

To fast for 24 hours, it is easiest if you begin at noon and finish at noon on the following day or fast from one dinner to the next.

Again, drink plenty of water.

As you begin to fast, you may experience some unpleasant side effects, such as headache, nausea, bloating, or irritability. These symptoms are part of the cleansing response and are often a result of toxins and waste matter being purged from the body which usually takes place within 12–36 hours.

If you experience these symptoms, you can cut back on your fluid intake and drink vegetable juices: carrot juice, carrot and celery mixes, carrot with celery, spinach, and broccoli. Carrot with a little apple juice, or a carrot, apple, and lemon juice mixture is good to facilitate the continuation of the cleansing. Six ounces of carrot juice, one ounce of apple, and 1/2 ounce of lemon juice will help keep the pH steady, slow the diarrhea, and keep the cleansing action going.

If you are feeling nauseated and bloated, it is an indication of two possibilities: (1) poisons are being released at a very rapid rate and may be backing up into the liver. Keeping the liver cleansed and flushed is extremely important. So it would be good to take ledum essential oil in a capsule at night or early morning. Ledum has a very strong effect on the liver and kidneys as a diuretic and a bile duct dilator.

The second reason for feeling ill is that the colon may not be eliminating as well because of spastic colon, loss of peristalsis (the wavelike motion of the intestines that moves waste matter out of the body), and/or from prolapsing with restrictions from kinks, loops, or twists in the colon. Hydrocolon therapy is a powerful treatment for cleansing the body and assisting in restoring peristalsis. You can call a colon hydrotherapist or buy a colima board to begin this therapy. In any case, you may also want to consult your health care professional.

Cleansing and Emotions

During cleansing you may have an unexpected emotional clearing. There are various essential oil blends designed to help control your emotions and modulate and facilitate the emotional release. Herbs, such as St. John's wort, kava (used with caution), and hops extract, are excellent for managing stress and negative emotions. The essential oils of valerian, Roman and German chamomile, and lavender, are exceptionally beneficial. Essential oil blends with tangerine, lavender, Roman chamomile, and blue tansy are calming and relaxing. Lemon oil is also calming. Most citrus oils containing aldehydes can be very calming in these situations. Vitamin B12 and folic acid are also important for emotional stability.

Ideally, these herbs or oils should be taken using oral infusion therapy (sprayed into the inside of the mouth where they can be most efficiently delivered into the blood).

The first 2–4 days of the fast are often the most difficult, since you will be overcoming the powerful psychological need to eat. As your body is cleansed of parasites and putrefying toxins, you will experience a sudden surge in energy and well-being. Tapeworms, pinworms, and roundworms often start to appear in your stools (after 4–6 days), and physical hunger will fade away. As the cleansing progresses, your mind will become sharper, your memory will improve, and your spirit will become more buoyant.

Remember: It is crucial to drink plenty of distilled water throughout the day, at least 8–10 glasses. Water is crucial for not only flushing out toxins, but maintaining the metabolic machinery of your cells and tissues in proper working condition.

The Complete Cleanse

It is difficult to control internal pollution with a simple one-time fix or a single magic-bullet type solution. Complete cleansing requires a battery of different solutions all targeted at specific systems of the body. Cleansing the liver needs different herbs, oils, and minerals than cleansing the colon which requires a different cleansing solution than the intestines.

Complete cleansing also requires a broad array of products that are effective against a wide variety of contaminants and microorganisms—not just one or two. Contaminants, like heavy metals, need a different set of tools to deactivate and purge them from the body than parasites do.

An important part of a complete cleansing program is essential oils. Highly antibacterial, antifungal, antiviral, and anti-inflammatory, essential oils help dissolve and chelate toxic chemicals and poisons in the body. They also promote digestive function by promoting the secretion and production of natural enzymes that enhance colon peristalsis.

CHAPTER 6

Producing Therapeutic-Grade Essential Oils

Organic Herb Farming

The key to producing oils that are of genuine therapeutic quality starts with the proper cultivation of the herbs in the field.

- Plants should be grown on virgin land uncontaminated by chemical fertilizers, pesticides, fungicides, or herbicides. They should also be grown away from nuclear plants, factories, interstates, highways, and heavily-populated cities, if possible.
- Because robust, healthy plants produce higher quality essential oils, the soil should be nourished with enzymes, minerals, and organic mulch. The mineral content of the soil is crucial to the proper development of the plant, and soils that lack minerals result in plants that produce inferior oils.
- Land and crops should be watered with deep-well, reservoir, or watershed water. Mountain stream water is best because of its purity and high mineral content. Municipally treated water or secondary run-off water from residential and commercial areas can introduce undesirable chemical residues into the plant and the essential oil.
- Different varieties of plants produce different qualities of oils. Only those cultivars that produce the highest quality essential oil should be selected.
- The timing of the harvest is one of the most important factors in the production of therapeutic-grade oils. If the plants are harvested at the wrong time of the season or even at the incorrect time of day, they may distill into a substandard essential oil. In some instances, changing harvest time, by even a few hours, can make a huge difference. For example, German chamomile harvested in the morning will produce an oil with far more azulene (a powerful anti-inflammatory compound) than chamomile harvested in the late afternoon.

Gary Young Lecturing at the Mona, Utah distillery, which is open to the public. Here he explains the first step of distilling: placing the herbs in the cookers. The rest of the process occurs on the lower level of this two-story operation.

- Other factors that should be taken into consideration during the harvest include the amount of dew on the leaves, the percentage of plant in bloom, and weather conditions during the two weeks prior to harvest.
- To prevent herbs from drying out prior to being distilled, distillers should be located as close to the field as possible. Transporting herbs to distillers hundreds or thousands of miles away heightens the risk of exposure to pollutants, dust, mold, and petrochemical residues.

Distillation

The temperature and pressure levels during steam distillation can enhance or destroy the value of the oil. The operator of the distiller must have a full understanding of the value of essential oils in order to produce quality oils. If the pressure or temperature is too high, it may change the molecular structure of the fragrance molecule, altering the chemical constituents. For example, the distilling process for lavender should not exceed three pounds of pressure, and the temperature should not exceed 245° F.

Steam Distillation

Essential oils can be extracted from the plant by a variety of methods, including solvent extraction, carbon-dioxide extraction, and steam distillation. Steam distillation actually takes three forms. The first uses just water, where plant material is placed in boiling water. The rising steam and oils are captured and then separated. Clove oil is distilled this way. There is also a combination water/steam method where boiling water and steam are pushed through and around the plant matter (this is how nutmeg essential oil is distilled). The final method is straight steam, where steam is pushed through the plant material, picking up the essential oils. Lavender is distilled this way.

In each of these processes, as the steam rises, it ruptures the oil membranes in the plant and releases the essential oil. The steam, carrying the essential oil molecules, rises to a condenser, where the oil-steam mixture condenses and reliquefies. As the steam condenses back to water, the lighter essential oil collects and floats on the top. This mixture is then sent to a separator where the oil is separated from the water. The remaining water is referred to as hydrosol or floral water.

There are many variants in steam distillation. Subtle differences in equipment and processing conditions can translate into huge differences in essential oil quality. The size and material of the cooking chamber, the type of condenser

Pressure/Temperature Chart for Distilling Several Therapeutic-Grade Essential Oils

Essential Oil	Starting Material	Oil Production	Optical Rotation	Pressure in pounds	Distilling Temp.	Distilling Time
Cypress	2000 lb	1 lb	24	0	220	24 hrs.
Pine	1000 lb	1 lb	2	0	180	8 hrs.
Myrtle	500 kl	1 kl	22	1-2	200	7-9 hrs.
Palmarosa	600 kl	1 kl	6	2	200	4 hrs.
Lemongrass	650 kl	17.5 kl	0	5	230	2.75 hrs.
Citronella	150 lb	1 lb	0	5	225	4.5 hrs.
Rosewood	500 kl	1 kl	-4	30	287	3 hrs.
Cinnamon	1300 lb	5 oz	0	5	225-235	9-24 hrs.
Clove	450 kl	5 lit	0	10	229	18 hrs.
Eucalyptus globulus	250 lb	1 lb	5	5	225	3-18 hrs.
Melaleuca alternifolia	1000 lb	10-15 lb	3	3	218	2-3 hrs.
Geranium	500 lb	6 lb	-8	1.2	200	1-3 hrs.

Explaining what happens after the essential oil is captured in steam in the cooker: The mixture is cooled in the condenser, the oil separates, and is then skimmed off.

and separator, and the degree of temperature and pressure can all have a huge impact on the oil. Distillation is as much a science as it is an art. If the pressure or temperature is too high, or if the cooking chambers are constructed from reactive materials, the oil may not be therapeutic grade.

Vertical steam distillation offers the greatest potential for protecting the therapeutic benefits and quality of essential oils. In ancient distillation, low pressure (5 pounds or lower) and low temperature were extremely important to produce the therapeutic benefits. Marcel Espieu, president of the Lavender Growers Association in Southern France, has long maintained that the best oil quality can only be produced when the pressure is zero pounds during distillation.

Temperature also has a distinct effect. At certain temperatures, the oil fragrance, as well as the chemical constituents, become altered. High pressures and high temperatures seem to cause a harshness in the oil. Even the oil pH and the electrical polarity are greatly affected.

For example, cypress requires a minimum of 24 hours of distillation at 265° F and 5 pounds of pressure to extract most of the therapeutically-active constituents. If distillation time is cut by only two hours, 18 to 20 constituents will be missing from the resulting oil.

Inspecting the stainless steel condensers and separators at the St. Maries, Idaho distillery.

However, most commercial cypress oil is distilled for only 2 hours and 15 minutes! This short distillation time allows the producer to cut costs and produces a cheaper oil, since money is saved on the fuel needed to generate the steam. It also causes less wear and tear on equipment. Sadly, it results in an oil with little or no therapeutic value.

In France, lavender produced commercially is often distilled for only 15 to 20 minutes at 155 pounds of pressure with a steam temperature approaching 350° F. Although this high temperature, high pressure oil costs less to produce and is easily marketed, it is of poor quality. It retains few, if any, of the therapeutic properties of high-grade lavender distilled at zero pounds of pressure for a minimum of 1 hour and 15 minutes.

In many large commercial operations, distillers introduce chemicals into the steam distillation process to increase the volume of oil produced. Chemical trucks may even pump solvents directly into the boiler water. This expands oil production by as much as 18 percent. These chemicals inevitably leach into the distilling water and mix with the essential oil, fracturing the molecular structure of the oil and altering both its fragrance and therapeutic value. These chemicals remain in the oil after it is sold because it is impossible to completely separate them from the oil.

This is where Gary Young is most at home, in the midst of an organic herb field at his Mona, Utah farm.

Mary Young lends a hand by driving the harvester at the St. Maries, Idaho herb farm.

Another way that essential oil producers increase the quantity of the oil extracted is through redistillation. This refers to the repeated distillation of the plant material to maximize the volume of oil by using second, third, and fourth stages of steam distillation. Each successive distillation generates a weaker and less potent essential oil. Such essential oils are also degraded due to prolonged exposure to water and heat used in the redistillation process. This water can hydrolize or oxidize the oil and begin to chemically break down the constituents responsible for its aroma and therapeutic properties.

Combining Traditional Steam Distillation with Modern Technology

Few people appreciate how chemically complex essential oils are. They are rich tapestries of literally hundreds of chemical components, some of which—even in small quantities—contribute important therapeutic benefits. The key to preserving as many as possible of these delicate aromatic constituents is to steam-distill plant material in small batches using low pressure and low heat. This is the traditional method of distillation that has been used for centuries in Europe but is being abandoned in favor of high-volume pressure cookers designed to operate at over 400° F and use over 50 pounds of pressure.

Even more important, the cooking chamber where the plants are distilled should be constructed of a non-reactive metal, preferably stainless steel, to reduce the possibility of the essential oil being chemically altered by more reactive metals such as aluminum or copper.

No solvents or synthetic chemicals should be used or added to the water used to generate steam because they might jeopardize the integrity of the essential oil. Even the addition of chemicals to water used in a closed-loop, heat-exchange system of the condenser can be risky, since there is no guarantee that they will be completely isolated from the essential oil. It is unfortunate that many essential oils distilled commercially are processed using boiler water laden with chemicals and descaling agents.

Absolutely no pesticides, herbicides, fungicides, or agricultural chemicals of any kind should be used in the cultivation of herbs earmarked for distillation. These chemicals—even in minute quantities—can react with the essential oil and degrade its purity and quality and render it therapeutically less effective. During distillation, pesticide residue leaches out of the plant material, with the extracted essential oil.

Essential Oil Production

Producing pure essential oils is very costly. It often requires several hundred or even thousands of pounds of raw plant material to produce a single pound of essential oil. For example, it can take 2–3 tons of melissa plant material to produce one pound of melissa oil. Its extremely low yield explains why it sells for $9,000 to $15,000 per kilo. It takes 5,000 pounds of rose petals to produce approximately one pint of rose oil. It is not difficult to understand why these oils are so expensive.

The vast majority of oils are produced for the perfume industry, which is only interested in their aromatic qualities. High pressure, high temperatures, and the use of chemical solvents are used in this distillation process to produce greater quantities of oil in a shorter time. To most people, these oils carry a pleasant aroma, but they lack true therapeutic properties. Many of the important chemical constituents necessary to produce therapeutic results are either flashed off with the high heat or are not released from the plant material.

Different Forms of Essential Oil Production

Expressed oils are pressed from the rind of fruits, such as grapefruit, lemon, lime, mandarin, orange, and tangerine. Rich in terpene alcohols, expressed oils are not technically "essential oils," even though they are highly regarded for their therapeutic properties. Expressed oils should only be obtained from organically grown crops, since pesticide residues can become highly concentrated in the oil.

Steam distillation is the oldest and traditional method of extraction. Plant material is inserted into a cooking chamber, and steam is passed through it. After the steam is collected and condensed, it is run through a separator to collect the oil.

Solvent-extraction involves the use of oil-soluble solvents, such as hexane, di-methylenechloride, and acetone.

Absolutes are technically not "essential oils" but are "essences." They are obtained from the grain alcohol extraction of a concrete, which is the solid waxy residue that is derived from the extraction of plant materials, usually flower petals. This method of extraction is used primarily for botanicals where the fragrance and therapeutic parts of the plant can only be unlocked using solvents. Jasmine and neroli are extracted this way.

A Summary of the Benefits of Therapeutic-Grade Essential Oils

1. Essential oils are small enough in molecular size that they can quickly penetrate the tissues of the skin.
2. Essential oils are lipid-soluble and are capable of penetrating cell membranes, even if the membranes have hardened because of an oxygen deficiency. According to Jean Valnet, MD, essential oils can affect every cell of the body within 20 minutes and are then metabolized like other nutrients.
3. Essential oils, according to researchers at the University of Vienna, stimulate blood flow, which increases oxygen and nutrient delivery.
4. Essential oils are some of the most powerful known antioxidants as determined by the ORAC test developed at Tufts University.
5. Essential oils are antibacterial, antifungal, anti-infectious, antimicrobial, antiparasitic, antiviral, and antiseptic. Some essential oils have been shown to destroy all tested bacteria and viruses.
6. Essential oils may detoxify the cells and blood in the body.
7. Essential oils containing sesquiterpenes have the ability to pass the blood-brain barrier.
8. Essential oils are aromatic, and when diffused, may provide air purification by:
   - Increasing ozone and negative ions in the area.
   - Eliminating odors from cooking, bacteria, mold, animals, and other sources.
   - Filling the air with a fresh, aromatic scent.
9. Essential oils promote emotional, physical, and spiritual well-being.

Gary showing his little son Jacob one of France's most beautiful lavender fields.

Gary and Mary Young touring a French distillery.

CHAPTER 7

Single Oils

This section describes over 90 single essential oils and includes botanical information, therapeutic and traditional uses, the chemical constituents of each oil, extraction method, safety data, and application instructions. Also included are ways to determine the purity of essential oils and how to maximize the shelf life of the oils.

How to be Sure Your Essential Oils are Therapeutic Grade

There are many ways to be sure if your essential oils are of the highest quality therapeutic grade. For a better idea of the quality of your oils, answer the following questions about your essential oil and essential oil supplier:

Are the fragrances subtle, rich, organic, and delicate? Do the fragrances of your oils vary slightly from batch to batch or bottle to bottle as an indication that they are pure and painstakingly distilled in small batches rather than industrially processed on a large scale?

Does your supplier send each batch of essential oils it receives through multiple chemical analyses before it is released?

Are these tests performed by independent labs who certify the results?

Does your supplier grow and distill its own organically grown herbs?

Are the distillation facilities part of the farm where the herbs are grown so they are freshly distilled, or do the herbs wait for many days to be processed, thereby losing their potency?

Does your supplier use low pressure and low temperature to distill essential oils, preserving all of their fragile chemical constituents? Are the distillation cookers fabricated from food-grade stainless steel alloys to reduce the likelihood of the oils chemically reacting with metal?

Does your supplier have representatives traveling worldwide to personally inspect the fields and distilleries where the herbs are grown and distilled at the time of harvest? Do they scrutinize the facilities to check that no synthetic chemicals are being used in any of these processes?

Do your essential oils comply with the AFNOR and ISO standards?

How to Maximize the Shelf Life of Your Essential Oils

The highest quality essential oils are bottled in **dark glass**. The reason for this is two-fold: glass is more stable than plastic and does not "breathe" the same way plastic does. Also, the darkness of the glass protects the oil from light that may chemically alter or degrade it over time.

After using an essential oil, keep the lid **tightly sealed**. Bottles that are improperly sealed can result in the loss of some of the lighter, lower-molecular-weight parts of the oil, especially the monoterpenes and sesquiterpenes. In addition, over time, oxygen in the air may react with and oxidize the essential oil.

Store essential oils **away from light**, especially sunlight. While the amber glass of the oil bottles does afford some protection against visible light, the darker the storage conditions, the longer your oil will last.

Store essential oils in a **cool location**. Excessive heat can alter the molecular structure of the oil the same way ultraviolet light can. This can lead to changes in the fragrance and therapeutic quality of the essential oil.

Single Oils Listings

The following information will acquaint you with the botanical and chemical makeup of 92 essential oils, along with directions for applying or diffusing each oil.

NOTE: When you read that an oil can be applied "neat," it means the oil can be placed directly on the skin without any dilution.

Angelica *(Angelica archangelica)*

Botanical Family: Apiaceae or Umbelliferae (parsley).

Plant Origin: France, Belgium.

Extraction Method: Steam distilled from roots.

Key Constituents:

Limonene [60–70%]
Alpha Pinene [5–8%]
Alpha and Beta Phellandrene [3–6%]

Action: Angelica is an anticoagulant, is sedating to the nervous system, and it reduces inflammation of the intestinal wall. Emotionally, it is calming, assisting in the release of pent-up negative feelings.

Traditional Uses: Known as the "holy spirit root" or the "oil of angels" by the Europeans, angelica's healing powers were so strong that it was believed to be of divine origin. From the time of Paracelsus, it was credited with the ability to protect from the plague. The stems were chewed during the plague of 1660 to prevent infection. When burned, the seeds and roots were thought to purify the air.

Indications: Bruises, colic, coughs, respiratory infections, indigestion, menopause, premenstrual tension, loss of appetite, and rheumatic conditions.

Application: Apply to Vita Flex points of the shoulders (see Chapter 10), on the bottom of the feet, or use in a cold air diffuser.

Fragrant Influence: Angelica is soothing and calming and helps release and let go of negative feelings by bringing memories back to the point of origin before trauma or anger was experienced.

Safety Data: If pregnant or under a doctor's care, consult your physician. Avoid if diabetic. Avoid direct sunlight after use (see note below).

Companion Oils: Patchouli, vetiver, clary sage, and most citrus oils.

NOTE: Because angelica contains bergopten, it may be photo-sensitizing and should not be applied to skin that will be exposed to direct sunlight or ultraviolet light within 3 days.

Anise *(Pimpinella anisum)*

Botanical Family: Umbelliferae (dainty, white-flowered annual).

Plant Origin: Turkey.

Extraction Method: Steam distillation from seeds (fruit).

Key Constituents:

Trans-Anethol [85–95%]
Methyl Chavicol [2–4%]

Action: Anise is antiseptic, antispasmodic, diuretic, and a stimulant.

Balsam Fir (See *Fir, Balsam*)

Basil *(Ocimum basilicum)*

Botanical Family: Lamiaceae or Labiatae (mint).

Plant Origin: Egypt, India, USA, France.

Extraction Method: Steam distilled from leaves, stems, and flowers.

Key Constituents:

Methyl Chavicol (estragol) [75-80%]
Linalol [1–5%]
1,8 Cineol (Eucalyptol) [1-5%]
Methyl Eugenol [1-5%]

Action: Basil is a powerful antispasmodic, is anti-infectious, antiviral, anti-inflammatory, a decongestant (veins, arteries of the lungs, prostate), and is antibacterial.

Traditional Uses: Used extensively in traditional Asian medicine, basil's name is derived from "*basileum*," the Greek name for "king." In the 16th century, the powdered leaves were inhaled to treat migraines and chest infections. The Hindu people put basil sprigs on the chests of the dead to protect them from evil spirits. Italian women wore basil to attract possible suitors.

Indications: Migraines, mental fatigue, and scanty menstrual periods.

Other Uses: Basil is relaxing to both striated and smooth muscles, soothing for insect bites, and stimulating to the sense of smell. It may help bronchitis and chest infections.

Application: Apply to tip of the nose, on the temples, and on the location of stings and bites. For mental fatigue, inhale first, then apply to the crown of the head, the forehead, the heart, and the navel. Basil may also be added to food or water as a dietary supplement.

Safety Data: If pregnant or under a doctor's care, consult your physician. Do not use if epileptic. Skin test for sensitivity.

Companion Oils: Bergamot, wintergreen or birch, cypress, geranium, lavender, lemongrass, and marjoram.

Selected Research:

Fyfe L, et al. "Inhibition of *Listeria monocytogenes* and *Salmonella enteriditis* by combinations of plant oils and derivatives of benzoic acid: the development of synergistic antimicrobial combinations." *Int J Antimicrob Agents*. 1997;9(3):195-9.

Wan J, et al. "The effect of essential oils of basil on the growth of *Aeromonas hydrophila* and *Pseudomonas fluorescens*." *J Appl Microbiol*. 1998;84(2):152-8.

Lachowicz KJ, et al. "The synergistic preservative effects of the essential oils of sweet basil (*Ocimum basilicum L.*) against acid-tolerant food microflora." *Lett Appl Microbiol*. 1998;26(3):209-14.

Bay Laurel (See *Laurus nobilis*)

Birch *(Betula alleghaniensis)*

(Very similar in chemistry to wintergreen)

Botanical Family: Betulaceae.

Plant Origin: USA, Canada, Scandinavia.

Extraction Method: Steam distilled from wood.

Key Constituent:

Methyl Salicylate [90+%]

Action: Birch is analgesic, antispasmodic, anti-inflammatory, a liver stimulant, and it supports bone function.

Traditional Uses: The American Indians and early European settlers flavored their tea with birch bark. Birch's main constituent, methyl salicylate, is also found in willow trees and is similar to the salicylic acid used in aspirin.

Indications: Arthritis, rheumatism, inflammation, muscular pain, tendonitis, hypertension, and cramps. Birch and wintergreen essential oil contain an active principle similar to cortisone that is beneficial for bone, muscle, and joint discomfort.

Other Uses: Birch essential oil may be helpful for cystitis, acne, bladder infection, gout, gallstones, edema, eczema, skin diseases, ulcers, and urinary tract disorders.

Application: Birch is safest to apply after diluting with a massage or vegetable oil. It also may be applied neat (undiluted) to the bottom of the feet. For baths, add 3–5 drops to bath water with 1/2 oz. of a bath or shower gel.

Fragrant Influence: Birch stimulates and increases awareness in all levels of the sensory system.

Safety Data: If pregnant or under a doctor's care, consult your physician. Do not use if epileptic. Skin test for allergies.

Companion Oils: Wintergreen, basil, cypress, geranium, juniper, lavender, lemongrass, marjoram, peppermint, and Roman chamomile.

NOTE: Be careful of your sources in obtaining either birch or wintergreen essential oils. There may be no true birch essential oil available worldwide. Additionally, much of the wintergreen sold today has been chemically extended and adulterated with synthetic methyl salicylate.

Bergamot *(Citrus bergamia)*

Botanical Family: Rutaceae (citrus).

Plant Origin: Italy, Ivory Coast.

Extraction Method: Pressed from the rind and rectified. Also produced by solvent extraction or vacuum distillation.

Key Constituents:

Limonene [30–45%]
Linalyl Acetate [22–36%]
Linalol [3–15%]
Gamma-Terpene [6–10%]
Beta-Pinene [5.5–9.5%]

Action: Bergamot is calming, antiseptic, anti-infectious, anti-inflammatory, antibacterial, and it provides hormonal support.

Traditional Uses: It is believed that Christopher Columbus brought bergamot to Bergamo in Northern Italy from the Canary Islands. A mainstay in traditional Italian medicine, bergamot has been used in the Middle East for hundreds of years for skin conditions associated with an oily complexion. Bergamot is responsible for the distinctive flavor of the renowned Earl Grey Tea, and was used in the first genuine eau de cologne.

Indications: Stress, loss of appetite, indigestion, agitation, depression, infection, inflammation, intestinal parasites, rheumatism, insomnia, vaginal candida, and it also is an insect repellent.

Other Uses: Bergamot may help bronchitis, cold sores, oily complexion, anxiety, nervous tension, coughs, urinary tract infections, respiratory infection, sore throat, thrush, and tonsilitis. Jean Valnet, MD, recommends it as an antidepressant and to regulate appetite.

Application: Diffuse, apply to the forehead, on the temples, and on the location of stings and bites. Apply where you would a deodorant. It may be added to food or water as a dietary supplement.

Fragrant Influence: Bergamot may help to relieve anxiety, stress, and tension, and has many constituents contributing refreshing, mood-lifting qualities.

Safety Data: If pregnant or under a doctor's care, consult your physician. **NOTE:** Bergamot is *very* photo-sensitizing and should NOT be applied to skin that will be exposed to direct sunlight or ultraviolet light within 3 days.

Black Pepper *(Piper nigrum)*

Botanical Family: Piperaceae.

Plant Origin: Madagascar, Egypt, India.

Extraction Method: Steam distilled from berries.

Key Constituents:

Beta Caryophyllene [25–35%]
Limonene [8–12%]
Sabinene [5–10%]
Alpha and Beta Pinenes [10–15%]

Action: Black pepper may help with toothache, is an expectorant, stimulates digestive secretions, reduces pain, and dispels fever.

Traditional Uses: Pepper was used by the Egyptians in mummification as evidenced by the discovery of black pepper in the nostrils and abdomen of Ramses II. It is reported that "mendicant monks of India" ate several black peppercorns a day to maintain their incredible stamina and energy.

Other Uses: This oil may increase cellular oxygenation, support the digestive glands, stimulate the endocrine system, increase energy, and help rheumatoid arthritis. It may also help with loss of appetite, chills, cholera, respiratory infections, indigestion, constipation, coughs, diarrhea, dysentery, influenza, nausea, neuralgia, poor circulation, poor muscle tone, quinsy, sprains, toothache, vertigo, viruses, and vomiting.

Application: Apply neat to the bottom of the feet. Dilute with a vegetable oil when applying topically elsewhere. Add to food as a flavoring or to rice milk as a dietary supplement.

Fragrant Influence: Black pepper is comforting and stimulating.

Safety Data: If pregnant or under a doctor's care, consult your physician. Skin test for irritation.

Companion Oils: Cumin, fennel, frankincense, lavender, marjoram, rosemary CT cineol, sandalwood, and other spice oils.

Selected Research: Unnikrishnan MC, et al. "Tumour reducing and anticarcinogenic activity of selected spices." *Cancer Lett.* 1990;51(1):85-9.

Blue Tansy (See Tansy, Blue)

Blue Cypress *(Callitris intratropica)*

Botanical Family: Cypressaceae.

Plant Origin: Australia.

Extraction Method: Steam distilled from the leaves and wood of the tree.

Key Constituents:

Alpha, Beta, and Gamma Eudesmols [18–30%]
Guaiol [8–18%]
Bulnesol [5–15%]
Alpha, Beta, and Delta Selinenes [5–10%]

Action: Blue cypress is anti-inflammatory, antiviral, effective against herpes simplex, herpes zoster, cold sores, and human papilloma virus. This essential oil is useful as an insect repellent. It also relieves abdominal cramps and minor aches and pains.

Traditional Uses: Blue cypress in ancient times was used for incense, perfume and embalming.

Cajeput *(Melaleuca leucadendra)*

Botanical Family: Myrtaceae (myrtle).

Plant Origin: Vietnam.

Extraction Method: Steam distilled from leaves and twigs.

Key Constituents:

Eucalyptol [50–65%]
Alpha-Terpineol [7–13%]
Limonene [3–8%]
Alpha Pinene [1–3%]

Action: Cajeput is antimicrobial, a mild analgesic, antispasmodic, antineuralgic, antiseptic (pulmonary, urinary, and intestinal), insecticidal, and can be used as an expectorant.

Traditional Uses: In Malaysia and other Indonesian islands, cajeput was used for respiratory infections, headaches, rheumatism, toothache, skin conditions, throat infections, and sore muscles. Cajeput derives its name from the Malaysian word for "white tree."

Indications: Arthritis, acne, respiratory infections, asthma, bronchitis, urinary complaints, coughs, cystitis, stiff joints, toothache, hay fever, bursitis, headaches, insect bites, intestinal problems, laryngitis, dysentery, psoriasis, rheumatism, sinusitis, oily skin, sore throat, and viral infections.

Application: Diffuse or rub on the bottom of the feet.

Safety Data: If pregnant or under a doctor's care, consult your physician. Use with caution. Do not use synthetic cajeput, as it could cause blistering and skin eruption. Skin test for sensitivity.

Companion Oils: Wintergreen or birch, *Eucalyptus radiata,* juniper, and peppermint.

Calamus *(Acorus calamus)*

Botanical Family: Araceae.

Plant Origin: India.

Extraction Method: Steam distilled from the root.

Key Constituents:

Alpha and Beta-Asarones [16–22%]
Shyobunone [5–10%]
Shyobunone Isomeres [7–13%]
Calamuscenone [6–12%]
Preisocalamendial [5–9%]

Action: Calamus can be used to help digestive problems, nervous complaints, and headaches, and is also used to increase the appetite.

Traditional Uses: Calamus was an herb traditionally used in Egypt and India to help improve mental focus, wisdom, and sexuality. In China it was used to aid in the recovery from stroke. Historically, Native Americans would hold a piece of calamus root in their mouths when running long distances to increase their endurance.

Application: Singers can use calamus to numb their throat so they can clear the phlegm, and keep singing.

Other Uses: Calamus can be used to help reduce the desire for tobacco. When rubbed on the feet, it may help with foot odor. It also helps with asthma, bronchitis, colic, memory loss, stroke, and depression.

Cardamom *(Elettaria cardamomum)*

Botanical Family: Zingiberaceae (ginger).

Plant Origin: Guatemala.

Extraction Method: Steam distilled from ripe fruit (seeds).

Key Constituents:

Alpha Terpinyl Acetate [45–55%]
1,8 Cineol (Eucalyptol) [16–24%]
Linalol [4–7%]
Limonene [1–3%]

Action: Cardamom is antispasmodic (neuro-muscular), antibacterial, an expectorant, and anti-infectious.

Traditional Uses: Cardamom has been used for paralysis, rheumatism, cardiac disorders, epilepsy, spasms, pulmonary disease, digestive, intestinal, and urinary complaints.

Indications: Indigestion, loss of appetite, coughs, debility, halitosis, mental fatigue, headaches, heartburn, nausea, and sciatica. Cardamom may also alleviate menstrual problems and irregularities.

Application: Diffuse, rub on the bottom of the feet, the stomach, the solar plexus, and the thighs.

Fragrant Influence: Cardamom is uplifting, refreshing, and invigorating.

Safety Data: If pregnant or under a doctor's care, consult your physician.

Companion Oils: Bergamot, cedarwood, cinnamon, cistus, clove, neroli, orange, rose, and ylang ylang.

Carrot Seed *(Daucus carota)*

Botanical Family: Apiaceae (Umbelliferae).

Plant Origin: France.

Extraction Method: Steam distilled from dried seeds.

Key Constituents:

Carotol [22.3–23%]
Alpha-Pinene [11.4–13%]
Sabinene [9.4–11]

Action: Carrot seed oil is antiseptic, carminative, diuretic, hepatic, a stimulant, vasodilator, and a smooth muscle relaxant.

Traditional Uses: Carrot seed oil was used for the treatment of eczema, psoriasis, and wrinkles and as an aid for dry skin. It is said to ease PMS, and has a tonic action on the liver and gallbladder. Carrot seed oil has been used for the treatment of jaundice.

Application: Apply topically.

Safety Data: Nontoxic and non-irritant. Avoid during pregnancy.

Cassia *(Cinnamomum cassia)*

Botanical Family: Lauraceae (laurel).

Plant Origin: China.

Extraction Method: Steam distilled from bark.

Key Constituents:

Trans-Cinnamaldehyde [70–88%]
Trans-O-Methoxycinnamaldehyde [3–15%]
Coumarin [1.5–4%]
Cinnamyl Acetate [0–6%]

Action: Cassia is antibacterial, antiviral, and antifungal.

Safety Data: If pregnant or under a doctor's care, consult your physician. (May cause skin irritation, if applied neat.)

NOTE: While its aroma is similar to cinnamon, cassia is chemically and physically quite different.

Cedarwood *(Cedrus atlantica)*

Botanical Family: Pinaceae (pine).

Plant Origin: Morocco, USA. *Cedrus atlantica* is the species most closely related to the biblical Cedars of Lebanon.

Extraction Method: Steam distilled from bark.

Key Constituents:

Alpha-Himachalene [10–20%]
Beta-Himachalene [35–55%]

Gamma-Himachalene [8–15%]
Delta-Cadinene [2–6%]

Action: Cedarwood is mildly antiseptic and may be effective against hair loss (alopecia areata), tuberculosis, bronchitis, gonorrhea, and skin disorders such as acne and psoriasis. It can reduce hardening of artery walls. It is high in sesquiterpenes which can stimulate the limbic region of the brain (the center of our emotions). It also may help stimulate the pineal gland, which releases melatonin, an antioxidant hormone associated with deep sleep.

Traditional Uses: Throughout antiquity, cedarwood has been used in medicines and cosmetics. The Egyptians used it for embalming the dead. It was used as both a traditional medicine and incense in Tibet, and for purification by Native Americans. It is recognized for its calming properties and is used to benefit the skin and underlying tissues.

Indications: Bronchitis, anger/hysteria, hair loss, arteriosclerosis, diuretic, tuberculosis, calming, nervous tension, and urinary infections.

Other Uses: Cedarwood may help with acne, anxiety, arthritis, respiratory congestion, coughs, cystitis, dandruff, psoriasis, sinusitis, skin diseases, and fluid retention. It may help open the pineal gland. It also helps to reduce oily skin.

Application: Diffuse or apply topically on location.

Safety Data: If pregnant or under a doctor's care, consult your physician.

Companion Oils: Bergamot, cypress, *Eucalyptus radiata,* juniper, and rosemary CT cineol.

Bible References: (See additional Bible references in Appendix C).

Leviticus 14:4— "Then shall the priest command to take for him that is to be cleansed two birds alive and clean, and cedar wood, and scarlet, and hyssop."

Leviticus 14:6— "As for the living bird, he shall take it, and the cedar wood, and the scarlet, and the hyssop, and shall dip them and the living bird in the blood of the bird [that was] killed over the running water."

Leviticus 14:49— "And he shall take to cleanse the house two birds, and cedar wood, and scarlet, and hyssop."

Selected Research:

Hay IC, et al. "Randomized trial of aromatherapy. Successful treatment for alopecia areata." *Arch Dermatol*. 1998;134(11):1349-52.

Celery Seed *(Apium graveolens)*

Botanical Family: Apiaceae (Umbelliferae).

Plant Origin: China, Hungary, India, USA.

Extraction Method: Steam distilled from dried seeds.

Key Constituents:

D-Limonene [60–65%]
Sedanolic Acid + Sedanolide [3–5%]

Action: Celery seed oil is an antioxidant, antiseptic, antispasmodic, diuretic, hepatic, carminative, and a stimulant.

Traditional Uses: Used for bladder and kidney complaints, menstrual problems, and digestive ailments. Celery seed oil has been found to have a liver regenerating effect.

Application: Apply topically. Add to food or rice milk as a dietary supplement or flavoring.

Safety Data: Nontoxic and non-irritating. Avoid during pregnancy.

Chamomile (German) *(Matricaria recutita)*

Botanical Family: Asteraceae or Compositae (daisy).

Plant Origin: USA, Egypt, Hungary.

Extraction Method: Steam distilled from flowers.

Key Constituents:

Chamazulene [2–5%]
Bisabolol Oxide A [32–42%]
Trans-Beta-Farnesene [18–26%]
Bisobol Oxide B [3–6%]
Cis Spiro Ether [4–8%]

Action: German chamomile is sedating, calming, anti-inflammatory, antispasmodic, and a decongestant. It supports digestive, liver, and gallbladder function, reduces scarring, and relieves allergies.

Traditional Uses: German chamomile has been highly esteemed for over 3,000 years and has been used for many types of skin conditions and stress-related complaints.

Indications: Insomnia, nervous tension, stress, bursitis, tendonitis, inflammation, carpal tunnel syndrome, headaches, acne, liver and gallbladder disease, parasites, and ulcers.

Other Uses: German chamomile is a cleanser of the blood, helps increase liver function and secretion, and supports the pancreas. German chamomile promotes the regeneration of skin and can be used for abscesses, burns, rashes, cuts, and dermatitis. It is also helpful for teething pains, acne, eczema, chronic gastritis, infected nails, cystitis, inflamed joints, menopausal problems, sores, skin disorders, stress-related complaints, toothaches, ulcers, and wounds.

Application: Diffuse, add to food or water as a dietary supplement, or apply topically on location. Among the gentlest oils used in aromatherapy, the chamomiles are suitable for use on children.

Fragrant Influence: Dispels anger, stabilizes emotions, and helps release emotions linked to the past. It may also be used to soothe and clear the mind.

Safety Data: If pregnant or under a doctor's care, consult your physician.

Companion Oils: Wintergreen or birch, fir, geranium, helichrysum, hyssop, lavender, lemongrass, marjoram, *Melaleuca alternifolia,* sandalwood, spearmint, and spruce.

Chamomile (Roman) *(Chamaemelum nobile)*

Botanical Family: Asteraceae or Compositae (daisy).

Plant Origin: USA, Egypt.

Extraction Method: Steam distilled from flowers.

Key Constituents:

Isobutyl Angelate + Isamyl Methacrylate [30–45%]
Isomyl Angelate [12–22%]
Methyl Allyl Angelate [6–10%]
Isobutyl n-Butyrate [2–9%]
2-Methyl Butyl Angelate [3–7%]

ORAC: 2,446 (Oxygen Radical Absorbance Capacity—an antioxidant test developed at Tufts University expressed as micromole Trolox equivalent [TE] per liter).

Action: Calming for preanesthesia and tension, antispasmodic, anti-inflammatory, antiparasitic, and skin regeneration.

Traditional Uses: Roman chamomile is used extensively in Europe for the skin. For centuries, mothers have used chamomile to calm crying children, ease earaches, reduce fevers, soothe stomachaches and indigestion, and relieve toothaches and teething pain.

Indications: Roman chamomile may help calm and relieve restlessness and tension. Its anti-infectious properties benefit cuts, scrapes, and bruises.

Other Uses: Roman chamomile neutralizes allergies and increases the ability of the skin to regenerate. It is a cleanser of the blood and also helps the liver discharge poisons. This oil may help with allergies, bruises, cuts, depression, insomnia, muscle tension, nerves (calming and promoting nerve health), restless legs, and skin conditions such as acne, dermatitis, eczema, rashes, and sensitive skin. It can effectively minimize irritability and nervousness in hyperactive children.

Application: Diffuse or apply topically on the bottom of the feet, the ankles, the wrists, or on location. Add to food or rice milk as a dietary supplement. Among the gentlest oils used in aromatherapy. All of the chamomiles are suitable for use on children.

Fragrant Influence: Because Roman chamomile is calming and relaxing, it can combat depression, insomnia, and stress. It minimizes anxiety, irritability, and nervousness. It may also dispel anger, stabilize the emotions, and help to release emotions that are linked to the past.

Safety Data: If pregnant or under a doctor's care, consult your physician. Test for skin sensitivity.

Companion Oils: Clary sage, geranium, lavender, or rose.

Cinnamon Bark *(Cinnamomum verum)*

Botanical Family: Lauraceae (laurel).

Plant Origin: Sri Lanka, Madagascar, India.

Extraction Method: Steam distilled from bark.

Key Constituents:

Trans-Cinnamaldehyde [40–50%]
Eugenol [20–30%]
Beta-Caryophyllene [3–8%]
Linalol [3–7%]

ORAC: 103,448.

Action: Cinnamon bark is highly antimicrobial, anti-infectious, and anti-bacterial for a wide spectrum of infections. It is antiviral, antifungal (candida), a general tonic, It increases blood flow when previously restricted, and is a light anticoagulant.

Traditional Uses: Cinnamon bark is one of the most antimicrobial essential oils. It has been produced in Sri Lanka for over 2,000 years. Research has found that pathogenic micro-organisms cannot live in the presence of cinnamon oil (Yousef, 1980).

Indications: Tropical infection, typhoid, and vaginitis.

Other Uses: Cinnamon oil may be beneficial for circulation, infections, coughs, exhaustion, respiratory infections, digestion, rheumatism, and warts. This oil also fights viral and infectious diseases and may be a sexual stimulant.

Application: Diffuse, apply topically on the bottom of the feet, the ankles, and the wrists. May be added to food or water as a dietary supplement. Because two of the chemical constituents found in cinnamon (cinnamaldehyde and eugenol) can burn the skin, dilute 1 drop of essential oil to 50 drops of a vegetable or massage oil before applying to the skin. Amount of dilution may vary depending on skin sensitivities.

NOTE: Cinnmaldehyde and eugenol found in cinnamon oil can cause dermal irritation. Repeated use can result in burning and extreme contact sensitization.

Safety Data: If pregnant or under a doctor's care, consult your physician. Skin test for sensitivity. Diffuse with caution; cinnamon may irritate the nasal membranes if it is inhaled directly from the diffuser.

Companion Oils: All citrus oils, frankincense, cypress, juniper, geranium, lavender, rosemary CT cineol, and all spice oils.

Bible Reference: (See additional Bible references in Appendix C.)

Exodus 30:23—"Take thou also unto thee principal spices, of pure myrrh five hundred shekels, and of sweet cinnamon half so much, even two hundred and fifty shekels, and of sweet calamus two hundred and fifty shekels…"

Proverbs 7:17—"I have perfumed my bed with myrrh, aloes, and cinnamon."

Song of Solomon 4:14—"Spikenard and saffron; calamus and cinnamon, with all trees of frankincense; myrrh and aloes, with all the chief spices:"

Selected Research:

Tantaoui-Elaraki A, et al. "Inhibition of growth and aflatoxin production in *Aspergillus parasiticus* by essential oils of selected plant materials." *J Environ Pathol Toxicol Oncol*. 1994;13(1):67-72.

Cistus *(Cistus ladanifer)* (known also as *Labdanum*)

Botanical Family: Cistaceae.

Plant Origin: France, Spain.

Extraction Method: Steam distilled from branches.

Key Constituents:

Alpha-Pinene [40–60%]
Camphene [2–5%]
Bornyl Acetate [3–6%]
Trans-Pinocarveol [3–6%]

ORAC: 38,648.

Action: Cistus is anti-infectious, antiviral, antibacterial, a powerful antihemorrhaging agent, helps reduce inflammation, and is a neurotonic for the sympathetic nervous system.

Traditional Uses: Cistus is also known as "rock rose" and has been studied for its effects on cell regeneration.

Indications: Bronchitis, respiratory infections, coughs, rhinitis, urinary infections, wounds, and wrinkles.

Other Uses: Cistus may strengthen and support the immune system (due to phenol action).

Application: Diffuse or apply topically mixed with a massage oil.

Fragrant Influence: Calming to the nerves, elevates the emotions.

Safety Data: If pregnant or under a doctor's care, consult your physician.

Companion Oils: Bergamot, clary sage, cypress, juniper, lavender, lavandin, patchouli, pine, sandalwood, and vetiver.

Citronella *(Cymbopogon nardus)*

Botanical Family: Poaceae or Gramineae (grasses).

Plant Origin: Sri Lanka, Philippines, Egypt.

Extraction Method: Steam distilled from leaves.

Key Constituents:

Geraniol [18–30%]
Limonene [5–10%]
Trans-Methyl Isoeugenol [4–10%]
Geranyl Acetate [5–10%]
Borneol [3–8%]

Action: Citronella is antibacterial, antifungal, anti-inflammatory, antiseptic, antispasmodic, and it is insecticidal, an insect-repellent, and a deodorant.

Traditional Uses: Various cultures have used this oil to treat intestinal parasites, digestive and menstrual problems, and also used it as a stimulant.

Indications: Headaches, respiratory infections, neuralgia, fatigue, and oily skin.

Other Uses: This oil can be used as an antiseptic to sanitize and deodorize surfaces. It makes an excellent insect repellent when combined with cedarwood.

Application: Diffuse or apply topically on the bottom of the feet or on location diluted with massage oil.

Safety Data: If pregnant or under a doctor's care, consult your physician. Repeated use can result in extreme contact sensitization. Skin test for sensitivity.

Companion Oils: Bergamot, cedarwood, geranium, lemon, orange, and pine.

Clary Sage *(Salvia sclarea)*

Botanical Family: Lamiaceae or Labiatae (mint).

Plant Origin: USA, France.

Extraction Method: Steam distilled from flowering plant.

Key Constituents: Contains more than 250 constituents

Linalyl Acetate [56–78%]
Linalol [7–24%]

Germacrene D [2–12%]
Sclareol [.4–3%]

Action: Clary sage is antidiabetic, helps reduce high cholesterol, is estrogen-like, supports hormones, is anti-infectious, antifungal, antispasmodic, relaxing, antibacterial, and may help with epilepsy, menopause, and PMS.

Traditional Uses: The name "clary" sage came from the nickname "clear eyes," given in the Middle Ages, because of its ability to cure eye conditions.

Indications: Bronchitis, cholesterol, hemorrhoids, hormonal imbalance, insomnia, intestinal cramps, menstrual cramps, PMS, premenopause, and weak digestion.

Other Uses: This oil may be used for menstrual problems, depression, headaches, dandruff, insect bites, insomnia, kidney disorders, dry skin, throat infections, ulcers, circulatory problems, and whooping cough.

Application: Diffuse or apply topically on the bottom of the feet, the ankles, and the wrists. May be added to food or rice milk as a dietary supplement.

Fragrant Influence: Enhances one's ability to dream and is very calming and stress-relieving.

Safety Data: If pregnant or under a doctor's care, consult your physician. Use caution with infants and children.

Companion Oils: Bergamot, cedarwood, lemon, orange, cypress, geranium, juniper, lavender, and sandalwood.

Clove *(Syzygium aromaticum)*

Botanical Family: Myrtaceae (myrtle).

Plant Origin: Madagascar, Spice Islands.

Extraction Method: Steam distilled from bud stems.

Key Constituents:

Eugenol [75–87%]
Eugenyl Acetate [.2-5%]
Beta-Caryophyllene [4-17%]

ORAC: 10,786,875.

Action: Clove is highly antimicrobial, antiseptic, analgesic, bactericidal, and is a powerful antioxidant. It is hemostatic (blood thinning) and is also anti-inflammatory.

Traditional Uses: The people on the island if Ternate were free from epidemics until the 16th century, when Dutch conquerors destroyed the clove trees that flourished on the islands. Many of the islanders died from the epidemics that followed.

Eugenol, clove's principal constituent, is used in the dental industry for the numbing of gums. Courmont et al. demonstrated that a solution of .05% eugenol from clove oil was sufficient to kill tuberculosis bacteria (Valnet, 1990)[1].

Indications: Infectious diseases, intestinal parasites, tuberculosis, respiratory infections, pain, toothache, scabies, and infected wounds.

Other Uses: According to Jean Valnet, MD, clove oil can prevent contagious disease and may treat arthritis, bronchitis, cholera, cystitis, dental infection, amoebic dysentery, diarrhea, tuberculosis, acne, fatigue, thyroid dysfunction, halitosis, headaches, hypertension, insect bites, nausea, neuritis, dermatitis, rheumatism, sinusitis, skin cancer, chronic skin disease, bacterial colitis, sores (speeds healing of mouth and skin sores), viral hepatitis, warts, and lymphoma.

Application: Diffuse or apply topically diluted with a vegetable or massage oil. Add 1–2 drops in 4 fl. oz. of water and use as a gargle. Apply neat on the palms of the hands, bottom of the feet, and on gums and teeth. One to two drops may be added to a glass of rice milk as a dietary supplement. For oral hygiene, rub directly on the gums surrounding an infected tooth. To break tobacco addiction, place a drop on tongue with finger. For tickling cough, put a drop on the back of the tongue.

Fragrant Influence: Clove may influence healing, serve as a mental stimulant, encourage sleep, stimulate dreams, and create a sense of protection and courage.

Safety Data: If pregnant or under a doctor's care, consult your physician. Repeated use can result in contact sensitization. Skin test for sensitivity. **CAUTION:** Clove essential oil can act as a blood thinner and should be avoided if taking a prescription blood thinner such as Warfarin™ or Coumarin™.

1. Valnet, Jean. Robert Tisserand, ed. *The Practice of Aromatherapy,* Healing Arts Press, Rochester, VT, 1990, page 47.

Companion Oils: Basil, bergamot, cinnamon bark, clary sage, grapefruit, lavender, lemon, nutmeg, orange, peppermint, rose, rosemary CT cineol, and ylang ylang.

Selected Research:

Nishijima H, et al. "Mechanisms mediating the vasorelaxing action of eugenol, a pungent oil, on rabbit arterial tissue." *Jpn J Pharmacol*. 1999 Mar;79(3):327-34.

Jayashree T, et al. "Antiaflatoxigenic activity of eugenol is due to inhibition of lipid peroxidation." *Lett Appl Microbiol*. 1999; 28(3):179-83.

Wie MB, et al. "Eugenol protects neuronal cells from excitotoxic and oxidative injury in primary cortical cultures." *Neurosci Lett*. 1997: 4;225(2):93-6.

Coriander *(Coriandrum sativum)*

Botanical Family: Apiaceae or Umbelliferae (parsley).

Plant Origin: Russia, India.

Extraction Method: Steam distilled from seeds.

Key Constituents:

Linalol [65–78%]
Alpha-Pinene [3–7%]
Camphor [4–6%]
Gamma-Terpinene [2–7%]
Limonene [2–5%]
Geranyl Acetate [1–3.5%)]
Geraniol [0.5–3%]

Action: Coriander is anti-inflammatory and has a sedative effect.

Traditional Uses: Coriander seeds were found in the ancient Egyptian tomb of Ramses II. This oil has been researched at Cairo University for its effects in lowering glucose and insulin levels and supporting pancreatic function[2]. It has also been studied for its effects in strengthening the pancreas.

Other Uses: Coriander may help with arthritis, diarrhea, respiratory infections, indigestion, digestive spasms, poor circulation, rheumatism,

2. Farag, RS, The Essential Oils of Coriander, Common Dill and Bitter Fennel and their Effects on Diabetic Rats, *Bull Fac of Agric*, University of Cairo, Vol. 43, No. 1 (Jan. 1992):31-44.

gout, infections (general), measles, headaches, nausea, muscular aches and pains, neuralgia, skin conditions (acne, psoriasis and dermatitis), and stress. It may also help during convalescence and after a difficult childbirth. Because of its estrogenic content, coriander may regulate and help control pain related to menstruation.

Application: Apply topically. May be added to food or water as a dietary supplement or flavoring.

Fragrant Influence: Soothing and calming.

Safety Data: If pregnant or under a doctor's care, consult your physician. Use sparingly, as coriander can be hamper mental function in larger doses.

Companion Oils: Bergamot, cinnamon, citronella, clary sage, cypress, ginger, jasmine, neroli, petitgrain, pine, sandalwood, and other spice oils.

Cumin *(Cuminum cyminum)*

Botanical Family: Apiaceae or Umbelliferae (parsley).

Plant Origin: Egypt.

Extraction Method: Steam distilled from seeds.

Key Constituents:

Cuminaldehyde [16–22%]
Gamma-Terpinene [16–22%]
Beta-Pinene [12–18%]
Para-Mentha-1,4-dien-7-al [25–35%]
Para-Cymene [3–8%]

Action: Cumin is antiviral, an immune stimulant, helps appetite and digestion, and acts as a liver regulator.

Traditional Uses: A tradition suggests that the ancient Hebrews used cumin as an antiseptic for circumcision.

Indications: Poor circulation, indigestion, digestive spasms, headaches, and migraines.

Other Uses: *Cuminum cyminum* is calming and a powerful support to the immune system. It may also help with wound healing and scars.

Application: Diffuse or apply topically. Dilution may be required. Skin test for sensitivity before using without a carrier oil.

Safety Data: If pregnant or under a doctor's care, consult your physician. Avoid direct sunlight for 12 hours after use.

Companion Oils: Cinnamon, frankincense, jasmine, myrrh, patchouli, rose, sandalwood, and ylang ylang.

Cypress *(Cupressus sempervirens)*

Botanical Family: Cupressaceae (cypress).

Plant Origin: France, Spain.

Extraction Method: Steam distilled from branches.

Key Constituents:

Alpha-Pinene [40–65%]
Beta-Pinene [0.5–3%]
Delta-3-Carene [12–25%]
Limonene [1.8–7%]
Myrcene [1–3.5%]

Action: Cypress improves circulation and supports the nerves and intestines. It is anti-infectious, antibacterial, antimicrobial, and strengthens blood capillaries. It also acts as an insect repellent.

Traditional Uses: Cypress is one of the oils most used for the circulatory system.

Indications: Arthritis, bronchitis, circulation, cramps, hemorrhoids, insomnia, intestinal parasites, menopausal problems, menstrual pain, pancreas insufficiencies, pulmonary infections, rheumatism, spasms, tuberculosis, throat problems, varicose veins, and fluid retention. Jean Valnet, MD, suggests that it may be helpful for some cancers.

Other Uses: This oil may be beneficial for asthma, strengthening blood capillary walls, reducing cellulite, supporting the circulatory system, and strengthening connective tissue. It may help with coughs, edema, improving energy, gallbladder ailments, bleeding gums, hemorrhaging, laryngitis, liver disorders, muscular cramps, nervous tension, nose bleeds, and ovarian cysts. It is outstanding when used in skin care, lessening scar tissue.

Application: Use topically with a massaging action toward the center of the body. Apply where you would wear a deodorant.

Fragrant Influence: Cypress helps ease the pain of loss. It creates a feeling of security, grounding, and it helps heal emotional trauma.

Safety Data: If pregnant or under a doctor's care, consult your physician.

Companion Oils: Bergamot, clary sage, juniper, lavender, lemon, orange, and sandalwood.

Bible Reference:

Isaiah 44:14—"He heweth him down cedars, and taketh the cypress and the oak, which he strengtheneth for himself among the trees of the forest: he planteth an ash, and the rain doth nourish it."

Dill *(Anethum graveolens)*

Botanical Family: Apiaceae or Umbelliferae (parsley).

Plant Origin: Austria, Hungary.

Extraction Method: Steam distilled from the whole plant.

Key Constituents:

Carvone [30–45%]
Limonene [15–25%]
Alpha- and Beta-Phellandrenes [20–35%]

Action: Dill is antispasmodic, antibacterial, an expectorant, and a stimulant.

Traditional Uses: The dill plant is mentioned in the Papyrus of Ebers from Egypt (1550 BC). Roman gladiators rubbed their skin with dill before each match. It is used in European hospitals.

Indications: Dill has been researched at Cairo University[3] for its effects in glucose and insulin levels and supporting pancreatic function.

Other Uses: This oil may help bronchial problems, liver deficiencies, indigestion, constipation, headaches, indigestion, and nervousness. It may also help normalize insulin levels, lower glucose levels, promote milk flow in nursing mothers, and support pancreatic function.

Application: Apply topically on the abdomen and the bottom of the feet. May be added to food or rice milk as a dietary supplement.

3. Farag, RS, The Essential Oils of Coriander, Common Dill and Bitter Fennel and their Effects on Diabetic Rats, *Bull Fac of Agric*, University of Cairo, Vol. 43, No. 1 (Jan. 1992):31-44.

Fragrant Influence: Dill calms the autonomic nervous system and, when diffused with Roman chamomile, may help calm fidgety children.

Safety Data: If pregnant or under a doctor's care, consult your physician.

Companion Oils: Nutmeg and citrus oils: lemon, orange, etc.

Douglas Fir (See Fir, Douglas)

Elemi *(Canarium luzonicum)*

Botanical Family: Burseraceae (frankincense).

Plant Origin: Philippines.

Extraction Method: Steam distilled from the gum of the tree.

Key Constituents:

Limonene [40–72%]
Alpha-Phellandrene [10–24%]
Sabinene [3–8%]
Elemol [1–25%]

Action: Elemi is antiseptic and antimicrobial.

Traditional Uses: Elemi has been used in Europe for hundreds of years in salves for skin, and is included in celebrated healing ointments, such as *baum paralytique*. Used by a 17th century physician, J. J. Wecker, on the battle wounds of soldiers, elemi belongs to the same botanical family as frankincense (*Boswellia carteri*) and myrrh (*Commiphora myrrha*). The Egyptians used elemi for embalming, and subsequent cultures discovered its benefits in skin care.

Indications: Sluggish glands, scarring, upset stomach, amoebic dysentery.

Other Uses: It is widely regarded today for soothing sore muscles, protecting and rejuvenating the skin, reducing wrinkles, and stimulating nerves. Its fragrance is very conducive to meditation.

Application: Apply topically or diffuse. It is one of the gentlest oils in aromatherapy, and suitable for use on children.

Safety Data: If pregnant or under a doctor's care, consult physician.

Eucalyptus citriodora *(Eucalyptus citriodora)*

Botanical Family: Myrtaceae (myrtle).

Plant Origin: China.

Extraction Method: Steam distilled from leaves.

Key Constituents:

Citronellal [75–85%]
Neo-Isopulegol + Isopulegol [0–10%]

Action: *Eucalyptus citriodora* is analgesic, antiseptic, antiviral, antibacterial, and antifungal as well as a deodorant, expectorant, and an insecticidal agent.

Traditional Uses: *Eucalyptus citriodora* has been used to perfume linen closets, and as an insect repellent, especially for cockroaches and silverfish.

Indications: Asthma, athlete's foot and other fungal infections, respiratory infections, cuts, dandruff, fevers, herpes, infectious skin conditions, laryngitis, scabs, shingles, sore throat, sores and wounds.

Application: Diffuse or rub on the bottom of the feet or on location.

Safety Data: If pregnant or under a doctor's care, consult your physician. **NOTE:** Do not take internally.

Eucalyptus dives *(Eucalyptus dives)*

Botanical Family: Myrtaceae (myrtle).

Plant Origin: Australia, Brazil.

Extraction Method: Steam distilled from leaves.

Key Constituents:

Alpha- and Beta-Phellandrene [23–30%]
Piperitone [35–45%]
Para-Cymene [6–10%]
Alpha-Thujen [2–6%]
Terpinene-4-ol [3–6%]

Action: This species has a different, more specific antibacterial action than other eucalyptus oils.

Application: Apply topically or diffuse. Avoid direct inhalation.

Safety Data: If pregnant or under a doctor's care, consult your physician.

Eucalyptus globulus *(Eucalyptus globulus)*

Botanical Family: Myrtaceae (myrtle).

Plant Origin: Australia, Brazil, China.

Extraction Method: Steam distilled from leaves.

Key Constituents:

1,8 Cineol (Eucalyptol) [58–80%]
Alpha-Pinene [10–22%]
Limonene [1–8%]
Para–Cymene [1–5%]
Trans-Pinocarveol [1–5%]
Aromadendrene [1–5%]
Globulol [0.5–1.5%]

ORAC: 24,157.

Action: *Eucalyptus globulus* is mucolytic, antimicrobial, antibacterial, antifungal (candida), antiviral, antiseptic and is an expectorant.

Traditional Uses: For centuries, Australian Aborigines used the disinfecting leaves of *E. globulus* to cover wounds. Shown by laboratory tests to be a powerful antimicrobial agent, it contains a high percentage of eucalyptol (a key ingredient in many antiseptic mouth rinses). Often used for the respiratory system, eucalyptus has also been investigated for its powerful insect repellent effects (Trigg, 1996). Eucalyptus trees have been planted throughout parts of North Africa to successfully block the spread of malaria. According to Jean Valnet, MD, a solution of 2 percent eucalyptus oil sprayed in the air will kill 70 percent of airborne staph bacteria[4]. Some doctors still use solutions of eucalyptus oil in surgical dressings.

Indications: Asthma, candida, coughs, diabetes, herpes, hypoglycemia, lungs, measles, headaches, respiratory infections, sinusitis, shingles, and tuberculosis.

Other Uses: This oil may be used for aches/pains, acne, allergies, arthritis, bronchitis, burns, respiratory infections, cystitis, endometriosis, gonorrhea, inflammation of the ear, eye, and sinus, and as decongestant. Also for malaria, rheumatism, respiratory infections, skin and throat infection/sores, ulcers, vaginitis, and wounds. *E. globulus* is helpful for increasing energy.

4. Jean Valnet, MD, *The Practice of Aromatherapy: A Classic Compendium of Plant Medicines & Their Healing Properties,* Healing Arts Press, Vermont, 1980, page 122.

Application: Apply topically, diffuse, or use in a humidifier. May be added to food or rice milk as a dietary supplement.

Fragrant Influence: It promotes health, well-being, purification, and healing.

Safety Data: If pregnant or under a doctor's care, consult your physician. **NOTE:** Do not take internally.

Companion Oils: Geranium, juniper, lavender, lemon, lemongrass, melissa, pine, sandalwood, and thyme.

Selected Research: Tovey ER, et al. "A simple washing procedure with eucalyptus oil for controlling house dust mites and their allergens in clothing and bedding." *J Allergy Clin Immunol*. 1997; 100(4):464-6.

Weyers W, et al. "Skin absorption of volatile oils. Pharmacokinetics." *Pharm Unserer Zeit*. 1989;18(3):82-6.

Zanker KS, et al. "Evaluation of surfactant-like effects of commonly used remedies for colds." *Respiration*. 1980;39(3):150-7.

Eucalyptus polybractea *(Eucalyptus polybractea)*

Botanical Family: Myrtaceae (myrtle).

Plant Origin: Australia.

Extraction Method: Steam distilled from leaves.

Key Constituents:

1,8 cineol (Eucalyptol) [91%]
Limonene [1.5%]
Para-Cymene [1.5%]
Alpha-Pinene [1.5%]

Action: *Eucalyptus polybractea* is anti-infectious, antiviral, antibacterial, anti-inflammatory, mucolytic, an expectorant, and an insect repellent.

Indications: Acne and cystitis.

Application: Diffuse, apply topically, or use in a humidifier.

Safety Data: If pregnant or under a doctor's care, consult your physician.

Eucalyptus radiata *(Eucalyptus radiata)*

Botanical Family: Myrtaceae (myrtle).

Plant Origin: Australia.

Extraction Method: Steam distilled from leaves.

Key Constituents:

Eucalyptol [60–75%]
Alpha-Terpineol [5–10%]
Limonene [4–8%]
Alpha-Pinene [2–6%]

Action: *Eucalyptus radiata* is anti-infectious, antibacterial, antiviral, anti-inflammatory, and expectorant.

Traditional Uses: An antimicrobial oil studied for its action against viruses, *Eucalyptus radiata* is used extensively for respiratory infections.

Indications: Conjunctivitis, vaginitis, acne, sinusitis, and bronchitis.

Other Uses: This oil, when combined with bergamot, has been used effectively on herpes simplex. It may also help with acne, bronchitis, ear inflammation, endometriosis, nasal and sinus congestion, sinusitis, and vaginitis.

Application: Diffuse, rub on the bottom of the feet or on location, or use in a humidifier.

Safety Data: If pregnant or under a doctor's care, consult your physician.

Fennel *(Foeniculum vulgare)*

Botanical Family: Apiaceae or Umbelliferae (parsley).

Plant Origin: Australia, Spain.

Extraction Method: Steam distilled from the crushed seeds.

Key Constituents:

Trans-Anethol [60–80%]
Fenchone + Linalol [12–16%]
Alpha-Pinene [3–5%]
Methyl Chavicol [2–5%]

Action: Fennel stimulates estrogen production, facilitates birthing, increases lactation, promotes digestion, reduces indigestion, supports the heart and respiratory system, expels worms, is stimulating to the circulatory and respiratory systems. It is antiseptic, antispasmodic, and analgesic.

Traditional Uses: Fennel was believed to ward off evil spirits and to protect against spells cast by witches during medieval times. Sprigs were hung over doors to fend off evil spirits. For hundreds of years, fennel seeds have been used as a digestive aid and to balance menstrual cycles. Recently it has been used in mouthwashes and toothpastes.

Indications: Cystitis, sluggish digestion, fluid retention, gout, intestinal parasites, intestinal spasms, nausea, menopause and pre-menopause problems.

Other Uses: Fennel oil may be used for indigestion, stimulating the cardiovascular and respiratory system, for constipation, digestion, balancing hormones, supporting pancreatic function, and PMS. It may break up fluids and toxins, and cleanse the tissues.

Application: Apply topically diluted with a vegetable or massage oil.

Safety Data: If pregnant or under a doctor's care, consult your physician. **NOTE:** Use caution if epileptic.

Companion Oils: Basil, geranium, lavender, lemon, rosemary CT cineol, and sandalwood.

Selected Reference: Fyfe L, et al. "Inhibition of *Listeria monocytogenes* and *Salmonella enteriditis* by combinations of plant oils and derivatives of benzoic acid: the development of synergistic antimicrobial combinations." *Int J Antimicrob Agents*. 1997;9(3):195-9.

Fir, Balsam *(Abies balsamea)*

Botanical Family: Pinaceae (pine)

Plant Origin: USA.

Extraction Method: Steam distilled from needles/branches.

Key Constituents:

Alpha-Pinene [28–49%]
Beta-Pinene [14–24%]
Camphene [13–20%]
Limonene [13–20%]

Action: Balsam fir is antitumoral, anticancerous, antioxidant, combats respiratory infections, and is antifungal. It may also ease the pain of arthritis and bursitis.

Safety Data: If pregnant or under a doctor's care, consult your physician. Skin test for sensitivity.

Fir, Douglas *(Pseudotsuga menziesii)*

Botanical Family: Abietaceae.

Plant Origin: USA.

Extraction Method: Steam distilled from needles/branches.

Key Constituents:

Alpha-Pinene [25–40%]
Beta-Pinene [7–15%]
Limonene [6–11%]
Bornyl Acetate [8–15%]

Action: Douglas fir is antitumoral, anticancerous, antifungal, is an antioxidant, and combats respiratory infections.

Safety Data: If pregnant or under a doctor's care, consult your physician. Skin test for sensitivity.

Fir, White *(Abies concolor)*

Botanical Family: Abietaceae.

Plant Origin: USA.

Extraction Method: Steam distilled from needles/branches.

Key Constituents:

Alpha-Phinene [8–12%]
Beta-Phinene [20–30%]
Camphene [7–15%]
Bornyl Acetate [13%]
Beta-Phellandrene [11–16%]
Delta-Cadinene [2–7%]

Action: White fir is anti-tumoral, anti-cancerous, anti-fungal, is an anti-oxidant, and combats respiratory infections.

Safety Data: If pregnant or under a doctor's care, consult your physician. Skin test for sensitivity.

Fleabane *(Conyza canadensis)*

Botanical Family: Asteraceae or Compositae (daisy).

Plant Origin: Canada.

Extraction Method: Steam distilled from stems, leaves, and flowers.

Key Constituents:

Limonene [60–75%]
Cis-Alpha-Bergamotene [5–11%]
Trans-Beta-Ocimene [3–7%]

Action: Stimulates liver and pancreas, is antirheumatic, antispasmodic, hormone-like, and is a cardiovascular dilator. Daniel Pénoël, MD, used it to treat children with retarded puberty.

Safety Data: If pregnant or under a doctor's care, consult your physician.

NOTE: This oil is still under study.

Frankincense *(Boswellia carteri)*

Botanical Family: Burseraceae (Frankincense).

Plant Origin: Somalia.

Extraction Method: Steam distilled from gum/resin.

Key Constituents:

Alpha-Pinene [28–49%]
Limonene [10–16%]
Sabinene [3–7%]
Myrcene [8–12%]
Beta-Caryophyllene [3–7%]
Alpha-Thuyene [4–8%]
Paracymene [2–5%]

Action: Expectorant, antitumoral, immunostimulant, and antidepressant.

Traditional Uses: Also known as "olibanum," or "Oil from Lebanon" the name frankincense is derived from the Medieval French word for "real incense." Frankincense is considered the "holy anointing oil" in the Middle East and has been used in religious ceremonies for thousands of years. It was well known during the time of Christ for its anointing and healing powers and was one of the gifts given to Christ at His birth. "Used to treat every conceivable ill known to man," frankincense was valued more than gold during ancient times, and only those with great wealth and abundance possessed it. Researchers today have discovered that the sequiterpenes in frankincense, help stimulate the limbic system of the brain (the center of emotions) as well as the hypothalamus, pineal and pituitary glands. The hypothalamus is the master gland of the human body, controlling the release of many hormones including thyroid and growth hormone. Frankincense is now being researched and used therapeutically in European hospitals and is being investigated for its ability to improve human growth hormone production.

Indications: Asthma, depression, and ulcers.

Other Uses: This oil may help with allergies, bites (insect and snake), bronchitis, cancer, respiratory infections, diphtheria, headaches, hemorrhaging, herpes, high blood pressure, inflammation, stress, tonsilitis, typhoid, and warts. It contains sesquiterpenes, enabling it to go beyond the blood brain barrier where it is elevating to the mind and helps to overcome stress and despair. It also increases the activity of leukocytes in defense of the body against infection.

Application: Diffuse or apply topically. May be added to food or rice milk as a dietary supplement.

Fragrant Influence: It increases spiritual awareness and promotes meditation. Frankincense may also help improve attitude and uplift spirits.

Safety Data: If pregnant or under a doctor's care, consult physician.

Companion Oils: All oils.

Bible Reference: There are over 52 references to frankincense—considering that "incense" is translated from the Hebrew/Greek "frankincense" and is referring to the same oil. (See additional Bible references in Appendix C.)

Exodus 30:34—"And the Lord said unto Moses, Take unto thee sweet spices, stacte, and onycha, and galbanum; these sweet spices with pure frankincense: of each shall there be a like weight:"

Leviticus 2:1—"And when any will offer a meat offering unto the Lord, his offering shall be of fine flour; and he shall pour oil upon it, and put frankincense thereon:"

Leviticus 2:2—"And he shall bring it to Aaron's sons the priests: and he shall take thereout his handful of the flour thereof, and of the oil thereof, with all the frankincense thereof; and the priest shall burn the memorial of it upon the altar, to be an offering made by fire, of a sweet savour unto the Lord:"

Selected Research:

Michie, C.A., et al. "Frankincense and myrrh as remedies in children." *J R Soc Med.* 1991;84(10):602-5.

Wang, L.G., et al. "Determination of DNA topoisomerase II activity from L1210 cells—a target for screening antitumor agents." Chung Kuo Yao Li Hsueh Pao. 1991;12(2):108-14.

Galbanum *(Ferula gummosa)*

Botanical Family: Apiaceae or Umbelliferae (parsley).

Plant Origin: Iran.

Extraction Method: Steam distilled from resin derived from stems and branches.

Key Constituents:

Alpha-Pinene [5–21%]
Beta-Phinene [40–70%]
Delta-3-Carene [2–16%]
Myrcene [2.5–3.5%]
Sabinene [0.3–3%]

Action: Galbanum is anti-infectious, a stimulant, supporting to the kidneys and menstruation, analgesic, and a light antispasmodic.

Traditional Uses: Mentioned in Egyptian papyri and the Old Testament (Exodus 30:34), galbanum was esteemed for its medicinal and spiritual properties. Dioscorides, an ancient Roman historian, records that galbanum was used for its antispasmodic, diuretic, and pain-relieving properties.

Indications: Abscesses, boils, wounds, inflammation.

Other Uses: Galbanum may also help with acne, asthma, bronchitis, chronic coughs, cramps, cuts, indigestion, muscular aches and pains, nervous tension, poor circulation, rheumatism, scar tissue, stress, and wrinkles.

Application: Apply topically. May be added to food or rice milk as a dietary supplement.

Fragrant Influence: Harmonic and balancing. It may help increase spiritual awareness and meditation.

Safety Data: If pregnant or under a doctor's care, consult physician.

Companion Oils: All oils.

Bible Reference: Exodus 30:34—"And the Lord said unto Moses, Take unto thee sweet spices, stacte, and onycha, and galbanum; these]sweet spices with pure frankincense: of each shall there be a like weight:"

Geranium *(Pelargonium graveolens)*

Botanical Family: Geraniaceae.

Plant Origin: Egypt, India.

Extraction Method: Steam distilled from leaves.

Key Constituents:

Citronellol + Nerol [35–50%]
Citronnellyl Formate [9–15%]
Geraniol [5–10%)
6,9-Guaiadene [4–8%]
Isomenthone [4–8%]

Action: Antispasmodic, antitumoral, adrenal cortex stimulant, anti-inflammatory, astringent, hemostatic (stops bleeding) anti-infectious, antibacterial, antifungal, revitalizes skin tissue, and dilates bile ducts for liver detoxification. Geranium balances the sebum, which is the fatty secretion in the sebaceous glands of the skin that keep the skin supple. Helps cleanse oily skin and restores and enlivens pale skin.

Traditional Uses: Geranium has been used for centuries for skin care.

Indications: Skin conditions (dermatitis, eczema, psoriasis, vitiligo), herpes, shingles, bleeding, tumor growths, and hormone imbalances.

Other Uses: This oil may be used for acne, burns, circulatory problems (improves blood flow), depression, gingivitis, liver problems, sterility, digestion, insomnia, menstrual problems, neuralgia (severe pain along the nerve), regenerating tissue and nerves, pancreas imbalances, ringworm, sore throats, and wounds. Jean Valnet, MD, recommends it for liver disorders and hepatitis.

Application: Diffuse and apply topically. May be added to food or rice milk as a dietary supplement. Apply where you would use a deodorant.

Fragrant Influence: It may help to release negative memories. It may also help ease nervous tension and stress, balance the emotions, lift the spirit, and foster peace, well-being, and hope.

Safety Data: If pregnant or under a doctor's care, consult physician.

Companion Oils: All oils.

Selected Research: Lis-Balchin, M, et al. "Antimicrobial activity of Pelargonium essential oils added to a quiche filling as a model food system." *Lett Appl Microbiol*. 1998;27(4):207-10.

Lis-Balchin, M, et al. "Comparative antibacterial effects of novel Pelargonium essential oils and solvent extracts." *Lett Appl Microbiol*. 1998;27(3):135-41.

Fang, HJ, et al. "Studies on the chemical components and anti-tumour action of the volatile oils from Pelargonium graveoleus." *Yao Hsueh Hsueh Pao*. 1989;24(5):366-71.

Ginger *(Zingiber officinale)*

Botanical Family: Zingiberaceae (ginger).

Plant Origin: China.

Extraction Method: Steam distilled from root.

Key Constituents:

Zingiberene + Alpha-Selinene [25–40%]
Beta-Sesquiphellandrene + Delta-Cadinene [7–14%]
Beta-Phellandrene + 1,8 Cineol (Eucalyptol) + Limonene [8–15%]
AR Curcumene [5–11%]

Action: Ginger is a digestive tonic, sexual tonic, reduces pain, and is an expectorant.

Traditional Uses: Ginger is used to combat the effects of motion sickness and has been studied for its gentle, simulating effects. Women in the West African country of Senegal weave belts of ginger root to restore their mates' sexual potency.

Indications: Arthritis, rheumatism, indigestion, digestive disorders, and motion sickness.

Other Uses: Ginger may be used for alcoholism, loss of appetite, arthritis, chills, respiratory infections, congestion, coughs, digestive disorders, infectious diseases, muscular aches/pains, nausea, rheumatism, sinusitis, sore throats, and sprains.

Application: Diffuse or apply topically. May be added to food or rice milk as a dietary supplement or flavoring.

Fragrant Influence: Gentle, stimulating, endowing physical energy, and courage.

Safety Data: If pregnant or under a doctor's care, consult your physician. Repeated use can possibly result in contact sensitization. Avoid direct sunlight after use.

Companion Oils: All spice oils, all citrus oils, *Eucalyptus radiata,* frankincense, geranium, myrtle, rosemary CT cineol, and spearmint.

Goldenrod *(Solidago canadensis)*

Botanical Family: Asteraceae.

Plant Origin: Canada.

Extraction Method: Steam distilled.

Key Constituents:

Germacrene D [22–35%]
Alpha-Pinene [10–18%]
Myrcene [8–15%]
Sabinene [5–11%]
Limonene [6–12%]

Action: Goldenrod is a diuretic, is anti-inflammatory, hepatic, mucolytic, a stimulant, and a tonic.

Traditional Uses: The genus name, "solidago," comes from the Latin *solide*, which means "to make whole." During the Boston Tea Party, when the English tea was dumped into Boston Harbor, Colonists drank goldenrod tea instead. This gave it the nickname "Liberty Tea."

Indications: Arthritis, asthma, candida, colds, cough, and hypertension.

Other Uses: Goldenrod helps to thin mucus secretions and relieve congested mucus membranes. It promotes urination, cleans the kidneys, reduces inflammation and prevents infection.

Application: Diffuse or apply topically on location. May be added to food or rice milk as a dietary supplement. Has been used as a wash or compress for wounds, for headaches and rheumatism, and as a gargle for sore throat, laryngitis and thrush.

Grapefruit *(Citrus* x *paradisi)*

Botanical Family: Rutaceae (citrus).

Plant Origin: USA.

(Grapefruit is a hybrid between *Citrus maxima* and *Citrus sinensis*.)

Extraction Method: Cold pressed from rind.

Key Constituents:

Limonene [88–95%]
Myrcene [1–4%]

Action: Grapefruit is antiseptic, disinfecting, detoxifying, and diuretic. Like many cold-pressed citrus oils, it has unique fat-dissolving characteristics. It is exceptionally cleansing for oily skin. Psychologically, it is an antidepressant and is emotionally uplifting.

Indications: Acne, cellulite, digestion, and fluid retention.

Other Uses: Grapefruit oil may help with depression, drug withdrawal, eating disorders, fatigue, jet lag, liver disorders, migraine headaches, premenstrual tension, and stress. It may also have a cleansing effect on the kidneys, the lymphatic system, and the vascular system.

Application: Diffuse or apply topically. Add to food or rice milk as a dietary supplement or flavoring.

Fragrant Influence: Refreshing and uplifting.

Safety Data: If pregnant or under a doctor's care, consult physician. **NOTE:** Grapefruit can be mildly photosensitizing. Avoid direct exposure to sunlight/UV rays for 3 days after using this oil topically.

Companion Oils: Basil, bergamot, cedarwood, German chamomile, cypress, frankincense, geranium, juniper, lavender, peppermint, rosemary CT cineol, rosewood, and ylang ylang.

Helichrysum *(Helichrysum italicum)*

Botanical Family: Asteraceae or Compositae (daisy).

Plant Origin: Yugoslavia, Corsica.

Extraction Method: Steam distilled from blossoms.

Key Constituents:

Neryl Acetate [25–35%]
Gamma-Curcuneme [9–15%]
Limonene [8–13%]
Neryl Propionate [3–7%]
Beta-Caryophyllene [1–5%]
Linalol [1–4%]
Nerol [2–5%]

ORAC: 17,420.

Action: Anticoagulant, anesthetic, dissolves hematomas (blood clots), mucolytic, expectorant, antispasmodic, stimulates liver, reduces scar tissue and skin discoloration. It balances blood pressure, chelates chemicals and toxins.

Traditional Uses: Helichrysum has been studied by European researchers for regenerating tissue and nerves and improving circulation and skin conditions.

Indications: Hematoma (swelling or blood-filled tumor), bleeding, arteriosclerosis, atherosclerosis, hypertension, congestive heart failure, cardiac arrhythmias, thrombosis, embolisms, liver disorders, phlebitis, sciatica, sinus infection, and skin conditions (eczema, dermatitis, psoriasis).

Other Uses: This oil may help blood circulation, hearing loss, pain (acute), respiratory conditions, scar tissue, and varicose veins. It may regenerate tissue, detoxify and stimulate liver cell function.

Application: Diffuse. Apply topically around the outside of the ear, the temples, the forehead, the back of the neck, or on location.

Fragrant Influence: It is uplifting to the subconscious.

Safety Data: If pregnant or under a doctor's care, consult physician.

Hyssop *(Hyssopus officinalis)*

Botanical Family: Lamiaceae or Labiatae (mint).

Plant Origin: France, Hungary.

Extraction Method: Steam distilled from stems/leaves.

Key Constituents:

Beta-pinene [13.5–23%]
Sabinene [2–3%]
Pinocamphone [5.5–17.5%]
Iso-Pinochamphone [34.5–50%]
Germacrene D [2–3%]
Limonene [1–4%]

Action: Anticatarrhal, mucolytic, a decongestant, an expectorant, is cleansing, purifying, and helps to reduce fats in the tissue. Hyssop raises low blood pressure, regulates menstrual flow, and increases perspiration.

Traditional Uses: While there is some uncertainty that *Hyssopus officinalis* is the same species of plant as the hyssop referred to in the Bible, there is no question that *H. officinalis* has been used medicinally for almost a millennium for its antiseptic, disinfecting, and anti-infectious properties. It has also been used for opening the respiratory system.

Indications: Anxiety, arthritis, asthma, bruises, respiratory infections, coughs, cuts, dermatitis, indigestion, fatigue, nervous tension, parasites (it expells worms), rheumatism, sore throats, viral infections, and wounds.

Application: Diffuse and apply topically. May be added to food or water as a dietary supplement.

Fragrant Influence: Stimulates creativity and meditation.

Safety Data: If pregnant or under a doctor's care, consult your physician. **NOTE:** Do not use if epileptic.

Companion Oils: All citrus oils, clary sage, fennel, geranium, myrtle, and sage.

Bible References: (See additional Bible references in Appendix C).

Exodus 12:22— "And ye shall take a bunch of hyssop, and dip it in the blood that is in the bason, and strike the lintel and the two side posts with the blood that is in the bason; and none of you shall go out at the door of his house until the morning."

Leviticus 14:4—"Then shall the priest command to take for him that is to be cleansed two birds alive and clean, and cedar wood, and scarlet, and hyssop:"

Leviticus 14:6—"As for the living bird, he shall take it, and the cedar wood, and the scarlet, and the hyssop, and shall dip them and the living bird in the blood of the bird that was killed over the running water:"

Jasmine *(Jasminum officinale)*

Botanical Family: Oleaceae (olive).

Plant Origin: India.

Extraction Method: Absolute extraction from flower petals. Jasmine is actually an "essence" not an essential oil. The flowers must be picked at night to maximize fragrance.

Key Constituents:

Benzyl Acetate [18–28%]
Benzyl Benzoate [14–21%]
Linalol [3–8%]
Phytol [6–12%]
Isophytol [3–7%]
Squalene [3–7%]

Action: Jasmine is beneficial for the skin, is uplifting, an antidepressant, and is stimulating.

Traditional Uses: Jasmine has been nicknamed as the "queen of the night" and "moonlight of the grove." For centuries, women have treasured jasmine for its beautiful, seductive fragrance.

Indications: Dry, oily, irritated, or sensitive skin, anxiety, stress, and depression.

Other Uses: This oil may help with eczema (when caused by emotions), frigidity, labor pains, laryngitis, lethargy (abnormal drowsiness), menstrual pain and problems, and stress. It is ideal for skin care.

Application: Diffuse and apply topically.

Fragrant Influence: Uplifting and stimulating in times of hopelessness and nervous exhaustion. It helps to reduce anxiety, apathy, depression, dilemmas that deal with relationships, indifference, and listlessness. When worn as a cologne, it increases excitability.

Safety Data: If pregnant or under a doctor's care, consult physician.

Companion Oils: Bergamot, frankincense, geranium, helichrysum, lemongrass, mandarin, melissa, orange, palmarosa, rose, rosewood, sandalwood, and spearmint.

NOTE: One pound of jasmine oil requires about 1,000 pounds of jasmine petals or 3.6 million fresh unpacked blossoms. The blossoms must be collected before sunrise, or much of the fragrance will have evaporated. The quality of the blossoms may also be compromised if they are crushed. A single pound of pure jasmine oil may cost between $1,200 to $4,500. In contrast, synthetic jasmine oils can be obtained for $3.50 per pound, but they obviously do not possess the same therapeutic qualities as the pure jasmine essence. The properties mentioned above are based on pure jasmine essence, not synthetic oil.

Juniper *(Juniperus communis* and *J. osteosperma)*

Botanical Family: Cupressaceae (cypress).

Plant Origin: USA.

Extraction Method: Steam distilled from berries, branches, and twigs.

Key Constituents:

Alpha-Pinene [20–40%]
Sabinene [3–18%]
Myrcene [1–6%]
Camphor [10–18%]
Limonene [3–8%]
Bornyl Acetate [12–20%]
Terpinene-4-ol [3–8%]

ORAC: 2,517.

Action: Juniper is antiseptic, astringent, a digestive stimulant, is purifying, and detoxifying. Juniper increases circulation through the kidneys and promotes excretion of uric acid and toxins.

Traditional Uses: Bundles of juniper berries were hung over doorways to ward off witches during medieval times. It has been used for centuries as a diuretic. Until recently, French hospital wards burned sprigs of juniper and rosemary to protect against infection.

Indications: Acne, dermatitis, eczema, depression, fatigue, liver problems, sore muscles, rheumatism, ulcers, urinary infections, fluid retention, and wounds.

Other Uses: Juniper oil may work as a detoxifier and a cleanser, as well as being beneficial for the skin. It may possibly assist with nerve regeneration.

Application: Diffuse or apply topically. May be added to food or rice milk as a dietary supplement.

Fragrant Influence: Juniper evokes feelings of health, love, and peace and may help to elevate one's spiritual awareness.

Safety Data: If pregnant or under a doctor's care, consult physician.

Companion Oils: Bergamot, all citrus oils, cypress, geranium, lavender, *Melaleuca alternifolia,* and rosemary CT cineol.

Bible Reference:

Job 30:45—"Who cut up mallows by the bushes, and juniper roots for their meat."

Selected Research:

Takacsova M, et al. "Study of the antioxidative effects of thyme, sage, juniper and oregano." *Nahrung*. 1995;39(3):241-3.

Laurus nobilis *(Laurus nobilis—Bay Laurel)*

Botanical Family: Lauraceae.

Plant Origin: France.

Extraction Method: Steam distilled from leaves.

Key Constituents:

Alpha-Pinene [4–10%]
Beta-Pinene [3–8%]
Sabinene [4–12%]
Linalol [4–16%]
1,8 Cineol (Eucalyptol) [35–50%]
Eugenol + Terpenyl Acetate [10–18%]

Action: *Laurus nobilis* is antiseptic, antimicrobial, an expectorant, mucolytic, anti-infectious, antibacterial (staph, strep, *E. coli*), and an anticoagulant.

Traditional Uses: Both the leaves and the black berries were also used to alleviate indigestion, and loss of appetite. During the Middle Ages, it was used for angina pectoris, asthma, gout, migraine, palpitations, and liver and spleen complaints.

Indications: Nerve damage, arthritis (rheumatoid), and oral infections.

Other Uses: Bay laurel may help with loss of appetite, asthmatic conditions, chronic bronchitis, hair loss (after an infection), lice, scabies, and viral infections.

Application: Diffuse or apply topically on the abdomen or on location.

Fragrant Influence: Bay laurel has been used as a fragrance component in cosmetics and perfumes.

Safety Data: If pregnant or under a doctor's care, consult your physician. Use in moderation.

Lavandin *(Lavandula* x *hybrida)*

Botanical Family: Lamiaceae or Labiatae (mint).

Extraction Method: Steam distilled from plant.

Key Constituents:

Linalyl Acetate [28–35%]
Linalol [30–38%]
Camphor [5–12%]
Limonene + 1,8 Cineol (Eucalyptol) [2–8%]
Borneol [2–6%]
Terpinene-4-ol [2–7%]
Lavandulyl Acetate [1–5%]

Action: Lavandin is antibacterial, antifungal, and a strong antiseptic. (See lavender for related properties.)

Traditional Uses: As suggested by its botanical name, *Lavandula* x *hybrida*, lavandin is a hybrid plant developed by crossing true lavender with spike lavender or aspic (*Lavandula latifolia*). It has been used to sterilize the animal cages in veterinary clinics and hospitals throughout Europe.

Indications: (There is not a long history of the therapeutic use of lavandin.)

Other Uses: Lavandin is best used as an antiseptic. Its greater penetrating qualities make it well suited to help with respiratory, circulatory, and muscular conditions.

Application: Diffuse or apply topically.

Fragrant Influence: It has the similar calming effects as lavender but is slightly harsher.

Safety Data: If pregnant or under a doctor's care, consult your physician. **NOTE:** Do not use for burns.

Companion Oils: Bergamot, cinnamon, citronella, clove, cypress, clary sage, geranium, lime, patchouli, pine, rosemary CT cineol, and thyme.

Lavender *(Lavandula angustifolia)*

Botanical Family: Lamiaceae or Labiatae (mint).

Plant Origin: USA, France.

Extraction Method: Steam distilled from flowering top.

Key Constituents:

Linalyl Acetate [24–45%]
Linalol [25–38%]
Cis-Beta-Ocimene [4–10%]
Trans-Beta-Ocimene [1.5–6%]
Terpinene-4-ol [2–6%]

ORAC: 3,669.

Action: Lavender is antiseptic, analgesic, antitumoral, anticonvulsant, anti-inflammatory, and a sedative. Lavender is beneficial for healing burns and cleansing cuts and wounds. It is ideal for skin care, since it prevents the build up of excess sebum, a skin oil that bacteria feed on. Lavender has also been clinically evaluated for its relaxing effects.

Traditional Uses: The French scientist René Gattefossé was the first to discover lavender's ability to promote tissue regeneration and speed wound healing when he was in a laboratory explosion where his arm was burned severely, developing gaseous gangrene. Today, lavender is one of the few essential oils still listed in the British Pharmacopoeia.

Indications: Burns (cell renewal), sunburns (including lips), dandruff, hair loss, allergies, convulsions, herpes, headaches, indigestion, insomnia, high blood pressure, menopausal conditions, nausea, phlebitis, tumors, premenstrual conditions, scarring (minimizes), skin conditions (acne, dermatitis, eczema, psoriasis, and rashes) and stretch marks. It may be used to cleanse cuts, bruises, and skin irritations.

Other Uses: Lavender is a universal oil with many different applications. It may also help arthritis, asthma, bronchitis, convulsions, depression, earaches, heart palpitations, high blood pressure, hives (urticaria), insect bites, laryngitis, nervous tension, respiratory infections, rheumatism, and throat infections.

Application: Diffuse or apply topically. Lavender has a wide range of uses. Safe for use on small children. May also be added to food or rice milk as a dietary supplement.

Fragrant Influence: Lavender is calming, relaxing, and balancing, both physically and emotionally.

Safety Data: If pregnant or under a doctor's care, consult physician.

Companion Oils: Most oils, especially citrus oils, chamomile, clary sage, and geranium.

Selected Research:

Larrondo JV, et al. "Antimicrobial activity of essences from labiates." *Microbios*. 1995; 82(332):171-2.

Guillemain J, et al. "Neurodepressive effects of the essential oil of *Lavandula angustifolia* Mill." *Ann Pharm Fr*. 1989;47(6):337-43.

Kim HM, et al. "Lavender oil inhibits immediate-type allergic reaction in mice and rats." *J Pharm Pharmacol*. 1999;51(2):221-6.

Ledum *(Ledum groenlandicum)*

Botanical Family: Ericaceae.

Plant Origin: North America.

Extraction Method: Steam distilled.

Key Constituents:

Limonene [20–35%]
Cis- and Trans-Paramenth1(7) 8 Diene 8-ol [12–17%]
Cis- and Trans-Paramenthatriene 1,3,8 [8–15%]

Action: Ledum is known to be anti-inflammatory, antitumoral, antibacterial, hepatoprotectant, a diuretic, and a decongestant.

Traditional Uses: Known colloquially as "Labrador tea," ledum is a strongly aromatic herb that has been used for centuries in folk medicine. The native people of Eastern Canada used this herb for tea, as a general tonic, and to treat a variety of kidney-related problems. Ledum has helped protect the native people of North America against scurvy for more than 5,000 years. The Cree Indians used it for fevers and colds.

Indications: Liver dysfunctions, hepatitis, cirrhosis, fatty liver, obesity, laryngitis, bronchitis, allergies, influenza, edema, and thyroid regulation.

Other Uses: Ledum can be used for all types of skin problems, for coughs, hoarseness, stomach discomfort, prostate infection, congested prostate, insomnia, and allergies.

Application: Diffuse or apply topically diluted 1 drop to 1 teaspoon of vegetable oil/carrier oil. As a dietary supplement dilute 1 drop of essential oil in 4 fluid ounces of rice milk.

Fragrant Influence: A strong aromatic.

Safety Data: If using topically, always dilute (one drop essential oil in one teaspoon vegetable oil).

Companion Oils: Frankincense, goldenrod, wintergreen or birch, lemon, and sage.

Lemon *(Citrus limon)*

Botanical Family: Rutaceae (citrus).

Plant Origin: USA, Italy.

Extraction Method: Cold pressed from rind. It takes 3,000 lemons to produce a kilo of oil.

Essential Oils and Learning

A university in Japan experimented with diffusing different oils in the office. When they diffused lemon, there were 54 percent fewer errors, with jasmine there were 33 percent fewer errors, and with lavender there were 20 percent fewer errors. When oils were diffused while studying and taking a test, test scores increased by as much as 50 percent.

Diffusing an essential oil while studying may also improve memory while taking a test. By inhaling the same aroma, the smell of the oil may encourage recall of facts or figures learned previously by bringing back the memory of what was studied.

Key Constituents:

Limonene [59–73%]
Gamma-Terpinene [6–12%]
Beta-Pinene [7–16%]
Alpha-Pinene [1.5–3%]
Sabinene [1.5–3%]

Action: Lemon is anti-infectious, antibacterial (spores), antiseptic, antiviral, and a disinfectant. Lemon improves microcirculation, promotes white blood cell formation, and improves immune function.

Traditional Uses: Lemon has antiseptic-like properties and contains compounds that have been studied for their effects on immune function. According Jean Valnet, MD,[5] the vaporized essence of lemon can kill meningococcus bacteria in 15 minutes, typhoid bacilli in one hour, *Staphylococcus aureus* in two hours, and *Pneumococcus* bacteria within three hours. Even a 0.2% solution of lemon oil can kill diphtheria bacteria in 20 minutes and inactivate tuberculosis bacteria. Lemon oil has been widely used in skin care to cleanse skin and reduce wrinkles.

Indications: Anemia, asthma, herpes, warts, shingles, bleeding, malaria, parasites, rheumatism, throat infection, ureter infections, and varicose veins.

Other Uses: Lemon oil may be beneficial for anxiety, blood pressure, digestive problems, respiratory infections, and sore throats. It helps promote leukocyte formation, improves memory, strengthens nails, cleans the skin, and promotes a sense of well-being. Lemon has shown to

5. Jean Valnet, MD, *The Practice of Aromatherapy: A Classic Compendium of Plant Essences & Their Healing Properties,* Healing Arts Press, Vermont, 1990, page 154.

have antidepressant effects in research done by Komori, et al., 1995. It serves as an effective insect repellent and works well in removing gum, wood stain, oil, and grease spots.

Application: Diffuse or add a few drops of lemon oil to 1 cup of pure water in a spray bottle to deodorize and sterilize the air. Add 5 drops of lemon oil and 2 drops of peppermint oil (*Mentha piperita*) to 1 cup of pure water, shake and spray for purification and for a refreshing, lifting aerosol. Add to food or rice milk as a dietary supplement or flavoring.

Fragrant Influence: It promotes clarity of thought and purpose, as well as health, healing, physical energy, and purification. Its fragrance is invigorating, enhancing, and warming.

Safety Data: If pregnant or under a doctor's care, consult your physician. **NOTE**: Lemon oil is photosensitizing, so avoid exposure to direct sunlight/UV rays for 3 days after applying topically.

Companion Oils: German chamomile, *Eucalyptus radiata,* fennel, frankincense, geranium, juniper, peppermint, sandalwood, and ylang ylang.

Lemongrass *(Cymbopogon flexuosus)*

Botanical Family: Poaceae or Gramineae (grass).

Plant Origin: India, Guatemala.

Extraction Method: Steam distilled from leaves.

Key Constituents:

Geranial [35–45%]
Geraniol [5–10%]
Neral [25–40%]
Trans-Beta-Caryophyllene [2–6%]

ORAC: 17,765.

Action: Lemongrass supports digestion, tones and helps regenerate connective tissues and ligaments, dilates blood vessels, strengthens vascular walls, promotes lymph flow, and is anti-inflammatory and sedative.

Traditional Uses: Lemongrass is used for purification and digestion. Research was published in *Phytotherapy Research* on topically applied lemongrass for its powerful antifungal properties.

Indications: Bladder infection, digestive disturbances, parasites, torn ligaments, edema, fluid retention, kidney disorders, and varicose veins.

Other Uses: Lemongrass oil may help improve circulation, digestion, and eyesight, as well as combat headaches, infections, respiratory problems, sore throats, and fluid retention. It aids in tissue regeneration.

Application: Diffuse or apply topically. Add to food or rice milk as a dietary supplement.

Fragrant Influence: Lemongrass promotes psychic awareness and purification.

Safety Data: If pregnant or under a doctor's care, consult your physician. Skin test for sensitivity/irritation.

Companion Oils: Basil, cedarwood, *Eucalyptus radiata,* geranium, lavender, *Melaleuca alternifolia*, and rosemary CT cineol.

Selected Research:

Pattnaik S, et al. "Antibacterial and antifungal activity of ten essential oils in vitro." *Microbios*. 1996;86(349):237-46.

Lorenzetti BB, et al. "Myrcene mimics the peripheral analgesic activity of lemongrass tea." *J Ethnopharmacol*. 1991;34(1):43-8.

Elson CE, et al. "Impact of lemongrass oil, an essential oil, on serum cholesterol." *Lipids*. 1989;24(8):677-9.

Mandarin *(Citrus reticulata)*

Botanical Family: Rutaceae (citrus).

Plant Origin: Madagascar, Italy, China.

Extraction Method: Cold pressed from rind.

Key Constituents:

Limonene [65–75%]
Gamma-Terpinene [16–22%]
Alpha-Pinene [2–3%]
Beta-Pinene [1.2–2%]
Myrcene [1.5–2%]

Action: Mandarin is a light antispasmodic, a digestive tonic (digestoid), is antiseptic, antifungal, and stimulates the gallbladder.

Traditional Uses: This fruit was traditionally given to Imperial Chinese officials named the Mandarins.

Other Uses: This oil may help acne, digestive problems, fluid retention, insomnia, intestinal problems, skin problems (congested and oily skin, scars, spots), tones the skin, diminishes stretch marks (when combined with either jasmine, lavender, sandalwood, and/or frankincense), calms nervous tension, and restlessness. Recommended for children and pregnant women because it is very gentle.

Application: Diffuse or apply topically.

Fragrant Influence: It is appeasing, gentle, and promotes happiness.

Safety Data: If pregnant or under a doctor's care, consult your physician. **NOTE:** Photo-sensitizing. Avoid direct sunlight for 3 days after use.

Companion Oils: Cinnamon, clove, lavender, neroli, nutmeg, citrus oils (lemon, orange, etc.) and spice oils.

Marjoram *(Origanum majorana)*

Botanical Family: Lamiaceae or Labiatae (mint).

Plant Origin: France.

Extraction Method: Steam distilled from leaves.

Key Constituents:

Terpinene-4-ol [25–35%]
Gamma-Terpinene [12–20%)
Linalol + Cis-4-Thujanol [3–8%]
Alpha-Terpinene [6–13%]
Sabinene [2–6%]

Action: Marjoram is anti-infectious, antibacterial, dilates blood vessels, regulates blood pressure, soothes muscles, promotes intestinal peristalsis, tones the parasympathetic nervous system, and supports the respiratory system.

Traditional Uses: Marjoram was known as the "herb of happiness" to the Romans and "joy of the mountains" to the Greeks. It was believed to increase longevity.

Indications: Aches, arthritis, asthma, bronchitis, indigestion, constipation, cramps, insomnia, migraine headaches, neuralgia, rheumatism, and sprains.

Other Uses: Marjoram may be relaxing and calming to the muscles that constrict and sometimes contribute to headaches. It may help anxiety, nervous tension, bruises, burns, sores, cuts, circulatory disorders, respiratory infections, fungal and viral infections, menstrual problems, ringworm, shingles, shock, sores, spasms, sunburns, and fluid retention.

Application: Diffuse or apply topically. Massage to calm stressed muscles. Add to food or rice milk as a dietary supplement or flavoring.

Fragrant Influence: Marjoram assists in calming the nerves.

Safety Data: If pregnant or under a doctor's care, consult physician.

Companion Oils: Bergamot, cedarwood, German chamomile, cypress, lavender, nutmeg, orange, rosemary CT cineol, rosewood, and ylang ylang.

Melaleuca alternifolia *(Melaleuca alternifolia)*

Botanical Family: Myrtaceae (myrtle).

Plant Origin: Australia.

Extraction Method: Steam distilled from leaves.

Key Constituents:

Gamma-Terpinene [10–28%]
Alpha-Terpinene [5–13%]
1,8 Cineol (Eucalyptol) [0–15%]
Alpha-Terpineol [1.5–8%]
Para-Cymene [0.5–12%]
Terpinenol-4 [30–45%]
Limonene [0.5–4%]
Aromadendrene [trace–7%]
Alpha-Pinene [1–6%]

Action: *Melaleuca alternifolia* (also called tea tree oil) is anti-infectious, antibacterial (large spectrum action of gram positive and gram negative bacteria), antifungal, antiviral, antiparasitic, antiseptic, anti-inflammatory, an immunostimulant, is cardiotonic, a decongestant of the veins, reduces phlebitis, is neurotonic, analgesic, and protects against radiation.

Traditional Uses: Highly regarded as an antimicrobial and antiseptic essential oil. It has high levels of terpinenol, which is the key active constituent.

Indications: Athlete's foot, fungal infections, bronchitis, respiratory infections, gum disease, rash, sore throat, sunburn, tonsilitis, and vaginal thrush.

Other Uses: This oil may help acne, burns, candida, cold sores, inflammation, viral infections, ingrown nails, warts, and wounds (promotes healing).

Application: Diffuse or apply topically. Safe for use on children and pets.

Fragrant Influence: *Melaleuca alternifolia* promotes cleansing and purity.

Safety Data: If pregnant or under a doctor's care, consult your physician. Repeated use can possibly result in contact sensitization.

Companion Oils: All citrus oils, cypress, *Eucalyptus radiata,* lavender, rosemary CT cineol, and thyme.

Selected Research: Syed TA, et al. "Treatment of toenail onychomycosis with 2% butenafine and 5% *Melaleuca alternifolia* (tea tree) oil in cream." *Trop Med Int Health*. 1999;4(4):284-7.

Hammer KA, et al. "In vitro susceptibilities of lactobacilli and organisms associated with bacterial vaginosis to *Melaleuca alternifolia* (tea tree) oil." Antimicrob Agents Chemother. 1999;43(1):196.

Concha JM, et al. 1998 William J. Stickel Bronze Award. "Antifungal activity of *Melaleuca alternifolia* (tea-tree) oil against various pathogenic organisms." *J Am Podiatr Med Assoc*. 1998;88(10):489-92.

Melaleuca ericifolia *(Melaleuca ericifolia)*

Botanical Family: Myrtaceae (myrtle).

Plant Origin: Australia.

Key Constituents:

Alpha-Pinene [5–10%]
1,8 Cineol + Beta-Phellandrene [18–28%]
Alpha-Terpineol [1–5%]
Para-Cymene [1–6%]
Linalol [34–45%]
Aromadendrene [2–6%]

Application: Diffuse or apply topically on the temples, wrists, throat, face, chest or on location. Dilute 4–8 drops in 30 ml. of a vegetable or massage oil for body massage.

Safety Data: If pregnant or under a doctor's care, consult physician.

Note: This oil is still under study. It is somewhat gentler than *Melaleuca alternifolia* and has been found beneficial for bronchitis, asthma, respiratory infection, cynitis, and sinus infection.

Melaleuca quinquenervia (Naouli) *(Melaleuca quinquenervia)*

Botanical Family: Myrtaceae (myrtle).

Plant Origin: Australia.

Extraction Method: Steam distilled from leaves and branches.

Key Constituents:

Limonene + 1,8 Cineol (Eucalyptol) [55–70%]
Alpha-Pinene [7–15%]
Beta-Pinene [2–6%]
Viridiflorol [2–6%]

Action: *Melaleuca quinquenervia* is male hormone-like, anti-inflammatory, anti-infectious, antibacterial, antiviral, and antiparasitic (kills amoeba and parasites in the blood).

Indications: Mucous in respiratory passages, the urinary tract, and genital organs and high blood pressure.

Other Uses: This oil may help with respiratory allergies, infections, and hemorrhoids.

Application: Diffuse or apply topically.

Fragrant Influence: *Melaleuca quinquenervia* is sweet and delicate.

Safety Data: If pregnant or under a doctor's care, consult your physician. Repeated use can possibly result in contact sensitization.

Melissa *(Melissa officinalis)*

Botanical Family: Lamiaceae or Labiatae (mint). Sometimes referred to as "lemon balm."

Plant Origin: USA, France.

Extraction Method: Steam distilled from leaves and flowers.

Key Constituents:

Geranial [25–35%]
Neral [18–28%]
Beta-Caryophyllene [12–19%]

Action: Melissa is calming, sedative, hypotensive (lowers blood pressure), fights against cholera, and is anti-inflammatory.

Traditional Uses: Melissa has powerful antimicrobial constituents. Anciently, melissa was used for nervous disorders and many different ailments dealing with the heart or the emotions. It was also used to promote fertility. Melissa was the main ingredient in Carmelite water, distilled in France since 1611 by the Carmelite monks.

Indications: Allergies, anxiety, asthma, bronchitis, chronic coughs, respiratory infections, cold-sore blisters, indigestion, depression, dysentery, eczema, fevers, hypertension, indigestion, insect bites, insomnia, menstrual problems, migraine, nausea, nervous tension, palpitations, throat infections, and vertigo.

Other Uses: Researchers in Germany reported that the application of a dried extract from *Melissa officinalis* resulted in remission of herpes simplex lesions and a prolongation of the interval to the next episode.[6]

Application: Diffuse or apply topically.

Fragrant Influence: Melissa brings out gentle characteristics within people. It is calming and uplifting and may help to balance the emotions. It may also help to remove emotional blocks and instill a positive outlook on life.

Safety Data: If pregnant or under a doctor's care, consult physician.

Companion Oils: Geranium, lavender, and other floral and citrus oils.

Selected Research: Yamasaki K, et al. "Anti-HIV-1 activity of herbs in Labiatae." *Biol Pharm Bull*. 1998;21(8):829-33.

Larrondo JV, et al. "Antimicrobial activity of essences from labiates." *Microbios*. 1995;82 (332):171-2.

Kucera LS, et al. "Antiviral activities of extracts of the lemon balm plant." *Ann NY Acad Sci*. 1965 Jul 30;130(1):474-82.

6. Koytchev, R, Balm mint extract (Lo-701) for topical treatment of recurring herpes libialis, *Phytomedicine,* 1999 Oct;6(4):225-30.

Mountain Savory *(Satureja montana)*

Botanical Family: Lamiaceae or Labiatae.

Plant Origin: France.

Extraction Method: Steam distilled from flowering plant.

Key Constituents:

Carvacrol [22–35%]
Thymol [14–24%]
Gamma-Terpinene [8–15%]
Carvacrol Methyl Ether [4–9%]
Beta-Caryophyllene [3–7%]

ORAC: 113,071.

Action: Mountain savory is strongly anti-infectious, antibacterial, antifungal, antiviral, antiparasitic, an immunostimulant, general tonic and stimulant.

Traditional Uses: Mountain savory has been used historically as a general tonic for the body.

Indications: Acute pain, sluggish nervous and circulatory systems.

Other Uses: Due to its high phenol content, mountain savory is a very strong antiseptic and has been used to hasten the formation of scabs, and to help with abscesses, burns, and cuts. It is also known to stimulate the adrenal gland. Recent research by Yamasaki suggests that the extract may have anti-HIV activity. (See reference below.)

Application: Diffuse or apply topically mixed with a vegetable or massage oil.

Fragrant Influence: It may produce strong psychological effects and may help revitalize and stimulate the nervous system. It is a powerful energizer and motivator.

Safety Data: If pregnant or under a doctor's care, consult your physician. Dilution is recommended when using topically. Always skin test for sensitivity.

Selected Research: Yamasaki K, et al. "Anti-HIV-1 activity of herbs in Labiatae." *Biol Pharm Bull*. 1998; 21(8):829-33.

Panizzi L, et al. "Composition and antimicrobial properties of essential oils of four Mediterranean Lamiaceae." *J Ethnopharmacol*. 1993;39(3):167-70.

Myrrh *(Commiphora myrrha)*

Botanical Family: Burseraceae (Frankincense).

Plant Origin: Somalia.

Extraction Method: Steam distilled from gum/resin.

Key Constituents:

Lindestrene [30–45%]
Curzerene [17–25%]
Furanoendesma-1,3-diene [4–8%]
Methoxyfuronogermacrene [5–9%]
Beta- and Gamma-Elemenes [3–6%]

Action: Myrrh is anti-infectious, antiviral, antiparasitic, hormone-like, anti-inflammatory, soothes skin conditions, is antihyperthyroid, and supports immune system.

Traditional Uses: The Arabian people used myrrh for many skin conditions such as chapped and cracked skin and wrinkles. It has one of the highest levels of sesquiterpenes, a class of compounds that has direct effects on the hypothalamus, pituitary, and amygdala, the seat of our emotions. Myrrh is widely used today in oral hygiene products.

Indications: Bronchitis, diarrhea, dysentery, hyperthyroidism, stretch marks, thrush, ulcers, vaginal thrush, and viral hepatitis.

Other Uses: This oil may also help asthma, athlete's foot, candida, coughs, eczema, digestion, fungal infection, gingivitis, gum infections, hemorrhoids, mouth ulcers, ringworm, sore throats, wounds, and wrinkles.

Application: Apply topically on location or in a massage. May be added to food or rice milk as a dietary supplement.

Fragrant Influence: Myrrh promotes spiritual awareness and is uplifting.

Safety Data: If pregnant or under a doctor's care, consult physician.

Companion Oils: Frankincense, lavender, patchouli, sandalwood, and all spice oils.

Bible References: (See additional Bible references in Appendix C.)

Genesis 37:25—"And they sat down to eat bread: and they lifted up their eyes and looked, and, behold, a company of Ishmeelites came from Gilead with their camels bearing spicery and balm and myrrh, going to carry it down to Egypt."

Genesis 43:11—"And their father Israel said unto them, If it must be so now, do this; take of the best fruits in the land in your vessels, and carry down the man a present, a little balm, and a little honey, spices, and myrrh, nuts, and almonds:"

Exodus 30:23—"Take thou also unto thee principal spices, of pure myrrh five hundred shekels, and of sweet cinnamon half so much, even two hundred and fifty shekels, and of sweet calamus two hundred and fifty shekels,"

Selected Research: Al-Awadi FM, et al. "Studies on the activity of individual plants of an antidiabetic plant mixture." *Acta Diabetol Lat.* 1987;24(1):37-41.

Dolara P, et al. "Analgesic effects of myrrh." *Nature*. 1996 Jan 4;379(6560):29.

Michie CA, et al. "Frankincense and myrrh as remedies in children." *J R Soc Med*. 1991;84(10):602-5.

Myrtle *(Myrtus communis)*

Botanical Family: Myrtaceae (myrtle).

Plant Origin: Tunisia, Morocco.

Extraction Method: Steam distilled from leaves.

Key Constituents:

Alpha-Pinene [45–60%]
1,8 Cineol (Eucalyptol) [17–27%]
Limonene [5–11%]
Linalol [2–5%]

Action: Myrtle is an expectorant, is anti-infectious, a liver stimulant, prostate decongestant, a light antispasmodic, a regulator for the thyroid and ovary, and a tonic for the skin.

Traditional Uses: Myrtle has been researched by Dr. Daniel Pénoël for normalizing hormonal imbalances of the thyroid and ovaries. It has also been researched for its soothing effects on the respiratory system.

Indications: Bronchitis, coughs, hypothyroidism, insomnia, sluggish thyroid, prostate congestion, respiratory tract ailments, sinus infection, tuberculosis, and ureter infections.

Other Uses: This oil may help anger, asthma, respiratory infections, cystitis, diarrhea, dysentery, impaired digestion, hemorrhoids, and hormonal imbalances. It may support the immune system, fight infections, sinusitis, infectious diseases, and pulmonary disorders, aid skin conditions (acne, blemishes, bruises, oily skin, psoriasis, etc.). Useful on children for chest complaints and coughs.

Application: Apply topically, diffuse, or use in a humidifier. Suitable for use on children.

Fragrant Influence: Elevating and euphoric.

Safety Data: If pregnant or under a doctor's care, consult physician.

Companion Oils: Bergamot, lavender, lemon, lemongrass, *Melaleuca alternifolia*, rosewood, rosemary CT cineol, spearmint, and thyme.

Bible Reference: (See additional Bible references in Appendix C.)

Nehemiah 8:15—"And that they should publish and proclaim in all their cities, and in Jerusalem, saying, Go forth unto the mount, and fetch olive branches, and pine branches, and myrtle branches, and palm branches, and branches of thick trees, to make booths, as it is written."

Isaiah 41:19—"I will plant in the wilderness the cedar, the shittah tree, and the myrtle, and the oil tree; I will set in the desert the fir tree, and the pine, and the box tree together:"

Isaiah 55:13—"Instead of the thorn shall come up the fir tree, and instead of the brier shall come up the myrtle tree: and it shall be to the Lord for a name, for an everlasting sign that shall not be cut off."

Neroli *(Citrus aurantium)*

Botanical Family: Rutaceae (citrus).

Plant Origin: Morocco, Tunisia.

Extraction Method: Absolute extraction from flowers of the orange tree.

Key Constituents:

Linalol [28–44%]
Limonene [9–18%]
Beta-Pinene [7–17%]
Linalyl Acetate [3–15%]
Trans-Ocimene [3–8%]

Alpha-Terpineol [2–5.5%]
Trans-Nerolidol [1–5%]
Myrcene [1–4%]

Action: Neroli is anti-infectious, antibacterial, antiparasitic, a digestive tonic, antidepressive, and hypotensive (lowers blood pressure).

Traditional Uses: Loved by the Egyptian people for its great attributes for healing the mind, body, and spirit.

Indications: Anxiety, depression, digestive spasms, fear, headaches, heart arrhythmia, hysteria, insomnia, nervous tension, palpitations, PMS, poor circulation, scars, shock, stress-related conditions, stretch marks, tachycardia, thread veins, and wrinkles.

Other Uses: Neroli may support the digestive system and fight bacteria, infections, parasites, and viruses. In support of the skin, neroli works at the cellular level to help shed the old skin cells and stimulate new cell growth. It is particularly beneficial for mature and sensitive skin.

Application: Diffuse or apply topically.

Fragrant Influence: As a natural tranquilizer, neroli has powerful psychological effects. It has been used successfully to treat depression, anxiety, and shock. It is calming and relaxing to body and spirit. It may also help to strengthen and stabilize the emotions and bring relief in seemingly hopeless situations. Neroli encourages confidence, courage, joy, peace, and sensuality.

Safety Data: If pregnant or under a doctor's care, consult physician.

Companion Oils: Cedarwood, geranium, jasmine, lavender, lemon, rose, and sandalwood.

Nutmeg *(Myristica fragrans)*

Botanical Family: Myristicaceae.

Plant Origin: Tunisia, Indonesia.

Extraction Method: Steam distilled from fruits and seeds.

Key Constituents:

Sabinene [14–29%]
Beta-Pinene [13–18%]
Alpha-Pinene [15–28%]

Limonene [2–7%]
Gamma-Terpinene [2–6%]
Terpinene-4-ol [2–6%]
Myristicine [5–12%]

Action: Nutmeg is antiseptic, antiparasitic, reduces pain, promotes normal menstruation, and improves circulation.

Traditional Uses: Nutmeg has been used historically to benefit circulation to muscles and joints, and relieve muscle pain. It also helps to support the nervous system, overcome fatigue, and support immune and nervous systems.

Indications: Appetite (loss of), chronic debility, digestion (helps with starchy foods and fats), gallstones, halitosis, and rheumatism.

Other Uses: This oil has adrenal cortex-like activity, which helps support the adrenal glands for increased energy. It may also help treat arthritis, bacterial infection, frigidity, gout, impotence, menstrual problems, nausea, severe nerve pain.

Application: Apply topically diluted with a vegetable or massage oil. Add to food or rice milk as a dietary supplement or flavoring.

Safety Data: If pregnant or under a doctor's care, consult your physician. **NOTE:** Do not use if epileptic. Dilute with massage oil or only apply a single undiluted drop at a time when applied topically.

Companion Oils: Cinnamon bark, clove, cypress, frankincense, lemon, *Melaleuca alternifolia,* melissa, orange, patchouli, and rosemary CT cineol.

Orange *(Citrus aurantium)*

Botanical Family: Rutaceae (citrus).

Plant Origin: USA, South Africa, Italy, China.

Extraction Method: Cold pressed from rind.

Key Constituents:

Limonene [85–90%]
Myrceme [0.5–3%]

ORAC: 18,898.

Action: Orange is calming, sedative, anti-inflammatory, antitumoral, anti-coagulant, and improves circulation.

Traditional Uses: Used historically for palpitation, scurvy, jaundice, bleeding, heartburn, and diarrhea.

Indications: Angina (false), cardiac spasm, insomnia, menopause, and tumor growth.

Other Uses: Orange oil may help appetite, bone density, bronchitis, respiratory infections, indigestion (dilute for infants; it helps them sleep), complexion (dull and oily), dermatitis, digestive system. Orange lowers high cholesterol, helps mouth ulcers, muscle soreness, tissue repair, fluid retention, and wrinkles.

Application: Diffuse, apply topically on location, or add to food or rice milk as a dietary supplement flavoring.

Fragrant Influence: Uplifting, works as an antidepressant.

Safety Data: If pregnant or under a doctor's care, consult your physician. **NOTE:** Photosensitive: Citrus oils should NOT be applied to skin that will be exposed to direct sunlight or UV light within 3 days.

Companion Oils: Cinnamon bark, clove, cypress, frankincense, geranium, juniper, lavender, nutmeg, and rosewood.

Selected Research:

Reddy BS, et al. "Chemoprevention of colon carcinogenesis by dietary perillyl alcohol." *Cancer Res.* 1997;57(3):420-5.

Oregano *(Origanum compactum)*

Botanical Family: Lamiaceae or Labiatae (mint).

Plant Origin: USA, Turkey, France.

Extraction Method: Steam distilled from leaves and flowers.

Key Constituents:

Carvacrol [60–75%]
Gamma-Terpinene [3.5–8.5%]
Para-Cymene [5.5–9%]
Beta-Caryophyllene [2–5%]
Myrcene [1–3%]
Thymol [0–5%]

ORAC: 153,007.

Action: Oregano is a powerful anti-infectious agent (for respiratory, intestines, genital, nerves, blood, and lymphatics) with large-spectrum action against bacteria, mycobacteria, fungi, viruses, and parasites. It is a general tonic and immune stimulant.

Indications: Asthma, bronchitis (chronic), mental disease, pulmonary tuberculosis, rheumatism (chronic), and whooping cough.

Other Uses: This oil may help respiratory infections, digestion problems, viral and bacterial pneumonia, respiratory system problems, balance metabolism, and strengthen the vital centers.

Application: Apply neat to bottom of feet. Dilute with a vegetable or massage oil if applying elsewhere on the skin. May be used undiluted in Raindrop Technique (see Chapter 11). Add to food or rice milk as a dietary supplement or flavoring.

Fragrant Influence: Creates a feeling of security.

Safety Data: Caution: High phenol can burn the skin. Dilute to 1 drop essential oil to 50 drops vegetable or massage oil for topical application other than the bottom of the feet. Use extra caution to avoid contact with all mucous membranes. If pregnant or under a doctor's care, consult your physician. Skin test for sensitivity.

Companion Oils: Basil, fennel, geranium, lemongrass, myrtle, pine, rosemary CT cineol, and thyme.

Palmarosa *(Cymbopogon martinii)*

Botanical Family: Poaceae or Gramineae (grass).

Plant Origin: India, Conoros.

Extraction Method: Steam distilled from leaves.

Key Constituents:

Geraniol [70–85%]
Geranyl Acetate [6–10%]
Linalol [3–7%]

Action: Palmarosa is antimicrobial, antibacterial, antifungal, antiviral, a uterine tonic, and cardiotonic.

Traditional Uses: Helps with skin problems. A relative of lemongrass, palmarosa is antimicrobial and supportive to the nerves and circulation.

Indications: This oil may be beneficial for rashes, candida, the cardiovascular system, the digestive and nervous systems, and in fighting infections. It is valuable for all types of skin problems because it stimulates new cell growth, regulates oil production, moisturizes, and speeds healing.

Application: Apply topically.

Fragrant Influence: Creates a feeling of security. It also helps to reduce stress and tension and promotes recovery from nervous exhaustion.

Safety Data: If pregnant or under a doctor's care, consult physician.

Companion Oils: Basil, fennel, geranium, lemongrass, myrtle, pine, rosemary CT cineol, and thyme.

Patchouli *(Pogostemon cablin)*

Botanical Family: Lamiaceae or Labiatae (mint).

Plant Origin: Indonesia, India.

Extraction Method: Steam distilled from flowers.

Key Constituents:

Patchoulol [25–35%]
Alpha-Bulnesene [14–20%]
Alpha-Guaiene + Seychellene [15-25%]
Alpha-Patchoulene [5–9%]

Action: Patchouli is soothing to digestion, a decongestant, is anti-inflammatory, anti-infectious, antimicrobial, antiseptic, and soothes wrinkled or chapped skin.

Traditional Uses: It is very beneficial for the skin and helps prevent wrinkles or chapped skin. It is a general tonic and stimulant and helps the digestive system. It also helps relieve itching.

Indications: Allergies, dermatitis, eczema, hemorrhoids, and tissue regeneration.

Other Uses: This oil helps the body eliminate toxic material. It may also curb appetite; it helps with acne; soothes insect bites; helps with cellulite, congestion, dandruff, depression, helps with weight control; relieves itching from hives; helps with skin conditions (chapped and loose skin); fluid retention; and weeping wounds.

Application: Diffuse or apply topically.

Fragrant Influence: It is sedating, calming, and relaxing, reducing anxiety. It may have some influence on sexual energy.

Safety Data: If pregnant or under a doctor's care, consult physician.

Companion Oils: Bergamot, clary sage, frankincense, geranium, ginger, lavender, lemongrass, myrrh, pine, rosewood, and sandalwood.

Peppermint (*Mentha piperita)*

Botanical Family: Lamiaceae or Labiatae (mint).

Plant Origin: North America.

Extraction Method: Steam distilled from leaves, stems, and flower buds.

Key Constituents:

Menthol [34–44%]
Menthone [12–20%]
Menthofurane [4–9%]
1,8 Cineol (Eucalyptol) [2–5%]
Pulegone [2–5%]
Menthyl Acetate [4–10%]

Action: Peppermint is anticarcinogenic, supports digestion, expels worms, is a decongestant, is anti-infectious, antibacterial, antifungal, mucolytic, a stimulant, is hypertensive, cardiotonic, stimulates the gallbladder, is a pain-reliever, an expectorant, and anti-inflammatory for the intestinal and urinary tract. It can heighten or restore the sense of taste by stimulating the trigeminal nerve.

Traditional Uses: Peppermint is one of the oldest and most highly regarded herbs for soothing digestion. Jean Valnet, MD, studied peppermint's effect on the liver and respiratory systems. Other scientists have also researched peppermint's role in affecting impaired taste and smell when inhaled. Dr. William N. Dember of the University of Cincinnati studied peppermint's ability to improve concentration and mental accuracy. Alan Hirsch, MD, studied peppermint's ability to directly affect the brain's satiety center (the ventromedial nucleus of the hypothalamus) which triggers a sensation of fullness after meals.

Indications: Asthma, bronchitis, candida, diarrhea, digestive problems, fever, halitosis, heartburn, hemorrhoids, hot flashes, indigestion, menstrual irregularity, headaches, motion sickness, nausea, tumor growth, respiratory infections, shock, itchy skin, throat infections, and varicose veins.

Other Uses: This oil may help arthritis, depression, skin conditions (eczema, psoriasis, dermatitis), food poisoning, headaches, hives, hysteria, inflammation, morning sickness, nerve regeneration, rheumatism, elevate and open sensory system, ease the pain of toothaches, and kills tuberculosis bacillus according to Jean Valnet, MD.

Application: Diffuse. Massage on the stomach or add to water or tea for supporting normal digestion. Apply to the bottom of the feet or rub on the temples to treat headaches. To improve concentration, alertness, and memory, place 2 drops on the tongue. Add to food as a flavoring and preservative.

Fragrant Influence: It is purifying and stimulating to the conscious mind.

Safety Data: If pregnant or under a doctor's care, consult your physician. Avoid contact with eyes, mucus membranes, or sensitive skin areas. Do not apply neat to a fresh wound or burn.

CAUTION: Always dilute when using on children's delicate skin.

Selected Research: Gobel H, et al. "Effect of peppermint and eucalyptus oil preparations on neurophysiological and experimental algesimetric headache parameters." *Cephalalgia*. 1994; 14(3):228-34.

Juergens UR, et al. "The anti-inflammatory activity of L-menthol compared to mint oil in human monocytes in vitro: a novel perspective for its therapeutic use in inflammatory diseases." *Eur J Med Res*. 1998; 3(12):539-45.

Samman MA, et al. "Mint prevents shamma-induced carcinogenesis in hamster cheek pouch." *Carcinogenesis*. 1998;19(10):1795-801.

Petitgrain *(Citrus aurantium)*

Botanical Family: Rutaceae (citrus).

Plant Origin: Italy.

Extraction Method: Steam distilled from leaves and twigs.

Key Constituents:

Linalyle Acetate [40–55%]
Linalol [15–30%]
Alpha-Terpineol [3.5–7.5%]
Geranyl Acetate [2–5%]
Geraniol [2–4.5%]

Action: Petitgrain is antispasmodic, anti-inflammatory, anti-infectious, and antibacterial.

Traditional Uses: Petitgrain derives its name from the extraction of the oil, which at one time was from the green unripe oranges when they were still about the size of a cherry.

Other Uses: This oil may help re-establish nerve equilibrium. It may also help with acne, fatigue, greasy hair, insomnia, and excessive perspiration.

Application: Diffuse or apply topically.

Fragrant Influence: Petitgrain is uplifting and helps to refresh the senses, clear confusion, reduce mental fatigue, and reduce depression. It may also stimulate the mind, support memory, and gladden the heart.

Safety Data: If pregnant or under a doctor's care, consult physician.

Companion Oils: Bergamot, cistus, clary sage, clove, geranium, jasmine, lavender, neroli, orange, palmarosa, and rosemary CT cineol.

Pine *(Pinus sylvestris)*

Botanical Family: Pinaceae (pine).

Plant Origin: Austria, Russia, Canada.

Extraction Method: Steam distilled from needles.

Key Constituents:

Alpha-Pinene [55–70%]
Beta-Pinene [3–8%]
Limonene [5–10%]
Delta-3-Carene [6–12%]

Action: Pine is hormone-like, antidiabetic, cortisone-like, a sexual stimulant, hypertensive (high blood pressure), anti-infectious, antifungal, and antiseptic.

Traditional Uses: Pine was first investigated by Hippocrates, the father of Western medicine, for its benefits to the respiratory system. In 1990, Dr. Pénoël and Dr. Franchomme described pine oil's antiseptic properties in their medical textbook. Pine is used in massage for stressed muscles and joints. It shares many of the same properties as *Eucalyptus globulus*, and the action of both oils is enhanced when blended. Native Americans stuffed mattresses with pine needles to repel lice and fleas. Pine was used to treat lung infections and even added to baths to revitalize those suffering from mental or emotional fatigue.

Indications: Asthma, pulmonary infections, bronchitis, diabetes, severe infections, rheumatoid arthritis, and sinusitis.

Other Uses: This oil may help dilate the respiratory system, particularly the bronchial tract. It may also help with respiratory infections, coughs, cuts, cysts, fatigue, gout, lice, nervous exhaustion, scabies, skin parasites, sores, stress, and urinary infection. Pine oil may also help increase blood pressure and stimulate the adrenal glands and the circulatory system. Pine oil is a good ingredient for any first aid kit.

Application: Diffuse or apply topically. Dilute to avoid possible skin irritation. Put two drops in the palms of the hands, place over mouth and nose, and inhale. Add 2–4 drops to warm bathwater. Disperse with a bath gel if desired.

Fragrant Influence: Pine helps soothe mental stress, relieve anxiety, freshen and deodorize a room, and revitalize the entire body.

Safety Data: If pregnant or under a doctor's care, consult your physician. Avoid oils adulterated with turpentine, a low-cost, but potentially hazardous filler.

Companion Oils: Cedarwood, *Eucalyptus radiata,* juniper, lavender, lemon, marjoram, *Melaleuca alternifolia,* and rosemary CT cineol.

Bible Reference: Nehemiah 8:15—"And that they should publish and proclaim in all their cities, and in Jerusalem, saying, Go forth unto the mount, and fetch olive branches, and pine branches, and myrtle branches, and palm branches, and branches of thick trees, to make booths, as it is written."

Isaiah 41:19—"I will plant in the wilderness the cedar, the shittah tree, and the myrtle, and the oil tree; I will set in the desert the fir tree, and the pine, and the box tree together:"

Isaiah 60:13—"The glory of Lebanon shall come unto thee, the fir tree, the pine tree, and the box together, to beautify the place of my sanctuary; and I will make the place of my feet glorious."

Ravensara *(Ravensara aromatica)*

Botanical Family: Lauraceae.

Plant Origin: Madagascar.

Extraction Method: Steam distilled from branches.

Key Constituents:

Limonene + Eucalyptol [50–65%)
Sabinene [6–12%]
Alpha-Terpineol [5–11%]
Alpha-Pinene [4–9%]
Beta-Pinene [1–5%]

Action: Ravensara is anti-infectious, antiviral, antibacterial, an expectorant, antimicrobial, and it supports the nerves and respiratory system.

Traditional Uses: Ravensara is referred to by the people of Madagascar as "the oil that heals."

Indications: Bronchitis, cholera, herpes, infectious mononucleosis, insomnia, muscle fatigue, rhinopharyngitis, shingles, sinusitis, viral hepatitis.

Other Uses: Ravensara may help asthma, cystitis, burns, cancer, respiratory infections, cuts, pneumonia, scrapes, viral infections, wounds, and it strengthens the respiratory system.

Application: Diffuse or apply topically.

Safety Data: If pregnant or under a doctor's care, consult physician.

Rose *(Rosa damascena)*

Botanical Family: Rosaceae.

Plant Origin: Bulgaria, Turkey.

Extraction Method: Steam distilled from flower (a two-part process).

Key Constituents:

Geraniol [12–28%]
Citronellol [34–44%]
Nerol [6–9%]
Phenylethylic Alcohol [0–2%]

Action: Rose is anti-inflammatory, prevents and reduces scarring, and balances and elevates the mind.

Traditional Uses: Rose has been used for the skin for thousands of years. The Arab physician, Avicenna, was responsible for first distilling rose oil, eventually authoring an entire book on the healing attributes of the rose water derived from the distillation of rose. Throughout much of ancient history, the oil was produced by enfleurage, a process of pressing the petals along with a vegetable oil to extract the essence. Today, however, almost all rose oils are solvent extracted.

NOTE: The Bulgarian *Rosa damascena* (high in citronellol) is very different from Morrocan *Rosa centifolia* (high in phenyl ethanol). They have different colors, aromas, and therapeutic actions.

Other Uses: This oil may help asthma, chronic bronchitis, herpes simplex, impotence, scarring, sexual debilities, skin diseases, and wrinkles.

Application: Diffuse or apply topically.

Fragrant Influence: The beautiful fragrance of rose is intoxicating and aphrodisiac-like. It helps bring balance and harmony, allowing one to overcome insecurities. It is stimulating and elevating to the mind, creating a sense of well-being.

Safety Data: If pregnant or under a doctor's care, consult physician.

Selected Research: Sysoev NP "The effect of waxes from essential oil plants on the dehydrogenase activity of the blood neutrophils in mucosal trauma of the mouth." *Stomatologiia* 1991;70(1):12-3.

Mahmood N, et al. "The anti-HIV activity and mechanisms of action of pure compounds isolated from Rosa damascena." *Biochim Biophys Res Commun*. 1996;229(1):73-9.

Rosemary *(Rosmarinus officinalis CT 1,8 cineol)*

Botanical Family: Labiatae.

Plant Origin: France, USA.

Extraction Method: Steam distilled from leaves.

Key Constituents:

1,8 Cineol (Eucalyptol) [38–55%]
Alpha-Pinene [9–14%]
Beta-Pinene [4–9%]
Camphor [5–15%]
Camphene [2.5–6%]
Borneol [1.5–5%]
Limonene [1–4%]

ORAC: 3,309.

Action: Rosemary is antifungal, antibacterial, antiseptic, antiparasitic, a general stimulant, enhances mental clarity, and supports nerves and endocrine gland balance.

Traditional Use: Rosemary was part of the "Marseilles Vinegar" or "Four Thieves Vinegar" used by grave-robbing bandits to protect themselves during the 15th century plague. The name of the oil is derived from the Latin words for dew of the sea (*ros* + *marinus*). According to folklore history, rosemary originally had white flowers; however, they turned red after the Virgin Mary laid her cloak on the bush. Since the time of ancient Greece (about 1000 BC), rosemary was burnt as incense. Later cultures believed that it warded off devils, a practice that eventually became adopted by the sick who then burned rosemary to protect against infection. Until recently, French hospitals used rosemary to disinfect the air.

Indications: Rheumatism, arthritis, myalgia, hepatitis, liver conditions, menstrual disturbances, hypertension (weak doses), hypotension (strong doses), indigestion, bronchitis, respiratory and lung infections, hair loss (alopecia areata), and asthma.

Other Uses: Rosemary improves concentration and stimulates the scalp.

Application: Diffuse, inhale, or apply topically on location. Add to food or rice milk as a dietary supplement or flavoring.

Fragrant Influence: Helps overcome mental fatigue and improves mental clarity and focus.

Safety Data: Epileptics should use with caution. If pregnant or under a doctor's care, consult physician.

Companion Oils: Basil, *Eucalyptus radiata*, lavender, marjoram, peppermint, and pine.

Selected Research: Larrondo JV, et al. "Antimicrobial activity of essences from labiates." *Microbios*. 1995; 82(332):171-2.

Panizzi L, et al. "Composition and antimicrobial properties of essential oils of four Mediterranean Lamiaceae." *J Ethnopharmacol*. 1993;39(3):167-70.

Diego MA, et al. "Aromatherapy positively affects mood, EEG patterns of alertness and math computations." *Int J Neurosci*. 1998; 96(3-4):217-24.

Rosemary Verbenon *(Rosmarinus officinalis CT verbenon)*

Botanical Family: Labiatae.

Plant Origin: France, USA.

Extraction Method: Steam distilled from leaves.

Key Constituents:

Alpha-Pinene [32–45%)
Limonene +1,8 Cineol (Eucalyptol) [7–13%]
Bornyl Acetate [6–11%]
Camphene [6–10%]
Camphor [3–7%]

Action: Rosemary verbenon is mucolytic, an expectorant, antispasmodic, antibacterial, antiseptic, and it balances the endocrine glands.

Traditional Uses: Rosemary verbenon has been used to lower cholesterol.

Indications: Respiratory infections, bronchitis, viral hepatitis, nervous tension, cardiac arrhythmia, cystitis, arthritis, and rheumatism.

Other Uses: Because of its lower camphor and higher verbenon content, this chemotype of rosemary is milder than the cineol chemotype and so is especially well-suited for chest, lung, and sinus infections. It is ideal for skin care, and can be used to combat hair loss.

Application: Diffuse, inhale, or apply topically on location. May also be added to food or rice milk as a dietary supplement.

Fragrant Influence: Less stimulating than rosemary CT cineol, rosemary verbenon can be clarifying for emotions and psychologically balancing.

Safety Data: Epileptics should use with caution. If pregnant or under a doctor's care, consult physician.

Companion Oils: Basil, *Eucalyptus radiata,* lavender, marjoram, peppermint, and pine.

Rosewood *(Aniba rosaeodora)*

Botanical Family: Lauraceae.

Plant Origin: Brazil.

Extraction Method: Steam distilled from wood.

Key Constituents:

Linalol [70–90%)
Alpha-Terpineol [2–7%]
Alpha-Copaene [trace–3%]
1,8 Cineol (Eucalyptol) [trace–3%]
Geraniol [0.5–2.5%]

Action: Rosewood is anti-infectious, antibacterial, antiviral, antiparasitic, antifungal, and soothing to the skin. It has been researched at Weber State University[7] in Ogden, Utah, for its inhibition rate against gram positive and gram negative bacterial growth.

Indications: Acne, candida, depression, eczema, oral infections, dry skin, and vaginitis.

Other Uses: This oil may create skin elasticity and is soothing to the skin. It is recognized for its ability to get rid of candida of the skin and slow the aging process. It may also be beneficial for cuts, nausea, tissue regeneration, and wounds. It helps to create a synergism with all other oils.

Application: Diffuse or apply topically.

Fragrant Influence: It is soothing and nourishing to the skin.

Safety Data: If pregnant or under a doctor's care, consult physician.

Sage *(Salvia officinalis)*

Botanical Family: Lamiaceae or Labiatae (mint).

Plant Origin: Spain, Croatia, France.

Extraction Method: Steam distilled from leaves and flowers.

Key Constituents:

Alpha-Thuyone [18–43%]
Beta-Thuyone [3–8.5%]

7. Chao, et al., Screening for Inhibitory Activity of Essential Oils on Selected Bacteria, Fungi, and Viruses, *J Essen Oil Res, Aug*. 2000.

1,8 Cineol (Eucalyptol) [5.5–13%]
Camphor [4.5–24.5%]
Camphene [1.5–7%]
Alpha-Pinene [1–6.5]
Alpha-Humulene [0–12%]

Action: Sage is an expectorant, is mucolytic, anti-infectious, fights against cholera, is estrogen-like, supports menstruation, prevents and reduces scarring, regulates circulation, soothes skin conditions and is a balancer and detoxifier of the body. Sage contains camphor, which balances estrogen levels, providing support during PMS and menopause.

Traditional Uses: Known as *herba sacra* or sacred herb by the ancient Romans, sage's name, *Salvia,* is derived from the word for "salvation." Sage has been used in Europe for oral infections and skin conditions. It has been recognized for its benefits in strengthening the vital centers and supporting metabolism.

Indications: Asthma, chronic bronchitis, sluggish digestion, gingivitis, glandular disorders, menstrual irregularity, and menopause.

Other Uses: This oil may help improve estrogen, progesterone, and testosterone balance. It activates the nervous system and adrenal cortex and may help with illness that is related to digestion and liver problems. It may also be beneficial for acne, arthritis, bacterial infections, dandruff, depression, eczema, fibrosis, hair loss, low blood pressure, mental fatigue, metabolism, respiratory problems, rheumatism, skin conditions, sores, and sprains. Sage strengthens the vital centers of the body, balancing the pelvic chakra where negative emotions from denial and abuse are stored.

Application: Diffuse or apply topically diluted with a vegetable or massage oil. Add to food or rice milk as a dietary supplement or flavoring.

Fragrant Influence: It is mentally stimulating and may help in coping with despair and mental fatigue.

Safety Data: If pregnant or under a doctor's care, consult your physician. Sage is an oral toxin due to thujone content. Do not use if epileptic. Use caution if suffering from high blood pressure.

Companion Oils: Bergamot, lavender, lemon, peppermint, lemongrass, pine, and rosemary CT cineol.

Sandalwood *(Santalum album)*

Botanical Family: Santalaceae (sandalwood).

Plant Origin: Indonesia, India.

Extraction Method: Steam distilled from wood.

Key Constituents:

Alpha-Santalol [47–55%]
Beta-Santalols [19–23%]

ORAC: 1,655.

Action: Sandalwood is high in sesquiterpenes that have been researched in Europe for their ability to stimulate the pineal gland and the limbic region of the brain, the center of emotions. The pineal gland is responsible for releasing melatonin, a powerful antioxidant that enhances deep sleep. Sandalwood is similar to frankincense oil in its support of nerves and circulation.

Traditional Uses: Sandalwood has been used for centuries in Ayurvedic medicine. It was used traditionally for skin revitalization, yoga, and meditation.

Indications: Bronchitis (chronic), herpes, cystitis, skin tumors.

Other Uses: Sandalwood helps with cystitis and urinary tract infections. It may also be beneficial for acne, depression, meditation, pulmonary infections, menstrual problems, nervous tension, and skin infection. It helps dry or dehydrated skin.

Application: Diffuse or apply topically. Add to food or rice milk as a dietary supplement or flavoring.

Fragrant Influence: Enhances deep sleep, may help remove negative programming from the cells.

Safety Data: If pregnant or under a doctor's care, consult your physician.

Companion Oils: Cypress, frankincense, lemon, myrrh, patchouli, spruce, and ylang ylang.

Selected References:

Benencia F, et al. "Antiviral activity of sandalwood oil against herpes simplex viruses-1 and -2." *Phytomedicine* 1999;6(2):119-23.

Dwivedi C, et al. "Chemopreventive effects of sandalwood oil on skin papillomas in mice." *Eur J Cancer Prev.* 1997;6(4):399-401.

Spearmint *(Mentha spicata)*

Botanical Family: Lamiaceae or Labiatae (mint).

Plant Origin: USA, Europe.

Extraction Method: Steam distilled from leaves.

Key Constituents:

Carvone [45–55%]
Cis-Dihydrocarvone [5–10%]
Limonene [15–25%]

ORAC: 5,398.

Action: Spearmint is anti-inflammatory, calming, astringent, antiseptic, mucolytic, stimulates the gallbladder, and promotes menstruation.

Traditional Uses: Spearmint oil has been used to help support the respiratory and nervous systems.

Indications: Bronchitis, candida, cystitis, and hypertension.

Other Uses: This oil may balance and increase metabolism. It may aid the glandular, nervous, and respiratory systems. It may also help with acne, stimulate a poor appetite, help bad breath, promote easier labor in childbirth, and help with depression, digestion, dry skin, eczema, headaches, intestines (soothes), menstruation (to slow heavy periods), nausea, sore gums, vaginitis, and excess weight.

Application: Diffuse or apply topically. Add to food or rice milk as a dietary supplement or flavoring.

Fragrant Influence: Spearmint's hormone-like activity may help open and release emotional blocks and bring about a feeling of balance and a lasting sense of well-being.

Safety Data: If pregnant or under a doctor's care, consult your physician.

Companion Oils: Basil, lavender, peppermint, and rosemary CT cineol.

Spikenard *(Nardostachys jatamansi)*

Botanical Family: Valerianaceae.

Plant Origin: India.

Extraction Method: Steam distilled from roots.

Key Constituents:

Calarene [22–35%]
Beta-Ionene [4–8%]
Beta-Maaliene [4–9%]
Aristoladiene [3–7%]

Action: Spikenard is antibacterial, antifungal, anti-inflammatory, a deodorant, relaxing, and a skin tonic.

Traditional Uses: Spikenard is highly regarded in India as a perfume, medicinal herb, and skin tonic. It was the one of the most precious oils in ancient times, used only by priests, kings, or high initiates. References in the New Testament describe how Mary of Bethany used a salve of spikenard to anoint the head of Jesus before the Last Supper.

Indications: The oil is known for helping in the treatment of allergic skin reactions.

Other Uses: Spikenard may also help with allergies, candida, indigestion, insomnia, menstrual difficulties, migraine, nausea, rashes, bacterial infections, stress, tachycardia, tension, and wounds that will not heal. According to Dietrich Gumbel, PhD[8] spikenard strengthens the heart and circulatory system.

Application: Apply to the abdomen or on location for soothing and calming action.

Fragrant Influence: Spikenard is relaxing, soothing, and helps nourish and regenerate the skin.

Safety Data: If pregnant or under a doctor's care, consult physician.

Companion Oils: Cistus, lavender, patchouli, pine, and vetiver.

Bible References: (See additional Bible references in Appendix C.)

Song of Solomon 1:12—"While the king sitteth at his table, my spikenard sendeth forth the smell thereof."

Song of Solomon 4:13—"Thy plants are an orchard of pomegranates, with pleasant fruits; camphire, with spikenard,"

Song of Solomon 4:14—"Spikenard and saffron; calamus and cinnamon, with all trees of frankincense; myrrh and aloes, with all the chief spices:"

8. Gumbel, Dietrich, PhD, *Principles of Holistic Therapy with Herbal Essences*, Medizinverlage Heidelberg Gmbh, 2nd Rev. edition (January 1993)

Spruce *(Picea mariana)*

Botanical Family: Pinaceae (pine).

Plant Origin: Canada.

Extraction Method: Steam distilled from leaves, needles, and twigs.

Key Constituents:

Bornyl Acetate [18–28%]
Camphene [17–25%]
Alpha-Pinene [12–19%]
Beta-Pinene [4–8%]
Delta-3-Carene [5–10%]
Limonene [2–7%]
Santene [1–5%]
Tricyclene [1–5%]

Action: Spruce is antispasmodic, anti-infectious, antiparasitic, antiseptic, anti-inflammatory, hormone-like, cortisone-like; a general tonic, and it stimulates thymus.

Traditional Uses: The Lakota Indians used spruce to strengthen their ability to communicate with the Great Spirit.

Indications: Arthritis, candida, hyperthyroidism, immune-depression, prostatitis and rheumatism.

Other Uses: Spruce may be beneficial for bone pain, glandular imbalances, aching joints, and sciatica pain. It may help support the nervous system and respiratory system, and can be stimulating to the pineal, thymus, and adrenal glands.

Application: Diffuse or apply topically. Add to food or rice milk as a dietary supplement or flavoring.

Fragrant Influence: Helps to open and release emotional blocks, bringing about a feeling of balance. It also helps the respiratory and nervous systems.

Safety Data: If pregnant or under a doctor's care, consult physician.

Companion Oils: Wintergreen or birch, *Eucalyptus radiata*, frankincense, helichrysum, and ravensara.

Tangerine *(Citrus nobilis)*

Botanical Family: Rutaceae (citrus).

Plant Origin: USA, South Africa.

Extraction Method: Cold pressed from rind.

Key Constituents:

Limonene [85–93%]
Beta-Phellandrene + Cis-Beta-Ocimene [2–5%]
Myrcene [1–4%]

Action: Tangerine promotes happiness, helps with anxiety and nervousness.

Indications: Diffuse or apply topically. Add to food or water as a dietary supplement or flavoring.

Other Uses: Tangerine may help dissolve cellulite, improve circulation, and help digestive system disorders, dizziness, anxiety, insomnia, irritability, liver problems, parasites, stretch marks (smooths when blended with lavender), and fluid retention.

Application: Diffuse or apply topically. Add to food or rice milk as dietary supplement or flavoring.

Fragrant Influence: Calming, helps with anxiety and nervousness.

Safety Data: If pregnant or under a doctor's care, consult physician.

Companion Oils: Basil, bergamot, German chamomile, clary sage, frankincense, geranium, grapefruit, lavender, lemon, and orange.

Tansy *(Tanacetum vulgare)*

Botanical Family: Asteraceae or Compositae (daisy).

Plant Origin: USA.

Extraction Method: Steam distilled from leaves.

Key Constituents:

Beta-Thujone [65–80%]
Camphor [3–8%]
Sabinene [1–4%]
Germacrene D [3–7%]

Action: Tansy is analgesic, antitumoral, believed to help stop bleeding, and is an immune stimulant.

Traditional Uses: This antimicrobial oil has been used extensively as an insect repellent. According to E. Joseph Montagna's PDR on herbal formulas, it may help numerous skin conditions and tone the entire system.

Indications: Respiratory infections, stomach conditions, arthritis, irritable bowel syndrome, aneurysm, bruises, diarrhea, freckles, and gout.

Application: Diffuse or apply topically.

Safety Data: If pregnant or under a doctor's care, consult your physician.

Companion Oils: Wintergreen or birch, clary sage, elemi, hyssop, myrtle, pine, valerian, and vetiver.

Tansy, Blue *(Tanacetum annuum)*

Botanical Family: Asteraceae or Compositae (daisy).

Plant Origin: Morocco, France.

Extraction Method: Steam distilled from leaves and flowers.

Key Constituents:

Camphor [1–17%]
Sabinene [10–17%]
Beta-Pinene [5–10%]
Myrcene [7–13%]
Alpha-Phellandrene [5–10%]
Para-Cymene [3–8%]
Chamazulene [3–6%]

Action: Blue tansy is anti-inflammatory, reduces pain, relieves itching, is sedating to the nerves, is an antihistamine, hypotensive (helps with low blood pressure), and has hormone-like effects.

Safety Data: If pregnant or under a doctor's care, consult physician.

Tarragon *(Artemisia dracunculus)*

Botanical Family: Asteraceae or Compositae (daisy).

Plant Origin: Slovenia, France,USA.

Extraction Method: Steam distilled from leaves.

Key Constituents:

Methyl Chavicol (Estragole) [68–80%]
Trans-Beta-Ocimene [6–12%]
Cis-Beta-Ocimene [6–12%]
Limonene [2–6%]

Action: Tarragon is a neuromuscular antispasmodic, is anti-inflammatory, anti-infectious, antifermentation, and reduces allergies.

Traditional Uses: Tarragon has been used in Europe for its antimicrobial and antiseptic functions.

Indications: Colitis, hiccups, intestinal spasms, parasites, rheumatic pain, sciatica.

Other Uses: Tarragon may be beneficial for abdominal discomfort and spasms, arthritis, digestive complaints, genital and urinary tract infection, nausea, premenstrual discomfort, and wounds. It may also balance the autonomic nervous system.

Application: Apply topically diluted with vegetable or massage oil. Add to food or rice milk as a dietary supplement or flavoring.

Safety Data: If pregnant or under a doctor's care, consult your physician. **NOTE:** Do not use if epileptic.

Companion Oils: German chamomile, clary sage, balsam fir, juniper, lavender, pine, rosewood, orange, and tangerine.

Thyme *(Thymus vulgaris CT thymol)*

Botanical Family: Lamiaceae or Labiatae (mint).

Plant Origin: USA, France.

Extraction Method: Steam distilled from leaves, stems, and flowers.

Key Constituents:

Thymol [37–55%]
Para-Cymene [14–28%]
Gamma-Terpinene [4–11%]
Linalol [3–6.5%]
Carvacrol [0.5–5.5%]
Myrcene [1–2.8%]

ORAC: 159,590.

Action: Thyme is highly antimicrobial, antifungal, antiviral, a uterine tonic, and cardiotonic.

Traditional Uses: Thyme has been used for respiratory problems, digestive complaints, the prevention and treatment of infection, gastritis, bronchitis, pertussis, asthma, laryngitis, and tonsilitis. The Egyptians used thyme for embalming.

Indications: Asthma, bronchitis, colitis, cystitis, dermatitis, anthrax, fatigue (general), pleurisy, psoriasis, sciatica, tuberculosis, vaginal candida.

Other Uses: This oil is a general tonic for the nerves and stomach. It may also help with bacterial infections, respiratory infections, circulation, depression, digestion, headaches, insomnia, rheumatism, urinary infections, and viruses along the spine (see Raindrop Technique in Chapter 11).

Application: Apply topically, diluted with a vegetable or massage oil. Add to food or rice milk as a dietary supplement or flavoring.

Fragrant Influence: Thyme may be beneficial in helping to overcome fatigue and exhaustion after illness.

Safety Data: If pregnant or under a doctor's care, consult your physician.

Companion Oils: Bergamot, citrus oil, cedarwood, juniper, *Melaleuca alternifolia,* oregano, and rosemary CT cineol.

Selected Research: Panizzi L, et al. "Composition and antimicrobial properties of essential oils of four Mediterranean Lamiaceae." *J Ethnopharmacol*. 1993;39 (3):167-70.

Youdim KA, et al. "Beneficial effects of thyme oil on age-related changes in the phospholipid C20 and C22 polyunsaturated fatty acid composition of various rat tissues." *Biochim Biophys Acta*. 1999;1438(1):140-6.

Inouye S, et al. "Antisporulating and respiration-inhibitory effects of essential oils on filamentous fungi." Mycoses. 1998;41(9-10):403-10.

Thyme Linalol *(Thymus vulgaris CT linalol)*

Botanical Family: Lamiaceae or Labiatae (mint).

Plant Origin: France.

Extraction Method: Steam distilled from leaves.

Key Constituents:

Linalol + Cis-4-Thujanol [30–40%]
Terpinene-4-ol [6–12%]
Myrcene [4–8%]
Para-Cymene [4–8%]
Gamma-Terpinene [4–8%]

Action: Thyme linalol is highly antimicrobial, antifungal, antiviral, a uterine tonic, and a cardiotonic (just as thyme CT thymol—but is is gentler).

Safety Data: If pregnant or under a doctor's care, consult your physician.

Companion Oils: Bergamot, all citrus oils, cedarwood, juniper, *Melaleuca alternifolia,* oregano, and rosemary CT cineol.

Tsuga *(Tsuga canadensis)*

Botanical Family: Pinaceae.

Plant Origin: Canada.

Extraction Method: Steam distilled from needles and twigs of the conifer tree commercially known as hemlock.

Key Constituents:

Alpha- and Beta-Pinenes [18–25%]
Camphene [12–18%]
Limonene + Beta-Phellandrene [3–7%]
Bornyl Acetate [28–38%]
Tricyclene [4–8%]
Myrcene [1–3%]

Action: Tsuga is analgesic, antirheumatic, an astringent, a blood cleanser, and a stimulant.

Uses: Treats coughs, respiratory conditions, kidney ailments, skin conditions, urinary infections, venereal diseases.

Application: Diffuse or apply topically diluted 1 drop of essential oil to 1 teaspoon of vegetable or massage oil. May be added to food or rice milk as a dietary supplement.

Safety Data: If pregnant or under a doctor's care, consult your physician. Repeated use can possibly result in contact sensitization.

Valerian *(Valeriana officinalis)*

Botanical Family: Valerianaceae.

Plant Origin: Belgium, Croatia, France.

Extraction Method: Steam distilled from root.

Key Constituents:

Borneol Acetate [32–44%]
Camphene + Alpha-Fenchene [24–34%[
Alpha-Pinene [4–8%]
Beta-Pinene [2–6%]
Isobicyclogermacrenol [3–6%]
Myrtenyl Acetate [1–5%]

Action: Valerian is sedative and tranquilizing to the central nervous system. Its warming properties can help with hypothermia.

Traditional Uses: For more than 30 years, valerian has been clinically investigated for its tranquilizing properties. Researchers have pinpointed sesquiterpenes as the active constituents that exerts a calming effect on the central nervous system. The German Commission E has pronounced valerian to be an effective treatment for restlessness and for sleep disturbances resulting from nervous conditions.

Other Uses: Because of its effect on the nervous system, it may help with insomnia, nervous indigestion, migraine, restlessness, and tension.

Application: Diffuse or apply topically, especially in a soothing massage. Add to food or rice milk as a dietary supplement.

Fragrant Influence: Calming, relaxing, grounding, and emotionally balancing; a sleep aid.

Safety Data: If pregnant or under a doctor's care, consult your physician. Repeated use can possibly result in contact sensitization.

Companion Oils: Cedarwood, lavender, mandarin, patchouli, petitgrain, pine, and rosemary CT cineol.

Selected Research:

Wagner J, et al. "Beyond benzodiazepines: alternative pharmacologic agents for the treatment of insomnia." *Ann Pharmacother*. 1998;32(6):680-91.

Vetiver *(Vetiveria zizanioides)*

Botanical Family: Poaceae or Gramineae (grass).

Plant Origin: Haiti, India.

Extraction Method: Steam distilled from root.

Key Constituents:

Alpha-Vetivone [3–6%]
Beta-Vetivone [3–6%]
Khusenol [6–11%]
Isovalencenol [11–15%]
Nootkatone [2–5%]
Khusimone [3–6%]

Action: Vetiver is antiseptic, antispasmodic, calming, grounding, a rubefacient (locally warming), a sedative (nervous system), and a stimulant (circulatory, production of red corpuscles).

Traditional Uses: It is well known for its anti-inflammatory properties and is traditionally used for arthritic symptoms.

Other Uses: Vetiver may help acne, anxiety, arthritis, cuts, depression (including postpartum), insomnia, rheumatism, stress, skin care (oily, aging, irritated).

Application: Diffuse or apply topically, especially in a soothing massage. May be added to food or rice milk as a dietary supplement.

Fragrant Influence: Vetiver has a heavy, earthy fragrance similar to patchouli with a touch of lemon. It is psychologically grounding, calming, and stabilizing. It helps one cope with stress and recover from emotional traumas and shocks.

Safety Data: If pregnant or under a doctor's care, consult your physician.

Companion Oils: Clary sage, jasmine, lavender, patchouli, rose, sandalwood, and ylang ylang.

Vitex *(Vitex negundo)*

Botanical Family: Lamiaceae or Labiatae (mint).

Plant Origin: Turkey.

Extraction Method: Steam distilled from the inner bark, small branches, and leaves of the chaste tree.

Key Constituents:

Beta-Caryophyllene [38–48%]
Limonene + 1,8 Cineol (Eucalyptol) [3–7%]
Sabinene [10–15%]
Caryophyllene Oxide [5–10%]
Longifolene + Alpha-Gurjunene [5–10%]

Traditional Uses: Vitex has been extensively researched in Europe for its effects on Parkinson's and other neurological disorders.

Application: Diffuse or apply topically diluted with vegetable or massage oil for massage. Rub 2–3 drops in the palms, cup over the nose and inhale. Add 2–4 drops to 1 teaspoon salt and dissolve in warm bath water.

Safety Data: If pregnant or under a doctor's care, consult physician.

NOTE: *Vitex negundo* essential oil is different from the extract of the chaste berry, which is used for PMS symptoms and hormone balance.

Western Red Cedar *(Thuja plicata)*

Botanical Family: Cupressaceae (Cypress).

Plant Origin: Canada.

Extraction Method: Steam distilled from leaves and twigs.

Key Constituents:

Alpha-Thujone [70–85%]
Beta-Thujone [5–9%]
Sabinene [2–5%]

Action: Western red cedar is antifungal, antibacterial, antiparasitic, a hair follicle stimulator, and an insect repellent.

Traditional Uses: It was used traditionally by the Native American Indians to help them enter a higher spiritual realm. They used it to stimulate the scalp and as an antimicrobial and antiseptic agent. It is an ingredient of cold-remedy salves used to clear the nose and chest.

Application: Diffuse. Apply on the crown of the head or on location.

Safety Data: If pregnant or under a doctor's care, consult your physician.

White Fir (See Fir, White)

Wintergreen *(Gaultheria procumbens)*

(Very similar in chemistry and action to birch)

Botanical Family: Ericaceae.

Plant Origin: China.

Extraction Method: Steam distilled from leaves.

Key Constituent:

Methyl salicylate [90+%]

Action: Wintergreen is antispasmodic, anti-inflammatory, and a liver stimulant.

Traditional Uses: Leaves have been chewed to increase respiratory capacity by Native Americans when running long distances and performing difficult labor. Settlers in early America had their children chew the leaves for several weeks each spring to prevent tooth decay. Wintergreen was used as a substitute for black tea during the Revolutionary War.

Indications: Arthritis, rheumatism, inflammation, muscular pain, tendonitis, hypertension, and cramps.

Other Uses: Wintergreen oil may be beneficial for cystitis, acne, bladder infection, gout, gallstones, edema, eczema, osteoporosis, skin diseases, ulcers, and urinary tract disorders. It contains an active principle similar to cortisone and is beneficial for bone, muscle, and joint discomfort.

Application: Apply neat to the bottom of the feet. Dilute with vegetable or massage oil when applying elsewhere. Add 3–5 drops to 1/2 fl. oz. of bath gel and add to bath water for soothing bath.

Fragrant Influence: It stimulates and increases awareness in all levels of the sensory system.

Safety Data: If pregnant or under a doctor's care, consult your physician. Do not use if epileptic. Skin test for allergies.

Companion Oils: Basil, birch, cypress, geranium, juniper, lavender, lemongrass, marjoram, peppermint, and Roman chamomile.

NOTE: Be careful of your sources in obtaining either birch or wintergreen essential oils. There may be no true birch essential oil available worldwide. Additionally, much of the wintergreen sold today has been chemically extended and adulterated with synthetic methyl salicylate.

Yarrow *(Achillea millefolium)*

Botanical Family: Asteraceae or Compositae (daisy).

Plant Origin: USA.

Extraction Method: Steam distilled from flowering top.

Key Constituents:

Chamazulene [12–19%]
Trans-Beta-Caryophyllene [4-8%]
Germacrene D [4–8%]
Camphor [4–9%]
Sabinene [3–7%]
Beta-Pinene [3–7%]
1,8 Cineol (Eucalyptol) [2–6%]

Action: Yarrow is anti-inflammatory, reduces indigestion, reduces or prevents scarring, and promotes the healing of wounds.

Traditional Uses: The Greek Achilles, hero of the Trojan War, was said to have used the yarrow herb to help cure the injury to his Achilles tendon. Yarrow was considered sacred by the Chinese, who recognized the harmony of the Yin and Yang energies within it. It has been said that the fragrance of yarrow makes possible the meeting of heaven and earth. Yarrow was used by Germanic tribes for the treatment of battle wounds.

Indications: Acne, appetite (lack of), bladder or kidney weakness, cellulite, respiratory infections, digestion (poor), menstrual problems, eczema, gallbladder inflammation, gastritis, gout, poor hair growth, headaches, hemorrhoids, hypertension, liver and menopause problems, neuritis, neuralgia, pelvic and urinary infections, prostatitis, rheumatism, sprains, sunburn, thrombosis, ulcers, vaginitis, varicose veins, and wounds.

Other Uses: Yarrow is a powerful decongestant of the prostate and helps to balance hormones.

Application: Diffuse or apply topically.

Fragrant Influence: Balancing highs and lows, both external and internal, yarrow may allow us to have our heads in the clouds while our feet remain firm on the ground. Its balancing properties may also make it useful during meditation. It is supportive to intuitive energies and helps reduce confusion and ambivalence.

Safety Data: If pregnant or under a doctor's care, consult physician.

Ylang Ylang *(Cananga odorata)*

Botanical Family: Annonaceae (custard-apple).

Plant Origin: The Indian Ocean island of Commores, Indonesia, Philippines.

Extraction Method: Steam distilled from flowers. Flowers are picked early in the morning to maximize oil yield. The highest quality oil is drawn from the first distillation. There are three further distillations which yield increasingly lower grades.

Key Constituents:

Germacrene D [15–20%]
Alpha-Farnesene [8–12%]
Benzyl Acetate [9–15%]
Benzyl Benzoate [3–6%]
Linalol [6–10%]
Methyl-Paracresol [5–9%]
Isoeugenol [3–5%]
Cinnamyl Acetate [3–5%]

Action: Ylang ylang is antispasmodic, it balances blood pressure, and regulates the heartbeat. It is used in hair preparations to promote thick, shiny, lustrous hair (it is also reported to help control split ends).

Traditional Use: Ylang ylang means "flower of flowers." Ylang ylang flowers have been used to cover the beds of newlywed couples on their wedding night.

Indications: Heart arrhythmias, cardiac problems, high blood pressure, anxiety, impotence, arterial hypertension, depression, mental fatigue, hair loss, labored breathing, insomnia, palpitations, insect bites, and tachycardia.

Other Uses: Ylang ylang may help balance male-female energies so one can move closer towards being in spiritual attunement and allowing greater focus of thoughts, filtering out the ever-present negative frequencies. It may help lower blood pressure, calm rapid breathing, balance equilibrium, ease frustration, balance heart function, help impotence and intestinal problems, shock, and skin problems.

Application: Diffuse or apply topically mixed with vegetable or massage oil. Add to food or rice milk as a dietary supplement or flavoring.

Fragrant Influence: Ylang ylang influences sexual energy and enhances relationships. It may help stimulate the adrenal glands. It is calming and relaxing and may also help with anger and possibly rage, and low self-esteem. It brings back the feeling of self-love, confidence, joy and peace.

Safety Data: If pregnant or under a doctor's care, consult your physician. Repeated use can possibly result in contact sensitization.

CHAPTER 8

Hydrosols

Hydrosols (also called floral waters) are aromatic water extracts that are a result of the steam distilling process that produces essential oils. As steam passes through the plant material, the plant or herb releases essential oil which is then separated out as the steam cools. The oil floats on the top of the water and is collected. The remaining water is laced with subtle traces of oil and contains beneficial water soluble phyto-compounds Hydrosols have properties that are similar to those of the essential oil, but in lower concentrations. They are gentle, fragrant, and suitable for all ages.

Many hydrosols are rehydrating, nurturing, and protective to the skin. They are also uniquely uplifting, calming, soothing, relaxing, and restorative.

CAUTION: Do not spray directly into ears or eyes.

How to Use:

1. Diffuse in a cool mist diffuser.
2. Spray into the air to freshen the home or office.
3. Spray in an airplane or other enclosed environment to sanitize stale air.
4. Spray on face to energize, and overcome fatigue and drowsiness.
5. Drink undiluted or diluted to taste with water or juice.
6. Spray on animals to deter pests.
7. Spray on plants to deter pests.

Some Common Hydrosols and Their Effects:

Basil—is stimulating, energizing, uplifting, and relaxing to the muscles.

Chamomile (German)—is relaxing and soothing for sore muscles, tendons, and ligaments. It also soothes skin irritations and swelling.

Clary Sage—supports the cells and hormones. It contains natural sclareol, which stimulates the body's production of estrogen. It may also help with headaches, dry skin, or coughs.

Eucalyptus—is antiseptic and well-suited for cleansing oily skin and soothing respiratory complications. It may also be used as an insect repellent.

Balsam Fir—is a detoxifier and an energizing and uplifting restorative.

Juniper—is stimulating to the nervous system and detoxifies and cleanses the skin.

Lavender—is soothing to the skin and calming. It can be sprayed on skin or misted in the air to promote sleep.

Melissa—is exquisitely relaxing and uplifting. Melissa has used to treat herpes sores. In lab tests, it has been shown to be antimicrobial against *Streptococcus haemolytica*, which can colonize in the throat and esophagus.

Peppermint—is uplifting, energizing, cooling, refreshing, and soothing to digestion.

Spearmint—is cooling and refreshing. It is excellent for cleansing blemished and oily skin, and soothing for digestion and headaches.

Tansy—brings mental uplift, a positive attitude, and a general feeling of well-being. It is antimicrobial and supports the cleansing of the lymphatic system.

Thyme—is antiseptic, cleansing, energizing, and stimulating to the scalp.

CHAPTER 9

Oil Blends

This section describes specific oil blends I created for both physical and emotional health. Each blend is formulated to maximize the synergistic effect when various single oil chemistries are combined. Synergy is a very real phenomenon where the interaction of two or more agents results in their combined effect being greater than the sum of their individual effects.

When these essential oil constituents come together in a carefully crafted blend, the enhancement of their properties is noticeable and measurable in physical, spiritual, and emotional benefits.

Abuse Relief Blend

This blend produces a beautiful fragrance that enables one to relax into a mental state where one may be able to release the trauma of sexual and/or ritual abuse. This blend also helps unlock other traumatic experiences such as physical and emotional abuse. It brings peace to the soul and freedom to go forward in life with joy.

Recipe:

- 40 drops ylang ylang
- 30 drops geranium
- 20 drops lavender
- 10 drops cedarwood
- 15 drops balsam fir
- 5 drops rose
- 16 drops orange
- 4 drops helichrysum

Ylang Ylang *(Cananga odorata)* helps bring about a sense of relaxation and may help balance male and female energies. It balances equilibrium and restores confidence and self-love.

Geranium *(Pelargonium graveolens)* helps release negative memories, thereby opening and elevating the mind.

Lavender *(Lavandula angustifolia)* has sedative and calming properties that help overcome headaches, stress, and nervous tension.

Cedarwood *(Cedrus atlantica)* has calming and purifying properties. This conifer oil was used by North American Indians to enhance their spiritual awareness and communication. It may help stimulate the pineal gland which is responsible for releasing melatonin, a hormone associated with deep sleep.

Balsam Fir *(Abies balsamea)* has antiseptic properties and also contains d-limonene, a powerful antioxidant.

Rose *(Rosa damascena)* appears to possess a very high biofrequency compared to other essential oils. It creates a sense of balance, harmony, and well-being, and elevates the mind. Rose promotes healthy skin, reduces scarring, and may help with chronic bronchitis, asthma, tuberculosis, sexual disabilities, frigidity, impotency, skin disease, ulcers, sprains, wrinkles, thrush, and gingivitis.

Orange *(Citrus aurantium)* is anti-inflammatory and improves circulation. It was believed to bring joy, peace, and happiness to those who possessed it. It is elevating to the mind and body.

Helichrysum *(Helichrysum italicum)* helps regenerate tissue and nerves and improve circulation. It is an anticoagulant, prevents phlebitis, helps regulate cholesterol, stimulates liver cell function, and may help to clean plaque and debris from the veins and arteries. Helichrysum is mucolytic, an expectorant, antispasmodic, and reduces scarring and discoloration. It may also stimulate nerve endings and improve conditions such as hearing loss. It may help release feelings of anger.

Safety Data: This blend may be irritating to those with sensitive skin. Avoid eye contact. In case of accidental eye contact, put a few drops of any pure vegetable oil in the eye and call your doctor if necessary. Never use water to dilute or rinse.

Application: Apply over energy centers and areas of abuse, on Vita Flex points (see Chapter 10), the navel, lower abdomen, temples, and nose.

Companion Oils: Trauma Blend, Mood Lifting Blend, and Spiritual Blend.

Anti-Aging Blend

This blend contains oils that rank among the most powerful antioxidants. When taken as a dietary supplement, it can promote longevity and prevent premature aging.

Recipe:

- 20 drops thyme
- 10 drops mandarin
- 7 drops clove

Thyme CT Thymol *(Thymus vulgaris CT thymol)* has been shown in studies to dramatically boost glutathione levels in the heart, liver, and brain. It also prevents lipid peroxidation or degradation of the fats found in many vital organs.[1] The oxidation of fats in the body is directly linked to accelerated aging.

Mandarin *(Citrus reticulata)* contains over 90 percent d-limonene, one of the most powerful anticancer compounds studied in recent years.

Clove *(Syzygium aromaticum)* has the highest known antioxidant power as measured by ORAC (oxygen radical absorbent capacity),[2] a test developed by researchers at Tufts University to accurately measure free radical scavenging ability.

Safety Data: This blend may be irritating to those with sensitive skin. Avoid eye contact. In case of accidental eye contact, put a few drops of any pure vegetable oil in the eye and call your doctor if necessary. Never use water to dilute or rinse.

Application: Dilute in a pure vegetable oil and apply topically. Be aware that citrus oils are photo-sensitizing so limit sun exposure after applying to skin. To use as a dietary supplement, dilute 1-3 drops in 4 fl. oz. of rice or almond milk. Can be taken in a vegetable capsule. Take 1–3 capsules a day with meals.

Companion Oil: Immune Blend.

1. Youdim KA, Deans SG, Dietary supplementation of thyme (Thymus vulgaris L.) essential oil during the lifetime of the rat: its effects on the antioxidant status in liver, kidney and heart tissues. *Mech Aging Dev.* 1999 Sep 8;109(3):163-75.
2. The ORAC (oxygen radical absorbent capacity) laboratory test was developed by Dr. Guohua Cao at the USDA Human Nutrition Center on Aging at Tufts University. This sensitive test measures the ability of antioxidants to absorb free radicals, known to cause aging. Both time and degree of inhibition are measured with this test.

Antibacterial Blend

This blend is formulated for diffusing to help purify the home and work environment. It cleanses the air and neutralizes mildew, cigarette smoke, and disagreeable odors. When applied directly to the skin, it may be used to cleanse cuts and scrapes and may help neutralize the poison of bites from spiders, bees, hornets, and wasps.

Recipe:

- 35 drops melaleuca
- 20 drops citronella
- 20 drops lemongrass
- 12 drops lavandin
- 10 drops rosemary

Melaleuca (*Melaleuca alternifolia*) is antiseptic, anti-infectious, antibacterial, antifungal, antiviral, antiparasitic, anti-inflammatory, immune-stimulating, a decongestant, a neurotonic, and may protect against radiation.

Citronella *(Cymbopogon nardus)* is antiseptic, antibacterial, antispasmodic, anti-inflammatory, insecticidal, and soothing to the tissues.

Lemongrass *(Cymbopogon flexuosus)* has strong antifungal properties when applied topically.

Lavandin *(Lavandula x hybrida)* is antifungal, antibacterial, a strong antiseptic, and a tissue regenerator.

Rosemary *(Rosmarinus officinalis CT 1,8 cineol)* is antiseptic, antimicrobial, and may be beneficial for skin conditions and dandruff. It may help fight candida and is anti-infectious, antispasmodic, balances the endocrine system, and is an expectorant. It helps overcome mental fatigue, stimulating memory and opening the conscious mind.

Safety Data: This blend may be irritating to those with sensitive skin. Avoid eye contact. In case of accidental eye contact, put a few drops of any pure vegetable oil in the eye and call your doctor if necessary. Never use water to dilute or rinse.

Application: Diffuse 15–30 minutes every 3–4 hours. Apply topically to disinfect and cleanse. Put a few drops on cotton balls and place the cotton in air vents in the home, car, hotel room, office, and other enclosed areas for purifying air and repelling insects.

Companion Oils: Antiseptic Blend and Antimicrobial Blend.

Antimicrobial Blend

This blend was created from research about a group of 15th-century thieves who rubbed oils and aromatics on themselves to avoid contracting the plague while they robbed the bodies of the dead and dying. When apprehended, these thieves disclosed the formula of herbs, spices, and oils they used to protect themselves in exchange for more lenient punishment.

The oils used in this blend are highly antiviral, antiseptic, antibacterial, antimicrobial, and help to protect the body against such illnesses as flu, colds, sinusitis, bronchitis, pneumonia, sore throats, etc.

Recipe:

- 30 drops rosemary
- 25 drops lemongrass
- 10 drops thyme
- 3 drops cinnamon bark

Rosemary *(Rosmarinus officinalis CT 1,8 cineol)* is antiseptic, antimicrobial, and may be beneficial for skin conditions and dandruff. It may help fight candida and is anti-infectious, antispasmodic, balances the endocrine system, and is an expectorant. It helps overcome mental fatigue, stimulating memory and opening the conscious mind.

Lemongrass *(Cymbopogon flexuosus)* has strong antifungal properties when applied topically. It is used for purification and digestion.

Thyme *(Thymus vulgaris CT thymol)* is highly antimicrobial and antifungal. Thyme has been used to treat respiratory problems[3] and digestive complaints, and can be used to prevent and treat infection, gastritis, bronchitis, pertussis, asthma, laryngitis, and tonsilitis. It may also help with bacterial infections, respiratory infections, circulation, depression, digestive problems, headaches, insomnia, rheumatism, urinary infections, and viruses along the spine.

Cinnamon Bark *(Cinnamomum verum)* is the oil of wealth from the Orient and part of the anointing oil formula the Lord gave Moses (Exodus 30:22-27). Cinnamon oil was regarded by the emperors of China and India to have great value; the emperors' wealth was measured by the amount of oil they possessed. Traditionally, it was thought to attract wealth and abundance. Physically, cinnamon bark oil has many attributes. It is anti-infectious, antibacterial, antiparasitic, antiviral, and antifungal. It is also a powerful purifier and oxygenator, and it enhances the action and the activity of other oils.

3. Inouye S, Yamaguchi H, Takizawa T. Screening of the antibacterial effects of a variety of essential oils on respiratory tract pathogens, using a modified dilution assay method. *J Infect Chemother* 2001 Dec;7(4):251-4

Safety Data: This blend may be irritating to those with sensitive skin. Avoid eye contact. In case of accidental eye contact, put a few drops of any pure vegetable oil in the eye and call your doctor if necessary. Never use water to dilute or rinse.

Application: Diffuse for 15–30 minutes every 3–4 hours at work or home environment. Apply to the bottoms of the feet. Dilute one drop in 5 drops of a vegetable or massage oil and massage over thymus. It is safest when applied to the bottoms of the feet, as it may create a burning sensation on the skin. It is best to dilute 20-80 with vegetable oil before applying topically. For headaches, put one drop on tongue and push tongue against the roof of the mouth.

Companion Oil: Immune Blend.

Antiseptic Blend

This blend has antiseptic-like properties when used topically for cleansing cuts, scrapes, burns, rashes, and bruised tissue. It may also help prevent growth of bacteria, fungus, or infection. Antiseptic Blend helps regenerate damaged tissue and fight infection and fungus. It is also very beneficial for animals such as horses, dogs, and cats in the same way it benefits humans.

Recipe:

- 20 drops melaleuca
- 20 drops naouli
- 15 drops lavender
- 10 drops rosemary

Melaleuca (*Melaleuca alternifolia)* is antiseptic, anti-infectious, antibacterial, antifungal, antiviral, antiparasitic, anti-inflammatory, immune-stimulating, a decongestant, a neurotonic, and protects against radiation.

Naouli *(Melaleuca quinquenervia)* is an anti-inflammatory to the respiratory system and urinary tract, tonic to the digestive system, antihypertensive, anti-infectious, antiviral, antiparasitic, and antibacterial. It has been used by European doctors for liver and pancreas deficiencies in children, viral hepatitis, colitis, ulcers, rheumatoid arthritis, hypertension of the arteries, and eczema.

Lavender *(Lavandula angustifolia)* is known as the universal oil because of its wide range of usage. It has sedative and calming properties that help overcome insomnia, tension, and stress.

Rosemary *(Rosmarinus officinalis* CT 1,8 cineol*)* is antiseptic, antimicrobial, and may be beneficial for skin conditions and dandruff. It may help fight candida and is anti-infectious, antispasmodic, balances the endocrine system, and is an expectorant. It helps overcome mental fatigue, stimulating memory and opening the conscious mind.

Safety Data: This blend may be irritating to those with sensitive skin. Avoid eye contact. In case of accidental eye contact, put a few drops of any pure vegetable oil in the eye and call your doctor if necessary. Never use water to dilute or rinse.

Application: Diffuse to dispel unpleasant odors or apply topically on areas where the skin is broken, including cuts, scrapes, burns, rashes, and infection. Put 1–2 drops on a piece of cotton and place the cotton in the ear for earaches.

Topical Treatment: This blend is best used layered with an ointment to seal the oils and keep wounds soft, thus promoting healing.

Antiviral Blend

This blend includes essential oils that have recently been scientifically documented to be highly effective against several different types of viruses ranging from human papilloma virus (HPV) to herpes simplex viruses. It works well in any application, from inhalation to ignestion to topical application. It is particularly helpful as a preventive during types when viral diseases are spreading, i.e. cold, flu, etc.

Recipe:

- 20 drops sandalwood
- 12 drops peppermint
- 8 drops tsuga
- 8 drops thyme thymol
- 8 drops melaleuca
- 8 drops ravensara
- 3 drops clove

Sandalwood *(Santalum album)* is high in sesquiterpenes, which have been researched for their ability to stimulate the pineal gland and the limbic region of the brain, the center of our emotions. The pineal gland is responsible for releasing melatonin, a hormone that enhances deep sleep. Used traditionally for skin revitalization, yoga, and meditation, sandalwood is similar to frankincense oil in its support of nerves and circulation.

Peppermint *(Mentha piperita)* is one of the oldest and most highly regarded herbs for soothing digestion. Jean Valnet, MD, studied the beneficial effects of peppermint on the liver and respiratory systems. Daniel Pénoël, MD, reports that it may help to reduce fevers, candida, nausea, and vomiting, and strengthen the respiratory system. Adding peppermint to drinking water helps cool body temperature during hot weather. This effect is caused by the menthol in peppermint. This compound stimulates the nervous system and may be stimulating for the mind.

Tsuga *(Tsuga canadensis)* treats coughs, respiratory conditions, kidney ailments, skin conditions, urinary infections, and venereal diseases.

Thyme *(Thymus vulgaris CT thymol)* is highly antimicrobial and antifungal. Thyme has been used to treat respiratory problems and digestive complaints, and can be used to prevent and treat infection, gastritis, bronchitis, pertussis, asthma, laryngitis, and tonsilitis. It may also help with bacterial infections, respiratory infections, circulation, depression, digestive problems, headaches, insomnia, rheumatism, urinary infections, and viruses along the spine.

Melaleuca (*Melaleuca alternifolia)* is antiseptic, anti-infectious, antibacterial, antifungal, antiviral, antiparasitic, anti-inflammatory, immune-stimulating, a decongestant, a neurotonic, and protects against radiation.

Ravensara *(Ravensara aromatica)* is referred to by the people of Madagascar as the oil that heals. It is antiseptic, anti-infectious, antiviral, antibacterial, antifungal, an expectorant and supporting to the nerves. Similar to clove and nutmeg, ravensara may aid the respiratory system and support the adrenal glands. It has been shown to help with flu, sinusitis, bronchitis, viral hepatitis, cholera, herpes, infectious mononucleosis, insomnia, muscle fatigue, and rhinopharyngitis.

Clove *(Syzygium aromaticum)* has the highest known antioxidant power as measured by ORAC (oxygen radical absorbent capacity), a test developed by researchers at Tufts University to accurately measure free radical scavenging ability.

Safety Data: This blend may be irritating to those with sensitive skin. Avoid eye contact. In case of accidental eye contact, put a few drops of any pure vegetable oil in the eye and call your doctor if necessary. Never use water to dilute or rinse.

Application: This blend is designed to fight a variety of common viral infections. It should be diluted for direct skin application unless applying to the bottom of the feet. Can be used in a diffusor for inhalation and can also be used in capsules for ingestion to fight internal viral infections.

Companion Oils: Antimicrobial Blend, Antibacterial Blend, Immune Blend

Brain Blend

Many of the oils in this blend contain high sesquiterpene compounds that have been shown to increase oxygen at receptor sites around the pineal, pituitary, and hypothalamus glands. They are responsible for the secretion of human growth hormone (hGH). Clinical research suggests that these oils may play a major role in dissolving petrochemicals known to plug the receptor sites and prevent receptivity. Brain Blend may help clear the "brain fog" that people experience due to exposure to synthetic petrochemicals in food, skin and hair care products, and heavy chemical-laden air. Brain Blend may increase mental potential and clarity, and long-term use may retard the aging process. It may also support and strengthen immune function. It is perfect for promoting deep concentration and channeling physical energy into mental energy.

Recipe:

- 30 drops balsam fir
- 15 drops frankincense
- 15 drops sandalwood
- 8 drops helichrysum
- 3 drops melissa

Balsam Fir *(Abies balsamea)* has antiseptic properties and also contains d-limonene, a powerful antioxidant.

Frankincense *(Boswellia carteri)* is considered a holy anointing oil in the Middle East and has been used in religious ceremonies for thousands of years. Containing sesquiterpenes, it helps stimulate the limbic part of the brain, which elevates the mind, helping to overcome stress and despair. Frankincense has a warming, elevating effect on the mind.

Sandalwood *(Santalum album)* is high in sesquiterpenes, which have been researched for their ability to stimulate the pineal gland and the limbic region of the brain, the center of our emotions. The pineal gland is responsible for releasing melatonin, a hormone that enhances deep sleep. Used traditionally for skin revitalization, yoga, and meditation, sandalwood is similar to frankincense oil in its support of nerves and circulation.

Helichrysum *(Helichrysum italicum)* helps improve circulation and stimulate optimum nerve function, properties which can lead to enhanced awareness and cognition. On an emotional level, its ability to help release feelings of anger can allow the mind to gain focus and concentration.

Melissa *(Melissa officinalis)* is a powerful, antimicrobial oil, yet it is very gentle and delicate because of the nature of the plant. It calms and balances the emotions and is very stimulating to the anterior pituitary and immune system.

Safety Data: This blend may be irritating to those with sensitive skin. Avoid eye contact. In case of accidental eye contact, put a few drops of any pure vegetable oil in the eye and call your doctor if necessary. Never use water to dilute or rinse.

Application: Diffuse or wear on neck, throat, and under the nose as a perfume or cologne. Massage 1–2 drops with a finger on the insides of cheeks in the mouth. Doing this 1–2 times a day will immediately improve the smell sensory cortex.

Companion Oils: Clarity Blend and Respiratory Blend.

Circulation Blend

This blend may support cardiovascular, lymphatic, and circulatory systems helping to lower high blood pressure, reduce stress, and alleviate hemorrhoids.

Recipe:

- 24 drops goldenrod
- 10 drops cypress
- 8 drops marjoram
- 4 drops ylang ylang

Goldenrod *(Solidago canadensis)*. The genus name, *solidago*, comes from the Latin *solide*, which means "to make whole." During the Boston Tea Party, when English tea was dumped into Boston Harbor, colonists drank goldenrod tea instead, which gave it the nickname "Liberty Tea." Goldenrod helps to thin mucus secretions and relieve congested mucus. It promotes urination, cleans the kidneys, reduces inflammation, and prevents infection.

Cypress *(Cupressus sempervirens)* is one of the oils used most for the circulatory and lymphatic systems. It may help alleviate edema, cellulite, varicose veins, and water retention. It is anti-infectious, antibacterial, antimicrobial, mucolytic, antiseptic, refreshing, and relaxing. It may help improve the cardiovascular system and circulation as well as help relieve other lymphatic and capillary problems.

Marjoram *(Origanum majorana)* is used for calming the respiratory system and soothing sore and aching muscles. Marjoram may have a sedative effect and calm nervous tension. Marjoram helps regenerate smooth muscle tissue, and assists in relieving spasms, sprains, bruises, and migraine headaches. It is antimicrobial, anti-infectious, antibacterial, antiseptic, and may work as a diuretic.

Ylang Ylang *(Cananga odorata)* has been used traditionally to balance heart function, having been used to treat tachycardia (rapid heart beat) and high blood pressure. Ylang ylang has also been used for insomnia, nervous depression, rage, and low self-esteem.

Safety Data: This blend may be irritating to those with sensitive skin. Avoid eye contact. In case of accidental eye contact, put a few drops of any pure vegetable oil in the eye and call your doctor if necessary. Never use water to dilute or rinse.

Application: Apply over the heart, on the feet, on the life line of the hand and under the ring finger, above the elbow, and behind the ring toe on the left foot. Dilute this blend 50-50 with a vegetable or massage oil for full body massage. It may also help to apply this blend along the spine from the first to the fourth thoracic vertebrae, which correspond to the cardiopulmonary nerves.

Companion Oils: Helichrysum, rosemary, ylang ylang, and Mood Lifting Blend.

Clarity Blend

This blend has been used to promote a clear mind and mental alertness. Rosemary and peppermint, found in this blend, have been used for years to improve mental activity and vitality.

Dr. William N. Dember of the University of Cincinnati discovered in his research[4] that inhaling peppermint oil increased the mental accuracy of the students tested by 28 percent. Clarity Blend may help keep one awake while driving and also keep one from going into shock during times of trauma.

Recipe:

- 40 drops cardamom
- 30 drops rosemary
- 10 drops vetiver
- 5 drops peppermint
- 5 drops geranium
- 3 drops basil

Cardamom *(Elettaria cardamomum)* is uplifting, refreshing, and invigorating. It may be beneficial for clearing confusion. In a study done by Dember, et al.,[5] cardamom was found to enhance performance accuracy.

Rosemary *(Rosmarinus officinalis CT verbenon)* is antiseptic, antimicrobial, and may be beneficial for skin conditions and dandruff. It may help fight candida and is anti-infectious, antispasmodic, balances the endocrine system, and is an expectorant. It helps overcome mental fatigue, stimulating memory and opening the conscious mind.

Vetiver *(Vetiveria zizanioides)* is well known for its anti-inflammatory properties and it is traditionally used for arthritic symptoms. Vetiver may also help acne, anxiety, arthritis, cuts, depression (including postpartum), insomnia, rheumatism, stress, and oily, aging, tired, or irritated skin.

Peppermint *(Mentha piperita)* is one of the oldest and most highly regarded herbs for soothing digestion. Jean Valnet, MD, studied the beneficial effects of peppermint on the liver and respiratory systems. Daniel Pénoël, MD, reports that it may help to reduce fevers, candida, nausea,[6] and vomiting, and

4. Dember WN, et al., Olfactory Stimulation and Sustained Attention, *Compendium of Olfactory*, (Avery N. Gilbert, Editor) 1995, pp. 39-46.

5. Dember, William N; Warm, Joel S; Parasuraman, Raja. Olfactory stimulation and sustained attention. In *Compendium of Olfactory Research, Explorations in Aroma-Chology: Investigating the Sense of Smell and Human Response to Odors 1982-1984*, Avery N. Gilbert (Ed.) 1995, Kendall/ Hunt Publishing Co., Dubuque, IA, 39-46

6. Pénoël, Daniel, MD Pénoël, Rose-Marie, *Natural Home Health Care Using Essential Oils*, Editions Osmobiose 1998, La Drome, France, pp. 136-7.

Clarity Blend Reveals Toxic Buildup

Those who get headaches from diffusing Clarity Blend may be suffering from significant petrochemical or heavy metal accumulation in the brain. This blend is rich in the essential oil of cardamom, which contains high levels of transphenol—a powerful molecule which tends to generate headaches in the presence of petrochemicals or heavy metals.

strengthen the respiratory system. Adding peppermint to drinking water helps cool body temperature during hot weather. This effect is caused by the menthol in peppermint. This compound stimulates the nervous system and may be stimulating for the mind.

Geranium *(Pelargonium graveolens)* assists in balancing hormones. It is antispasmodic, anti-inflammatory, anti-infectious, antibacterial, antifungal, and stimulates the liver and pancreas. This oil is uplifting and has been used to treat anxiety.

Basil *(Ocimum basilicum)* can be relaxing to smooth muscles as well as the involuntary muscles of the heart and digestive system. It may soothe insect bites from bees, wasps, and spiders. It has been found to alleviate mental fatigue, spasms, rhinitis, and help when there is a loss of smell due to nasal congestion.

Safety Data: This blend may be irritating to those with sensitive skin. Avoid eye contact. In case of accidental eye contact, put a few drops of any pure vegetable oil in the eye and call your doctor if necessary. Never use water to dilute or rinse.

Application: Diffuse, mix with Epson salt and put in bath water, or put 2–5 drops on a cotton ball and put cotton in home and car air vents. Apply on temples, wrists, back of neck, and feet. Apply on the brain Vita Flex points on the feet (large toe).

Companion Oils: Energy Blend (when overly tired), Brain Blend, lemon, and peppermint.

Digestive Blend

These oils are blended to assist in relieving digestive problems such as an upset stomach, belching, heartburn, and bloating. Massage a drop or two on the outer ear to help alleviate morning sickness. Digestive Blend has been found to rid animals of parasites after application to their feet. It may also help dispel parasites by massaging and placing a compress across the animal's stomach.

Recipe:

- 30 drops anise
- 25 drops rosemary
- 10 drops tarragon
- 8 drops ginger
- 8 drops fennel
- 3 drops blue tansy

Anise *(Pimpinella anisum)* is antispasmodic, antiseptic, stimulates the increase of bile from the liver, expels worms, increases lactation, and helps calm gall bladder contractions. It may help with painful menstruation and irregularity, problems with menopause, dyspepsia, spastic colitis, flatulence, indigestion, lung congestion, vomiting, asthmatic bronchitis, and intestinal pain. According to Gattefossé, it is a good digestive aid.

Rosemary *(Rosmarinus officinalis CT verbenon)* is antiseptic, antimicrobial, and may be beneficial for skin conditions and dandruff. It may help fight candida and is anti-infectious, antispasmodic, balances the endocrine system, and is an expectorant. It helps overcome mental fatigue, stimulating memory and opening the conscious mind.

Tarragon *(Artemisia dracunculus)* has been used in Europe for its antimicrobial and antiseptic functions. It helps to reduce dyspepsia, intestinal spasms, and urinary tract infection. It may ease digestion, abdominal pain, and spasms. It may also reduce premenstrual discomfort and nerve pain. It is antispasmodic, anti-inflammatory, anti-infectious, antiviral, antibacterial, and prevents fermentation.

Ginger *(Zingiber officinale)* is used for relief from motion sickness, arthritis, rheumatism, sprains, muscle aches and pains, congestion, coughs, sinusitis, sore throats, diarrhea, flatulence, colic, indigestion, loss of appetite, stomachache, fever, flu, chills, and infectious disease.

Fennel *(Foeniculum vulgare)* is antiseptic and stimulating to the circulatory and respiratory systems. It is antispasmodic, antiseptic, and used for flatulence and vomiting. It is stimulating to the cardiovascular and respiratory systems. With its hormone-like activity, it may help facilitate childbirth and increase lactation after birthing. Fennel has been used to soothe the stomach and is offered in other countries after meals to aid digestion.

Blue Tansy (*Tanacetum annuum*) may help cleanse the liver and calm the lymphatic system, thus helping one to overcome anger and negative emotions and promote a feeling of self-control. European research shows that it works as an antihistamine, anti-inflammatory, and stimulant for the thymus gland. It is also effective in relieving dermatitis, arthritis, sciatica, tuberculosis, and allergies.

Safety Data: This blend may be irritating to those with sensitive skin. Avoid eye contact. In case of accidental eye contact, put a few drops of any pure vegetable oil in the eye and call your doctor if necessary. Never use water to dilute or rinse.

Application: Apply to the stomach & intestine Vita Flex points (see Chapter 10) on the feet. Massage a drop or two on outer ear to help alleviate morning sickness. Add 1–2 drops to 8 ounces of water as a dietary supplement. In case of an upset stomach, Digestive Blend may be applied on location. Massage 2–3 drops on the paws of animals to expel parasites. Parasites may also be dispelled by massaging or placing a compress across the animal's stomach.

Companion Oils: Peppermint and spearmint.

Emotional Release Blend

This oil blend may stimulate a sense of harmony and balance within the mind and body, and help release anger and memory trauma from the cells of the liver bringing about a sense of peace and emotional well-being. Letting go of negative emotions and releasing frustration enables one to progress in a positive way, both mentally and physically.

Recipe:

- 20 drops German chamomile
- 10 drops ledum
- 30 drops ylang ylang
- 25 drops geranium
- 15 drops sandalwood

German Chamomile *(Matricaria recutita)* has been a highly respected oil for over 3,000 years and has been used for helping skin conditions such as dermatitis, boils, acne, rashes, and eczema. It is also used for hair care, burns, cuts, toothaches, teething pains, inflamed joints, menopausal problems, insomnia, migraine headaches, and stress-related complaints.

Ledum *(Ledum groenlandicum)* is anti-inflammatory, antitumoral, antibacterial, diuretic, hepatoprotectant, and decongestant. Ledum is a strongly aromatic herb that has been used for centuries in folk medicine. The native people of Eastern Canada used this herb for tea, as a general tonic, and to treat a variety of kidney-related problems. Ledum has helped protect the native people of North America against scurvy for thousands of years. The Cree Indians used it for fevers and colds.

Ylang Ylang *(Cananga odorata)* helps bring about a sense of relaxation and may help balance male and female energies. It balances equilibrium and restores confidence and self-love.

Geranium *(Pelargonium graveolens)* stimulates nerves and assists in balancing hormones. Its aromatic influence helps release negative memories, thereby opening and elevating the mind.

Sandalwood *(Santalum album)* is high in sesquiterpenes, which have been researched for their ability to stimulate the pineal gland and the limbic region of the brain, the center of our emotions. The pineal gland is responsible for releasing melatonin, a hormone that enhances deep sleep. Used traditionally for skin revitalization, yoga, and meditation, sandalwood is similar to frankincense oil in its support of nerves and circulation.

Safety Data: This blend may be irritating to those with sensitive skin. Avoid eye contact. In case of accidental eye contact, put a few drops of any pure vegetable oil in the eye and call your doctor if necessary. Never use water to dilute or rinse.

Application: Apply over the liver or as a compress. Massage on the bottom of the feet and apply behind the ears. May be worn as a perfume or cologne.

Companion Oil: Liver Blend.

Energy Blend

Traditionally, the oils in this blend were used for increasing vitality, circulation, and alertness in the body. When used together with Clarity Blend, it may help one stay awake while driving late at night.

Recipe:

- 40 drops rosemary
- 30 drops balsam fir
- 20 drops juniper
- 10 drops nutmeg
- 10 drops pepper
- 3 drops blue tansy

Rosemary *(Rosmarinus officinalis CT 1,8 cineol)* is antiseptic, antimicrobial, and may be beneficial for skin conditions and dandruff. It may help fight candida and is anti-infectious, antispasmodic, balances the endocrine system, and is an expectorant. It helps overcome mental fatigue, stimulating memory and opening the conscious mind.

Balsam Fir *(Abies balsamea)* has antiseptic properties and also contains d-limonene, a powerful antioxidant.

Juniper *(Juniperus communis* or *J. osteosperma)* may work as a detoxifier and cleanser, and promotes improved nerve and kidney function. It is also beneficial for the skin, reducing dermatitis, eczema, and acne. It elevates spiritual awareness, creating feelings of love and peace.

Nutmeg *(Myristica fragrans)* has adrenal cortex-like activity, which helps support the adrenal glands for increased energy. It may help with difficulties related to circulation, aches and pains in muscles and joints related to stress, arthritis, and gout. Nutmeg may also help with digestive problems. It is antiseptic, antiparasitic, analgesic, and a neurotonic.

Pepper, Black *(Piper nigrum)* stimulates the endocrine system and increases energy while increasing cellular oxygenation. It is anti-inflammatory which may soothe deep tissue muscle aches. It is an expectorant, supportive to the digestive glands, and has been traditionally used for rheumatoid arthritis.

Blue Tansy (*Tanacetum annuum*) may help cleanse the liver and calm the lymphatic system thus helping one to overcome anger and negative emotions and promote a feeling of self-control. European research shows that it works as an antihistamine, anti-inflammatory, and stimulant for the thymus gland, reducing dermatitis, arthritis, sciatica, tuberculosis, and allergies.

Safety Data: This blend may be irritating to those with sensitive skin. Avoid eye contact. In case of accidental eye contact, put a few drops of any pure vegetable oil in the eye and call your doctor if necessary. Never use water to dilute or rinse.

Application: Diffuse or apply on the wrists, temples, back of the neck, or behind ears as a perfume or cologne. Add to warm bath water after mixing in Epsom salt or bath gel. Dilute 50-50 with a vegetable or massage oil for an uplifting body massage. Massage on Vita Flex points of the feet. Simple diffusion can be achieved by applying a few drops on a cotton ball and placing the cotton in the air vent of a car or on the heat registers of the home or hotel room.

Companion Oils: Clarity Blend and Brain Blend.

Energy Balance Blend

This blend helps balance energies within the body, giving courage, confidence, and self-esteem. It has been found to help the muscles of the body self-correct, improving balance and alignment and relieving pain. The oils in this blend empower the physical and spiritual bodies to overcome fear and opposition when facing adversity. They help build courage, confidence, and self-esteem. This blend has been touted as a "chiropractor in a bottle." It has improved scoliosis for some in as little as 30 minutes, while other individuals require several applications

Recipe:

- 15 drops spruce
- 7 drops frankincense
- 6 drops blue tansy
- 2 drops rosewood
- 1 drop balsam fir

Spruce *(Picea mariana)* helps to open and release emotional blocks, bringing about a feeling of balance and grounding. Spruce is anti-infectious, antiseptic, and anti-inflammatory

Frankincense *(Boswellia carteri)* is considered a holy anointing oil in the Middle East and has been used in religious ceremonies for thousands of years. Containing sesquiterpenes, it helps stimulate the limbic part of the brain, which elevates the mind, helping to overcome stress and despair. It is also used in European medicine to combat depression.

Blue Tansy (*Tanacetum annuum*) may help cleanse the liver and calm the lymphatic system, helping one to overcome anger and negative emotions and thereby promote a feeling of self-control. Its primary constituents are limonene and sesquiterpenes. European research shows that it works as an antihistamine, anti-inflammatory, and stimulant for the thymus gland reducing dermatitis, arthritis, sciatica, tuberculosis, and allergies.

Rosewood *(Aniba rosaeodora)* is soothing and nourishing to the skin. It has been researched at Weber State University for its inhibition rate against gram positive and gram negative bacterial growth.[7] This oil is soothing, creates skin elasticity, and helps the skin rid itself of irritations and problems such as candida. It is anti-infectious, antibacterial, antifungal, antiviral, and antiparasitic.

Balsam Fir *(Abies balsamea)* has antiseptic properties and also contains d-limonene, a powerful antioxidant.

7. Chao, S et al., Screening for Inhibitory Activity of Essential Oils on Selected Bacteria, Fungi, and Viruses, *J Essen Oil Res, Sept./Oct.* 2000.

Safety Data: This blend may be irritating to those with sensitive skin. Avoid eye contact. In case of accidental eye contact, put a few drops of any pure vegetable oil in the eye and call your doctor if necessary. Never use water to dilute or rinse.

Application: Apply 4–6 drops on the bottoms of the feet. Put on the wrists, the chest, and at the base of the neck, or along the spine as used in the Raindrop Technique (see Chapter 11). When applying the oils along the spine, apply Energy Balance Blend first and let it work for 5–10 minutes before applying other oils. This blend may be worn as a perfume or cologne.

Female Blend

This blend helps relieve PMS symptoms and menstrual discomforts including cramping and irregular periods. It may also be used for mood swings and headaches caused by hormonal imbalances.

Recipe:

- 30 drops clary sage
- 20 drops fennel
- 20 drops marjoram
- 5 drops jasmine
- 8 drops sage

Clary Sage *(Salvia sclarea)* balances the hormones. It contains natural sclareol, a phytoestrogen that mimics estrogen function. It may help with menstrual cramps, PMS, pre-menopause symptoms, and circulatory problems.

Fennel *(Foeniculum vulgare)* is antiseptic and stimulating to the circulatory and respiratory systems. It is antispasmodic, antiseptic, and used for flatulence and vomiting. It is stimulating to the cardiovascular and respiratory systems. With its hormone-like activity, it may help facilitate childbirth and increase lactation after birthing. Fennel has been used to soothe the stomach and is offered in other countries after meals to aid digestion.

Marjoram *(Origanum majorana)* is used for calming the respiratory system and soothing sore and aching muscles. Marjoram helps regenerate smooth muscle tissue, and also assists in relieving spasms and migraine headaches and calming the nerves. It is antimicrobial, anti-infectious, antibacterial, antiseptic and may work as a diuretic. Marjoram aids in relief of menopause symptoms as well as painful periods.

Jasmine *(Jasminum officinale)* is beneficial for dry, greasy, irritated, or sensitive skin. It is used for muscle spasms, sprains, coughs, laryngitis, frigidity, depression, and nervous exhaustion. Jasmine has also been used for prostate problems and impotence.

Sage *(Salvia officinalis)* is estrogen-like, supports menstruation, prevents and reduces scarring, regulates circulation, soothes skin conditions and is a balancer and detoxifier of the body. Sage contains camphor, which balances estrogen levels, providing support during PMS and menopause.

Safety Data: This blend may be irritating to those with sensitive skin. Avoid eye contact. In case of accidental eye contact, put a few drops of any pure vegetable oil in the eye and call your doctor if necessary. Never use water to dilute or rinse.

Application: Apply to the Vita Flex points (see Chapter 10) on the feet and around the ankles, both inside and out. Dilute 50-50 with a vegetable or massage oil for application on other locations. May also be applied as a warm compress over the lower abdomen, across the lower back, or on any painful location. Diffuse directly or with a diffuser.

Companion Oils: Pain Relief Blend, Male Blend, jasmine, and clary sage.

Glandular Blend

This blend may help overall vitality. It contains oils associated with hormonal balance, improving and balancing metabolism, and weight control. It may also help alleviate hot flashes in women.

Recipe:

- 40 drops spearmint
- 30 drops myrtle
- 30 drops Fleabane
- 10 drops sage
- 8 drops geranium
- 5 drops nutmeg

Spearmint *(Mentha spicata)* helps support the respiratory and nervous systems. With its hormone-like activity, it may help open and release emotional blocks and bring about a feeling of balance. This oil may aid the respiratory, nervous, and glandular systems. Spearmint is antispasmodic, anti-infectious, antiparasitic, antiseptic, and anti-inflammatory. It has also been used to increase metabolism to burn fat.

Myrtle *(Myrtus communis)* may help normalize hormonal imbalances of the thyroid and ovaries. It may help the respiratory system with chronic coughs and tuberculosis. Myrtle is suitable to use for coughs and chest complaints with children, and may support immune function in fighting cold, flu, and infectious disease.

Fleabane *(Conyza canadensis)* stimulates the liver and pancreas, is anti-rheumatic, antispasmodic, and hormone-like. Daniel Pénoël, MD, used it to treat children with retarded puberty. It is also known as "fleabane."

Sage *(Salvia officinalis)* has been used in Europe for skin conditions such as eczema, acne, dandruff, and hair loss. It has been recognized for its ability to strengthen the vital centers. It may help in relieving depression and mental fatigue. Sage contains sclareol, which stimulates the body to produce its own estrogen. It contains natural estrogenic compounds that help relieve PMS symptoms. The Lakota Indians used it for purification and healing. Sage is used to dispel negative emotions from sexual abuse and denial, and as a complete body tonic for healing and strength.

Geranium *(Pelargonium graveolens)* assists in balancing hormones. It is antispasmodic, relaxant, anti-inflammatory, anti-infectious, antibacterial, antifungal, and stimulates the liver and pancreas.

Nutmeg *(Myristica fragrans)* helps support the adrenal glands for increased energy. It may help with difficulties related to circulation. It may also help relieve aches and pains in muscles and joints related to stress, arthritis, and gout. Nutmeg may also help with digestive problems such as flatulence, indigestion, and nausea. It is antiseptic, antiparasitic, and a neurotonic.

Safety Data: This blend may be irritating to those with sensitive skin. Avoid eye contact. In case of accidental eye contact, put a few drops of any pure vegetable oil in the eye and call your doctor if necessary. Never use water to dilute or rinse.

Application: Dilute 50-50 and apply over the lower back, thyroid, kidneys, liver, feet, and glandular areas. It may also be applied to the Vita Flex points on the feet for these same areas of the body.

Companion Oils: Energy Blend, ledum, peppermint, and myrtle.

Headache Blend

This blend contains oils that were traditionally used to relieve headaches, nausea, depression, and problems related to migraine headaches.

Recipe:

- 10 drops peppermint
- 10 drops basil
- 8 drops marjoram
- 3 drops helichrysum

Peppermint *(Mentha piperita)* is one of the oldest and most highly regarded herbs for soothing digestion. Jean Valnet, MD, studied the beneficial effects of peppermint on the liver and respiratory systems. Other scientists have researched its effect on impaired taste and smell as well as improved concentration and mental accuracy. Alan Hirsch, MD, studied its ability to directly affect the brain's satiety center, triggering a sensation of fullness after meals, which may help in weight loss by curbing the appetite. Daniel Pénoël, MD, reports that it may help to reduce fevers, candida, nausea, vomiting, and strengthen the respiratory system. Adding peppermint oil to drinking water helps cool body temperature during hot weather.

Basil *(Ocimum basilicum)* can be relaxing to smooth muscles as well as the involuntary muscles of the heart and digestive system. It may soothe insect bites from bees, wasps, and spiders. Basil has been found to alleviate mental fatigue, spasms, rhinitis, and help when there is a loss of smell due to nasal congestion.

Marjoram *(Origanum majorana)* is used for calming the respiratory system and soothing sore and aching muscles. Marjoram helps regenerate smooth muscle tissue, and also assists in relieving spasms and migraine headaches and calming the nerves. It is antimicrobial, anti-infectious, antibacterial, and antiseptic, and may work as a diuretic.

Helichrysum *(Helichrysum italicum)* helps regenerate tissue and nerves and improves circulation. It is an anticoagulant, prevents phlebitis, helps regulate cholesterol, stimulates liver cell function, and may help clean plaque and debris from the veins and arteries. It is mucolytic, an expectorant, antispasmodic, and reduces scarring and discoloration. It may also stimulate nerve endings and improve conditions such as hearing loss. It may help release feelings of anger promoting forgiveness.

Safety Data: This blend may be irritating to those with sensitive skin. Avoid eye contact. In case of accidental eye contact, put a few drops of any pure vegetable oil in the eye and call your doctor if necessary. Never use water to dilute or rinse.

Application: Most effective when inhaled. Rub 2 drops in the palms of the hands, cup over the nose and inhale. Massage several drops at the base of the skull, and on the back of the neck. Apply to the forehead, crown, shoulders, temples, and Vita Flex points on the feet.

Companion Oils: Muscle Relaxing Blend, Clarity Blend, and Pain Relief Blend.

Immune Blend

This is a powerful blend for building, strengthening, and protecting the body and supporting the immune system. Diffusing Immune Blend protects the home environment, especially during the seasons of cold and flu. Immune Blend has been found to help with symptoms of lupus and also inner ear infections.

Recipe:

- 30 drops mountain savory
- 10 drops thyme
- 20 drops lemon
- 20 drops ravansara
- 5 drops oregano
- 5 drops cumin
- 5 drops tansy

Mountain Savory *(Satureja montana)* is antimicrobial and immune stimulating. It is antiviral, antibacterial, antifungal, antiparasitic, and a general tonic for the body.

Thyme *(Thymus vulgaris CT thymol)* is highly antimicrobial and antifungal. Thyme has been used for respiratory problems, digestive complaints, the prevention and treatment of infection, gastritis, bronchitis, pertussis, asthma, laryngitis, and tonsilitis. It may also help with bacterial infections, respiratory infections, poor circulation, depression, digestion, headaches, insomnia, rheumatism, urinary infections, and viruses along the spine.

Lemon *(Citrus limon)* has antiseptic-like properties and contains compounds that have been studied for their effects on immune function. It increases microcirculation, which may improve vision. It may serve as an insect repellent and may be beneficial for the skin. It has been found to promote leukocyte formation, dissolve cellulite, increase lymphatic function, and promote a sense of well-being. Its fragrance is stimulating and invigorating.

Ravensara *(Ravensara aromatica)* is referred to by the people of Madagascar as the oil that heals. It is antiseptic, anti-infectious, antiviral, antibacterial, antifungal, an expectorant and supporting to the nerves. Similar to clove and nutmeg, ravensara may aid the respiratory system and support the adrenal glands. It has been shown to help with flu, sinusitis, bronchitis, viral hepatitis, cholera, herpes, infectious mononucleosis, insomnia, muscle fatigue, and rhinopharyngitis.

Oregano *(Origanum compactum)* is one of the most powerful antimicrobial essential oils. Laboratory research at Weber State University[8] showed it to have a 99 percent kill rate against *in vitro* colonies of *Streptococcus pneumoniae*, a microorganism responsible for many kinds of lung and throat infections. This oil is antiviral, antibacterial, antifungal, and antiparasitic.

Cumin *(Cuminum cyminum)*, commonly found in Egypt, helps with digestion and supports the immune system. It is antiseptic, antispasmodic, and carminative.

Tansy *(Tanacetum vulgare*) is antiviral, anti-infectious, antibacterial, and fights cold, flu, and infections. According to E. Joseph Montagna's *Herbal Desk Reference*, tansy may improve weakness of the kidneys, heart, joints, and digestive system, and may help tone the entire body system.

Safety Data: This blend may be irritating to those with sensitive skin. Avoid eye contact. In case of accidental eye contact, put a few drops of any pure vegetable oil in the eye and call your doctor if necessary. Never use water to dilute or rinse.

Application: Diffuse daily for 15–30 minutes every 3–4 hours or as needed. Massage on the bottom of the feet. Dilute 20-80 and apply Raindrop-style along the spine as needed. May also be rubbed on the throat and chest. Apply 2–3 drops to the thymus. Put 1 drop on a piece of cotton and place the cotton in the ear for earaches.

Companion Oils: Alternate with Antimicrobial Blend. Other single oils may be added for extra strength: rosewood, melissa, oregano, clove, cistus, frankincense, and mountain savory.

8. Horne D, et al., Antimicrobial effects of essential oils on Streptococcus pneumoniae. *Journal of Essential Oil Research,* (September/October 2001). 13, 387-392.

Liver Blend

The oils in this blend have been known to support liver and lymphatic system detoxification. Negative emotions such as anger and hate are stored in the liver, creating toxicity and leading to sickness and disease. Liver Blend also helps break addictions to substances such as coffee, alcohol, drugs, and tobacco.

Recipe:

- 30 drops Roman chamomile
- 20 drops ledum
- 10 drops carrot seed
- 10 drops celery seed
- 8 drops German chamomile

Roman Chamomile *(Chamaemelum nobile)* may calm and relieve restlessness, tension, insomnia, and muscle tension. Chamomile helps heal cuts, scrapes, and bruises, and is anti-infectious. It may relieve allergies and expel toxins from the liver. It is used extensively in Europe for skin care.

Ledum *(Ledum groenlandicum)* is anti-inflammatory, antitumoral, antibacterial, diuretic, hepatoprotectant, and decongestant. Ledum is a strongly aromatic herb that has been used for centuries in folk medicine. The native people of Eastern Canada used this herb for tea, as a general tonic, and to treat a variety of kidney-related problems. Ledum has helped protect the native people of North America against scurvy for thousands of years. The Cree Indians used it for fevers and colds.

Carrot Seed *(Daucus carota)* is widely used in European folk medicine for the treatment of jaundice and hepatic disorders. It has a tonic action on the liver and gallbladder.

German Chamomile *(Matricaria recutita)* has been a highly respected oil for over 3,000 years and has been used for helping skin conditions such as dermatitis, boils, acne, rashes, and eczema. It is also used for hair care, burns, cuts, toothaches, teething pains, inflamed joints, menopausal problems, insomnia, migraine headaches, and stress-related complaints.

Celery Seed *(Apium graveolens)* has been used traditionally to treat arthritis and muscle spasm. With antibacterial and diuretic properties, celery seed oil has been used to help flush bacteria and minerals that can cause kidney and bladder stones. Lab animal studies have shown that celery seed prevents liver damage caused by toxic chemicals. Do not use this oil if you are pregnant.

Safety Data: This blend may be irritating to those with sensitive skin. Avoid eye contact. In case of accidental eye contact, put a few drops of any pure vegetable oil in the eye and call your doctor if necessary. Never use water to dilute or rinse.

Application: Apply over the liver or use as a hot compress. Massage the Vita Flex points on the feet or dilute with a vegetable or massage oil and apply Raindrop-style along the spine.

Companion Oil: Digestive Blend.

Male Blend

This blend is beneficial for both men and women. It may help to decongest the prostate and promote greater hormonal balance. Some women have found that it reduces hot flashes. (Generally, Male Blend helps women age 30 and older, and Female Blend is for younger women.)

Recipe:

- 30 drops clary sage
- 30 drops fennel
- 20 drops sage
- 10 drops yarrow
- 5 drops peppermint

Clary Sage *(Salvia sclarea)* balances the hormones. It contains natural sclareol, a phytoestrogen that mimics estrogen function. It may help with menstrual cramps, PMS, pre-menopause symptoms, circulatory problems.

Fennel *(Foeniculum vulgare)* is antispasmodic, antiseptic, and stimulating to the circulatory and respiratory systems. With its hormone-like activity, it may help facilitate childbirth and increase lactation after birthing.

Sage *(Salvia officinalis)* has been used in Europe for skin conditions such as eczema, acne, and dandruff. It has been recognized for its benefits of strengthening the vital centers. It may help in relieving depression and mental fatigue. Sage contains sclareol, which stimulates the body to produce its own estrogen. Like its cousin clary sage, sage is known for supporting the body during PMS and menopause. The Lakota Indians used sage for purification and healing, and to dispel negative emotions from denial and sexual abuse, as well as a complete body tonic for healing and strength.

Yarrow *(Achillea millefolium)* decongests the prostate and balances hormones. It is anti-inflammatory, reduces scarring, and helps with nerve inflammation.

Peppermint *(Mentha piperita)* is one of the oldest and most highly regarded herbs for soothing digestion. Jean Valnet, MD, studied the beneficial effects of peppermint on the liver and respiratory systems. Daniel Pénoël, MD, reports that it may help to reduce fevers, candida, nausea, vomiting, and strengthen the respiratory system. Adding peppermint oil to drinking water helps cool body temperature during hot weather.

Safety Data: This blend may be irritating to those with sensitive skin. Avoid eye contact. In case of accidental eye contact, put a few drops of any pure vegetable oil in the eye and call your doctor if necessary. Never use water to dilute or rinse.

Application: Apply to Vita Flex points on the ankles. Massage over the lower pelvis or apply as a hot compress directly on other areas of concern.

Companion Oils: Glandular Blend, clary sage, and sage.

Mood Lifting Blend

This exotic blend inspires feelings of self-love and confidence and brings joy to the heart. It inspires romance and may help overcome grief and depression.

Recipe:

- 40 drops bergamot
- 40 drops ylang ylang
- 30 drops rosewood
- 20 drops geranium
- 10 drops jasmine
- 5 drops rose

Bergamot *(Citrus bergamia)* has been used in the Middle East for hundreds of years for acne, boils, cold sores, eczema, insect bites, psoriasis, scabies, varicose veins, ulcers, sore throat, thrush, oily complexion, infectious disease, and depression. It balances hormones, calms emotions, and relieves anxiety, stress, and tension.

Ylang Ylang *(Cananga odorata)* helps bring about a sense of relaxation and may help balance male and female energies. It balances equilibrium and restores confidence and self-love.

Rosewood *(Aniba rosaeodora)* is soothing and nourishing to the skin. It has been researched at Weber State University for its inhibition rate against gram positive and gram negative bacterial growth.[9] This oil is soothing, creates skin elasticity, and helps the skin rid itself of irritations and problems such as candida. It is anti-infectious, antibacterial, antifungal, antiviral, and antiparasitic.

Geranium *(Pelargonium graveolens)* assists in balancing hormones. It is antispasmodic, anti-inflammatory, anti-infectious, antibacterial, antifungal, and stimulates the liver and pancreas.

Jasmine *(Jasminum officinale)* is beneficial for dry, greasy, irritated, or sensitive skin. It is used for muscle spasms, sprains, coughs, laryngitis, frigidity, depression, and nervous exhaustion.

Rose *(Rosa damascena)* appears to possess a very high biofrequency compared to other essential oils. It creates a sense of balance, harmony, and well-being, and elevates the mind. Rose promotes healthy skin, reduces scarring, and may help with chronic bronchitis, asthma, tuberculosis, sexual disabilities, frigidity, impotency, skin disease, ulcers, sprains, wrinkles, thrush, and gingivitis.

Safety Data: This blend may be irritating to those with sensitive skin. Avoid eye contact. In case of accidental eye contact, put a few drops of any pure vegetable oil in the eye and call your doctor if necessary. Never use water to dilute or rinse.

Application: Diffuse or use as a perfume or cologne. Apply directly over the heart, thymus, temples, and wrists. Add to bath water. Dilute with a vegetable or massage oil for a full-body massage. Put two drops on a wet cloth and put the cloth in the dryer for fragrancing.

Companion Oil: Clarity Blend.

9. Chao, et al., Screening for Inhibitory Activity of Essential Oils on Selected Bacteria, Fungi, and Viruses, *J Essen Oil Res, Aug*. 2000.

Muscle Relaxing Blend

This special blend may help relax, calm, and relieve tight, sore, tired, and aching muscles resulting from sports injuries, fatigue, or stress. It may also help to relieve headaches or charlie horses.

Recipe:

- 25 drops balsam fir
- 15 drops basil
- 10 drops marjoram
- 8 drops spruce
- 4 drops wintergreen

Balsam Fir *(Abies balsamea)* has antiseptic properties and also contains d-limonene, a powerful antioxidant.

Basil *(Ocimum basilicum)* can be relaxing to smooth muscles and the involuntary muscles of the heart and digestive system. The name, "basil," is derived from the Greek word, *basilicon*, meaning a "royal" ointment or remedy. It may soothe insect bites from bees, wasps, and spiders. Basil has been found to alleviate mental fatigue, muscle spasms, and rhinitis, and help when there is a loss of smell due to nasal congestion.

Marjoram *(Origanum majorana)* is used for calming the respiratory system and soothing sore and aching muscles. Marjoram helps regenerate smooth muscle tissue, and assists in relieving spasms, sprains, bruises, migraine headaches, and calming the nerves. It is antimicrobial, anti-infectious, antibacterial, antiseptic, and may work as a diuretic.

Spruce *(Picea mariana)* helps the respiratory and nervous systems. It is anti-infectious, antiseptic, and anti-inflammatory. Its aromatic influences help to open and release emotional blocks, bringing about a feeling of balance and grounding.

Wintergreen *(Gaultheria procumbens)* leaves have been chewed by Native Americans to increase respiratory capacity when running long distances and performing difficult labor. Settlers in early America had their children chew the leaves for several weeks each spring to prevent tooth decay. Wintergreen was used as a substitute for black tea during the Revolutionary War. It contains an active principle similar to cortisone and is beneficial for bone, muscle, and joint discomfort.

Safety Data: This blend may be irritating to those with sensitive skin. Avoid eye contact. In case of accidental eye contact, put a few drops of any pure vegetable oil in the eye and call your doctor if necessary. Never use water to dilute or rinse.

Application: Apply on location to muscles, neck, and feet as an aid to relaxation. Dilute with a vegetable or massage oil for a body massage.

Companion Oils: Basil, elemi, spruce, wintergreen or birch, helichrysum, tansy, and marjoram.

Pain Relief Blend

This blend was created to help heal an injury where ligaments were severely torn. It helps reduce inflammation, which increases circulation and healing and reduces pain. Many people have found relief from arthritis symptoms, sports injuries, sprains, muscle spasms, bumps, and bruises, with this blend.

Recipe:

- 30 drops balsam fir
- 10 drops helichrysum
- 5 drops peppermint
- 1 drop oregano

Balsam Fir *(Abies balsamea)* has antiseptic properties and also contains d-limonene, a powerful antioxidant.

Helichrysum *(Helichrysum italicum)* helps regenerate tissue and nerves and improve circulation. It is an anticoagulant, prevents phlebitis, helps regulate cholesterol, stimulates liver cell function, and may help clean plaque and debris from the veins and arteries. Helichrysum is mucolytic, an expectorant, antispasmodic, and reduces scarring and discoloration. It may also stimulate nerve endings and improve conditions such as hearing loss. It may help release feelings of anger and thereby promote forgiveness.

Oregano *(Origanum compactum)* is one of the most powerful antimicrobial essential oils. Laboratory research at Weber State University showed it to have a 99 percent kill rate against *in vitro* colonies of *Streptococcus pneumoniae*, a microorganism responsible for many kinds of lung and throat infections.[10] Oregano is antiviral, antibacterial, antifungal, and antiparasitic.

10. Horne D, et al., Antimicrobial effects of essential oils on Streptococcus pneumoniae. *Journal of Essential Oil Research,* (September/October 2001). 13, 387-392.

Peppermint *(Mentha piperita)* is one of the oldest and most highly regarded herbs for soothing digestion. Jean Valnet, MD, studied the beneficial effects of peppermint on the liver and respiratory systems. Daniel Pénoël, MD, reports that it may help to reduce fevers, candida, nausea, vomiting, and strengthen the respiratory system. Adding peppermint oil to drinking water helps cool body temperature during hot weather.

Safety Data: This blend may be irritating to those with sensitive skin. Avoid eye contact. In case of accidental eye contact, put a few drops of any pure vegetable oil in the eye and call your doctor if necessary. Never use water to dilute or rinse.

Application: Apply to the bottom of the feet first, working the Vita Flex points, and then topically on location. Rub on the temples, the back of the neck, the forehead, or use as a compress on the back. Apply on location for sore muscles, cramps, bruises, or wherever there is discomfort after exercise.

Companion Oils: Antiseptic Blend and wintergreen or birch (for bone pain).

Respiratory Blend

This combination gives strength in fighting respiratory disease and infections; and may help alleviate symptoms of tuberculosis, asthma, and pneumonia.

Recipe:

- 30 drops ravensara
- 25 drops eucalyptus radiata
- 20 drops eucalyptus australiana
- 18 drops ponderosa pine
- 16 drops myrtle
- 10 drops cypress
- 5 drops peppermint

Ravensara *(Ravensara aromatica)* is referred to by the people of Madagascar as the oil that heals. It is antiseptic, anti-infectious, antiviral, antibacterial, antifungal, an expectorant, and supporting to the nerves. Similar to clove and nutmeg, ravensara may aid the respiratory system. It has been shown to help with flu, sinusitis, bronchitis, herpes, infectious mononucleosis, and rhinopharyngitis.

Eucalyptus *(Eucalyptus radiata)* may have a profound antiviral effect upon the respiratory system. It may also help reduce inflammation of the nasal mucous membrane.

Eucalyptus *(Eucalyptus radiata var. australiana)* is antiviral, antibacterial, and antifungal.

Ponderosa Pine *(Pinus ponderosa)* opens and disinfects the respiratory system, particularly the bronchial tract. It has been used since the time of Hippocrates to support respiratory function and fight infection. According to Daniel Pénoël, MD, pine is one of the best oils for bronchitis and pneumonia.

Myrtle *(Myrtus communis)* may help normalize hormonal imbalances of the thyroid and ovaries. It may help the respiratory system with chronic coughs and tuberculosis. Myrtle is suitable to use for coughs and chest complaints with children, and may support immune function in fighting cold, flu, and infectious disease.

Cypress *(Cupressus sempervirens)* promotes blood circulation and lymph flow. It is anti-infectious, antibacterial, antimicrobial, mucolytic, antiseptic, refreshing, and relaxing.

Peppermint *(Mentha piperita)* is useful for many kinds of respiratory conditions, including bronchitis and pneumonia. High in menthol and menthone, it helps suppress coughs and clears lung and nasal congestion.

Safety Data: This blend may be irritating to those with sensitive skin. Avoid eye contact. In case of accidental eye contact, put a few drops of any pure vegetable oil in the eye and call your doctor if necessary. Never use water to dilute or rinse.

Application: Diffuse Massage on the Vita Flex points on the feet. Apply topically over the throat and lung area. Put a few drops on your pillow at night. Use in a retention enema diluted 20-80 with a vegetable oil and retain during the night.

Companion Oils: Antimicrobial Blend and Antiseptic Blend.

Romance Blend

This blend has a beautiful and romantic fragrance that is extremely uplifting, refreshing, and arousing. It promotes the excitement of experiencing new heights of self-expression and awareness. Romance Blend is also very nourishing and hydrating for the skin.

Recipe:

- 30 drops geranium
- 30 drops rosewood
- 15 drops ylang ylang
- 10 drops myrrh
- 10 drops black pepper

Geranium *(Pelargonium graveolens)* helps release negative memories, thereby opening and elevating the mind.

Rosewood *(Aniba rosaeodora)* is soothing and nourishing to the skin. It has been researched at Weber State University for its inhibition rate against gram positive and gram negative bacterial growth. This oil is soothing, creates skin elasticity, and helps the skin rid itself of irritations and problems such as candida. Rosewood is anti-infectious, antibacterial, antifungal, antiviral, and antiparasitic.

Ylang Ylang *(Cananga odorata)* helps bring about a sense of relaxation and may help balance male and female energies. It balances equilibrium and restores confidence and self-love.

Myrrh *(Commiphora myrrha)* is referenced throughout the Bible, constituting a part of a holy anointing formula given to Moses (Exodus 30:22-27). It has one of the highest levels of sesquiterpenes, a class of compounds that can stimulate the hypothalamus, pituitary, and amygdala, the control center for emotions and hormone release in the brain. Myrrh has been used in eastern countries to enhance the feeling of spirituality or euphoria.

Black Pepper *(Piper nigrum)* stimulates the endocrine system and increases energy while increasing cellular oxygenation. It is anti-inflammatory and may soothe deep tissue muscle aches. It has been traditionally used to treat rheumatoid arthritis.

Safety Data: This blend may be irritating to those with sensitive skin. Avoid eye contact. In case of accidental eye contact, put a few drops of any pure vegetable oil in the eye and call your doctor if necessary. Never use water to dilute or rinse.

Application: Apply on location, dilute with a vegetable or massage oil for body massage, or add to a bath or shower gel. Use with a compress over the abdomen, or wear as a perfume or cologne.

Companion Oil: Mood Lifting Blend.

Spiritual Blend

This blend combines oils traditionally used by the Native Americans to increase spirituality, enhancing prayer and inner awareness. This blend brings us closer to our spiritual connection.

Recipe:

- 40 drops cedarwood
- 30 drops balsam fir
- 15 drops sandalwood
- 15 drops frankincense
- 5 drops myrrh

Cedarwood *(Cedrus atlantica)* has calming and purifying properties. High in sesquiterpenes which can stimulate the limbic part of the brain (the center of our emotions), this conifer oil has been used by North American Indians to enhance spiritual awareness and communication. Cedarwood may also help stimulate the pineal gland, which releases melatonin, a hormone that enhances deep sleep.

Balsam Fir *(Abies balsamea)* has antiseptic properties and also contains d-limonene, a powerful antioxidant.

Sandalwood *(Santalum album)* is high in sesquiterpenes, which have been researched for their ability to stimulate the pineal gland and the limbic region of the brain, the center of our emotions. Used traditionally for skin revitalization, yoga, and meditation, sandalwood is similar to frankincense oil in its support of nerves and circulation.

Frankincense *(Boswellia carteri)* is considered a holy anointing oil in the Middle East and has been used in religious ceremonies for thousands of years. Containing sesquiterpenes, it helps stimulate the limbic part of the brain, which elevates the mind, helping to overcome stress and despair. Frankincense has a warming, elevating effect on the mind.

Myrrh *(Commiphora myrrha)* is referenced throughout the Bible, constituting a part of a holy anointing formula given to Moses (Exodus 30:22-27). It has one of the highest levels of sesquiterpenes, a class of compounds that can stimulate the hypothalamus, pituitary, and amygdala, the control center for emotions and hormone release in the brain. Myrrh has been used in eastern countries to enhance the feeling of spirituality or euphoria.

Safety Data: This blend may be irritating to those with sensitive skin. Avoid eye contact. In case of accidental eye contact, put a few drops of any pure vegetable oil in the eye and call your doctor if necessary. Never use water to dilute or rinse.

Application: Diffuse during times of meditation and prayer, also apply 2–3 drops to a cotton ball and put in the home or office air vent. Wear on the back of the neck, the sides of the forehead, the crown of the head, the bottom of the feet, or along the spine.

Stress Reduction Blend

This gentle fragrance is specifically designed for diffusing. It promotes relaxation and a deep sense of peace, helping to dampen tensions and uplift spirits. When massaged on the bottom of the feet, it can be a wonderful prelude to a peaceful night's rest. It may calm overactive and hard-to-manage children. The oils in this blend have historically been used to help reduce depression, anxiety, stress, and insomnia. This blend, along with a mineral supplement, may be a healthy alternative to Ritalin.

Recipe:

- 30 drops lavender
- 20 drops Roman chamomile
- 10 drops tangerine
- 5 drops cistus

Lavender *(Lavandula angustifolia)* is known as the universal oil because of its wide range of usage. It has sedative and calming properties that help overcome insomnia, tension, and stress.

Roman Chamomile *(Chamaemelum nobile)* may calm and relieve restlessness, tension, insomnia, and muscle tension. Chamomile helps heal cuts, scrapes, and bruises, and is anti-infectious. It may relieve allergies and expel toxins from the liver. It is used extensively in Europe for skin care.

Cistus *(Cistus ladanifer)* is also known as "rock rose" and has been studied for its effects on the regeneration of cells.

Tangerine *(Citrus nobilis)* contains esters and aldehydes that are sedating and calming, helping with anxiety and nervousness.

Safety Data: May be irritating to those with sensitive skin. Avoid eye contact. In case of accidental eye contact, put a few drops of any pure vegetable oil in the eye and call your doctor if necessary. Never use water to dilute or rinse.

Application: Diffuse, wear as a perfume, or apply on the bottom of the feet, the wrists, and outside of the ears. Mix with a bath gel and put in a warm bath. Dilute with a vegetable or massage oil for a body massage.

Companion Oils: Lavender (for insomnia) and chamomile (for calming).

Trauma Blend

Trauma Blend may help release buried emotional trauma as well as upsets due to accidents, the death of a loved one, assault, abuse, etc. This blend of calming, grounding essential oils can help purge stress and uproot traumas that cause fatigue, anger, restlessness, and a weakened immune response.

Recipe:

- 20 drops Kaffir lime
- 20 drops davana
- 16 drops lavender
- 15 drops frankincense
- 12 drops cedarwood
- 10 drops spruce
- 5 drops rose
- 6 drops tsuga

Kaffir lime *(Citrus hystrix)* is anti-infectious, antiseptic, a neurotonic, and a liver decongestant. With its hormone-like properties, it helps underactive sexual glands. The constituents of aldehydes, esters, and coumarins make it calming and sedating.

Davana *(Artemisia pallens)* is high in sesquiterpenes which are supporting to the immune system. It is mucolytic, antispasmodic, works to reduce painful scarring, and helps overcome anxiety.

Lavender *(Lavandula angustifolia)* has sedative and calming properties that can help overcome insomnia, headaches, stress, and nervous tension.

Frankincense *(Boswellia carteri)* is considered a holy anointing oil in the Middle East and has been used in religious ceremonies for thousands of years. Frankincense is believed to help stimulate the limbic part of the brain, which elevates the mind, helping to overcome stress and despair. It is used in European medicine to combat depression.

Cedarwood *(Cedrus atlantica)* has calming and purifying properties. High in sesquiterpenes which can stimulate the limbic part of the brain (the center of our emotions), this conifer oil has been used by North American Indians to enhance spiritual awareness and communication. Cedarwood may also help stimulate the pineal gland, which releases melatonin, a hormone that enhances deep sleep.

Spruce *(Picea mariana)* helps to open and release emotional blocks, bringing about a feeling of balance and grounding. Spruce is anti-infectious, antiseptic, and anti-inflammatory.

Rose *(Rosa damascena)* appears to possess a very high biofrequency compared to other essential oils. It creates a sense of balance, harmony, and well-being, and elevates the mind.

Tsuga *(Tsuga canadensis)* treats coughs, respiratory conditions, kidney ailments, skin conditions, urinary infections, and venereal diseases.

Safety Data: This blend may be irritating to those with sensitive skin. Avoid eye contact. In case of accidental eye contact, put a few drops of any pure vegetable oil in the eye and call your doctor if necessary. Never use water to dilute or rinse.

Application: Diffuse or apply a few drops to the bottom of the feet, on the chest, behind the ears, on the forehead, and at the nape of the neck. Apply along the spine Raindrop-style.

Companion Oils: Stress Reduction Blend and Mood Lifting Blend.

Gary Young uses the Vita Flex Technique to apply essential oils on an elderly Tarahumara woman in Mexico.

CHAPTER 10

Vita Flex Technique

Vita Flex Technique means "vitality through the reflexes." It is a specialized form of hand and foot massage that is exceptionally effective in delivering the benefits of essential oils throughout the body. It is said to have originated in Tibet thousands of years ago, and was perfected in the 1960s by Stanley Burroughs long before acupuncture was popular in Western medicine.

It is based on a complete network of reflex points that stimulate all the internal body systems. Essential oils are applied to contact points, and energy is released through electrical impulses created by contact between the fingertips and reflex points.This electrical charge follows the nerve pathways to a break or clog in the electrical circuit usually caused by toxins, damaged tissues, or loss of oxygen. As with acupressure there are hundreds of Vita Flex reflex points throughout the human body, encompassing the entire realm of body and mind, that are capable of releasing many kinds of tension, congestion, and imbalances.

In contrast to the steady stimulation of Reflexology, Vita Flex uses a rolling and releasing motion that involves placing all four fingers flat on the skin, rolling onto the fingertips, and continuing over onto the fingernail using medium pressure. Then moving forward about half the width of the finger, this rolling and releasing technique is continually repeated until the Vita Flex point, or area, is covered. This movement is repeated over the area three times.

Combine this technique with 1-3 drops of essential oil applied to those areas of the feet that correspond to the system of the body you wish to support (see the diagram on the next page). Rapid and extraordinary results are experienced when combining essential oils with Vita Flex stimulation, as it increases the effect of both.

The diagram that follows the Vita Flex charts shows the nervous system connection to the spine for the electrical points throughout the body.

Vita Flex Points

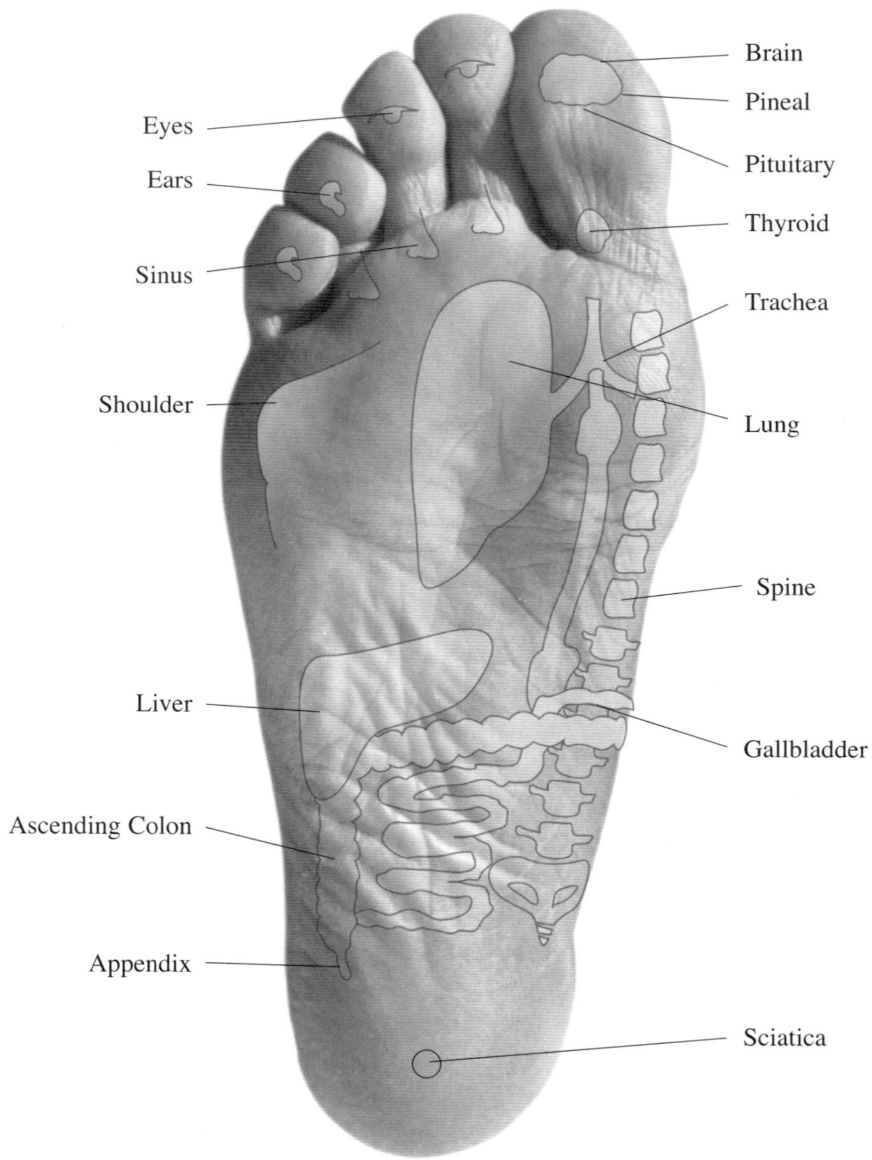

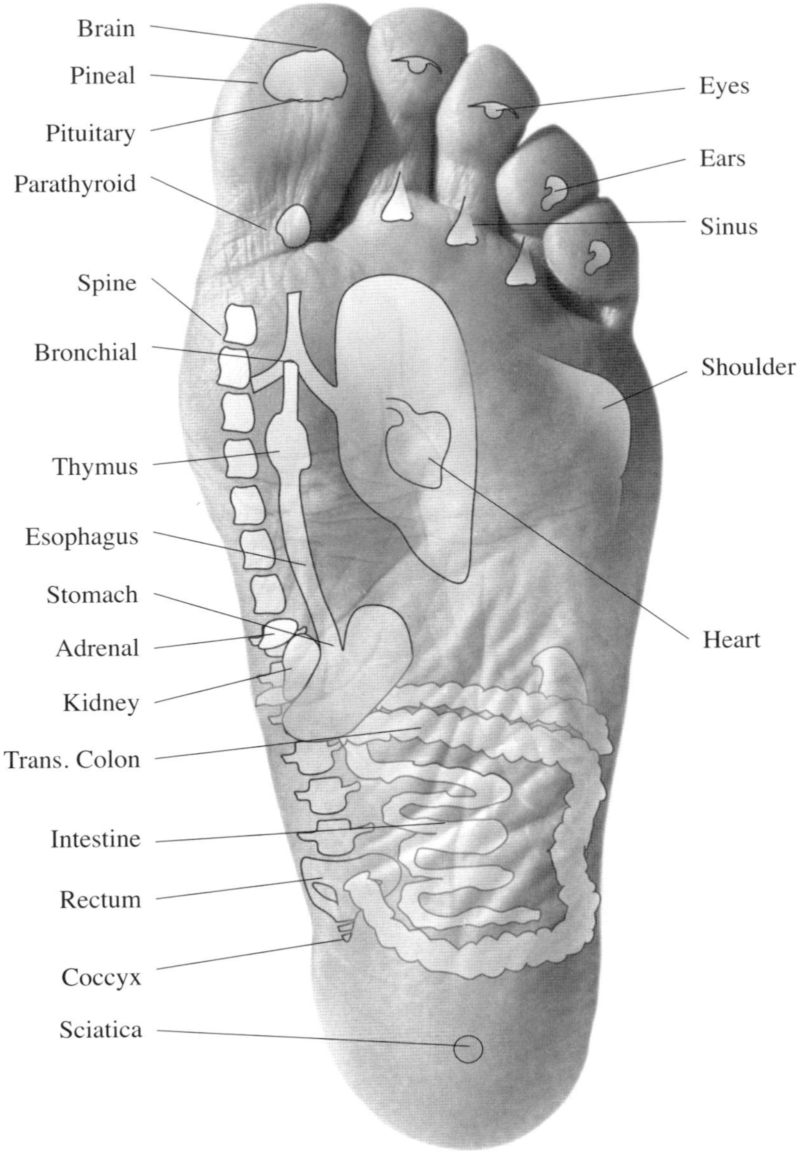
Brain
Pineal
Pituitary
Parathyroid
Spine
Bronchial
Thymus
Esophagus
Stomach
Adrenal
Kidney
Trans. Colon
Intestine
Rectum
Coccyx
Sciatica
Eyes
Ears
Sinus
Shoulder
Heart

Nervous System Connection Points

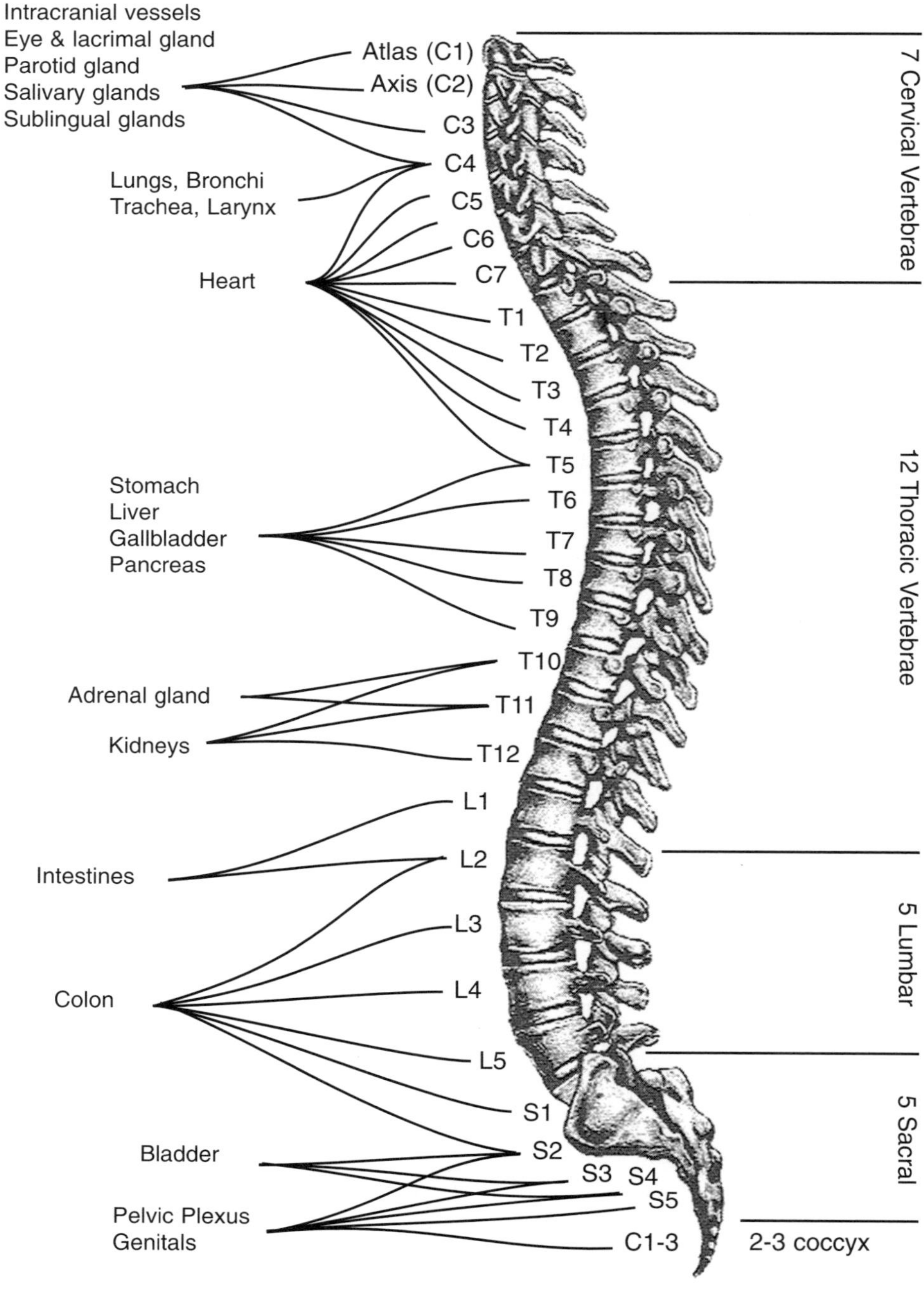

CHAPTER 11

Raindrop Technique®

I developed the Raindrop Technique® (RT) during the 1980s based on my research with essential oils as antimicrobial agents, and prompted by some fascinating information I learned from an elder among the Lakota Indian Nation in South Dakota. He related to me that several generations ago, his ancestors regularly migrated north across the Canadian border into the northern regions of Saskatchewan and Manitoba, where they often witnessed the Aurora Borealis, or Northern Lights. When the Aurora Borealis was on display, those who were ill or had complicated health problems would stand facing the dancing lights and hold their hands out toward the lights and inhale deeply. Their belief was that the air was charged with healing energy from the Aurora Borealis. Mentally, they would "inhale" this energy into their spine and then out through nerve pathways to afflicted areas of the body.

As reported by this elder, this process stimulated an incredible healing effect for many of his ancestors. I don't know if this is where the effleurage I teach (feathered finger stroking) first originated, but it became associated with this tradition after the borders were closed and the Lakota could no longer migrate north. Restricted to their reservations, they began practicing this energy process mentally, coupled with light stroking to facilitate the spreading of energy through the body. While I have not been able to further substantiate this tradition, it did provide the promptings that gave birth to the design and development of Raindrop Technique (RT). Since 1989, RT has received an enormous amount of praise from users around the world for its ability to help ameliorate spinal abnormalities such as scoliosis and kyphosis, and facilitate tissue cleansing.

RT is based on the idea—now being explored in a number of scientific studies—that many types of scoliosis and spinal misalignments are caused by viruses or bacteria that lie dormant along the spine. These pathogens create inflammation, which, in turn, contorts and disfigures the spinal column.

RT is a powerful, non-invasive tool for assisting the body in correcting defects in the curvature of the spine by utilizing the antiviral, antibacterial, and anti-inflammatory action of several key essential oils. During the years that it has been practiced, it has resolved numerous cases of scoliosis, kyphosis, and chronic back pain. Further, it has eliminated the need for back surgery for hundreds of people. By integrating Vita Flex and massage, the power of essential oils brings the body into structural and electrical alignment.

Consistent with the French Model

The use of undiluted essential oils in RT is consistent with the French model for aromatherapy—which is the most extensively practiced and studied model in the world. With over 40 years of experience using essential oils clinically, the French have consistently recommended neat (undiluted) use of essential oils. An illustrious roster of 20th century French physicians provides convincing evidence that undiluted essential oils have a valuable place in the therapeutic arsenal of clinical professionals. René Gattefossé, PhD; Jean Valnet, MD; Jean-Claude Lapraz, MD; Daniel Pénoël, MD; and many others have long attested to the safe and effective use of undiluted essential oils and the dramatic and powerful benefits they can impart. According to Dr. Pénoël, "What happens when we use [essential oils] without diluting them? With many current essential oils, nothing dangerous or serious can happen."

In the case of Raindrop Technique®, the use of certain undiluted essential oils typically causes minor reddening and "heat" in the tissues. Normally, this is perfectly safe and not something to be overly concerned about. Blondes, redheads, and persons whose systems are toxic are more susceptible to this temporary reddening. Should the reddening or heat become excessive, it can be remedied within a minute or two by the immediate application of several drops of pure, quality vegetable oil to the affected area. This effectively dilutes the oils and the warming effect. Temporary mild warming is normal for RT. Typically it is even milder than that of many capsicum creams or sports ointments. Indeed, rather than being a cause of concern, this warming indicates that positive benefits are being imparted. In cases where the warmth or heat exceeds the comfort zone of the recipient, as mentioned before, the facilitator can apply any pure vegetable oil to the area until the comfort level is regained and reddening dissipates (usually within 2 minutes).

NOTE: If a rash should appear, it is an indication of a chemical reaction between the oils and synthetic compounds in the skin cells and interstitial fluid of the body (usually from conventional personal care products). Some misconstrue this as an allergic reaction, when in fact the problem is not caused by an allergy but rather by foreign chemicals already imbedded in the tissues.

A number of medical professionals throughout the United States have adopted RT in their clinical practice and have found it to be an outstanding resource for aiding sciatica, scoliosis, kyphosis, and chronic back pain. Ken Krieger, DC, a chiropractor practicing in Scottsdale, Arizona, states, "As a chiropractor, I believe that the dramatic results of RT are enough for me to rewrite the books on scoliosis." Similarly, Terry Friedmann, MD, of Westminster, Colorado, states that "these essential oils truly represent a new frontier of medicine; they have resolved cases that many professionals had regarded as hopeless."

Do Infections Cause Scoliosis and Sciatica?

A growing amount of scientific research shows that certain microorganisms lodge near the spinal cord and contribute to deformities. Studies at Western General Hospital in Edinburgh, Scotland, linked virus-like particles to idiopathic scoliosis.[1,2] Researchers at the University of Bonn have also found the varicella zoster virus can lodge in the spinal ganglia throughout life.[3]

Research in 2001 further corroborated the existence of infectious microorganisms as a cause of spine pain and inflammation. Alistair Stirling and his colleagues at the Royal Orthopedic Hospital in Birmingham, England, found that 53 percent of patients with severe sciatica tested positive for chronic, low-grade infection by gram-negative bacteria (particularly *Propionibacterium acnes*) which triggered inflammation near the spine. Stirling suggested that the reason these bacteria had not been identified earlier was because of the extended time required to incubate disc material (7 days).[4]

The tuberculosis mycobacterium has also been shown to contribute to spinal disease and possibly deformations. Research at the Pasteur Institute in France, published in *The New England Journal of Medicine*, documented increasing numbers of patients showing evidence of spinal disease (Pott's disease) caused by tuberculosis.[5, 6, 7, 8]

1. Green RJ, Webb JN, Maxwell MH. The nature of virus-like particles in the paraxial muscles of idiopathic scoliosis. *J Pathol*. 1979 Sep;129(1):9-12.
2. Webb JN, Gillespie WJ. Virus-like particles in paraspinal muscle in scoliosis. *Br Med J*. 1976 Oct 16;2(6041):912-3.
3. Wolff MH, Buchel F, Gullotta F, Helpap B, Schneweiss KE. Investigations to demonstrate latent viral infection of varicella-Zoster virus in human spine ganglia. *Verh Dtsch Ges Pathol*. 1981;65:203-7.
4. Stirling AL, et al., Association between sciatica and Propionibacterium acnes. *Lancet* 2001:V357.
5. Nagrath SP, Hazra DK, Pant PC, Seth HC. Tuberculosis spine—a diagnostic conundrum. Case report. *J Assoc Physicians India*. 1974 May;22(5):405-7.
6. Jenks PJ, Stewart B. Images in clinical medicine. Vertebral tuberculosis. *N Engl J Med*. 1998 June 4;338(23):1677.
7. Monaghan D, Gupta A, Barrington NA. Case report: Tuberculosis of the spine—an unusual presentation. *Clin Radiol*. 1991 May;43(5):360-2.
8. Petersen CK, Craw M, Radiological differentiation of tuberculosis and pyogenic osteomyelitis: a case report. *J Manipulative Physiol Ther*. 1986 Mar;9(1):39-42.

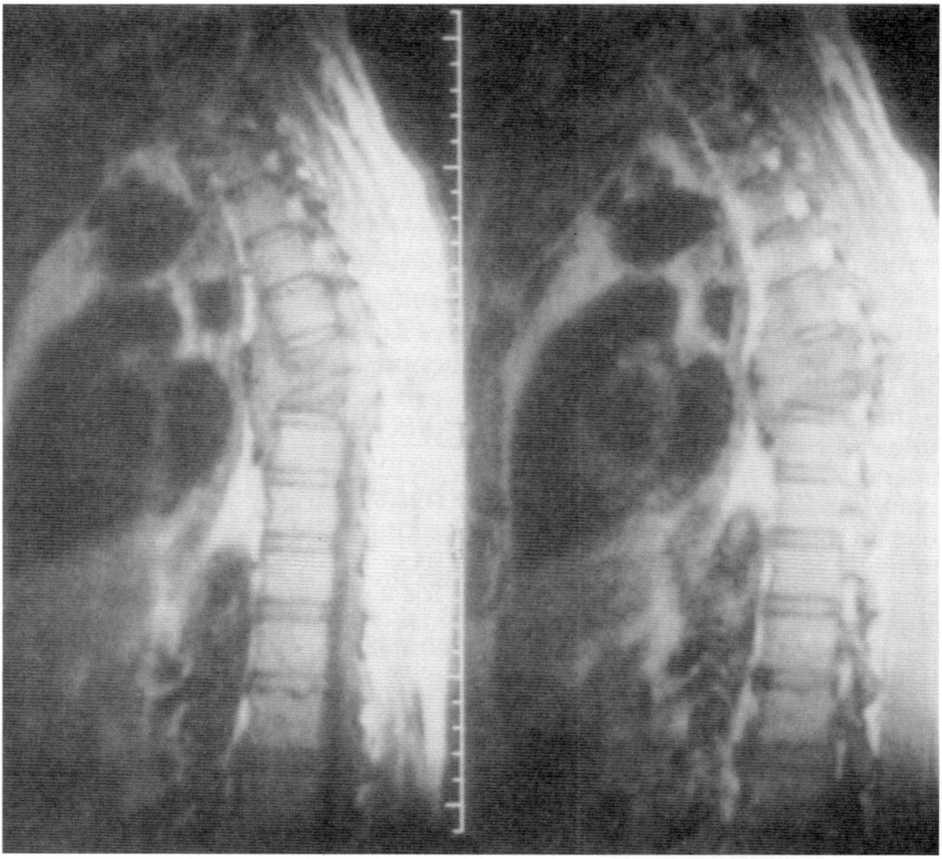

Example of kyphosis (hunchback) caused by an infectious microorganism (tuberculosis) in the spine. The above X-rays show two views of the spine of a 62 year-old man with a 3-month history of increasing back pain and inflammation due to kyphosis. The problem had become so severe that he could no longer walk unaided; however, there was no history of tuberculosis. The X-rays show the collapse of the seventh thoracic vertebra. He subsequently underwent back surgery to help correct the problem. Specimens taken during the surgery did not immediately show a bacterial infection, but after 12 weeks of incubation, the presence of Mycobacterium tuberculosis was detected, confirming the original diagnosis of spinal tuberculosis.

Source: Jenks, Peter J. and Stewart, Bruce. Images in Clinical Medicine. Vertebral Tuberculosis. *New England Journal of Medicine*, 1998 June 4, 338 (23);1677.

In addition, vaccines made from live viruses have been linked to spinal problems. A 1982 study by Pincott and Taff found a connection between oral poliomyelitis vaccines and scoliosis.[9]

9. Pinott JR, Taffs LF. Experimental scoliosis in primates: a neurological cause. *J Bone Joint Surg Br.* 1982;64(4):503-7.

Powerful Infection-Fighters

Essential oils are some of the most powerful inhibitors of microbes known, and as such are an important new weapon in combating many types of tissue infections. A 1999 study by Marilena Marino and colleagues found that thyme oil exhibited strong action against stubborn gram-negative bacteria.[10] Similarly, basil essential oil also demonstrated strong bactericidal action against microorganisms *Aeromonas hydrophila* and *Pseudomonas fluorescens*.[11] A study at the Central Food Technological Institute in Mysore, India, found that a large number of essential oil components had tremendous germ-killing effects, inhibiting the growth of *Staphylococcus*, *Micrococcus*, *Bacillus,* and *Enterobacter* strains of bacteria. These compounds included menthol (found in peppermint), eucalyptol (found in rosemary, eucalyptus, and geranium), linalool (found in marjoram), and citral (found in lemongrass).[12] A 2001 study I conducted with Diane Horne, Sue Chao, and colleagues at Weber State University in Ogden, Utah, found that oregano, thyme, peppermint, and basil exhibited very strong antimicrobial effects against pathogens such as *Streptococcus pneumoniae*, a major cause of illness in young children and death in elderly- and immune-weakened patients.[13] Many other studies confirm these findings.[14]

The ability of essential oils to penetrate the skin quickly and pass into body tissues to produce therapeutic effects has also been studied. Hoshi University researchers in Japan found that cyclic monoterpenes (including menthol, which is found in peppermint) are so effective in penetrating the skin that they can actually enhance the absorption of water-soluble drugs.[15] North Dakota State University researchers have similarly found that cyclic monoterpenes such as limonene and other terpenoids such as menthone and eugenol easily pass through the dermis, magnifying the penetration of pharmaceutical drugs such as tamoxifen.[16]

It is interesting to note that many essential oils used in RT—in addition to being highly antimicrobial—are also among those classified as GRAS (Generally Regarded As Safe) for internal use by the U.S. Food and Drug

10. Marino M, Bersani C, Comi G. Antimicrobial activity of the essential oils of Thymus vulgaris L. measured using a bioimpedometric method. *Journal of Food Protection,* Vol. 62, No. 9, 1999 pp. 1017-1023.

11. Wan J, Wilcock A, Coventry MJ. The effect of essential oils of basil on the growth of Aeromonas fluorescens. *Journal of Applied Microbiology,* 1998, 84, 152-158.

12. Beuchat LR. Antimicrobial properties of spices and their essential oils. Center for Food Safety and Quality Enhancement, Department of Food Science and Technology, University of Georgia, Griffin, Georgia.

13. Horne D, et al., Antimicrobial effects of essential oils on Streptococcus pneumoniae. *Journal of Essential Oil Research,* (September/October 2001). 13, 387-392.

14. Moleyar V, Narasimham P. Antibacterial activity of essential oil components. *International Journal of Food Microbiology,* Vol. 16 (1992) 337-32.

15. Obata Y, et al. Effect of pretreatment of skin with cyclic monoterpenes on permeation of diclofenac in hairless rat. *Biol Pharm Bull*. 1993 Mar;16(3)312-4.

16. Zhao K, Singh J. Mechanisms of percutaneous absorption of tamoxifen by terpenes: eugenol, d-limonene and menthone. *Control Release*. 1998. Nov 13;55(2-3)253-60.

Administration. These include basil, marjoram, peppermint, oregano, and thyme. These and many other GRAS essential oils have a decades-long history of being consumed as foods or flavorings with virtually no adverse reactions.

In sum, RT is one of the safest, noninvasive techniques available for spinal health. It is also an invaluable tool to promote healing from within using topically applied essential oils.

Introduction to the Technique

My Raindrop Technique® uses a sequence of highly antimicrobial essential oils synergistically combined to simultaneously kill the responsible viral agents and reduce inflammation. The principle single oils used include: oregano (*Origanum compactum*), thyme (*Thymus vulgaris*), basil or balsam fir (*Ocimum basilicum* or *Abies balsamea*), cypress (*Cupressus sempervirens*), wintergreen or birch (*Gaultheria procumbens* or *Betula alleghaniensis*), marjoram (*Origanum majorana*), and peppermint (*Mentha piperita*).

The oils are dispensed like little drops of rain from a height of about six inches above the back and very lightly massaged along the vertebrae and back muscles. Although the entire process takes about 45 minutes to complete, the oils will continue to work in the body for up to one week following treatment, with continued re-alignment taking place during this time.

One caution: RT is not a cure-all or a magic bullet. A healthy balanced body is the result of a well-rounded program of exercise and proper diet. Health is everything we do, say, hear, see, and eat. RT is only one tool to help restore balance in the body. Healthy eating habits and a positive, open mind will also help prepare the body and skin to accept the oils better and more rapidly.

Although this technique is explained as simply as possible, you may want to contact Essential Science Publishing to purchase a demonstration video. Every step of the technique is carefully demonstrated in an actual hands-on presentation. You can order the video by visiting the ESP website at www.essentialscience.net or by calling toll-free 800-336-6308. Viewing this video and following the outline presented here will make this revolutionary technique easy to understand and easy to put into practice.

If you intend to offer the Raindrop Technique® as a service, please be advised that some states require that you be a licensed massage therapist, aesthetician or chiropractor prior to offering any service where physical touch is involved. Please check the regulations for your jurisdiction.

The Raindrop Technique®

It is recommended that RT be performed in a quiet, semi-darkened area free of distractions. Soft and relaxing music will make the recipient more comfortable. The temperature should be cool enough to prevent sweating, but warm enough to be comfortable as the recipient's back and legs will be exposed. In describing the technique, "facilitator" refers to the person giving the Raindrop Technique; "recipient" refers to the person receiving it.

For This Technique, You Will Need:

1. Massage table (ideally) or a comfortable, flat surface for the recipient to lie on. The surface should be high enough that the facilitator can perform the technique without back strain. It is best to cover the surface with sheets or towels that are expendable as several of the oils may stain certain fabrics. Also, some of the oils can react with the vinyls used to cover massage tables so be sure vinyl surfaces are covered well.
2. Two medium-sized towels and a twin-sized bed sheet. The towels will be used to make a warm compress; the sheet to protect the modesty of the recipient.
3. Easy access to hot water.
4. Timer, clock, or watch.
5. A stable tray on which to place oils (and instructions, if needed) near the receiver.
6. Each of the 10 oils listed throughout this chapter. (Seven single oils, two blends and a vegetable or massage oil.)

Preparation

- Both the facilitator and the recipient should remove all jewelry. This includes watches, pendants, chains, rings, bracelets, belts, earrings, etc.
- The facilitator should wear clothing that is loose and comfortable, and may wish to remove their shoes.
- The recipient should be draped in a bed sheet or towel, or dressed in hospital gown-attire so the facilitator can apply essential oils to the shoulders, neck, back, legs, and feet of the recipient.

- The facilitator should make sure their fingernails are clipped and filed down as short as possible to prevent unintentionally scratching the recipient's skin, particularly when doing the Vita Flex Technique.
- The facilitator should make sure fingernails are free of fingernail polish (essential oils remove many polishes and lacquers).
- Only perform RT if you are feeling healthy, energized, and emotionally/ mentally clear and focused.
- For optimum results, the recipient should drink extra purified or distilled water for the first few days following RT. This will aid the body in flushing toxins from the tissues.

NOTE: Facilitators may choose to apply frankincense to themselves (on wrists, shoulders, neck, and top of the head) to help counter any negative energies coming from the recipient.

To begin:

- The recipient should lie on their back, face up on the massage table with the head resting in the face cradle.
- The recipient should lie as straight as possible with the hips flat on the table. The arms should rest alongside the body.
- The facilitator should keep constant physical contact with the recipient to prevent feelings of insecurity, anxiousness, or abandonment.
- Check for evenness of feet and in the length of the legs. Hold recipient's ankles just below the shin bone (with the right hand on the left ankle and the left hand on the right ankle) with the index finger of each hand touching the center of the outside ankle bone. While holding the ankles in this position, the thumbs of the facilitator should be even with one another. Unevenness could indicate a pelvic rotation or structural misalignment.

STEP 1 – Apply Energy Balance Blend to feet and shoulders

Oregano, thyme, and Energy Balance Blend are the foundation oils for all Raindrop Technique work. The technique always begins with the application of Energy Balance Blend to the feet and shoulders. This is one of the most important steps for a successful RT because it works on the physical, electrical, spiritual, and emotional levels, supporting the physical and energy alignment of the body. The key to using this oil blend is patience. Once the frequencies begin to balance, a structural alignment will much more likely begin to occur.

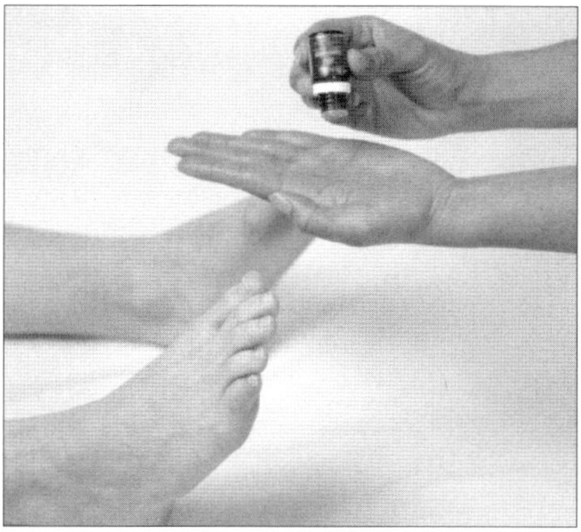

Fig. A — Putting Energy Balance Blend in the hand

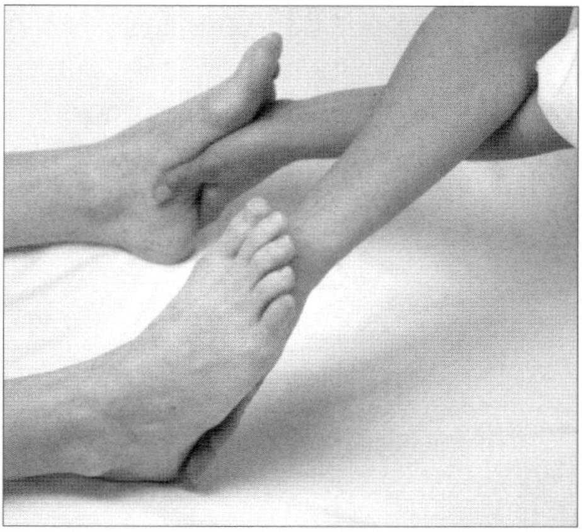

Fig. B — Placing hands on the recipient's feet

This first step forms the foundation for everything that follows.

- According to energy medicine principles, female energy relates to the left side of the body, male energy to the right side. So this application begins differently for males and females.
- Put 6 drops of Energy Balance Blend into your left hand and apply to the left foot first if the recipient is a woman (See Fig. A); put the oil in the right hand and apply to the right foot first if the recipient is a man. Then apply the oil on the other foot.

STEP 2 - Place hands on recipient's feet and shoulders

Step 2 works best if there are two facilitators: one to hold the feet, the other to make contact at the shoulders. However, if you are working by yourself, the application works well just holding the feet, which is the most important. You may kneel or sit while holding the feet or shoulders of the recipient. You should be in a comfortable position to maintain contact for several minutes.

- Cross your hands and place your palms as flat as possible against the soles of the receiver's feet. This hand crossing enables the facilitator to place the right palm on the right foot and the left palm on the left foot. The facilitator should hold this position for at least 5 minutes. (See Fig. B)
- If two facilitators are available, the second should sit or stand at the recipient's head and apply three drops of Energy Balance Blend to each shoulder. The right palm is placed on the recipient's right shoulder and left palm is placed on the left shoulder at the same time (without crossing arms). There must be as much palm-to-shoulder contact as possible.

- Let your mind be free and peaceful. Encourage the recipient to take deep breaths, inhaling and exhaling deeply and slowly, so they can engage in their own healing. The recipient may feel a little heat or tingling on the feet, or an energy working up through the legs to the back, even moving as high as the head. Some facilitators may feel their hands become warm or tingly. Sometimes the facilitator may feel a pulsating effect. The facilitator should try to feel the energy coming through the recipient's feet. Look for:

    - Temperature chang
    - A "pulsing" feeling
    - Subtle vibration

    Once you feel energy and it is equal in both feet, you can release.

The vertebrae can achieve some realignment with this initial application alone. However, if there are people present with hidden negative attitudes, the results may be less than optimal. Only perform the RT if you are feeling healthy, energized, and emotionally/mentally clear and focused.

CAUTION: If there is a fold in the skin on the back of the neck or elsewhere, please note that essential oils can accumulate there. Be aware of this as you proceed, and if the recipient notices a burning sensation in a skin fold, be prepared to add a high quality vegetable (cold-pressed virgin olive, almond, hazelnut, or fractionated coconut oil) or massage oil there.

STEP 3 – Apply seven essential oils to the feet

In this step we will apply the seven single oils in a specific order to the spinal Vita Flex area of the soles of the feet (see chart on pages 204-205) using the Vita Flex Technique. The seven oils in their application sequence are:

- **Oregano** has potent antimicrobial and anti-inflammatory properties.
- **Thyme** is highly antimicrobial, inhibiting the growth of infectious micro-organisms. It easily penetrates the skin and travels throughout the body.
- **Basil** or **Balsam Fir**: Basil has antispasmodic properties that relax muscles. It is also anti-inflammatory and antimicrobial. Balsam fir is an excellent substitute for basil and is less irritating to sensitive skin.
- **Cypress** oil improves circulation, relieves spasms and swelling, and helps heal damaged tissue.
- **Wintergreen** or **Birch** are virtually identical chemically. They are anti-inflammatory and analgesic (pain-relieving) due to their high methyl salicylate content. They are excellent for bones and joints.

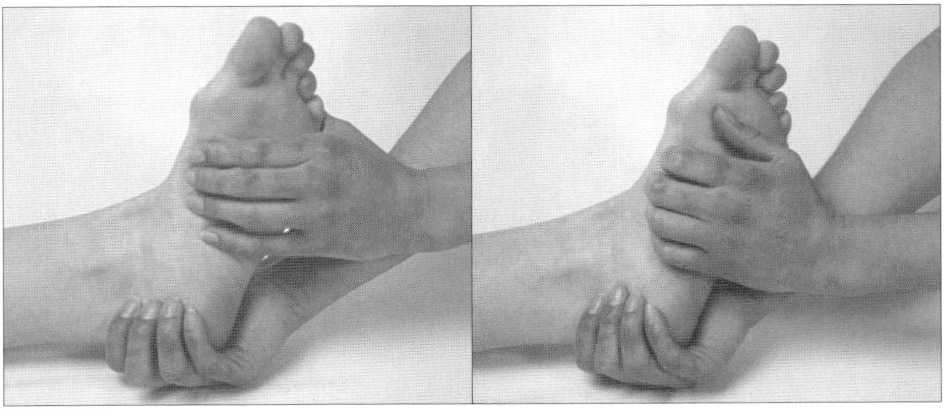

Fig. C — Applying thyme to the Vita Flex points of the foot

NOTE: Be careful of your sources in obtaining either of these oils. It is my experience in the market that there is very little natural birch essential oil available worldwide. Additionally, much of the wintergreen sold today has been chemically extended and adulterated with synthetic methyl salicylate.

- **Marjoram** oil is antispasmodic and muscle-relaxing.
- **Peppermint** enhances the effects of all the preceding essential oils. It also has pain-killing and antimicrobial properties, stimulating circulation and cooling inflamed tissue.

The procedure for this portion of RT involves a series of substeps as follows:

A. Place **2-3 drops of oregano** (small feet require only 1-2 drops of essential oil) in the palm of the left hand. Dip the fingertips of the right hand in the oil, stir clockwise three times and apply along the spine Vita Flex points of the right foot (see chart on pages 204-205). This is the area along the bottom inside edge of the foot from the heel to the tip of the big toe. Massage with Vita Flex Technique the full length of this area three times. Remember to use the right hand for both oil application and Vita Flex massage on the right foot. (See Fig. C)

B. Place **2-3 drops of thyme** essential oil in the palm of the left hand. Dip two fingertips of the right hand in the oil, stir clockwise three times and apply—just as above with oregano oil—along the spinal Vita Flex area of the right foot. Massage along the full length of this spinal area using the Vita Flex Technique once to apply the oil, then two more times.

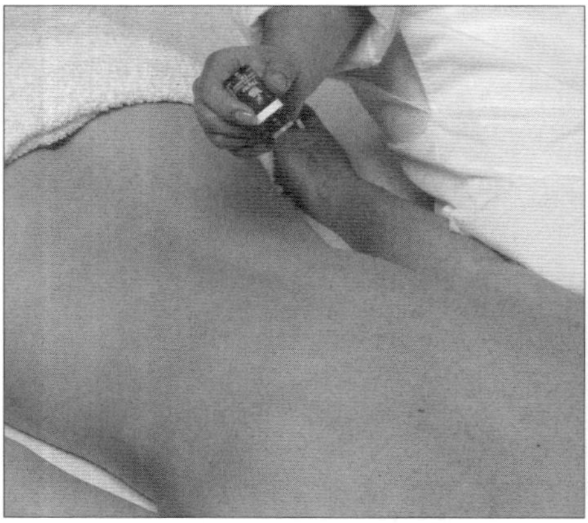

Fig. D — Applying oregano and thyme to the spine

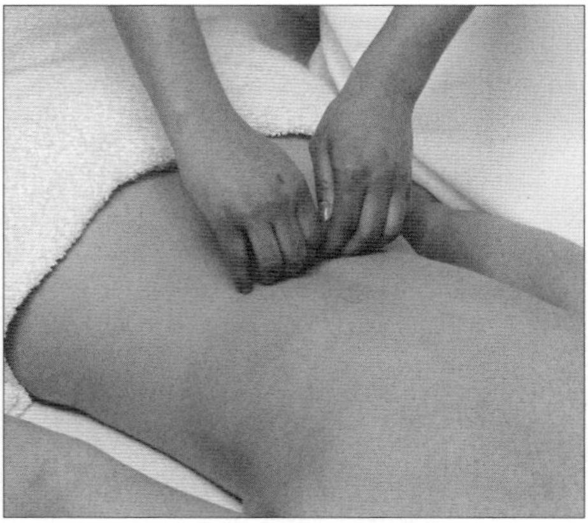

Fig. E — Brush strokes up the spine

C. Place **2-3 drops of basil or balsam fir** in the same manner as above on the right foot.

D. Place **2-3 drops of cypress** in the same manner as above on the right foot.

E. Place **2-3 drops of wintergreen or birch** in the same manner as above on the right foot.

F. Place **2-3 drops of marjoram** in the same manner as above on the right foot

G. Place **2-3 drops of peppermint** in the same manner as above on the right foot.

Repeat steps A-G, on the left foot, placing the oils in the palm of the right hand and applying them and doing Vita Flex on the left foot with the left hand.

STEP 4 - Apply oregano and thyme to spine

- Have the recipient turn over on their stomach to expose the back. Do this carefully to protect the recipient's modesty.
- Hold the bottle six inches above the skin and evenly space **2-4 drops of oregano oil** along the center of the spine from bottom to top (sacrum to atlas). (See Fig. D)
- Immediately after applying oregano, with 6-inch brush-like strokes, brush the backs of your fingertips along the spine as you "feather up" the back from the sacrum (base of spine) to the atlas (hair line on back of neck). Repeat this feathering process two more times. (See Fig. E)

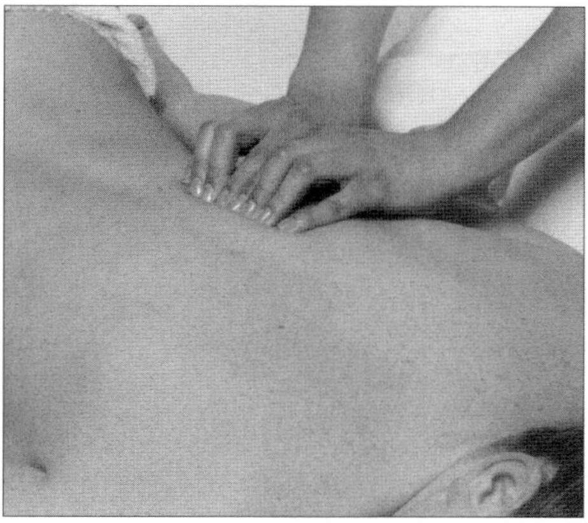

Fig. F — Easing muscles away from spine

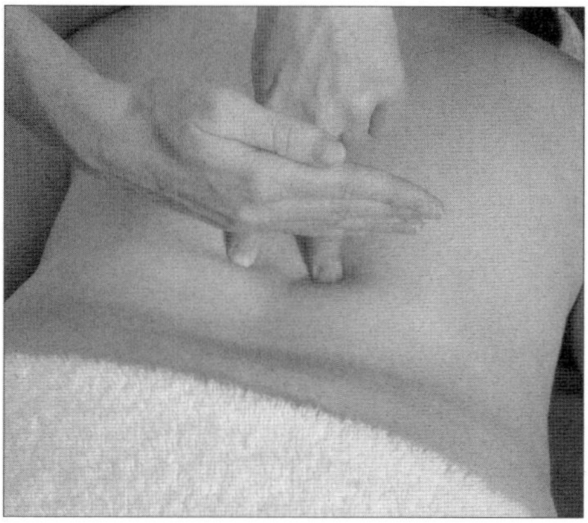

Fig. G — Two fingers straddling spine

- In the same way as above, evenly space **3-5 drops of thyme oil** along the center of the spine from bottom to top. Feather in the thyme just as you did for oregano.

CAUTION: More is not better. If there is a slight warming or burning sensation along the spine or on the neck, apply a pure vegetable or massage oil. The high phenol content of oregano and thyme essential oils can produce excess warming or reddening to the skin, particularly with fair-skinned people. Following the application of thyme and oregano, if the recipient becomes uncomfortable with burning sensations, apply 5-10 drops of vegetable or massage oil over affected areas.

NOTE: For more information about each of the Raindrop Technique oils, refer to the single oils and oil blend chapters of this book.

STEP 5 - Apply basil or balsam fir; massage spinal muscles using circular motions

- Evenly drop **6-10 drops** of basil or balsam fir evenly along the center of the spine.
- Spread the oil over the back by using the feathering technique described in step 4.
- In small circular clockwise motions (using the pads of the fingertips of both hands placed side by side) massage the muscles on each side of the spine. Start at the sacrum and work up to the atlas, using the fingertips to gently push or pull the tissue away from the spine. After finishing one side of the spine, start on the other side. Do not work directly on the spine, but on the muscles on either side of the spine. Do not apply direct pressure to the vertebrae. Repeat this step two more times. (See Fig. F)

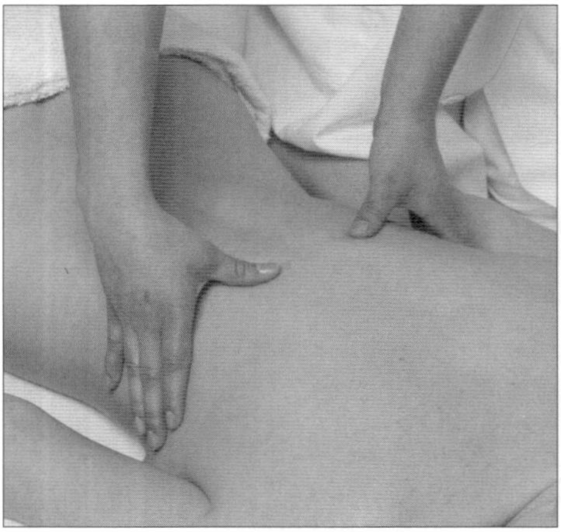

Fig. H — Thumb-rolling up spine (Down position)

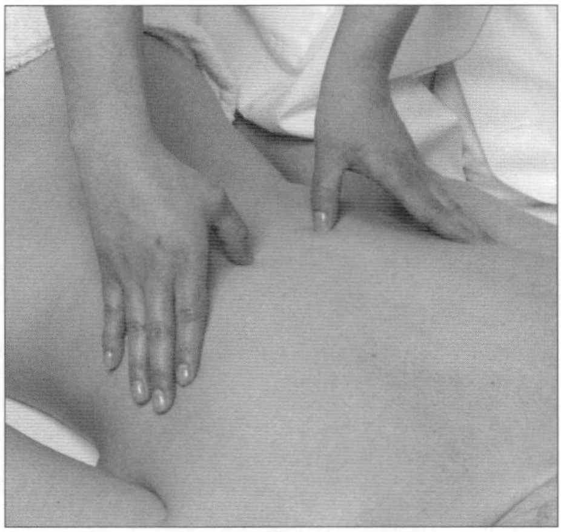

Fig. I — Thumb-rolling up spine (Up position)

STEP 6 – Apply cypress and do a finger straddle/hand "saw" massage

- Evenly drop **6-10 drops** of cypress along the center of the spine.
- Spread the oil over the spine and spinal muscles using the feathering technique described in Step 4.
- Stand on the recipient's left side (right side if the facilitator is left handed) near the shoulder area, facing the recipient's feet. Straddle the spine at the sacrum (base) with the index and middle fingers of the non-dominant hand. Place the bottom edge of the dominant hand (ulnar or pinky side down) just below the middle joints of the two straddling fingers. (See Fig. G)

Simultaneously perform the following two motions:

1. Apply moderate downward pressure with the straddling fingers while pulling them slowly to the atlas (top) of the spine.
2. Using an equal downward pressure, "Saw" the dominant hand back and forth, using short, rapid 1-inch strokes, moving the two straddling fingers back and forth as you slide them up the spine. all the way to the hairline.

   Repeat this step two more times.

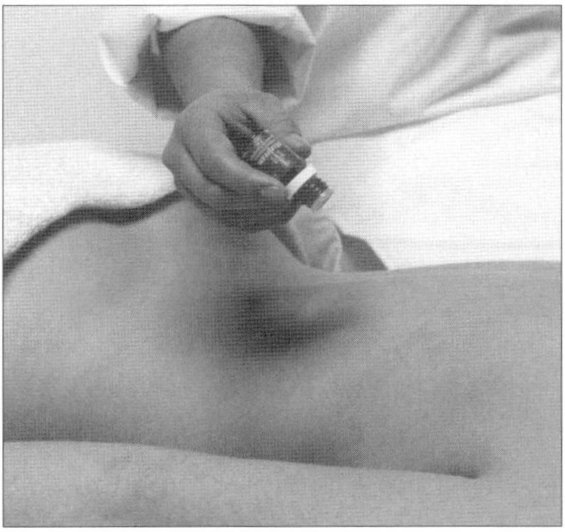

Fig. J — Applying basil, wintergreen or birch, cypress, marjoram, and peppermint to muscles on each side of spine

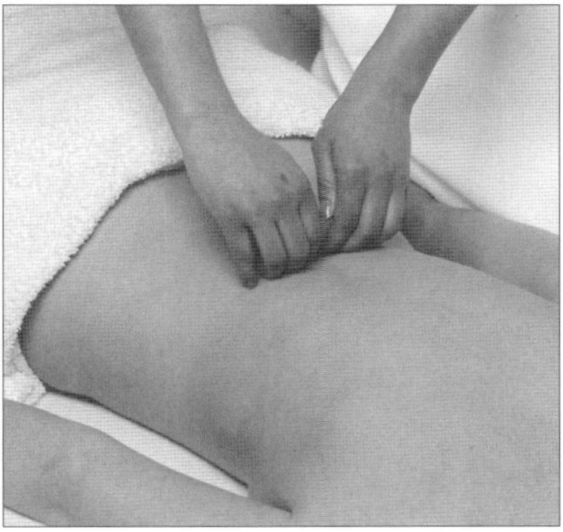

Fig. K — Brush strokes up the back muscles

STEP 7 – Apply wintergreen or birch and thumb-roll up the spine

- Evenly drop **6-10 drops** of wintergreen or birch along the center of the spine.
- Spread the oil over the spine and spinal muscles using the feathering technique described in Step 4.
- With your thumbs one inch apart on either side of the spine, use the Vita Flex method of thumb-rolling to work up the spine a thumbwidth at a time, from the sacrum to the atlas. Apply mild pressure. You may want to offset your thumbs by one inch to avoid bumping thumbs on the inward roll. Continue to roll your thumbs lightly over onto the nails and then release. Repeat this step two more times. (See Figs. H and I)

STEP 8 – Apply marjoram and peppermint to spinal muscles using flared feather strokes

In this step we apply the last two essential oils—in the sequence listed—to the muscles along either side of the spine and feather them to the rib and shoulders areas of the back. The two oils are marjoram and peppermint.

- Evenly drop (Raindrop-style) **6-10 drops** (depending on the length of the recipient's spine) of marjoram onto the muscles along **each side** of the spine (12-20 drops total). (See Fig. J)
- After applying marjoram, with the nail side of your fingertips, use **6-inch** brush-like strokes to feather the oil up the spine from the sacrum to the atlas. Repeat this step two more times. (See Fig. K)

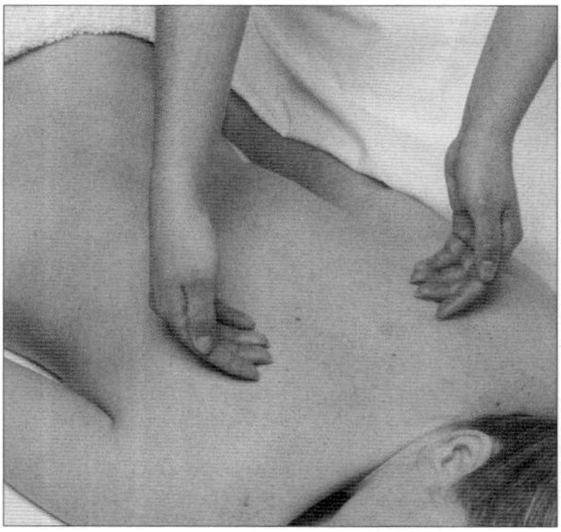

Fig. L — "Feathering up" the back over muscles next to the spine

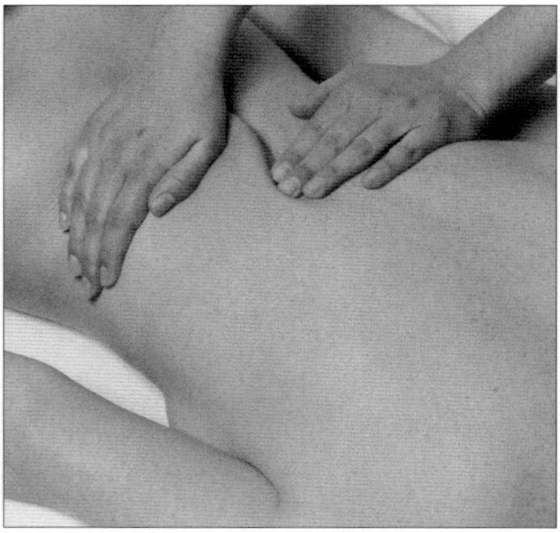

Fig. M — Palm rub massage on the back

- Then, extending the feather strokes (about 8 inches), lightly flare the fingertips out towards the sides of the back as you feather up the spine. Flare right hand to the right side of the back, and the left hand to the left side of the back, moving all the way to the side of the rib cage. Repeat this step two more times. This light stroking, or feathering, is called "effleurage." (See Fig. L)
- Starting at the sacrum, do a second set of flared feather strokes moving up the **full length** of the spine to the atlas (the hairline on the back of the neck). Flare your fingertips out over the shoulders and neck when you reach the atlas. Repeat this two more more times, for a total of three times.
- Apply and feather a total of **6-10 drops** of peppermint essential oil using the same process.

STEP 9 - Apply Muscle Relaxing Blend to the back

The Muscle Relaxing Blend contains several highly antispasmodic essential oils that help relax sore, tense, or inflamed muscles.

- Apply at least **6-8 drops of Muscle Relaxing Blend** over the entire length of **each side** of the spine (12-16 drops total). Feather in the blend as in Step 8, then, using circular motions with the flat of the hands, gently massage into the back muscles. Include the areas along the outer edges of the rib cage and shoulders that have not been previously worked.

STEP 10 – Massage entire back and neck with a quality vegetable or massage oil, finishing with palm rub

This application helps to seal in the essential oils, enhancing penetration.

- Put **12-20 drops of vegetable or massage oil** (depending on the size of the back), in your palm to warm the oil before spreading onto the muscles of the entire back and back of the neck. Use a gentle massage to evenly spread the massage oil.
- Place both hands on the receiver's back, palms down, near the base of the spine, one hand close to you, one hand on the far side of the back. Then slide the palms, with mild downward pressure, in opposite directions from the far side of the back to the near side, working slowly up the back toward the neck. Continue this alternating back and forth massage up to the nape of the neck. (See Fig. M) Do this massage up and down the back three times.

STEP 11 – Apply Energy Balance Blend to the spine

Apply **6-10 drops of Energy Balance Blend**, raindrop-style, along the center of the spine, from the sacrum to the atlas. Feather in the blend as in Step 8. Gently massage into the spine and spinal muscles using circular motions with the flats of your hands, moving from the sacrum to the atlas. Repeat two more times.

STEP 12 – Apply moist warm towel; perform back press

CAUTION: ***Special care must be taken with this step because the back can become hot!*** The heat will usually build slowly and peak in about 3-8 minutes, before cooling down to the point where it feels quite pleasant. The greater the inflammation and viral infection along the spine, the hotter the area along the spine will become.

If the heat becomes uncomfortable, place a dry, folded towel **between** the back and the damp towel (see first point below). If the warming sensation continues to be uncomfortable, remove all towels and massage the area with 10-15 drops of vegetable or massage oil.

- Soak one of the towels in warm water, wring it out, fold it in thirds, and lay it along the entire length of the spine.
- Place the other dry towel (folded in half) over the wet towel.
- Allow the heat from the wet towel to penetrate, usually about 8–10 minutes. If the heat fades before 8 minutes are up, it may be helpful to apply the warm moist towel a second time.

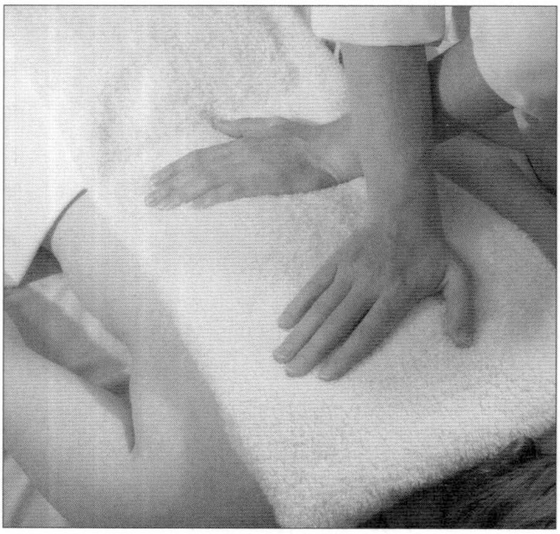

Fig. N — Back Press

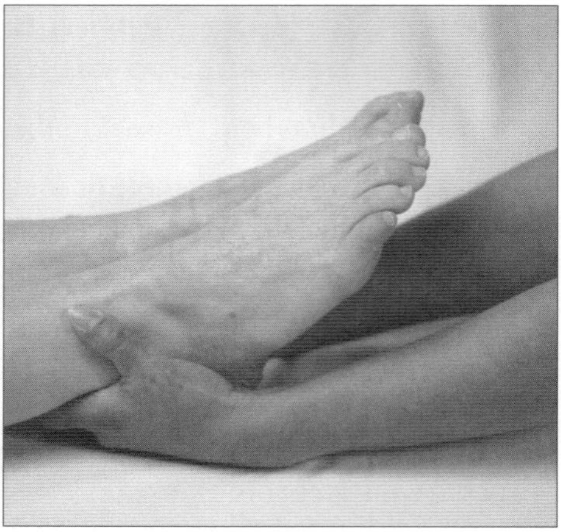

Fig. O — Stretching the spine

- Pay very close attention to the recipient's comfort. Ask questions.
- After the warmth of the oils has subsided (from 8–15 minutes), with the towels still in place, perform the back press by crossing the hands and placing them 1-2 inches apart at the base of the back. Gently press the hands down and away from each other, vibrating the hands and spreading them slightly. Repeat this process of pressing, vibrating and spreading the hands 3-5 times, each time starting further up the spine, until reaching the top of the spine (See Fig. N). Repeat this step two more times.

STEP 13 - Remove towels and inspect spine

- Remove the towels. Make sure the person is lying with their head snug in the head cradle of the massage table and with their spine straight (hips aligned with shoulders).
- Check the spine. Corrections may or may not be visible. Results may take several days to take full effect. You may need to perform another technique at a later time.

STEP 14 - Gently stretch the back and neck

- Have the recipient turn over onto their back. Be careful to keep the receiver covered to protect modesty.
- If you are working alone, hold the ankles firmly and apply light pressure to stretch the back as shown (See Fig. O). If there is a second facilitator, they

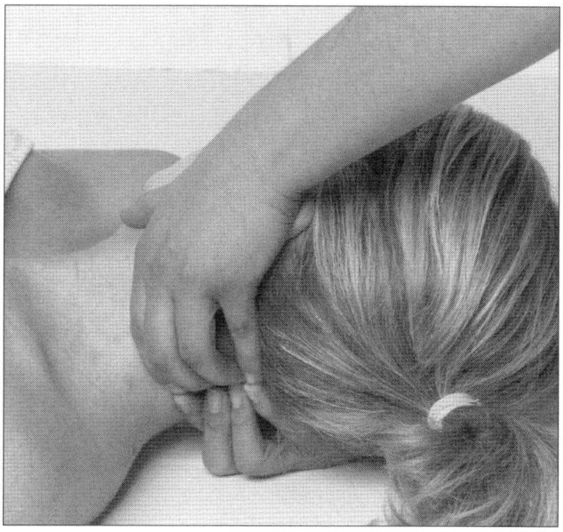

Fig. P — Finger placement for cranial hold stretch

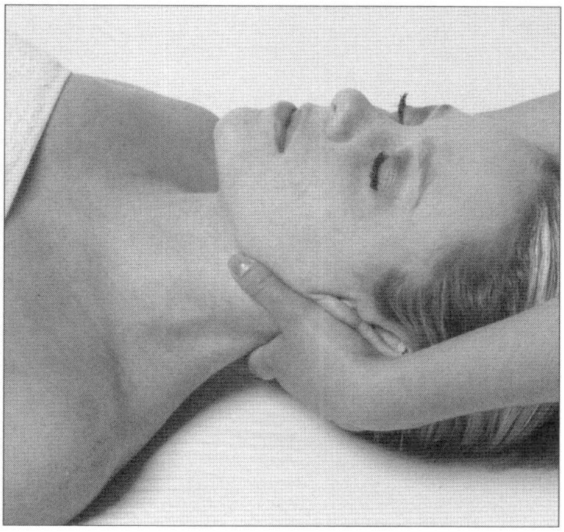

Fig. Q — Cranial hold

NOTE: People with advanced rheumatoid arthritis, high blood pressure, or Down Syndrome should avoid neck stretching. In such cases, consult a health care professional regarding steps 14 and 15 of the Raindrop Technique.

should hold the ankles while you cradle the individual's head in your hands (see cranial hold below), place your thumbs around the chin, and gently lift and ease back to create slight tension. Hold for 3 seconds, then release for 3 seconds. Repeat three times.

Best results are achieved when two people perform this stretching step: one gently tensioning the neck while the other holds the legs. If there is only one facilitator, this step can be done in two sequential steps—ankles first, then neck.

STEP 14A – Finger placement for cranial hold

- Place both hands under the recipient's neck, with the fingers touching each other and the thumbs just below the jaw. (See Fig. P)

STEP 14B – Basic cranial hold

- Gently pull the recipient's head back from the torso using the cranial hold. Pull back gently for 3 seconds, then release for 3 seconds. Repeat this cycle slowly and gently three times. Check with the recipient during this process to verify that they are not experiencing any pain. If there is pain, immediately discontinue the stretch. (See Fig. Q)

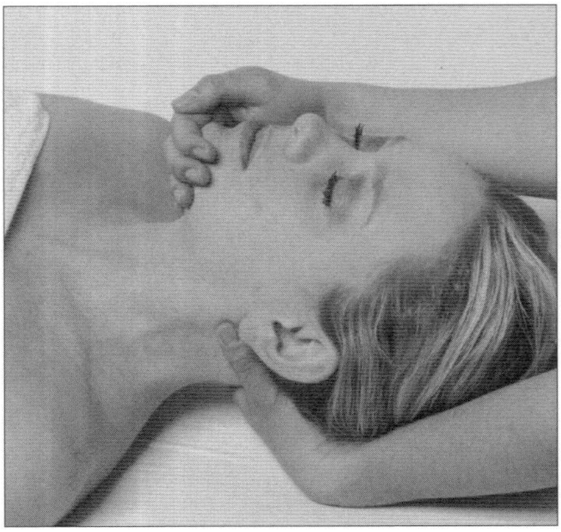

Fig. R — Holding chin during modified cranial hold

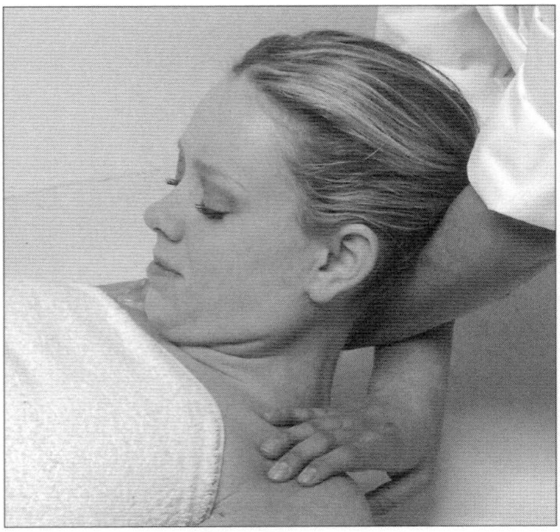

Fig. S — Neck Flex

STEP 14C - Modified cranial hold

This is an alternate version of the cranial hold, which differs in the hand placement on the receiver's head.

- Hold the recipient's head with one hand under the neck, palm up, and the other hand cradling the receiver's chin. Gently create tension in the neck by slowly pulling the head away from the torso. Hold for 5 seconds, then release for 5 seconds. Repeat two more times. (See Fig. R)
- Do not pull too hard. An assistant, if available, can anchor the feet while you gently tension the neck.

STEP 15 - Neck Flex

- Kneel or sit so that your shoulders are parallel to the recipient's shoulders.
- Cross your arms and place your hands (palm side down) on the recipient's shoulders (left hand on the right shoulder and visa versa).
- Make sure the recipient's tongue is not between their teeth.
- Raise your elbows in order to gently lift and stretch the recipient's neck until their chin touches the chest.
- Repeat this step two more times. (See Fig. S)
- For optimum results, the recipient should drink extra purified or distilled water for the first few days following RT. This will aid the body in flushing toxins from the tissues.

Customizing Raindrop Technique® to Address Specific Health Issues

Raindrop Technique can be customized to address different health issues that are not directly related to back problems. Lung infections, digestive complaints, hormonal problems, liver insufficiencies, and other problems can all be dealt with by substituting standard RT essential oils with other oils that are specifically targeted for that body system.

As a rule, when customizing RT, you will generally want to start with the Energy Balance Blend, oregano, and thyme. These three oils form the basis or "hub" of all Raindrop applications. (For extra antiviral effect, add mountain savory.) The other essential oils such as basil, wintergreen, marjoram, thyme, or cypress can be omitted or replaced by essential oils specific for the condition being treated.

For example, if a lung infection is present, basil and wintergreen should be replaced with ravensara, cypress replaced with *Eucalyptus radiata*, and marjoram replaced with mountain savory. (See diagram on next page)

There are several variations to the basic Raindrop Technique. These variations are not easy to explain and require class instruction and demonstration.

SUMMARY:

Raindrop Technique (RT) is a powerful tool that assists both professionals and lay people to achieve true balance in the body. Out of the thousands of RT sessions that I and others have performed, I have witnessed hundreds of instances where the results were amazingly profound and immediate. Let me mention just a few:

A young man from Denver, Colorado who suffered from chronic scoliosis was able—for the first time in eight years—to fully bend over after the application of RT. With an overhead camera televising an image of his spine as he bent over, an audience of over 400 watched the vertebrae in his spine literally move into place. When he stood up, he was measured and had gained an inch in height.

Another case involved a professional model in her early 40s, who had developed early adult-onset scoliosis. She had to alter clothing so it would fit properly for modeling sessions. She wasn't able to sit still for any length of time. After receiving RT from me, her spine straightened to such a degree that she, too, gained an inch in height. She followed up with more RT in the next few months and reported that all discomfort was gone. She now dances and rides horses pain-free.

BRAIN
cardemom, peppermint,
Clarity Blend,
Headache Blend,
Stress-reduction Blend
HEART/
CIRCULATION
clove, nutmeg,
goldenrod, cypress,
Circulation Blend
JOINTS/BONES
wintergreen, spruce,
helichrysum,
Pain Relief Blend
LIVER
ledum, carrot seed,
German chamomille,
Liver Blend
Energy
Balance Blend,
oregano,
thyme
LONGEVITY
thyme, frankincense,
Anti-Aging Blend
LUNG
ravensara, eucalyptus
radiata, myrtle,
Respiratory Blend,
Antiseptic Blend
COLON/
DIGESTION
tarragon, fennel,
cumin, spearmint,
Digestive Blend
HORMONE
BALANCE
clary sage, fleabane,
Glandular Blend,
Female Blend,
Male Blend

It is quite common that individuals with scoliosis who receive RT will gain 1/2 an inch or more in stature from a single application. Many others have reported pain relief, congestion relief, and cold and flu relief as a result of RT. This is why RT has captured so much interest among those involved in the healing arts.

I have conducted RT on my own five-day-old infant son. I used only one drop of each oil. I applied it to my fingers and massaged it into the fingers first, so that only trace amounts of the oils were applied to the skin. Children can benefit from RT, but it is critical to adjust the amount of oil used in proportion to their body size. Amounts should be adjusted to reflect the difference in body size relative to an adult.

Every person is biochemically different, and what works for one may not work for another. Different body types respond to the applications in ways you may not expect. Learn to be sensitive to the person on whom you are working so that you can respond to their needs.

The question is often asked, "How long do the effects of this application last?" Again, I have found that each person responds differently. Generally speaking, a high level of health and proper diet are key factors, as are exercise and attitude. The effects of one application may last several months for one person, but for another it may be necessary to have repeated applications weekly until the body begins to respond. The goal is to retrain the tissues of the body. This may take a few weeks or even a full year.

Spinal alignment may have a completely different look when the individual is lying down, rather than sitting. There is more torque on the spine in a sitting or standing position, so these are the positions in which X-rays are usually taken. The spine may appear to be totally corrected when the receiver is lying down, but then appear to be crooked when they are in a sitting position. This variance is normal and may be apparent until a total retraining of the muscles occurs. The object is to achieve proper alignment in all positions.

CHAPTER 12

Lymphatic Pump

Maintaining lymph circulation is one of the keys to keeping the immune system adequately functioning. This technique is designed to promote lymph circulation. It is an excellent tool for those who are sedentary or bedridden.

1. With the recipient lying on their back, hold one leg with one hand just above ankles with your palm on the underside of the leg (covering the Achille's tendon).
2. Place the other hand on the bottom of the recipient's foot with your palm over the ball of their feet and your fingers curled around their toes.
3. Push the top of the recipient's foot away from you. (See Fig. A)

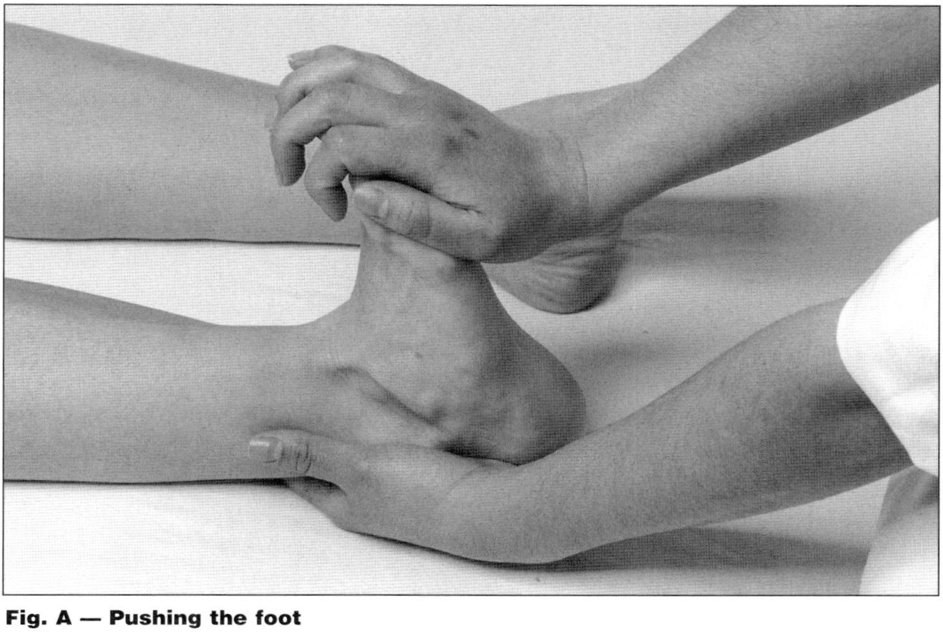

Fig. A — Pushing the foot

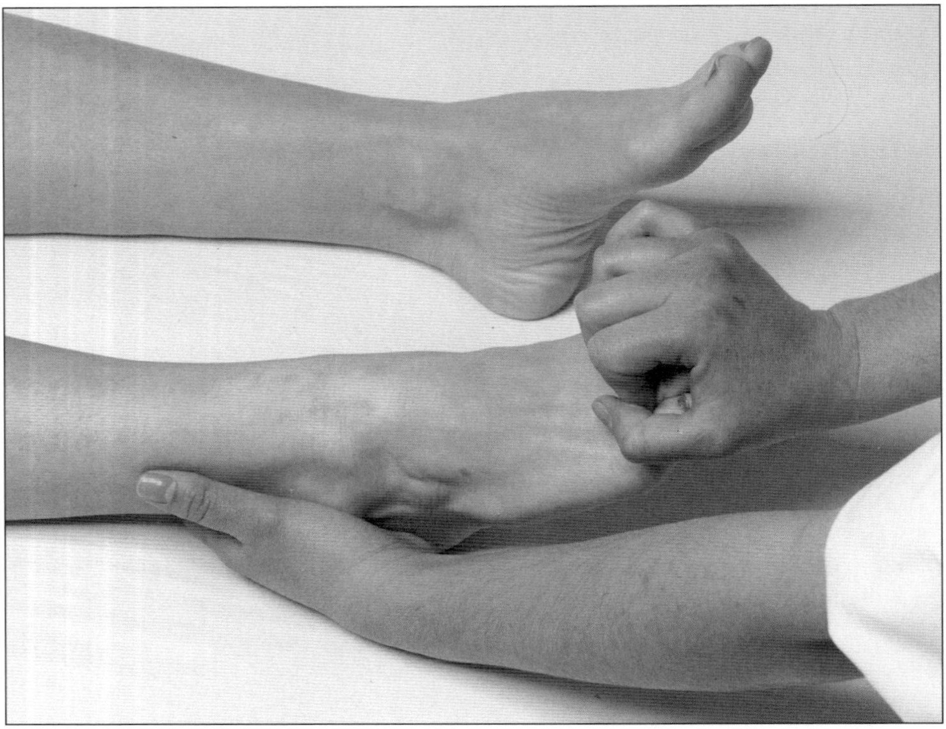

Fig. B — Pulling the foot

4. Then, pull the recipient's foot toward you by the toes until the ball of the foot is as close to the table as possible. (See Fig. B)
5. Check with the recipient during the pump to verify that the muscles in their feet are not being overextended. This should be an active process, but not a painful one.
6. Pull and push their foot using this "pumping motion" at least 10 times on each leg for maximum benefit. Note that their entire body should move during each step of the Lymphatic Pump.

CHAPTER 13

Auricular Aroma Technique

I developed Auricular Aroma Technique, the integration of essential oils with standard auricular technique, after using essential oils in an acupuncture application in my clinic. I found that using essential oils in conjunction with acupuncture was extremely beneficial. I also found that acupuncture stimulation with essential oils was noticeably greater than either acupuncture or essential oil application by themselves.

Acupuncture with essential oils seems to enhance benefits substantially. As I left my first clinical practice and began researching, farming, and teaching, I knew I could not continue the practice of acupuncture, so I started developing a technique that everyone could use. That technique is called auricular probe technique, using a small, pen-shaped instrument with a rounded end to apply the oils to the acupuncture meridians or Vita Flex points on the ears. This concept can be used in both the emotional and physical realm.

For working the spine and dealing with neurological problems that exist because of spinal cord injury, auricular probe technique was found to be extremely beneficial to deliver the oils to the exact location of the neurological damage.

Auricular probe technique is a program that I have been researching, developing, and teaching to doctors. It has shown tremendous potential and will grow to be a well-known modality in the future.

Emotional Ear Chart

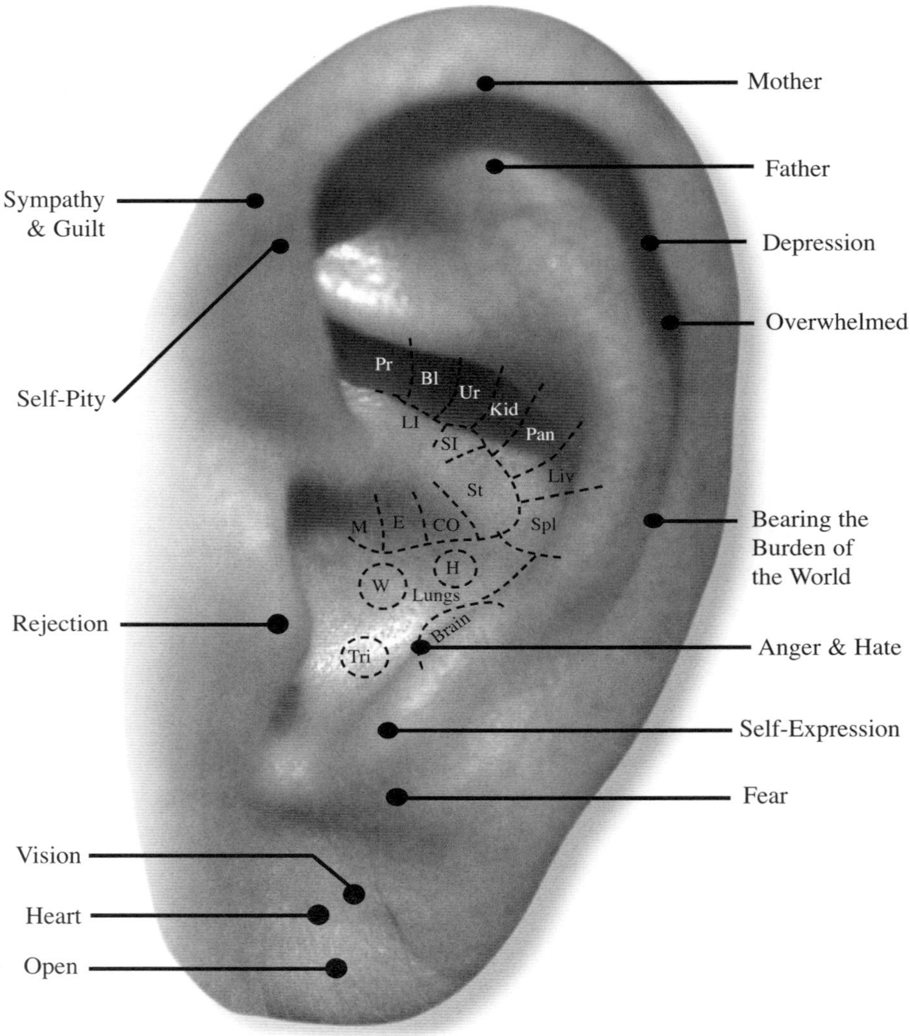

Physical Ear Chart

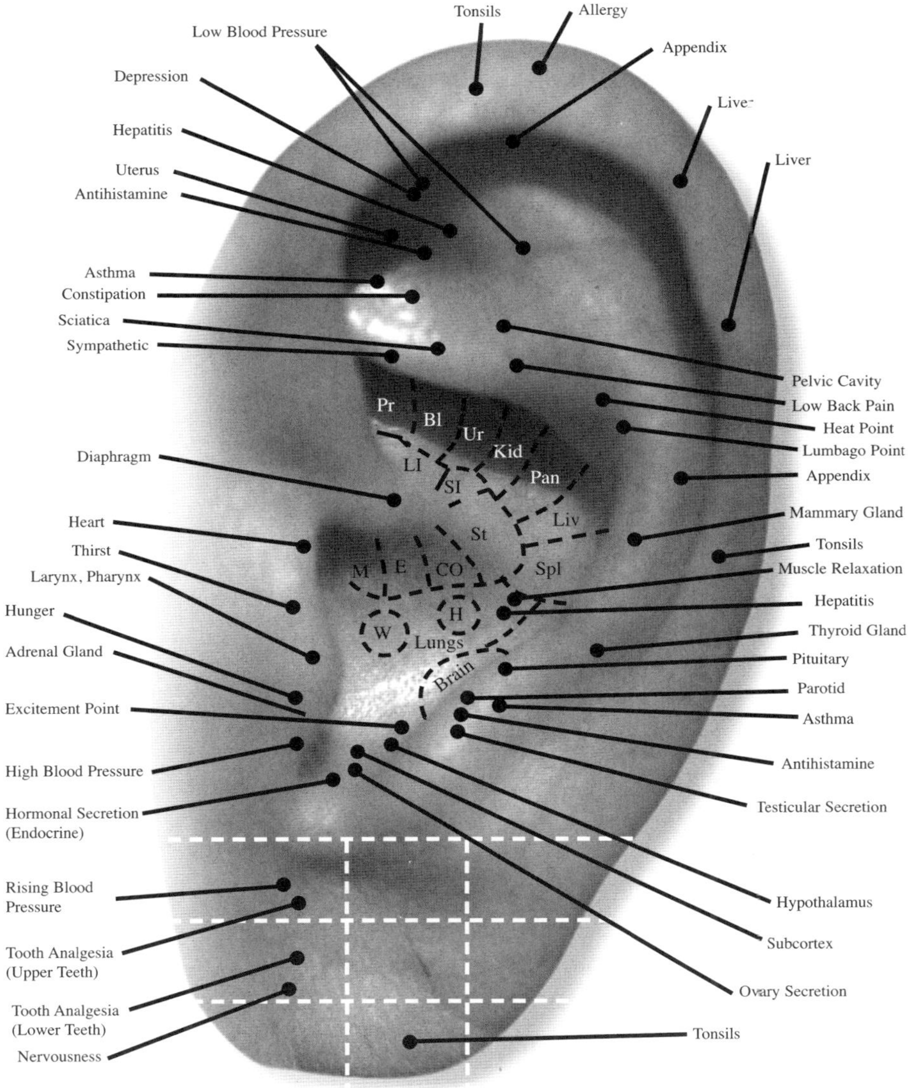

M	Mouth	LI	Large Intestine	Pan	Pancreas, Gall Bladder
E	Esophagus	Pr	Prostate	Liv	Liver
CO	Cardiac Orifice	Bl	Bladder	Spl	Spleen
St	Stomach	Ur	Ureter	H	Heart
SI	Small Intestine	Kid	Kidney	W	Windpipe, Trachea

CHAPTER 14

Emotional Response with Essential Oils

Today, we live in a society of emotional turmoil. There is more focus on emotional behavior and psychological conditions of the body now than at any time in our history. Many doctors are recognizing the possibility that a number of diseases are caused by emotional problems that link back to infancy and perhaps even to the womb. These emotional problems may have compromised our immune system or genetic structuring, causing children to become allergic to something that the mother ingested while pregnant.

Essential oils play an important role in assisting people to move beyond these emotional barriers. The aldehydes and esters of certain essential oils are very calming and sedating to the central nervous system (including both the sympathetic and parasympathetic systems). These substances allow us to relax instead of letting anxiety build up in our body. Anxiety creates an acidic condition that activates the transcript enzyme which then transcribes that anxiety on the RNA template and stores it in the DNA. That emotion then becomes a predominant factor in our lives from that moment on.

When we encounter an emotionally charged situation, instead of being overwhelmed by it, we can diffuse essential oils, put them in our bath, or wear them as cologne. The aromatic molecules will absorb into the bloodstream from the nasal cavity to the limbic system. They will activate the amygdala (the memory center for fear and trauma) and sedate and relax the sympathetic/parasympathetic system. The oils help support the body in minimizing the acid that is created so that it does not initiate a reaction with the transcript enzyme.

Because essential oils affect the amygdala and pineal gland in the brain, they can help the mind and body by releasing emotional trauma and sharpening focus.

People have many distractions in today's fast-paced world. Essential oils may assist people to stay centered in their goals. Those who are struggling to retain or remember information can breathe the essential oils of peppermint, cardamom, or rosemary to stimulate the brain and memory functions for better concentration. Those who find it difficult to stay focused can breathe the essential oils of galbanum, frankincense, sandalwood, and melissa. These oils are extremely beneficial for clarifying one's purpose. For emotional clearing and release, the combination of essential oils called Emotional Release is especially helpful.

Oils For Emotional Application

Abuse

Single Oils: Geranium, ylang ylang, sandalwood.

Blends: Abuse Relief
Mood Lifting
Stress Reduction
Trauma
Energy Balance

Agitation

Single Oils: Bergamot, cedarwood, clary sage, frankincense, geranium, juniper, lavender, myrrh, marjoram, rosewood, rose, ylang ylang, sandalwood.

Blends: Stress Reduction
Mood Lifting
Energy Balance

Anger

Single Oils: Bergamot, cedarwood, Roman chamomile, frankincense, lavender, lemon, marjoram, myrrh, orange, rose, sandalwood, ylang ylang.

Blends: Emotional Release
Energy Balance
Mood Lifting
Trauma

Anxiety

Single Oils: Orange, Roman chamomile, ylang ylang, lavender.

Blends: Energy Balance
Stress Reduction
Mood Lifting

Apathy

Single Oils: Frankincense, geranium, marjoram, jasmine, orange, peppermint, rosewood, rose, sandalwood, thyme, ylang ylang.

Blends: Mood Lifting
Energy Balance

Argumentative

Single Oils: Cedarwood, Roman chamomile, eucalyptus, frankincense, jasmine, orange, thyme, ylang ylang.

Blends: Stress Reduction
Mood Lifting
Energy Balance
Emotional Release

Boredom

Single Oils: Cedarwood, spruce, Roman chamomile, cypress, frankincense, juniper, lavender, rosemary CT cineol, sandalwood, thyme, ylang ylang, black pepper.

Blends: Energy Balance
Energy

Concentration

Single Oils: Cedarwood, cypress, juniper, lavender, lemon, basil, helichrysum, myrrh, orange, peppermint, rosemary CT cineol, sandalwood, ylang ylang.

Blends: Clarity
Brain

Confusion

Single Oils: Cedarwood, spruce, cypress, peppermint, frankincense, geranium, ginger, juniper, marjoram, jasmine, rose, rosewood, rosemary CT cineol, basil, sandalwood, thyme, ylang ylang.

Blends: Clarity
Energy Balance
Brain

Day-Dreaming

Single Oils: Ginger, spruce, lavender, helichrysum, lemon, myrrh, peppermint, rosewood, rose, rosemary CT cineol, sandalwood, thyme, ylang ylang.

Blends: Energy Balance
Brain
Energy

Depression

Single Oils: Frankincense, lemon, sandalwood, geranium, lavender, angelica, orange, grapefruit, ylang ylang.

Blends: Energy Balance
Mood Lifting
Brain

Despair

Single Oils: Cedarwood, spruce, clary sage, frankincense, lavender, geranium, lemon, orange, lemongrass, peppermint, spearmint, rosemary CT cineol, sandalwood, thyme, ylang ylang.

Blends: Mood Lifting
Energy Balance

Despondency

Single Oils: Bergamot, clary sage, cypress, geranium, ginger, orange, rose, rosewood, sandalwood, ylang ylang.

Blends: Stress Reduction
Spiritual
Energy Balance
Mood Lifting
Trauma

Disappointment

Single Oils: Clary sage, frankincense, geranium, ginger, juniper, lavender, spruce, orange, thyme, ylang ylang.

Blends: Mood Lifting
Energy Balance

Discouragement

Single Oils: Bergamot, cedarwood, frankincense, geranium, juniper, lavender, lemon, orange, spruce, rosewood, sandalwood.

Blends: Energy Balance
Spiritual
Mood Lifting

Fear

Single Oils: Bergamot, clary sage, Roman chamomile, cypress, geranium, juniper, marjoram, myrrh, spruce, orange, sandalwood, rose, ylang ylang.

Blends: Energy Balance
Trauma

Forgetfulness

Single Oils: Cedarwood, Roman chamomile, frankincense, rosemary CT cineol, basil, sandalwood, peppermint, thyme, ylang ylang.

Blends: Clarity
Energy Balance
Brain

Frustration

Single Oils: Roman chamomile, clary sage, frankincense, ginger, juniper, lavender, lemon, orange, peppermint, thyme, ylang ylang, spruce.

Blends: Energy Balance
Stress Reduction

Grief/Sorrow

Single Oils: Bergamot, Roman chamomile, clary sage, *Eucalyptus globulus,* juniper, lavender.

Blends: Energy Balance
Mood Lifting
Emotional Release
Trauma
Spiritual

Guilt

Single Oils: Roman chamomile, cypress, juniper, lemon, marjoram, geranium, frankincense, sandalwood, spruce, rose, thyme.

Blends: Energy Balance
Emotional Release
Spiritual

Irritability

Single Oils: All oils except eucalyptus, peppermint, black pepper.

Blends: Energy Balance
Stress Reduction
Mood Lifting

Jealousy

Single Oils: Bergamot, eucalyptus, frankincense, lemon, marjoram, orange, rose, rosemary CT cineol, thyme.

Blends: Energy Balance
Mood Lifting
Emotional Release

Mood Swings

Single Oils: Bergamot, clary sage, sage, geranium, juniper, fennel, lavender, peppermint, rose, jasmine, rosemary CT cineol, lemon, sandalwood, spruce, yarrow, ylang ylang.

Blends: Stress Reduction
Energy Balance
Female
Male
Mood Lifting
Brain

Obsessiveness

Single Oils: Clary sage, cypress, geranium, lavender, marjoram, rose, sandalwood, ylang ylang, helichrysum.

Blend: Energy Balance

Panic

Single Oils: Bergamot, Roman chamomile, frankincense, lavender, marjoram, wintergreen or birch, myrrh, rosemary CT cineol, sandalwood, thyme, ylang ylang, spruce.

Blends: Energy Balance
Stress Reduction
Trauma

Resentment

Single Oils: Jasmine, rose, tansy.

Blends: Mood Lifting
Spiritual

Restlessness

Single Oils: Angelica, bergamot, cedarwood, basil, frankincense, geranium, lavender, orange, rose, rosewood, ylang ylang, spruce.

Blends: Stress Reduction
Energy Balance
Spiritual Blend

Shock

Single Oils: Helichrysum, basil, Roman chamomile, myrrh, ylang ylang, rosemary CT cineol.

Blends: Clarity
Energy Balance
Spiritual
Mood Lifting
Trauma
Brain

Gary interviews an elderly Vilcabamba Indian woman in Ecuador with the assistance of an interpreter.

Gary is backpacking into a remote Tarahumara village in Mexico to study the health secrets of these native people.

CHAPTER 15

Longevity and Essential Oils

Essential oils and aromatics were some of the most highly prized natural medicines of the ancient world. References to cassia, clove, frankincense, myrrh, spikenard, cinnamon, and rosemary appear in many historical writings, including the Old and New Testaments as well as the writings of Hippocrates, Avicenna, and ancient Egyptian hieroglyphics.

Intriguing new research offers a tantalizing glimpse into the far-reaching potential of essential oils like thyme (*Thymus vulgaris*) to reverse or slow the aging process by acting as powerful antioxidants that protect tissues and organs from oxidative stress and damage. Other oils, such as clove (*Syzygium aromaticum*) and lemon *(Citrus limon)* have not only been shown to act as powerful antioxidants, but also to protect cellular DNA from damage and to act as potent antiseptics with broad-spectrum germ-killing properties.

What Causes Aging?

There is still some controversy concerning the cause of aging and premature death. Some researchers believe that declining levels of hormones from the pituitary and hypothalamus are the culprits. Others point an accusing finger at the crosslinking of collagen, a key protein of the soft tissues that constitutes a third of all protein in the body. Still others blame the buildup of lipofuscin, a brownish pigment that accumulates inside the cells, particularly nerve and heart muscle cells.[1]

However, the oxidative stress/free radical theory of aging is the most persuasive and substantiated. This rationale posits that aging is caused by cumulative oxidative stress to the cell walls, receptors, and DNA. Rogue electrons that are generated from normal metabolic and immune functions

1. Hayflick, L. *How and Why We Age*. Ballantine Books, New York, 1994.

Essential Oils vs. Fatty Oils

Fatty oils are very different from essential oils. Fatty oils, such as cottonseed, almond, olive, corn, sunflower, and canola oil, are usually pressed from a seed or fruit. They are greasy in texture and have little odor, being simple mixtures of several different fatty acids (ie., capric, stearic, and oleic).

In contrast, essential oils are usually steam distilled from leaves, flowers, roots, and bark. They have strong odors and are not greasy. Because many are lighter than water, they float and tend to evaporate very easily. Essential oils are complex mosaics of hundreds of aromatic molecules (ie., terpenes, sesquiterpenes, and phenols) that usually have a ring-like structure.

CAPRIC FATTY ACID
(from coconut oil)

Methyl end | Acid end

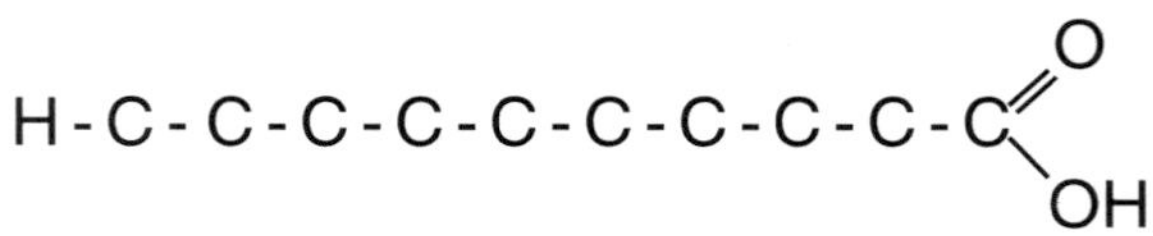

THYMOL
(from thyme ess. oil)

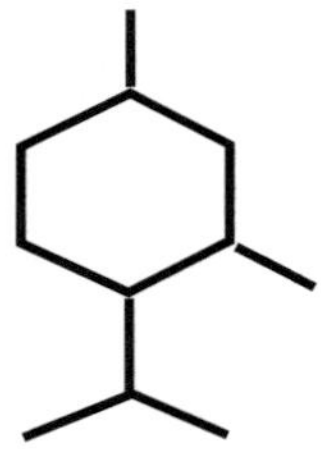

attack proteins and disrupt DNA, eventually overwhelming the natural repair abilities of the body and sometimes leading to disease and death.[2,3,4]

While many researchers have focused on damage to the DNA (the blueprint for cellular operations) as the cause of aging, few have appreciated how devastating free radical damage can be to fats—especially the unstable polyunsaturated fatty acids (PUFAs) that form the phospholipid membranes of almost every cell in the body. When these fatty membranes are attacked by free radicals, ion transport and hormone receptors are disrupted.[5] As cell membranes become less fluid, they lose their ability to function normally. This can hasten the onset of tissue and organ damage and lead to premature death.

2. Harmon, D, Ageing: a theory based on free radical and radiation chemistry. *J. Gerontology* 11, (1956): 298-300.
3. Harmon, D, Free radical theory of ageing: Effect of free radical inhibitors on the mortality rate of male LAFmice. *J. Gerontology* 23 (1968): 476-482.
4. Harmon, D, Free radical theory of ageing: Effect of the amount and degree of unsaturation of dietary fat on mortality rate. *J. Gerontology* 26 (1971): 451-457.
5. Stubbs CD & Smith AD, The modification of mammalian membrane polyunsaturated fatty acid composition in relation to membrane fluidity and function. *Biochimica et Biophysica Acta* 779, (1984)89-137.

One of the most easy-to-understand examples of the detrimental effects of cell membrane brittleness occurs in the blood vessel walls. As the blood vessels lose their flexibility, the risk of hypertension (high blood pressure) increases, as does the incidence of arteriosclerosis.

Why does free radical damage escalate with age? Because antioxidant protection declines as we grow older. Free radical scavengers such as superoxide dismutase (SOD) and glutathione peroxidase chart a steady decline along with other antioxidants. This means that the older body is less efficient in neutralizing free radicals and combating the oxidative damage that gradually weakens and eventually destroys key organs.

Levels of polyunsaturated fats such as DHA (decosahexaenoic acid) are also crucial for healthy brain and eye function. DHA occurs in unusually high concentrations in the cerebral cortex—the most advanced part of the brain structure where logic and reasoning take place. When DHA becomes oxidized and loses its double bonds because of free radical attacks, brain and cognitive function can deteriorate. This can lead to memory loss, dementia, and even death. By protecting fats like DHA from free radical attack, hydrolysis, or oxidation, brain health can be significantly improved.[6,7,8,9]

The crux of the problem is that DHA and other long chain PUFAs are very unstable and are vulnerable to chemical alteration and oxidation. This means that the antioxidant systems of the body must work overtime to protect them in order to sustain health. An even greater problem is that the liver slows down PUFA production with age, so it becomes less and less able to replace through desaturase activities the dwindling supply of PUFA needed to sustain the brain, tissues, and other organs.[10]

Thus the longevity of the organism is strongly linked to preserving the integrity of the polyunsaturated fats that comprise cells, nerves, and other tissues. Preventing the degradation of these fats from free radical damage can forestall the signs of accelerated aging.

---

6. Barja de Quiroga G, et al., Antioxidant defences and peroxidation in liver and brain of aged rats. *Biochemical Journal* 272 (1990), 247-250.

7. Lamptey MS & Walker BL, A possible dietary role for linolenic acid in the development of the young rat. Journal of Nutrition 106, (1976) 86-93.

8. Okuyama H, Minimum requirements of n-3 and n-6 essential fatty acids for the function of the central nervous system and for the prevention of chronic disease. *Proceedings of the Society for Experimental Biology and Medicine* 200, (1992) 174-176.

9. Yamamoto N, et al, Effects of dietary alpha-linolenate/linolenate balance of brain lipid composition and learning ability of rats. *Journal of Lipid Research* 28, (1987) 144-151.

10. Bourre et al., Function of dietary polyunsaturated fatty acids in the nervous system. *Prostaglandins, Leukotrienes, and Essential Fatty Acids* 48 (1993): 5-15.

Preserving the Integrity of Fats *In Vitro*

In the late 1980s, Dr. Radwan Farag of the biochemistry department of the University of Cairo was among the first to show *in vitro* how selected essential oils were able to significantly slow the rancidity (oxidation) of fatty oils such as cottonseed oil. He dosed samples of cottonseed oil with 200 ppm of thyme oil (55.7% thymol and 36% p-cymene) and 400 ppm of clove oil (85.3% eugenol). After comparing the essential oil-treated samples with untreated control samples, he found that both thyme and clove oil afforded significant protection against rancidity to the cottonseed oil as determined by lowered peroxide and TBA values. Thyme oil generated a 20% reduction in rancidity while clove oil triggered almost a 30% drop.[11]

A second study by Dr. Farag and his colleagues showed that essential oils such as thyme, clove, rosemary (*Rosmarinus officinalis*), and sage (*Salvia officinalis*) arrested the oxidation of linoleic acid, a polyunsaturated omega-6 fatty acid.[12]

In addition, Dr. Farag demonstrated the safety of these essential oils *in vivo*. When he added thyme and clove oils to rat feed rations at up to six times the minimum concentration needed to stall fat oxidation, none of the rats studied suffered any negative side effects. Essential oil-fed rats exhibited no difference in protein, cholesterol, and liver enzyme levels (SGPT, SGOT) when compared with a control group.[13]

Thyme and Clove Essential Oil Slow the Oxidation of Cottonseed Oil

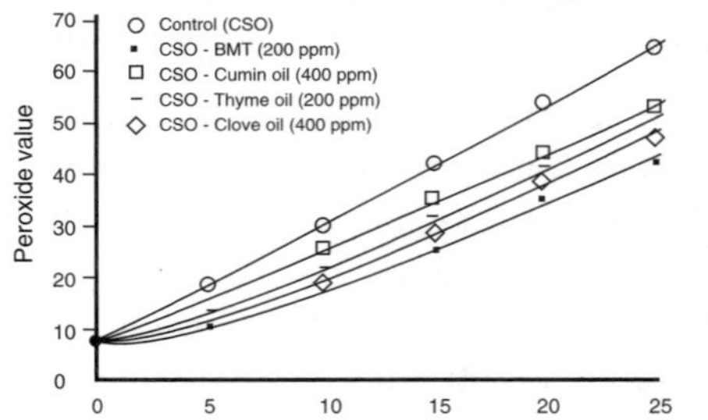

Farag et al., 1989

Protecting Fats and Phospholipids in Animals

Almost a decade after Farag's groundbreaking research, another series of more intensive *in vivo* studies were begun at the Scottish Agricultural College in the United Kingdom and the Semmelweis University of Medicine in Hungary. In these clinical trials, researchers found that daily lifelong feeding of thyme and clove oils to laboratory animals preserved key antioxidant levels in the liver,

11. Farag et al., Antioxidant activity of some spice essential oils on linoleic acid oxidation in aqueous media. *JAOCS* June 1989;66: 792-799.
12. Farag et al., Inhibitory effects of individual and mixed pairs of essential oils on the oxidation and hydrolysis of cottonseed oil and butter. *FASC*, 1989; 40: 275-279.
13. Farag et al., Safety evaluation of thyme and clove essential oils as natural antioxidants. *Afr J Agr Sci*. 1991;18: 169-17.

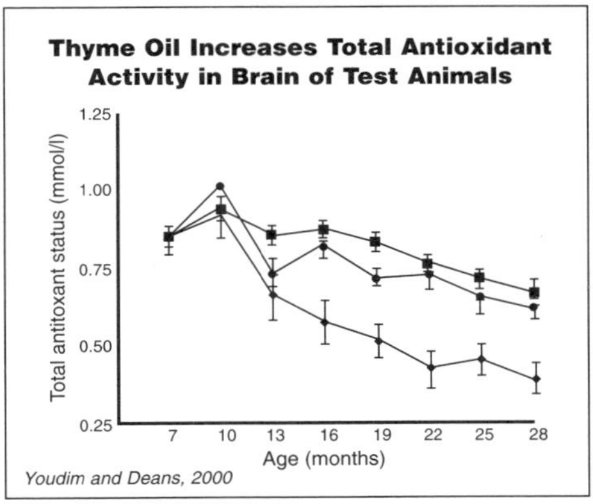

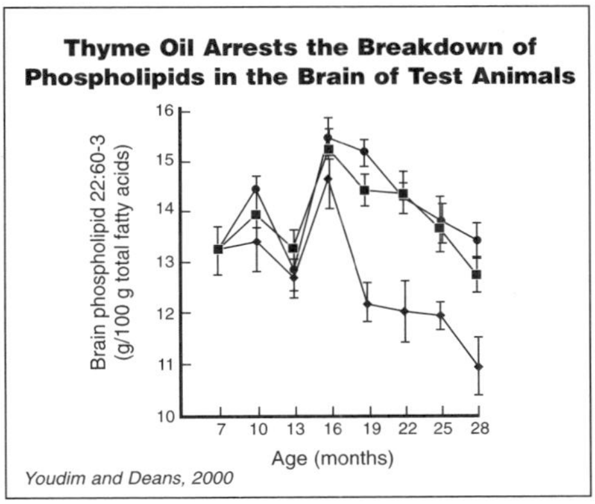

kidneys, heart, and brain. Even more importantly, essential oils arrested the oxidation and destruction of long-chain PUFAs throughout the organism.

One of the first studies to document these remarkable antioxidant effects was conducted at the Semmelweis University of Medicine in 1993. Researchers fed different groups of mice with daily doses of 0.72 mg of essential oils including thyme (*Thymus vulgaris*), clove (*Syzygium aromaticum*), nutmeg (*Myristica fragrans*), and pepper (*Piper nigrum*). Groups of younger mice (6 months old) were treated for five weeks, while groups of 22 month-old mice were treated for 21 weeks. Following treatment, the livers of the animals were examined for levels of C20 and C22 polyunsaturated fatty acids, which declines substantially during the animal's lifetime.

The results were phenomenal. According to the researchers, "dietary administration of the volatile oils to the aging mice had a marked effect on fatty acid distribution by virtually restoring the proportions of the polyunsaturated fatty acids within the phospholipids to the levels observed in young mice."

Another randomized, controlled animal study at Semmelweis University in 1997 showed that these same essential oils—thyme, clove, nutmeg, and pepper—restored DHA in the eyes to much younger levels. As a long-chain polyunsaturated fatty acid (PUFA) that is very fragile and easily oxidized, DHA is absolutely crucial for normal eye health. Declining levels of DHA have been directly linked to heightened risk of age-related macular degeneration, the leading cause of blindness in old age.[14,15]

In this case, dietary supplementation of just 3.9 mg per day of essential oils to laboratory animals over a 17-month period was sufficient to markedly slow DHA loss in their eyes.

14. Rotstein et al., Effects of aging on the composition and metabolism of docosahexaenoate-containing lipids of retina. *Lipids*, 1987 Apr;22(4):253-60.

15. Neuringer M & Connor WE, N-3 fatty acids in the brain and retina: evidence for their essentiality. *Nutrition Reviews* 44, 285-294.

Preserving Brain Function

The brain is another organ where DHA is essential to health. Karesh Youdim and his colleagues at the Scottish Agricultural College tested the ability of essential oils to preserve DHA levels in the brain of 100 animal subjects. Feeding them a daily dose (42.5 mg/K of body weight) of thyme oil (48% thymol) over the course of their lifetime (28 months), the researchers achieved stunning results: Thyme oil dramatically slowed age-related DHA and PUFA degradation in the brain. In other words, the essential oil of thyme was able to partially prevent brain aging through protection of essential fatty acids. An analysis of the data showed that the DHA levels in 28 month-old animals' brains was almost the same as that of 7 month-olds. In human terms, this was equivalent to an 80-year-old having the brain chemistry of a 20-year-old![16]

Thyme oil supplements also slowed the decline of total brain antioxidant levels that occurs with age. Lifelong supplementation with thyme oil in laboratory rats resulted in antioxidant levels dropping by only 29%, compared with a 45% fall for untreated animals.

Even more startling is the fact that thyme essential oil also preserved levels of PUFAs in the animals' hearts, livers, and kidneys, while at the same time raising total antioxidant levels—including key antioxidants such as glutathione peroxidase and superoxide dismutase. This was accomplished by feeding laboratory rats daily thyme oil supplements (42.5 mg/K of body weight) throughout their lives.[17]

Clove Oil Affords Protection Against Cancer

Clove oil also has potent antioxidant-boosting properties. Animal studies conducted at LKT Laboratories in Minneapolis, Minnesota, found that five compounds within clove oil significantly increased levels of GST (glutathione S-transferase), one of the most important detoxifying enzymes in the human body that is critical for neutalizing potential cancer-causing chemicals. Just 60 mg of each of the five compounds (b-caryophyllene, b-caryophyllene oxide, a-humulene, a-humulene epoxide I, and eugenol) fed to rats over the course of six days (3 doses of 20 mg each) resulted in a doubling of GST activity in the liver and a quadrupling of GST level in the small bowel mucosa. The authors concluded that "these sesquiterpenes show promise as potential anticarcinogenic agents."[18]

16. Youdim KA, et al., Effect of thyme oil and thymol dietary supplementation on the antioxidant status and fatty acid composition of the ageing rat brain. *Br J Nutr.* 2000 Jan;83(1):87-93.

17. Youdim KA, Deans SG., Dietary supplementation of thyme (Thymus vulgaris L.) essential oil during the lifetime of the rat: its effects on the antioxidant status in liver, kidney and heart tissues. *Mech Ageing Dev.* 1999 Sep 8;109(3):163-75.

18. Zheng GQ, et al. Sesquiterpenes from clove (Eugenia caryophyllata) as potential anticarcinogenic agents. *J Nat Prod.* 1992 Jul;55(7):999-1003.

Thyme Oil Raises Antioxidant Levels in the Heart

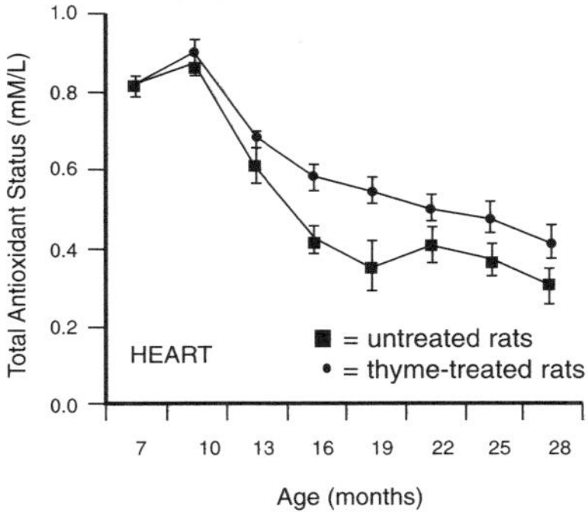

Thyme Oil Raises Antioxidant Levels in the Liver

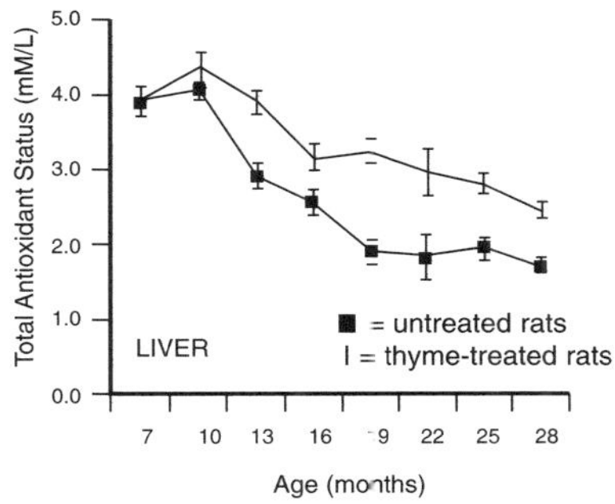

How 5 Constituents in Clove Oil Raise Glutathione Levels

Compound	Liver Levels of GST	Small Bowel Levels of GST
Control	0.74	0.25
Compound 1	1.92	0.75
Compound 2	2.13	1.20
Compound 3	1.47	0.63
Compound 4	1.54	0.81
Compound 5	1.26	0.59

Zheng et al., 1992.

Thyme Oil Raises Antioxidant Levels in the Kidneys

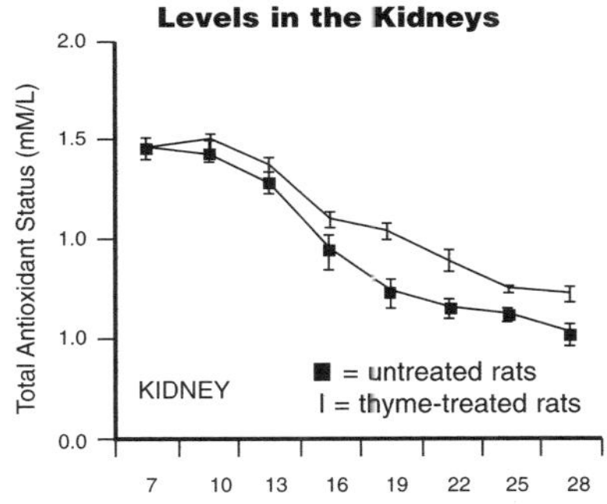

Youdim, 1999

Many other researchers have shown that clove essential oil exhibits pronounced antitumoral and DNA-protectant effects.[19,20]

Essential oils may do more than just raise antioxidant levels and block damage to PUFAs. They may also protect cellular DNA from damage that can eventually lead to mutations and subsequent tumor growth. In a 1986 study, Yokota et al., found that a diet including 5% eugenol (the chief constituent in clove oil) helped protect test animals against the mutagenic and cancer-causing affects of the chemical benzo[a]pyrene.[21]

19. Rompelberg et al. Antimutagenicity of eugenol in the rodent bone marrow micronucleus test. *Mutat Res*. 1995 Feb;346(2):69-75.
20. Sukumaran et al. Inhibition of tumour promotion in mice by eugenol. *Indian J Physiol Pharmacol*. 1994 Oct;38(4):306-8.
21. Yokota H, et al., Suppressed mutagenicity of benzo[a]pyrene by the liver S9 fraction and microsomes from eugenol-treated rats. *Mutat Res*. 1986 Dec;172(3):231-6.

Potent Weapons Against Microbes

Another method by which aromatics and essential oils may exert a life-lengthening effect is through their ability to inhibit the growth of bacteria, fungi, and viruses. Some bacteria, such as *Chlamydia pneumoniae* have been implicated as one of the true causes of heart disease. Viruses, such as HIV and hepatitis, have resulted in liver failure and premature death. Fungi like *Candida albicans* have been implicated in cancer due to their secretion of mycotoxins.

I conducted one of the most comprehensive studies to probe the powerful antimicrobial effects of essential oils with Sue Chao at Weber State University. Using disc diffusion assays, we tested the killing power of 67 different essential oils against a variety of yeast, molds, gram negative bacteria, and gram positive bacteria. Cinnamon, clove, thyme, peppermint, oregano, and mountain savory exerted the strongest antimicrobial properties.[22]

The following year we tested the ability of thyme, oregano, and clove essential oils to destroy colonies of *Streptococcus pneumoniae*, the bacteria responsible for many types of throat, sinus, and lung infections.[23]

Essential Oils: Treatments for Arthritis, Heart Disease, and More

A growing body of clinical research during the last several decades indicates that essential oils have enormous potential to treat conditions ranging from acne to obesity.

Peppermint *(Mentha piperita)* has been reviewed for its ability to block pain, relieve headaches[24], combat indigestion[25], boost mental alertness[26,27], induce weight loss[28], kill lice[29], and inhibit tumor growth.[30]

22. Chao, et al., Screening for Inhibitory Activity of Essential Oils on Selected Bacteria, Fungi, and Viruses. *Journal of Essential Oil Research*, 1997.
23. Chao et al., Antimicrobial Effects of Essential Oils on Streptococcus pneumoniae. *JEOR,* 2001.
24. Gobel et al. Effect of peppermint and eucalyptus oil preparations on neurophysiological and experimental algesimetric headache parameters. *Cephalalgia*. 1994 Jun;14(3):228-34; 182.
25. Dalvi et al. Effect of peppermint oil on gastric emptying in man: a preliminary study using a radiolabelled solid test meal. *Indian J Physiol Pharmacol*. 1991 Jul;35(3):212-4.
26. Dember WN, et al., Olfactory Stimulation and Sustained Attention, *Compendium of Olfactory*, (Avery N. Gilbert, Editor) pp. 39-46.
27. Miltner et al. Emotional qualities of odors and their influence on the startle reflex in humans. *Psychophysiology*. 1994 Jan;31(1):107-10.
28. Hirsch, Alan. *A Scentsational Guide to Weight Loss*. Rockport, MA: Element, 1997.
29. Veal L. The potential effectiveness of essential oils as a treatment for headlice, Pediculus humanus capitis. *Complement Ther Nurs Midwifery*. 1996 Aug;2(4):97-101.
30. Russin, et al. Inhibition of rat mammary carcinogenesis by monoterpenoids. *Carcinogenesis*. 1989 Nov;10(11):2161-4.

Melaleuca *(Melaleuca alternifolia)* has been used to treat acne[31], kill fungi[32], and inhibit bacteria growth.[33,34]

Lavender *(Lavandula angustifolia)* fights travel sickness[35], reduces atherosclerosis[36], protects blood vessels[37], acts as a local anaesthetic[38], and has anticonvulsant properties.[39]

Clove *(Syzygium aromaticum)* has been researched for its action against tooth decay[40] as well as its antifungal[41] and anticonvulsant activities.[42]

Rosemary *(Rosmarinus officinalis)* has been shown to enhance alertness[43], combat fungi such as *Candida albicans*, and act as an antioxidant.[44]

Orange *(Citrus aurantium)* halts fungus infection[45,46] and inhibits tumor formation.[47] Limonene, an important component of orange and lemon oil has demonstrated similar tumor-suppressing effects in studies at Indiana University.[48]

31. Bassett et al. A comparative study of tea-tree oil versus benzoylperoxide in the treatment of acne. *Med J Aust*. 1990 Oct 15;153(8):455-8.
32. Nenoff et al. Antifungal activity of the essential oil of Melaleuca alternifolia (tea tree oil) against pathogenic fungi in vitro. *Skin Pharmacol*. 1996;9(6):388-94.
33. Cox et al. The mode of antimicrobial action of the essential oil of Melaleuca alternifolia (tea tree oil). J *Appl Microbiol*. 2000 Jan;88(1):170-5.
34. Carson et al. Antimicrobial activity of the major components of the essential oil of Melaleuca alternifolia. *J Appl Bacteriol*. 1995 Mar;78(3):264-9.
35. Bradshaw et al. Effects of lavender straw on stress and travel sickness in pigs. *J Altern Complement Med*. 1998 Fall;4(3):271-5.
36. Nikolaevskii et al. Effect of essential oils on the course of experimental atherosclerosis. *Patol Fiziol Eksp Ter*. 1990 Sep-Oct;(5):52-3.
37. Siurein S A. Effects of essential oil on lipid peroxidation and lipid metabolism in patients with chronic bronchitis]. *Klin Med* (Mosk). 1997;75(10):43-5.
38. Ghelardini et al. Local anaesthetic activity of the essential oil of Lavandula angustifolia. *Planta Med*. 1999 Dec;65(8):700-3
39. Elisabetsky et al. Anticonvulsant properties of linalool in glutamate-related seizure models. *Phytomedicine*. 1999 May;6(2):107-13.
40. Cai and Wu .Compounds from Syzygium aromaticum possessing growth inhibitory activity against oral pathogens. *J Nat Prod*. 1996 Oct;59(10):987-90.
41. Covello et. al. Determination of eugenol in the essence of "Eugenia caryophyllata". Titration in non-aqueous solvent and comparison with other methods of analysis. *Boll Chim Farm*. 1966 Nov;105(11):799-806.
42. Pourgholami M.H. et.al. Evaluation of the anticonvulsant activity of the essential oil of Eugenia caryophyllata in male mice. *J Ethnopharmacol*. 1999 Feb;64(2):167-71.
43. Diego Migul A. et al. Aromatherapy positively affects mood, EEG patterns of alertness and math computations. *Int J Neurosci*. 1998 Dec;96(3-4):217-24.
44. Lopez-Bote et. al. Effect of dietary administration of oil extracts from rosemary and sage on lipid oxidation in broiler meat. *Br Poult Sci*. 1998 May;39(2):235-40.
45. Ramadan W. et. al. Oil of bitter orange: new topical antifungal agent. *Int J Dermatol*. 1996 Jun 35(6):448-9.
46. Alderman G, and Elmer H., Inhibition of Growth and Aflatoxin Production of Aspergillus Parasiticus by Citrus Oils. *Z. Leb. Unt-Forsch* 1976: 353-58.
47. Wattenberg L.W. et. al. Inhibitory effects of 5-(2-pyrazinyl)-4-methyl-1,2-dithiol-3-thione (Oltipraz) on carcinogenesis induced by benzo[a]pyrene, diethylnitrosamine and uracil mustard. *Carcinogenesis*. 1986 Aug;7(8):1379-81.
48. Crowell P. L. Prevention and therapy of cancer by dietary monoterpenes. *J Nutr*. 1999 Mar;129(3):775S-778S.

Basil *(Ocimum basilicum)* has been shown to have anticancer properties.[49]

Eucalyptus *(Eucalyptus radiata)* has been studied for reducing inflammation[50], improving cerebral blood flow[51] , inhibiting Candida growth[52] , and treating bronchitis.[53]

Many other documented benefits of aromatics have been recorded in recent medical literature.[54-66]

Longevity Nutrition

During the last five years, I have traveled throughout the world investigating the regions inhabited by most long-lived peoples on earth: the Ningxia province in China, Hunzaland in Pakistan, southern Ecuador, the Talish Mountain region of Azerbaijan, and the Tarahumara valley of central Mexico. After intensively examining the dietary habits of these cultures, I found one common denominator: an active lifestyle and a mineral-rich diet exceptionally high in antioxidant foods, such as wolfberries and apricots.

49. Aruna, K. and V.M. Sivaramakrishnan. "Anticarcinogenic Effects of the Essential Oils from Cumin, Poppy and Basil." *Food Chem Toxicol*. 1992;30(11):953-56.
50. Juergens et. al. The anti-inflammatory activity of L-menthol compared to mint oil in human monocytes in vitro: a novel perspective for its therapeutic use in inflammatory diseases. *Eur J Med Res*. 1998 Dec 16;3(12):539-45.
51. Nasel et.al. Functional imaging of effects of fragrances on the human brain after prolonged inhalation. *Chem Senses*. 1994 Aug;19(4):359-64.
52. Steinmetz et. al.,Transmission and scanning electronmicroscopy study of the action of sage and rosemary essential oils and eucalyptol on Candida albicans. *Mycoses*. 1988 Jan;31(1):40-51.
53. Ulmer et. al., [Chronic obstructive bronchitis. Effect of Gelomyrtol forte in a placebo-controlled double-blind study]. Fortschr Med. 1991 Sep 20;109(27):547-50.
54. Cao G, et al, Antioxidant capacity in different tissues of young and old rats. *Proceedings of the society for Experimental Biology and Medicine* 211(1996), 359-365.
55. Chao et al., Antimicrobial Effects of Essential Oils on Streptococcus pneumoniae. *JEOR*, 2001.
56. Deans SG, et al, Natural antioxidants from aromatic and medicinal plants. *Role of Free Radicals in Biological Systems*, pp. 159-165 (1993a) [J Feher, A Blazovics, B Matkovics and M Mezes, editors]. Budapest: Akademiai Kiado.
57. Farag et. al. Acute hepatic damage in rats impairs metharbital metabolism. *Pharmacology*. 1987;34(4):181-91.
58. Halliwell B & Gutteridge JMC, *Free Radicals in Biology and Medicine*, 2nd Edition. (1989), Oxford: Clarendon Press.
59. Inhibition of growth and aflatoxin production of Aspergillus parasiticus by citrus oils. *Z Lebensm Unters Forsch*. 1976 Apr 28;160(4):353-8.
60. Kaplan RJ & Greenwood CE, Dietary saturated fatty acids and brain function. *Neurochemistry Research* 23, (1989)615-626.
61. Ramadan W. et. al. Oil of bitter orange: new topical antifungal agent. *Int J Dermatol*. 1996 Jun;35(6):448-9.
62. Recsan Z, et al, Effect of essential oils on the lipids of the retina in the aging rat: a possible therapeutic use. *J Ess Oil Res* 9, (1997) 53-56.
63. Scott BL & Bazan NG, Membrane docosahexaenoate is supplied to the developing brain and retina by the liver. *Proceedings of the National Academy of Sciences USA* 86, (1989) 2903-2907.
64. Socci DJ, et al, Chronic antioxidant treatment improves the cognitive performance in aged rats. *Brain Research* 693, (1995) 88-94.
65. Wahnon R, et al, Age and membrane fluidity. *Mechanisms of Ageing and Development* 50, (1989) 249-255.
66. Youdim KA, et al., Effect of thyme oil and thymol dietary supplementation on the antioxidant status and fatty acid composition of the ageing rat brain. *Br J Nutr*. 2000 Jan;83(1):87-93.

Gary Young interviews a 103-year-old doctor of Chinese traditional medicine who is still practicing in Yingchung, Ningxia, China.

This Chinese woman from the Ningxia province is 121 years old and still works daily in her garden. Gary Young is holding the fifth generation of her family.

In particular, I found that Chinese wolfberries (Ningxia variety) and potassium-rich apricots were two foods consumed by people routinely reaching 110 and 120 years of age.

In my book, *Longevity Secrets,* I discussed the scientific reasons why these foods may confer important anti-aging properties. This is certainly due to their extremely high content of essential minerals such as magnesium and potassium, as well as a their rich supply of potent natural antioxidants.

Research also indicates that foods high in antioxidants, such as wolfberries, blueberries, strawberries, raspberries, and spinach can dramatically increase glutathione levels and actually reverse the signs of aging.

A new test developed by USDA researchers at Tufts University in Boston, Massachusetts, has been able to identify the highest known antioxidant foods. Known as ORAC (oxygen radical absorbance capacity), this test is the first of its kind to measure both time and degree of free radical inhibition.

The Ningxia wolfberry was documented to have the highest ORAC score of any food tested. A special variety grown on the Yellow River in the Ningxia Province of central China, the Ningxia cultivar is very different from any other type of wolfberry. Among the 17 types of wolfberry identified, the Ningxia wolfberry has by far the highest levels of immune-stimulating polysaccharides. It also possesses over 33 times the antioxidant power of oranges and an incredible 120 times the antioxidant potential of carrots. In addition, the Chinese wolfberry is one of the most nutrient-dense foods known, rich in many vitamins and minerals including calcium, magnesium, B vitamins, and vitamin C.

A diet high in antioxidants can combat the free radical damage in the body that is associated with premature aging and degenerative diseases.

The Hunza People—Limited Caloric Intake

The Hunzakuts living in the remote Hunza Valley in northern Pakistan are renowned for their longevity. The Hunzakuts (as they call themselves) routinely live past ages 100, 110 and even 120. They also share another remarkable trait: the near absence of degenerative disease.

It is known that the diet of the Hunza people is high in potassium and low in sodium. Apricots, barley, millet, and buckwheat are the main staples of their diet along with mineral-rich water with a pH of 8.5. But there is yet another unusual factor that may protect the health of the Hunza people and increase their longevity: their limited food intake.

Gary traveled onto the high mountains of Pakistan to meet and interview the Hunzakut people renowned for their longevity.

Because the land provides just enough food to cover their basic caloric expenditures, the Hunzakuts rarely indulge in overeating. In fact, prior to the construction of the Korakoram Highway, they annually endured near-fasting conditions for several weeks each spring, a time when the previous year's food was depleted and the current year's harvests had not yet begun.

Restricted caloric intake such as fasting can have powerful effects on longevity because it increases blood levels of growth hormone which is one of the most significant anti-aging hormones to be identified during the last two decades. Secreted by the pituitary gland, growth hormone production steadily declines with age. By age 70, the human body produces less than one-tenth of the growth hormone it did at age 20.

Clinical studies have repeatedly shown that growth hormone production is stimulated by low glucose levels. Because fasting depresses glucose levels, it leads to a surge in natural growth hormone production (Khansari et al., 1991).

Other studies have shown that the practice of caloric restriction (providing all necessary nutrients but limiting calorie intake) results in increased longevity and postponement of disease. Clive McCay at Cornell University showed that rats fed a diet low in calories but high in vitamins, minerals, and nutrients lived up to *twice as long* as rats fed on a regular diet (McCay et al., 1939). Ray Walford of the University of California in Los Angeles found that in studies on mice, the greater the reduction in calories, the longer the animal lived—as long as the vitamin and mineral content remained constant and the calories consumed did not drop below 40 percent of the normal (Walford et al., 1987).

While in Azerbaijan in 2001, Gary Young met several healthy and active citizens who were 100 years of age and older. An unusual example was Mrs. Chefer Guyzi Gulleva who told Gary she was 130 years old. She is shown above with Gary and some of her descendants, including her son (sitting to her right) who was reportedly born when she was 71 years old. At the time this photo was taken, he was 59. The family produced her Russian passport (shown below) as documentation of her birth in 1870.

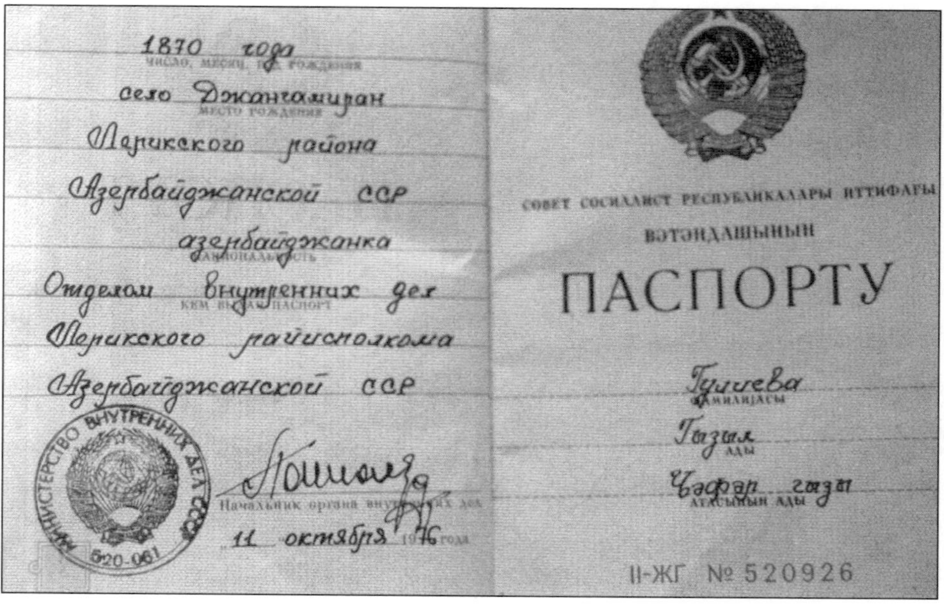

CHAPTER 16

Application Methods & Reference Guide

How Essential Oils Work

Essential oils can work through topical application, inhalation, ingestion, or rectal/vaginal retention.

Topical application is certainly the simplest and most common means of using essential oils. According to researcher Jean Valnet, MD, an essential oil that is directly applied to the skin can pass into the bloodstream and diffuse throughout the tissues in 20 minutes or less. More recent studies have also documented the ability of essential oils to penetrate the stratum corneum (the upper layer of skin) to reach the subdermal tissues and blood vessels beneath. (Huang et al., 1999; Ogiso et al., 1995.)

Some of the compounds in essential oils that work synergistically to enhance permeation include alpha-pinene (frankincense, valerian, basil, cistus), beta-pinene (galbanum, hyssop, rosemary), alpha-terpineol (bay laurel, *Melaleuca ericifolia*, ravensara), 1,8-cineol (*Eucalyptus globulus*, *E. radiata*, *E. dives*, rosemary) d-limonene (balsam fir, tangerine, orange, lemon, grapefruit), and menthol (peppermint).

Inhalation is an effective means of therapeutically using and delivering an essential oil, particularly to the nasal passages, throat, and lungs. The fragrance of an essential oil can have a positive influence on both the mind and body due to its ability to stimulate the brain's limbic system (a group of subcortical structures including the hypothalamus, the hippocampus, and the amygdala). This can produce powerful effects on everything from emotional balance and energy levels to appetite control, heart, and immune function. Additionally, many studies confirm the antiviral and antibacterial effects of essential oils which can have a direct impact on disease.

Dietary use (ingestion) of essential oils may be one of the most effective ways of unlocking their health benefits. Many essential oils have been used as food flavorings or as a part of patent medicines for centuries, endowing them with a long history of safe use. Recent research shows that certain essential oils have very high ORAC scores making them act as potent antioxidants that can actually raise antioxidant levels in the body and prevent premature aging. (ORAC is oxygen radical absorbant capacity, a test developed by researchers at Tufts University to accurately measure free radical scavenging ability.)

Many of the oils listed in this book are classified as "GRAS" by the U.S. Food and Drug Administration. This means they are "generally regarded as safe" for human consumption. A list of GRAS oils appears in Appendix B.

Retaining essential oils internally both rectally and vaginally is proving to be the most efficient means of getting essential oils into the internal tissues of the body. This application is especially effective when trying to help the organs of the lower abdomen, including the prostate, uterus, colon and small intestine. Breaking research, particularly in Europe, is validating the effectiveness of essential oils in treating diseases and disorders in these organs.

How to Mix Oils and Blends

The essential oils and blends that are listed in this section for each specific condition can be used either separately or together. By combining a single oil with another recommended single oil or blend, a synergistic or additive effect is produced that frequently results in a stronger total effect than the sum of the actions produced by each oil or blend separately. Any two to four of the listed single oils could be combined to produce a blend.

How to Choose an Essential Oil

The first consideration, of course, is the purity of the oil you choose. You may see some inventive grading systems for "therapeutic-grade" essential oils. Some may be marked "Grade A." But this is a USDA designation for grading eggs, butter, cheese, and meat. There is no grading system for essential oils in the United States other than conforming to the European ISO/AFNOR standards. Many oils are marketed as gas chromatography-, and mass spectrum-

Consult Your Health Care Professional

Consult your health care professional about any serious disease or injury. Do not attempt to self-diagnose or prescribe any natural substances such as essential oils for health conditions that require professional attention.

How to Tap the Full Therapeutic Potential of Essential Oils

An outstanding way to tap the full therapeutic potential of essential oils is to combine them with bath salts and use them in the shower. Specially designed shower heads are available that can be filled with essential oils and bath salts. As the water passes through the mixture, it disperses the essential oils into the spray, creating a fragrant, antiseptic spa.

tested. But who is setting the standard to be measured by these tests? Again, the world standard is set by ISO/AFNOR. A company founded in India in 1999 offers an EOBBD or HEBBD certification but an Internet search failed to locate any more information about this vague certification. Don't accept substandard or perfume-grade oils.

As you read below, the essential oils listed for a specific condition are not intended to be a comprehensive or complete list; they are merely a starting point. Other oils that are not listed may also be effective.

In addition, the essential oils are not listed in any particular order. This is because one oil might be more compatible with one person's chemistry than another's for aromatic purposes and skin sensitivity, not necessarily for physical response. If results are not felt within a few hours with the first oil, try another oil, blend, or combination.

How to Use Essential Oils

Essential oils should be used in moderation as they are highly concentrated. The safest application is with Vita Flex or acupressure-point applications on the feet. Vita Flex is a Tibetan form of reflexology which I feel is more valuable than regular reflexology as it doesn't put constant pressure on a contact point. Vita Flex application of essential oils generates a tremendous response that sometimes produces noticeable effects within 1 to 3 minutes. It is recommended that most essential oils be diluted in vegetable oil prior to topical or internal application (particularly if you have not used essential oils previously). You will find specific guidelines on dilution rates in the Application Methods chart that follows.

When using essential oils topically, first do a skin test with 1 drop of essential oil on the inside of the upper arm. Wait up to 30 minutes to determine sensitivity. Use no more than 10-20 drops during one topical application.

Many essential oils can be used as dietary supplements, and a list of these oils (recognized as GRAS or Generally Regarded As Safe) appears in Appendix B. All essential oils should be diluted prior to oral use unless directed by a physician or one trained in the oral use of essential oils. No more than 2-4 drops should be consumed at one time (in a single serving) unless indicated otherwise. The simplest way to dilute essential oils for ingestion is to mix a drop in one-fourth of a teaspoon of half rice milk and maple syrup. (Alternatively, goat's milk and agave syrup can also be used.) Traditionally, a drop or two of oil was placed on a piece of bread and then ingested. To avoid strong or unpleasant tastes, essential oils are commonly swallowed in gelatin capsules, as explained in Application Methods below.

How to Convert

1 drop	= approximately 60 mg
1 ml	= 1/5 teaspoon = approximately 20 drops = fills one 00 capsule
5 ml	= 1 teaspoon = approximately 80 drops
15 ml	= 1 tablespoon = 1/2 fluid ounce
240 ml	= 1 cup (depends on product)
30 ml	= 1 fluid ounce
28 grams	= 1 ounce

When using essential oils always increase fluid intake because the oils can accelerate the detoxification process in the body. If you are not taking in adequate fluids, toxins could recirculate causing nausea, headaches, etc.

Avoid Petrochemicals

Exercise caution when applying essential oils to skin that has been exposed to cosmetics, personal care products, or soaps and cleansers containing synthetic or petroleum-based chemicals. Essential oils may react with such chemicals and cause skin irritation, nausea, or headaches.

Essential oils can also react with toxins built up in the body from chemicals in food, water, and the work environment. If you experience a reaction to essential oils, reduce the amount of oils you are using and immediately start a liver/colon cleanse. (See cleansing information in Chapter 5.) Be sure you are drinking enough pure water—at least one and a half times your body weight in ounces each day.

Petroleum-based chemicals and toxins are dissolved in the body by many of the essential oil molecules like phenols and terpenes. The chemical gases from these toxins are released into the blood which can result in a reaction. If the reaction continues, change the location where you are using the oils and apply oils only on the soles of the feet. You will want to continue to eliminate the poisons by flushing them from your body.

A Definition and Tip for Safe Use:

- When you read that an oil can be applied "neat," it means the oil can be placed directly on the skin without any dilution.
- Skin-test the essential oil as it will be applied (neat or diluted) on a small patch of skin. If any redness or irritation results, cleanse skin thoroughly and reapply. If skin irritation persists, discontinue using the oil or oil blend at that location and work primarily through the soles of the feet.

How to Use This Reference Guide

This Guide has two parts, which must be used together in order to correctly and safely develop regimens for essential oil treatment.

The first part of the guide is a list of 18 standard application methods found on the next two pages. For each of these applications, dilution rates, mixtures and procedures are listed in detail. Each application has a key word in all capital letters.

The second part of the guide comprises the rest of the chapter and includes headings for some 300 different diseases and health problems with listings of essential oils and blends which are appropriate for those conditions. At the end of each heading is a section titled "APPLICATIONS." Within this applications section is a listing of keywords for the applications that are appropriate and effective for that condition. <u>It is important to note that only keywords are listed. Readers must return to the application methods guide on the next two pages to get the full detail of how to use the oils.</u>

As explained in earlier sections of this book, essential oils are very concentrated natural substances—easily 100 times more concentrated than the natural herbs they come from. So dilution of an essential oil is an important part of using it therapeutically. Some essential oils are so mild that dilution is simply not necessary, even for use on infants. Others are so strong that dilution is mandatory. (See Appendix F for a list of recommended safe dilutions for all the oils mentioned in this book).

Here is an example of how to develop a treatment program using the two parts of the guide. Let's say that you are experiencing a sore throat and want to know what you can do to treat that condition with essential oils.

Step 1: Locate the topic in the large Personal Guide

In this case, the heading you are looking for is a subhead located under the main heading of THROAT INFECTION. It is found on page 499.

Step 2: Note the recommended essential oils to be used.

In this case, the section on Sore Throat lists 10 single oils, 3 standard blends, and 2 custom blends that all can be used in the application methods listed. This listing shows all possible oils, but <u>only 1-3 oils or blends should be used for treatment at any given time.</u> You will need to select 1-3 oils or blends that you will use based on availability, budget and aroma (some oils are strong enough that you may not want to be using or wearing them at work.)

Step 3: Make a list of the possible methods listed in the APPLICATIONS section.

In this case, quite a variety of methods is listed. Altogether 10 different application methods are listed, ranging from Direct Inhalation to Raindrop Technique. (Not all conditions this many applications.) Most recommend only one or two. The 10 applications for a sore throat are intended to show all possible applications of essential oils for treating that condition.

Usually only 1-3 different applications should be used at any given time. This is a matter of both convenience and safety. If someone were to attempt all 10 applications for a sore throat at once, it would require an enormous investment of time, be extremely inconvenient and would put more essential oil in that person's body than is needed or helpful.

Step 4: Using the key words listed, select 1-3 application(s) that are most appropriate for your schedule, your budget and your lifestyle.

Clearly you will have to know a little bit about each application in order to make this choice. That is why it is important to read through all the application methods before using the main part of the guide. When in doubt about the exact procedure of an application, refer back to the detailed applications listing on the next two pages.

Step 5: Make a written personal regimen that includes the 1-3 oils and the 1-3 application methods you will be using. This will save you from having to look up everything each time you do an application.

Step 6: Make sure you understand the proper dilution levels.

If you do not properly link oils with applications, you could make a mistake here. For example, one of the applications for sore throat is Direct Inhalation, in which the oils are used in their 'neat,' or undiluted state. However, for Topical Application to the skin, the dilution rate is 50-50 or 1 part essential oil to 1 part vegetable oil.

Step 7: Be faithful with your regimen.

Essential oils are wonderful, natural, healing substances, and they work extremely well with the body's own defenses to solve a problem. However, they are not drugs, and they may not always work in seconds, or even minutes. Sometimes it can take hours or even days to see the improvement.

Basic Application Methods

NOTE: Please read this information carefully as all directions in the following personal guide section will refer to the 18 methods outlined here.

TOPICAL APPLICATION (On the skin surface)

- NEAT: Apply neat (undiluted) as directed to affected area. (See Appendix F)
- DILUTE 50-50: 1 part essential oil (s) to 1 part vegetable or massage oil. (See Appendix F)
- DILUTE 20-80: 1 part essential oil(s) to 4 parts vegetable or massage oil. (See Appendix F)
- VITA FLEX: Apply 1-3 drops neat to the Vita Flex points on the feet as directed. See Vita Flex chart found in Chapter 10 for point locations.
- COMPRESS: Dilute 1 part essential oil(s) with 4 parts vegetable oil and apply 8-10 drops on affected area. Cover with a HOT, moist hand towel. Then cover the moist towel with a dry towel for 10-15 minutes. Can also use a cool, moist hand towel instead of a hot one, to create a COLD compress.
- BATH SALT: Mix thoroughly 10-15 drops of essential oil into 2 tablespoons of Epsom salt or baking soda. Dissolve in warm bathwater as tub is filling and soak for at least 20 minutes before using soap or shampoo; or place in special shower head designed to hold salt/essential oil mixture and shower for 10 minutes.
- BODY MASSAGE: Apply diluted in a 20:80 ratio (20% essential oils to 80% massage oil) in a full-body massage.
- RAINDROP Technique: (See Chapter 11)

RETENTION

- RECTAL: Dilute the recommended essential oil(s) in 10:90 ratio (1 part essential oil to 9 parts cold-pressed vegetable oil), insert 1-2 tablespoons in rectum with a bulb syringe and retain up to 8 hours or overnight.
- TAMPON: Dilute the recommended essential oil(s) in 10:90 ratio (1 part essential oil to 9 parts cold-pressed vegetable oil). Apply 1-2 tablespoons to a tampon and insert into vagina (for internal infection) OR apply to a sanitary pad (for external lesions). Retain up to 8 hours or overnight. Use only tampons or sanitary pads made with organic cotton.

ORAL

- GARGLE: Add 2-3 drops essential oil with 4 tablespoons purified water, shake or mix vigorously. Gargle for 30 seconds.
- TONGUE: Apply 1 drop of essential oil neat to the back of the tongue with cotton swab or fingertip. Retain, allowing oil to combine with saliva, for at least 1 minute, then swallow. Note: this should NOT be done with essential oils which have a red application code. (See Appendix F)

INHALATION

- DIFFUSION: Diffuse neat in a cold-air diffuser (cold air diffusers are not designed to handle vegetable oils and they may clog the mechanism).
- DIRECT: Apply 2-3 drops of essential oil(s) to the palm of one hand; rub palms together; cup hands over nose and mouth (being careful not to touch the skin near your eyes) and inhale vapors deeply 6-8 times.
- VAPOR: Run hot, steaming water into a sink or large bowl. Water should be at least 2 inches deep to retain heat for a few minutes. Drape a towel over your head, covering the hot water also, enclosing your face over the steaming water. Add 3-6 drops of essential oils(s) into the hot water. Inhale vapors as deeply as possible several times, through the nose, as they rise with the steam. Recharge vapors with additional hot water.

INGESTION

- CAPSULE: Unless directed otherwise, use a clean medicine dropper to fill the larger half of an empty gelatin capsule (available at health food stores) with essential oil(s); then fill the remainder with high quality vegetable oil and take as directed.

  There are two basic dosages used for capsules, indicated by capsule size. '00' size capsules (which contain a 400 mg dose when filled with a 50-50 dilution of essential oil) and '0' size capsules (which contain a 200 mg dose when filled with a 50-50 dilution of essential oil). If '0' size capsules are not readily available, you can half fill '00' size capsules.
- RICE MILK: Add the essential oil to rice milk and take as directed. Use 3-5 drops in 1/2 cup of rice milk. Goat milk may be substituted for rice milk.
- MAPLE SYRUP: Add the essential oil to Grade B Maple Syrup. Use 3 drops in 1 tsp. maple syrup. Hold in mouth for 30 seconds before swallowing. Agave syrup (a low-glycemic natural sweetener derived from the Agave plant) can be substituted for maple syrup.

Reference Guide

ABSCESS (Skin)

(See SKIN DISORDERS)

ABSENTMINDEDNESS

(See BRAIN DISORDERS)

Single Oils:

Peppermint *(Mentha piperita)*
Cardamom*(Elettaria cardamomum)*
Vetiver *(Vetiveria zizanioides)*
Frankincense *(Boswellia carteri)*
Sandalwood *(Santalum album)*
Rosemary cineol *(Rosmarinus officinalis CT 1,8 cineol)*
Melissa *(Melissa officinalis)*
Balsam fir *(Abies balsamea)*
Basil *(Ocimum basilicum)*

Blends:

Clarity Blend
Brain Blend
Headache Blend

Applications:

INHALATION:	DIFFUSION: 15 minutes every 2 hours, as needed
	DIRECT: 2-3 times per day, as needed
TOPICAL:	NEAT, 1-2 drops on temples and/or back of neck, as needed

ABUSE (Mental and Physical)

The trauma from mental and physical abuse can result in self-defeating behavior that undermines success later in life. Through their powerful effect on the limbic system of the brain (the center or stored memories and emotions), essential oils can help release pent up trauma, emotions, or memories.

Single Oils:

Geranium *(Pelargonium graveolens)*
Balsam fir *(Abies balsamea)*
Frankincense *(Boswellia carteri)*
Sandalwood *(Santalum album)*
Melissa *(Melissa officinalis)*

Blends:

Abuse Relief Blend
Trauma Blend
Emotional Release Blend
Mood Lifting Blend
Brain Blend
Energy Balance Blend

Abuse Relief Blend and Trauma Blend are primarily for physical abuse; the other blends are primarily intended for emotional abuse issues, but they can be interchanged.

Applications:

INHALATION:	DIFFUSION: 15 minutes every 2 hours, as needed
	DIRECT: 2-3 times per day, as needed
TOPICAL:	NEAT, 1-2 drops on temples and/or back of neck as needed. Also apply 2-3 drops on the Vita Flex liver points of the foot. Also apply a trace under the nose

ACID/ALKALINE BALANCE

(See FUNGAL INFECTIONS)

ACIDOSIS

(See FUNGAL INFECTIONS)

Acidosis is a condition where the pH of the intestinal tract and the blood become excessively acidic. This can promote the growth of pathogenic fungi like candida and exacerbate yeast infections. Eventually this condition can lead to many forms of chronic and degenerative disease. Essential oils have been shown to reduce the fungi that often contribute to candidiosis.

To raise pH, avoid acid-ash foods, overuse of antibiotics, and monitor the pH of the saliva (6.4-6.5), urine (5.5-5.5), and blood (7.3-7.6).

Single Oils:
Peppermint *(Mentha piperita)*
Tansy *(Tanacetum vulgare)*
Clove *(Syzygium aromaticum)*
Lemon *(Citrus limon)*

Blends:
Digestive Blend

Applications:

INGESTION:	CAPSULE, 00 size, 2 per day between meals, if possible, otherwise with meals

ACQUIRED IMMUNE DEFICIENCY SYNDROME

(See AIDS)

ACNE

(See SKIN DISORDERS)

ADD

(See ATTENTION DEFICIT DISORDER)

ADDICTIONS

Many food and chemical dependencies, such as addictions to tobacco, caffeine, drugs, alcohol, and sugar may originate in the liver. Cleansing and detoxifying the liver is a crucial first step toward breaking free of these addictions.

Trace mineral and mineral deficiencies can also play a part in some addictions. Magnesium, potassium, calcium, and zinc should all be included in the diet.

Blends:
Stress Reduction Blend
Liver Blend

(See Liver and Smoking cessation)

Applications:

INHALATION:	DIFFUSION: 15 minutes every 2 hours, as needed DIRECT: 2-3 times per day, as needed
TOPICAL:	NEAT, 1-2 drops on temples and/or back of neck 4 times a day COMPRESS: warm compress over liver

ADDISON'S DISEASE

(See ADRENAL GLAND IMBALANCE)

ADRENAL GLAND IMBALANCE

The adrenal glands consist of two sections: an inner part called the medulla produces stress hormones and an outer part called the cortex secretes critical hormones called glucocorticoids and aldosterone. Because of these hormones, the cortex has a far greater impact on overall health than the medulla does.

Why are aldosterone and glucocorticoids so important? Because they directly affect blood pressure and mineral content and help regulate the conversion of carbohydrates into energy.

Addison's Disease

In cases like Addison's disease, adrenal cortex hormones are no longer produced or are severely limited. This can lead to life-threatening fluid and mineral loss unless these hormones are replaced.

If adrenal insufficiency is accompanied by a lack of thyroid hormone, the condition is known as Schmidt's syndrome.

Supporting the Adrenal Glands

Add essential oils to 1/4 teaspoon of massage oil and apply as a warm compress over the adrenal glands (located on top of the kidneys).

- 3 drops clove
- 3 drops nutmeg
- 7 drops rosemary cineol

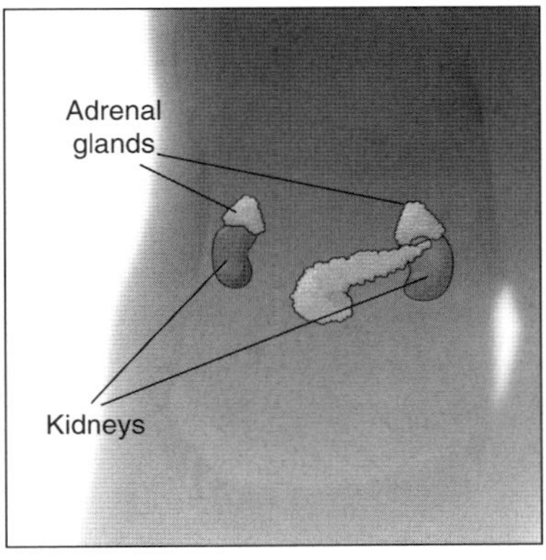

Symptoms:
- Severe fatigue
- Lightheadedness when standing
- Nausea
- Depression/irritability
- Craving salty foods
- Loss of appetite
- Muscle spasms
- Dark, tan-colored skin

Essential oils can play a part in correcting deficiencies in adrenal cortex function. Nutmeg, for example, has adrenal-like activity that raises energy levels.

Single Oils:

Nutmeg *(Myristica fragrans)*
Black pepper *(Piper nigrum)*

Blends:

Glandular Blend
Mood Lifting Blend
Energy Blend

The following essential oil blend is designed to be used with a cool compress for adrenal support:
- 4 drops nutmeg
- 3 drops clove
- 7 drops rosemary cineol
- 20 drops massage oil or a vegetable oil.

Applications:

TOPICAL:	COMPRESS, warm, over the adrenal gland area (on back, over the kidneys)
INGESTION:	CAPSULE, 00 size, 2 per day

Cushing's disease

Cushing's disease is the opposite of Addison's disease: It is characterized by the overproduction of adrenal cortex hormones. While these hormones are crucial to sound health in normal amounts, their unchecked overproduction can cause as much harm as underproduction. This results in the following symptoms:

Slow wound healing
Low resistance to infection
Obesity
Acne
Moon-shaped face
Easily-bruised skin
Weak or wasted muscles
Osteoporosis

Although Cushing's disease can be caused by a malfunction in the pituitary, it is usually triggered by excessive use of immune-suppressing corticosteroid medications—such as those used for asthma and arthritis. Once these are discontinued, the disease will abate.

Single Oils:
Lemon *(Citrus limon)*
Peppermint *(Mentha piperita)*
Fleabane *(Conyza canadensis)*

Blends:
Immune Blend
Antimicrobial Blend

Applications:

TOPICAL:	COMPRESS, warm, over the adrenal gland area (on back, over the kidneys)
INGESTION:	CAPSULE, 00 size, 2 per day

AGENT ORANGE EXPOSURE

(See LIVER)

AGITATION

Single Oils:
Lavender *(Lavandula angustifolia)*
Orange *(Citrus aurantium)*
Roman chamomile *(Chamaemelum nobile)*

Blends:
Stress Reduction Blend
Mood Lifting Blend

Applications:

INHALATION:	DIFFUSION: 15 minutes every 2 hours, as needed DIRECT: 2-3 times per day, as needed
TOPICAL:	NEAT, 1-2 drops on temples and/or back of neck VITA FLEX, 1-2 drops on brain and heart points

AIDS (Acquired Immune Deficiency Syndrome)

The AIDS virus attacks and infects immune cells critical to the function of normal immunity.

Essential oils such as lemon, cistus, thyme, lavender have immune building properties. In May 1994, Dr. Radwan Farag of Cairo University demonstrated that cumin seed oil had an 88 to 92 percent inhibition effect against HIV, a precursor to the AIDS virus.

Single Oils:

Cistus *(Cistus ladanifer)*
Lemon *(Citrus limon)*
Cumin *(Cuminum cyminum)*

Blends:

Brain Blend
Energy Balance Blend
Antimicrobial Blend
Immune Blend

Applications:

Use the following regimen:

1. Energy Balance Blend and Antimicrobial Blend: 4-6 drops on the feet daily for 3 weeks.
2. Immune Blend: 6 drops daily in capsules
3. Raindrop Technique: 2 times weekly.

ALLERGIES

(See ASTHMA)

Allergies can be triggered by food, pollen, environmental chemicals, dander, dust, and insect bites and can impact:

Respiration—wheezing, labored breathing
Mouth—swelling of the lips or tongue, itching lips

Digestive tract—diarrhea, vomiting, cramps
Skin—rashes, dermatitis
Nose—sneezing, congestion

Food Allergies

Food *allergies* are different from food *intolerances*. The former involves an immune system reaction, whereas the latter involves a gastrointestinal reaction (far more common). For example, peanuts often produce a lifelong allergy in adults due to peanut proteins being targeted by immune system antibodies as foreign invaders. In contrast, the intolerance of pasteurized cow's milk that causes cramping and diarrhea is due to the inability to digest lactose (milk sugar) because of a lack of the enzyme lactase.

Food allergies are often associated with the consumption of peanuts, shellfish, tree nuts, wheat, cow's milk, eggs, and soy. Infants and children are far more susceptible to food allergies than adults, due to the immaturity of their immune and digestive systems.

Hay fever (allergic rhinitis)

Hay fever is an allergic reaction triggered by airborne allergens (pollen, animal hair, feathers, dust mites) that cause the release of histamines and subsequent inflammation of nasal passages and sinus-related areas. Allergies resemble asthma, which manifests in the chest and lungs.

Symptoms: Inflammation of the nasal passages, sinuses, and eyelids that causes sneezing, runny nose, watery, red, itchy eyes, and wheezing.

Single Oils:
Lavender *(Lavandula angustifolia)*
Ledum *(Ledum groenlandicum)*
Roman chamomile *(Chamaemelum nobile)*
Nutmeg *(Myristica fragrans)*

Blends:
Energy Balance Blend
Digestive Blend

Applications:

INHALATION:	DIFFUSION: 15 minutes every 2 hours, as needed
	DIRECT: 2-3 times per day, as needed
INGESTION:	CAPSULE, 00 size, 2 times per day

ALOPECIA AREATA (Baldness)

Alopecia is an inflammatory hair-loss disease that is the second-leading cause of baldness in the U.S. A randomized, double-blind study at the Aberdeen Royal Infirmary in Scotland found that certain essential oils were extremely effective in combating this disease (Hay et al., 1998; Kalish, 1999).

Single Oils:

Thyme thymol *(Thymus vulgaris CT thymol)*
Rosemary cineol *(Rosmarinus officinalis CT 1,8 cineol)*
Lavender *(Lavandula angustifolia)*
Cedarwood *(Cedrus atlantica)*

Applications:

TOPICAL: DILUTE 20-80, dilute 5 drops essential oils in 20 drops olive, grapeseed or fractionated coconut oil and massage into scalp before retiring nightly

ALZHEIMER'S

(See BRAIN DISORDERS)

ANALGESIC

Single Oils:

Roman chamomile *(Chamaemelum nobile)*
Balsam fir *(Abies balsamea)*
Elemi *(Canarium luzonicum)*
Wintergreen or birch *(Gaultheria procumbens or Betula alleghaniensis)*
Clove *(Syzygium aromaticum)*
Peppermint *(Mentha piperita)*
Lavender *(Lavandula angustifolia)*
Lemongrass *(Cymbopogon flexuosus)*
Tansy *(Tanacetum vulgare)*

Blends:

Pain Relief Blend
Antimicrobial Blend

Additional simple blends for pain relief:

- Equal parts helichrysum and clove,
- Equal parts tea tree oil *(Melaleuca alternifolia)* and rosemary CT cineol,
- Equal parts wintergreen or birch, spruce and black pepper,
- 3 parts *Melaleuca alternifolia* with 5 parts rosemary CT cineol

Applications:

TOPICAL:	NEAT or DILUTE 50-50, 1-2 drops on affected area

ANEURYSM

(See CARDIOVASCULAR CONDITIONS)

Aneurysms are weak spots on the blood vessel wall which balloon out and may eventually rupture. In cases of brain aneurysms, a bursting blood vessel can cause a hemorrhagic stroke, which can result in death or paralysis (with a fatality rate of over 50 percent).

See your physician for treatment if you have, or suspect you have, an aneurysm.

Some essential oils support the cardiovascular system. Cypress strengthens capillary and vascular walls. Helichrysum helps dissolve blood clots.

Single Oils:

Helichrysum *(Helichrysum italicum)*
Sandalwood *(Santalum album)*
Tansy *(Tanacetum vulgare)*
Cypress *(Cupressus sempervirens)*

Blends:

Circulation Blend
Brain Blend

Aneurysm blend:

- 5 drops cypress
- 2 drops helichrysum
- 3 drops of frankincense

Applications:

TOPICAL:	DILUTE 50-50, on affected area 3-5 times per day
INHALATION:	DIFFUSER, 15 minutes, 4-6 times per day
INGESTION:	CAPSULE, 00 size, 2 per day

ANOREXIA

(See ADDICTIONS)

While psychotherapy remains indispensable for anorexia, the inhalation of essential oils may alter emotions enough to effect a change in the underlying psychology or disturbed-thinking pattern which supports this self-destructive behavior. This is accomplished by the ability of fragrance to directly impact the emotional hub inside the brain.

Many people with anorexia believe they don't deserve to be healthy or loved unless they are "slender."

Anorexia nervosa is an eating disorder characterized by total avoidance of food and virtual self-starvation. It may or may not be accompanied by bulimia (binge-purge behavior).

Single Oils:

Tarragon *(Artemisia dracunculus)*
Mandarin *(Citrus reticulata)*
Orange *(Citrus aurantium)*
Lemon *(Citrus limon)*
Ginger *(Zingiber officinale)*

Blends:

Energy Balance Blend
Brain Blend

Applications:

INHALATION:	DIFFUSION: 15 minutes every 2 hours, as needed
	DIRECT: 2-3 times per day, as needed
TOPICAL:	NEAT, 1-2 drops on temples and/or back of neck 4 times a day
	COMPRESS: warm compress over liver

ANTHRAX

Caused by the bacteria *Bacillus anthracis*, anthrax is one of the oldest and deadliest diseases known. There are three predominant types: the external form acquired from contact with infected animal carcasses, an internal form contracted by eating meat from an infected animal, and the deadly type which comes from breathing airborne anthrax spores. One fatal internal version is battlefield anthrax, which is the most lethal variety. It has been bioengineered as a biological weapon. When airborne anthrax bacteria invade the lungs, it is 90 percent fatal unless antibiotics are administered at the very beginning of the infection. Often anthrax goes undiagnosed until it is too late for antibiotics.

External varieties of anthrax may be contracted by exposure to animal hides and wool. While vaccination and antibiotics have stemmed anthrax infection in recent years, new strains have developed that are resistant to all counter measures.

According to Jean Valnet, MD, thyme oil is extremely effective for killing the anthrax bacillus[1]. Two highly antimicrobial phenols in thyme essential oil, carvacrol and thymol, are responsible for this action.

Single Oils:
Thyme *(Thymus vulgaris)*
Oregano *(Origanum compactum)*
Clove *(Syzygium aromaticum)*
Cinnamon *(Cinnamomum verum)*
Rosewood *(Aniba rosaeodora)*

Blends:
Antimicrobial Blend

Applications: (Preventive)

TOPICAL:	DILUTE 20-80, on hands and exposed skin areas
INHALATION:	DIFFUSER, 5 minutes 4-6 times per day to purify air
INGESTION:	CAPSULE, 00 size, 4 times per day

ANTISEPTIC

Single Oils:
Rosemary cineol *(Rosmarinus officinalis CT 1,8 cineol)*
Rosemary verbenon *(Rosmarinus officinalis CT verbenon)*
Thyme thymol *(Thymus vulgaris CT thymol)*
Eucalyptus (all types)
Mountain savory *(Satureja montana)*
Tea tree oil *(Melaleuca alternifolia)*
Lavandin *(Lavandula x hybrida)*
Lemon *(Citrus limon)*
Lemongrass *(Cymbopogon flexuosus)*

1 Jean Valnet, MD, *The Practice of Aromatherapy: A Classic Compendium of Plant Medicines & Their Healing Properties,* Healing Arts Press, 1990, p. 197.

Cinnamon *(Cinnamomum verum)*
Clove *(Syzygium aromaticum)*
Oregano *(Origanum compactum)*

Blends:

Antibacterial Blend
Antiseptic Blend
Antimicrobial Blend

Applications:

TOPICAL:	DILUTE according to application code (Appendix F) and apply to affected area 2 to 10 times daily as needed.

APPETITE, LOSS OF

Single Oils:

Bergamot *(Citrus bergamia)*
Ginger *(Zingiber officinale)*
Spearmint *(Mentha spicata)*
Orange *(Citrus aurantium)*
Nutmeg *(Myristica fragrans)*

Ginger stimulates digestion and improves appetite.

Applications:

INHALATION:	DIFFUSER, 10 minutes, 3-5 times per day
	DIRECT: 3-5 times per day, as needed
INGESTION:	CAPSULE, 00 size, 1 per day

ARTERIOSCLEROSIS

Single Oils:

Helichrysum *(Helichrysum italicum)*
Clove *(Syzygium aromaticum)*
Thyme thymol *(Thymus vulgaris CT thymol)*
Wintergreen or birch *(Gaultheria procumbens* or *Betula alleghaniensis)*
Orange *(Citrus aurantium)*
Frankincense *(Boswellia carteri)*

Blends:

Anti-Aging Blend

Applications:

INGESTION:	CAPSULE, 00 size, 2 per day

The Power of Smell

Unlike other senses (such as sight, hearing, touch, and taste) the sense of smell can exert a direct effect on the limbic system of the brain, the hormonal and emotional center of the brain. This enables essential oils (through their aroma) to affect many types of neurological, emotional, or behavioral problems, including autism, ADD, cerebral palsy.

ARTHRITIS

Osteoarthritis

Osteoarthritis involves the breakdown of the cartilage that forms a cushion between two joints. As this cartilage is eroded, the two bones of the joint start rubbing together and wearing down. (In contrast, rheumatoid arthritis is caused from a swelling and inflammation of the synovial membrane, the lining of the joint.

Researchers have linked the increasing risk of many degenerative diseases to nutrient deficiencies, including a lack of sufficient minerals and trace minerals.

Nutmeg, a source of myristicin, has been researched for its anti-inflammatory effects in several studies. It works by inhibiting proinflammatory prostaglandins when taken internally or applied topically. Clove exhibits similar action.

Chamazulene, the blue sesquiterpene in German chamomile, blue yarrow and blue tansy also shows strong anti-inflammatory activity when used both topically and orally.

Single Oils:

Wintergreen or birch *(Gaultheria procumbens* or *Betula alleghaniensis)*
Helichrysum *(Helichrysum italicum)*
Balsam fir *(Abies balsamea)*
Spruce *(Picea mariana)*
German chamomile *(Matricaria recutita)*
Rosemary cineol *(Rosmarinus officinalis CT 1,8 cineol)*
Oregano *(Origanum compactum)*
Clove *(Syzygium aromaticum)*
Nutmeg *(Myristica fragrans)*
Blue tansy *(Tanacetum annuum)*
Elemi *(Canarium luzonicum)*
Peppermint *(Mentha piperita)*

Blends:

Muscle Relaxing Blend
Pain Relief Blend

Applications:

TOPICAL:	DILUTE according to application code (Appendix F) and apply 4-8 times per day, as needed. Oils can also be applied undiluted and followed with massage oil
INGESTION:	CAPSULE, 00 size, 3 times per day

Rheumatoid Arthritis

Rheumatoid arthritis is a painful inflammatory condition of the joints marked by swelling, thickening and inflammation of the synovial membrane lining the joint. (By contrast, osteoarthritis is characterized by breakdown of the joint cartilage without swelling or inflammation.)

Rheumatoid arthritis is classified as an autoimmune disease because it is caused by the body's own immune system attacking the joints.

Other factors can aggravate arthritis such as:

- Deficiencies of minerals and other nutrients
- Microbes and toxins
- Lack of water intake

Essential oils constitute some of the most effective treatments for combating arthritis pain and combating infections (if present). Peppermint has been studies for its ability to kill pain by blocking substance P and calcium channels (Gobel et al., 1994).

In cases where arthritis is caused by infectious organisms, such as *Borrelia burgdorferi,* (Lyme disease), *chlamydia,* and *salmonella,* essential oils may counteract and prevent infection, especially when diffused or applied topically. Highly antimicrobial oils include: mountain savory, rosemary CT cineol, *Melaleuca alternifolia* and oregano.

Additionally, a supplement commonly known as MSM has been documented to be one of the most effective natural supplements for reducing the pain associated with rheumatism and arthritis. The subject of a number of clinical studies, MSM was used extensively by Ronald Lawrence, MD, in his clinical practice to dramatically reduce rheumatic and arthritic symptoms.

Single oils:

Wintergreen or birch *(Gaultheria procumbens* or *Betula alleghaniensis)*
Spruce *(Picea mariana)*
Cypress *(Cupressus sempervirens)*
Peppermint *(Mentha piperita)*
Mountain savory *(Satureja montana)*
Marjoram *(Origanum majorana)*
Rosemary cineol *(Rosmarinus officinalis CT 1,8 cineol)*
Oregano *(Origanum compactum)*
Helichrysum *(Helichrysum italicum)*
Thyme thymol *(Thymus vulgaris CT thymol)*
Nutmeg *(Myristica fragrans)*

Blends:

Muscle Relaxing Blend
Pain Relief Blend

Applications:

TOPICAL:	DILUTE according to application code (see Appendix F) and apply to affected area
	COMPRESS: Cold, 1-2 times daily
INGESTION:	CAPSULE, 00 size, 2 times per day

ASTHMA

(See also ALLERGIES)

During an asthma attack, the bronchials (air tubes) in the lungs become swollen and clogged with a thick, sticky mucus. The muscles of the air tubes will also begin to constrict or tighten. This results in very difficult or labored breathing. If an attack is severe, it can actually be life-threatening.

Many asthma attacks are triggered by an allergic reaction to pollen, skin particles, dandruff, cat or dog dander, dust mites, and foods such as eggs, milk, flavorings, dyes, and preservatives. Asthma can also be triggered by respiratory infection, exercise, stress, and psychological factors.

For asthma-related problems essential oils are most effective when they are mixed with a carrier oil and retained in the rectum overnight. Use *Eucalyptus radiata, Eucalyptus citriodora,* myrtle, balsam fir, or frankincense.

Many reference works report that essential oils should not be inhaled for asthma-related problems. Instead, the oils could be applied to the soles of the feet or ingested (if they are GRAS - Generally Regarded As Safe—see Appendix B).

In the years that I have been working with essential oils, I have never seen anyone with asthma develop a problem inhaling them. In fact, many people have experienced temporary relief from asthma by inhaling certain essential oils but this must be done under a doctor's supervision.

Single Oils:

Hyssop *(Hyssopus officinalis)*
Hyssopus officinalis var. decumbens

Blends:

Digestive Blend
Respiratory Blend

Applications:

TOPICAL:	VITA FLEX, lung and throat points, 2-6 times daily
INGESTION:	CAPSULE, 00 size, 1 per day

ATHLETE'S FOOT

(See FOOT PROBLEMS)

ATTENTION DEFICIT DISORDER (ADD)

Attention deficit disorder may be caused by mineral deficiencies in the diet. Improper intake of magnesium and potassium, as well as other trace minerals, is linked to many kinds of similar cognitive disturbances.

The use of fragrance and essential oils can have a significant effect in mitigating the problems of ADD through their effect on the limbic system of the brain.

Single Oils:

Vetiver *(Vetiveria zizanioides)*
Cedarwood *(Cedrus atlantica)*
Peppermint *(Mentha piperita)*
Sandalwood *(Santalum album)*
Cardamom *(Elettaria cardamomum)*
Ledum *(Ledum groenlandicum)*
Lavender *(Lavandula angustifolia)*

Blends:

Brain Blend
Mood Lifting Blend

Applications:

INHALATION: DIFFUSER, 15 minutes 4-8 times per day
DIRECT, 4-8 times per day

AUTISM

Autism is a neurologically based developmental disorder that is four times more common in boys than girls. It is characterized by:

- Social ineptness (loner)
- Nonverbal and verbal communication difficulties
- Repetitive behavior (rocking, hair twirling)
- Self injurious behavior (head-banging)
- Very limited or peculiar interests
- Reduced or abnormal responses to pain, noises, or other outside stimuli

Autism is being increasingly linked to certain vaccinations, the MMR being most often cited by researchers. British researcher Andrew Wakefield, MD suggests single shots for children for measles, mumps,and rubella (instead of the MMR combined shot) until further research is done.

Until very recently, children were receiving large doses of mercury (from thimerosal, a vaccine preservative, comprised of 49.6% mercury) that were well above the limit recommended by the EPA. Some success in reversing autism has resulted from mercury detoxification along with nutritional supplementation.

Some researchers believe that gastrointestinal disorders are linked in some way to the brain dysfunctions that cause autism in children (Horvath et al., 1998). In fact, there have been several cases of successful treatment of autism using pancreatic enzymes.

Stimulation of the limbic region of the brain may also help treat autism. Aromas from essential oils have a powerful ability to stimulate this part of the brain since the sense of smell (olfaction) is tied directly into the mind's emotional and hormonal centers. As a result the aroma of an essential oil has the potential to exert a powerful influence on disorders such as ADD and autism.

Single Oils:

Frankincense *(Boswellia carteri)*
Sandalwood *(Santalum album)*
Eucalyptus globulus
Melissa *(Melissa officinalis)*
Vetiver (*Vetiveria zizanioides)*
Cedarwood *(Cedrus atlantica)*

Blends:
Energy Balance Blend
Brain Blend
Clarity Blend
Stress Reduction Blend

Applications:

DIFFUSION:	DIFFUSER, 15 minutes, 4-6 times daily DIRECT, 4-6 times daily

BACK INJURIES AND PAIN

(See SPINE INJURIES AND PAIN)

BALDNESS

(see also ALLOPECIA AREATA)

Male pattern baldness is often a result of excess conversion of testosterone to dihydrotestosterone through the enzyme 5-alpha-reductase. It can also be caused by a condition called allopecia areata.

Singles:
Fleabane *(Conyza canadensis)*
Peppermint *(Mentha piperita)*
Black Pepper *(Piper nigrum)*

Applications:

TOPICAL:	DILUTE 20-80, massage into scalp before retiring. (For this application fractionated coconut oil is recommended as the diluting vegetable oil. It's finer structure is more readily absorbed into the scalp.)

BELL'S PALSY

(See NERVE DISORDERS)

BITES

(See INSECT BITES)

BLADDER INFECTION

(See URINARY/BLADDER INFECTION)

BLEEDING

(See HEMORRHAGING)

BLEEDING GUMS

(See PERIODONTAL DISEASE)

BLISTERS

Single Oils:

Tea tree oil *(Melaleuca alternifolia)*
Lavender *(Lavandula angustifolia)*
Melissa *(Melissa officinalis)*
German chamomile *(Matricaria recutita)*
Cistus *(Cistus ladanifer)*

Blends:

Antibacterial Blend
Spiritual Blend
Antiseptic Blend

Applications:

TOPICAL: DILUTE 50-50, apply to blistered area 3-5 times daily, as needed

BLOOD CLOTS

(See also CIRCULATION or CARDIOVASCULAR CONDITIONS)

Blood clots (also known as embolisms) can form anywhere in the body. If they block a blood vessel in the brain, they can cause a stroke; if they obstruct a coronary artery, they can cause an ischemic heart attack.

Those who have thicker blood or suffer from narrowed blood vessels due to diabetes, arteriosclerosis, atherosclerosis, or hypertension, are far more likely to suffer serious or fatal consequences from a blood clot.

Helichrysum is especially effective for preventing blood clot formation and promoting the dissolution of the clot. Natural blood thinners, such as clove oil, can also be effective. Clove oil occurs in high concentrations in the Antimicrobial Blend.

Single Oils:

Helichrysum *(Helichrysum italicum)*
Clove *(Syzygium aromaticum)*

Nutmeg *(Myristica fragrans)*
Lemon *(Citrus limon)*
Orange *(Citrus aurantium)*
Grapefruit *(Citrus x paradisi)*
Tangerine *(Citrus reticulata)*

Blends:
Antimicrobial Blend
Pain Relief Blend

Applications:

TOPICAL:	DILUTE 50-50, on location 4-6 times daily
	COMPRESS, warm, for 15 minutes 2 times per day
INGESTION:	CAPSULE, 00 size, 3 times per day between meals
	RICE MILK: 2 times per day

Additional application option:

- Massage equal parts lemon, lavender and helichrysum on location, with or without hot packs.

BLOOD PRESSURE, HIGH (Hypertension)

(See CARDIOVASCULAR CONDITIONS)

BLOOD PRESSURE, LOW (Hypotension)

(See CARDIOVASCULAR CONDITIONS)

BOILS

Single Oils:
Rosemary cineol *(Rosmarinus officinalis CT 1,8 cineol)*
Lavender *(Lavandula angustifolia)*
German chamomile *(Matricaria recutita)*
Peppermint *(Mentha piperita)*
Tea tree oil *(Melaleuca alternifolia)*
Naioli *(Melaleuca quinquinervia)*
Nutmeg *(Myristica fragrans)*

Blends:
Antimicrobial Blend

Applications:

TOPICAL:	DILUTE 50-50, 2-3 drops on location 3-6 times per day
INGESTION:	CAPSULE, 00 size, 3 times per day

BONE (Bruised, Broken)

Single Oils:

Wintergreen or birch *(Gaultheria procumbens* or *Betula alleghaniensis)*
Spruce *(Picea mariana)*
Balsam fir *(Abies balsamea)*
Cypress *(Cupressus sempervirens)*
Elemi *(Canarium luzonicum)*
Rosemary cineol *(Rosmarinus officinalis CT 1,8 cineol)*
Clove *(Syzygium aromaticum)*
Ginger *(Zingiber officinale)*

Blends:

Muscle Relaxing Blend
Pain Relief Blend
Mood Lifting Blend

Another blend for bone health and healing:

- 8 drops balsam fir
- 6 drops helichrysum
- 1 drop oregano

NOTE: Apply oils very gently on break locations.

Applications:

TOPICAL:	DILUTE 50-50, apply 3-5 drops gently on location COMPRESS, Cold, 2-5 times per day

Seeing the Big Picture Can Produce Big Results

When selecting oils, particularly for injuries, think through the cause and type of injury and select oils for each segment. For instance, a broken bone could encompass muscle damage, nerve damage, ligament strain or tear, inflammation, infection, bone injury, and possibly an emotion. Select an oil or oils for each perceived problem and apply in rotation or prepare a blend to cover all of them. The emotion may be shock, anger, guilt, or the person may have had pain for a long time and needed to release or relieve it. They may need some joy in their lives, etc. Work through all factors of the injury.

Bone Pain

Single Oils:

Wintergreen or birch *(Gaultheria procumbens* or *Betula alleghaniensis)*
Balsam fir *(Abies balsamea)*
White fir *(Abies concolor)*
Helichrysum *(Helichrysum italicum)*

Blends:

Pain Relief Blend

Applications:

TOPICAL: DILUTE 50-50, apply 3-5 drops gently on location
COMPRESS, Cold, 2-5 times per day

Additional regimens:

Broken bone blend:
- 10 drops wintergreen or birch
- 3 drops helichrysum
- 2 drops lemongrass
- 3 drops pine
- 4 drops balsam fir

Prior to casting, apply a few drops of the above blend to the local area neat. If there is any sign of skin sensitivity or irritation, be prepared to apply a small amount of vegetable or massage oil.

Bone Mending Blend #1
- 8 drops helichrysum
- 4 drops clove
- 2 drops tansy or lemongrass
- 12 drops wintergreen or birch
- 6 drops pine or white fir

Dilute the above in 1 teaspoon of vegetable or massage oil and apply on location

Bone Mending Blend #2:
- 10 drops wintergreen or birch
- 8 drops marjoram
- 4 drops cypress
- 2 drops peppermint
- 1 drop basil

Dilute the above in 1 teaspoon of vegetable or massage oil and apply on location

BRAIN DISORDERS

(Also see NEUROLOGICAL DISEASES)

The fragrance of many essential oils exerts a powerful stimulus on the limbic system—a part of the brain located on the margin of the cerebral cortex, including the amygdala, hippocampus, and hypothelous which interact directly with the thalamus and hypothalamus. Acting together, these glands and brain components combined are the seat of memory, emotions, and sexual arousal, and govern aggressive behavior.

The ability of essential oils to pass the blood-brain barrier gives them enormous therapeutic potential against such neurological diseases like Parkinson's, Alzheimer's, Lou Gehrig's, and MS.

Over 4 million Americans suffer from Alzheimer's. Alzheimer's was found to nearly double in subjects with high levels of homocysteine in the Framingham Study. Aluminum continues to be linked to Alzheimer's yet older Americans are urged to get yearly flu shots which contain aluminum as an adjuvant. Pepper, grapefruit, and fennel oils have been found to stimulate brain activity.[2] Peppermint oil has proven effective in protecting against stresses and toxins in brain cells.[3]

Richard M. Restak, MD, a leading neurologist in Washington, D.C., stated that maintaining normal synaptic firing would forestall many types of neurological deterioration in the body. (See his book, *Older & Wiser,* Berkley Books, 1999, pp. 172-173.)

Essential oils high in sesquiterpenes, such as vetiver, cedarwood, patchouli, vitex, German chamomile, myrrh, melissa, sandalwood, and frankincense cross the blood-brain barrier. The following oils are all general cerebral stimulants:

Single Oils:

Cedarwood *(Cedrus atlantica)*
Vetiver *(Vetiveria zizanioides)*
Sandalwood *(Santalum album)*
Ginger *(Zingiber officinale)*
Nutmeg *(Myristica fragrans)*
Vitex *(Vitex negundo)*
German chamomile *(Matricaria recutita)*

2. Haze S, Sakai K, Gozu Y, "Effects of fragrance on sympathetic activity in normal adults," *Jpn J Pharmacol* 2002 Nov;903):247-53.
3. Koo HN et al., "Inhibition of heat shock-induced apoptosis by peppermint oil in astrocytes," *J Mol Neurosci* 2001 Dec;17(3):391-6.

Eucalyptus globulus
Helichrysum *(Helichrysum italicum)*
Spikenard *(Nardostachys jatamansi)*
Frankincense *(Boswellia carteri)*
Fleabane *(Conyza canadensis)*

Blends:
Brain Blend
Energy Balance Blend
Circulation Blend

Applications:

TOPICAL:	NEAT: As needed, apply 1-2 drops directly onto the brain reflex centers as needed. These points include the forehead, temples, and mastoids (the bones just behind the ears). Apply oils and mild direct pressure to the brainstem area (center top of neck at base of skull), and work down the spine. VITA FLEX: apply 1-2 drops to brain points on feet each day RAINDROP: once every two weeks

Impaired Concentration

Single Oils:
Basil *(Ocimum basilicum)*
Lemon *(Citrus limon)*
Peppermint *(Mentha piperita)*
Cardamom *(Elettaria cardamomum)*

Blends:
Brain Support Blend
Clarity Blend
Energy Balance Blend

Applications:

TOPICAL:	NEAT, apply 1-2 drops to brain reflex centers (see above application), as needed
INHALATION:	DIRECT, 2-4 times per day, as needed

Impaired Memory

Essential oils improve memory by stimulating an opening of emotional blocks.

Peppermint improves mental concentration and memory. Dr. William N. Dember conducted a study at the University of Cincinnati in 1994 showing that inhaling peppermint increased mental accuracy by 28 percent.

The fragrance of diffused oils such as lemon have also been reported to increase memory retention and recall.

Single Oils:

Peppermint *(Mentha piperita)*
Rosemary cineol *(Rosmarinus officinalis CT 1,8 cineol)*
Vetiver *(Vetiveria zizanioides)*
Basil *(Ocimum basilicum)*
Rose *(Rosa damascena)*
Lemon *(Citrus limon)*
Cardamom *(Elettaria cardamomum)*

Blends:

Brain Blend
Clarity Blend
Headache Blend
Energy Blend

Memory Recipe 1:
- 5 drops basil
- 10 drops rosemary cineol
- 2 drops peppermint
- 4 drops helichrysum

Memory Recipe 2:
- 4 drops lavender
- 3 drops geranium
- 3 drops rosewood
- 3 drops rosemary cineol
- 2 drops tangerine
- 1 drop spearmint
- 2 drops tansy

Right Brain vs. Left Brain

The left brain is logical, rational, and judgmental. The right brain is artistic and creative.

I believe essential oils heighten right brain activity and increase left brain integration.

Reminder!

Be sure the essential oils you use are high quality essential oils which meet European ISO/AFNOR standards. Oils that come from a second, third, or even ninth distilling have lost most therapeutic benefits and are suitable only for perfumery. Oils that have been extended with synthetic chemicals may actually be harmful to the body.

Applications:

TOPICAL:	DILUTE 20-80, apply 1-3 drops on temples, forehead, mastoids (bone behind ears), and/or brainstem (back of neck)
INHALATION:	DIRECT, 2-6 times per day, as needed

NOTE: Vascular cleansing will allow better and improved blood flow, enhancing distribution of oxygen and nutrients to all organs, including the brain (See VASCULAR CLEANSING).

Stroke

There are two kinds of strokes: thrombotic strokes and hemorrhagic strokes. Thrombotic strokes are caused from a blood clot lodging in a cerebral blood vessel and cutting blood supply to a part of the brain. A hemorrhagic stroke is caused by an aneurysm, or a weakness in the blood vessel wall that balloons out and ruptures, spilling blood into the surrounding brain tissue.

Thrombotic Stroke:

(See BLOOD CLOTS)

Single Oils:

Helichrysum *(Helichrysum italicum)*
Peppermint *(Mentha piperita)*
Clove *(Syzygium aromaticum)*
Grapefruit *(Citrus x paradisi)*
Tangerine *(Citrus reticulata)*
Sandalwood *(Santalum album)*

Blends:

Antimicrobial Blend
Circulation Blend
Immune Blend
Brain Blend
Clarity Blend

Applications:

TOPICAL: DILUTE 50-50, apply 1-3 drops on back of neck, temples, forehead, and base of throat just above clavicle notch.
VITA FLEX, apply 1-3 drops on brain points of the feet

INGESTION: RICE MILK, twice a day
CAPSULE, 00 size, 2 times per day

Hemorrhagic Stroke:

(See HEMORRHAGING or BRUISING)

The essential oil of cypress may help strengthen vascular walls.

Single Oils:

Cypress *(Cupressus sempervirens)*
Helichrysum *(Helichrysum italicum)*

Applications:

INGESTION: RICE MILK, twice a day
CAPSULE, 00 size, 2 times per day

BREASTFEEDING

Dry or Cracked nipples

Single Oils:

Lavender *(Lavandula angustifolia)*
Myrrh *(Commiphora myrrha)*
Geranium *(Pelargonium graveolens)*
Sandalwood *(Santalum album)*
Helichrysum *(Helichrysum italicum)*

Blends:

Energy Balance Blend

Applications:

TOPICAL: DILUTE 50-50 and massage over breast and on Vita Flex points of the feet

Improve Lactation

Single Oils:

Geranium *(Pelargonium graveolens)*
Fennel *(Foeniculum vulgare)*
Sage *(Salvia officinalis)*

Blends:
Mood Lifting Blend

Applications:

TOPICAL: DILUTE 50-50 and massage over breast and on Vita Flex points of the feet.

NOTE: Do not use fennel longer than 10 days at a time, as it will excessively increase flow through the urinary tract.

Mastitis (Infected Breast)

Single Oils:
Manuka *(Leptospermum scoparium)*
Clove *(Syzygium aromaticum)*
Thyme thymol *(Thymus vulgaris CT thymol)*
Rosemary cineol *(Rosmarinus officinalis CT 1,8 cineol)*

Applications:

TOPICAL: DILUTE 20-80 and massage over breast and on Vita Flex points of the feet.

Breast Blend:
- 10 drops tangerine
- 10 drops lavender

Mix in 1 teaspoon of vegetable or massage oil. Rub on the breasts and under armpits twice daily.

BRONCHITIS

(See LUNG INFECTIONS)

BRUISING

(See BLOOD CLOTS)

Essential oils can help speed the healing of bruises and reduce the risk of blood clot formation. Oils like cypress help to strengthen capillary walls, while oils like *Amyris balsamifera* and helichrysum help speed the reabsorption of the blood that has collected in the tissue.

Essential oils such as clove and nutmeg have been clinically shown to reduce platelet stickiness and tendency to aggregate or clump. This property can be very useful in reducing bruising due to excess thrombosis.

Single Oils:

Helichrysum *(Helichrysum italicum)*
Cypress *(Cupressus sempervirens)*
Balsam fir *(Abies balsamea)*
Clove *(Syzygium aromaticum)*
Nutmeg *(Myristica fragrans)*
Amyris *(Amyris balsamifera)*

Blends:

Bruise Recipe 1:
- 5 drops helichrysum
- 4 drops lavender
- 3 drops cypress
- 3 drops lemongrass
- 3 drops geranium

Bruise Recipe 2:
- 6 drops clove
- 4 drops black pepper
- 3 drops peppermint
- 2 drops marjoram
- 2 drops geranium
- 2 drops cypress

Applications:

TOPICAL: NEAT or DILUTE 50-50, apply 1-3 drops on bruised area, 2-5 times daily. Helichrysum is especially beneficial in healing bruises when applied neat on location
COMPRESS, cold, on location, 2-4 times daily, as needed

BURNS

(See SKIN DISORDERS or SHOCK)

There are three types of burns:

- First-degree burns only damage the outer layer of the skin.
- Second-degree burns damage both the outer layer and the underlying layer known as the dermis.
- Third-degree burns not only destroy or damage both skin layers but also damage underlying tissues.

Burns can be caused by the sun's rays, chemicals, electricity, radiation, or heat. Thermal burns are the most common type.

The Deadly Dehydration of Burns

The reason that burns tend to swell and blister is due to fluid loss from the damaged blood vessels. This is why it is important to keep the burn well hydrated and to drink plenty of water.

In cases of serious burns, fluid loss can become so severe that it sends the victim into shock and requires intravenous transfusions of saline solution to bring up blood pressure.

Balsam fir, lavender and helichrysum are tissue regenerators and reduce scarring and skin discoloration.

NOTE: All burns can be serious, therefore, seek medical attention. If the burn is large or severe, the individual may go into shock. Inhaling oils may help reduce the shock. (See SHOCK)

Recent clinical experience at the Young Life Research Institute of Natural Medicine showed that balsam fir causes no irritation to the skin when used for burn conditions, and it is now being used on children at the clinic – in addition to lavender-because of its gentle qualities.

After a burn has started to heal and is drying and scabbing, use a body lotion with a few drops of balsam fir or lavender oil to keep skin soft and to promote faster healing.

First-degree burns/Sunburn

While we all need sun exposure for our bodies to create vitamin D, sunburn can be a definite health risk. The best prevention for sunburn is to avoid prolonged exposure to the sun. When you do go outdoors for more than 15 minutes, try to select a sunscreen or sunblock without skin-damaging petrochemicals.

A natural solution used by fur trappers in centuries past was mink oil. If you choose, balsam fir or lavender essential oil, added to mink oil would be an excellent option for skincare.

In the event of a sunburn, essential oils such as balsam fir and lavender can offer amazing pain-relieving and healing benefits.

Single Oils:

Balsam fir *(Abies balsamea)*
Lavender *(Lavandula angustifolia)*
Helichrysum *(Helichrysum italicum)*
Melissa *(Melissa officinalis)*

Blends:

Antiseptic Blend

Applications:

TOPICAL:	NEAT OR DILUTE 50-50, 1-3 drops on burn location will almost immediately cool tissue and reduce inflammation. Apply 3-6 times daily, or as needed.

Second-Degree burns/Blisters

(See BLISTERS)

Third-Degree Burns

For third-degree burns, seek immediate medical attention.

BURSITIS

Bursitis is in an inflammation of the bursa, which are small, fluid-filled sacs located near the joints. Bursa act as shock absorbers when muscles or tendons come into contact with bone. As the bursa become swollen, they result in pain, particularly when the affected joint is used.

Bursitis can be caused by injury, infection, or arthritis, and usually involves the joints of the knees, elbows, shoulders, and Achilles tendon. Occasionally bursitis can occur in the base of the big toe. Bursitis may signal the beginning of arthritis.

Single Oils:

Balsam fir *(Abies balsamea)*
Marjoram *(Origanum majorana)*
Basil *(Ocimum basilicum)*
Lavender *(Lavandula angustifolia)*
Black pepper *(Piper nigrum)*
German chamomile *(Matricaria recutita)*
Peppermint *(Mentha piperita)*
Wintergreen or birch *(Gaultheria procumbens* or *Betula alleghaniensis)*
Tansy *(Tanacetum vulgare)*
Elemi *(Canarium luzonicum)*

Blends:

Pain Relief Blend

Applications:

TOPICAL:	NEAT or DILUTE 50-50, apply 2-4 drops to affected area/joint 3-5 times daily, or as needed to soothe pain COMPRESS, cold, around affected joint 1-3 times daily.

CANCER

NOTE: No cancer treatment should be undertaken without consulting a licensed medical practitioner. The essential oil applications listed here can be used to complement the effectiveness of conventional cancer therapies. These essential oil applications should continue until the cancer is in remission.

Essential oils rich in limonene such as lemon, orange, tangerine, and balsam fir have been shown in animal studies to have potent anticarcinogenic effects. According to a study at the University of Indiana[4], "monoterpenes appear to act through multiple mechanisms in the chemoprevention and chemotherapy of cancer." Studies using 1-15 grams a day of limonene in very advanced cancer patients resulted in almost 20% of the patients going into remission.

Limonene seems to work even more effectively as a cancer-preventative. Cancers in their earliest stages respond much better than cancers in more advanced growth.

Recent cell-culture studies indicated that sandalwood essential oil inhibits growth by up to 90% of several different types of cancer cells (cervical, breast, skin, and prostate) while having little or no harmful effects on normal cells. Sandalwood showed excellent action even at very small concentrations (100 ppm). Tsuga, thyme thymol, and thyme linalol also showed low normal cell toxicity and strong anticancer action.

As a cancer preventative, any of the listed oils can be taken, diluted 50-50 in a 00 capsule, one per day, as a dietary supplement.

To enhance the action of essential oils, cancer requires strong cleansing and fasting programs. All cancers are best treated in the early stages by alternating and varying the essential oils used each week, so the cancer cells do not build up a resistance to the treatment.

4. Crowell P. Prevention and therapy of cancer by dietary monoterpenes. J Nutr. 1999 Mar;129(3):775S-778S.

The following are regarded generally as anti-cancerous oils.

Single Oils:

Helichrysum *(Helichrysum italicum)*
Lemon *(Citrus limon)*
Orange *(Citrus aurantium)*
Tangerine *(Citrus reticulata)*
Sandalwood *(Santalum album)*
Lavender *(Lavandula angustifolia*
Clove *(Syzygium aromaticum)*
Thyme linalol *(Thymus vulgaris CT linalol)*
Balsam fir *(Abies balsamea)*
Tsuga *(Tsuga canadensis)*

Blends:

Immune Blend
Energy Balance Blend (for emotions related to the disease)

Another simple anti-cancer blend:

- 12 drops frankincense
- 5 drops lavender
- 6 drops helichrysum

Applications:

TOPICAL:	NEAT or DILUTE 50-50, apply direct on skin cancers, cancerous nodes, 1-3 drops several times daily VITA FLEX, 1-3 drops on points relevant for internal cancers RAINDROP, 2-3 times per month, substituting anti-cancerous oils for the five optional Raindrop oils (see Chapter 11)
INGESTION:	CAPSULE, 00 size, 2 capsules 2-4 times daily
RETENTION:	RECTAL, 3 times per week using a 20-80 dilution

Brain Tumors

Single Oils:

Frankincense *(Boswellia carteri)*
Lemon *(Citrus limon)*
Orange *(Citrus aurantium)*
Tangerine *(Citrus reticulata)*
Clove *(Syzygium aromaticum)*

Applications:

TOPICAL:	NEAT or DILUTE 50-50, if needed, apply 2-4 drops to temples, forehead and back of neck 2-6 times daily
INGESTION:	CAPSULE, 00 size, 2 capsules 2-4 times daily

Additional regimens:

- Inhale frankincense using DIRECT method 6-10 times daily and massage frankincense on brainstem and carotid arteries. Apply 1 drop of frankincense on the roof of the mouth and the buccal cavity (inside of cheeks) with your finger.
- Mix 4 drops frankincense and 5 drops Immune Blend and massage on the neck 4 times daily.
- Mix 15 drops frankincense and 6 drops clove in 1 tablespoon vegetable oil and apply 4-6 times daily on the brain stem (spine at base of skull), temples, mastoids (behind the ears), forehead, and crown (top of head).
- Put 10 drops frankincense and 1 drop clove in diffuser. Sit in front of the diffuser and breathe vapors for at least 15 minutes, 3 times a day. If you get a headache or feel nauseated, reduce to what is tolerable, but do not discontinue use.

Bone Cancer

Single Oils:

Frankincense *(Boswellia carteri)*
Lemon *(Citrus limon)*
Orange *(Citrus aurantium)*
Tangerine *(Citrus reticulata)*
Clove *(Syzygium aromaticum)*

Blends:

Immune Blend

Applications:

TOPICAL:	DILUTE 50-50, massage on location and on spine 1-4 times daily
INGESTION:	CAPSULE, 00 size, 2 capsules 1-3 times daily RICE MILK, 4-6 times daily

Bone cancer blend:

- 15 drops frankincense
- 6 drops clove
- 1 tablespoon vegetable or massage oil

Massage 4-6 drops on location 3-5 times daily

Apply 2-3 drops each of frankincense and Immune Blend on the spine, 3 times daily.

Breast Cancer

The use of topically applied natural progesterone (20 mg per day) can dramatically reduce the risk of breast cancer. Eighty-five percent of all breast cancers are ductal cancers, and natural progesterone has been shown to slow the growth of ductal cells that promote cancer growth. In addition, new research indicates that some essential oils can dramatically inhibit cancer growth while leaving normal cells unharmed.

Studies at the Young Life Research Institute of Natural Medicine show that ledum, balsam fir, tsuga, lavender, clove, and frankincense may be effective in treating breast cancer.

To enhance the action of essential oils, cancer requires strong cleansing and fasting programs. Cancer is best treated in its early stages by alternating and varying the essential oils used each week, so the cancer cells do not build up a resistance to the treatment.

For a cancer preventative, dilute up to 20 drops of either orange, sandalwood, myrtle, or tsuga in 1 tablespoon of olive oil, put in 00-size capsule and take one daily as a dietary supplement.

Single Oils:

Sandalwood *(Santalum album)*
Myrtle *(Myrtus communis)*
Tsuga *(Tsuga canadensis)*
Lavender *(Lavandula angustifolia)*
Clove *(Syzygium aromaticum)*
Lemon *(Citrus limon)*
Orange *(Citrus aurantium)*
Tangerine *(Citrus reticulata)*
Frankincense *(Boswellia carteri)*
Myrrh *(Commiphora myrrha)*

Blends:

Brain Blend

Applications:

TOPICAL:	DILUTE 50-50, apply 4-10 drops on location daily
	VITA FLEX: apply 1-3 drops to breast Vita Flex points (see location in breast cancer regimen below)
INGESTION:	CAPSULE, 00 size, 1 capsule 2-4 times daily
	RICE MILK, 2-4 times daily

Additional breast cancer regimen:

A. Massage 1-3 drops frankincense on breast Vita Flex point on feet, which is on top of the foot at the base of the three middle toes. Continue massaging the Vita Flex areas after applying the oil (see Vita Flex Technique in chapter 10).

B. Layer on location 15 drops frankincense, 10 drops lavender, and 3 drops clove. Apply oils and massage daily for 4 days, then rest for 4 days. Repeat as necessary.

C. Put 6 drops of frankincense and 4 drops ledum in a 00-size capsule, fill remainder with vegetable oil. Take 1-3 capsules daily.

D. Diffuse frankincense and Brain Blend for 15 minutes 2-5 times daily

Cervical Cancer

The use of topically applied natural progesterone creams can dramatically reduce the risk of cervical cancer, especially in postmenopausal women. In addition, new research indicates that some essential oils can significantly inhibit cancer growth while leaving normal cells unharmed.

Single Oils:

Tsuga *(Tsuga canadensis)*
Thyme linalol *(Thymus vulgaris CT linalol)*
Galbanum *(Ferula gummosa)*
Patchouli *(Pogostemon cablin)*
Sandalwood *(Santalum album)*
Douglas fir *(Pseudotsuga menziesii*
Hyssop *(Hyssopus officinalis)*
Nutmeg *(Myristica fragrans)*
Sage *(Salvia officinalis)*

Applications:

INGESTION:	CAPSULE, 1 capsule 2-4 times daily
RETENTION:	TAMPON, 3 times per week

Colon Cancer

To enhance the action of essential oils, cancer requires strong cleansing and fasting programs. Cancer is best treated in its early stages by alternating and varying the essential oils used each week, so the cancer cells do not build up a resistance to the treatment.

For a cancer preventative, mix up to 20 mg of these essential oils in 1 tablespoon of vegetable oil, and put in 00 size gel caps. Take one per day.

The gastritis associated with *H. pylori* infection is closely associated with gastric cancers.[5] Highly antiseptic oils can kill *Helicobacter pylori* that causes the infection. These oils include oregano, mountain savory, *Melaleuca alternifolia*, *Backhyousia citriodora,* and thyme thymol.

Single Oils:

Clove *(Syzygium aromaticum)*
Frankincense *(Boswellia carteri)*
Ledum *(Ledum groenlandicum)*
Orange *(Citrus aurantium)*
Tsuga *(Tsuga canadensis)*
Lavender *(Lavandula angustifolia)*

Applications:

INGESTION: CAPSULE, 00 size, 1 capsule 3-5 times daily
RICE MILK, 2-4 times daily

Colon cancer regimen:

Day 1: Put 10 drops of frankincense and 10 drops tsuga in a 00 capsule, fill with vegetable oil. Take 3 times during the day.

Day 2: Put 16 drops frankincense and 3 drops clove in a 00 capsule, fill with vegetable oil. Take 3 times during the day.

Day 3: Put 10 drops frankincense and 10 drops lavender in a 00 capsule, fill with vegetable oil. Take 3 times a day.

Day 4: Put 10 drops frankincense and 10 drops ledum in a 00 capsule, fill with vegetable oil. Take 3 times during the day.

Days 5-8: Repeat the above 4-day cycle

Day 9-12: Rest for 4 days

Day 13: Restart the program

5. Uemura N, Okamoto S, Yamamoto S, "H. pylori infection and development of gastric cancer," *Keio J Med* 2002 Dec;51 Suppl 2:63-8.

Hodgkin's Disease

Single Oils:

Clove *(Syzygium aromaticum)*
Lavender *(Lavandula angustifolia)*
Frankincense *(Boswellia carteri)*
Cistus *(Cistus ladanifer)*
Bay laurel *(Laurus nobilis)*

Applications:

TOPICAL:	NEAT or DILUTE 50-50 on location 2-4 times daily or as needed
INGESTION:	CAPSULE, 00 size, 1 capsule 3-5 times daily

Leukemia

Single Oils:

Frankincense *(Boswellia carteri)*
Clove *(Syzygium aromaticum)*
Lavender *(Lavandula angustifolia)*

Blends:

Antimicrobial Blend

Applications:

TOPICAL:	BODY MASSAGE, apply very gently. Do not do deep tissue massage.
INGESTION:	CAPSULE, 00 size, 1 capsule 3-5 times daily

Liver Cancer

Cleansing is extremely important since an optimally functioning liver is necessary to rid the body of toxins. Anger and hate are stored in the liver and cause extreme toxicity and eventually trigger disease.

Single Oils:

Frankincense *(Boswellia carteri)*
Lavender *(Lavandula angustifolia)*
Lemon *(Citrus limon)*
Orange *(Citrus aurantium)*
Tangerine *(Citrus reticulata)*
Thyme thymol *(Thymus vulgaris CT thymol)*

Blends:

Liver Blend

Applications:

TOPICAL:	NEAT or DILUTE 50-50 if needed, 2-6 drops over liver area 2-4 times daily COMPRESS, warm, over liver area nightly VITA FLEX, massage 1-3 drops on liver Vita Flex points of feet
INGESTION:	CAPSULE, 00 size, 1 capsule 3-5 times daily

Liver Cancer regimen:

Liver Cancer blend:
- 30 drops frankincense
- 20 drops lavender
- 10 drops tsuga
- 10 drops ledum
- 4 tablespoons castor oil

Apply 20-30 drops of this mixture over the liver area, then cover with a warm moist towel for 20 minutes as a compress, 5 nights per week.

Also, fill 00-size capsules with this mixture and take 1 capsule 3-5 times daily

Lung Cancer

Strong cleansing and fasting programs are required in cancer cases, to enhance the action of the essential oils. All cancers are best treated in the earliest stages. The action of the essential oils is further enhanced by alternating and varying the oils used every week, so the cancer cells do not build up a resistance to the treatment.

Single Oils:
Ledum *(Ledum groenlandicum)*
Orange *(Citrus aurantium)*
Frankincense *(Boswellia carteri)*
Balsam fir *(Abies balsamea)*

Blends:
Respiratory Blend

Lung cancer blend #1:
- 4 drops frankincense
- 3 drops sage
- 3 drops myrrh
- 3 drops clove
- 2 drops ravensara
- 2 drops hyssop

Lung cancer blend #2:

- 6 drops Respiratory Blend
- 5 drops clove
- 4 drops myrrh
- 5 drops frankincense
- 2 drops sage

Applications:

INHALATION:	DIFFUSER, 15 minutes 3-5 times daily
INGESTION:	CAPSULE, 00 size, 1 capsule 3 times daily
RETENTION:	RECTAL, nightly, retain for 8 hours

Lung Cancer Regimen:

Day 1a: Begin diffusing frankincense and Respiratory Blend.

Day 1b: Use 10 drops frankincense, 10 drops Respiratory Blend and 1 teaspoon olive oil in a retention enema. Retain overnight.

Day 2: Use 10 drops frankincense, 10 drops lavender and 1 teaspoon olive oil in a retention enema.

Day 3: Use 20 drops frankincense and 1 teaspoon olive oil in retention enema.

Day 4: Use 10 drops frankincense, 10 drops Respiratory Blend and 1 teaspoon olive oil in a retention enema.

Rest 2 days before continuing. If no improvement detected, do not rest.

Alternate oils for retention enema use (add any one of the following oils to 1 teaspoon of olive oil):

- *Eucalyptus globulus:* 10 drops
- Frankincense: 10 drops
- Peppermint and frankincense: 5 drops
- Balsam fir: 20 drops
- Cypress: 10 drops

Diffuse regularly during the day the same oil combinations (neat) that are used in the retention enema for that night.

Rub Immune Blend up the spine, daily. Apply warm compress on back and chest twice daily.

Lymphoma (Cancer of Lymph Nodes)

Strong cleansing and fasting programs are required in cancer cases, to enhance the action of the essential oils. All cancers are best treated in the earliest stages. The action of the essential oils is further enhanced by alternating and varying the oils used every week, so the cancer cells do not build up a resistance to the treatment.

Both Hodgkin's disease and non-Hodgkin's disease are characterized by swollen lymph gland nodes, generally first appearing on the neck, armpit, or groin.

Lymphoma may be caused from petrochemical pollution in the air and water. After prolonged exposure, toxins such as benzene, styrene, and toluene begin to accumulate in the lymphatic system, eventually triggering cellular mutations and cancer.

Symptoms for non-Hodgkin's lymphoma
- Generally ill, loss of appetite, loss of weight, fever, and night sweats.

Symptoms of Hodgkin's lymphoma
- Fever, fatigue, weakness, itching.

Single Oils:

Frankincense *(Boswellia carteri)*
Myrrh *(Commiphora myrrha)*
Clove *(Syzygium aromaticum)*
Sage *(Salvia officinalis)*

Blends:

Immune blend

Lymphoma blend #1:
- 10 drops frankincense
- 5 drops clove or myrrh
- 3 drops tsuga

Lymphoma blend #2:
- 15 drops frankincense
- 6 drops clove

Applications:

TOPICAL:	NEAT or DILUTE 50-50 if needed. Apply 2-4 drops on swollen nodes daily. Rub along spine 2-3 times daily BODY MASSAGE, 2-3 times weekly
RETENTION:	RECTAL, nightly, will bring faster results than topical applications

Melanoma (Skin Cancer)

Melanoma is the most lethal form of skin cancer. It tends to aggressively spread and metastasize, quickly colonizing the lymph nodes and internal organs. It has a high fatality rate.

A sudden change in the appearance of an old mole or the appearance of red lesions, may indicate melanoma. If you suspect that you have melanoma or any skin cancer, you should immediately contact your physician.

Single Oils:

Frankincense *(Boswellia carteri)*
Tsuga *(Tsuga canadensis)*
Orange *(Citrus aurantium)*
Lavender *(Lavandula angustifolia)*
Tansy *(Tanacetum vulgare)*
Tea tree oil *(Melaleuca alternifolia)*

Blends:

Emotional Release Blend
Liver Blend
Glandular Blend
Antibacterial Blend

Applications:

TOPICAL:	NEAT, apply 2-6 drops on location 3-5 times daily
INGESTION:	CAPSULE, 00 size, 1 capsule 2 times daily RICE MILK: 2-4 times daily

Ovarian Cancer

Single Oils:

Lemon *(Citrus limon)*
Orange *(Citrus aurantium)*
Tangerine *(Citrus reticulata)*

Frankincense *(Boswellia carteri)*
Myrrh *(Commiphora myrrha)*
Geranium *(Pelargonium graveolens)*

Blends:
Immune Blend

Applications:

TOPICAL:	NEAT, 3-5 drops up the spine, on the feet, just below the navel and on the throat. Do this application daily
INGESTION:	CAPSULE, 00 size, 1 capsule 3 times daily
	RICE MILK, 2-4 times daily
RETENTION:	TAMPON, nightly

Rectal/Vaginal Retention Regimen:

Use the following recipe for alternating rectal and vaginal implants. Use as vaginal retention implant the first night and as rectal retention enema the second night. Alternate for 6 days. Rest 3 days. Repeat.

- 15 drops frankincense
- 5 drops myrrh
- 6 drops geranium
- 1 tablespoon olive oil

Prostate Cancer

Many prostate cancers may be testosterone-dependent, so it may be necessary to avoid taking anything that can raise testosterone levels, such as DHEA or androstenedione. New cell-culture research indicates that some essential oils can inhibit cancer growth by up to 90 percent while leaving normal cells unharmed.

Single Oils:
Ledum *(Ledum groenlandicum)*
Frankincense *(Boswellia carteri)*
Myrrh *(Commiphora myrrha)*
Orange (*Citrus aurantium*)
Balsam fir *(Abies balsamea)*
Cumin *(Cuminum cyminum)*

Blends:
Male Blend

Applications:

TOPICAL:	DILUTE 50-50, 1-3 drops between the rectum and scrotum 1-3 times daily
	VITA FLEX: 1-3 drops on reproductive Vita Flex points on feet
INGESTION:	CAPSULE, 00 size, 1 capsule 3 times daily
	RICE MILK, 2-4 times daily
RETENTION,	RECTAL, nightly

Prostate Regimen:

The following regimen reduced PSA (prostate specific antigen) counts 70 percent in 2 months:

- 10 drops frankincense
- 5 drops myrrh
- 3 drops sage

Use the above blend for the following three Applications:

a. Mix the above amounts of essential oils with 1 tablespoon olive oil and use nightly as rectal retention enema.

b. Massage 1-3 drops neat on Vita Flex reproductive points (ankles) on both feet.

c. Dilute 50-50 with vegetable oil and apply 2-4 drops topically between the rectum and the scrotum twice daily.

Uterine Cancer

Environmental pollutants become lodged in tissues, such as the breasts, thyroid, ovaries, and uterus. Many chemicals mimic or imitate our natural hormones and can fit the hormone receptors, blocking hormones out, thus tricking and over-stimulating these organs. This can become a major source of cancer of the breast, uterus, ovaries, and lymph nodes.

(Same program as OVARIAN CANCER, listed above)

CANDIDA

(See FUNGAL INFECTIONS)

CANKER SORES

These tend to occur because of stress, illness, weakened immune system, or injury caused by such things as hot food, rough brushing of teeth, or dentures.

Single Oils:

Melissa *(Melissa officinalis)*
Sage *(Salvia officinalis)*
Blue cypress *(Callitris intratropica)*
Clove *(Syzygium aromaticum)*
Lavender *(Lavandula angustifolia)*

Blends:

Antimicrobial Blend
Antiviral Blend

Applications:

TOPICAL:	NEAT, 1 drop applied gently with fingertip to canker sore 3-5 times daily
ORAL:	GARGLE, 2-4 times daily
INGESTION:	SYRUP, 2-4 times daily

CARDIOVASCULAR CONDITIONS

Blood Pressure, High

Single Oils:

Lavender *(Lavandula angustifolia)*
German chamomile *(Matricaria recutita)*
Goldenrod *(Solidago canadensis)*
Clove *(Syzygium aromaticum)*
Roman chamomile *(Chamaemelum nobile)*
Ylang ylang *(Cananga odorata)*
Cypress *(Cupressus sempervirens)*
Helichrysum *(Helichrysum italicum)*

Blends:

Circulation Blend
Muscle Relaxing Blend
Stress Reduction Blend

Applications:

TOPICAL:	DILUTE 20-80, full body massage once a day
INHALATION:	DIFFUSER, 20 minutes, 3 times a day
INGESTION:	CAPSULE, 00 size, 1 per day

Additional regimens:

1. For 3 minutes, massage 1-2 drops each of Circulation Blend and ylang ylang on heart Vita Flex point and over the heart and carotid arteries. Blood pressure will begin to drop within 5 to 20 minutes. Monitor blood pressure and reapply as required. Lemon and helichrysum can also be used.
2. Inhalation of jasmine may reduce anxiety and therefore, lower blood pressure.

Blood Pressure, Low

Single Oils:

Sage *(Salvia officinalis)*
Pine *(Pinus sylvestris)*
Rosemary cineol *(Rosmarinus officinalis CT 1,8 cineol)*

Blends:

Circulation Blend
Glandular Blend
Mood Lifting Blend

Applications:

TOPICAL:	DILUTE 20-80, full body massage once a day
INHALATION:	DIFFUSER, 20 minutes, 3 times a day
INGESTION:	CAPSULE, 00 size, 1 per day

Additional regimens:

1. Use 1 drop each of Circulation Blend and rosemary on heart Vita Flex points; for massage, dilute 50-50 with vegetable oil.
2. Place 3 drops each of Circulation Blend and rosemary in a 00-size capsule, fill with vegetable oil, and take once daily.

High Cholesterol

Helichrysum is a chelator that lowers and regulates cholesterol and reduces blood clotting. (For tips on application, see Heart Vita Flex under BLOOD PRESSURE.)

Circulation Blend regulates and lowers blood pressure and breaks down plaque on the blood vessel walls.

Single Oils:

Rosemary cineol *(Rosmarinus officinalis CT 1,8 cineol)*
Clove *(Syzygium aromaticum)*
Roman chamomile *(Chamaemelum nobile)*
Spikenard *(Nardostachys jatamansi)*
Helichrysum *(Helichrysum italicum)*
Nutmeg *(Myristica fragrans)*

Blends:

Clarity Blend
Circulation Blend
Immune Blend
Liver Blend

Applications:

TOPICAL:	NEAT or DILUTE 50-50 if needed, apply 2-4 drops at pulse points where arteries are close to the surface (wrists, inside elbows, base of throat). Also rub 6-10 drops along spine 2 times daily BODY MASSAGE, 2 times weekly
INGESTION:	CAPSULE, 00 size, 1 capsule 3 times daily RICE MILK, 1-2 times daily

Cholesterol reducing blend:

- 4 drops rosemary cineol
- 5 drops Roman chamomile
- 3 drops helichrysum
- 5 drops onion oil *(Allium cepa)*

Rub this blend along the spine twice daily. Alternate this spine application with Immune Blend every other day.

Dilute this blend with 1 tablespoon vegetable oil and put in 00 size capsules and take 3 times daily.

Hardening of the Arteries

Single Oils:

Helichrysum *(Helichrysum italicum)*
Cypress *(Cupressus sempervirens)*

Blends:

Circulation Blend

Applications:

TOPICAL:	BODY MASSAGE, 2 times weekly
INGESTION:	CAPSULE, 00 size, 3 times daily

Phlebitis (inflammation of veins)

Helichrysum prevents phlebitis. Helichrysum blended with lavender also gives excellent results for this problem.

Single Oils:

German chamomile *(Matricaria recutita)*
Roman chamomile *(Chamaemelum nobile*
Helichrysum *(Helichrysum italicum)*
Lavender *(Lavandula angustifolia)*
Geranium *(Pelargonium graveolens)*

Blends:

Circulation Blend

Applications:

TOPICAL:	NEAT, 2-4 drops on location 2-4 times daily
	COMPRESS, cold, on location, 2-4 times daily

CARPAL TUNNEL SYNDROME

(See NERVE DISORDERS)

CATARACTS

(See EYE DISORDERS)

CELLULITE

Cellulite is one of the harder types of fats to dissolve in the body. Cellulite is an accumulation of old fat cell clusters that solidify and harden as the surrounding tissue loses its elasticity.

Excess fat is undesirable for two reasons:

1. The extra weight puts an extra load on all body systems, particularly the heart and cardiovascular system, as well as the joints (knees, hips, spine etc).

2. Toxins and petrochemicals (pesticides, herbicides, metallics) tend to accumulate in fatty tissue. This can contribute to hormone imbalance, neurological problems, and a higher risk of cancer.

Essential oils such as ledum, tangerine and grapefruit may help reduce fat cells. Cypress enhances circulation to support the elimination of fatty deposits. The essential oils of lemongrass and spearmint also may help support fat metabolism.

Cellulite is slow to dissolve, so target areas should be worked for a month or more in conjunction with weight training, a weight loss program, and drinking purified water—one-and-a-half times the body weight in ounces each day. Be patient. You should begin to see results in 4 to 6 weeks when using the oils in combination with a muscle-building and weight-loss regime.

Single Oils:

Rosemary cineol *(Rosmarinus officinalis CT 1,8 cineol)*
Grapefruit *(Citrus x paradisi)*
Tangerine *(Citrus nobilis)*
Cypress *(Cupressus sempervirens)*
Fennel *(Foeniculum vulgare)*
Juniper *(Juniperus communis* or *J. osteosperma)*
Spearmint *(Mentha spicata)*
Lemongrass *(Cymbopogon flexuosus)*

Blends:

Glandular Blend.

Cellulite Blend #1:

- 5 drops rosemary cineol
- 10 drops grapefruit
- 2 drops cypress

Cellulite Blend #2:

- 10 drops grapefruit
- 5 drops lavender
- 3 drops helichrysum
- 3 drops patchouli
- 4 drops cypress

Cellulite Blend #3 (For Bath):

- 5 drops juniper
- 3 drops orange
- 3 drops cypress
- 3 drops lemon

Mix together with 2 tablespoons Epsom salt or baking soda and dissolve in warm bath water.

Applications:

TOPICAL:	DILUTE 50-50, massage 2-6 drops on cellulite locations at least 3 times daily, especially before exercising BATH SALT: 2-4 times weekly

CHEMICAL SENSITIVITY REACTION

Environmental poisoning and chemical sensitivity are becoming a major cause of discomfort and disease. Strong chemical compounds, such as insecticides, herbicides, and formaldehyde found in paints, glues, cosmetics, and fingernail polish, enter the body easily. Symptoms include indigestion, upper and lower gas, poor assimilation, poor electrolyte balance, rashes, hypoglycemia, allergic reaction to foods and other substances, along with emotional mood swings, fatigue, irritability, lack of motivation, lack of discipline and creativity.

Single Oils:

Frankincense *(Boswellia carteri)*
Sandalwood *(Santalum album)*

Blends:

Antibacterial Blend
Clarity Blend
Brain Blend
Liver Blend

Applications:

TOPICAL:	DILUTE 50-50, on affected locations, 2-4 times daily
INGESTION:	CAPSULE, 00 size, 1-3 capsules daily

(See VASCULAR CLEANSING)

How Pollutants Contribute to Cancer

The pollutants to which we are exposed accumulate in tissues such as the breasts, thyroid, ovaries, and uterus. Some of these chemicals can mimic or imitate natural hormones, thereby activating hormone receptors that overstimulate glands. This can increase the risk of hormone-dependent cancers, such as breast and uterine cancer.

Absorption of Chemicals on Hands

Handling refuse or any type of contaminant without protective gloves may cause discoloration of hands as well as dangerous chemical exposure.

Use good rubber gloves and change them often or at least wash them out with strong soap, rinse well, and dry well. If hands become discolored through chemical absorption, soak them in a solution of 3 percent hydrogen peroxide, available at most drug stores. This helps remove chemicals from the skin.

Single Oils:
Lavender *(Lavandula angustifolia)*
Lemon *(Citrus limon)*

Blends:
Antibacterial Blend

Applications:

TOPICAL:	NEAT, Rub 3-7 drops lavender, lemon, or Antibacterial Blend on hands, then cover with clean cotton gloves or wrap lightly with cotton bandages all night.

CHICKEN POX

Single Oils:
Lavender *(Lavandula angustifolia)*
Tea tree oil *(Melaleuca alternifolia)*
Melissa *(Melissa officinalis)*

Blends:
Antiviral Blend

Applications:

TOPICAL:	Mix 20 drops of essential oils (using any of the above single oils) in 1 tablespoon of calamine lotion (or dilute 50-50 in vegetable oil) and dab on spots

CHOLECYSTITIS

(See GALLBLADDER INFECTION.)

Inflammation of the gallbladder is usually due to obstruction of the gallbladder (bile) outlet with symptoms ranging from mild edema and congestion to severe infection and perforation.

CHOLERA

Cholera is an acute diarrheal disease caused by an enterotoxin produced by a gram negative bacteria called *Vibrio cholerae*. Severe cases are marked by vomiting, muscle cramps and constant watery diarrhea which can result in serious fluid loss, saline depletion, acidosis and shock. The disease is typically found in India and Southeast Asia and is spread by feces-contaminated water and food. If you suspect cholera, you should immediately seek professional medical advice.

A recent study shows lemon products such as freshly squeezed juice, peel, and essential oil, act as a biocide against *V. cholerae* with no harmful side effects.[6]

Single Oils:

Lemon *(Citrus limon)*
Clove *(Syzygium aromaticum)*
Thyme thymol *(Thymus vulgaris CT thymol)*
Rosemary cineol *(Rosmarinus officinalis CT 1,8 cineol)*
Oregano *(Origanum compactum)*

Applications:

INGESTION: CAPSULE, 00 size, 1 capsule 3 times daily with meals

CHOLESTEROL (High)

(See CARDIOVASCULAR CONDITIONS)

CHRONIC FATIGUE SYNDROME

(See EPSTEIN-BARR VIRUS)

CIRCULATION DISORDERS

(See BLOOD CLOTS AND CARDIOVASCULAR CONDITIONS)

Good circulation is undoubtedly the foundation of good health; however, sluggish or inadequate circulation can result in tissue toxicity, starvation, and eventually, cellular death. The damage that poor or inadequate circulation can cause is best illustrated in the gangrene that often develops in the legs and arms of many advanced diabetic patients. Because the blood cannot efficiently circulate through these areas, parts of the tissues literally rot away.

Essential oils may be extremely useful for promoting circulation. For example, myrtle, lemon, and cypress have been used to strengthen and dilate capillaries

6. de Castillo et al., "Bactericidal activity of lemon juice and lemon derivatives against Vibrio cholerae," *Biol Pharm Bull* 2000 Oct;23(10):1235-8.

and increase circulation. Helichrysum and clove are natural blood thinners, balancing the viscosity or thickness of the blood, and they amplify the effects of cypress. Marjoram relaxes muscles and dilates blood vessels, while nutmeg acts as a circulatory stimulant. Goldenrod is a vein decongestant.

Essential oils such as clove and citrus rind oils (lemon and orange, etc.) can enhance circulation through their ability to reduce the thickness or viscosity of blood.

Single Oils:

Goldenrod *(Solidago canadensis)*
Helichrysum *(Helichrysum italicum)*
Marjoram *(Origanum majorana)*
Cypress *(Cupressus sempervirens)*
Myrtle *(Myrtus communis)*
Orange *(Citrus aurantium)*
Grapefruit *(Citrus x paradisi)*
Clove *(Syzygium aromaticum)*
Peppermint *(Mentha piperita)*
Geranium *(Pelargonium graveolens)*
Nutmeg *(Myristica fragrans)*

Blends:

Circulation Blend
Energy Blend
Pain Relief Blend

Applications:

TOPICAL:	DILUTE 50-50, 2-4 drops on affected area 2-3 times daily. Also apply over carotid arteries and pulse points, wherever arteries are close to the skin surface BODY MASSAGE, 2-3 times weekly, start at feet and work up to heart
INGESTION:	CAPSULE, 0 size, 1 capsule twice daily

To Improve Circulation

Circulation Blend #1:

- 5 drops basil
- 8 drops marjoram
- 10 drops cypress
- 3 drops peppermint

Circulation Blend #2:
- 2-3 drops basil
- 1-2 drops marjoram
- 1 drop peppermint

Circulation Blend #3:
- 3 drops basil
- 2 drops peppermint
- 4 drops cypress
- 8 drops marjoram
- 10 drops wintergreen or birch

These recipes are best diluted with 1 teaspoon vegetable or massage oil and massaged on location.

COLD SORES (Herpes Simplex Type I)

Single Oils:

Tea tree oil *(Melaleuca alternifolia)*
Lavender *(Lavandula angustifolia)*
Sandalwood *(Santalum album)*
Peppermint *(Mentha piperita)*
Tansy *(Tanacetum vulgare)*
Melissa *(Melissa officinalis)*
Ravensara *(Ravensara aromatica)*
Thyme *(Thymus vulgare)*

Studies have shown that neat applications of melissa to be effective against Herpes Simplex Type I and herpes labialis. The healing period was shortened, the spread of infection prevented, and symptoms such as itching, tingling, and burning were lessened.[7,8]

Peppermint and *Melaleuca alternifolia* oils have also been studied for positive effects on the pain of herpes.[9,10]

7. Dimitrova et al., "effect of Melissa officinalis L. extracts," Acta Microbiol Bulg 1993;29-:65-72.
8. Koytchev R, et al., "Balm mint extract (Lo-701) for topical treatment of recurring herpes labialis," Phytomedicine 1999 Oct;6(4):225-30.
9. Davies SJ, Harding LM, Baranowski AP, "A novel treatment of postherpetic neuralgia using peppermint oil," *Clin J Pain* 2002 May-Jun;18(3):200-2
10. Carson CF et al., "Melaleuca alternifolia (tea tree) oil gel (6%) for the treatment of recurrent herpes labialis," *J Antimicrob Chemother* 2001 Sep;48(3):450-1.

Blends:

Antibacterial Blend
Antiseptic Blend
Antiviral Blend

Applications:

TOPICAL:	NEAT, apply one drop as soon as a cold sore starts, 5-10 times daily DILUTE 50-50, a dilution will help to reduce discomfort or drying of the skin when applying essential oils to an open sore

COLDS

(See also INFECTION, SINUS INFECTION, THROAT INFECTION)

The best treatment for a cold is prevention. Because many essential oils have strong antimicrobial properties, they can be diffused to prevent the spread of airborne bacteria and viruses. Essential oils and blends such as Antimicrobial Blend, Antibacterial Blend, and Respiratory Blend are very effective in helping the body fight against colds.

The antiviral oils are powerful prophylactic agents for protection against colds. These include basil, hyssop, rosemary cineol, bergamot, *Eucalyptus radiata, Melaleuca alternifolia,* clove, oregano, cistus, thyme, and mountain savory.

Single Oils:

Peppermint *(Mentha piperita)*
Thyme thymol *(Thymus vulgaris CT thymol)*
Bay laurel *(Laurus nobilis)*
Oregano *(Origanum compactum)*
Rosewood *(Aniba rosaeodora)*
Eucalyptus radiata
Tea tree oil *(Melaleuca alternifolia)*
Ravensara *(Ravensara aromatica)*
Rosemary cineol *(Rosmarinus officinalis CT 1,8 cineol)*
Rosemary verbenon *(Rosmarinus officinalis CT verbenon)*
Mountain savory *(Satureja montana)*

Blends:

Antiseptic Blend
Respiratory Blend
Immune Blend
Antimicrobial Blend
Antiviral Blend

How Essential Oils Benefit the Respiratory Tract

- Myrrh is very effective for throat problems and hoarseness.
- Pine dilates and opens bronchial tubes.
- Respiratory Blend strengthens the respiratory system, dilates and opens the pulmonary tract, and fights respiratory infections.
- Rose, sage, and sandalwood help chronic bronchitis.
- One of the most effective therapeutic applications for respiratory problems is diluted essential oils injected with a Fleet enema syringe into the rectum and retained overnight.

Cold Blend #1:
- 2 drops lemon
- 4 drops *Eucalyptus radiata*
- 6 drops rosemary verbenon
- 4 drops peppermint
- 3 drops cypress

Cold Blend #2:
- 5 drops rosemary verbenon
- 4 drops Respiratory Blend
- 4 drops frankincense
- 1 drop oregano
- 2 drops peppermint

Applications:

INHALATION:	DIRECT, 3-5 times daily, or as needed
	VAPOR, 2-3 times daily, as needed
INGESTION:	SYRUP, 3-6 times daily
ORAL:	GARGLE, 3-6 times daily
TOPICAL:	DILUTE 50-50, massage 1-3 drops on each of the following areas: forehead, nose, cheeks, lower throat, chest and upper back, 1-3 times daily
	VITA FLEX, massage 1-3 drops on Vita Flex points on the feet.
	RAINDROP Technique, 1-2 times weekly
	BATH SALT, (see below)

Bath Blend for relief of cold symptoms:

- 2 drops *Eucalyptus radiata*
- 6 drops frankincense
- 3 drops helichrysum

- 6 drops spruce
- 15 drops ravensara
- 1 drop wintergreen or birch

Stir above essential oils into 1/2 cup Epsom salt or baking soda, then add mixture to hot bath water while tub is filling. Soak in hot bath until water cools.

For head cold/sinus congestion:

(See also SINUS INFECTION)

Single Oils:

Ledum *(Ledum groenlandicum)*
German chamomile *(Matricaria recutita)*
Eucalyptus radiata
Frankincense *(Boswellia carteri)*
Pine *(Pinus sylvestris)*
Peppermint *(Mentha piperita)*
Rosemary cineol *(Rosmarinus officinalis 1,8 CT cineol)*
Balsam fir *(Abies balsamea)*
Ravensara *(Ravensara aromatica)*
Lemon *(Citrus limon)*

Blends:

Respiratory Blend
Antiseptic Blend
Antiviral Blend

Sinus congestion recipe:

- 4 drops Respiratory Blend
- 4 drops frankincense
- 4 drops lemon

Applications:

INHALATION:	DIRECT, 3-5 times daily, or as needed
	VAPOR, 2-3 times daily, as needed
INGESTION:	SYRUP, 3-6 times daily
ORAL:	GARGLE, 3-6 times daily
TOPICAL:	DILUTE 50-50, massage 1-3 drops on each of the following areas: forehead, nose, cheeks, lower throat, chest and upper back, 1-3 times daily
	VITA FLEX, massage 1-3 drops on Vita Flex points on the feet.
	RAINDROP Technique, 1-2 times weekly
	BATH SALT, daily

Congestive Cough

(See also THROAT INFECTION, LUNG INFECTION)

Single Oils:

Eucalyptus globulus
Goldenrod *(Solidago canadensis)*
Ledum *(Ledum groenlandicum)*
Ravensara *(Ravensara aromatica)*
Cedarwood *(Cedrus atlantica)*
Marjoram *(Origanum majorana)*
Spruce *(Picea mariana)*
Hyssop *(Hyssopus officinalis)*

Blends:

Respiratory Blend
Stress Reduction Blend
Antiseptic Blend

Applications:

INGESTION:	SYRUP, 2-4 times daily
INHALATION:	DIRECT, 3-6 times daily, as needed
	VAPOR, 1-3 times daily, as needed
ORAL:	GARGLE, 4-6 times daily
TOPICAL:	COMPRESS, warm, 1-2 daily, over chest, over throat, and on upper back

COLITIS, ULCERATIVE

Also known as ileitis or proctitis, ulcerative colitis is marked by the inflammation of the top layers of the lining of the large intestine (colon). It is different from both irritable bowel syndrome (which has no inflammation) and Crohn's disease (which occurs deeper in the colon wall).

The inflammation and ulcerous sores that are characteristic of ulcerative colitis occur most frequently in the lower colon and rectum and occasionally throughout the entire colon.

Symptoms include: fatigue, nausea, weight loss, loss of appetite, bloody diarrhea, loss of body fluids and nutrients, frequent fevers, abdominal cramps, arthritis, liver disease and skin rashes.

Single Oils:

Peppermint *(Mentha piperita)*
Spearmint *(Mentha spicata)*
Tarragon *(Artemisia dracunculus)*

Anise seed oil *(Pimpinella anisum)*
Fennel *(Foeniculum vulgare)*

Blends:
Digestive Blend

Applications:

INGESTION:	CAPSULE, 00 size, 1 capsule 3-4 times daily SYRUP, 3-4 times daily
TOPICAL:	DILUTE 50-50, massage 3-6 drops to lower abdomen area 2-4 times daily

COLITIS, VIRAL

In cases where colitis is caused by a virus rather than a bacteria, the following treatments are recommended:

Single Oils:
Melissa *(Melissa officinalis)*
Oregano *(Origanum compactum)*
Blue cypress *(Callitris intratropica)*
Cumin *(Cuminum cyminum)*
Tea tree oil *(Melaleuca alternifolia)*
Melaleuca quinquinervia
Lemongrass *(Cymbopogon flexuosus)*
Tarragon *(Artemisia dracunculus)*

Blends:
Digestive Blend
Antiseptic Blend
Antibacterial Blend
Antimicrobial Blend
Antivital Blend

Applications:

INGESTION:	CAPSULE, 00 size, 1 capsule 2-3 times daily
TOPICAL:	DILUTE 50-50, massage 4-6 drops over colon area 2-4 times daily VITA FLEX, 1-3 drops on colon Vita Flex points RAINDROP, 1-2 times weekly. COMPRESS, warm, diluted 20-80, using equal parts helichrysum and Digestive Blend, over colon area
RETENTION:	RECTAL, use the formula below in a rectal implact 3 times weekly

Viral colitis Blend:

- 3 drops myrrh
- 3 drops *Melaleuca quinquinervia*
- 2 drops Antibacterial Blend
- 2 drops Roman chamomile
- 2 drops cumin
- 2 drops Digestive Blend

Mix with 1 Tablespoon vegetable oil.

COMA

Single Oils:

Frankincense *(Boswellia carteri)*
Sandalwood *(Santalum album)*
Cypress *(Cupressus sempervirens)*
Black pepper *(Piper nigrum)*
Peppermint *(Mentha piperita)*

Blends:

Trauma Blend
Energy Balance Blend

Applications:

INHALATION:	DIFFUSER, 15 minutes 5-7 times daily
TOPICAL:	DILUTE 50-50, 3-5 drops on temples, neck and shoulders

CONFUSION

Single Oils:

Peppermint *(Mentha piperita)*
Lemon *(Citrus limon)*
Rosemary cineol *(Rosmarinus officinalis CT 1,8 cineol)*
Basil *(Ocimum basilicum)*
Cardamom *(Elettaria cardamomum)*

Blends:

Clarity Blend
Brain Blend
Headache Blend

Applications:

INHALATION:	DIRECT, 2-3 times daily, or as needed

(See BRAIN DISORDERS/ALZHEIMER'S)

CONNECTIVE TISSUE (Ligaments, Tendons)

Connective tissue is an essential part of every structure in the body.

Tendonitis, (often called "Tennis Elbow" and "Golfer's Elbow"), is a torn or inflamed tendon. Tenosynovitis, sometimes called "Trigger Finger," is a tendon being restricted by its sheath (particularly thumbs and fingers) by being swollen and inflamed. Repetitive use or infection may be the cause.

Helichrysum and lemongrass make a powerful combination for reducing pain and repairing torn ligaments. Lavender with lemongrass, and marjoram with lemongrass work well together for inflamed tendons.

NOTE: For sprains, use cold packs. For any serious sprain or constant pain, always consult a health care professional. Any time there is tissue damage, there is always inflammation, which needs to be reduced first.

When selecting oils, particularly for injuries, think through the cause and type of injury and select oils for each segment. For instance, tendonitis could encompass muscle damage, nerve damage, ligament strain or tear, inflammation, infection, fever on location, and possibly an emotion. Therefore, select an oil or oils for each perceived problem and apply in rotation or prepare a blend to cover all problems. The emotional distress may be anger or guilt.

Single Oils:

Basil *(Ocimum basilicum)*
Lemongrass *(Cymbopogon flexuosus)*
Marjoram *(Origanum majorana)*
Helichrysum *(Helichrysum italicum)*
Wintergreen or birch *(Gaultheria procumbens* or *Betula alleghaniensis)*
Cypress *(Cupressus sempervirens)*
Peppermint *(Mentha piperita)*

Blends:

Muscle Relaxing Blend
Pain Relief Blend
Circulation Blend

The following list shows singles and blends best suited to the particular trouble spots involved with connective tissue.

Bone:

Wintergreen or birch *(Gaultheria procumbens* or *Betula alleghaniensis)*
Spruce *(Picea mariana)*
Pain Relief Blend

Muscle:
Basil *(Ocimum basilicum)*
Marjoram *(Origanum majorana)*
Pain Relief Blend

Ligament:
Lemongrass *(Cymbopogon flexuosus)*
Elemi *(Canarium luzonicum)*
Tansy *(Tanacetum vulgare)*
Pain Relief Blend

Spasms:
Basil *(Ocimum basilicum)*
Lemongrass *(Cymbopogon flexuosus)*
Helichrysum *(Helichrysum italicum)*
Muscle Relaxing Blend
Pain Relief Blend
Circulation Blend

How to Speed Healing

With any damaged tissue, circulation should be increased to promote healing. The essential oil of cypress can increase circulation.

Anytime there is tissue damage, there is always inflammation which should be addressed first.

Knee Cartilage Injury

Single Oils:
Peppermint *(Mentha piperita)*
Balsam fir *(Abies balsamea)*
Douglas fir *(Pseudotsuga menziesii)*
Wintergreen or birch *(Gaultheria procumbens* or *Betula alleghaniensis)*

Blends:
Cartilage Blend:
- 9 drops lemongrass
- 10 drops marjoram
- 12 drops ginger

Applications:
TOPICAL: DILUTE 50-50, massage 4-6 drops on knee 3 times daily. For swelling, elevate and apply ice packs

Tendonitis

Tendonitis Blend #1:
- 10 drops basil
- 8 drops wintergreen or birch
- 6 drops cypress
- 3 drops peppermint

Tendonitis Blend #2 (for pain relief):
- 10 drops rosemary cineol
- 10 drops *Eucalyptus radiata*
- 10 drops peppermint

Applications:

TOPICAL:	NEAT or DILUTE 50-50, as required. Gently massage 3-5 drops on affected areas, 2-4 times daily

Sprain or Torn Ligament

Sprain Blend
- 5 drops lemongrass
- 15 drops Muscle Relaxing Blend

Applications:

TOPICAL:	NEAT or DILUTE 50-50, as required. Gently massage 3-5 drops on affected areas, 2-4 times daily

CONSTIPATION

The principle causes of constipation are inadequate fluid intake and low fiber consumption. Eliminating these causes in the diet is a mandatory first step. Constipation can eventually lead to diverticulosis and diverticulitis, conditions common among older people. Certain essential oils have demonstrated their ability to improve colon health through supporting intestinal flora, stimulating intestinal motility and peristalsis, fighting infections and eliminating parasites.

(see also DIVERTICULOSIS and DIVERTICULITIS)

Why Constipation Can Produce Problems Later in Life

The reason constipation creates diverticulosis is due to the fact that the muscles of the colon must strain to move an overly-hard stool, which puts excess pressure on the colon. Eventually weak spots in the colon walls form, resulting in the creation of abnormal pouches called diverticula.

These pouches can also be created by parasites which burrow and embed in the lining of the colon wall and lay eggs there. It's always wise to consider treating for parasites when diverticula are present.

Single Oils:

Ginger *(Zingiber officinale)*
Peppermint *(Mentha piperita)*
Fennel *(Foeniculum vulgare)*
Tarragon *(Artemisia dracunculus)*
Anise seed *(Pimpinella anisum)*

Blends:

Digestive Blend

Applications:

INGESTION:	CAPSULE , 00 size, 1 capsule 2-3 times daily
	RICE MILK, 2-4 times daily

CONVULSIONS

(See BRAIN DISORDERS)

Monitor diet. Discontinue sugar and dairy products, fried and processed foods.

Blends:

Brain Blend
Energy Balance Blend

Applications:

INHALATION:	DIRECT, 4-5 times daily
	DIFFUSER, 20 minutes 2-3 times daily
TOPICAL:	NEAT, apply 2-4 drops at base of skull, across the neck and top of the spine (C1-C6 vertebrae) and on bottom of feet (for relief only)

COUGHS

(See LUNG INFECTIONS, COLDS)

CRAMPS (Abdominal)

(See DIGESTIVE PROBLEMS)

CRAMPS (Muscle)

(See MUSCLES)

CROHN'S DISEASE

(See COLITIS, ULCERATIVE)

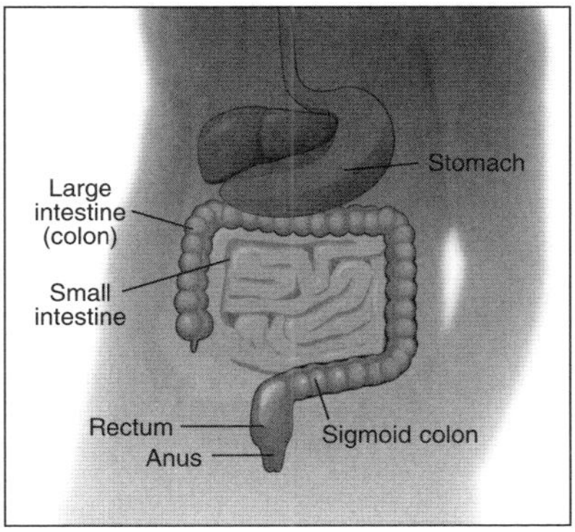

Crohn's disease creates inflammation, sores, and ulcers on the intestinal wall. These sores occur deeper than ulcerative colitis. Moreover, unlike other forms of colitis, Crohn's disease can also occur in other areas of the body including large intestine, appendix, stomach, and mouth.

Symptoms include:

- Abdominal cramping
- Lower right abdominal pain
- Diarrhea
- A general sense of feeling ill

Attacks may occur once or twice a day for life. If the disease continues for years, it can cause deterioration of bowel function, leaking bowel, poor absorption of nutrients, loss of appetite and weight, intestinal obstruction, severe bleeding, and increased susceptibility to intestinal cancer.

Some researchers believe that Crohn's disease is caused by an overreacting immune system and is actually an autoimmune disease (where the immune system mistakenly attacks the body's own tissues).

Single Oils:

Peppermint *(Mentha piperita)*
Nutmeg *(Myristica fragrans)*

Blends:

Digestive Blend
Raindrop Technique on the spine with Immune Blend.

Applications:

INGESTION:	CAPSULE, 0 size, 3 times daily
	RICE MILK, 2-4 times daily
TOPICAL:	RAINDROP Technique 1-2 times weekly, using Immune Blend

CUSHING'S DISEASE

(See ADRENAL GLAND IMBALANCE)

CUTS

(See WOUNDS, SCRAPES AND CUTS)

CYSTITIS

(See URINARY TRACT/BLADDER INFECTION)

DANDRUFF

Dandruff may be caused from allergies, parasites, and or chemicals.

Single Oils:

Tea tree oil *(Melaleuca alternifolia)*
Cedarwood *(Cedrus atlantica)*
Lavender *(Lavandula angustifolia)*
Balsam fir *(Abies balsamea)*
Western red cedar *(Thuja plicata)*
Rosemary cineol *(Rosmarinus officinalis CT 1,8 cineol)*
Sage *(Salvia officinalis)*

Blends:

Antiseptic Blend

It was shown that *Melaleuca alternifolia* was successful in treating dandruff and other fungal infections (Nenoff, P et al., 1996).

Applications:

TOPICAL: DILUTE 20-80, massage 1 tablespoon into the scalp for at least two minutes every other day before retiring at night

DECONGESTANTS

(See COLDS, MUCUS)

DENTAL

Essential oils make excellent oral antiseptics, analgesics and anti-inflammatories. Clove essential oils has been used in mainstream dentistry for decades to numb the gums and help prevent infections.

Prior to visiting the dentist, rub a drop or two of clove and Pain Relief Blend on gums and jaw. (Clove may interfere with bonding of crowns so keep it off teeth if this procedure is planned.)

For dental pain and infection control

Single Oils:

Wintergreen or birch *(Gaultheria procumbens* or *Betula alleghaniensis)*
Helichrysum *(Helichrysum italicum)*
Tea tree oil *(Melaleuca alternifolia)*
Eucalyptus radiata
Clove *(Syzygium aromaticum)*
Thyme *(Thymus vulgaris)*
Oregano *(Origanum compactum)*

Blends:

Pain Relief Blend
Antimicrobial Blend
Respiratory Blend

Applications:

TOPICAL: DILUTE 50-50, apply 1-2 drops on gums and around teeth. Repeat as needed. Just before having teeth pulled, rub 1-2 drops of helichrysum, Antimicrobial Blend and Respiratory Blend around gums

DEODORANT

Excessive body odor indicates putrefaction in the system and possibly poor digestion from the lack of enzymes in the digestive tract. It can also be caused by hormone imbalances and candida infections.

The essential oils of lavender, lavandin, citronella, geranium, and melaleuca inhibit proliferation of odor-causing bacteria on the skin.

Single Oils:

Lavender *(Lavandula angustifolia)*
Geranium *(Pelargonium graveolens)*
Citronella *(Cymbopogon nardus)*
Clove *(Syzygium aromaticum)*
Eucalyptus globulus
Tea tree oil *(Melaleuca alternifolia)*
Myrtle *(Myrtus communis)*

Blends:

Female Blend
Glandular Blend

Mood Lifting Blend
Antiseptic Blend
Male Blend

Applications:

TOPICAL:	DILUTE 50-50, apply 2-4 drops under arms on the skin. Put 2 drops on a washcloth when washing. BATH SALT, daily

Deodorant Recipe:

- 4 ounces of unscented talcum powder
- 2 ounces of baking soda
- 3 drops lavender oil or geranium oil

Mix well. Use under arms, on the feet (or in shoes).

DEPRESSION

(See INSOMNIA)

Diffusing or directly inhaling essential oils can have an immediate positive impact on moods. Olfaction is the only sense that can have direct effects on the limbic region of the brain. Studies at the University of Vienna[11] have shown that some essential oils and their primary constituents (cineol) can stimulate blood flow and activity in the emotional regions of the brain.

Clinical studies at the Department of Psychiatry at the Mie University of Medicine showed that lemon not only reduced depression but reduced stress when inhaled (Komori et al., 1995).

Single Oils:

Eucalyptus globulus
Lemon *(Citrus limon)*
Jasmine *(Jasminum officinale)*
Frankincense *(Boswellia carteri)*

Blends:

Mood Lifting Blend
Energy Balance Blend

Applications:

INHALATION:	DIFFUSER, 20 minutes 3 times daily DIRECT, 2 minutes 4 times daily

11. Nasel et al., Functional imaging of effects of fragrances on the human brain after prolonged inhalation, *Chem Senses,* 1995 Jun;20(3):349-50.

Postpartum Depression

Single Oils:

Vetiver *(Vetiveria zizanioides)*
Lemon *(Citrus limon)*
St. John's wort *(Hypericum perforatum)*
Cedarwood *(Cedrus atlantica)*
Sandalwood *(Santalum album)*

Blends:

Trauma Blend
Mood Lifting Blend
Stress Reduction Blend

Applications:

INHALATION: DIFFUSER, 20 minutes 3 times daily
DIRECT, 2 minutes 4 times daily

DERMATITIS

(See ECZEMA/DERMATITIS under SKIN DISORDERS)

DIABETES—BLOOD SUGAR IMBALANCE

The pancreas produces insulin, which enables the body to use glucose. If there is no insulin, or not enough insulin is produced, the body cannot regulate the sugar levels in the body. This disorder is called diabetes mellitus, which causes low energy and abnormally high blood glucose (sugar).

Single Oils:

Coriander *(Coriandrum sativum)*
Cinnamon *(Cinnamomum verum)*
Fennel *(Foeniculum vulgare)*
Dill *(Anethum graveolens)*
Cypress *(Cupressus sempervirens)*
Clove *(Syzygium aromaticum)*

Blends:

Glandular Blend
Liver Blend
Digestive Blend

Applications:

INGESTION: CAPSULE, 0 size, 3 times daily

DIGESTION PROBLEMS

Any of the following indicate that the digestive system is not functioning properly:

- Rumbling or gurgling sounds in the abdomen
- Heartburn (may be a possible indication of candida)
- Constipation and diarrhea
- Constant hunger or fatigue after eating
- Food intolerance or food allergies
- Intestinal parasites

Poor bowel function is linked to enzyme deficiency, low fiber, insufficient liquid, bad diet, stress, food-borne illness, and candida. Essential oils detoxify the digestive tract and enhance intestinal motility and peristalsis.

Cramps (stomach)

Single Oils:

Rosemary cineol *(Rosmarinus officinalis CT 1,8 cineol)*
Ginger *(Zingiber officinale)*
Basil *(Ocimum basilicum)*

Applications:

INGESTION:	CAPSULE, 0 size, 1 capsule twice daily RICE MILK, 1-3 times daily
TOPICAL:	DILUTE 50-50, apply 6-10 drops over stomach area 2 times daily COMPRESS, warm, 1-2 times daily VITA FLEX, 1-3 drops on stomach Vita Flex points of feet

Diarrhea (due to infection)

Nutmeg has been shown to have powerful action against diarrhea in a number of medical studies.[12,13]

Single Oils:

Peppermint *(Mentha piperita)*
Ginger (*Zingiber officinale)*
Mountain savory *(Satureja montana)*
Oregano *(Origanum compactum)*

12. Weiss HJ, et al., "The effect of salicylates on the hemostatic properties of platelets in man," *J Clin Invest* 1968 Sep;47(9):2169-80.
13. Fawell WN, Thompson G, "Nutmeg for diarrhea of medullarly carcinoma of thyroid," *N Eng J Med* 1973 Jul 12;289(2):108-9.

Clove *(Syzygium aromaticum)*
Nutmeg *(Myristica fragrans)*
Lemon *(Citrus limon)*

Blends:
Antimicrobial Blend
Digestive Blend

Diarrhea detox blend:
- 4 drops lemon
- 3 drops mountain savory
- 2 drops oregano

Applications:

INGESTION:	CAPSULE, 0 size, 1 capsule twice daily RICE MILK, 1-3 times daily
TOPICAL:	DILUTE 50-50, apply 6-10 drops over stomach area 2 times daily COMPRESS, warm, 1-2 times daily VITA FLEX, 1-3 drops on stomach Vita Flex points of feet

Gas, Flatulence:

Single Oils:
Peppermint *(Mentha piperita)*
Tarragon *(Artemisia dracunculus)*
Nutmeg *(Myristica fragrans)*
Anise seed *(Pimpinella anisum)*
Fennel *(Foeniculum vulgare)*
Ledum *(Ledum groenlandicum)*

Blends:
Digestive Blend

Applications:

INGESTION:	CAPSULE, 0 size, 1 capsule twice daily
TOPICAL:	DILUTE 50-50, apply 6-10 drops over stomach area 2 times daily COMPRESS, warm, 1-2 times daily VITA FLEX, 1-3 drops on stomach Vita Flex points of feet

Heartburn

Lemon juice is one of the best remedies for heartburn. Place several drops in water and sip slowly. Ingesting lemon juice and/or essential oils slows the production of digestive acids in the stomach.

Single Oils:
Peppermint *(Mentha piperita)*
Ginger *(Zingibar officinale)*
Spearmint *(Mentha spicata)*
Lemon *(Citrus limon)*

Blends:
Digestive Blend

Heartburn recipe:

- 2 drops basil
- 2 drops tansy
- 8 drops lemon
- 3 drops sandalwood

Applications:

INGESTION:	CAPSULE, 0 size, 1 capsule twice daily
	RICE MILK, 1-3 times daily, as needed
TOPICAL:	DILUTE 50-50, apply 6-10 drops over stomach area 2 times daily
	VITA FLEX, 1-3 drops on stomach Vita Flex points of feet

Hiccups

(see HICCUPS)

Indigestion

Singles:
Peppermint *(Mentha piperita)*
Fennel *(Foeniculum vulgare)*
Ginger *(Zingiber officinale)*
Cumin *(Cuminum cyminum)*
Spearmint *(Mentha spicata)*
Nutmeg *(Myristica fragrans)*
Orange *(Citrus aurantium)*
Grapefruit *(Citrus x paradisi)*

Blends:
Digestive Blend

Applications:

INGESTION:	CAPSULE, 0 size, 1 capsule twice daily
	RICE MILK, 1-3 times daily
TOPICAL:	DILUTE 50-50, apply 6-10 drops over stomach area 2 times daily
	COMPRESS, warm, 1-2 times daily
	VITA FLEX, 1-3 drops on stomach Vita Flex points of feet

Nausea

(See NAUSEA)

DIPHTHERIA

(See also THROAT INFECTIONS)

An acute infectious disease caused by toxigenci strains of *Corynebacterium diphtheriae*, acquired by contact with an infected person or carrier. It is usually confined to the upper respiratory tract, and characterized by the formation of a tough *false membrane* attached firmly to the underlying tissue that will bleed if forcibly removed. In the most serious infections the membrane begins in the tonsil area and may spread to the uvula, soft palate and pharyngeal wall, followed by the larynx, trachea, and bronchial tree where it may cause life-threatening bronchial obstructions.

Single Oils:
Goldenrod *(Solidago canadensis)*
Thyme thymol *(Thymus vulgaris CT thymol)*
Eucalyptus radiata
Clove *(Syzygium aromaticum)*

Applications:

INHALATION:	DIRECT, 6-8 times daily
INGESTION:	CAPSULE, 00 size, 1 capsules 2 times daily

DISINFECTANT

(See ANTISEPTIC)

DIVERTICULOSIS / DIVERTICULITIS

Diverticulosis is one of the most common conditions in the U.S. It is caused by a lack of fiber in the diet. Diverticulosis is characterized by small, abnormal pouches (diverticula) that bulge out through weak spots in the wall of the intestine. It is estimated that half of all Americans from age 60 to 80 have diverticulosis.

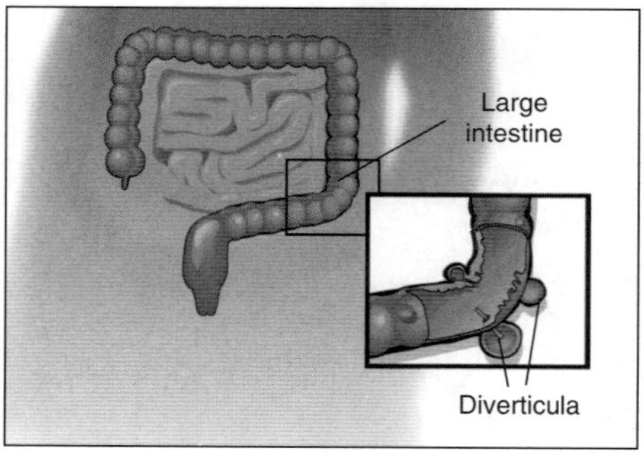

Symptoms:
- Cramping
- Bloating
- Constipation

One of the easiest ways to resolve this condition is by increasing fiber intake to 20-30 grams daily. Peppermint oil stimulates contractions in the colon.

While diverticulosis involves the condition of merely having colon abnormalities, diverticulitis occurs when these abnormalities or diverticula become infected or inflamed. Diverticulitis is present in 10 to 25 percent of people with diverticulosis.

Symptoms (in addition to those listed above, include)
- Tenderness on lower left side of abdomen
- Fever and chills

Many of these symptoms are similar to those of irritable bowel syndrome. (See IRRITABLE BOWEL SYNDROME)

Single Oils:

Patchouli *(Pogostemon cablin)*
Anise seed *(Pimpinella anisum)*
Tarragon *(Artemisia dracunculus)*
Rosemary cineol *(Rosmarinus officinalis CT 1,8 cineol)*
Fennel *(Foeniculum vulgare)*
Peppermint *(Mentha piperita)*
Mountain savory *(Satureja montana)*
Oregano *(Origanum compactum)*
Thyme linalol *(Thymus vulgaris CT linalol)*

Blends:

Digestive Blend
Antiseptic Blend

Recipe 1:

- 15 drops Digestive Blend
- 5 drops Antiseptic Blend

Recipe 2:

- 10 drops Digestive Blend
- 12 drops frankincense

Applications:

INGESTION:	CAPSULE, enteric coated, 0 size, 1 capsule 2-3 times daily.
	MAPLE SYRUP, 1-3 times daily.
TOPICAL:	DILUTE 50-50, 3-5 drops on lower abdomen twice daily.
	VITA FLEX, 2-4 drops on intestinal Vita Flex points on feet 2-3 times daily.
	COMPRESS, warm, twice daily
RETENTION:	RECTAL, nightly before retiring, retain overnight.

DIZZINESS

Single Oils:

Cypress *(Cupressus sempervirens)*
Tangerine *(Citrus reticulata)*
Peppermint *(Mentha piperita)*
Basil *(Ocimum basilicum)*
Cardamom *(Elettaria cardamomum)*

Blends:

Circulation Blend
Clarity Blend
Brain Blend
Antimicrobial Blend

Applications:

INHALATION:	DIRECT, 1-2 minutes as needed
TOPICAL:	NEAT, 1-3 drops on temples, back of neck and shoulders, as needed
	VITA FLEX, 1-3 drops on brain Vita Flex points of feet

If blood circulation is a factor, see Circulation.

DYSENTERY

Any of several disorders marked by inflammation of the intestines, especially of the colon, and attended by pain in the abdomen and frequent stools containing blood and mucus. Causes include chemicals, bacteria, protozoa and parasites.

(see DIARRHEA)

Single Oils:

Lemon *(Citrus limon)*
Mountain savory *(Satureja montana)*
Oregano *(Origanum compactum)*
Tansy *(Tanacetum vulgare)*
Peppermint *(Mentha piperita)*

Blends:

Antimicrobial Blend
Digestive Blend
Antiviral Blend

Applications:

INGESTION: CAPSULE, 00 size, 1 capsule three times daily

DYSPEPSIA

(See DIGESTIVE PROBLEMS)

EAR PROBLEMS

Ear Ache

Single Oils:

Thyme linalol *(Thymus vulgaris CT linalol)*
Lavender *(Lavandula angustifolia)*
Tea tree oil *(Melaleuca alternifolia)*
Rosemary cineol *(Rosmarinus officinalis CT 1,8 cineol)*
Helichrysum *(Helichrysum italicum)*
Roman chamomile *(Chamaemelum nobile)*
Ravensara *(Ravensara aromatica)*
Peppermint *(Mentha piperita)*
Eucalyptus radiata

Blends:
Antiseptic Blend
Antibacterial Blend
Pain Relief Blend
Antimicrobial Blend (diluted)
Immune Blend

Applications:

TOPICAL: DILUTE 50-50 in warm olive oil. Apply 2 drops to a cotton swab. Using the swab, apply traces to the skin AROUND the opening of the ear, but not in it. Put 2-3 drops of the diluted essential oil on a piece of cotton and place it carefully over the ear opening. Leave in overnight. Additional relief may be obtained by placing a warm compress over the ear
VITA FLEX, massage 1-2 drops on ear lobes and on ear Vita Flex points of the feet

NOTE: Never put essential oils directly into the ear. Ear pain can be very serious. Always seek medical attention if pain persists.

Ear Mites

Single Oils:
Eucalyptus radiata
Tea tree oil *(Melaleuca alternifolia)*

Blends:
Antibacterial Blend

Applications:

TOPICAL: DILUTE 50-50 in warm olive oil. Apply 2 drops to a cotton swab. Using the swab, apply traces to the skin AROUND the opening of the ear, but not in it. Put 2-3 drops of the diluted essential oil on a piece of cotton and place it carefully over the ear opening. Leave in overnight. Additional relief may be obtained by placing a warm compress over the ear
VITA FLEX, massage 1-2 drops on ear lobes and on ear Vita Flex points of the feet

NOTE: Never put essential oils directly into the ear.

Perforated Eardrum

Single Oils:
Lavender *(Lavandula angustifolia)*

Blends:
Antiseptic Blend

Applications:

TOPICAL: Use cotton swab soaked in lavender to apply essential oil to the outside area around the ear canal opening. Repeat, alternating lavender with Antiseptic Blend. Put 2-3 drops of neat essential oil on cotton ball, leave in ear overnight.

NOTE: Never put essential oils directly into the ear.

ECZEMA

(See ECZEMA/DERMATITIS under SKIN DISORDERS)

EDEMA (Swelling)

(see KIDNEY DISORDERS, WATER RETENTION)

Swelling—particularly around the ankles—is noticeable when fluids accumulate in the tissue. This puffiness under the skin and around the ankles is more apparent at the end of the day when fluids settle to the lowest part of the body. A potassium deficiency can worsen swelling, so the first recourse is to increase potassium intake.

Single Oils:
Ledum *(Ledum groenlandicum)*
German chamomile *(Matricaria recutita)*
Cedarwood *(Cedrus atlantica)*
Wintergreen or birch *(Gaultheria procumbens* or *Betula alleghaniensis)*
Peppermint *(Mentha piperita)*
Lavender *(Lavandula angustifolia)*
Grapefruit *(Citrus x paradisi)*
Juniper *(Juniperus communis* or *J. osteosperma)*
Orange *(Citrus aurantium)*
Fennel *(Foeniculum vulgare)*
Geranium *(Pelargonium graveolens)*
Clove *(Syzygium aromaticum)*

Blends:

Circulation Blend
Glandular Blend
Digestive Blend

Edema Blend #1:
- 10 drops tangerine
- 5 drops cypress
- 10 drops lemon or 3 drops juniper

Edema Blend #2:
- 10 drops wintergreen or birch
- 6 drops fennel
- 2 drops tansy
- 3 drops patchouli
- 10 drops tangerine

Applications:

TOPICAL:	DILUTE 50-50, massage 3-5 drops into affected area 2-3 times daily COMPRESS, cold, 1-2 times daily VITA FLEX, massage 1-3 drops on bladder Vita Flex point on foot
INGESTION:	CAPSULE, 0 size, twice a day

Morning and Evening Edema regimen:

Morning Blend:
- 10 drops tangerine
- 10 drops cypress

Evening Blend:
- 8 drops geranium
- 5 drops cypress
- 5 drops helichrysum

Dilute each blend 50-50 in vegetable or massage oil and rub on legs from the feet up the legs. Use Morning Blend in the a.m.; Evening Blend in the p.m. Do this for one week

EMOTIONAL TRAUMA

The effect of heavy emotional trauma can disrupt the stomach and digestive system. (See DIGESTION.)

Also see Chapter 14: Emotional Response and Essential Oils

Single Oils:

Frankincense *(Boswellia carteri)*
Lavender *(Lavandula angustifolia)*
Lemon *(Citrus limon)*
German chamomile *(Matricaria recutita)*
Kaffir lime *(Citrus hystrix)*
Rose *(Rosa damascena)*
Galbanum *(Ferula gummosa)*
Valerian *(Valeriana officinalis)*

Blends:

Emotional Release Blend
Energy Balance Blend
Stress Reduction Blend
Trauma Blend

Applications:

INHALATION:	DIRECT, 3-4 times daily, as needed
TOPICAL:	NEAT, apply 1-2 drops to crown of head and forehead. Best if applied in a quiet, darkened room
	VITA FLEX, massage 1-3 drops on heart Vita Flex points
INGESTION:	SYRUP, 1-2 times daily

Additional regimens:

Place 1-3 drops of Emotional Release Blend over the thymus and rub in gently. Apply up to 3 times daily as needed.

Blend equal parts frankincense and Energy Balance Blend and apply 1-2 drops neat on temples, forehead, crown and back of neck before retiring. Use for 3 nights.

ENDOCRINE SYSTEM

The endocrine system encompasses the hormone-producing glands of the body. These glands cluster around blood vessels and release their hormones directly into the bloodstream. The pituitary gland exerts a wide range of control over the hormonal (endocrine) system and is often called the master gland. Other glands include the pancreas, adrenals, thyroid and parathyroid, ovaries, and testes. The limbic system lies along the margin of the cerebral cortex (brain) and is the hormone-producing system of the brain. It includes the amygdala, hippocampus, pineal, pituitary, thalamus, and hypothalamus.

Essential oils increase circulation to the brain. This enables the pituitary and other glands to secrete neural transmitters and hormones that support the endocrine and immune systems.

The thyroid is one of the most important glands for regulating the body systems. The hypothalamus plays an even more important role, since it not only regulates the thyroid, but the adrenals and the pituitary gland as well.

The following oils are endocrine supportive

Single Oils:

Fleabane *(Conyza canadensis)*
Helichrysum *(Helichrysum italicum)*
Lemon verbena *(Lippia citriodora)*
Nutmeg *(Myristica fragrans)*
Clove *(Syzygium aromaticum)*
Rosemary cineol *(Rosmarinus officinalis CT 1,8 cineol)*
Spearmint *(Mentha spicata)*

Blends:

Glandular Blend
Energy Blend

Applications:

INGESTION:	CAPSULE, 0 size, 2 capsules per day
INHALATION:	DIRECT, three times daily
	DIFFUSER, 15 minutes 3 times daily
TOPICAL:	VITA FLEX, massage 1-3 drops on Vita Flex points for the glands on feet

Additional regimen:

Place 1-2 drops of Glandular Blend on the tongue, the roof of the mouth, the thyroid and adrenals, and the Vita Flex points for these glands on the feet.

EPILEPSY

Single Oils:

Clary sage *(Salvia sclarea)*
Jasmine *(Jasminum officinale)*

Blends:

Energy Balance Blend
Brain Blend

Applications:

INHALATION:	DIRECT, 4 times per day as needed.
TOPICAL:	DILUTE 50-50, apply 1-3 drops on back of neck and behind ears 2-3 times daily
	VITA FLEX, massage 2-4 drops on brain Vita Flex points on feet

NOTE: If epileptic, avoid basil, wintergreen or birch, fennel, hyssop, tansy, sage, nutmeg, tarragon and rosemary cineol.

EPSTEIN-BARR VIRUS

(See HYPOGLYCEMIA, FATIGUE, THYROID, ADRENAL)

Generally associated with Chronic Fatigue Syndrome. Symptoms include indigestion, upper and lower gas, poor assimilation, poor electrolyte balance, allergic reaction to foods and other substances, emotional mood swings, fatigue, irritability, and a lack of motivation, discipline, and creativity.

Hypoglycemia is a precursor and can render the body susceptible to the Epstein-Barr virus. Controlling hypoglycemia may reduce or eliminate many symptoms of Epstein-Barr/Chronic Fatigue Syndrome.

Singles Oils:

Thyme thymol *(Thymus vulgaris CT thymol)*
Clove *(Syzygium aromaticum)*
Grapefruit *(Citrus x paradisi)*
Nutmeg *(Myristica fragrans)*
Blue tansy *(Tanacetum annuum)*
Mountain savory *(Satureja montana)*
Oregano *(Origanum compactum)*

Blends:
Immune Blend
Glandular Blend
Antimicrobial Blend
Antiviral Blend

Applications:

INGESTION:	CAPSULE, 00 size, 1 capsules 3 times daily
TOPICAL:	RAINDROP Technique, weekly with Immune Blend
INHALATION:	DIRECT, 4-5 times daily

EXPECTORANT

(See MUCUS)

EYE DISORDERS

In 1997, Dr. Terry Friedmann, MD eliminated his need for glasses after using sandalwood and juniper around the opening of his eyes above the eyebrow and around cheeks only (being careful never to get oil into eyes).

NOTE: Never place oils in eyes or on eyelids.

Blocked Tear Ducts

Single Oils:
Lavender *(Lavandula angustifolia)*

Applications:
1 drop lavender oil rubbed over the bridge of the nose may provide relief.

Cataracts and Glaucoma

Cataracts are a clouding of the eye lens that often comes with aging. Glaucoma is a condition caused by an abnormal buildup of intraocular pressure in the eye.

Single Oils:
Clove *(Syzygium aromaticum)*

Clove oil is the most powerful known antioxidant and when taken internally it can slow or prevent both cataracts and glaucoma.

APPLICATION:

INGESTION:	CAPSULE, 0 size, 2-3 times daily

Blends:

Eye Blend #1:
- 10 drops lemongrass
- 5 drops cypress
- 3 drops *Eucalyptus radiata*

Eye Blend #2:
- 10 drops lemon
- 5 drops cypress
- 3 drops *Eucalyptus radiata*

Applications:

TOPICAL: DILUTE 20-80, apply 2-4 drops in a wide circle around the eye, being careful not get any oil in the eye or on the eyelid, 1-3 times daily. This may also help with puffiness. Also apply on temples and eye Vita Flex points on the feet and hands (the undersides of your two largest toes and your index, and middle fingers).

NOTE: If essential oils should ever accidentally get into the eyes, dilute with a pure vegetable oil. NEVER rinse with water.

FAINTING

(See SHOCK)

Single Oils:

Peppermint *(Mentha piperita)*
Sandalwood *(Santalum album)*
Cardamom *(Elettaria cardamomum)*
Spearmint *(Mentha spicata)*

Blends:

Clarity Blend
Brain Blend

Applications:

INHALATION: DIRECT, 1-2 times as needed

FATIGUE

(See also HYPOGLYCEMIA, FUNGAL INFECTIONS, EPSTEIN- BARR VIRUS THYROID IMBALANCES or ADRENAL GLAND IMBALANCES)

A lack of energy can be due to a host of factors, including low thyroid hormone activity or adrenal hormone imbalance. Other factors may also play a part, including diabetes, cancer, and other conditions.

Single Oils:

Lemongrass *(Cymbopogon flexuosus)*
Juniper *(Juniperus communis* or *J. osteosperma)*
Basil *(Ocimum basilicum)*
Lemon *(Citrus limon)*
Peppermint *(Mentha piperita)*
Rosemary cineol *(Rosmarinus officinalis CT 1,8 cineol)*
Nutmeg *(Myristica fragrans)*
Black pepper *(Piper nigrum)*

Blends:

Energy Balance Blend
Mood Lifting Blend
Energy Blend

Applications:

TOPICAL:	DILUTE 50-50, 2-4 drops at base of throat, temples, back of neck VITA FLEX, massage 1-3 drops on relevant Vita Flex points on feet
INHALATION:	DIRECT, 2-4 times daily
INGESTION:	SYRUP, 1-3 times daily

Mental Fatigue

Single Oils:

Black pepper *(Piper nigrum)*
Sage *(Salvia officinalis)*
Peppermint *(Mentha piperita)*
Nutmeg *(Myristica fragrans)*

Blends:

Energy Blend
Energy Balance Blend

Applications:

INHALATION:	DIRECT, 1-2 times as needed
TOPICAL:	DILUTE 50-50, massage 2-4 drops on temples, forehead, crown and back of neck, as needed

FEVER

Fevers are one of the most powerful healing responses orchestrated by the human body, and are especially valuable in fighting infectious diseases. However, if fever raises body temperature excessively (over 104°F) then neurological damage can occur.

Some essential oils are very cooling when applied to the skin and can help reduce fevers. Because of its menthol content, peppermint is used predominately for fever control.

Single Oils:

Peppermint *(Mentha piperita)*
Lavender *(Lavandula angustifolia)*
Ledum *(Ledum groenlandicum)*
Balsam fir *(Abies balsamea)*

Blends:

Immune Blend

Fever Blend recipe

- 10 drops lavender
- 8 drops peppermint
- 3 drops *Eucalyptus radiata*
- 3 drops sandalwood
- 1 drop rosemary

Applications:

TOPICAL:	DILUTE 50-50, apply 1-3 drops to forehead, temples and back of neck.
INGESTION:	RICE MILK, Sip slowly, 1-2 times as needed CAPSULE, 00 size, 1-2 capsules daily, as needed SYRUP, dissolve 1 tsp of syrup/essential oil mixture in an 8 oz. glass of cool water and sip slowly.
INHALATION:	DIRECT, 3-4 times, as needed

FIBROIDS

Fibroids are fairly common benign tumors of the female pelvis that are composed of smooth muscle cells and fibrous connective tissue. Fibroids are not cancerous and neither develop into cancer nor increase a women's cancer risk in the uterus.

Fibroids can have a diameter as small as 1 mm or as large as 8 inches. They can develop in clusters or alone as a single knot or nodule.

Fibroids frequently occur in premenopausal women and are seldom seen in young women who have not begun menstruation. Fibroids usually stabilize or even regress in women who have been through menopause.

Single Oils:

Frankincense *(Boswellia carteri)*
Inula *(Inula graveolens)*
Cistus *(Cistus ladanifer)*
Lavender *(Lavandula angustifolia)*
Tansy *(Tanacetum vulgare)*
Oregano *(Origanum compactum)*
Helichrysum *(Helichrysum italicum)*

Blends:

Energy Balance Blend
Glandular Blend

Applications:

INGESTION:	CAPSULE, 0 size, twice daily
TOPICAL:	COMPRESS, warm, on lower abdomen, daily

FIBROMYALGIA

Fibromyalgia is a autoimmune disorder of soft tissues. (In contrast, arthritis occurs in the joints.) Symptoms include general body pain, in some parts worse than others, usually brought on by short periods of exercise. The pain is ubiquitous and continuous. It interrupts sleep patterns so that the fourth stage of sleep is never attained, and thus the body cannot rejuvenate and heal. Fibromyalgia is an acid condition in which the liver is toxic (see LIVER DISORDERS).

Single Oils:

German chamomile *(Matricaria recutita)*
Nutmeg *(Myristica fragrans)*
Balsam fir *(Abies balsamea)*

Blends:

Pain Relief Blend
Immune Blend

Fibromyalgia Blend #1:
- 8 drops balsam fir
- 6 drops white fir
- 4 drops wintergreen or birch
- 2 drops spruce

Fibromyalgia Blend #2:
- 10 drops Pain Relief Blend
- 8 drops wintergreen or birch
- 8 drops marjoram
- 6 drops spruce

Applications:

TOPICAL:	DILUTE 50-50, gently massage 2-4 drops on pain locations
	COMPRESS, warm, on pain location, 3 times weekly
	BODY MASSAGE, weekly
	RAINDROP Technique, adding Immune blend, weekly
INGESTION:	CAPSULE, 0 size, twice daily

FLATULENCE

(See DIGESTIVE PROBLEMS)

FLU (Influenza)

The antiviral oils are powerful prophylactic agents for protection against the flu. These include basil, hyssop, rosemary cineol, bergamot, *Eucalyptus radiata, Melaleuca alternifolia,* clove, oregano, cistus, thyme, and mountain savory.

Single Oils:

Tea tree oil *(Melaleuca alternifolia)*
Basil *(Ocimum basilicum)*
Cistus *(Cistus ladanifer)*
Thyme *(Thymus vulgaris)*
Clove *(Syzygium aromaticum)*
Oregano *(Origanum compactum)*
Mountain savory *(Satureja montana)*
Oregano *(Origanum compactum)*
Eucalyptus radiata
Myrtle *(Myrtus communis)*
Peppermint *(Mentha piperita)*

Blends:

Immune Blend
Digestive Blend
Antimicrobial Blend
Antiviral Blend

Applications:

INGESTION:	RICE MILK, 2-4 times daily
	CAPSULE, 00 size, 1 capsule 3 times daily
INHALATION:	DIRECT, 2-4 times daily
TOPICAL:	DILUTE 50-50, 2-4 drops on chest, stomach or lower back, as needed, 2-3 times daily
	RAINDROP Technique, 1-2 times weekly
	COMPRESS, warm, over lower abdomen, 1-2 times daily
	BATH SALT, (see below)

Flu Recipe for bath

- 2 drops *Eucalyptus radiata*
- 6 drops frankincense
- 3 drops helichrysum
- 6 drops spruce
- 15 drops ravensara
- 1 drop wintergreen or birch

Stir above essential oils into 1/4 cup Epsom salt or baking soda, then add mixture to hot bath water while tub is filling. Soak in hot bath until water cools.

FOOD POISONING

Food poisoning is caused by a variety of food-borne pathogens, including *listeria*, *shigella*, *E. coli* and *salmonella*. The antibacterial properties of essential oils are such that—unlike antibiotics—they can kill off these pathogens without significantly disrupting beneficial intestinal flora.

Single Oils:

Tarragon *(Artemisia dracunculus)*
Thyme thymol *(Thymus vulgaris CT thymol)*
Clove *(Syzygium aromaticum)*
Oregano *(Origanum compactum)*
Patchouli *(Pogostemon cablin)*

Blends:
Digestive Blend
Antibacterial Blend
Antimicrobial Blend

Applications:

INGESTION: CAPSULE, 00 size, 2 capsules, 2-3 times per day until symptoms end

FOOT PROBLEMS

Athlete's Foot

Athlete's foot is a fungal infection of the skin similar to ringworm (See FUNGAL INFECTIONS). This fungus thrives in the warm, moist environment to which many feet are subjected.

The best remedy is to keep feet cool and dry and avoid wearing tight-fitting shoes or heavy natural (ie. cotton) socks. Wear sandals, shoes, and socks woven from a light, breathable fabric.

It is especially important to control this fungus infection during showering or bathing, since the moist, warm environment favors the growth of the *Tinea* culture responsible for athlete's foot. Antifungal essential oils such as tea tree and Antiseptic Blend can be added to bath salts and used in a dispenser shower head to create a mild, antifungal shower.

Single Oils:
Tea tree oil *(Melaleuca alternifolia)*
Balsam fir *(Abies balsamea)*
Lavender *(Lavandula angustifolia)*
Peppermint *(Mentha piperita)*
Manuka *(Leptospermum scoparium)*
Lemongrass *(Cymbopogon flexuosus)*

Blends:
Antiseptic Blend
Antimicrobial Blend

Athlete's foot blend #1:

- 8 drops *Melaleuca alternifolia*
- 2 drops lavender

Athlete's foot blend #2:
- 8 drops *Melaleuca alternifolia*
- 4 drops peppermint
- 2 drops mountain savory

Applications:

TOPICAL:	NEAT or DILUTE 50-50 as needed. Apply 5-7 drops to affected areas between toes and around toenails BATH SALT, daily

Blisters on Feet

(see BLISTERS)

Bunions

Bunions are caused from bursitis at the base of a toe. (See BURSITIS)

Bunion Recipe:
- 6 drops *Eucalyptus radiata*
- 3 drops lemon
- 4 drops ravensara
- 1 drop wintergreen or birch

Applications:

TOPICAL:	NEAT or DILUTE 50-50, if needed. Apply 2-4 drops over bunion area, twice daily

Sore Feet

Single Oils:

Peppermint *(Mentha piperita)*
Balsam fir *(Abies balsamea)*
Lavender *(Lavandula angustifolia)*
Helichrysum *(Helichrysum italicum)*
Wintergreen or birch *(Gaultheria procumbens* or *Betula alleghaniensis)*

Blends:

Antiseptic Blend
Pain Relief Blend

Applications:

TOPICAL: DILUTE 50-50, massage 6-9 drops onto each foot
COMPRESS, warm, for added effect and penetration
BATH SALT, mix 10 drops essential oil in 1 tbsp Epsom salt and add to hot water in a basin large enough for footbath

FRIGIDITY

(See SEXUAL DYSFUNCTIONS)

FUNGAL INFECTIONS (Candida)

Fungi and yeast feed on decomposing or dead tissues. They exist everywhere: inside our stomachs, on our skin, and out on the lawn. When kept under control, the yeast and fungi populating our bodies are harmless and digest what our bodies cannot or do not use.

When we feed the naturally occurring fungi in our bodies too many acid-ash foods, such as sugar, animal proteins, and dairy products, the fungal populations grow out of control. This condition is known as systemic candidiasis and is marked by fungi invading the blood, gastrointestinal tract, and tissues.

Fungal cultures such as candida excrete large amounts of poisons called mycotoxins as part of their life cycles. These poisons must be detoxified by the liver and immune systems. Eventually they can wreak enormous damage on the tissues and organs and are believed to be an aggravating factor in many degenerative diseases, such as cancer, arteriosclerosis, and diabetes.

Symptoms of Systemic Fungal Infection:

- Fatigue/low energy
- Low resistance to illness
- Unbalanced blood sugar
- Irritability
- Indigestion
- Diarrhea/constipation
- Rectal or vaginal itch
- Overweight
- Allergies
- Headaches
- Mood swings
- Colitis and ulcers
- Urinary tract infections

Single Oils:

Tea tree oil *(Melaleuca alternifolia)*
Juniper *(Juniperus communis* or *J. osteosperma)*
Ravensara *(Ravensara aromatica)*
Thyme thymol *(Thymus vulgaris CT thymol)*

> **Using Raindrop Technique to Purge Pathogenic Fungi**
>
> Pathogenic microorganisms have a tendency to hibernate along the spinal cord and in the lymphatic system. The body has the ability to hold them in a suspended state for long periods of time. When the immune system becomes compromised from stress, fatigue or other factors, they can be released and manifest illness and disease.
>
> Oregano, thyme, or hyssop along the spine using Raindrop Technique may help to drive the dormant fungi out of the spinal fluid.
>
> Additionally, lymphatic pump therapy will revitalize a sluggish lymphatic system to better combat pathogenic fungi. (see Chapter 12)

Lemongrass *(Cymbopogon flexuosus)*
Rosemary cineol *(Rosmarinus officinalis CT 1,8 cineol)*
Cumin *(Cuminum cyminum)*
Peppermint *(Mentha piperita)*
Palmarosa *(Cymbopogon martinii)*
Rosewood *(Aniba rosaeodora)*
Cistus *(Cistus landanifer)*

Blends:

Antiseptic Blend
Respiratory Blend
Immune Blend
Antibacterial Blend
Antimicrobial Blend

Applications:

TOPICAL:	DILUTE 50-50 or 20-80, as needed, massage 3-4 drops on thymus (at the clavical notch which is at the front center of the collarbone at base of throat) to stimulate the immune system. Also apply to bottoms of the feet, and on the chest; massage 5-10 drops on stomach
	VITA FLEX, massage 2-3 drops on relevant Vita Flex points of feet
	BATH SALT, daily
INGESTION:	CAPSULE, 0 size, 1 capsule 2-3 times daily between meals
	RICE MILK, 3 times daily between meals

Ringworm and Skin Candida

The ringworm fungus infects the skin causing scaly round itchy patches. It is infectious and can be spread from an animal or human host alike. Skin candida is a fungal infection that can erupt almost anywhere on the skin. It shows up in various places, such as behind the knees, inside the elbows, behind the ears, on temple area, and between the breasts.

Single Oils:

Tea tree oil *(Melaleuca alternifolia)*
Lavender *(Lavandula angustifolia)*
Rosemary cineol *(Rosmarinus officinalis CT 1,8 cineol)*
Geranium *(Pelargonium graveolens)*
Rosewood *(Aniba rosaeodora)*
Myrrh *(Commiphora myrrha)*

Blends:

Antiseptic Blend
Respiratory Blend

Ringworm Blend:

- 3 drops *Melaleuca alternifolia*
- 3 drops spearmint
- 1 drop peppermint
- 1 drop rosemary

Skin Candida Blend:

- 2 drops tansy
- 10 drops *Melaleuca alternifolia*
- 1 drop oregano
- 2 drops patchouli

Combating Ringworm

Using antifungal essential oils while bathing or showering is especially important because fungal infections thrive in moist, warm environments. Essential oils like *Melaleuca alternifolia* or Antiseptic Blend can easily be added to bath salts or Epsom salts to combat fungal infections.

There are specially designed shower heads that can be filled with bath salts and essential oils. As the water passes over the mixture, it disperses the essential oils and salts into the shower spray, creating an antiseptic spa.

Applications:

TOPICAL:	NEAT, massage 2-4 drops over affected area, then layer on a sealing antiseptic ointment, 2-4 times daily, In severe cases, use 35 percent food-grade hydrogen peroxide to clean infected areas before applying Antiseptic Blend. Saturate gauze with oils and wrap the infected area.

Thrush (Candida albicans)

Thrush is a fungal infection of the mouth and throat marked by creamy, curd-like patches in the oral cavity. Even though it appears in the mouth, thrush is usually a sign of systemic fungal overgrowth throughout the body. Thrush can usually be treated locally through the use of antifungal essential oils.

Single Oils:

Cinnamon *(Cinnamomum verum)*
Clove *(Syzygium aromaticum)*
Peppermint *(Mentha piperita)*
Rosemary cineol *(Rosmarinus officinalis CT 1,8 cineol)*
Lemongrass *(Cymbopogon flexuosus)*
Rosewood *(Aniba rosaeodora)*
Orange *(Citrus aurantium)*
Lavender *(Lavandula angustifolia)*

Blends:

Antimicrobial Blend
Antiseptic Blend
Antibacterial Blend
Immune Blend

Applications:

TOPICAL:	DILUTE 50-50 or 20-80, as needed, massage 3-4 drops on thymus (at the clavical notch which is at the front center of the collarbone at base of throat) to stimulate the immune system. Also apply 1-3 drops to bottoms of the feet, and on the chest; massage 5-10 drops on stomach
	VITA FLEX, massage 2-3 drops on relevant Vita Flex points of feet
INGESTION:	CAPSULE, 0 size, 1 capsule 2-3 times daily between meals
	RICE MILK, 3 times daily between meals

NOTE: the above applications are for adults, not infants. In cases of infants with thrush, consult a medical professional first.

Vaginal Yeast Infection

Vaginal yeast infections are usually caused from overgrowth of fungi like *Candida albicans*. These naturally occurring intestinal yeast and fungi are normally kept under control by the immune system, but when excess sucrose is consumed or antibiotics are used, these organisms convert from relatively harmless yeast into an invasive, harmful fungus that secretes toxins as part of its life cycle.

Vaginal yeast infections are just one symptom of systemic fungal infestation. While the yeast infection can be treated locally, the underlying problem of systemic candidiasis may still remain unless specific dietary and health practices are used.

Essential oils like *Melaleuca alternifolia, M. quinquenervia* and *Thymus vulgaris* have been documented to have highly antifungal activity. Good results have been obtained on vaginal yeast infections using these oils in douches.

Single Oils:

Lavender *(Lavandula angustifolia)*
Manuka *(Leptospermum scoparium)*
Tea tree oil *(Melaleuca alternifolia)*
Rosemary cineol *(Rosmarinus officinalis CT 1,8 cineol)*
Rosewood *(Aniba rosaeodora)*
Peppermint *(Mentha piperita)*
Spearmint *(Mentha spicata)*
Mountain savory *(Satureja montana)*
Thyme linalol *(Thymus vulgaris CT linalol)*

Blends:

Antiseptic Blend
Antibacterial Blend

Vaginal Yeast Infection Blend #1

- 14 drops Antibacterial Blend
- 10 drops frankincense
- 6 drops mountain savory

Vaginal Yeast Infection Blend #2:

- 10 drops juniper
- 10 drops lavender
- 10 drops *Melaleuca alternifolia*

Vaginal Yeast Infection Blend #3:

- 12 drops *Melaleuca alternifolia*
- 6 drops Antibacterial Blend
- 12 drops juniper

Applications:

RETENTION:	TAMPON, nightly for 5-10 days, as needed
INGESTION:	CAPSULE, 00 size, 1 capsule 3 times daily

GALLBLADDER INFECTION

The gallbladder stores bile created by the liver and releases it through the biliary ducts into the duodenum to promote digestion. Bile is extremely important for fat digestion and the absorption of vitamins such as A, D, and E.

When bile flow is obstructed due to gallstones or inflamed due to infection, serious consequences can ensue, including poor digestion, jaundice, and severe abdominal pain.

Single Oils:

Lemon *(Citrus limon)*
Ledum *(Ledum groenlandicum)*
Carrot seed *(Daucus carota)*
Celery seed *(Leptospermum scoparium)*
Juniper *(Juniperus communis* or *J. osteosperma)*
German chamomile *(Matricaria recutita)*

Blends:

Liver Blend

Applications:

INGESTION:	CAPSULE, 00 size, 1 capsule 3 times daily
TOPICAL:	NEAT, apply 6-10 drops over gallbladder area, 2-3 times daily
	COMPRESS, warm, 2-3 times daily
	VITA FLEX, massage 1-3 drops on liver Vita Flex points of the feet

GALLSTONES

When bile contains excessive cholesterol, bilirubin, or bile salts, gallstones can form. Stones made from hardened cholesterol account for the vast majority of gallstones, while stones made from bilirubin, the brownish pigment in bile, constitute only about 20 percent of gallstones.

Gallstones can block both bile flow and the passage of pancreatic enzymes. This can result in inflammation in the gallbladder (cholecystitis) or pancreas (pancreatitis) and jaundice. In some cases, gallstones can be life-threatening, depending where they are lodged.

Several studies have shown that limonene effectively and safely dissolves gallstones. Research at the Yamamato Surgical Hospital as well as the Kagawa Medical School in Japan demonstrated the use of limonene as a non-invasive treatment for gallstones in 8 patients. Limonene is found in large quantities in lemon, orange, grapefruit, tangerine, and mandarin essential oils. (Uchida et al., 1994; Yamamoto et al., 1993; Igimi et al., 1992; Vergunst et al., 1991.)

Single Oils:

Orange *(Citrus aurantium)*
Mandarin *(Citrus reticulata)*
Grapefruit *(Citrus paradisi)*
Juniper *(Juniperus communis* or *J. osteosperma)*
Nutmeg *(Myristica fragrans)*

Blends:

Liver Blend

Gall Bladder Blend:

- 2 drops ledum
- 1 drop Roman chamomile
- 1 drop lavender
- 1 drop rosemary cineol
- 1 drop geranium
- 1 drop juniper

Applications:

INGESTION:	CAPSULE: 0 size, 2 per day for 2 weeks.
TOPICAL:	DILUTE 50-50, massage 6-10 drops over gallbladder twice daily COMPRESS, 2-3 times daily VITA FLEX, massage 1-3 drops on liver Vita Flex points of feet

Risk Factors For Gallstones

- Being overweight. Obesity decreases gallbladder emptying and results in a significantly higher risk for gallstones.
- Being over 60 years old
- Being female and middle-aged (age 20-60)
- Using excess estrogen from hormone replacement or birth control pills.
- Using cholesterol-lowering drugs. While these drugs can lower cholesterol in the bloodstream, they can raise cholesterol in the gallbladder.
- Being diabetic. Diabetics suffer higher levels of triglycerides, which can increase the likelihood of getting gallstones.
- Rapid weight loss forces the liver to pump out extra cholesterol, which can become concentrated in the bile.

GANGRENE

Gangrene is the death or decay of living tissue caused by a lack of blood supply. A shortage of blood can result from a blood clot, arteriosclerosis, frostbite, diabetes, infection, or some other obstruction in the arterial blood supply. Gas gangrene (also known as acute or moist gangrene) occurs when tissues are infected with *Clostridium* bacteria. Unless the limb is amputated or treated with antibiotics, the gangrene can be fatal.

The part of the body affected with gangrene displays the following symptoms:

- Coldness
- Dark in color
- Looks rotten/decomposed
- Putrid smell

Other symptoms include:
- Fever
- Anemia

Dr. René Gattefossé suffered gaseous gangrene as a result of burns from a chemical explosion at the turn of the century. He successfully engineered his own recovery with the use of pure lavender oil.

NOTE: As with all serious medical conditions, consult your health care professional immediately if you suspect gangrene.

Single Oils:

Oregano *(Origanum compactum)*
Lavender *(Lavandula angustifolia)*
Mountain savory *(Satureja montana)*
Thyme *(Thymus vulgaris)*
Ravensara *(Ravensara aromatica)*
Cistus *(Cistus ladanifer)*
Blue cypress *(Callitris intratropica)*

Blends:

Antimicrobial Blend
Immune Blend
Antiseptic Blend

Applications:

TOPICAL:	DILUTE 20-80, apply 2-4 drops on affected area, 3-5 times daily
	COMPRESS, warm, 3 times daily, every other day

GASTRITIS

(See DIGESTIVE PROBLEMS)

Gastritis occurs when the stomach's mucosal lining becomes inflamed and the cells become eroded. This can lead to bleeding ulcers and severe digestive disturbances. Gastritis may be caused by excess acid production in the stomach, alcohol consumption, stress, and fungal or bacterial infections.

Symptoms of gastritis:

- Weight loss
- Abdominal pain
- Cramping

Single Oils:

Tarragon *(Artemisia dracunculus)*
Peppermint *(Mentha piperita)*
Fennel *(Foeniculum vulgare)*

Blends:

Digestive Blend

Applications:

INGESTION:	CAPSULE, 0 size, twice daily for 7 days
TOPICAL:	COMPRESS, warm, as needed

GINGIVITIS, PYORRHEA

(See PERIODONTAL DISEASE)

Essential oils are of the best treatments against gum diseases such as gingivitis and pyorrhea. Clove oil, for example, is used as dental disinfectant; and the active principle in clove oil, eugenol, is one of the best-studied germ-killers available. Manuka is also highly anti-bacterial.

GLAUCOMA

(See EYE DISORDERS)

Common among people over 30 years of age, glaucoma is an eye disease in which escalating pressure within the fluid of the eye eventually damages the optic nerve and causes blindness. Many people are unaware that they have the disease until their peripheral vision is permanently lost.

Glaucoma usually develops in middle age or later, although glaucoma in newborns, children, and teenagers can occur.

GOUT

(See KIDNEY DISORDERS) (for pain see JOINT STIFNESS & PAIN)

Gout is a disease marked by abrupt, temporary bouts of joint pain and swelling that are most evident in the joint of the big toe. It can also affect the wrist, elbow, knee, ankle, hand, and foot. As the disease progresses, pain and swelling in the joints become more frequent and chronic, with deposits called "tophi" appearing over many joints, including the elbows and on ears.

Gout is characterized by accumulation of uric acid crystals in the joints caused by excess uric acid in the blood. Uric acid is a byproduct of the breakdown of protein that is normally excreted by the kidneys into the urine. To reduce uric acid concentrations, it is necessary to support the kidneys, adrenal, and immune functions. It is also necessary to detoxify by cleansing and drinking plenty of fluids.

Excess alcohol, allergy-producing foods, or strict diets can cause outbreaks of gout. Foods rich in purines, such as wine, anchovies, and animal liver, can also cause gout.

Single Oils:

Geranium *(Pelargonium graveolens)*
Ledum *(Ledum groenlandicum)*
Carrot seed *(Daucus carota)*
Celery seed *(Leptospermum scoparium)*
Juniper *(Juniperus communis* or *J. osteosperma)*
Roman chamomile *(Chamaemelum nobile)*
Lemon *(Citrus limon)*

Blends:

Pain Relief Blend
Liver Blend

Gout Blend:

- 10 drops geranium
- 8 drops juniper
- 5 drops rosemary cineol
- 3 drops Roman chamomile
- 4 drops lemon
- 8 drops *Melaleuca alternifolia*

Applications:

INGESTION:	CAPSULE, 0 size, 1 capsules 3 times daily for 10 days, then rest 4 days, repeat as needed RICE MILK, 3 times daily
TOPICAL:	NEAT, gently massage 1-3 drops on affected joints 2-3 times daily

GRAVE'S DISEASE

(See THYROID)

GUM DISEASE

(See PERIODONTAL DISEASE)

HAIR AND SCALP PROBLEMS

Sulfur is the single most important mineral for maintaining the strength and integrity of the hair and hair follicle.

Cedarwood helps augment natural hair color. Clary sage supports the hair follicle. Lavender in shampoo helps to balance skin pH, decongest the lymphatics, and stimulate circulation. Rosemary adds body and conditions the hair.

Single Oils:

Rosemary cineol *(Rosmarinus officinalis CT 1,8 cineol)*
Lavender *(Lavandula angustifolia)*
Clary sage *(Salvia sclarea)*
Cedarwood *(Cedrus atlantica)*
Basil *(Ocimum basilicum)*
Ylang Ylang *(Cananga odorata)*
Juniper *(Juniperus communis* or *J. osteosperma)*
Sandalwood *(Santalum album)*
Lemon *(Citrus limon)*
Cypress *(Cupressus sempervirens)*
Rosewood *(Aniba rosaeodora)*

Blends:

Blend for Dry Hair

- 2 drops ylang ylang
- 8 drops rosewood
- 4 drops geranium

Blend for Oily Hair

- 6 drops patchouli
- 2 drops lavender
- 6 drops lemon

Applications:

TOPICAL: DILUTE 20-80, massage 1 tsp into the scalp vigorously and thoroughly for 2-3 minutes; leave on scalp for 60-90 minutes. (An excellent time to do this would be during an exercise routine). Mix 2-4 drops of essential oils with 1-2 teaspoons of shampoo to wash hair after exercising.

A rinse to help restore the acid mantle of the hair:

- 1 drop rosemary cineol,
- 1 tsp. pure apple cider vinegar
- 8 oz. water.

Use as a final rinse on hair. Rub 1 or 2 drops on as hairdressing or on hairbrush to prevent static electricity.

Premature Graying

This condition is thought to be from a deficiency of biotin, an important B vitamin.

Sandalwood oil retards graying. Rosewood will lighten hair color.

Dandruff

Single Oils:
Tea tree oil *(Melaleuca alternifolia)*
Rosemary cineol *(Rosmarinus officinalis CT 1,8 cineol*)
Cedarwood *(Cedrus atlantica)*

Blends:

Dandruff Blend
- 5 drops lemon
- 1 drop rosemary cineol or sage
- 1 drop lavender

Applications:

TOPICAL: DILUTE 50-50, massage 1 tsp into the scalp vigorously and thoroughly for 2-3 minutes; leave on scalp for 60-90 minutes. (An excellent time to do this would be during an exercise routine). Mix 2-4 drops of essential oils with 1-2 teaspoons of shampoo to wash hair after exercising.

Hair Loss

(See ALOPECIA AREATA)

Hair loss is caused by hormonal imbalances (such as abnormal increase in testosterone), or auto-immune conditions (as in the case of alopecia areata).

Essential oils are excellent for cleansing, nourishing, and strengthening the hair follicle and shaft. Rosemary (cineol chemotype) encourages hair growth.

Single Oils:

Lavender *(Lavandula angustifolia)*
Rosemary cineol *(Rosmarinus officinalis CT 1,8 cineol)*
Cedarwood *(Cedrus atlantica)*
Sandalwood *(Santalum album)*
Clary sage *(Salvia sclerea)*

Blends:

Hair loss prevention blend #1:

- 3 drops rosemary cineol
- 5 drops lavender
- 4 drops cypress
- 2 drops clary sage
- 2 drops juniper

Add 10 drops of the above blend to 1 tsp. of fractionated coconut oil and massage into the scalp where it is balding; then rub gently into the remainder of the scalp. This works best when done at night.

Hair loss prevention blend #2:

- 10 drops cedarwood
- 8 drops rosemary cineol
- 10 drops sandalwood
- 10 drops lavender

Hair loss prevention blend #3:

- 6 drops rosemary cineol
- 8 drops ylang ylang
- 12 drops cedarwood
- 12 drops clary sage

Applications:

TOPICAL: DILUTE 50-50, massage 1 tsp. into the scalp vigorously and thoroughly for 2-3 minutes; leave on scalp for 60-90 minutes. (An excellent time to do this would be during an exercise routine). Mix 2-4 drops of essential oils with 1-2 teaspoons of shampoo to wash hair after exercising

HALITOSIS (Bad Breath)

Persistent bad breath or gum disease, may be a sign of poor digestion or other health problems.

(See DIGESTION PROBLEMS and GUMS).

Single Oils:

Nutmeg *(Myristica fragrans)*
Clove *(Syzygium aromaticum)*
Cinnamon *(Cinnamomum verum)*

Spearmint *(Mentha spicata)*
Peppermint *(Mentha piperita)*
Tarragon *(Artemisia dracunculus)*

Blends:
Antimicrobial Blend

Bad Breath Blend:
- 4 drops spearmint
- 2 drops mandarin
- 2 drops cinnamon

Disinfectant mouthwash:
- 3 drops peppermint
- 2 drops lemon
- 2 drops clove
- 1 drop tea tree oil

Applications:

ORAL:	GARGLE, 2-4 times daily as needed
	TONGUE, 2-4 times daily as needed

HASHIMOTO'S THYROIDITIS

(See THYROID)

HEAD LICE

Headlice treatments contain many questionable chemicals. A safe alternative can be found using essential oils. Studies in Iceland showed the effectiveness against headlice of the essential oils of aniseed, cinnamon leaf, red thyme, tea tree *(Melaleuca alternifolia)*, peppermint, and nutmeg in shampoo and rinse solutions.[14]

Single Oils:
Eucalyptus radiata
Lavender *(Lavandula angustifolia)*
Peppermint *(Mentha piperita)*
Thyme *(Thymus vulgaris)*
Geranium *(Pelargonium graveolens)*

14. Veal L, "The potential effectiveness of essential oils as a treatment for headlice, Pediculus humanus capitis," *Complement Ther Nurs Midwifery* 1996 Aug;2(4):97-101.

Blends:

Head lice oil blend:

- 4 drops *Eucalyptus radiata*
- 2 drop lavender
- 2 drop geranium

Applications:

TOPICAL: DILUTE 50-50, 1 tsp. applied to scalp. Massage into entire scalp, cover with disposable shower cap and leave for at least 1/2 hour. Then shampoo and rise well. Use the rinse below.

Head lice rinse:

- 2 drops *Eucalyptus radiata*
- 2 drops lavender
- 2 drops geranium
- 1/2 oz. vinegar
- 8 oz. water

Mix into a container with a lid. Shake vigorously, then pour over hair making sure every strand is rinsed. This should be done leaning over bathtub or sink. This is not recommended if you are still in the bathtub as lice may cling to other body hairs. Dry naturally. Repeat daily until lice and eggs are gone.

HEADACHES

Headaches can be due to hormone imbalances, stress, sugar imbalance (hypoglycemia), deyhdration, or shortage of oxygen. Essential oils are known to improve circulation, helping to bring more oxygen to cells.

(see also PREMENSTRUAL SYNDROME, STRESS, HYPOGLYCEMIA)

Single Oils:

Peppermint *(Mentha piperita)*
Balsam fir *(Abies balsamea)*
German chamomile *(Matricaria recutita)*
Roman chamomile *(Chamaemelum nobile)*
Lavender *(Lavandula angustifolia)*
Basil *(Ocimum basilicum)*
Eucalyptus globulus
Valerian *(Valeriana officinalis)*
Spearmint *(Mentha spicata)*
Lemon *(Citrus limon)*
Rosemary cineol *(Rosmarinus officinalis CT 1,8 cineol)*

Blends:

Headache Blend
Brain Blend
Clarity Blend
Pain Relief Blend

Alternate headache blend #1:

- 4 drops tansy
- 5 drops Roman chamomile
- 2 drops peppermint
- 2 drops lavender
- 1 drop basil
- 3 drops rosemary cineol

Alternate headache blend #2:

- 2 drops tansy
- 1 drop Roman chamomile
- 3 drops spearmint
- 7 drops lavender

Applications:

INHALATION:	DIFFUSER, 15 minutes 3-5 times daily DIRECT, 3-8 times daily as needed
TOPICAL:	DILUTE 50-50, apply 1-3 drops on back of neck, behind ears, on temples, on forehead, and under nose. Be careful to keep away from eyes and eyelids.
ORAL:	TONGUE, place a drop on the tongue then push against the roof of the mouth

Hormonal Imbalance Headache

(see PREMENSTRUAL SYNDROME)

Migraines (vascular-type headaches)

Many migraine headaches may be due to colon congestion or poor digestion.

(see DIGESTION PROBLEMS)

Single Oils:

Helichrysum *(Helichrysum italicum)*
Sandalwood *(Santalum album)*
Rosemary cineol *(Rosmarinus officinalis CT 1,8 cineol)*
Basil *(Ocimum basilicum)*

> **Headache from Diffusing Clarity Blend and Brain Blend**
>
> People who get an instant headache from diffusing usually have a blockage related to heavy metals or synthetic chemicals from cosmetics and other topical chemicals.
>
> **Single Oils:** Helichrysum with rosemary cineol, mountain savory.
>
> **Blends:** Circulation Blend, Headache Blend, and Clarity Blend.
>
> Apply helichrysum, rosemary CT cineol, Circulation Blend. and Headache Blend to the arteries in the neck or along upper parts of wrists or on other pulse points where arteries are closest to the surface of the skin.

Peppermint *(Mentha piperita)*
Lavender *(Lavandula angustifolia)*
German chamomile *(Matricaria recutita)*
Eucalyptus radiata
Marjoram *(Origanum majorana)*

Blends:
Headache Blend
Clarity Blend

Applications:

TOPICAL:	NEAT, Apply 1-2 drops to temples, at base of neck, in center of forehead, and at nostril openings. Also massage on thumbs and big toes
INHALATION:	DIRECT, as needed

Tension Headache (see Stress)

Single Oils:
Balsam fir *(Abies balsamea)*
Lavender *(Lavandula angustifolia)*
Marjoram *(Origanum majorana)*
Lemongrass *(Cymbopogon flexuosus)*
Rosemary cineol *(Rosmarinus officinalis CT 1,8 cineol)*
Peppermint *(Mentha piperita)*
Valerian *(Valeriana officinalis)*
Cardamom *(Elettaria cardamomum)*

Blends:

Headache Blend
Muscle Relaxing Blend

Applications:

TOPICAL: DILUTE 50-50, apply 1-2 drops around the hairline, on the back of the neck, and across the forehead. Be careful not to use too much, as it will burn if any oil drips near eyes. If this should occur, dilute with a pure vegetable oil. Never with water.

Sinus-Related Headache

(see SINUS INFECTION)

Single Oils:

Rosemary cineol *(Rosmarinus officinalis CT 1,8 cineol)*
Melaleuca ericifolia
Eucalyptus radiata
Lavender *(Lavandula angustifolia)*
Lemon *(Citrus limon)*
Geranium *(Pelargonium graveolens)*

Blends:

Antiseptic Blend

Sinus headache blend:

- 5 drops *Melaleuca ericifolia*
- 9 drops rosemary cineol
- 2 drops bergamot
- 7 drops lavender
- 3 drops lemon
- 4 drops geranium

Applications:

INHALATION: DIRECT, 1-4 times hourly, as needed

HEARING IMPAIRMENT

Single Oils:

Helichrysum *(Helichrysum italicum)*
Juniper *(Juniperus communis* or *J. osteosperma)*
Peppermint *(Mentha piperita)*

Geranium *(Pelargonium graveolens)*
Lavender *(Lavandula angustifolia)*
Basil *(Ocimum basilicum)*

Blends:
Antibacterial Blend
Immune Blend
Antiseptic Blend

Applications:

TOPICAL: NEAT, (1) apply 1 drop essential oil on a cotton ball, then place it carefully in the opening of the ear canal. Retain overnight. Do NOT place oils directly in the ear canal.
NEAT, (2) massage 1-2 drops on each ear lobe, behind the ears, and down the jaw line (along the Eustachian tube).

Hearing Vita Flex Regimen

- Apply 1-2 drops neat helichrysum to the area OUTSIDE the opening to the ear canal with fingertip or cotton swab. Do NOT put oil inside the ear canal
- After applying the helichrysum, hold ear lobes firmly and pull in circular motion 10 times to help stimulate absorption and circulation in the ear canal.

Tinnitus (ringing in the ears)

Single Oils:
Helichrysum *(Helichrysum italicum)*
Juniper *(Juniperus communis* or *J. osteosperma)*
Geranium *(Pelargonium graveolens)*
Peppermint *(Mentha piperita)*
Lavender *(Lavandula angustifolia)*
Basil *(Ocimum basilicum)*

Applications:

TOPICAL: NEAT, massage 1-2 drops on temples and forehead and back of neck. Additionally, apply 1 drop each on tips of toes and fingers, so that the oils get into the Vita Flex pathways. (A change in hearing can often be noticed within 15-20 minutes.) Also, do the Hearing Vita Flex regimen described above.
VITA FLEX, Do the hearing regimen described above

HEART

Many people do not understand how someone relatively healthy, with low cholesterol levels, suffers a heart attack with no explanation. The explanation is actually inflammation.

Inflammation of the heart is caused when blood vessels leading to the heart are clogged and damaged. This released a protein into the bloodstream called C-reactive protein. The level of this protein indicates the degree of inflammation in the linings of the arteries. Certain essential oils have been documented to be excellent for reducing inflammation. German chamomile contains azulene, a blue compound with highly anti-inflammatory properties. Peppermint is also highly anti-inflammatory. Other oils also have anti-inflammatory properties such as helichrysum, spruce, birch or wintergreen, and valerian. Clove, nutmeg and wintergreen are natural blood thinners and help reduce blood clotting.

Magnesium, the most important mineral for the heart, acts as a smooth muscle relaxant and supports the cardiovascular system. Magnesium will act as a natural calcium channel blocker for the heart, lowering blood pressure and dilating the heart blood vessels (according to Terry Friedmann, MD).

Heart Vita Flex

As in all cases of serious medical conditions, you should immediately seek professional medical help if you suspect a heart condition or heart attack. Stimulating the heart Vita Flex centers can provide aid and relief until a medical professional arrives. The foot Vita Flex point related to the heart is on the sole of the left foot, on the ring toe (second toe) and behind the knuckle. The hand Vita Flex point related to the heart is in the palm of the left hand, one inch below the ring finger joint (at the lifeline). A secondary heart point is on the outside of the left upper arm (approximately 2 inches up the arm from the elbow crease), not on the muscle but up under the muscle. If a second person is present, have them use their thumbs to firmly press these two points alternately for 3 minutes, in a kind of pumping action, while you work the heart point on the left foot. Start with the foot point first; then go to the hand and arm, if possible.

Angina

Single Oils:

Ginger *(Zingiber officinale)*
Goldenrod *(Solidago canadensis)*

Blends:

Circulation Blend
Stress Reduction Blend

Applications:

TOPICAL:	NEAT, massage 1-3 drops over heart area 1-3 times daily. Also apply to left chest, left shoulder and back of neck VITA FLEX, massage 1 drop each of 2 or 3 of the recommended oils on heart Vita Flex points on foot, hand, and arm

Fibrillation

Arrhythmia is any variation from a normal heartbeat. Atrial fibrillation is a specific arrhythmia that occurs when the upper heart chambers contract at a rate of over 300 pulsations per minute. The lower chambers cannot keep this pace, so efficiency is reduced and not enough blood is pumped. Palpitations, a feeling that the heart is beating irregularly, more strongly, or more rapidly than normal, is the most common symptom.

Single Oils:

Ylang ylang *(Cananga odorata)*
Marjoram *(Origanum majorana)*
Goldenrod *(Solidago canadensis)*
Valerian *(Valeriana officinalis)*
Lavender *(Lavandula angustifolia)*
Rosemary verbenon *(Rosmarinus officinalis CT verbenon)*
Tansy *(Tanacetum vulgare)*

Blends:

Circulation Blend
Mood Lifting Blend
Stress Reduction Blend

Applications:

TOPICAL:	NEAT, massage 1-3 drops over heart area 1-3 times daily VITA FLEX, massage 1 drop each of 2 or 3 of the recommended oils on heart Vita Flex points on foot, hand, and arm
INHALATION:	DIRECT, as often as needed to bring calm

Heart Attack (Myocardial Infarction)

(See BLOOD CLOTS)

A heart attack is an interruption of the blood supply to an area of the heart. Depending on the size of the area affected, it can be mild or severe. **NOTE:** Contact your physician immediately if you suspect a heart attack.

Single Oils:

Goldenrod *(Solidago canadensis)*
Thyme thymol *(Thymus vulgaris CT thymol)*
Lavender *(Lavandula angustifolia)*
Roman chamomile *(Chamaemelum nobile)*
Helichrysum *(Helichrysum italicum)*
Tansy *(Tanacetum vulgare)*
Clove *(Syzygium aromaticum)*
Nutmeg *(Myristica fragrans)*

Blends:

Circulation Blend
Energy Balance Blend
Stress Reduction Blend
Pain Relief Blend

Applications:

TOPICAL: NEAT, apply 1-2 drops to heart Vita Flex points on foot, hand, and arm as described at beginning of this heading. If there is not enough time to remove shoes to get at the feet, apply the 'pumping' action to left hand and arm points. Using 1-2 drops of Circulation Blend on each point will increase effectiveness and may even revive an individual having a heart attack while waiting for medical attention.

Tachycardia

A form of arrhythmia in which the heart rate suddenly increases to 160 beats per minute or faster. Marjoram and Circulation Blend stimulate regeneration of smooth muscle tissue, particularly in the heart, which may help counteract both tachycardia (rapid heartbeat) or bradycardia (slow heartbeat).

Single Oils:

Goldenrod *(Solidago canadensis)*
Lavender *(Lavandula angustifolia)*
Marjoram *(Origanum majorana)*
Ylang ylang *(Cananga odorata)*
Tansy *(Tanacetum vulgare)*

Blends:

Circulation Blend
Stress Reduction Blend
Mood Lifting Blend

Applications:

TOPICAL:	NEAT, massage 1-3 drops over heart area 1-3 times daily VITA FLEX, massage 1 drop each of 2 or 3 of the recommended oils on heart Vita Flex points on foot,
INHALATION:	DIRECT, as often as needed to bring calm

Tonic—Stimulant

Single Oils:

Goldenrod *(Solidago canadensis)*
Anise seed *(Pimpinella anisum)*
Mandarin *(Citrus reticulata)*
Rosemary cineol *(Rosmarinus officinalis CT 1,8 cineol)*
Peppermint *(Mentha piperita)*
Thyme *(Thymus vulgaris)*
Marjoram *(Origanum majorana)*

Blends:

Circulation Blend

Applications:

TOPICAL:	NEAT, massage 1-3 drops over heart area 1-3 times daily VITA FLEX, massage 1 drop each of 2 or 3 of the recommended oils on heart Vita Flex points on foot, hand, and arm
INHALATION:	DIRECT, as often as needed to bring calm

HEARTBURN

(See HEARTBURN under DIGESTION PROBLEMS)

HEMATOMA

(See BLOOD CLOTS)

A hematoma is a tumor-like mass of coagulated blood, caused by a break in the blood vessel or capillary wall. Essential oils such as helichrysum or geranium are excellent for balancing blood viscosity and dissolving clots. Clove oil and citrus rind oils such as lemon and grapefruit exert a mild blood-thinning effect that can help speed the dissolution of the clot.

Those who bruise easily are usually low in vitamin C, which may be caused by insufficient intake or poor absorption.

Single Oils:

Cypress *(Cupressus sempervirens)*
Helichrysum *(Helichrysum italicum)*
Wintergreen or Birch *(Gaultheria procumbens* or *Betula alleghaniensis)*
Lemon *(Citrus limon)*
Nutmeg *(Myristica fragrans)*
Grapefruit *(Citrus x paradisi)*
Clove *(Syzygium aromaticum)*

Blends:

Circulation Blend
Pain Relief Blend

Additional blend:

- 6 drops helichrysum
- 4 drops German chamomile
- 4 drops geranium
- 3 drops cypress

Applications:

INGESTION:	CAPSULE, 0 size, 1 capsule 2-3 times daily for 14 days
TOPICAL:	DILUTE 50-50, apply 2-4 drops on location 2-3 times daily COMPRESS, warm, 1-2 times daily on location

HEMORRHAGING

Essential oils that are topically applied or used on pressure bandages are excellent for slowing bleeding and initiating healing.

Single Oils:
Helichrysum *(Helichrysum italicum)*
Geranium *(Pelargonium graveolens)*
Cistus *(Cistus ladanifer)*
Lavender *(Lavandula angustifolia)*
Cypress *(Cupressus sempervirens)*
Myrrh *(Commiphora myrrha)*
Hyssop *(Hyssopus officinalis)*

Blends:
Circulation Blend
Pain Relief Blend

Applications:
TOPICAL: COMPRESS, cold, as needed
NEAT, 1-2 drops on location for small wounds

HEMORRHOIDS

Single Oils:
Cypress *(Cupressus sempervirens)*
Helichrysum *(Helichrysum italicum)*
Myrrh *(Commiphora myrrha)*
Lemon *(Citrus limon)*
Spikenard *(Nardostachys jatamansi)*
Basil *(Ocimum basilicum)*
Peppermint *(Mentha piperita)*

Blends:
Muscle Relaxing Blend
Circulation Blend
Pain Relief Blend

Hemorrhoid Blend #1:
- 4 drops of helichrysum
- 2 drops cypress
- 1 drop of basil

Hemmorhoid Blend #2:
- 3 drops cypress
- 2 drops helichrysum
- 10 drops myrtle

Applications:

TOPICAL:	DILUTE 50-50, apply 3-5 drops on location. This may sting, but usually brings relief with one or two applications.
RETENTION:	RECTAL, once every other day for 6 days.

HEPATITIS

(See HEPATITIS under LIVER)

HERPES

(See SEXUALLY TRANSMITTED DISEASES)

HICCUPS

Hiccups are usually caused by irritated nerves of the diaphragm, possibly caused from a full stomach or indigestion. (See DIGESTIVE PROBLEMS)

Stimulate the Vita Flex point for hiccups by placing one drop of cypress and one drop of tarragon on the end of the index finger. Place the finger against the esophagus in the clavicle notch in the center, and curl inwards and down, like you're curling down inside the throat, and release.

Cypress or tarragon either topically applied or taken as a dietary supplement may relax intestinal spasms, nervous digestion, and hiccups.

Single Oils:

Cypress *(Cupressus sempervirens)*
Tarragon *(Artemesia dracunculus)*
Peppermint *(Mentha piperita)*

Applications:

TOPICAL:	DILUTE 50-50, apply 3-5 drops to chest and stomach areas.
INGESTION:	CAPSULE, 0 size, 1 capsule twice daily RICE MILK, 2-4 times daily may relax intestinal spasms, nervous digestion and chronic hiccups

HIVES

(See ITCHING under SKIN DISORDERS)

Hives refer to a generalized itching or dermatitis that can be due to allergies, damaged liver, chemicals, or other factors.

Single Oils:
Peppermint *(Mentha piperita)*
Patchouli *(Pogostemon cablin)*

Applications:

TOPICAL:	DILUTE 50-50, 2-4 drops on location as needed COMPRESS, cold, as needed

HORMONE IMBALANCE

(See HORMONE IMBALANCE under PREMENSTRUAL SYNDROME)

HOT FLASHES

(See MENOPAUSE)

HUNTINGTON'S CHOREA

(See NEUROLOGICAL DISEASES)

HYPERACTIVITY

Single Oils:
Lavender *(Lavandula angustifolia)*
Cedarwood *(Cedrus atlantica)*
Vetiver *(Vetiveria zizanioides)*
Roman chamomile *(Chamaemelum nobile)*
Peppermint *(Mentha piperita)*
Valerian *(Valeriana officinalis)*

Applications:

INHALATION:	DIRECT, 5 times daily for 30 days, off 5 days, then repeat

HYPERPNOEA

Abnormally fast, labored breathing.

Single Oils:

Ylang ylang *(Cananga odorata)*

Applications:

TOPICAL:	NEAT, 2-3 drops on solar plexus, base of throat and back of neck, as needed.

HYPERTENSION

(see CARDIOVASCULAR CONDITIONS)

HYPOGLYCEMIA

Hypoglycemia may also be caused by low thyroid function (See THYROID).

Excessive consumption of sugar or honey will also cause reactive hypoglycemia, in which a rapid rise in blood sugar is followed by abnormally low levels.

In some cases, hypoglycemia may be a precursor to candida, allergies, chronic fatigue syndrome, depression, and chemical sensitivities.

Signs of hypoglycemia (low blood sugar) include:

- Fatigue, drowsiness, and sleepiness after meals
- Headache or dizziness if periods between meals are too long
- Craving for sweets
- Allergic reaction to foods
- Palpitations, tremors, sweats, rapid heart beat
- Inattentiveness, mood swings, irritability, anxiety, nervousness, inability to cope with stress, and feelings of emotional depression
- Lack of motivation, discipline, and creativity
- Hunger that cannot be satisfied

Often people with some of these symptoms are misdiagnosed as suffering either chronic fatigue or neurosis. Instead, they may be hypoglycemic.

To treat chronic hypoglycemia, it may be necessary to first treat an underlying candida or yeast overgrowth (See FUNGAL INFECTIONS).

Essential oils may reduce hypoglycemic symptoms by helping to normalize sugar cravings and supporting and stabilizing sugar metabolism in the body.

Single Oils:

Lavender *(Lavandula angustifolia)*
Cinnamon *(Cinnamomum verum)*
Cumin *(Cuminum cyminum)*
Clove *(Syzygium aromaticum)*
Thyme thymol *(Thymus vulgaris CT thymol)*
Coriander *(Coriandrum sativum)*
Lemon verbena *(Lippia citriodora)*
Dill *(Anethum graveolens)*

Blends:

Antimicrobial Blend
Liver Blend
Digestive Blend

Applications:

INGESTION:	CAPSULE, 00 size, 1 capsule daily (especially with coriander, dill and thyme)
INHALATION:	DIRECT, 2-5 times daily as needed

IMPOTENCE

(See SEXUAL DYSFUNCTIONS)

Impotence (the inability to perform sexually) can be caused by physical limitations (an accident or injury) or psychological factcrs (inhibitions, trauma, stress, etc). In males, impotence is often linked to problems with the prostate or prostate surgery.

(See PROSTATE PROBLEMS).

If impotence is related to psychological trauma or unresolved emotional issues, it may be necessary to deal with these issues before any meaningful progress can be made. (See TRAUMA)

There is an extensive historical basis for the ability of fragrance to amplify desire and create a mood that can overcome frigidity or impotence. In fact, aromas such as rose, ylang ylang and jasmine have been used since antiquity to attract the opposite sex and create a romantic atmosphere.

Modern research has shown that the fragrance of some essential oils can stimulate the emotional center of the brain. This may explain why essential oils have the potential to help people overcome impotence when emotional inhibitions are involved.

Single Oils:

Ylang ylang *(Cananga odorata)*
Clary sage *(Salvia sclarea)*
Sandalwood *(Santalum album)*
Frankincense *(Boswellia carteri)*
Myrrh *(Commiphora myrrha)*
Ginger *(Zingiber officinale)*
Nutmeg *(Myristica fragrans)*
Rose *(Rosa damascena)*
Jasmine *(Jasminum officinale)*

Blends:

Energy Balance Blend

Applications:

INHALATION:	DIRECT, 2-4 times daily
TOPICAL:	VITA FLEX, 1-3 drops on reproductive Vita Flex points of feet
	BODY MASSAGE, 1-2 times weekly

INDIGESTION

(See DIGESTIVE PROBLEMS)

INFECTION (Bacterial and Viral)

Diffusing essential oils is one of the best ways to prevent the spread of airborne bacteria and viruses. Many essential oils, such as oregano, mountain savory, and rosemary cineol, exert highly antimicrobial effects and can effectively eliminate many kinds of pathogens.

Viruses and bacteria have a tendency to hibernate along the spine. (See citations noted in Raindrop Technique, Chapter 11.) The body may hold a virus in a suspended state for long periods of time. When the immune system is compromised, these viruses may be released and then manifest into illness. Raindrop Technique along the spine helps reduce inflammation and kill the microorganism.

Oregano and thyme are the standard anti-infectious oils for Raindrop application. However, other oils may also be used and may be more desirable for some people. Immune Blend, Respiratory Blend, and Antibacterial Blend, for example, all work well in the Raindrop application method.

(See COLDS, LUNG-, SINUS-, AND THROAT INFECTION)

How to Stimulate the Immune System

Apply Antimicrobial Blend to bottom of feet.

Apply Immune Stimulating Blend (below) on the throat and chest.

Apply 5 drops of Antimicrobial Blend in 1 teaspoon vegetable or massage oil and massage 5-6 drops on the thymus gland (located in upper chest area), 2-3 times daily

Immune Stimulating Blend:
- 10 drops lemon
- 8 drops oregano
- 5 drops mountain savory

Single Oils:

Mountain savory *(Satureja montana)*
Rosemary cineol *(Rosmarinus officinalis CT 1,8 cineol)*
Lemongrass *(Cymbopogon flexuosus)*
Spruce *(Picea mariana)*
Clove *(Syzygium aromaticum)*
Thyme thymol *(Thymus vulgaris CT thymol)*
Oregano *(Origanum compactum)*
Rosewood *(Aniba rosaeodora)*
Sage *(Salvia officinalis)*
Cistus *(Cistus ladanifer)*
Melaleuca alternifolia

To Kill Airborne Viruses and Bacteria

Periodically alternate diffusing Immune Blend and Antimicrobial Blend.

Topically apply 1 drop *Melaleuca alternifolia* and 1 drop rosemary cineol to stem infection.

Single Oils: *Melaleuca alternifolia* with cinnamon, clove, thyme, oregano, ravensara, or frankincense.

Blends: Melaleuca with Antimicrobial Blend.

Blends:

Antibacterial Blend
Antiseptic Blend
Antimicrobial Blend
Immune Blend
Respiratory Blend
Digestive Blend
Antiviral Blend

Applications:

TOPICAL:	DILUTE 20-80, 4-6 drops on location 2-3 times daily RAINDROP Technique, 1-2 times weekly
INGESTION:	CAPSULE, 00 size, 1 capsule twice daily

INFERTILITY

Single Oils:

Clary sage *(Salvia sclarea)*
Anise seed *(Pimpinella anisum)*
Fennel *(Foeniculum vulgare)*
Blue yarrow *(Achillea millefolium)*
Geranium *(Pelargonium graveolens)*

Blends:

Female Blend
Male Blend
Romance Blend

Applications:

INGESTION:	CAPSULE, 0 size, twice daily
TOPICAL:	NEAT, for females, apply 2-4 drops to the lower back and lower abdomen areas VITA FLEX: 1-3 drops applied to the reproductive Vita Flex points on hands and feet (These are the inside of wrists, inside and outside of the upper foot on either side of the anklebone, and along the achilles tendon)

INFLAMMATION

Inflammation can be caused by various conditions: bacteria, poor diet, chemicals, hormonal imbalance, or physical injury.

Certain essential oils have been documented to be excellent for reducing inflammation. German chamomile contains azulene, a blue compound with highly anti-inflammatory properties. Peppermint is also highly anti-inflammatory. Other oils also have anti-inflammatory properties such as helichrysum, spruce, birch or wintergreen, and clove.

There are different types of inflammation for which one oil might be better than another:

Myrrh and helichrysum: inflammation due to tissue/capillary damage, bruising.

Roman chamomile and lavender: inflammation due to bacterial infection.

Ravensara, hyssop and thyme: inflammation caused by viral infection.

Single Oils:

Wintergreen or birch *(Gaultheria procumbens* or *Betula alleghaniensis)*
Helichrysum *(Helichrysum italicum)*
Clove *(Syzygium aromaticum)*
Nutmeg *(Myristica fragrans)*
Lavender *(Lavandula angustifolia)*
Ravensara *(Ravensara aromatica)*
Thyme thymol *(Thymus vulgaris CT thymol)*
German chamomile *(Matricaria recutita)*
Roman chamomile *(Chamaemelum nobile)*
Cypress *(Cupressus sempervirens)*
Myrrh *(Commiphora myrrha)*
Hyssop *(Hyssopus officinalis)*
Peppermint *(Mentha piperita)*
Spruce *(Picea mariana)*

Blends:

Antibacterial Blend
Pain Relief Blend
Muscle Relaxing Blend
Antiseptic Blend
Immune Blend

Anti-inflammation blend #1:
- 10 drops fir
- 6 drops *Melaleuca alternifolia*
- 4 drops German chamomile
- 2 drops peppermint
- 2 drops lemongrass

Anti-inflammation blend #2:
- 6 drops frankincense
- 6 drops fir
- 6 drops *Eucalyptus citriodora*
- 4 drops ravensara
- 3 drops wintergreen or birch
- 1 drop peppermint

Applications:

TOPICAL:	DILUTE 50-50, 2-4 drops on inflammed area COMPRESS, cold, 1-3 times daily as needed
INGESTION:	CAPSULE, 0 size, 2 times daily

INSECT BITES

(See INSECT REPELLENT)

Because of their outstanding antiseptic and oil-soluble properties, essential oils are ideal for treating most kinds of insect bites. Essential oils such as lavender and peppermint reduce insect bite-induced itching and infection.

Singles oils:

Lavandin *(Lavandula x hybrida)*
Eucalyptus globulus
Citronella *(Cymbopogon nardus)*
Tea tree oil *(Melaleuca alternifolia)*
Peppermint *(Mentha piperita)*
German chamomile *(Matricaria recutita)*
Rosemary cineol *(Rosmarinus officinalis CT 1,8 cineol)*

Blends:

Antibacterial Blend
Antiseptic Blend
Pain Relief Blend

Blend for stings and bites:

- 10 drops lavandin
- 1 drop thyme
- 2 drops cistus
- 4 drops *Eucalyptus radiata*
- 3 drops Roman or German chamomile

Applications:

TOPICAL:	NEAT, (or DILUTE 50-50) apply 1-2 drops on bite location 2-4 times daily

Bee Stings

Single Oils:

Lavandin *(Lavandula x hybrida)*
Tansy *(Tanacetum vulgare)*

Blends:

Bee sting Blend:

- 2 drops lavandin
- 1 drop helichrysum
- 1 drop German chamomile
- 1 drop wintergreen or birch

Applications:

TOPICAL:	NEAT, per regimen below

Bee sting regimen:

- Flick or scrape stinger out with credit card or knife, taking care not to squeeze the venom sack.
- Apply 1-2 drops Antibacterial Blend, Antiseptic Blend, lavender, or tansy on location. Repeat until the venom spread has stopped.
- Apply lavandin with or without one or more of the single oils listed, 2-3 times daily until redness abates. Pain Relief Blend may be substituted for Antibacterial Blend.

Black Widow Spider Bite

Get victim to an emergency care facility immediately. Rub 1 drop lavandin every 2 minutes over the bite until you reach the hospital.

Brown Recluse Spider Bite

The bite of this spider causes a painful redness and blistering which progresses to a gangrenous slough of the affected area. Seek medical attention immediately.

Blends:
Antibacterial Blend

Blend Recipe:
- 1 drop lavandin
- 1 drop helichrysum
- 1 drop Antiseptic Blend

Applications:
TOPICAL: NEAT, 1 drop of either of the two blends above every minute until you reach medical treatment

Chiggers (Mites)

Single Oils:
Tea tree oil *(Melaleuca alternifolia)*
Lavender *(Lavandula angustifolia)*

Blends:
Respiratory Blend
Antibacterial Blend

Applications:
TOPICAL: NEAT, 2-6 drops depending on size of affected area 3-5 times daily

Ticks

Single Oils:
Thyme *(Thymus vulgaris)*
Oregano *(Origanum compactum)*
Peppermint *(Mentha piperita)*

Blends:
Respiratory Blend

Applications:
TOPICAL: NEAT, Apply 1 drop neat thyme or oregano to tick to loosen from skin. Apply 1 drop neat Antibacterial Blend on site to detoxify wound. Apply 1 drop neat peppermint every 5 minutes for 50 minutes to reduce pain and infection

INSECT REPELLENT

Single Oils:

Tansy *(Tanacetum vulgare)*
Eucalyptus radiata
Palmarosa *(Cymbopogon martinii)*
Geranium *(Pelargonium graveolens)*
Rosemary cineol *(Rosmarinus officinalis CT 1,8 cineol)*
Peppermint *(Mentha piperita)*
Citronella *(Cymbopogon nardus)*
Lemongrass *(Cymbopogon flexuosus)*
Thyme *(Thymus vulgaris)*

Blends:

Antibacterial Blend
Antimicrobial Blend
Antiseptic Blend

Applications:

TOPICAL: DILUTE 20-80, apply as needed

Insect Repellant Blend:

- 6 drops peppermint
- 6 drops *Melaleuca alternifolia*
- 9 drops *Eucalyptus radiata*

Using Essential Oils As Insect Repellents

Mosquito-repellent: Lemon, peppermint, *Eucalyptus radiata*, lemongrass.

Moth-repellent: Patchouli.

Horse-fly-repellent: Tansy floral water.

Cockroach-repellent: Mix 10 drops peppermint and 5 drops cypress in 1/2 cup salt water. Shake well and spray where roaches live.

Silverfish-repellent: *Eucalyptus radiata*, *Eucalyptus citriodora*.

To repel insects, essential oils can be diffused or put on cotton balls or cedar chips (for use in closets or drawers).

INSOMNIA

Insomnia may be caused by bowel or liver toxicity, poor heart function, negative memories and trauma, depression, mineral deficiencies, hormone imbalance, or underactive thyroid.

The fragrance of many essential oils can exert a powerful calming effect on the mind through their influence on the limbic region of the brain.

Single Oils:

Lavender *(Lavandula angustifolia)*
Cedarwood *(Cedrus atlantica)*
Lemon *(Citrus limon)*
German chamomile *(Matricaria recutita)*
Roman chamomile *(Chamaemelum nobile)*
Mandarin *(Citrus reticulata)*
Valerian *(Valeriana officinalis)*
Cypress *(Cupressus sempervirens)*
St. John's wort *(Hypericum perforatum)*
Balsam fir *(Abies balsamea)*
Rosemary verbenon *(Rosmarinus officinalis CT verbenon)*

Blends:

Stress Reduction Blend
Energy Balance Blend
Muscle Relaxing Blend

Insomnia Blend:

- 12 drops orange
- 8 drops lavender
- 4 drops balsam fir
- 3 drops geranium
- 2 drops Roman chamomile

Applications:

INHALATION: DIFFUSER, for 30-60 minutes at bedtime

TOPICAL: NEAT, apply 1-3 drops to shoulders, stomach and on bottoms of feet. Apply 1-3 drops of neat oil on a cotton towel and place on or near your pillow.
BATH SALT: just before retiring

(See DEPRESSION, THYROID IMBALANCE)

INFLUENZA

(See FLU)

IRRITABLE BOWEL SYNDROME

(See DIGESTIVE PROBLEMS)

Irritable bowel syndrome (IBS) is a common disorder of the intestines marked by the following symptoms:

- Cramps
- Gas and bloating
- Constipation
- Diarrhea and loose stools

IBS may be caused by a combination of stress and a high-fat diet. Fatty foods worsen symptoms by increasing the intensity of the contractions in the colon, thereby worsening symptoms. Coffee, chocolate and milk products, in particular, seem to have the most negative effect on IBS sufferers.

IBS is not the same as colitis, mucous colitis, spastic colon, and spastic bowel. Unlike colitis, IBS does not involve any inflammation and is actually called a "functional disorder" because it presents no obvious, outward signs of disease.

A number of medical studies have documented that peppermint oil (in enteric-coated capsules) is beneficial in treating irritable bowel syndrome and decreases pain.[15, 16, 17]

Single Oils:

Peppermint *(Mentha piperita)*
Anise seed *(Pimpinella anisum)*
Fennel *(Foeniculum vulgare)*

Blends:

Digestive Blend

Applications:

INGESTION: CAPSULE, 0 size, 1 capsule twice a day
RICE MILK, 2-4 times daily
SYRUP, 2-4 times daily

15. Weydert JA, et al., "Systematic review of treatments for recurrent abdominal pain," *Pediatrics* 2003 Jan;111(1):e1-11.
16. Logan AC, Beaulne TM, "The treatment of small intestinal bacterial overgrowth with enteric-caoated peppermint oil: a case report," *Altern Med Rev,* 2002 Oct;7(5):410-7.
17. Sagduyu K, "Peppermint oil for irritable bowel syndrome," *Psychosomatics* 2002 Nov-Dec;43(6):508-9.

ITCHING

(See SKIN DISORDERS or FUNGAL INFECTIONS)

JAUNDICE

(See LIVER)

Jaundice refers to the yellowing of the skin that is a result of a stressed or damaged liver.

Single Oils:

Ledum *(Ledum groenlandicum)*
Amyris *(Amyris balsamifera)*
Carrot seed *(Daucus carota)*
Thyme thymol *(Thymus vulgaris CT thymol)*
German chamomile *(Matricaria recutita)*
Geranium *(Pelargonium graveolens)*

Blends:

Liver Blend
Emotional Release Blend

Applications:

INGESTION:	CAPSULE, 0 size, once a day, using Liver Blend
TOPICAL:	COMPRESS, warm, 2-3 times daily over the liver

JOINT STIFFNESS AND PAIN

(see also PAIN, ARTHRITIS and CONNNECTIVE TISSUE)

Single Oils:

Douglas fir *(Pseudotsuga menziesii)*
Balsam fir *(Abies balsamea)*
Elemi *(Canarium luzonicum)*
German chamomile *(Matricaria recutita)*
Wintergreen or birch *(Gaultheria procumbens* or *Betula alleghaniensis)*
Cypress *(Cupressus sempervirens)*
Spruce *(Picea mariana)*
Peppermint *(Mentha piperita)*
Helichrysum *(Helichrysum italicum)*
Pine *(Pinus sylvestris)*

Blends:

Pain Relief Blend
Muscle Relaxing Blend
Circulation Blend

Joint Pain Blend #1:

- 10 drops helichrysum
- 2 drops rosemary cineol
- 5 drops marjoram
- 5 drops lavender

Joint Pain Blend #2:

- 8 drops spruce
- 5 drops Douglas fir
- 5 drops helichrysum
- 4 drops wintergreen or birch
- 2 drops German chamomile
- 4 drops elemi

Applications:

TOPICAL:	DILUTE 50-50, massage 3-6 drops on location, repeat as often as needed to control pain VITA FLEX: apply to appropriate Vita Flex points on the feet. Repeat as needed

JUVENILE DWARFISM

Dwarfism is caused by insufficient production of growth hormone by the pituitary. The essential oil *Conyza canadensis* was used by Daniel Pénoël, MD, in his clinical practice for reversing retarded maturation.

Single Oils:

Fleabane *(Conyza canadensis)*

Blends:

Brain Blend

Brain Blend stimulates the limbic system.

Applications:

TOPICAL:	DILUTE 50-50, massage 3-4 drops over base of throat (over thymus gland) and on back of neck (over brain stem) 2-3 times daily
INGESTION:	CAPSULE, 00 size, 1 capsule twice a day

KIDNEY DISORDERS

The kidneys remove waste products from the blood, control blood pressure, and create red blood cells. The kidneys filter over 200 quarts of blood each day and remove over 2 quarts of waste products and water which flow into the bladder as urine through tubes called ureters.

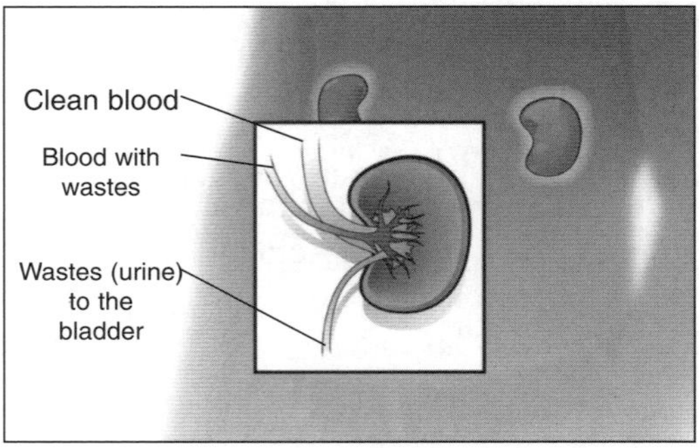

Strong kidneys are essential for good health. Inefficient or damaged kidneys can result in wastes accumulating in the blood and causing serious damage.

High blood pressure can be a cause and a result of chronic kidney failure, since kidneys are central to blood regulation (see BLOOD PRESSURE, HIGH).

Symptoms of poor kidney function include:

- Infrequent or inefficient urinations
- Swelling, especially around the ankles
- Labored breathing due to fluid accumulation in chest

Diuretic (To Increase Urine Flow)

Single Oils:

Ledum *(Ledum groenlandicum)*
Rosemary cineol *(Rosmarinus officinalis CT 1,8 cineol)*
Juniper *(Juniperus communis* or *J. osteosperma)*
Fennel *(Foeniculum vulgare)*
Anise *(Pimpinella anisum)*
Lemongrass *(Cymbopogon flexuosus)*
Grapefruit *(Citrus x paradisi)*
Geranium *(Pelargonium graveolens)*
Sage *(Salvia officinalis)*

Blends:

Liver Blend
Glandular Blend
Digestive Blend

Detoxifing the Kidneys

Essential oils can assist in detoxification due to their unique lipid-soluble properties.

Blends:

- Helichrysum with juniper or fennel.
- Helichrysum with Digestive Blend, Liver Blend, or Glandular Blend.

Place 1-3 drops in water and take as a dietary supplement three times a day. Apply as a compress over kidneys and bladder.

Applications:

INGESTION:	CAPSULE, 0 size, 3 times daily
TOPICAL:	DILUTE 50-50, massage 6-8 drops over kidney area on back COMPRESS, warm, 1-2 times daily

NOTE: Do not use fennel longer than 7 days at a time, since it aggressively increases flow through the urinary tract.

Edema (Swelling)

(see EDEMA, WATER RETENTION)

Kidney Infection/Inflammation (Nephritis)

Kidney inflammation can be caused by structural components, such as poor diet, or bacterial infection from *Escherichia coli, Staphylococcus aureus, Enterobacter,* and *Klebsiellabacteri*.

Abnormal proteins trapped in the glomeruli can also cause inflammation and damage to these tiny filtering units. This is called *glomerulonephritis*. This disease can be acute (flaring up in a few days), or chronic (taking months or years to develop). The mildest forms may not show any symptoms except through a urine test. At more advanced stages, urine appears smokey (as small amounts of blood are passed) and eventually red as more blood is excreted—the signs of impending kidney failure. As with all serious conditions, you should always consult a health care professional if you suspect a kidney infection of any kind.

Symptoms:

- Feeling of unwellness
- Drowsiness
- Back pain
- Nausea
- Smokey or red-colored urine

Damage to the glomeruli (tiny filtering units in the kidneys) caused by bacterial infections is called *pyelonephritis*. To control and reduce infection, drink a gallon of water mixed with 8 oz. of pure cranberry juice daily and use the following essential oils:

Single Oils:

Myrrh *(Commiphora myrrha)*
Cypress *(Cupressus sempervirens)*
Geranium *(Pelargonium graveolens)*
Tangerine *(Citrus nobilis)*
Marjoram *(Origanum majorana)*
Juniper *(Juniperus communis* or *J. osteosperma)*

Blends:

Antimicrobial Blend
Liver Blend
Circulation Blend

Applications:

INGESTION:	CAPSULE, 00 size, twice daily for 10 days
	RICE MILK, 2-4 times daily
TOPICAL:	COMPRESS, cold, 1-2 times daily over kidney area
	VITA FLEX, massage 1-3 drops on kidney Vita Flex points on feet

Kidney Compress regimen:

Kidney Compress Blend:

- 10 drops juniper
- 10 drops tangerine
- 6 drops geranium
- 3 drops helichrysum

Mix the above oils with 1 tsp vegetable or massage oil and massage 6-10 drops of the mixture on the back over the kidney area. Apply a COLD compress over the kidneys for one night.

> **Strengthen the Kidneys**
>
> - Drink 8 to 16 oz. raw cranberry juice and 8 ounces of water with the juice of 1/2 lemon, three times a day.
> - Drink plenty of other liquids, preferably distilled water.

The following night do another COLD compress over the kidneys using 10 drops Immune Blend in 1/4 tsp. vegetable or massage oil. Each night, massage the kidney Vita Flex points on the feet. Repeat, if needed.

Kidney Stones

A kidney stone is a solid piece of material that forms in the kidney from mineral or protein-breakdown products in the urine. Occasionally, larger stones can become trapped in a ureter, the bladder, or the urethra, which can block urine flow causing intense pain.

There are four types of kidney stones: Stones made from calcium (the most common type), stones made from magnesium and ammonia (a struvite stone), stones made from uric acid, and stones made from cystine (the most rare).

Some of the symptoms of kidney stones include:

- Persistent, intense, penetrating pain in back or side
- A burning sensation during urination
- Blood in the urine
- Bad-smelling or cloudy urine
- Fainting

It is important to drink plenty of water (at least 12 eight-ounce glasses daily) to help pass or dissolve a kidney stone.

Single Oils:

Wintergreen or birch *(Gaultheria procumbens* or *Betula alleghaniensis)*
Geranium *(Pelargonium graveolens)*
Juniper *(Juniperus communis* or *J. osteosperma)*
Helichrysum *(Helichrysum italicum)*
Fennel *(Foeniculum vulgare)*
Lemongrass *(Cymbopogon flexuosus)*

Blends:

Kidney Stone Blend #1:

- 5 drops rosemary cineol
- 5 drops geranium
- 5 drops juniper
- 1 Tbsp. agave or maple syrup
- 1/2 lemon
- 8 oz. distilled water

Emulsify oils in one tablespoon agave or maple syrup, add the juice from one-half a lemon, and 8 ounces of warm water and drink on empty stomach. Do this 2-3 times daily until stone passes.

Kidney Stone Blend #2:

- Mix 2 Tbsp. olive oil with 8 oz. apple juice in a container, shake vigorously, then drink, 2 to 3 times daily until stone passes.

Kidney Stone Compress Blend:

- 10 drops juniper
- 10 drops geranium
- 10 drops *Eucalyptus radiata*

Dilute with 1 tsp vegetable or massage oil. Apply 6-10 drops over kidney area and apply a hot compress for 30 minutes once a day. Massage juniper and geranium on bottom of the feet twice a day.

Applications:

INGESTION:	CAPSULE, 00 size, twice daily
	RICE MILK, 2-4 times daily
TOPICAL:	COMPRESS, warm, over kidney area 1-2 times daily
	VITA FLEX, massage 1-3 drops on kidney Vita Flex points of feet

Kidney Stone Regimen:

Use either Blend #1 or Blend #2 (not both) and supplement with kidney stone compresses daily to facilitate passing of the stone.

Ureter Infections

The ureter is the duct from the kidney to the bladder.

Single Oils:

Lemon *(Citrus limon)*
Myrtle *(Myrtus communis)*
Oregano *(Origanum compactum)*

Applications:

INGESTION:	CAPSULE, 00 size, twice daily for 10 days
	RICE MILK, 2-4 times daily
TOPICAL:	VITA FLEX, massage 1-3 drops on kidney Vita Flex points on feet.

KNEE CARTILAGE INJURY

(See CONNECTIVE TISSUE)

LEUKEMIA

(See CANCER)

LEG ULCERS

(See SKIN DISORDERS)

LIVER

The liver is one of the most important organs in the body, playing a major role in detoxifying the body. When the liver is damaged, due to excess alcohol consumption, viral hepatitis, or poor diet, an excess of toxins can build up in the blood and tissues that can result in degenerative disease and death.

Symptoms of stress or diseased liver include:

- Jaundice (abnormal yellow color of the skin). This may be the only visible sign of liver disease.
- Nausea
- Loss of appetite
- Dark-colored urine
- Yellowish or grey-colored bowel movements
- Abdominal pain or ascites, a swelling of the abdomen caused by an accumulation of fluid
- Itching, dermatitis, or hives
- Disturbed sleep caused by the build up of unfiltered toxins in blood
- General fatigue and loss of energy
- Lack of sex drive

Detoxification of Liver and Gall Bladder

Single Oils:

Ledum *(Ledum groenlandicum)*
Kaffir lime *(Citrus hystrix)*
Blue yarrow *(Achillea millefolium)*
Celery seed *(Apium graveolens)*
Helichrysum *(Helichrysum italicum)*
Mandarin *(Citrus reticulata)*
Cardamom *(Elettaria cardamomum)*
Geranium *(Pelargonium graveolens)*
Carrot seed *(Daucus carota)* vegetable oil
German chamomile *(Matricaria recutita)*
Roman chamomile *(Chamaemelum nobile)*

Blends:

Liver Blend
Digestive Blend
Glandular Blend

Additional Liver Blend:

- 2 drops German chamomile
- 3 drops helichrysum
- 10 drops orange
- 5 drops rosemary cineol

Gall Bladder Blend:

- 2 drops Roman chamomile
- 2 drops German chamomile

Applications:

INGESTION:	CAPSULE, 0 size, twice daily RICE MILK, 2-4 times daily
TOPICAL:	COMPRESS, warm, over the liver 1-2 times daily VITA FLEX, massage 1-3 drops on liver Vita Flex point of foot RAINDROP Technique 1-2 times weekly

> European research suggests that helichrysum dilates the liver ducts and facilitates the release of toxins and poisons from the system.
>
> —Salvatore Battaglia, *The Complete Guide to Aromatherapy,* Perfect Potion, Australia, 1997, page 162.

Hepatitis

Viral hepatitis is a serious, life-threatening disease of the liver which results in scarring (cirrhosis) and eventual organ destruction and death. There are several different kinds of hepatitis: Hepatitis A (spread by contaminated food, water, or feces) and hepatitis B and C (spread by contaminated blood or semen).

Symptoms include jaundice, weakness, loss of appetite, nausea, brownish or tea-colored urine, abdominal discomfort, fever and whitish bowel movements.

Single Oils:
Ledum *(Ledum groenlandicum)*
Celery seed *(Apium graveolens)*
Ravensara *(Ravensara aromatica)*
German chamomile *(Matricaria recutita)*
Thyme thymol *(Thymus vulgaris CT thymol)*
Clove *(Syzygium aromaticum)*

Blends:
Liver Blend
Emotional Release Blend
Immune Blend
Antimicrobial Blend

Applications:

INGESTION:	CAPSULE, 0 size, 3 times daily RICE MILK, 2-4 times daily
TOPICAL:	DILUTE 50-50, apply 1-3 drops on carotid arteries (on right and left side of throat just under jaw bone on either side) COMPRESS, warm, over liver 1-2 times daily VITA FLEX, massage 1-3 drops on liver Vita Flex point of foot RAINDROP Technique 2-3 times weekly

NOTE: Avoid citrus juices.

LIVER CANCER

(See CANCER)

LIVER SPOTS (Senile Lentigenes)

Single Oils:
Tansy *(Tanacetum vulgare)*

APPLICATION:

TOPICAL:	DILUTE 50-50, apply 2-4 drops over affected area 4 times daily for 2 weeks

(See SKIN DISORDERS)

LOU GEHRIG'S DISEASE (ALS)

Lou Gehrig's Disease is another name for Amyotrophic Lateral Sclerosis (ALS), a degenerative nerve disorder. ALS affects the nerve fibers in the spinal cord which control voluntary movement. Muscles require continuous stimulation by their associated nerves to maintain their tone. Removal or deadening of these nerves results in muscular atrophy. The lack of control forces the muscles to spasm, resulting in twitching and cramps. The sensory pathways are unaffected so feeling is never lost in the afflicted muscles.

(See NEUROLOGICAL DISEASES)

LUMBAGO (Lower Back Pain)

(See SPINE INJURIES AND PAIN)

LUNG INFECTION

Bronchitis

Bronchitis is characterized by inflammation of the bronchial tube lining accompanied by a heavy mucus discharge. Bronchitis can be caused by an infection or exposure to dust, chemicals, air pollution, or cigarette smoke.

When bronchitis occurs regularly over a long period (i.e. 3 months out of the year for several years) it is known as chronic bronchitis. It can eventually lead to emphysema.

Symptoms:
- Persistent, hacking cough
- Mucus discharge from the lungs
- Difficulty breathing

Avoiding air pollution is an easy way to reduce bronchitis symptoms. In cases where bronchitis is caused by a bacteria or virus, the inhalation of highly antimicrobial essential oils may help combat the infection. Heavy mucus may increase after eating foods containing processed sugar or flour.

Single Oils:

Rosemary cineol *(Rosmarinus officinalis CT 1,8 cineol)*
Eucalyptus radiata or *Eucalyptus citriodora*
Ravensara *(Ravensara aromatica)*
Thyme *(Thymus vulgaris)*
Wintergreen or birch *(Gaultheria procumbens* or *Betula alleghaniensis)*
Spruce *(Picea mariana)*
Helichrysum *(Helichrysum italicum)*
Spearmint *(Mentha spicata)*
Myrtle *(Myrtus communis)*
Balsam fir *(Abies balsamea)*

Blends:

Immune Blend
Respiratory Blend
Antiseptic Blend
Antibacterial Blend

Bronchitis Blend:

- 2 drops sage
- 4 drops myrrh
- 5 drops clove
- 6 drops ravensara
- 15 drops frankincense

NOTE: Essential oil blends work especially well in respiratory applications.

Applications:

TOPICAL:	DILUTE according to application code (Appendix F). Apply 2-6 drops to neck and chest as needed. COMPRESS, warm, on neck, chest and upper back areas 1-3 times daily VITA FLEX, on lung points of feet
ORAL:	GARGLE, hourly, or as needed
INHALATION:	DIRECT, 5-10 times daily as needed DIFFUSER, 15 minutes, 3-10 times daily as needed. Alternate oils/blends each time. Also diffuse at night during sleep VAPOR, 2-4 times daily as needed
RETENTION	RECTAL: Using any of the recommended blends, combine 20 drops with 1 tablespoon olive oil. Insert into rectum with bulb syringe and retain throughout the night. Repeat nightly for 2-3 days.

Pneumonia

Single Oils:

Goldenrod *(Solidago canadensis)*
Tea tree oil *(Melaleuca alternifolia* or *M. ericifolia)*
Rosemary cineol *(Rosmarinus officinalis CT 1,8 cineol)*
Ravensara *(Ravensara aromatica)*
Eucalyptus globulus and *E. radiata*
Mountain savory *(Satureja montana)*
Thyme thymol *(Thymus vulgaris CT thymol)*
Wintergreen or birch *(Gaultheria procumbens* or *Betula alleghaniensis)*
Hyssop *(Hyssopus officinalis)*
Spearmint *(Mentha spicata)*

Blends:

Respiratory Blend
Antiseptic Blend
Immune Blend
Antimicrobial Blend

Pneumonia Blend:

- 10 drops rosemary cineol
- 8 drops ravensara
- 8 drops frankincense
- 2 drops oregano
- 2 drops peppermint

Applications:

TOPICAL:	DILUTE according to application code (Appendix F). Apply 2-6 drops to neck and chest as needed. COMPRESS, warm, on neck, chest and upper back areas 1-3 times daily VITA FLEX, on lung points of feet RAINDROP Technique 1-2 times weekly
INGESTION:	CAPSULE, 00 size, two per day for 10 days
INHALATION:	DIRECT, 5-10 times daily as needed DIFFUSER, 15 minutes, 3-10 times daily as needed. Alternate oils/blends each time. Also diffuse at night during sleep. VAPOR, 2-4 times daily as needed
RETENTION:	RECTAL, using any of the recommended blends, combine 20-30 drops with 1 tablespoon olive oil. Insert with bulb syringe, retain overnight, nightly for 5-10 days as needed.

Whooping Cough

This is a contagious disease affecting the respiratory system particularly in children. Lungs become infected, as the air passages become clogged with thick mucus. Over the course of several days, the condition worsens, resulting in long coughing bouts (up to 1 minute). The continual coughing makes breathing difficult and labored.

Single Oils:

Rosemary cineol *(Rosmarinus officinalis CT 1,8 cineol)*
Lavender *(Lavandula angustifolia)*
Lemongrass *(Cymbopogon flexuosus)*
Thyme thymol *(Thymus vulgaris CT thymol)*
Myrtle *(Myrtus communis)*
Petitgrain *(Citrus aurantium)*
Nutmeg *(Myristica fragrans)*
Oregano *(Origanum compactum)*
Tea tree oil *(Melaleuca alternifolia)*

Blends:

Antimicrobial Blend
Antiseptic Blend
Antibacterial Blend
Immune Blend
Respiratory Blend

Applications:

TOPICAL: DILUTE 20-80, apply 2-4 drops to neck and chest as needed.
COMPRESS, warm, on neck, chest and upper back areas 1-3 times daily
VITA FLEX, on lung points of feet

INHALATION: DIRECT, 5-10 times daily as needed
DIFFUSER, 15 minutes, 3-10 times daily as needed. Alternate oils/blends each time. Also diffuse at night during sleep.
VAPOR, 2-4 times daily as needed

NOTE: Whooping cough usually affects children; because of their more sensitive skin, it is wise to use the 20-80 dilution rate for all essential oils used on children, except those with a "neat" application code (see Appendix F). Start with low concentrations until response is observed.

LUPUS

Lupus is an autoimmune disease characterized by several different varieties: *Lupus vulgaris* and *Lupus erythematosus* (discoid and systemic).

- *Lupus vulgaris* is characterized by lesions that form on skin. Brownish lesions may form on the face and become ulcerous and form scars.
- *Lupus erythematosus* (discoid) is characterized by scaly red patches on the skin and oval or butterfly-shaped lesions on the face. It is milder than the systemic type.
- Systemic *Lupus erythematosus* is more serious than discoid lupus. It inflames the connective tissue in any part of the body, including the joints, muscles, skin, blood vessels, membranes surrounding the lungs and heart, and occasionally the kidneys and brain.

Single Oils:

Cypress *(Cupressus sempervirens)*
Lemongrass *(Cymbopogon flexuosus)*

Blends:

Immune Blend
Energy Balance Blend
Glandular Blend
Mood Lifting Blend

Lupus Blend:

- 30 drops cypress
- 30 drops lemongrass
- 30 drops Glandular Blend

Applications:

TOPICAL: BODY MASSAGE, once every other day
RAINDROP Technique, 1-2 times weekly

Lupus Regimen:

Do the following daily:

1. BATH SALT, using Glandular Blend, add 30 drops to 1/2 cup Epsom salt or baking soda and add to hot bath. Soak for 30 minutes.
2. VITA FLEX: Massage Glandular Blend on bottoms of the feet; follow two hours later with foot massage using Antimicrobial Blend.
3. TOPICAL: Massage 10-15 drops Immune Blend over liver and on feet 2-3 times daily.

LYME DISEASE and ROCKY MOUNTAIN SPOTTED FEVER

These viral infections are both caused by the bite of an infected tick. Lyme Disease is caused by the microorganism *Borrelia burgdorferi*. Rocky Mountain Spotted Fever is caused by the bacteria *Rickettsiz ricketsii*.

(See TICK BITES under INSECT BITES)

Single Oils:

Thyme thymol *(Thymus vulgaris CT thymol)*
Oregano *(Origanum compactum)*
Clove *(Syzygium aromaticum)*
Blue cypress *(Callitris intratropica)*
Melissa *(Melissa officinalis)*

Blends:

Pain Relief Blend
Antiseptic Blend
Antimicrobial Blend
Immune Blend

Applications:

INGESTION: CAPSULE, 00 size, 1 capsule 3 times daily

LYMPHATIC SYSTEM

Essential oils have long been known to aid in stimulating and detoxifying the lymphatic system.

Single Oils:

Ledum *(Ledum groenlandicum)*
Sandalwood *(Santalum album)*
Helichrysum *(Helichrysum italicum)*
Myrtle *(Myrtus communis)*
Grapefruit *(Citrus x paradisi)*
Lemongrass *(Cymbopogon flexuosus)*
Cypress *(Cupressus sempervirens)*
Tangerine *(Citris nobilis)*

Blends:

Antimicrobial Blend
Circulation Blend
Energy Blend

Applications:

TOPICAL: DILUTE 50-50, massage 2-4 drops on sore lymph glands and under arms.
RAINDROP Technique weekly or as needed
COMPRESS, warm, over affected areas 1-2 times daily

Lymphatic Cleanse:
- 4 drops sandalwood
- 3 drops cypress
- 4 drops orange
- 2 drops grapefruit

Mix in 1 Tbsp of Grade B maple or agave syrup. Add to 1/2 gallon distilled water. Drink daily.

LYMPHOMA

(See CANCER)

M.C.T. (Mixed Connective Tissue) DISEASE

(see LUPUS)

M.C.T. is an autoimmune disease similar to lupus in which the connective tissue in the body becomes inflamed and painful. This condition is usually due to poor assimilation of protein and mineral deficiencies.

Single Oils:

Rosemary cineol *(Rosmarinus officinalis CT 1,8 cineol)*
Nutmeg *(Myristica fragrans)*
Clove *(Syzygium aromaticum)*
Lemongrass *(Cymbopogon flexuosus)*
Marjoram *(Origanum majorana)*
Peppermint *(Mentha piperita)*
Wintergreen or birch *(Gaultheria procumbens* or *Betula alleghaniensis)*
Cypress *(Cupressus sempervirens)*

Blends:

Immune Blend
Energy Balance Blend
Mood Lifting Blend

MCT Blend (for aches and discomfort):
- 10 drops basil
- 8 drops wintergreen or birch
- 6 drops cypress
- 3 drops peppermint

Applications:

TOPICAL: DILUTE 50-50, massage 4-8 drops on affected location 2-3 times daily
VITA FLEX, massage 1-3 drops on liver Vita Flex points of the feet
RAINDROP Technique, weekly or as needed.
Rub 2-4 drops of Immune Blend over the liver and on liver Vita Flex Points on the bottom of the right foot 2-3 times daily. This has been reported to help lupus, which is similar to M.C.T.

MALARIA

Malaria is a serious disease contracted from several species of *Anopheles* mosquitoes. While malaria is largely confined to the continent of Africa, an increasing number of cases have arisen in the U.S. If not treated, malaria can be fatal. As with all serious medical conditions, you should consult immediately with a health professional if you suspect malaria.

Symptoms:
- Fever
- Chills
- Anemia

The best defense against malaria is to use insect repellents effective against *Anopheles* mosquitoes. Once a person has contracted the disease, oils such as lemon and thyme can help amplify immune response.

Single Oils:

Lemon *(Citrus limon)*
Thyme *(Thymus vulgare)*
Bay laurel *(Laurus nobilis)*

Applications:

INGESTION: 3-6 drops lemon oil to 1 tsp agave and 8 oz water and sip when an outbreak is impending.

(See INSECT REPELLENT and INSECT BITES)

MALE HORMONE IMBALANCE

Single Oils:

Rosemary cineol *(Rosmarinus officinalis CT 1,8 cineol)*
Sage *(Salvia officinalis)*
Fennel *(Foeniculum vulgare)*
Ylang ylang *(Cananga odorata)*
Geranium *(Pelargonium graveolens)*
Blue yarrow *(Achillea millefolium)*

Blends:

Male Blend

Applications:

INGESTION: CAPSULE, 0 size, once a day

MEASLES

A highly contagious viral disease caused by parmyxovirus. It enters through the respiratory tract and passes into the lymphatic system, causing myalgia, malaise, cough, steadily mounting fever, and ultimately the characteristic measles rash typically starting behind the ears and spreading down the trunk and onto the extremities.

(see also LYMPHATIC SYSTEM)

Single Oils:

Lavender *(Lavandula angustifolia)*
Roman chamomile *(Chamaemelum nobile)*
Tea tree oil *(Melaleuca alternifolia)*
Clove *(Syzygium aromaticum)*
Thyme *(Thymus vulgaris CT thymol)*
German chamomile *(Matricaria recutita)*

Blends:

Immune Blend

Measles Blend:

- 15 drops lavender
- 15 drops Roman chamomile
- 5 drops *Melaleuca alternifolia*

Applications:

TOPICAL:	DILUTE 50-50, apply on spots, as needed. BATH SALT, soak at least 30 minutes daily. Mix 6 drops essential oils into 1 pint of water, shake well, and sponge patient down once a day

MEMORY

(See BRAIN DISORDERS)

MENTAL FATIGUE

(See FATIGUE)

METAL TOXICITY (Aluminum)

Aluminum is a very toxic metal that can cause serious neurological damage in the human body—even in minute amounts. Aluminum has been implicated in Alzheimer's disease.

People unwittingly ingest aluminum from their cookware, beverage cans, and antacids. Even deodorants have aluminum compounds. The first step toward reducing aluminum toxicity in the body is to avoid these types of aluminum-based products.

Single Oils:

Clove *(Syzygium aromaticum)*
Helichrysum *(Helichrysum italicum)*
Kaffir lime *(Citrus hystrix)*

Blends:

Pain Relief Blend

Applications:

INGESTION:	CAPSULE, 00 size, twice daily
TOPICAL:	RAINDROP Technique, weekly

MONONUCLEOSIS (Infectious)

Similar to cytomegalovirus, infectious mononuceosis is most often caused by the Epstein-Barr virus, also a cause of chronic fatigue syndrome.

See CHRONIC FATIGUE SYNDROME)

Single Oils:

Ravensara *(Ravensara aromatica)*
Hyssop *(Hyssopus officinalis)*
Thyme thymol *(Thymus vulgaris CT thymol)*
Mountain savory *(Satureja montana)*
Frankincense *(Boswellia carteri)*

Blends:

Antimicrobial Blend
Respiratory Blend

Mononucleosis Blend:

- 3 drops Antimicrobial Blend
- 3 drops thyme
- 3 drops mountain savory
- 2 drops ravensara

Applications:

INGESTION:	CAPSULE, 00 size, 1 capsule twice daily
TOPICAL:	RAINDROP Technique twice a week
	VITA FLEX, massage 3-6 drops on bottom of feet twice daily

MORNING SICKNESS

(See NAUSEA)

MOTION SICKNESS

(See NAUSEA)

MUCUS (Excess)

Many oils are natural expectorants; helping tissues discharge mucus, soft and hard plaque, and toxins.

Single Oils:

Frankincense *(Boswellia carteri)*
Ledum *(Ledum groenlandicum)*
Lavender *(Lavandula angustifolia)*
Helichrysum *(Helichrysum italicum)*
Eucalyptus radiata
Peppermint *(Mentha piperita)*
Lemon *(Citrus limon)*
Cypress *(Cupressus sempervirens)*
Marjoram *(Origanum majorana)*
Myrtle *(Myrtus communis)*
Rosemary cineol *(Rosmarinus officinalis CT 1,8 cineol)*

Blends:

Digestive Blend
Respiratory Blend
Antibacterial Blend

Expectorant Blend:

- 3 drops marjoram
- 3 drops ledum
- 1 drop lavender

Applications:

INHALATION:	DIRECT, 3-5 times daily
	DIFFUSER, 20 minutes 3 times daily
INGESTION:	CAPSULE, 0 size, 1 capsule twice a day
TOPICAL:	DILUTE 50-50, apply 2-4 drops on the T4 and T5 thoracic vertebrae (at the neck-to-shoulder intersection), 3-5 times daily
	VITA FLEX, massage on relevant Vita Flex points on the feet

MULTIPLE SCLEROSIS (MS)

(See NEUROLOGICAL DISEASES)

MUMPS

An acute, contagious, febrile disease marked by painful swelling and inflammation of the parotid glands and other salivary glands. The causative agent is a paromyxovirus, spread by direct contact, airborne droplets and urine.

Single Oils:

Thyme thymol *(Thymus vulgaris CT thymol)*
Manuka *(Leptospermum scoparium)*
Thyme linalol *(Thymus vulgaris CT linalol)*
Melissa *(Melissa officinalis)*
Ravensara *(Ravensara aromatica)*
Myrrh *(Commiphora myrrha)*
Blue cypress *(Callitris intratropica)*
Wintergreen or birch *(Gaultheria procumbens* or *Betula alleghaniensis)*

Blends:

Respiratory Blend
Antimicrobial Blend

Applications:

TOPICAL:	DILUTE 50-50, 2-4 drops behind the ears 4 times daily
	COMPRESS, warm, 1-3 times daily around throat and jaw
	RAINDROP Technique 1-2 times weekly
INGESTION:	CAPSULE, 00 size, 1 capsule twice a day

MUSCLES (Sore, Tight, Bruised, etc.)

Bruised Muscles (see Bruising)

To slow blood clot formation and to increase circulation, use cypress and helichrysum.

Single Oils:

Clove *(Syzygium aromaticum)*
German chamomile *(Matricaria recutita)*
Helichrysum *(Helichrysum italicum)*
Wintergreen or birch *(Gaultheria procumbens* or *Betula alleghaniensis)*
Cypress *(Cupressus sempervirens)*
Lavender *(Lavandula angustifolia)*
Geranium *(Pelargonium graveolens)*
Peppermint *(Mentha piperita)*

Blends:

Muscle Relaxing Blend
Pain Relief Blend

Applications:

TOPICAL: DILUTE 50-50, apply 2-4 drops to bruised area 3 times daily.

Sequence of application for bruise treatment:

- When a bruise displays black and blue discoloration and pain, start with helichrysum, wintergreen or birch, balsam fir, or oregano
- Once the pain and inflammation begin to decrease, use cypress, basil and Muscle Relaxing Blend to enhance the muscle relaxation
- Then follow with peppermint to stimulate the nerves and reduce inflammation
- Finally, finish with cold packs

Cramps and Charlie Horses

Magnesium and calcium deficiency or inadequate calcium metabolism may contribute to muscle cramps and charlie horses.

Single Oils:

Rosemary cineol *(Rosmarinus officinalis CT 1,8 cineol)*
Cypress *(Cupressus sempervirens)*
Marjoram *(Origanum majorana)*
Lavender *(Lavandula angustifolia)*
Elemi *(Canarium luzonicum)*
German chamomile *(Matricaria recutita)*

Blends:

Muscle Relaxing Blend
Pain Relief Blend

Applications:

TOPICAL: DILUTE 50-50, massage 2-4 drops on cramped muscle 3 times daily.

Inflammation Due to Injury

Tissue damage is usually accompanied by inflammation. Reduce inflammation by massaging with anti-inflammatory oils

Single Oils:

Peppermint *(Mentha piperita)*
German chamomile *(Matricaria recutita)*
Myrrh *(Commiphora myrrha)*
Wintergreen or birch *(Gaultheria procumbens* or *Betula alleghaniensis)*
Marjoram *(Origanum majorana)*
Clove *(Syzygium aromaticum)*
Roman chamomile *(Chamaemelum nobile)*

Blends:

Muscle Relaxing Blend

Muscle Injury Blend:

- 12 drops white fir
- 10 drops *Melaleuca alternifolia*
- 8 drops lavender
- 6 drops marjoram
- 3 drops yarrow
- 3 drops spearmint
- 2 drops peppermint

APPLICATION:

TOPICAL: DILUTE 50-50, massage 2-4 drops on inflamed muscle 3 times daily.

Inflammation Due to Infection

Single Oils:

Ravensara *(Ravensara aromatica)*
Hyssop *(Hyssopus officinalis)*
Melaleuca quinquinervia
Blue cypress *(Callitris intratropica)*

Applications:

TOPICAL: NEAT or DILUTE 50-50, massage 2-4 drops on inflamed muscle 3 times daily
COMPRESS, cold, 1-3 times daily

Sore Muscles

Single Oils:

Nutmeg *(Myristica fragrans)*
Elemi *(Canarium luzonicum)*
Marjoram *(Origanum majorana)*
Black pepper *(Piper nigrum)*
Basil *(Ocimum basilicum)*
Spruce *(Picea mariana)*
Roman chamomile *(Chamaemelum nobile)*
Wintergreen or birch *(Gaultheria procumbens* or *Betula alleghaniensis)*
Rosemary cineol *(Rosmarinus officinalis CT 1,8 cineol)*
Peppermint *(Mentha piperita)*

Blends:

Muscle Relaxing Blend
Stress Reduction Blend
Headache Blend

Sore Muscle Blend #1:

- 8 drops juniper
- 10 drops wintergreen or birch
- 8 drops lemon
- 4 drops rosemary cineol
- 8 drops lavender

Sore Muscle Blend #2:

- 9 drops cypress
- 8 drops rosemary cineol
- 8 drops lavender
- 2 drops elemi
- 2 drops valerian

Applications:

TOPICAL: DILUTE 50-50, massage 4-6 drops into sore muscle 3 times daily.
COMPRESS, warm, 1-3 times daily

Tight, Spasmed or Torn Muscles

Single Oils:

Elemi *(Canarium luzonicum)*
Wintergreen or birch *(Gaultheria procumbens* or *Betula alleghaniensis)*
Balsam fir *(Abies balsamea)*
Peppermint *(Mentha peperita)*
Basil *(Ocimum basilicum)*
White fir *(Abies concolor)*
Lemongrass *(Cymbopogon flexuosus)*
Marjoram *(Origanum majorana)*

Blends:

Muscle Relaxing Blend
Pain Relief Blend

Tight Muscle Blend:

- 6 drops marjoram
- 4 drops cypress
- 4 drops wintergreen or birch
- 3 drops valerian
- 1 drop helichrysum

Muscle Spasm Blend:

- 4 drops ravensara
- 10 drops Muscle Relaxing Blend
- 3 drops black pepper

Torn Muscle Blend:

- 8 drops balsam fir
- 8 drops sandalwood
- 7 drops Douglas fir
- 5 drops hyssop
- 4 drops lemongrass
- 5 drops helichrysum
- 4 drops wintergreen or birch
- 2 drops vetiver
- 1 drop tansy

Applications:

TOPICAL: DILUTE 50-50, massage 4-6 drops into affected muscle 3-5 times daily.
COMPRESS, alternate cold and hot, 2-4 times daily

Weakness in Muscle

Single Oils:
Ravensara *(Ravensara aromatica)*
Douglas fir *(Pseudotsuga menziesii)*
Lemongrass *(Cymbopogon flexuosus)*
Juniper *(Juniperus communis* or *J. osteosperma)*
Nutmeg *(Myristica fragrans)*

Blends:
Energy Blend

Applications:

TOPICAL:	DILUTE 50-50, massage 4-6 drops into weak muscle 3 times daily

MUSCULAR DYSTROPHY

Single Oils:
Pine *(Pinus sylvestris)*
Lavender *(Lavandula angustifolia)*
Marjoram *(Origanum majorana)*
Lemongrass *(Cymbopogon flexuosus)*

Blends:
Muscle Relaxing Blend
Pain Relief Blend

Applications:

TOPICAL:	DILUTE 50-50, massage 5-8 drops along spine 3 times daily RAINDROP Technique, weekly

NAILS (Brittle or Weak)

Poor or weak nails, often containing ridges, indicate a sulfur deficiency.

Single Oils:
Frankincense *(Boswellia carteri)*
Myrrh *(Commiphora myrrha)*
Lemon *(Citrus limon)*

Nail Blend:
- 2 drops frankincense
- 2 drops myrrh
- 2 drops lemon

Applications:

TOPICAL:	NEAT, 1-3 drops on nails and at base of nails 3 times per week

NARCOLEPSY

A chronic ailment consisting of uncontrollable, recurrent attacks of drowsiness and sleep during daytime. May be aggravated by hypothalamus dysregulation or thyroid hormone deficiency.

(see THYROID)

Single Oils:

Fleabane *(Conyza canadensis)*
Rosemary cineol *(Rosmarinus officinalis CT 1,8 cineol)*
Black pepper *(Piper nigrum)*
Cinnamon bark *(Cinnamomum verum)*

Blends:

Brain Blend

Applications:

INHALATION:	DIRECT, 4-8 times daily as needed
TOPICAL:	DILUTION 50-50, apply 1-2 drops on temples, behind ears, back of neck, on forehead, and under nostrils, as needed

NAUSEA

Patchouli oil contains compounds that are extremely effective in preventing vomiting due to their ability to reduce the gastrointestinal muscle contractions associated with vomiting (Yang et al., 1999). Peppermint has long been a traditional remedy for motion-induced nausea.

Single Oils:

Tansy *(Tanacetum vulgare)*
Nutmeg *(Myristica fragrans)*
Peppermint *(Mentha piperita)*
Patchouli *(Pogostemon cablin)*
Ginger *(Zingiber officinale)*

Blends:
Digestive Blend

Applications:

TOPICAL:	DILUTE 50-50, massage 1-3 drops behind each ear (mastoids) and over navel 2-3 times hourly COMPRESS, warm, over stomach, as needed
INHALATION:	DIRECT, 4-6 times hourly as needed
ORAL:	TONGUE, 1-4 times as needed

Morning Sickness

Single Oils:
Peppermint *(Mentha piperita)*
Spearmint *(Mentha spicata)*

Blends:
Digestive Blend

Applications:

TOPICAL:	DILUTE 50-50, massage 1-3 drops behind each ear (mastoids) and over navel 2-3 times hourly COMPRESS, warm, over stomach, as needed
INHALATION:	DIRECT, 4-6 times hourly as needed
ORAL:	TONGUE, 1-4 times as needed

Motion Sickness

Single Oils:
Patchouli *(Pogostemon cablin)*
Lavender *(Lavandula angustifolia)*
Peppermint *(Mentha piperita)*
Ginger *(Zingiber officinale)*
Spearmint *(Mentha spicata)*

Blends:
Digestive Blend
Energy Blend
Liver Blend

Applications:

TOPICAL:	DILUTE 50-50, massage 1-3 drops behind each ear (mastoids) and over navel 2-3 times hourly
	COMPRESS, warm, over stomach, as needed
INHALATION:	DIRECT, 4-6 times hourly as needed
ORAL:	TONGUE, 1-4 times as needed
INGESTION:	RICE MILK, 1-2 times as needed

Motion Sickness Preventive:
Mix 4 drops peppermint and 4 drops ginger in 1 oz. vegetable or massage oil. Rub 6-10 on chest and stomach before traveling.

NERVE DISORDERS

Nerve disorders usually involve peripheral or surface nerves and include neuritis, neuropathy, neuralgia, Bell's palsy, and carpal tunnel syndrome. In contrast, neurological disorders are usually associated with deep neurological disturbances in the brain, and these conditions include Lou Gehrig's disease, MS, and cerebral palsy. (See NEUROLOGICAL DISEASES)

Single Oils:

Peppermint *(Mentha piperita)*
Lavender *(Lavandula angustifolia)*
Cedarwood *(Cedrus atlantica)*
German chamomile *(Matricaria recutita)*
Roman chamomile *(Chamaemelum nobile)*
Sage *(Salvia officinalis)*
Rosemary cineol *(Rosmarinus officinalis CT 1,8 cineol)*
Spruce *(Picea mariana)*
Tangerine *(Citrus reticulata)*
Sandalwood *(Santalum album)*

Blends:

Energy Balance
Stress Reduction Blend

General blend for nerve disorders:
- 2 drops peppermint
- 10 drops juniper
- 1 drop geranium
- 8 drops marjoram
- 4 drops helichrysum

Applications:

TOPICAL: NEAT or DILUTE 50-50 as required, apply 2-4 drops to affected area 3-5 times daily

Bell's Palsy

A type of neuritis, marked by paralysis on one side of the face and inability to open or close the eyelid.

Single Oils:

Peppermint *(Mentha piperita)*
Helichrysum *(Helichrysum italicum)*
Juniper *(Juniperus communis* or *J. osteosperma)*

Blends:

Muscle Relaxing Blend
Pain Relief Blend

Applications:

TOPICAL: NEAT, massage 1-3 drops on the facial nerve, which is in front and behind the ear and any areas of pain 3-5 times daily until symptoms end

Carpal Tunnel Syndrome

Nerves pass through a tunnel formed by wrist bones (known as carpals) and a tough membrane on the underside of the wrist that binds the bones together. The tunnel is rigid, so if the tissues within it swell for some reason, they press and pinch the nerves creating a painful condition known as carpal tunnel syndrome. This condition is primarily sports-related or due to activities that involve strenuous or repeated use of wrists. A similar but less common condition can occur in the ankle (tarsal tunnel syndrome), or elbow.

Single Oils:

Peppermint *(Mentha piperita)*
Basil *(Ocimum basilicum)*
Wintergreen or birch *(Gaultheria procumbens* or *Betula alleghaniensis)*
Cypress *(Cupressus sempervirens)*
Marjoram *(Origanum majorana)*
Helichrysum *(Helichrysum italicum)*
Lemongrass *(Cymbopogon flexuosus)*

Blends:

Pain Relief Blend

Carpal Tunnel Blend:

- 5 drops wintergreen or birch
- 3 drops cypress
- 1 drop peppermint
- 2 drops marjoram
- 3 drops lemongrass

Applications:

TOPICAL:	NEAT or DILUTE 50-50 as required, apply 2-4 drops to affected area 3-5 times daily COMPRESS, cold, on location 2-3 times daily

Neuralgia

Neuralgia is pain from a damaged nerve. It can occur in the face, spine, or elsewhere. This reoccuring pain can be traced along a nerve pathway. Carpal tunnel syndrome is a specific type of neuralgia. The primary symptom is temporary sharp pain in the peripheral nerve(s).

Single Oils:

Marjoram *(Origanum majorana)*
Helichrysum *(Helichrysum italicum)*
Peppermint *(Mentha piperita)*
Juniper *(Juniperus communis* or *J. osteosperma)*
Nutmeg *(Myristica fragrans)*

Blends:

Pain Relief Blend
Liver Blend

Applications:

TOPICAL:	NEAT or DILUTE 50-50 as required, apply 2-4 drops to affected area 3-5 times daily COMPRESS, cold, on location 2-3 times daily
INHALATION:	DIRECT, Stress Reduction Blend 2-4 times daily

Neuritis

Neuritis is a painful inflammation of the peripheral nerves.

It is usually caused by prolonged exposure to cold temperature, heavy-metal poisoning, diabetes, vitamin deficiencies (beriberi and pellagra), and infectious diseases such as typhoid fever and malaria.

Symptoms:

- Pain
- Burning
- Numbness or tingling
- Muscle weakness or paralysis

Single Oils:

Peppermint *(Mentha piperita)*
Lavender *(Lavandula officinalis)*
Juniper *(Juniperus communis* or *J. osteosperma)*
Oregano *(Origanum compactum)*
Thyme thymol *(Thymus vulgaris CT thymol)*
Blue yarrow *(Achillea millefolium)*
Clove *(Syzygium aromaticum)*

Blends:

Energy Balance Blend
Muscle Relaxing Blend
Stress Reduction Blend

Applications:

TOPICAL:	NEAT or DILUTE 50-50 as required, apply 2-4 drops to affected area 3-5 times daily COMPRESS, cold, on location 2-3 times daily
INHALATION:	DIRECT, Stress Reduction Blend 2-4 times daily

Neuropathy

Neuropathy refers to actual damage to the peripheral nerves.

Damage to these peripheral nerves (other than spinal or those in the brain), generally starts as tingling in hands and feet and slowly spreads along limbs to the trunk.

Numbness, sensitive skin, neuralgic pain, weakening of muscle power can all develop in varying degrees. Most common causes include complications from diabetes (diabetic neuropathy), alcoholism, vitamin B12 deficiency, tumors, too many pain killers, exposure and absorption of chemicals, metallics, pesticides, and many other causes.

B vitamins and minerals such as magnesium, calcium, potassium, and organic sulfur are important in repairing nerve damage and quenching pain from inflamed nerves.

Conyza canadensis may boost production of pregnenolone and human growth hormone. Pregnenolone aids in repairing damage to the myelin sheath.[18] Juniper also may help in supporting nerve repair.

If paralysis is the problem, a regeneration of up to 60 percent may be possible. If, however, the nerve damage is too severe, treatment may not help. If the damage starts to reverse, there will be pain. Apply a few drops of Pain Relief Blend neat on location.

Symptoms:
- Tingling or numbness
- Gangrene

Single Oils:

Peppermint *(Mentha piperita)*
Fleabane *(Conyza canadensis)*
Juniper *(Juniperus communis* or *J. osteosperma)*
Blue yarrow (*Achillea millefolium*)
Goldenrod *(Solidago canadensis)*
Helichrysum *(Helichrysum italicum)*
Lemongrass *(Cymbopogon flexuosus)*

Blends:

Muscle Relaxing Blend
Pain Relief Blend
Stress Reduction Blend

Neuropathy blend #1:
- 10 drops juniper
- 10 drops geranium
- 10 drops helichrysum

Neuropathy blend #2:
- 15 drops geranium
- 10 drops helichrysum
- 6 drops cypress
- 10 drops juniper
- 5 drops peppermint

18. Baulieu E, Schumacher M, Progesterone as a neuroactive neurosteriod, with special reference to the effect of progesterone on myelination, *Steroids* 2000 Oct-Nov;65(10-11):605-12.

Applications:

TOPICAL:	NEAT or DILUTE 50-50 as required, apply 2-4 drops to affected area 3-5 times daily COMPRESS, cold, on location 2-3 times daily
INHALATION:	DIRECT, Stress Reduction Blend 2-4 times daily

NERVOUS FATIGUE

Nervous fatigue can cause motor skill problems.

Single Oils:

St. John's wort *(Hypericum perforatum)*
Blue yarrow *(Achillea millefolium)*
Juniper *(Juniperus communis* or *J. osteosperma)*
Geranium *(Pelargonium graveolens)*
Goldenrod *(Solidago canadensis)*
Helichrysum *(Helichrysum italicum)*
Thyme thymol *(Thymus vulgaris CT thymol)*
Peppermint *(Mentha piperita)*

Blends:

Brain Blend
Clarity Blend

Applications:

INHALATION:	DIRECT, 4-8 times daily as needed
TOPICAL:	DILUTION 50-50, apply 1-2 drops on temples, behind ears, back of neck , on forehead, and under nostrils, as needed

NERVOUS SYSTEM (Autonomic)

The autonomic nervous system controls involuntary activities such as heartbeat, breathing, digestion, glandular activity, and contraction and dilation of blood vessels.

The autonomic nervous system is composed of two parts that balance and complement each other: the parasympathetic and sympathetic nervous systems.

The sympathetic nervous system has stimulatory effects and is responsible for secreting stress hormones such as adrenaline and noradrenaline.

The parasympathetic nervous system has relaxing effects and is responsible for secreting acetylcholine which slows the heart and speeds digestion.

To Stimulate Parasympathetic Nervous System:

Single Oils:

Lavender *(Lavandula angustifolia)*
Patchouli *(Pogostemon cablin)*
Rose *(Rosa damascena)*
Marjoram *(Origanum majorana)*

Blends:

Energy Balance Blend
Immune Blend
Stress Reduction Blend

Applications:

INHALATION:	DIRECT, 1-2 times daily, as needed
INGESTION:	CAPSULE, 0 size, 1 capsule twice daily
TOPICAL:	RAINDROP Technique, biweekly

To Stimulate Sympathetic Nervous System:

Single Oils:

Peppermint *(Mentha piperita)*
Fennel *(Foeniculum vulgare)*
Grapefruit *(Citris x paradisi)*
Ginger *(Zingiber officinale)*
Eucalyptus radiata
Black pepper *(Piper nigrum)*

Blends:

Clarity Blend
Brain Blend

Applications:

INHALATION:	DIRECT, 1-2 times daily, as needed
INGESTION:	CAPSULE, 0 size, 1 capsule twice daily
TOPICAL:	RAINDROP Technique, biweekly

NEUROLOGICAL DISEASES

Juniper promotes nerve function. Frankincense may help clear the emotions of fear, anger and depression, which are common with people who have these neurological diseases.

Mood Lifting Blend will help people work through the psychological and emotional aspects of the disease.

Sulfur deficiency is very prevalent in these neurological diseases.

Vitex has been shown to reduce the symptoms of Central Nervous System disorders in animal studies.[19]

Single Oils:

Frankincense *(Boswellia carteri)*
Helichrysum *(Helichrysum italicum)*
Oregano *(Origanum compactum)*
Sage *(Salvia officinalis)*
Juniper *(Juniperus communis* or *J. osteosperma)*
Rosemary cineol *(Rosmarinus officinalis CT 1,8 cineol)*
Clove *(Syzygium aromaticum)*
Cardamom *(Elettaria cardamomum)*
Vitex *(Vitex negundo)*

Blends:

Mood Lifting Blend
Brain Blend
Clarity Blend

Neurological Blend:

- 1 drop rosemary cineol
- 1 drop helichrysum
- 1 drop ylang ylang
- 1 drop clove (clove must always be diluted in a vegetable oil)

Applications:

INHALATION:	DIRECT, 3-4 times daily
	DIFFUSER, 30 minutes, 2-3 times daily
TOPICAL:	DILUTE 50-50, 1-3 drops on brain reflex points on forehead, temples and mastoids (just behind ears). Use a direct pressure application, massaging 6-10 drops of diluted oil from the base of the skull down the neck and down the spine. Put a few drops of the oil on a loofah brush and rub along the spine vigorously. RAINDROP Technique, 3 times monthly, but use a cold compress instead of a warm one

NOTE: Never use hot packs for neurological problems. Always use cold packs to reduce pain and inflammation. In other words, reduce the temperature of the affected area.

19. Gupta M, Mazumder UK, Bhawal SR, "CNS activity of Vitex negundo Linn. in mice," *Indian J Exp Biol* 1999 Feb;37(2):143-6.

Huntington's Chorea

Huntington's Chorea is a degenerative nerve disease that generally becomes manifest in middle age. It is marked by uncontrollable body movements, which are followed—and occasionally preceded—by mental deterioration.

[Not to be confused with Sydenham's chorea (often called St. Vitus Dance, chorea minor, or juvenile chorea) which affects children, especially females, usually appearing between the ages of 7 and 14. The jerking symptoms eventually disappear.]

Single Oils:

Peppermint *(Mentha piperita)*
Juniper *(Juniperus communis* or *J. osteosperma)*
Basil *(Ocimum basilicum)*

Blends:

Muscle Relaxing Blend

Blend:

- 5 drops peppermint
- 10 drops juniper
- 3 drops basil
- 5 drops Muscle Relaxing Blend

Applications:

INHALATION:	DIRECT, 3-4 times daily DIFFUSER, 30 minutes, 2-3 times daily
TOPICAL:	DILUTE 50-50, 1-3 drops on brain reflex points on forehead, temples and mastoids (just behind ears). Use a direct pressure application, massaging 6-10 drops of diluted oil from the base of the skull down the neck and down the spine. Put a few drops of the oil on a loofah brush and rub along the spine vigorously. RAINDROP Technique, 3 times monthly, but use a cold compress instead of a warm one

NOTE: Never use hot packs for neurological problems. Always use cold packs to reduce pain and inflammation. In other words, reduce the temperature of the affected area.

Multiple Sclerosis (MS)

Multiple Sclerosis is a progressive, disabling disease of the nervous system (brain and spinal cord) in which inflammation occurs in the central nervous system. Eventually, the myelin sheaths protecting the nerves are destroyed, resulting in a slowing or blocking of nerve transmission.

MS is an autoimmune disease, in which the body's own immune system attacks the nerves. Some researchers believe that MS is triggered by a virus, while others make a case that it has a strong genetic or environmental component.

Symptoms:
- Muscle weakness in extremities
- Deteriorating coordination and balance
- Numbness or prickling sensations
- Poor attention or memory
- Speech impediments
- Incontinence
- Tremors
- Dizziness
- Hearing loss

Single Oils:

Juniper *(Juniperus communis* or *J. osteosperma)*
Blue yarrow *(Achillea millefolium)*
Helichrysum *(Helichrysum italicum)*
Geranium *(Pelargonium graveolens)*
Peppermint *(Mentha piperita)*
Thyme linalol *(Thymus vulgaris CT linalol)*
Oregano *(Origanum compactum)*
Wintergreen or birch *(Gaultheria procumbens* or *Betula alleghaniensis)*
Cypress *(Cupressus sempervirens)*
Marjoram *(Origanum majorana)*

Blends:

Energy Balance Blend
Muscle Relaxing Blend

MS Blend:
- 10 drops helichrysum
- 10 drops peppermint
- 10 drops rosemary cineol
- 5 drops basil eugenol

Maintaining MS Status Quo

One of the simplest ways to keep MS symptoms from worsening is to keep the body cool and avoiding any locations or physical activities which heat the body (including hot showers or exercise). Cold baths and swimming are two of the best activities for relieving symptoms.

Applying heat is the worst thing to do for MS. If an MS patient is suffering a worsening of symptoms, lower their body temperature (by up to 3 degrees F) by laying them on a table, covering them with a sheet, ice, shower curtain, and blankets (in that order). Work the feet with oils and watch for benefits.

Applications:

INHALATION: DIRECT, 3-4 times daily
DIFFUSER, 30 minutes, 2-3 times daily

TOPICAL: DILUTE 50-50, 1-3 drops on brain reflex points on forehead, temples and mastoids (just behind ears). Use a direct pressure application, massaging 6-10 drops of diluted oil from the base of the skull down the neck and down the spine. Put a few drops of the oil on a loofah brush and rub along the spine vigorously. RAINDROP Technique, 3 times monthly, but use a cold compress instead of a warm one.

MS Regimen (to be performed daily):

1. Layer neat applications of 4-6 drops of helichrysum, juniper, geranium and peppermint, Raindrop-style, along the spine. Lightly massage oils in the direction of the MS paralysis. For example, if it is in the lower part of the spine, massage down; if it is in the upper part of the spine, massage up. Follow the application with 30 minutes of cold packs (change cold packs as needed)
2. Apply 4-6 drops Energy Balance Blend on the spine. If the MS affects the legs rub down the spine; if it affects the neck, rub on the spine.
3. Apply 2-3 drops each of cypress and juniper to the back of the neck, then cover with 2-3 drops of Muscle Relaxing Blend.

To give additional emotional support to the person with MS symptoms, use Emotional Release Blend. Be patient. Overcoming MS is a long-term endeavor.

Parkinson's Disease

Parkinson's Disease involves the deterioration of specific nerve centers in the brain and affects more men than women by a ratio of 3:2. The main symptom is tremors, an involuntary shaking of hands, head, or both. Other symptoms include rigidity, slowed movement, and loss of balance. In many cases these are accompanied by a continuous rubbing together of thumb and forefinger, stooped posture, mask-like face, trouble swallowing, depression, and difficulty performing simple tasks. These symptoms may all be seen at different stages of the disease. The tremors are most severe when the affected part of the body is not in use. There is no pain or other sensation, other than a decreased ability to move. Symptoms appear slowly, in no particular order.

Single Oils:

Juniper *(Juniperus communis* or *J. osteosperma)*
Peppermint *(Mentha piperita)*
Vitex *(Vitex negundo)*

Blends:

Stress Reduction Blend
Energy Balance Blend

Applications:

INHALATION:	DIRECT, 3-4 times daily DIFFUSER, 30 minutes, 2-3 times daily
TOPICAL:	DILUTE 50-50, 1-3 drops on brain reflex points on forehead, temples and mastoids (just behind ears). Use a direct pressure application, massaging 6-10 drops of diluted oil from the base of the skull down the neck and down the spine. Put a few drops of the oil on a loofah brush and rub along the spine vigorously. RAINDROP Technique, 3 times monthly, but use a cold compress instead of a warm one.

NIGHT SWEATS

(See PREMENSTRUAL SYNDROME)

Single Oils:

Sage *(Salvia officinalis)*
Clary sage *(Salvia sclarea)*
Blue yarrow *(Achillea millefolium)*

Blends:
Male Blend
Glandular Blend

Applications:

TOPICAL:	DILUTE 50-50, apply 3-5 drops over lower abdomen and back of neck before retiring VITA FLEX, apply 2-3 drops to heart, to brain and to liver Vita Flex points on feet

NOSE

Nosebleeds

Nosebleeds usually are not serious. However, if bleeding does not stop in a short time or is excessive or frequent, consult your doctor.

Single Oils:
Helichrysum *(Helichrysum italicum)*
Geranium *(Pelargonium graveolens)*
Lavender *(Lavandula angustifolia)*
Lemon *(Citrus limon)*
Cypress *(Cupressus sempervirens)*

Blends:
Nosebleed Blend:
- 2 drops helichrysum
- 2 drops lavender
- 2 drops cypress

Applications:

INHALATION:	DIRECT, 1-3 times, as needed
TOPICAL:	NEAT, apply 1-3 drops on and around nose and on back of neck

Nosebleed regimen:

Wrap a pea-sized piece of ice in tissue paper; apply 1 drop of helichrysum, lavender or cypress to the tissue and push it up under the center of the upper lip, so it is sitting near the base of the nose. Hold this 'ice-tissue' in place for 1-2 minutes with pressure from the upper lip. This almost always immediately stops a nosebleed.

Dry Nose

Single Oils:

Lavender *(Lavandula angustifolia)*
Lemon *(Citrus limon)*
Peppermint *(Mentha piperita)*
Myrrh *(Commiphora myrrha)*
Tea tree oil *(Melaleuca alternifolia)*

Blends:

Nose Blend:

- 2 drops lavender
- 1 drop myrrh

Applications:

INHALATION:	DIRECT, 3-5 times daily as needed
	DIFFUSER, 20 minutes 3 times daily and before retiring
TOPICAL:	DILUTE 50-50, apply 1-2 drops to nostril walls with cotton swab twice daily

Nasal Irrigation Regimen:

Rosemary and tea tree oils can be used in a saline solution for very effective nasal irrigation that clears and decongests sinuses. As recommended by Daniel Pénoël, MD, the saline solution is prepared as follows:

- 12 drops rosemary cineol
- 4 drops tea tree
- 8 tablespoons very fine salt (salt flower)

The essential oils are mixed thoroughly in the fine salt and kept in a sealable container. For each nasal irrigation session, 1 teaspoon of this salt mixture is dissolved into

- 1 1/2 cups distilled water

This oils/salt/water solution is then placed in the tank of an oral irrigator to irrigate the nasal cavaties, which is done while bending over a sink. This application has brought surprisingly positive results in treating latent sinusitus and other nasal congestion problems.

Loss of Smell

Single Oils:

Basil *(Ocimum basilicum)*
Peppermint *(Mentha piperita)*
Rosemary cineol *(Rosmarinus officinalis CT cineol)*
Goldenrod *(Solidago canadensis)*
Frankincense *(Boswellia carteri)*

Applications:
INHALATION: DIRECT, 3 times daily

Nasal Irrigation Regimen: (see above)

Polyps (Nasal)

Single Oils:
Citronella *(Cymbopogon nardus)*

Blends:
Antibacterial Blend

Applications:
TOPICAL: DILUTE 50-50, carefully apply 1 drop on location inside the nostrils with a cotton swab 1-3 times daily

OBESITY

(see DEPRESSION)

Diffusing or directly inhaling essential oils can have an immediate positive impact on moods and appetites. Olfaction is the only sense that can have direct effect on the limbic region of the brain. Studies at the University of Vienna have shown that some essential oils and their primary constituents can stimulate blood flow and activity in the emotional centers of the brain.[20]

Fragrance influences the satiety center in the brain in such a manner that frequent inhalation of pleasing aromas can significantly reduce appetite. Dr. Alan Hirsch, in his landmark studies, showed dramatic weight loss in research subjects using aromas from peppermint oil and vanilla absolute to curb food cravings.[21]

Single Oils:
Peppermint *(Mentha piperita)*
Jasmine *(Jasminum officinale)*
Ylang Ylang *(Cananga odorata)*
Vanilla absolute

Blends:
Mood Lifting Blend

Applications:
INHALATION: DIRECT, as often as needed

20. Nasel, C. et al. "Functional imaging of effects of fragrances on the human brain after prolonged inhalation." Chemical Senses. 1994;19(4):359-64

21. Hirsch AR. Inhalation of Odorants for Weight Reduction, *Int J Obes,* 1994, page 306

OTITIS MEDIA

(See EAR INFECTION)

OVARIAN AND UTERINE CYSTS

(See CANCER)

Single Oils:

Frankincense *(Boswellia carteri)*
Geranium *(Pelargonium graveolens)*
Tea tree oil *(Melaleuca alternifolia)*
Oregano *(Origanum compactum)*
Cypress *(Cupressus sempervirens)*

Blends:

Antiseptic Blend
Female Blend
Male Blend

Female Cyst Blend #1:

- 5-10 drops frankincense
- 5 drops basil

Female Cyst Blend #2:

- 5-10 drops frankincense
- 5-10 drops geranium
- 5-10 drops cypress

Applications:

RETENTION:	TAMPON, nightly for 4 nights. NOTE: if irritation occurs, discontinue use for 3 days before resuming use.
TOPICAL:	COMPRESS, warm, on location, as needed VITA FLEX, massage 1-3 drops on the reproductive Vita Flex points, located around the anklebone, on either side of the foot. Work from the ankle bone down to the arch of the foot.

PAIN

One of the most effective essential oils for blocking pain is peppermint. A study by Gobel et al., in 1994, showed that peppermint blocks calcium channels and substance P, important factors in the transmission of pain signals. Other essential oils also have unique pain-relieving properties, including helichrysum, balsam fir and Douglas fir.

(See ARTHRITIS or HEADACHES)

Chronic Pain

Single Oils:
Peppermint *(Mentha piperita)*
Helichrysum *(Helichrysum italicum)*
Spruce *(Picea mariana)*
Wintergreen or birch *(Gaultheria procumbens* or *Betula alleghaniensis)*
Ginger *(Zingiber officinalis)*
Clove *(Syzygium aromaticum)*
Elemi *(Canarium luzonicum)*
Oregano *(Origanum compactum)*
Douglas fir *(Pseudotsuga menziesii)*
Balsam fir *(Abies balsamea)*
Rosemary cineol *(Rosmarinus officinalis CT 1,8 cineol)*

Blends:
Pain Relief Blend
Muscle Relaxing Blend

Applications:

INGESTION:	CAPSULE, 0 size, 1 capsule 2 times per day
TOPICAL:	DILUTE 50-50, 2-4 drops on location as needed
	COMPRESS, warm, on location as needed

Bone-Related Pain

Single Oils:
Wintergreen or birch *(Gaultheria procumbens* or *Betula alleghaniensis)*
Cypress *(Cupressus sempervirens)*
Balsam fir *(Abies balsamea)*
Spruce *(Picea mariana)*
Pine *(Pinus sylvestris)*
Peppermint *(Mentha piperita)*
Helichrysum *(Helichrysum italicum)*

Blends:
Pain Relief Blend

Applications:

TOPICAL:	DILUTE 50-50, 2-4 drops on location as needed VITA FLEX, apply to relevant points on feet, repeat as needed

Muscle-Related Pain

Single Oils:
Basil *(Ocimum basilicum)*
Peppermint *(Mentha piperita)*
Rosemary verbenon *(Rosmarinus officinalis CT verbenon)*
Marjoram *(Origanum majorana)*

Blends:
Pain Relief Blend
Muscle Relaxing Blend

Applications:

TOPICAL:	DILUTE 50-50, 2-4 drops on location as needed VITA FLEX, apply to relevant points on feet, repeat as needed

For Inflammation Pain

(see INFLAMMATION)

Trauma-related Pain

Single Oils:
Sandalwood *(Santalum album)*
Geranium *(Pelargonium graveolens)*

Blends:
Trauma Pain Relief Blend:

- 12 drops Douglas fir
- 10 drops *Melaleuca alternifolia*
- 8 drops lavender
- 6 drops marjoram
- 3 drops spearmint
- 2 drops peppermint

How to Use Essential Oils for Pain Control

Pain Relief Blend is powerful for pain reduction. When applied on location or to the Vita Flex points on the feet, it can act within seconds. Balsam fir, birch and wintergreen are also effective against pain.

Applications:

TOPICAL: DILUTE 50-50, 2-4 drops on location, 2-4 times daily. Also massage around hairline and on the tops of the toes.
COMPRESS, warm, on location as needed

Joint Pain

(see JOINT STIFFNESS)

PANCREATITIS

Pancreatitis is an inflammation of the pancreas that can be either acute or chronic. Acute pancreatitis can be caused by a sudden blockage in the main pancreatic duct, which results in enzymes becoming backed-up and literally digesting the pancreas unless remedied. Chronic pancreatitis occurs more gradually, with attacks recurring over weeks or months.

Symptoms:

- Abdominal pain, muscle aches, vomiting, abdominal swelling, sudden hypertension, jaundice, rapid weight loss, and fever.

In the case of acute pancreatitis, a total fast for at least 4-5 days is one of the safest and most effective methods of treatment. In the case of infection, fasting should be combined with immune stimulation.

Single Oils:

Geranium *(Pelargonium graveolens)*
Vetiver *(Vetiveria zizanioides)*
Peppermint *(Mentha piperita)*
Mountain savory *(Satureja montana)*
Oregano *(Origanum compactum)*

Blends:

Immune Blend
Antimicrobial Blend

Applications:

RETENTION:	RECTAL, 3 times a week
TOPICAL:	RAINDROP Technique, once a week
INGESTION:	CAPSULE, 0 size, 1 capsule 3 times a week

PARASYMPATHETIC NERVOUS SYSTEM

(See NERVOUS SYSTEM—AUTONOMIC)

PARASITES, INTESTINAL

(see FOOD POISONING)

Many types of parasites use up nutrients, while giving off toxins. This can leave the body depleted, nutritionally deficient, and susceptible to infectious disease.

Occasionally parasites can lie dormant in the body and then become active due to ingestion of a particular food or drink. This can result in the appearance and disappearance of symptoms even though parasites are still present.

The parasite, *Cryptosporidium parrum,* may be present in many municipal or tap waters. To remove, water must be distilled or filtered using a .3 micron filter.

Symptoms:
- Fatigue
- Weakness
- Diarrhea
- Gas and bloating
- Cramping
- Nausea
- Irregular bowel movements.

The first step to controlling parasites is beginning a fasting or cleansing program. A colon cleanse is particularly important. (See cleansing information in Chapter 5.)

Single Oils:

Tarragon *(Artemisia dracunculus)*
Anise seed *(Pimpinella anisum)*
Tansy *(Tanacetum vulgare)*
Basil *(Ocimum basilicum)*
Peppermint *(Mentha piperita)*
Ginger *(Zingiber officinale)*
Lemongrass *(Cymbopogon flexuosus)*
Nutmeg *(Myristica fragrans)*
Fennel *(Foeniculum vulgare)*

Juniper *(Juniperus communis* or *J. osteosperma)*
Clove *(Syzygium aromaticum)*
Mountain savory *(Satureja montana)*
Thyme thymol *(Thymus vulgaris CT thymol)*

Blends:
Digestive Blend
Liver Blend

Blend for parasite retention enema:
- 10 drops ginger
- 10 drops Digestive blend
- 1 tablespoon vegetable oil

Applications:

INGESTION:	CAPSULE, 00 size, 3 times a week
	RICE MILK, 1-3 times daily
TOPICAL:	COMPRESS, warm, over intestinal area, 2 times week
	VITA FLEX: massage up to 6 drops to the instep area on both feet (small intestine and colon Vita Flex points)
RETENTION:	RECTAL, use nightly for 7 nights, then rest for 7 nights. Repeat this cycle 3 times to eliminate all stages of parasite development

PERIODONTAL DISEASE

Periodontal disease is an infection of the gum and bone that hold the teeth in place. In advanced stages, this disease leads to painful chewing problems and even tooth loss.

Gingivitis and Pyorrhea

Single Oils:
Mountain savory *(Satureja montana)*
Clove *(Syzygium aromaticum)*
Tea tree oil *(Melaleuca alternifolia)*
Peppermint *(Mentha piperita)*
Wintergreen or birch *(Gaultheria procumbens* or *Betula alleghaniensis)*
Thyme thymol *(Thymus vulgaris CT thymol)*
Oregano *(Origanum compactum)*

Blends:
Antimicrobial Blend

Applications:

ORAL:	GARGLE, up to 10 times daily as needed

Gum Infection

Single Oils:
Mountain savory *(Satureja montana)*
Clove *(Syzygium aromaticum)*
Cinnamon *(Cinnamomum verum)*
Peppermint *(Mentha piperita)*
Wintergreen or birch *(Gaultheria procumbens* or *Betula alleghaniensis)*
Myrrh *(Commiphora myrrha)*

Blends:
Antimicrobial Blend
Antiseptic Blend

Applications:

ORAL:	GARGLE, 3-10 times daily, as needed
TOPICAL:	DILUTE 50-50, apply 1-2 drops on gums twice a day

Mouth Ulcers

Single Oils:
Myrrh *(Commiphora myrrha)*
Oregano *(Origanum compactum)*
Tea tree oil *(Melaleuca alternifolia)*

Blends:
Antimicrobial Blend
Antiseptic Blend

Applications:

ORAL:	GARGLE, 3-10 times daily, as needed
TOPICAL:	DILUTE 50-50, apply 1-2 drops on gums twice a day

If mouth ulcers are due to leukemia, saturate gauze with Antimicrobial Blend. Place gauze between gums and inner cheek skin and change gauze pads morning and evening. Massage abscessed area with Antimicrobial Blend. Irrigate mouth with mouthwash.

PERSPIRATION (Excessive)

Excessive perspiration may indicate adrenal and thyroid problems or diabetes. Sage helps regulate sweating.

Single Oils:

Geranium *(Pelargonium graveolens)*
Rosewood *(Aniba rosaeodora)*
Sage *(Salvia officinalis)*
Nutmeg *(Myristica fragrans)*

Blend:

Antibacterial Blend
Glandular Blend
Energy Blend

Applications:

INGESTION:	CAPSULE, 0 size, 1 capsule twice a day
TOPICAL:	DILUTE 20-80, apply 2-4 drops under arms daily

PH BALANCE

(See ACIDOSIS)

PHLEBITIS—THROMBOSIS

(See CARDIOVASCULAR CONDITIONS)

Phlebitis refers to inflammation of a blood vein. Symptoms include pain and tenderness along the course of the vein, discoloration of the skin, inflammatory swelling, joint pain, and acute edema below the inflammed site.

Thrombosis is the formation, development, or existence of a blood clot (thrombus) within the vascular system. This is a life-saving process when it occurs during hemorrhage. It is a life-threatening event when it occurs at any other time because the clot can block a vessel and stop the blood supply to an organ or part.

Single Oils:

Helichrysum *(Helichrysum italicum)*
Clove *(Syzygium aromaticum)*
Orange *(Citrus aurantium)*
Goldenrod *(Solidago canadensis)*
Tansy *(Tanacetum vulgare)*
Lavender *(Lavandula angustifolia)*

Applications:

INGESTION:	CAPSULE, 0 size, 1 capsule daily
TOPICAL:	DILUTE 50-50, apply 5-7 drops on location or over the heart, 3 times daily RAINDROP Technique, weekly

PLAQUE

(See CARDIOVASCULAR CONDITIONS)

PLEURISY

(see CARDIOVASCULAR CONDITIONS)

Inflammation of the pleura, or outer membranes covering the lungs and the thoracic cavity.

Single Oils:

Ravensara *(Ravensara aromatica)*
Thyme *(Thymus vulgaris)*

Blends:

Respiratory Blend
Immune Blend

Applications:

TOPICAL:	DILUTE 20-80, massage 5-7 drops on neck and chest 2-3 times daily COMPRESS, warm, on neck, chest and upper back areas, daily VITA FLEX, 1-3 drops on lung Vita Flex points of feet daily RAINDROP Technique, 1-2 times weekly

PNEUMONIA

(See LUNG INFECTION)

POLIO

Polio (Poliomylitis) is an acute infectious disease usually manifested in epidemics and caused by a virus. It creates an inflammation of the gray matter of the spinal cord. It is characterized by fever, sore throat, headache, and vomiting, sometimes stiffness of the neck and back. If it develops into the major illness, it can involve paralysis and atrophy of groups of muscles ending in contraction and permanent deformity.

Single Oils:

Frankincense *(Boswellia carteri)*
Melaleuca quinquinervia
Wintergreen or birch *(Gaultheria procumbens* or *Betula alleghaniensis)*
Melissa *(Melissa officinalis)*
Sandalwood *(Santalum album)*
Ravansara *(Ravansara aromatica)*
Blue cypress *(Callitris intratropica)*

Blends:

Polio Blend:

- 2 drops lemon
- 10 drops ylang ylang
- 7 drops frankincense
- 10 drops wintergreen or birch
- 7 drops myrtle
- 8 drops cypress
- 15 drops myrrh
- 10 drops tarragon
- 6 drops sage

Applications:

INGESTION: CAPSULE, 0 size, twice daily

PREMENSTRUAL SYNDROME (PMS)

PMS is one of the most common hormone-related conditions in otherwise healthy women. Women can experience a wide range of symptoms for 10 to 14 days before menstruation, and even 2 to 3 days into menstruation. These symptoms include mood swings, fatigue, headaches, breast tenderness, abdominal bloating, anxiety, depression, confusion, memory loss, sugar cravings, cramps, low back pain, irritability, weight gain, acne, and oily skin and hair. Causes may be hormonal, nutritional, psychological, and the stress of the Western culture. Essential oils have demonstrated an ability to balance and harmonize hormones and reduce negative symptoms safely. Specifically, sage, fennel, and clary sage have an estrogen-like action that improves estrogen, progesterone, and testosterone balance.

Single Oils:

Hops *(Humulus iupulus)*
Clary sage *(Salvia sclarea)*
Sage *(Salvia officinalis)*
Anise seed *(Pimpinella anisum)*
Fennel *(Foeniculum vulgare)*
Vitex *(Vitex negundo)*
Geranium *(Pelargonium graveolens)*
Blue yarrow *(Achillea millefolium)*

Blends:

Female Blend
Male Blend
Glandular Blend

Applications:

INHALATION:	DIRECT, 3-6 times daily
TOPICAL:	DILUTE 50-50, apply 4-6 drops to forehead, crown of head, soles of feet, lower abdomen and lower back 1-3 times daily
	VITA FLEX, massage 2-4 drops on reproductive Vita Flex points of feet
	COMPRESS, warm, daily, on lower back or lower abdomen
ORAL:	TONGUE, 1 drop of Glandular Blend on the tongue and then hold the tongue against the roof of the mouth, 2-4 times daily

Hormone Imbalance

Single Oils:

Geranium *(Pelargonium graveolens)*
Clary sage *(Salvia sclarea)*

Blends:

Female Blend
Male Blend

Hormone Balancing Blend #1:
- 10 drops fennel
- 10 drops clary sage
- 8 drops hyssop
- 4 drops helichrysum
- 6 drops ylang ylang

Hormone Balancing Blend #2:
- 5 drops bergamot
- 5 drops geranium

Applications:

TOPICAL:	DILUTE 50-50, apply 4-6 drops to forehead, crown of head, soles of feet, lower abdomen and lower back 1-3 times daily VITA FLEX, massage 3-6 drops on reproductive Vita Flex points of feet COMPRESS, warm, daily, on lower back or lower abdomen

Endometriosis

This is when the uterine lining develops on the outer wall of the uterus, ovaries, fallopian tubes, vagina, intestines, or on the abdominal wall. These fragments cannot escape like the normal uterine lining, which is shed during menstruation. Because of this, fibrous cysts often form around the misplaced uterine tissue. Symptoms can include abdominal or back pain during menstruation or pain that often increases after the period is over. Other symptoms may include heavy periods and pain during intercourse.

Single Oils:

Fennel *(Foeniculum vulgare)*
Clary sage *(Salvia sclarea)*

Blends:

Female Blend

Applications:

TOPICAL:	COMPRESS, warm, over uterus area, 2-3 times weekly VITA FLEX, massage 2-4 drops on reproductive Vita Flex points on feet
INGESTION:	CAPSULE, 0 size, twice daily for 2 weeks following menses

Menstrual Cramps

Single Oils:

Clary sage *(Salvia sclarea)*
Rosemary cineol *(Rosmarinus officinalis CT 1,8 cineol)*
Hops *(Humulus iupulus)*
Sage *(Salvia officinalis)*
Lavender (Lavandula angustifolia)
Roman chamomile *(Chamaemelum nobile)*
Cypress *(Cupressus sempervirens)*
Tarragon *(Artemisia dracunculus)*
Vitex *(Vitex negundo)*

Blends:

Female Blend
Glandular Blend

Blend for Menstrual Cramp Relief:

- 10 drops Female blend
- 4 drops hops *(Humulus iupulus)*

Applications:

TOPICAL:	COMPRESS, warm, over uterus area, 2-3 times weekly
	VITA FLEX, massage 2-4 drops on reproductive Vita Flex points on feet
INGESTION:	CAPSULE, 0 size, twice daily for 2 weeks prior to menses

Irregular Periods

Single Oils:

Sage *(Salvia officinalis)*
Fennel *(Foeniculum vulgare)*
Clary Sage *(Salvia sclarea)*

Blends:

Female Blend

Period Regulator Blend #1:

- 5 drops peppermint
- 9 drops fleabane
- 16 drops clary sage
- 11 drops sage
- 5 drops jasmine

Period Regulator Blend #2:
- 10 drops chamomile
- 10 drops fennel

Applications:

TOPICAL:	DILUTE 50-50, apply 4-6 drops to forehead, crown of head, soles of feet, lower abdomen, and lower back 1-3 times daily VITA FLEX, massage 3-6 drops on reproductive Vita Flex points of feet COMPRESS, warm, daily, on lower back or lower abdomen

Excessive Bleeding Blend
- 10 drops helichrysum
- 10 drops geranium

Applications:

TOPICAL:	DILUTE 50-50, massage 4-6 drops around ankles, lower back, and lower stomach, 1-3 times daily as needed.

PROSTATE CANCER

(See CANCER)

PROSTATE PROBLEMS

Scientists are tracing the higher incidence of hormone-dependent cancers including cancer of the breast, prostate and testis to exposure to endocrine disrupters in the environment.[22] Petrochemical contamination from DDT, PCB, pesticides, the phlate DBP, and synthetic steroids in meat, are implicated in interfering with hormone receptors, rendering them unable to function properly, eventually leading to cancer.

For prostate concerns, peppermint acts as an anti-inflammatory to the prostate. Fatty oils such as pumpkin seed oil have been shown in animal studies to act to reduce prostate swelling.[23]

22. Skakkebaek NE, "Endocrine disrupters and testicular dysgenesis syndrome," *Horm Res* 2002;57 Suppl 2:43.
23. Zhang X, et al., "Effect of the extracts of pumpkin seeds on the urodynamics of rabbits: an experimental study," *J Tongji Med Univ* 1994:14(4):235-8.

Single Oils:

Oregano *(Origanum compactum)*
Frankincense *(Boswellia carteri)*
Myrrh *(Commiphora myrrha)*
Orange *(Citrus aurantium)*
Balsam Fir *(Abies balsamea)*
Cumin *(Cuminum cyminum)*
Thyme linalol *(Thymus vulgaris CT linalol)*
Peppermint *(Mentha piperita)*
Pumpkin seed oil (fatty oil) *(Cucurbita pepo)*

Blends:

Male Blend
Hormone Blend
Glandular Blend

Prostate Blend:

- 10 drops frankincense
- 5 drops myrrh
- 3 drops sage

Applications:

TOPICAL:	DILUTE 20-80, apply 2-4 drops between the rectum and scrotum twice daily. Male Blend works especially well here
	VITA FLEX, massage 4-6 drops on Vita Flex reproductive points on the feet twice daily
RETENTION:	RECTAL, nightly for 7 days; rest 7 days, then repeat

Benign Prostate Hyperplasia (BPH)

Almost all males over age 50 have some degree of prostate hyperplasia, a condition which worsens with age. BPH can severely restrict urine flow and result in frequent, small urinations. Two herbs which are extremely effective for treating this condition are saw palmetto and *Pygeum africanum*. The mineral zinc is also important for normal prostate function and prostate health. The hormone-like activity of some essential oils can support a nutritional regimen to reduce BPH swelling.

Single Oils:

Ledum *(Ledum groenlandicum)*
Frankincense *(Boswellia carteri)*
Myrrh *(Commiphora myrrha)*
Orange *(Citrus aurantium)*
Balsam fir *(Abies balsamea)*
Cumin *(Cuminum cyminum)*

Blends:

Male Blend

Applications:

TOPICAL:	DILUTE 50-50, 1-3 drops between the rectum and scrotum 1-3 times daily
	VITA FLEX: 1-3 drops on reproductive Vita Flex points on feet
INGESTION:	CAPSULE, 00 size, 1 capsule 3 times daily
	RICE MILK, 2-4 times daily
RETENTION,	RECTAL, 3 times per week, at night

PBH Specific Regimen:
The following regimen reduced PSA (prostate specific antigen) counts 70 percent in 2 months: PSA counts typically rise when BPH occurs.

- 10 drops frankincense
- 5 drops myrrh
- 3 drops sage

Use the above blend for the following three applications simultaneously:

a. Mix the above amounts of essential oils with 1 tablespoon olive oil and use 3 times weekly as overnight rectal retention enema.
b. Massage 1-3 drops neat on Vita Flex reproductive points on both feet daily
c. Dilute 50-50 with vegetable oil and apply 2-4 drops topically between the rectum and the scrotum daily.

Prostatitis

Prostatitis is inflammation of the prostate, a more serious condition that can present symptoms similar to those of benign prostate hyperplasia: frequent urinations, restricted flow, etc.

Single Oils:

Rosemary cineol *(Rosmarinus officinalis CT 1,8 cineol)*
Myrtle *(Myrtus communis)*
Thyme linalol *(Thymus vulgaris CT linalol)*
Tsuga *(Tsuga canadensis)*
Peppermint *(Mentha piperita)*

Blends:

Male Blend
Hormone Blend
Glandular Blend

Prostatitis Blend:

- 10 drops frankincense
- 5 drops myrrh
- 3 drops sage

Applications:

INGESTION:	CAPSULE, 0 size, twice daily
RETENTION:	RECTAL, 3 times per week, at night
TOPICAL:	DILUTE 20-80, apply 1-3 drops to the area between the rectum and the scrotum daily
	VITA FLEX, massage 4-6 drops on reproductive Vita Flex points on feet

PSORIASIS

(See SKIN DISORDERS)

RESTLESS LEG SYNDROME

Single Oils:

Oregano *(Origanim compactum)*
Basil *(Ocimum basilicum)*
Marjoram *(Origanum majorana)*
Lavender *(Lavandula angustifolia)*
Cypress *(Cupressus sempervirens)*
Roman chamomile *(Chamaemelum nobile)*
Peppermint *(Mentha piperita)*

Blends:

Stress Reduction Blend
Muscle Relaxing Blend

Applications:

INHALATION:	DIRECT, 6-8 times daily as needed DIFFUSER, 20 minutes, 4 times daily
TOPICAL:	RAINDROP Technique, weekly

RHEUMATIC FEVER

Rheumatic fever results from a *Streptococcus* infection that primarily strikes children (usually before age 14). It can lead to inflammation that damages the heart muscle and valves.

Rheumatic fever is caused by the same genus of bacteria that causes strep throat and scarlet fever. Diffusing essential oils can help reduce the likelihood of contracting the disease. Essential oils such as mountain savory, rosemary cineol, *Melaleuca alternifolia,* thyme, and oregano, have powerful antimicrobial effects.

In cases where a child is already infected, the use of essential oils through the Raindrop Technique may be appropriate.

Single Oils:

Mountain savory *(Satureja montana)*
Peppermint *(Mentha piperita)*
Thyme linalol *(Thymus vulgaris CT linalol)*
Rosemary verbenon *(Rosmarinus officinalis CT verbenon)*
Tea tree oil *(Melaleuca alternifolia)*
Clove *(Syzygium aromaticum)*
Oregano *(Origanum compactum)*

Blends:

Antimicrobial Blend
Immune Blend

Applications:

INHALATION:	DIFFUSER, 1 hour, 3 times daily
TOPICAL:	DILUTE 50-50, massage 3-5 drops on bottoms of feet and on carotid artery spots under ear lobes RAINDROP Technique, once weekly

RINGWORM

(See FUNGAL INFECTIONS)

SALMONELLA

(See FOOD POISONING, and INFECTION)

SCABIES

Scabies are caused by arachnids known as itch mites, tiny parasites that burrow into the skin, usually in the fingers and genital areas. The most common variety, *Sarcoptes scabiei,* can quickly infest other people. Although it only lives six weeks, it continually lays eggs once it gets into the skin.

Essential oils have been studied for their ability to not only repel insects, but also kill them and their eggs as well. Because many oils are nontoxic to humans, they make excellent treatments to combat scabies infestations.

Single Oils:

Citronella *(Cymbopogon nardus)*
Peppermint *(Mentha piperita)*
Palmarosa *(Cymbopogon martinii)*
Lavandin *(Lavandula x hybrida)*
Eucalyptus globulus
Black pepper *(Piper nigrum)*
Ginger *(Zingiber officinale)*

Blends:

Digestive Blend
Antibacterial Blend
Stress Reduction Blend

Applications:

TOPICAL: NEAT, or DILUTE 50-50 if needed, apply 2-4 drops on location, 3 times daily
DILUTE 20-80, massage thoroughly 1 tsp. into scalp at night before retiring. To treat hair or scalp, add 2-4 drops of essential oil to 1 tsp. of shampoo.

SCAR TISSUE

Some essential oils may be valuable for reducing or minimizing the formation of scar tissue:

Single Oils:

Helichrysum *(Helichrysum italicum)*
Lavender *(Lavandula angustifolia)*
Cypress *(Cupressus sempervirens)*

Elemi *(Canarium luzonicum)*
Blue yarrow *(Achillea millefolium)*
Rose *(Rosa damascena)*
Cistus *(Cistus ladanifer)*
Myrrh *(Commiphora myrrha)*
Sandalwood *(Santalum album)*

Blends:

Scar Prevention Blend:
- 4 drops helichrysum
- 6 drops lavender
- 8 drops myrrh
- 2 drops sandalwood

Applications:

TOPICAL: NEAT, gently apply 2-6 drops over wound or cut daily until healed

SCIATICA

(See SPINE INJURIES and PAIN)

SCHIZOPHRENIA

A neurological disease that involves identity confusion. Onset is typically between the late teens and early 30's. Abnormal neurological findings may show a broad range of dysfunction including slow reaction time, poor coodination, abnormalities in eye tracking, and impaired sensory gating. Typically schizophrenia involves dysfunction in one or more areas such as interpersonal relations, work, education, or self-care. Some case are believed to be caused by viral infection.

Single Oils:

Peppermint *(Mentha piperita)*
Cardamom *(Elettaria cardamomum)*
Cedarwood *(Cedrus atlantica)*
Vetiver *(Vetiveria zizanioides)*
Melissa *(Melissa officinalis)*
Frankincense *(Boswellia carteri)*
Rosemary cineol *(Rosmarinus officinalis CT 1,8 cineol)*

Blends:
Brain Blend
Clarity Blend
Energy Balance Blend
Headache Blend

Applications:

INHALATION:	DIRECT, 4-6 times daily
TOPICAL:	RAINDROP Technique, once weekly

SCLERODERMA

Also known as systemic sclerosis, scleroderma is a non-infectious, chronic, autoimmune disease of the connective tissue. Caused by an over-production of collagen, the disease can involve either the skin or internal organs and can be life-threatening. Scleroderma is far more common among women than men.

Single Oils:
Frankincense *(Boswellia carteri)*
Roman chamomile *(Chamaemelum nobile)*
German chamomile *(Matricaria recutita)*
Lavender *(Lavandula angustifolia)*
Patchouli *(Pogostemon cablin)*
Sandalwood *(Santalum album)*
Myrrh *(Commiphora myrrha)*

Blends:
Antiseptic Blend

Scleroderma Blend #1:
- 3 drops Roman chamomile
- 3 drops lavender
- 3 drops patchouli

Scleroderma Blend #2:
- 4 drops sandalwood
- 4 drops myrrh

Applications:

TOPICAL:	DILUTE 50-50, massage 4-6 drops on location 3 times daily. Alternate between blend #1 and blend #2 (above) each day

SCOLIOSIS

(See SPINE INJURIES and Chapter 11: Raindrop Technique)

Scoliosis is an abnormal lateral or side-to-side curvature or twist in the spine. It is different from hyperkyphosis (hunchback) or hyperlordosis (swayback) which involve excessive front-to-back accentuation of existing spine curvatures.

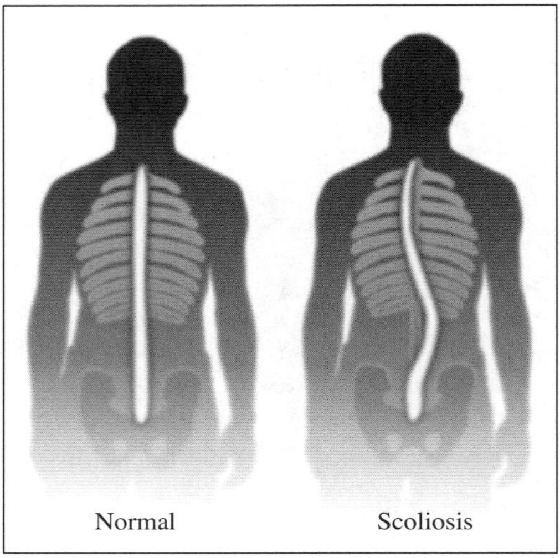

While a few cases of scoliosis can be attributed to congenital deformities (such as MS, cerebral palsy, Down's syndrome, or Marfan's syndrome), the vast majority of scoliosis types are of unknown origin.

Some medical professionals believe that scoliosis may be caused by persistent muscle spasms that pull the vertebrae off the spine, out of alignment. Others, and a growing body of research which are documenting this hypothesis, believe that it begins with hard-to-detect inflammation along the spine caused by latent viruses. (See citations in Chapter 11.)

Symptoms:

- When bending forward, the left side of the back is higher or lower than the right side (the patient must be viewed from the rear).
- One hip may appear to be higher or more prominent than the other.
- Uneven shoulders or scapulas (shoulder blades).
- When the arms are hanging loosely, the distance between the left arm and left side is different than the distance between the right arm and right side.

The Raindrop Technique is proving to be one of the most effective therapies for straightening spines misaligned due to scoliosis.

> Chiropractors are finding that their spinal manipulations take less time and effort, and the results last longer if they first apply 4-6 drops of Energy Balance Blend to the bottom of each foot.

Single Oils:

Oregano *(Origanum compactum)*
Thyme *(Thymus vulgaris)*
Basil *(Ocimum basilicum)*
Wintergreen or birch *(Gaultheria procumbens* or *Betula alleghaniensis)*
Cypress *(Cupressus sempervirens)*
Marjoram *(Origanum majorana)*
Peppermint *(Mentha piperita)*

Blends:

Muscle Relaxing Blend
Pain Relief Blend

Applications:

TOPICAL: RAINDROP Technique, 3-5 times monthly
DILUTE 50-50, as a supplement to Raindrop Technique, apply 3-6 drops along spine daily or as needed

SEIZURES

(See BRAIN DISORDERS or EPILEPSY)

Single Oils:

Frankincense *(Boswellia carteri)*
Sandalwood *(Santalum album)*
Melissa *(Melissa officinalis)*
Jasmine *(Jasminum officinale)*
Basil *(Ocimum basilicum)*

Blends:

Energy Balance Blend
Muscle Relaxing Blend
Stress Reduction Blend
Brain Blend

Applications:

TOPICAL: DILUTE 50-50, massage 10 drops into scalp 3 times daily to help reduce risk of seizure. Supplement with inhalation therapy below

INHALATION: DIRECT, 3-5 times daily

Remove all forms of sugar, artificial colors, and artificial flavors from diet. Avoid using all personal care products with ammonium-based compounds.

Seizure Regimen (do all the following):

- Massage 4-6 drops Energy Balance Blend on bottoms of feet daily
- Diffuse Stress Reduction Blend for 30 minutes 4 times a day
- Massage 4-6 drops Mood Lifting Blend over heart daily
- Do a Raindrop Technique on spine weekly.

SEXUAL DYSFUNCTION

(See IMPOTENCE)

Lack of Libido (Frigidity)

For Womem:

Single Oils:

Geranium *(Pelargonium graveolens)*
Ylang ylang *(Cananga odorata)*
Clary sage *(Salvia sclarea)*
Jasmine *(Jasminum officinale)*
Nutmeg *(Myristica fragrans)*
Rose *(Rosa damascena)*

Blends:

Romance Blend
Female Blend

For Men:

Single Oils:

Myrrh *(Commiphora myrrha)*
Black pepper *(Piper nigrum)*
Pine *(Pinus sylvestris)*
Ylang ylang *(Cananga odorata)*
Ginger *(Zingiber officinale)*
Nutmeg *(Myristica fragrans)*

Blends:

Mood Lifting Blend
Male Blend

Applications:

INHALATION:	DIRECT, 3-5 times daily
TOPICAL:	DILUTE 50-50, massage 4-6 drops on neck, shoulders and lower abdomen, 1-3 times daily

Excessive Sexual Desire

Single Oils:

Marjoram *(Origanum majorana)*
Lavender *(Lavandula angustifolia)*
St. John's wort *(Hypericum perforatum)*

Blends:

Stress Reduction Blend

Applications:

INHALATION:	DIRECT, 3-5 times daily
TOPICAL:	DILUTE 50-50, massage 4-6 drops on neck, shoulders and lower abdomen, 1-3 times daily

SEXUALLY TRANSMITTED DISEASES

Herpes Simplex Type II

The Herpes Simplex Virus Type 2, is transmitted by sexual contact and results in sores or lesions. Four to seven days after contact with an infected partner, tingling, burning, or persistent itching usually heralds an outbreak. One or two days later, small pimple-like bumps appear over reddened skin. The itching and tingling continue, and the pimples turn into painful blisters, which burst, bleeding with a yellowish pus. Five to seven days after the first tingling, scabs form, and healing begins.

Antiviral essential oils have generally been very effective in treating herpes lesions and reducing their onset. Oils such as *Melaleuca alternifolia,* melissa, and rosemary (verbenon) have been successfully used for this purpose by Daniel Pénoël, MD in his clinical practice. A study at the University of Buenos Aires found that sandalwood essential oil inhibited the replication of Herpes Simplex viruses-1 and -2.[24]

Those with herpes should avoid diets high in the amino acid L-arginine, substituting instead L-lysine. Lysine retards the growth of the virus. Foods such as amaranth are very high in lysine.

Single Oils:

Sandalwood *(Santalum album)*
Blue cypress *(Callitris intratropica)*
Melissa *(Melissa officinalis)*
Ravensara *(Ravensara aromatica)*
Tea tree oil *(Melaleuca alternifolia)*

24. Benencia F, et al. "Antiviral activity of sandalwood oil against herpes simplex viruses-1 and -2." *Phytomedicine.* 1999;6(2):119-23

Oregano *(Origanum compactum)*
Thyme thymol *(Thymus vulgaris CT thymol)*
Cumin *(Cuminum cyminum)*
Rosemary cineol *(Rosmarinus officinalis CT cineol)*
Blue cypress *(Callitris intratropica)*

Blends:

Antiseptic Blend
Antimicrobial Blend
Antibacterial Blend
Antiviral Blend

Herpes Blend #1:
- 1 drop lavender
- 1 drop tea tree oil

Herpes Blend #2:
- 2 drops sage
- 2 drops melissa
- 4 drops ravensara
- 2 drops lavender

Applications:

TOPICAL: NEAT, apply Herpes Blend #1 (above) on lesion as soon as it appears. Apply 1-2 drops of neat oil daily, alternating between the above herpes blend and Antiseptic Blend each day.
RAINDROP, 1-2 treatments

RETENTION: TAMPON, for additional vaginal treatment of herpes, use Herpes Blend #2 (above), diluted 20-80 in tampon/pad application nightly. If tampon/pad stings after 5 minutes, remove and change dilution rate to 10-90.

Genital Warts

Warts are a form of viral infection caused by the human papillomavirus (HPV), of which there are more than 60 different types.

One type of HPV virus is among the most common forms of sexually transmitted disease. Up to 24 million Americans may be currently infected with HPV, usually spread through sexual contact. HPV lives only in genital tissue. HPV can later lead to cervical cancer in women.

Single Oils:

Oregano *(Origanum compactum)*
Melissa *(Melissa officinalis)*
Thyme thymol *(Thymus vulgaris CT thymol)*
Tansy *(Tanacetum vulgare)*
Blue cypress *(Callitris intratropica)*
Tea tree oil *(Melaleuca alternifolia)*
Melaleuca ericifolia
Lavender *(Lavandula angustifolia)*

Blends:

Antiseptic Blend
Antimicrobial Blend
Immune Blend

Applications:

TOPICAL:	NEAT or DILUTE 50-50, 1-3 drops 2 times a day for 10 days
RETENTION:	TAMPON, nightly

Gonorrhea and Syphilis

NOTE: Seek immediate professional medical attention if you suspect you may have these diseases.

Single Oils:

Oregano *(Origanum compactum)*
Melissa *(Melissa officinalis)*
Blue cypress *(Callitris intratropica)*
Thyme thymol *(Thymus vulgaris CT thymol)*
Mountain savory *(Satureja montana)*
Cinnamon *(Cinnamomum verum)*

Blends:

Antimicrobial Blend

Applications:

INGESTION:	CAPSULE, 00 size, 1 capsule 2 times a day for 15 days

SHINGLES (Herpes Zoster)

Shingles is an active (generally short-lived) viral infection of the central nervous system that affects certain areas of the skin. This usually starts with fatigue, fever, chills, and at times, intestinal upset. On the third to fourth day, the affected skin area becomes excessively sensitive. On the fourth or fifth day, small painful blisters erupt along the nerve pathway and crust over. Normally these heal in about 5 days without further problems. One attack usually provides immunity for life. However, for many people, particularly the elderly, pain can persist for months, even years.

The virus that causes shingles is *Varicella zoster*, which also causes chicken pox. A childhood bout with chicken pox leaves many viruses dormant in sensory (skin) nerves. If the immune system is compromised from things such as severe emotional stress, illness, or long-term use of corticosteroids, the dormant viruses may become active and start to infect the pathway of the skin nerves.

NOTE: Occurrences of shingles around the eyes or on the forehead can cause blindness. Consult an ophthalmologist (eye doctor) immediately if such outbreaks occur.

Single Oils:

Elemi *(Canarium luzonicum)*
Tansy *(Tanacetum vulgare)*
Melaleuca alternifolia
Ravensara *(Ravensara aromatica)*
Oregano *(Origanum compactum)*
Blue cypress *(Callitris intratropica)*
Sandalwood *(Santalum album)*
Mountain savory *(Satureja montana)*
Thyme thymol *(Thymus vulgaris CT thymol)*
Peppermint *(Mentha piperita)*
Tamanu *(Calophyllum inophyllum)* (a fatty acid oil)

Essential Oils vs. Shingles

Equal amounts of ravensara and *Calophyllum inophyllum* (tamanu, a fatty acid oil) applied to a shingles outbreak have produced dramatic improvement and complete remission within 7 days (*Alternative Medicine, The Definitive Guide*, p. 56, 971).

Blends:

Antiviral Blend

Shingles blend #1:
- 10 drops German chamomile
- 5 drops lavender
- 4 drops sandalwood
- 2 drops geranium

Shingles blend #2:
- 10 drops sandalwood
- 5 drops blue cypress
- 4 drops peppermint
- 2 drops ravensara

APPLICATION:

TOPICAL: DILUTE 50-50, apply 6-10 drops on affected area, back of neck and down the spine 1-3 times daily. COMPRESS, alternating warm and cold, on spine, 1-3 times daily

Shingles regimen:

A. Layering in Raindrop Technique style, apply 3-4 drops each of oregano, mountain savory and thyme along the spine

B. Apply 15-20 drops vegetable or massage oil to the spine, massage briefly over the oils, then cover the skin with a dry towel and apply a warm pack for 15-20 minutes).

NOTE: Be cautious about warming. If the back becomes too hot, remove the warm pack immediately and add more vegetable or massage oil to cool.

C. Remove the warm pack and towel and layer 4-8 drops each of juniper, geranium and peppermint along the spine

D. Put the dry towel back over the skin and apply an ice pack for 30 minutes.

SHOCK

Shock can be described as a state of profound depression of the vital processes associated with reduced blood volume and pressure. The blood rushes to the vital organs after trauma.

It may be caused by the sudden stimulation of the nerves and convulsive contraction of the muscles caused by the discharge of electricity. Other causes include sudden trauma, terror, surprise, horror, or disgust.

Symptoms or signs:

- Irregular breathing
- Low blood pressure
- Dilated pupils
- Cold and sweaty skin
- Weak and rapid pulse
- Dry mouth
- Weak knees, dizziness

Any injury that results in the sudden loss of substantial amounts of fluids can trigger shock.

Shock can also be caused by allergic reactions (anaphylactic shock), infections in the blood (septic shock), or emotional trauma (neurogenic shock).

Shock should be treated by covering the victim with a blanket and elevating the victim's feet unless there is a head or upper torso injury. Inhaling essential oils can also help—especially in cases of emotional shock.

Single Oils:

Cardamom *(Elettaria cardamomum)*
Helichrysum *(Helichrysum italicum)*
Peppermint *(Mentha piperita)*
Tea tree oil *(Melaleuca alternifolia)*
Frankincense *(Boswellia carteri)*
Basil *(Origanum basilicum)*

Blends:

Clarity Blend
Trauma Blend
Energy Balance Blend

Applications:

INHALATION:	DIRECT, 1-2 drops
TOPICAL:	DILUTE 50-50, rub 1-2 drops on temples, back of neck, and under nose.

NOTE: When applying essential oil to the temples be careful not to get the oil too close to the eyes.

SINUS INFECTION

(See also COLDS, THROAT INFECTION)

Congestion (Sinus)

Single Oils:

Sandalwood *(Santalum album)*
Goldenrod *(Solidago canadensis)*
Ledum *(Ledum groenlandicum)*
Balsam fir *(Abies balsamea)*
Ravensara *(Ravensara aromatica)*
Thyme linalol *(Thymus vulgaris CT linalol)*
Eucalyptus radiata
Tea tree oil *(Melaleuca alternifolia)*
Peppermint *(Mentha piperita)*
Fennel *(Foeniculum vulgare)*
Rosemary cineol *(Rosmarinus officinalis CT 1,8 cineol)*

Blends:

Digestive Blend
Respiratory Blend
Antiviral Blend

Applications:

INHALATION:	DIRECT, 3-5 times daily, or as needed
	VAPOR, 2-3 times daily, as needed
INGESTION:	SYRUP, 3-6 times daily
ORAL:	GARGLE, 3-6 times daily
TOPICAL:	DILUTE 50-50, massage 1-3 drops on each of the following areas: forehead, nose, cheecks, lower throat, chest and upper back, 1-3 times daily
	VITA FLEX, massage 1-3 drops on Vita Flex points on the feet.
	RAINDROP Technique, 1-2 times weekly
	BATH SALT, daily

Nasal Irrigation Regimen:

Rosemary and tea tree oils can be used in a saline solution for very effective nasal irrigation that clears and decongests sinuses. As recommended by Daniel Pénoël, MD, the saline solution is prepared as follows:

- 12 drops rosemary cineol
- 4 drops tea tree
- 8 tablespoons very fine salt (salt flower)

The essential oils are mixed thoroughly in the fine salt and kept in a sealable container. For each nasal irrigation session, 1 teaspoon of this salt mixture is dissolved into

- 1 1/2 cups distilled water

This oils/salt/water solution is then placed in the tank of an oral irrigator to irrigate the nasal cavaties, which is done while bending over a sink. This application has brought surprisingly positive results in treating latent sinusitus and other nasal congestion problems.[25]

Sinusitis

Essential oils such as *Eucalyptus radiata* and ravensara strengthen the respiratory system, open the pulmonary tract, and fight respiratory infection.

Single Oils:

Clove *(Syzygium aromaticum)*
Ravensara *(Ravensara aromatica)*
Myrtle *(Myrtus communis)*
Cypress *(Cupressus sempervirens)*
Lemon *(Citrus limon)*
Eucalyptus radiata
Eucalyptus globulus
Tea tree oil *(Melaleuca alternifolia)*
Thyme linalol *(Thymus vulgaris CT linalol)*
Rosemary verbenon *(Rosmarinus officinalis CT verbenon)*

Blends:

Respiratory Blend
Antimicrobial Blend
Immune Blend
Antibacterial Blend

Sinusitis Blend: (Swab inside of nostrils)

- 3 drops *Melaleuca ericifolia*
- 3 drops Respiratory Blend

Applications:

INHALATION:	DIRECT, 3-5 times daily
TOPICAL:	DILUTE 50-50, apply 1-2 drops to a cotton swab, and swab inside of nostrils 3 times daily. The Sinusitis blend is ideal for this method.
ORAL:	GARGLE, 2-5 times daily

25. Pénoël, Daniel, MD. and Rose Marie, *Natural Home Health Care Using Essential Oils*, Essential Science Publishing, 1998. pp. 166-167

Nasal Irrigation Regimen: (see under Congestion)

Rhinitis (Inflammation of the mucous membranes of the nose)

Single Oils:

Basil *(Ocimum basilicum)*
Eucalyptus radiata
Tea tree oil *(Melaleuca alternifolia)*
Ravensara *(Ravensara aromatica)*

Blends:

Respiratory Blend
Antiseptic Blend

Applications:

INHALATION:	DIRECT, 4-8 times daily
TOPICAL:	NEAT, apply 2-4 drops on forehead and bridge of nose, being careful not to get oils in or near eyes or eyelids.

Rhinopharyngitis

Single Oils:

Eucalyptus radiata
Thyme *(Thymus vulgaris)*
Ravensara *(Ravensara aromatica)*

Blends:

Respiratory Blend
Antimicrobial Blend

Applications:

TOPICAL:	DILUTE, 50-50, apply just under jawbone
INHALATION:	DIRECT, 4-8 times daily
ORAL:	GARGLE, 2-5 times daily

SKIN DISORDERS

Our skin is our armor and the largest absorbent organ of the body. Protecting the skin environment is essential. Many chemical molecules are too large to be absorbed and lay on the surface of the skin, causing irritation, resulting in rashes, itching, blemishes, flaky and dry skin, dandruff, and allergies. Essential oils are soluble through lipids in the skin and are easily absorbed.

Many skin conditions may be related to dysfunctions of the liver. It may be necessary to cleanse, stimulate, and condition the liver and colon for 30 to 90 days before the skin begins to improve.

Single Oils:

Tea tree oil *(Melaleuca alternifolia)*
Blue cypress *(Callitris intratropica)*
Thyme thymol *(Thymus vulgaris CT thymol)*
Peppermint *(Mentha piperita)*
Lavender *(Lavandula angustifolia)*
German chamomile *(Matricaria recutita)*
Rosemary cineol *(Rosmarinus officinalis CT 1,8 cineol)*
Mountain savory *(Satureja montana)*
Palmarosa *(Cymbopogon martinii)*
Patchouli *(Pogostemon cablin)*
Rosewood *(Aniba rosaeodora)*
Juniper *(Juniperus communis* or *J. osteosperma)*
Ravensara *(Ravensara aromatica)*
Oregano *(Origanum compactum)*

Blends:

Antiseptic Blend
Antibacterial Blend
Immune Blend
Antimicrobial Blend

Applications:

TOPICAL: DILUTE 50-50 or 20-80 depending upon application code in Appendix F, apply on location 1-3 times daily

Abscesses:

Skin abscesses are small pockets of pus that collect under the skin. They are usually caused by a bacterial or fungal infection.

Single Oils:

Thyme *(Thymus vulgaris)*
Myrrh *(Commiphora myrrha)*
Frankincense *(Boswellia carteri)*
Wintergreen or birch *(Gaultheria procumbens* or *Betula alleghaniensis)*

Applications:

TOPICAL: DILUTE 50-50, apply on location 1-3 times daily

Acne

Acne results from an excess accumulation of dirt and sebum around the hair follicle and the pores of the skin. This accumulation may be due to an over-production of sebum, an oily substance that is secreted by the sebaceous glands in the hair follicles. As the pores and hair follicles become congested, bacteria begins to feed on the sebum. This leads to inflammation and infection around the hair follicle and the formation of a pimple or a pus-filled blackhead.

One of the most common forms of acne, *Acne vulgaris,* occurs primarily in adolescents due to hormone imbalances which stimulate the creation of sebum.

Acne in adults can be also be caused by hormone imbalances, as well as use of chlorinated compounds, endocrine system imbalances, or poor dietary practices, including too much sugar. Heavy or greasy makeup can also contribute to acne.

Stress may also play a role. According to research conducted by Dr. Toyoda in Japan, acne is a direct result of physical and emotional stress[26].

Essential oils constitute outstanding treatments of acne due to their ability to dissolve hardened sebum, kill bacteria, and preserve the acid mantle of the skin. Because essential oils may be slightly drying to the skin when applied neat, it may be necessary to dilute them with grapeseed oil or a massage oil to keep the skin hydrated.

A clinical study[27] found that *Melaleuca alternifolia* is equally effective as benzoyl peroxide for treating acne but with fewer side effects.

Single Oils:

Tea tree oil *(Melaleuca alternifolia)*
Geranium *(Pelargonium graveolens)*
Vetiver *(Vetiveria zizanioides)*
Sandalwood *(Santalum album)*
Lavender *(Lavandula angustifolia)*
Lemongrass *(Cymbopogon flexuosus)*
German chamomile *(Matricaria recutita)*
Rosewood *(Aniba rosaeodora)*
Cedarwood *(Cedrus atlantica)*
Eucalyptus radiata
Orange *(Citrus aurantium)*
Neroli *(Citrus aurantium)*

26. Toyoda M, Morohashi M, "Pathenogenesis of acne," *Med Electron Microse* 2001 Mar;34(1):29-40.

27. Bassett IB, et al. "A comparative study of tea-tree oil versus benzoyl peroxide in the treatment of acne." *Med J Aust.* 1990;153(8):455-8.

Blends:

Antiseptic Blend
Antibacterial Blend
Liver Blend
Glandular Blend

Applications:

TOPICAL:	NEAT or DILUTE 50-50 as required. Gently massage 3-5 drops into oily areas daily. Alternate oils daily for maximum effect

Athlete's Foot

(see FOOT PROBLEMS)

Burns

(See BURNS)

Chapped, Dry, or Cracked Skin

Body lotions combined with essential oils are very effective for rehydrating the skin of chapped hands and maintaining the natural pH balance of the skin.

Single Oils:

Roman chamomile *(Chamaemelum nobile)*
Neroli *(Citrus aurantium)*
Rose *(Rosa damascena)*
Palmarosa *(Cymbopogon martinii)*
Sandalwood *(Santalum album)*
Rosewood *(Aniba rosaeodora)*
Lavender *(Lavandula angustifolia)*
Spikenard *(Nardostachys jatamansi)*
Myrrh *(Commiphora myrrha)*

Blends:

Chapped skin blend:
- 1 drop rosewood
- 1 drop patchouli
- 1 drop geranium

Dry skin blend:
- 1 drop rose
- 1 drop Roman chamomile
- 1 drop sandalwood

Essential oils that help the skin

To rejuvenate and heal skin:
- Rosewood

To prevent and retard wrinkles:
- Lavender, spikenard, and myrrh

To regenerate the skin
- Geranium, helichrysum, and spikenard

To restore skin elasticity
- Rosewood, lavender
- Ylang ylang with lavender

To combat premature aging of the skin
Mix the following recipe into 1 tablespoon of high grade, unperfumed skin lotion and apply on location twice daily.

- 6 drops rosewood
- 4 drops geranium
- 3 drops lavender
- 2 drops frankincense

Applications:

TOPICAL: DILUTE 20-80 in a quality, unperfumed lotion base or other high grade emolient, skin oil, apply on location as often as needed

Clogged Pores

Single Oils:

Lemon *(Citrus limon)*
Melaleuca ericifolia
Orange *(Citrus aurantium)*
Geranium *(Pelargonium graveolens)*

Blends:

Antibacterial Blend

Applications:

TOPICAL: NEAT, apply 2-4 drops to affected area and remove with cotton ball

Diaper Rash

Single Oils:

Lavender *(Lavandula angustifolia)*
Helichrysum *(Helichrysum italicum)*
German chamomile *(Matricaria recutita)*
Cypress *(Cupressus sempervirens)*

Applications:

TOPICAL: DILUTE, 50-50, apply on location 2-4 times daily

Eczema/Dermatitis

Eczema and dermatitis are both inflammations of the skin and are most often due to allergies, but also can be a sign of liver disease (See LIVER).

Dermatitis usually results from external factors, such as sunburn or contact with poison ivy, metals (wristwatch, earrings, jewelry, etc.). Eczema can result from internal factors, such as irritant chemicals, soaps and shampoos, allergy to wheat (gluten), etc. It can also be exacerbated by hormonal factors. In both dermatitis and eczema, skin becomes red, flaky, and itchy; small blisters may form and, if broken by scratching, can become infected.

Single Oils:

Lavender *(Lavandula angustifolia)*
Juniper *(Juniperus communis* or *J. osteosperma)*
Ledum *(Ledum groenlandicum)*
Kaffir lime *(Citrus hystrix)*
Celery seed oil *(Leptospermum scoparium)*
Cistus *(Cistus ladanifer)*
Roman chamomile *(Chamaemelum nobile)*
German chamomile *(Matricaria recutita)*
Geranium *(Pelargonium graveolens)*
Rosewood *(Aniba rosaeodora)*
Thyme thymol *(Thymus vulgaris CT thymol)*

Blends:

Liver Blend
Antibacterial Blend
Antiseptic Blend

Applications:

TOPICAL: DILUTE 50-50, apply as needed on location

Freckles

Single Oils:

Tansy *(Tanacetum vulgare)*

Applications:

TOPICAL: Dilute 4-6 drops in 1/2 teaspoon of high grade, unperfumed skin lotion. Spread lightly over freckle areas. Use 2-3 times a week

Fungal Infection

(see FUNGAL INFECTIONS)

Single Oils:

Oregano *(Origanum compactum)*
Tea tree oil *(Melaleuca alternifolia)*
Melaleuca ericifolia

Blends:

Antiseptic Blend:

Antifungal skin blend:

- 10 drops patchouli
- 4 drops lavender
- 2 drops German chamomile
- 5 drops lemon

Applications:

TOPICAL: DILUTE 50-50, apply on location, 3-5 times daily

Itching

Itching can be due to dry skin, dermatitis, impaired liver function, allergies, or over-exposure to chemicals or sunlight.

Single Oils:

Peppermint *(Mentha piperita)*
Oregano *(Origanum compactum)*
Lavender *(Lavandula angustifolia)*
Helichrysum *(Helichrysum italicum)*
Nutmeg *(Myristica fragrans)*
German chamomile *(Matricaria recutita)*

Blends:
Muscle Relaxing Blend

Applications:

TOPICAL:	DILUTE 50-50, apply on location as needed

Melanoma (See cancer)

Moles

To remove moles: Apply 1 drops of oregano neat, directly on the mole, 1-3 times a day.

Poison Oak / Poison Ivy

Single Oils:

Peppermint *(Mentha piperita)*
Eucalyptus dives
German chamomile *(Matricaria recutita)*
Lemongrass *(Cymbopogon flexuosus)*
Tansy *(Tanacetum vulgare)*
Tea tree oil *(Melaleuca alternifolia)*
Rosemary cineol *(Rosmarinus officinalis CT 1,8 cineol)*
Basil *(Ocimum basilicum)*
Eucalyptus dives

Blends:
Antimicrobial Blend

Applications:

TOPICAL:	DILUTE 50-50, apply 4-6 drops to affected areas twice daily COMPRESS: Cold, apply on affected area twice daily

Psoriasis

Psoriasis is a non-infectious skin disorder that is marked by skin lesions that can occur in limited areas (such as the scalp) or that can cover up to 80-90 percent of the body.

The overly rapid growth of skin cells is the primary cause of the lesions associated with psoriasis. In some cases, skin cells grow four times faster than normal, resulting in the formation of silvery layers that flake off.

Symptoms:

- Occurs on elbows, chest, knees, and scalp.
- Slightly elevated reddish lesions covered with silver-white scales.
- The disease can be limited to one small patch or can cover the entire body.
- Rashes subside after exposure to sunlight.
- Rashes recur over a period of years.

Single Oils:

Roman chamomile *(Chamaemelum nobile)*
Tea tree oil *(Melaleuca alternifolia)*
Patchouli *(Pogostemon cablin)*
Helichrysum *(Helichrysum italicum)*
Rose *(Rosa damascena)*
German chamomile *(Matricaria recutita)*
Lavender *(Lavandula angustifolia)*

Blends:

Antiseptic Blend
Liver Blend

Psoriasis blend:

- 2 drops patchouli
- 2 drops Roman chamomile
- 2 drops lavender
- 2 drops Antiseptic Blend

Applications:

TOPICAL:	NEAT, apply 2-4 drops to affected area twice daily. Can be added to regular skin lotion. COMPRESS: warm, 3 times a week
INGESTION:	CAPSULE, 0 size, 1 per day

Sagging Skin

Single Oils:

Lavender *(Lavandula angustifolia)*
Helichrysum *(Helichrysum italicum)*
Patchouli *(Pogostemon cablin)*
Cypress *(Cupressus sempervirens)*

Blends:

Skin firming blend (morning):
- 10 drops tangerine
- 10 drops cypress

Skin firming blend (evening):
- 8 drops geranium
- 5 drops cypress
- 5 drops helichrysum
- 1 drop peppermint

Applications:

TOPICAL: NEAT or DILUTE 50-50, massage 4-6 drops on affected area daily

Stretch Marks

Essential oils can be invaluable companions during pregnancy. Oils like lavender and myrrh may help reduce stretch marks and improve the elasticity of the skin. Stretch marks are most commonly associated with pregnancy, but can also occur during growth spurts and periods of rapid weight gain.

Single Oils:

Lavender *(Lavandula angustifolia)*
Frankincense *(Boswellia carteri)*
Elemi *(Canarium luzonicum)*
Spikenard *(Nardostachys jatamansi)*
Geranium *(Pelargonium graveolens)*
Myrrh *(Commiphora myrrha)*

Applications:

TOPICAL: NEAT or DILUTE 50-50, apply on affected areas 2 times daily

Skin Ulcers and Bedsores

Single Oils:

Rosewood *(Aniba rosaeodora)*
Helichrysum *(Helichrysum italicum)*
Roman chamomile *(Chamaemelum nobile)*
Vetiver *(Vetiveria zizanioides)*

Patchouli *(Pogostemon cablin)*
Myrrh *(Commiphora myrrha)*
Lavender *(Lavandula angustifolia)*
Vetiver *(Vetiveria zizanioides)*

Blends:
Antiseptic Blend
Antibacterial Blend
Pain Relief Blend

Applications:

TOPICAL: NEAT or DILUTE 50-50, apply 4-6 drops on affected areas 2 times daily

Vitiligo

A skin disorder marked by patches of skin devoid of skin pigmentation.

Single Oils:
Vetiver *(Vetiveria zizanioides)*
Sandalwood *(Santalum album)*
Myrrh *(Commiphora myrrha)*

Blends:
Antibacterial Blend
Antiseptic Blend

Applications:

TOPICAL: NEAT, apply 2-4 drops on location, 2 times a day

Wrinkled or Rough Skin

Single Oils:
Frankincense *(Boswellia carteri)*
Helichrysum *(Helichrysum italicum)*
Cypress *(Cupressus sempervirens)*
Rose *(Rosa damascena)*
Lavender *(Lavandula angustifolia)*
Patchouli *(Pogostemon cablin)*
Sage *(Salvia officinalis)*
Geranium *(Pelargonium graveolens)*
Rosewood *(Aniba rosaeodora)*
Sandalwood *(Santalum album)*

Blends:

Wrinkle Blend:
- 5 drops sandalwood
- 5 drops helichrysum
- 5 drops geranium
- 5 drops lavender
- 5 drops frankincense

Applications:

TOPICAL:	DILUTE 50-50 in high grade, unperfumed body lotion or an emollient vegetable oil and apply on location as needed

NOTE: Be careful not to get lotion or oils near the eyes.

SLEEP DISORDERS

(See INSOMNIA)

Single Oils:

Lavender *(Lavandula angustifolia)*
Valerian *(Valeriana officinalis)*
Goldenrod *(Solidago canadensis)*
Marjoram *(Origanum majorana)*
Roman chamomile *(Chamaemelum nobile)*
Orange *(Citrus aurantium)*

Blends:

Stress Reduction Blend
Spiritual Blend

Applications:

INGESTION:	CAPSULE, 0 size, 1 per day
INHALATION:	DIRECT, 1-3 times before bed
	DIFFUSER: 30 minutes before bed

SMOKING CESSATION

(see ADDICTIONS)

Single Oils:

Cinnamon *(Cinnamomum verum)*
Clove *(Syzygium aromaticum)*
Nutmeg *(Myristica fragrans)*

Blends:

Liver Blend
Stress Reduction Blend
Antimicrobial Blend

Applications:

INHALATION: DIRECT, whenever the urge for a cigarette arises
DIFFUSE: 30 minutes, 3 times a day

SNAKE BITES

Single Oils:

Clove *(Syzygium aromaticum)*

Applications:

TOPICAL: DILUTE 50-50, Apply 4-6 drops on location
Get medical attention immediately

SNORING

Rub 4-6 drops thyme diluted 50-50 on the feet at bedtime.

SORE THROAT

(See THROAT INFECTION, COLDS)

SPASTIC COLON

(See DIGESTION PROBLEMS)

SPINA BIFIDA

Spina bifida (SB) is a defect in which the spinal cord of the fetus fails to close during the first month of pregnancy. This results in varying degrees of permanent nerve damage, paralysis in lower limbs, and incomplete brain development.

SB has three different variations:

- The most severe form is Myelomeningocele. The spinal cord and its protective sheath (known as the meninges) protrude from an opening in the spine.
- The next most severe form is Meningocele. Only the meninges protrude from the opening in the spine.

- The mildest form is Occulta. It is characterized by malformed vertebrae. Symptoms of this disease range from bowel and bladder dysfunctions to excess buildup in the brain of cerebrospinal fluid.

The easiest way to prevent SB is with folic acid supplementation (at least 400 mcg daily) by all women of child-bearing age.

To reduce symptoms:

Single Oils:
Mountain savory *(Satureja montana)*
Helichrysum *(Helichrysum italicum)*
Thyme *(Thymus vulgaris)*
Tea tree oil *(Melaleuca alternifolia)*

Blends:
Antiseptic Blend
Antimicrobial Blend

Applications:
TOPICAL: RAINDROP weekly
COMPRESS, warm, 2 times a week

SPINE INJURIES AND PAIN

According to numerous chiropractors, the Raindrop Technique using therapeutic-grade essential oils is revolutionizing the treatment of many types of back pain, spine inflammation, and vertebral misalignments (see chapter on RAINDROP TECHNIQUE).

All of the essential oils described in this chapter can be used effectively in a Raindrop Application as well as in traditional massage therapy.

The following essential oils, blends, and supplements and are used for supporting the structural integrity of the spine and reducing discomfort:

Single Oils:
Wintergreen or birch *(Gaultheria procumbens* or *Betula alleghaniensis)*
Douglas fir *(Pseudotsuga menziesii)*
Balsam fir *(Abies balsamea)*
Spruce *(Picea mariana)*
Peppermint *(Mentha piperita)*
Marjoram *(Origanum majorana)*
Basil *(Ocimum basilicum)*

Blends:

Energy Balance Blend
Muscle Relaxing Blend
Antimicrobial Blend
Pain Relief Blend

Applications:

TOPICAL:	DILUTE 50-50, 6-10 drops on location twice a day or as needed COMPRESS, warm,1-2 times daily (if not inflammed) RAINDROP, 3 times a month for one month

Backache

Single Oils:

Lavender *(Lavandula angustifolia)*
German chamomile *(Matricaria recutita)*
Basil *(Ocimum basilicum)*
Peppermint *(Mentha piperita)*
Geranium *(Pelargonium graveolens)*
Elemi *(Canarium luzonicum)*

Blends:

Backache blend:

- 5 drops clary sage
- 5 drops lavender
- 5 drops chamomile

Pointer Technique for Nerve Damage

The "pointer technique" may also be used on the foot Vita Flex points.

If there is nerve damage, apply about 6 drops of peppermint along the spine, starting at the hips and ending at the neck, using Raindrop Technique. Starting at the bottom of the spine, use a small-nosed pointer (about the size of a pencil but with a round end).

Stimulate each vertebra between each rib on the vertebra knuckles all the way up on each side of the spine. Use medium pressure and a rocking motion for 1-10 seconds at each location. Then follow the same procedure once more up the center of the spine directly on each vertebra.

Applications:

TOPICAL:	NEAT, apply 2-4 drops to aching area 1-3 times daily as needed COMPRESS: warm, if there is no inflammation; cold, if there is inflammation, 1-2 times daily RAINDROP, weekly for 3 weeks

Calcification of Spine

Single Oils:

Geranium *(Pelargonium graveolens)*
Rosemary cineol *(Rosmarinus officinalis CT 1,8 cineol)*
Eucalyptus radiata
Ravensara *(Ravensara aromatica)*
Oregano *(Origanum compactum)*
Vetiver *(Vetiveria zizanioides)*
Elemi *(Canarium luzonicum)*

Blends:

Respiratory Blend

Applications:

TOPICAL:	RAINDROP, 3 times a month

Herniated Disk /Disc Deterioration

For this situation, it is best to consult a specialist. For temporary relief until medical attention can be given:

Single Oils:

Helichrysum *(Helichrysum italicum)*
Spruce *(Picea mariana)*
Basil eugenol *(Ocimum basilicum CT eugenol)*
Thyme *(Thymus vulgaris)*
Melissa *(Melissa officinalis)*

Blends:

Pain Relief Blend
Muscle Relaxing Blend

Applications:

TOPICAL:	DILUTE 50-50, apply on location for pain relief COMPRESS: Cold, on location as needed RAINDROP, weekly

Lumbago (Lower back pain)

Chronic lower back pain can have many causes, including a damaged or pinched nerve (neuralgia) or a congested colon.

Single Oils:
Marjoram *(Origanum majorana)*
Nutmeg *(Myristica fragrans)*
Basil *(Ocimum basilicum)*
Wintergreen or birch *(Gaultheria procumbens* or *Betula alleghaniensis)*
Helichrysum *(Helichrysum italicum)*
German chamomile *(Matricaria recutita)*
Elemi *(Canarium luzonicum)*
Peppermint *(Mentha piperita)*

Blends:
Pain Relief Blend

Applications:

TOPICAL:	DILUTE 50-50, 6-10 drops on location twice a day or as needed COMPRESS, warm, 1-2 times daily (if not inflammed) RAINDROP, 3 times a month

Neck Pain and Stiffness

Single Oils:
Basil *(Ocimum basilicum)*
Marjoram *(Origanum majorana)*
Helichrysum *(Helichrysum italicum)*
Wintergreen or birch *(Gaultheria procumbens* or *Betula alleghaniensis)*
Douglas fir *(Pseudotsuga menziesii)*
Balsam fir *(Abies balsamea)*
Nutmeg *(Myristica fragrans)*
Elemi *(Canarium luzonicum)*
Peppermint *(Mentha piperita)*

Blends:
Neck stiffness blend:
- 5 drops basil
- 5 drops marjoram
- 3 drops lavender

How to Make Your Own High-Powered Massage Oil

Add these formulas to 4 oz. of vegetable or massage oil to create a custom muscle-toning formula.

Massage Oil #1:

- 10 drops wintergreen or birch
- 10 drops balsam fir
- 10 drops marjoram
- 8 drops elemi
- 8 drops vetiver
- 5 drops helichrysum
- 5 drops cypress
- 5 drops peppermint

Massage Oil #2:

- 20 drops wintergreen or birch
- 15 drops marjoram
- 10 drops juniper
- 10 drops cypress
- 6 drops spruce

Neck pain Blend:

- 2 drops helichrysum
- 10 drops wintergreen or birch
- 8 drops cypress
- 15 drops basil
- 4 drops peppermint

Applications:

TOPICAL: DILUTE 50-50, apply 4-6 drops to neck area and massage 1-3 times daily, as needed
COMPRESS: warm, on neck area, once a day or as needed (if no inflammation)

Sciatica

Sciatica is a type of lower back pain that radiates from the lumbar spine area (above the hips) down the back side of the leg. Sciatica is caused from neuralgia (nerve pain) or neuritis (nerve inflammation) originating from the sciatic nerve, which travels from the lower leg to lower back and is the longest nerve in the human body with branches throughout the legs and feet.

Acute sciatica has a sudden onset and is usually triggered by a misaligned vertebra pressing against the sciatic nerve due to accident, injury, pregnancy, or inflammation.

Symptoms:
- Lower back pain
- Swelling or stiffness in a leg
- Loss of sensation in a leg
- Muscle wasting in a leg

Single Oils:
Helichrysum *(Helichrysum italicum)*
Peppermint *(Mentha piperita)*
Nutmeg *(Myristica fragrans)*
Thyme thymol *(Thymus vulgaris CT thymol)*
Spruce *(Picea mariana)*
Wintergreen or birch *(Gaultheria procumbens* or *Betula alleghaniensis)*
Basil *(Origanum basilicum)*
Rosemary cineol *(Rosmarinus officinalis CT 1,8 cineol)*
Clove *(Syzygium aromaticum)*

Blends:
Pain Relief Blend
Muscle Relaxing Blend

Applications:

TOPICAL:	DILUTE 50-50, 6-10 drops on location twice a day or as needed
	COMPRESS, warm,1-2 times daily (if not inflammed)
	RAINDROP, 3 times a month

SPRAIN

(See CONNECTIVE TISSUE)

Single Oils:
Wintergreen or birch *(Gaultheria procumbens* or *Betula alleghaniensis)*
Balsam fir *(Abies balsamea)*
Lemongrass *(Cymbopogon flexuosus)*
Basil *(Ocimum basilicum)*
Pine *(Pinus sylvestris)*
Spruce *(Picea mariana)*
Cypress *(Cupressus sempervirens)*
Peppermint *(Mentha piperita)*

Blends:
Pain Relief Blend

Applications:

TOPICAL:	DILUTE 50-50, apply 4-6 drops on location 3-5 times daily COMPRESS: cold, on location, 2 times daily

STOMACH ACHE

(See DIGESTION PROBLEMS)

STRESS

Single Oils:

Lavender *(Lavandula angustifolia)*
Roman chamomile *(Chamaemelum nobile)*
Blue tansy *(Tanacetum annuum)*
German chamomile *(Matricaria recutita)*
Marjoram *(Origanum majorana)*
Rose *(Rosa damascena)*
Sandalwood *(Santalum album)*
Frankincense *(Boswellia carteri)*
Cedarwood *(Cedrus atlantica)*

Blends:

Energy Balance Blend
Mood Lifting Blend

Applications:

INHALATION:	DIRECT, as needed DIFFUSER, 30 minutes 1-3 times daily
INGESTION:	CAPSULE, 0 size, 2 times a day
TOPICAL:	DILUTE 50-50, apply on temples, neck, and shoulders twice daily, or as needed BATH SALT, daily

STRETCH MARKS

(See SKIN DISORDERS)

STROKE

(See BRAIN DISORDERS)

SUNBURN

(See BURNS)

SYMPATHETIC NERVOUS SYSTEM

(See NERVOUS SYSTEM—AUTONOMIC)

TACHYCARDIA

(See CARDIOVASCULAR CONDITIONS)

TENDONITIS

(See CONNECTIVE TISSUE)

TEETHING PAIN

(See TOOTHACHE)

TEETH GRINDING

(see STRESS)

Single Oils:
Lavender *(Lavandula angustifolia)*
Valerian *(Valeriana officinalis)*

Blends:
Stress Reduction Blend

Applications:

INHALATION:	DIRECT, 1-3 times daily and before retiring DIFFUSER, 30 minutes twice a day and before retiring
TOPICAL:	NEAT, massage 1-3 drops each of lavender and valerian on bottoms of feet before retiring

THROAT INFECTION

Cough

Single Oils:
Cypress *(Cupressus sempervirens)*
Eucalyptus polybractea
Eucalyptus radiata
Eucalyptus globulus
Lemon *(Citrus limon)*
Frankincense *(Boswellia carteri)*
Ravensara *(Ravensara aromatica)*
Thyme *(Thymus vulgaris)*

Oregano *(Origanum compactum)*
Peppermint *(Mentha piperita)*
Myrrh *(Commiphora myrrha)*
Cedarwood *(Cedrus atlantica)*

Blends:

Antimicrobial Blend
Antiseptic Blend
Respiratory Blend

Cough Blend #1:

- 2 drops cypress
- 1 drop *Eucalyptus polybractea*

Cough Blend #2:

- 2 drops *Eucalyptus globulus*
- 2 drops lemon

Heavy Cough Blend:

- 3 drops frankincense
- 3 drops lemon
- 2 drops ravensara
- 1 drop thyme

Applications:

INHALATION:	DIRECT, 3-6 times daily VAPOR, 2-3 times daily
INGESTION:	RICE MILK, 2-4 times daily. It is beneficial to heat the rice milk and sip slowly for more soothing relief. SYRUP, 3-5 times daily
ORAL:	TONGUE, 2-6 times daily or as often as needed GARGLE, 4-8 times daily
TOPICAL:	DILUTE 50-50, apply 1-3 drops to throat, chest and back of neck 2-4 times daily VITA FLEX, apply 1-3 drops to lung Vita Flex points RAINDROP Technique, weekly

Dry Cough

Mix 2 drops lemon and 3 drops *Eucalyptus radiata* with 1 tsp. agave or maple syrup. Dissolve this mixture into 4 oz. of warm distilled water, and sip slowly. Repeat as often as needed for relief.

Laryngitis

Put 1 drop Antiseptic Blend and 1 drop lemon in 1/2 tsp. agave or maple syrup. Hold in back of mouth for 1-2 minutes, then swallow. Repeat as needed.

Sore Throat

Single Oils:

Cypress *(Cupressus sempervirens)*
Eucalyptus radiata
Lemon *(Citrus limon)*
Frankincense *(Boswellia carteri)*
Ravensara *(Ravensara aromatica)*
Thyme *(Thymus vulgaris)*
Oregano *(Origanum compactum)*
Peppermint *(Mentha piperita)*
Myrrh *(Commiphora myrrha)*
Sage *(Salvia officinalis)*

Blends:

Antimicrobial Blend
Antiseptic Blend
Respiratory Blend

Sore Throat Blend #1:

- 2 drops thyme
- 2 drops cypress
- 1 drop *Eucalyptus radiata*
- 1 drop peppermint
- 1 drop myrrh

Sore Throat Blend #2:

- 2 drops *Eucalyptus globulus*
- 5 drops lemon
- 2 drops wintergreen or birch

Applications:

INHALATION:	DIRECT, 3-6 times daily VAPORS, 2-3 times daily
INGESTION:	RICE MILK, 2-4 times daily. It is beneficial to heat the rice milk and sip slowly for more soothing relief. SYRUP, 3-5 times daily
ORAL:	TONGUE, 2-6 times daily or as often as needed GARGLE, 4-10 times daily
TOPICAL:	DILUTE 50-50, apply 1-3 drops to throat, chest and back of neck, 2-4 times daily COMPRESS, warm, on chest area, 2-3 times daily VITA FLEX, apply 1-3 drops to lung Vita Flex points RAINDROP Technique, 1-2 weekly

Strep Throat

Single Oils:

Kaffir lime *(Citrus hystrix)*
Mountain savory *(Satureja montana)*
Thyme thymol *(Thymus vulgaris CT thymol)*
Lavender *(Lavandula angustifolia)*
German chamomile *(Matricaria recutita)*
Myrtle *(Myrtus communis)*
Tea tree oil *(Melaleuca alternifolia)*
Rosemary cineol *(Rosmarinus officinalis CT 1,8 cineol)*
Oregano *(Origanum compactum)*
Eucalyptus globulus

Blends:

Antiseptic Blend
Antibacterial Blend
Immune Blend
Respiratory Blend
Digestive Blend

Applications:

INHALATION:	DIRECT, 3-6 times daily VAPOR, 2-3 times daily DIFFUSER, 30 minutes 4-5 times daily and at night
INGESTION:	RICE MILK, 2-4 times daily. It is beneficial to heat the rice milk and sip slowly for more soothing relief. SYRUP, 3-5 times daily

ORAL:	TONGUE, 2-6 times daily or as often as needed GARGLE, 4-8 times daily
TOPICAL:	DILUTE 50-50, apply 1-3 drops to throat, chest and back of neck 2-4 times daily COMPRESS, warm, on chest area, 2-3 times daily VITA FLEX, apply 1-3 drops to lung Vita Flex points RAINDROP Technique, 1-2 weekly

Strep Throat Vita Flex Regimen

- 1 drop cinnamon
- 6 drops lavender or German chamomile
- 2 drops hyssop

Massage 1-3 drops neat on the lung Vita Flex points of the feet; or, mix the above recipe with 1 teaspoon vegetable or massage oil and apply topically on the throat.

THRUSH

(see FUNGAL INFECTIONS)

THYROID

Located at the base of the neck just below the Adam's apple, the thyroid is the energy gland of the human body. It produces T3 and T4 thyroid hormones that control the body's metabolism. The thyroid also controls other vital functions such as digestion, circulation, immune function, hormone balance, and emotions.

The thyroid gland is actually controlled by the pituitary gland which signals the thyroid when to produce thyroid hormone. The pituitary gland, in turn, is directed by chemical signals sent by the hypothalamus gland which monitors hormone levels in the bloodstream.

A lack of thyroid hormone does not necessarily mean that the thyroid is not functioning properly (although in many cases, this may be the case). In some instances, the pituitary may be malfunctioning because of its failure to release sufficient TSH (thyroid stimulating hormone) to spur the thyroid to make thyroid hormone.

Other cases of thyroid hormone deficiency may be due to the hypothalamus failing to release sufficient TRH (thyrotropin releasing hormone) to stimulate the pituitary (which in turn stimulates the thyroid).

In cases where thyroid hormone deficiency is caused by a malfunctioning pituitary or hypothalamus, better results may be achieved by using essential oils that stimulate the pituitary or hypothalamus such as cedarwood.

People with type A blood have more of a tendency to have weak thyroid function.

Hyperthyroid (Graves Disease)

Graves disease is an autoimmune disease which results in an excess of thyroid hormone production. When the thyroid becomes overactive and produces excess thyroid hormone, the following symptoms occur:

- Anxiety
- Restlessness
- Insomnia
- Premature gray hair
- Diabetes mellitus
- Arthritis
- Vitiligo (loss of skin pigment)

Single Oils:

Myrrh *(Commiphora myrrha)*
Spruce *(Picea mariana)*
Blue tansy *(Tanacetum annuum)*
Lemongrass *(Cymbopogon flexuosus)*

Blends:

Glandular Blend

Applications:

TOPICAL:	DILUTE 50-50, apply 3-5 drops over the thyroid (lower front of the neck on both sides of the trachea), 1-3 times daily
	VITA FLEX, apply 1-3 drops on the thyroid Vita Flex points of the feet (located on the inside edge of the ball of the foot, just below the base of the big toe.)
INGESTION:	CAPSULE, 0 size, 1 capsule twice a day

Hypothyroid (Hashimoto's disease)

When the thyroid is underactive and produces insufficient thyroid hormone. Approximately 40 percent of the U.S. population suffers from this disorder, and these people tend to also suffer hypoglycemia (low blood sugar).

Hashimoto's disease, like Graves disease, is an autoimmune condition affecting the thyroid.

The following symptoms occur:

- Fatigue
- Yeast infections (Candida)
- Lack of energy
- Reduced immune function
- Poor resistance to disease
- Recurring infections

(see HYPOGLYCEMIA).

Single Oils:
Ledum *(Ledum groenlandicum)*
Lemongrass *(Cymbopogon flexuosus)*
Myrtle *(Myrtus communis)*
Peppermint *(Mentha piperita)*
Spearmint *(Mentha spicata)*
Myrrh *(Commiphora myrrha)*
Clove *(Syzygium aromaticum)*

Blends:
Glandular Blend

Applications:

TOPICAL:	DILUTE 50-50, apply 3-5 drops over the thyroid (lower front of the neck on both sides of the trachea), 1-3 times daily VITA FLEX, apply 1-3 drops on the thyroid Vita Flex points of the feet (located on the inside edge of the ball of the foot, just below the base of the big toe.)
INGESTION:	CAPSULE, 0 size, 1 capsule twice a day

TINNITIS (Ringing in Ears)

(See HEARING IMPAIRMENT)

TOOTHACHE

(See PERIODONTAL DISEASE)

Clove and eugenol were used in the care of teeth and gums throughout history. German chamomile can be used for teething pains. Essential-oil-enhanced toothpaste and mouthwash can be very helpful.

NOTE: For small children, dilute these oils (20:80 ratio) in vegetable oil.

Single Oils:

Clove *(Syzygium aromaticum)*
Wintergreen or birch *(Gaultheria procumbens* or *Betula alleghaniensis)*
German chamomile *(Matricaria recutita)*
Tea tree oil *(Melaleuca alternifolia)*
Peppermint *(Mentha piperita)*

Blends:

Antimicrobial Blend

Applications:

TOPICAL:	DILUTE 50-50, apply on affected tooth and gum area as needed
ORAL:	GARGLE, 4-6 times daily or as needed

TONSILLITIS

(See THROAT INFECTONS, COLDS)

The tonsils are infection-fighting lymphatic tissues (immune cells) that surround the throat. When these become infected with streptococcal bacteria they become inflamed, causing a condition known as tonsilitis.

It become popular in the 1960s and 1970s to have the tonsils removed when they became infected. However, tonsillectomies have become much less frequent as researchers have discovered the important role tonsils play in fighting infectious diseases and optimizing immune response.

The pharyngeal tonsils located at the back of the throat (known as the adenoids) can also become infected—a condition known as adenitis.

Single Oils:

Clove *(Syzygium aromaticum)*
Goldenrod *(Solidago canadensis)*
Oregano *(Origanum compactum)*

Mountain savory *(Satureja montana)*
Ravensara *(Ravensara aromatica)*
Thyme *(Thymus vulgaris)*

Applications:

ORAL:	GARGLE, 4-6 times daily
TOPICAL:	DILUTE 50-50, apply 2-4 drops on upper throat just below jawbone directly below earlobe, 2-4 times daily

TOXEMIA

(See INFECTION)

When toxins or bacteria begin to accumulate in the bloodstream, a condition called toxemia is created. Best results are achieved by eliminating all sugar, white flour, breads, pasta, and fried foods.

Single Oils:

Clove *(Syzygium aromaticum)*
Tangerine *(Citrus reticulata)*
Orange *(Citrus aurantium)*
Cypress *(Cupressus sempervirens)*

Blends:

Antibacterial Blend

Applications:

INGESTION:	CAPSULE, 00 size, 1 capsule 2 times a day

TRAUMA (Emotional)

(See SHOCK)

Emotional trauma can be generated from events that involve loss, bereavement, accidents, or misfortunes. Essential oils, through their ability to tap the emotional and memory center of the brain, may facilitate the processing and release of emotional trauma in a way that minimizes psychological turmoil.

Blends:

Trauma Blend
Emotional Release Blend
Energy Balance Blend

Applications:

TOPICAL:	DILUTE 50-50, massage 2-4 drops to temples, forehead, crown and shoulders 1-3 times daily
INHALATION:	DIRECT, 1-3 times daily as needed

TUBERCULOSIS

(See LUNG INFECTION)

Tuberculosis (TB) is a highly contagious lung disease caused by *Mycobacterium tuberculosis*. The germs are spread via coughs, sneezes, and physical contact. The most worrisome aspect of this disease is its latency. Those infected may harbor the germ for years, yet display no outward or visible signs of infection. However, when their immune systems become challenged or downregulated due to stress, candida, diabetes, corticosteroid use, or other factors, the bacteria can become reactivated and develop into full-blown TB.

Because many essential oils have broad-spectrum antimicrobial properties, they can be diffused to prevent the spread of airborne bacteria like *Mycobacterium tuberculosis*. Essential oils and blends such as Antimicrobial Blend, Antibacterial Blend, and Respiratory Blend are extremely effective for killing this type of germs.

Many essential oils have also been shown to be immune-stimulating. Lemon oil has been shown increase lymphocyte production—a pivotal part of the immune system (Valnet, 1990).

Single Oils:

Ravensara *(Ravensara aromatica)*
Rosemary cineol *(Rosmarinus officinalis CT 1,8 cineol)*
Cinnamon *(Cinnamomum verum)*
Thyme thymol *(Thymus vulgaris CT thymol)*
Eucalyptus radiata or *E. globulus*
Sandalwood *(Santalum album)*
Clove *(Syzygium aromaticum)*
Oregano *(Origanum compactum)*
Mountain savory *(Satureja montana)*
Peppermint *(Mentha piperita)*
Spearmint *(Mentha spicata)*
Myrtle *(Myrtus communis)*

Blends:

Respiratory Blend
Antimicrobial Blend
Immune Blend

Applications:

INHALATION:	DIFFUSE, 1 hour, twice a day and at night. DIRECT, 3-5 times daily
TOPICAL:	DILUTE 50-50, apply 6-10 drops on chest and upper back 1-3 times daily COMPRESS, warm, on chest and upper back, twice daily
INGESTION:	CAPSULE, 00 size, 1 capsule 3 times a day for 10 days

Tuberculosis Specific Regimen:

1. Diffuse Respiratory Blend as often as possible during the day
2. Mix the following in 2 tablespoons vegetable oil. Insert into rectum with bulb syringe and retain overnight. Do this nightly for 7 nights, then rest 4 nights. Repeat.
   - 2 drops sage
   - 4 drops myrrh
   - 5 drops clove
   - 6 drops ravensara
   - 15 drops frankincense
3. Rub 4-6 drops of Antimicrobial Blend on the bottom of the feet nightly
4. Rub 6-8 drops Immune Blend up the spine and apply a warm compress on back twice a day.

TUMORS

(See CANCER)

TYPHOID FEVER

Typhoid fever is an infectious disease caused by a bacteria known as *Salmonella typhi*. Usually contracted through infected food or water, typhoid is common in lesser-developed countries.

Some people infected with typhoid fever display no visible symptoms of disease, while others become seriously ill. Both people who recover from typhoid fever and those who remain symptomless are carriers for the disease, and can infect others through the bacteria they shed in their feces.

To avoid contracting typhoid fever—especially when traveling overseas—it is essential to drink purified or distilled water and eat thoroughly cooked foods. Fresh vegetables can be carriers of the bacteria, especially if they have been irrigated with water that has come into contact with human waste.

Symptoms:

- Sustained, high fever (101° to 104° F)
- Stomach pains
- Headache
- Rash of reddish spots
- Impaired appetite
- Weakness

Single Oils:

Ravensara *(Ravensara aromatica)*
Cinnamon *(Cinnamomum verum)*
Peppermint *(Mentha piperita)*
Black pepper *(Piper nigrum)*
Mountain savory *(Satureja montana)*
Clove *(Syzygium aromaticum)*
Thyme *(Thymus vulgaris)*

Applications:

INGESTION: CAPSULE, 00 size, 1 capsule twice a day for 10 days

ULCERS (Stomach)

(see DIGESTION PROBLEMS)

Ulcers may be caused by *Helicobacter pylori* (bacteria). Several gastro-duodenal diseases include gastritis and gastric or peptic ulcers.

Single Oils:

Clove *(Syzygium aromaticum)*
Cinnamon *(Cinnamomum verum)*
Tea tree oil *(Melaleuca alternifolia)*
Oregano *(Origanum compactum)*
Thyme *(Thymus vulgaris)*

Blends:

Antimicrobial Blend
Respiratory Blend

Applications:

INGESTION: CAPSULE, 0 size, 1 capsule 3 times a day for 20 days

URINARY TRACT/BLADDER INFECTION

Infections and inflammation of the urinary tract are caused by bacteria that travel up the urethra. This disorder is more common in women than men because of the woman's shorter urethra. If the infection travels up the ureters and reaches the kidneys, kidney infection can result.

(See KIDNEY DISORDERS)

Symptoms:

- Frequent urge to urinate with only a small amount of urine coming out
- Strong smelling urine
- Blood in urine
- Burning or stinging during urination

Bladder infection (known as cystitis or interstitial cystitis) is marked by the following symptoms:

- Tenderness or chronic pain in bladder and pelvic area
- Frequent urge to urinate
- Pain intensity fluctuates as bladder fills or empties
- Symptoms worsen during menstruation

Single Oils:

Oregano *(Origanum compactum)*
Mountain savory *(Satureja montana)*
Tea tree oil *(Melaleuca alternifolia)*
Thyme thymol *(Thymus vulgaris CT thymol)*
Cistus *(Cistus ladanifer)*
Juniper *(Juniperus communis* or *J. osteosperma)*
Rosemary cineol *(Rosmarinus officinalis CT 1,8 cineol)*
Clove *(Syzygium aromaticum)*

Blends:

Digestive Blend
Respiratory Blend
Antibacterial Blend
Antiseptic Blend

Applications:

INGESTION: CAPSULE, 0 size, 1 capsule two times a day
TOPICAL: COMPRESS, warm, over bladder, 1-2 times a day

UTERINE CANCER

(See CANCER)

VAGINAL INFECTION

(See FUNGAL INFECTIONS)

Single Oils:

Myrrh *(Commiphora myrrha)*
Mountain savory *(Satureja montana)*
Oregano *(Origanum compactum)*
Tea tree oil *(Melaleuca alternifolia)*
Thyme thymol *(Thymus vulgaris CT thymol)*

Blends:

Antiseptic Blend

Applications:

RETENTION: TAMPON, 3 times a week

VAGINAL YEAST INFECTION

(See FUNGAL INFECTIONS)

VARICOSE VEINS (Spider Veins)

The blue color of varicose veins is congealed blood in the surrounding tissue from hemorrhaging of capillaries around the veins. This blood has to be dissolved and re-absorbed.

If you suspect a clot has developed in a vein, rub cypress and helichrysum neat on location and get immediate professional medical attention.

Helichrysum helps dissolve coagulated blood in surrounding tissue.

Cypress strengthens capillary walls.

Tansy improves weak veins.

Single Oils:

Helichrysum *(Helichrysum italicum)*
Basil *(Ocimum basilicum)*
Cypress *(Cupressus sempervirens)*
Wintergreen or birch *(Gaultheria procumbens* or *Betula alleghaniensis)*
Peppermint *(Mentha piperita)*
Lemon *(Citrus limon)*

Blends:

Circulation Blend
Muscle Relaxing Blend

Varicose Vein blend #1:
- 3 drops basil
- 1 drop wintergreen or birch
- 1 drop cypress
- 1 drop helichrysum

Varicose Vein blend #2:
- 2 drops helichrysum
- 2 drops of cypress

Applications:

TOPICAL: NEAT, apply 2-4 drops on location, massaging toward the heart, 3-6 times daily

Nightly Varicose Vein Regimen (legs):

A. Apply 1-3 drops Varicose Vein Blend #1 neat on location. Rub very gently towards heart with smooth strokes along the vein, then up and over the vein until the oil is absorbed. Repeat with blend #2.
B. Apply 6 drops tangerine and 6 drops cypress to the area. Gently massage until absorbed.
C. Do the lymphatic pump procedure described in Chapter 12.
D. Follow with a soft massage of the whole leg using 10-15 drops of Circulation Blend, diluted 50-50
E. Wrap and elevate the leg. It is best to do this at night before retiring and to gradually elevate the foot off the bed, an inch more each night, until it is 4 inches higher than the head.
F. Wear support hose during the daytime. It may take up to a year to achieve desired results.

VASCULAR CLEANSING

We absorb heavy metals from air, water, food, skin care products, mercury fillings in teeth, etc. These chemicals lodge in the fatty tissues of the body, which, in turn, give off toxic gases that may cause allergic symptoms. Cleansing the body of these heavy metals is extremely important to have a healthy immune function, especially if we have amalgam dental fillings.

Drink at least 64 ounces of distilled or pure spring water daily to flush toxins and chemicals out of the body.

Single Oils:
Helichrysum *(Helichrysum italicum)*
Cypress *(Cupressus sempervirens)*
Frankincense *(Boswellia carteri)*
German chamomile *(Matricaria recutita)*
Lemongrass *(Cymbopogon flexuosus)*

Blends:
Circulation Blend

Vascular cleansing blend:
- 10 drops juniper
- 10 drops cypress
- 10 drops lemongrass

Applications:

TOPICAL:	DILUTE 50-50, apply 4-6 drops to under arms, kidney area and bottoms of feet, 1-3 times daily
	RAINDROP Technique, 1-3 times monthly
INGESTION:	CAPSULE, 0 size, 1 capsule once a day

(See CIRCULATION PROBLEMS)

VITILIGO

(See SKIN DISORDERS)

WARTS, GENITAL

(See SEXUALLY TRANSMITTED DISEASES)

WATER RETENTION

Water retention is usually a result of hormonal imbalances that trigger excess fluid retention in the body. Correcting hormone imbalances or using natural diuretics can both help.

Single Oils:

Clary sage *(Salvia sclarea)*
Tarragon *(Artemisia dracunculus)*
Peppermint *(Mentha piperita)*
Juniper *(Juniperus communis* or *J. osteosperma)*
Fennel *(Foeniculum vulgare)*
Geranium *(Pelargonium graveolens)*

Blends:

Female Blend
Digestive Blend

Applications:

TOPICAL:	DILUTE 50-50, Apply to affected areas 2-4 times daily
INGESTION:	CAPSULE, 00 size, 3 times per day

WHOOPING COUGH

(LUNG INFECTION)

WOUNDS, SCRAPES, OR CUTS

Lavender can be used undiluted to disinfect wounds, scrapes, and cuts. Roman chamomile is also very mild and non-toxic; it is an excellent pain reliever and remedy for scratches, chapped and dry skin. Add Roman chamomile to a sealing ointment for a healing first aid salve.

When selecting oils for surface injuries, treat the whole person, not just the cut. Think through the cause and type of injury and select oils for each aspect of the trauma. For instance, a wound could encompass muscle damage, nerve damage, ligament damage, inflammation, infection, bone injury, fever, and possibly an emotion. Therefore, select an oil or blend that treats each aspect.

Single Oils:

Lavender *(Lavandula angustifolia)*
Tea tree oil *(Melaleuca alternifolia)*
Rosemary cineol *(Rosmarinus officinalis CT 1,8 cineol)*
Eucalyptus globulus
Cypress *(Cupressus sempervirens)*
Wintergreen or birch *(Gaultheria procumbens* or *Betula alleghaniensis)*
Thyme thymol *(Thymus vulgaris CT thymol)*
Oregano *(Origanum compactum)*
German chamomile *(Matricaria recutita)*
Lavandin *(Lavandula x hybrida)*
Mountain savory *(Satureja montana)*
Peppermint *(Mentha piperita)*

Blends:

Antibacterial Blend
Antiseptic Blend
Antimicrobial Blend

Bruise and scrape blend: (may be used on infants and children):

- 3 drops helichrysum
- 3 drops lavender

Infected cuts blend:

- 7 drops geranium
- 5 drops peppermint
- 10 drops *Melaleuca alternifolia*
- 8 drops orange

Applications:

TOPICAL: DILUTE 50-50, apply 2-6 drops on location, 1-4 times daily as needed

NOTE: Peppermint may sting when applied to an open wound. To reduce discomfort, dilute with lavender oil or mix in a sealing ointment before applying. When applied to a wound or cut that has a scab, peppermint will soothe, cool, and reduce inflammation in damaged tissue.

First-Aid Spray

- 5 drops lavender
- 3 drops *Melaleuca alternifolia*
- 2 drops cypress

Mix above oils thoroughly in 1/2 teaspoon of salt. Add this to 8 ounces of distilled water and shake vigorously. Put in a spray bottle. Spray minor cuts and wounds before applying bandage. Repeat 2-3 times daily for 3 days. Complete the healing process by applying a drop or two of tea tree oil to the wound daily for the next few days.

To reduce bleeding

Single Oils:

Rose Hip Seed Oil *(Rosa mosqueta)*
Rose *(Rosa damascena)*
Helichrysum *(Helichrysum italicum)*
Lemon *(Citrus limon)*
Geranium *(Pelargonium graveolens)*
Cypress *(Cupressus sempervirens)*

Blends:

Antiseptic Blend
Antibacterial Blend

Wound compress blend:

- 5 drops geranium
- 5 drops lemon
- 5 drops German chamomile

Applications:

TOPICAL: COMPRESS, cold, 1-2 times until bleeding stops

Melaleuca alternifolia (Tea tree oil)

During World War II, melaleuca was found to have very strong antibacterial properties and worked well in preventing infection in open wounds. Antiseptic Blend is a blend containing two types of melaleuca oil, making it an exceptional antiseptic and tissue regenerator.

To reduce scarring:

Single Oils:

Rose hip seed oil *(Rosa mosqueta)*
Frankincense *(Boswellia carteri)*
Lemongrass *(Cymbopogon flexuosus)*
Lavender *(Lavandula angustifolia)*
Geranium *(Pelargonium graveolens)*
Helichrysum *(Helichrysum italicum)*
Myrrh *(Commiphora myrrha)*

Blends:

Scar Prevention Blend #1:

- 10 drops helichrysum
- 6 drops lavender
- 8 drops lemongrass
- 4 drops patchouli

Scar Prevention Blend #2:

- 3 drops lavender
- 3 drops lemongrass
- 3 drops geranium

Applications:

TOPICAL:	DILUTE 50-50, apply 2-4 drops on wound, 2-5 times daily

To promote healing:

Single Oils:

Patchouli *(Pogostemon cablin)*
Lavender *(Lavandula angustifolia)*
Neroli *(Citrus aurantium)*
Myrrh *(Commiphora myrrha)*
Helichrysum *(Helichrysum italicum)*
Sandalwood *(Santalum album)*
Tansy *(Tanacetum vulgare)*

Blends:

Antiseptic blend
Antibacterial blend

Applications:

TOPICAL:	DILUTE 50-50, apply 2-4 drops on wound 2-5 times daily.

To disinfect:

Single Oils:

Thyme thymol *(Thymus vulgaris linalol and thymol)*
Tea tree oil *(Melaleuca alternifolia)*
Mountain savory *(Satureja montana)*

Blends:

Antiseptic blend
Antibacterial blend

Applications:

TOPICAL:	DILUTE 50-50, apply 2-4 drops on wound 2-5 times daily.

WORMS

(See PARASITES)

WRINKLES

(See SKIN DISORDERS)

YEAST INFECTION

(See HORMONES, FUNGAL INFECTION)

References

Alderman G, and Elmer H. Inhibition of Growth and Aflatoxin Production of Aspergillus Parasiticus by Citrus Oils. *Z Lebensm Unters Forsch*. 1976 Apr 28;160(4):353-8.

Aqel MB. "Relaxant effect of the volatile oil of Rosmarinus officinalis on tracheal smooth muscle." *J Ethnopharmacol*. 1991;33(1-2):57-62.

Aruna K, and Sivaramakrishnan VM. Anticarcinogenic Effects of Essential Oils from Cumin, Poppy, and Basil. *Phytotherapy Research* 1996, 577-79.

Aruna K and Sivaramakrishnan VM. "Anticarcinogenic Effects of the Essential Oils from Cumin, Poppy and Basil." *Food Chem Toxicol*. 1992;30(11):953-56.

Azizan A, et al. "Mutagenicity and antimutagenicity testing of six chemicals associated with the pungent properties of specific spices as revealed by the Ames Salmonella/microsomal assay." *Arch Environ Contam Toxicol*. 1995;28(2):248-58.

Barja de Quiroga G, et al. Antioxidant defenses and peroxidation in liver and brain of aged rats. *Biochemical Journal* 272 (1990), 247-250.

Bassett IB, et al. "A comparative study of tea-tree oil versus benzoylperoxide in the treatment of acne." *Med J Aust*. 1990;153(8):455-8.

Becker, MD, Robert O. *The Body Electric*. New York: Wm. Morrow, 1985.

Belaiche, MD, Paul. *Traité de Phytothérapie Et D'Aromathérapie*. Paris: Maloine, 1979.

Belvi Viktor. *Aromatherapy*. New York: Avon Books, 1993.

Benencia F, et al. "Antiviral activity of sandalwood oil against herpes simplex viruses-1 and -2." *Phytomedicine*. 1999;6(2):119-23

Bernardis LL, et al. "The lateral hypothalamic area revisited: ingestive behavior." *Neurosci Biobehav Rev*. 20(2):189-287 (1996).

Bilgrami KS, et al. "Inhibition of aflatoxin production & growth of Aspergillus flavus by eugenol & onion & garlic extracts." *Indian J Med Res*. 1992;96:171-5.

Bradshaw RH, et al. "Effects of lavender straw on stress and travel sickness in pigs." *J Altern Complement Med*. 1998;4(3):271-5.

Brodal A. *Neurological Anatomy in Relation to Clinical Medicine*. New York: Oxford University Press, 1981.

Buchbauer G, et al. "Aromatherapy: evidence for sedative effects of the essential oil of lavender after inhalation." *Z Naturforsch* [C]. 1991;46(11-12):1067-72.

Cai and Wu. Compounds from Syzygium aromaticum possessing growth inhibitory activity against oral pathogens. *J Nat Prod*. 1996 Oct;59(10):987-90.

Cao G, et al. Automated assay of oxygen radical absorbance capacity with the COBAS FARA II. *Clin Chem*. 1995 Dec;41(12 Pt 1):1738-44.

Carson CF, et al. "Antimicrobial activity of the major components of the essential oil of Melaleuca alternifolia." *J Appl Bacteriol*. 1995;78(3):264-9.

Chao et al. Antimicrobial Effects of Essential Oils on Streptococcus pneumoniae. *JEOR*, 2001.

Chao, et al. Screening for Inhibitory Activity of Essential Oils on Selected Bacteria, Fungi, and Viruses. *Journal of Essential Oil Research*, Sept./Oct. 2000.

Chopra, MD, Deepak. *Quantum Healing*. New York: Bantam Books, 1989.

Compendium of Olfactory Research. Edited by Avery N. Gilbert. Dubuque, IA: Kendall Hunt Publishing, 1995.

Concha JM, et al. 1998 William J. Stickel Bronze Award. "Antifungal activity of Melaleuca alternifolia (tea-tree) oil against various pathogenic organisms." *J Am Podiatr Med Assoc*. 1998;88(10): 489-92

Cornwell S, et al. "Lavender oil and perineal repair." *Mod Midwife* 1995;5(3):31-3.

Covello et al. Determination of eugenol in the essence of "Eugenia caryophyllata." Titration in non-aqueous solvent and comparison with other methods of analysis. *Boll Chim Farm*. 1966 Nov;105(11):799-806.

Courmont P, Morel A, et Bay I. "Sur le pourvoir infertilisant de quel ques essences végétables vis-à-vis du bacille tuberculeux humain." *C R Soc Biol*, 1927.

Cox et al. The mode of antimicrobial action of the essential oil of Melaleuca alternifolia (tea tree oil). J Appl Microbiol. 2000 Jan;88(1):170-5.

Crowell P. Prevention and therapy of cancer by dietary monoterpenes. *J Nutr*. 1999 Mar;129(3):775S-778S.

Dakhil MA, Morsy TA. The larvicidal activities of the peel oils of three citrus fruits against Culex pipiens. *J Egypt Soc Parasitol*. 1999 Aug;29(2):347-52.

Dalvi et al. Effect of peppermint oil on gastric emptying in man: a preliminary study using a radiolabelled solid test meal. *Indian J Physiol Pharmacol*. 1991 Jul;35(3):212-4.

Darom David. *Beautiful Plants of the Bible*, Israel: Palphot, Ltd.

Deans SG, et al. Natural antioxidants from aromatic and medicinal plants. In *Role of Free Radicals in Biological Systems*, pp. 159-165 (1993a) [J Feher, A Blazovics, B Matkovics and M Mezes, editors]. Budapest: Akademiai Kiado.

Delaveau P, et al. "Neuro-depressive properties of essential oil of lavender." *C R Seances Soc Biol Fil*. 1989;183(4):342-8.

Dember WN, et al. Olfactory Stimulation and Sustained Attention, *Compendium of Olfactory*, (Avery N. Gilbert, Editor) 1995, pp. 39-46.

Didry N, et al. "Activity of thymol, carvacrol, cinnamaldehyde and eugenol on oral bacteria." *Pharm Acta Helv*. 1994;69(1):25-8.

Diego MA, et al. "Aromatherapy positively affects mood, EEG patterns of alertness and math computations." *Int J Neurosci*. 1998 Dec;96 (3-4):217-24.

Dimitrova et al., "Antiherpes effect of Melissa officinalis L. extracts," *Acta Microbiol Bulg* 1993;29-:65-72.

Dolara P, et al. "Analgesic effects of myrrh." *Nature*. 1996 Jan 4;379(6560):29.

Doss Besada. *The Story of Abu Simbel*. Essex, England: Longman Group UK Limited, 1973.

Dunn C, et al. "Sensing an improvement: an experimental study to evaluate the use of aromatherapy, massage and periods of rest in an intensive care unit." *J Adv Nurs*. 1995;21(1):34-40.

Dwivedi C, et al. "Chemopreventive effects of sandalwood oil on skin papillomas in mice." *Eur J Cancer Prev*. 1997;6(4):399-401.

Elisabetsky, et al. Anticonvulsant properties of linalool in glutamate-related seizure models. *Phytomedicine*. 1999 May;6(2):107-13.

Elson CE, et al. "Impact of lemongrass oil, an essential oil, on serum cholesterol." *Lipids*. 1989;24(8):677-9.

Fang HJ, et al. "Studies on the chemical components and anti-tumour action of the volatile oils from Pelargonium graveoleus." *Yao Hsueh Hsueh Pao*. 1989;24(5):366-71.

Faoagali JL, et al. "Antimicrobial effects of melaleuca oil." *Burns*. 1998;24(4):383.

Farag et al. Acute hepatic damage in rats impairs metharbital metabolism. *Pharmacology*. 1987;34(4):181-91.

Farag et al. Antioxidant activity of some spice essential oils on linoleic acid oxidation in aqueous media. *JAOCS* June 1989;66: 792-799.

Farag et al. Inhibitory effects of individual and mixed pairs of essential oils on the oxidation and hydrolysis of cottonseed oil and butter. *FASC*, 1989; 40: 275-279.

Farag et al. Safety evaluation of thyme and clove essential oils as natural antioxidants. *Afr J Agr Sci*. 1991;18: 169-175,

Farag, PhD, Radwan S. "Safety Evaluation of Thyme and Clove Essential Oils as Natural Antioxidants." *African Journal of Agricultural Sciences*, Vol. 18, No. 1. Gisa, Egypt: Cairo University, 1991.

Fleming T, Ed. *PDR for Herbal Medicines*, Medical Economics Company, Inc., Montvale, NJ (1998).

Fyfe L, et al. "Inhibition of Listeria monocytogenes and Salmonella enteriditis by combinations of plant oils and derivatives of benzoic acid: the development of synergistic antimicrobial combinations." *Int J Antimicrob Agents*. 1997;9(3):195-9.

Garrison Omar. *Tantra: The Yoga of Sex*. New York: Harmony Books, 1964.

Gattefossé René-Maurice. *Gattefossé's Aromatherapy*. Saffron Walden, UK: C.W. Daniel & Co., 1993.

Ghelardini et al. Local anaesthetic activity of the essential oil of Lavandula angustifolia. *Planta Med*. 1999 Dec;65(8):700-3.

Gobel et al. Effect of peppermint and eucalyptus oil preparations on neurophysiological and experimental algesimetric headache parameters. *Cephalalgia*. 1994 Jun;14(3):228-34; 182.

Guenther Ernest. *The Essential Oils*. Florida: Malabar, 1950.

Guillemain J, et al. "Neurodepressive effects of the essential oil of Lavandula angustifolia Mill." *Ann Pharm Fr*. 1989;47(6):337-43.

Gumbel D. *Principles of Holistic Therapy with Herbal Essences*, Haug International, Brussels, Belgium (1993).

Hammer KA, et al. "In vitro susceptibilities of lactobacilli and organisms associated with bacterial vaginosis to Melaleuca alternifolia (tea tree) oil." *Antimicrob Agents Chemother*. 1999;43(1):196.

Hammer KA, et al. "Susceptibility of transient and commensal skin flora to the essential oil of Melaleuca alternifolia (tea tree oil)." *Am J Infect Control*. 1996;24(3):186-9.

Hammer KA, Carson CF, Riley TV, In-vitro activity of essential oils, in particular Melaleuca alternifolia (tea tree) oil and tea tree oil products, against Candida spp. J Antimicrob Chemother 1998 Nov;42(5):591-5.

Hasan HA, et al. "Inhibitory effect of spice oils on lipase and mycotoxin production." *Zentralbl Mikrobiol*. 1993;148(8):543-8.

Hausen BM, et al. "Comparative studies of the sensitizing capacity of drugs used in herpes simplex." *Derm Beruf Umwelt*. 1986;34(6):163-70.

Hay IC, et al. "Randomized trial of aromatherapy. Successful treatment for alopecia areata." *Arch Dermatol*. 1998; 134(11):1349-52.

Hayflick L. *How and Why We Age*. Ballantine Books, New York, 1994.

Hirsch Alan. "Inhalation of 2 acetylpyridine for weight reduction." *Chemical Senses* 18:570 (1993).

Hirsch Alan. *A Scentsational Guide to Weight Loss*. Rockport, MA: Element, 1997.

Hirsch AR. Inhalation of Odorants for Weight Reduction, *Int J Obes,* 1994, page 306

Horne D, et al. Antimicrobial effects of essential oils on Streptococcus pneumoniae, *J Essen Oil R,* Sept./Oct. 2001, 387-392.

Igimi et al., "A useful cholesterol solvent for medical dissolution of gallstones." Gastroenterol Jpn 1992 Aug;27(4):536-45.

Inouye S, et al. "Antisporulating and respiration-inhibitory effects of essential oils on filamentous fungi." *Mycoses*. 1998;41(9-10):403-10.

Jayashree T, et al. "Antiaflatoxigenic activity of eugenol is due to inhibition of lipid peroxidation." *Lett Appl Microbiol*. 1999; 28(3):179-83.

Jones MM and Basinger MA. Restrictions on the applicability of mixed ligand chelate therapy (MLC) in acute cadmium intoxication. *Res Commun Chem Pathol Pharmacol*. 1979 Jun;24(3):525-31.

Juergens UR, et al. "The anti-inflammatory activity of L-menthol compared to mint oil in human monocytes in vitro: a novel perspective for its therapeutic use in inflammatory diseases." *Eur J Med Res*. 1998; 3(12):539-45.

Kim HM, et al. "Lavender oil inhibits immediate-type allergic reaction in mice and rats." *J Pharm Pharmacol*. 1999;51(2):221-6.

Koytchev R, et al., "Balm mint extract (Lo-701) for topical treatment of recurring herpes labialis," *Phytomedicine* 1999

Oct;6(4):225-30.Kucera LS, et al. "Antiviral activities of extracts of the lemon balm plant." *Ann NY Acad Sci*. 1965 Jul 30;130(1):474-82.

Kulieva ZT. "Analgesic, hypotensive and cardiotonic action of the essential oil of the thyme growing in Azerbaijan." *Vestn Akad Med Nauk SSSR*. 1980;(9):61-3.

Lachowicz KJ, et al. "The synergistic preservative effects of the essential oils of sweet basil (Ocimum basilicum L.) against acid-tolerant food microflora." *Lett Appl Microbiol*. 1998;26(3):209-14.

LaDoux, MD, Joseph. Rationalizing Thoughtless Emotions. *Insight*, Sept. 1989.

Larrondo JV, et al. "Antimicrobial activity of essences from labiates." *Microbios*. 1995; 82(332): 171-2.

Lis-Balchin M, et al. "Antimicrobial activity of Pelargonium essential oils added to a quiche filling as a model food system." *Lett Appl Microbiol*. 1998;27(4):207-10.

Lis-Balchin M, et al. "Comparative antibacterial effects of novel Pelargonium essential oils and solvent extracts." *Lett Appl Microbiol*. 1998;27(3): 135-41.

Lopez-Bote, et al. "Effect of dietary administration of oil extracts from rosemary and sage on lipid oxidation in broiler meat." *Br Poult Sci*. 1998 May;39(2):235-40.

Lorenzetti BB, et al. "Myrcene mimics the peripheral analgesic activity of lemongrass tea." *J Ethnopharmacol*. 1991;34(1):43-8.

Mahmood N, et al. "The anti-HIV activity and mechanisms of action of pure compounds isolated from Rosa damascena." *Biochem Biophys Res Commun*. 1996;229(1):73-9.

Mailhebiau Philippe. *La Nouvelle Aromathérapie*. Editions. France: Jakin, 1994.

Mangena T, et al. "Comparative evaluation of the antimicrobial activities of essential oils of Artemisia afra, Pteronia incana and Rosmarinus officinalis on selected bacteria and yeast strains." *Lett Appl Microbiol*. 1999;28(4):291-6.

Masquelier J. *Radical Scavenging Effect of Proanthocyanidins*. Paris, 1986.

Maury Marguerite. *The Secret and Life of Youth*. Saffon Waldon, UK: C.W. Daniels & Co., 1995.

McGuffin M, et al. *Botanical Safety Handbook*, CRC Press, Boca Raton, FL (1997)

Meeker HG, et al. "The antibacterial action of eugenol, thyme oil, and related essential oils used in dentistry." *Compendium*. 1988;9(1):32, 34-5, 38 passim.

Meunier Christiane. *Lavandes & Lavandins*. Aix-en-Provence, France: Chaudoreille, 1985.

Michie CA, et al. "Frankincense and myrrh as remedies in children." *J R Soc Med*. 1991;84(10): 602-5.

Miltner, et al. Emotional qualities of odors and their influence on the startle reflex in humans. *Psychophysiology*. 1994 Jan;31(1):107-10.

Modgil R, et al. "Efficacy of mint and eucalyptus leaves on the physicochemical characteristics of stored wheat against insect infestation." *Nahrung*. 1998;42(5):304-8.

Moleyar V, et al. "Antibacterial activity of essential oil components." *Int J Food Microbiol*. 1992;16(4): 337-42.

Momchilova AM. *330 Years of Bulgarian Rose Oil*. Sofia, Bulgaria, 1994.

Montagna FJ. *HDR Herbal Desk Reference* Kendall/Hunt Publishing Company, Dubuque, IA (1979).

Murray M. *Encyclopedia of Nutritional Supplements*, Prima Publishing, Rocklin, CA (1996).

Nagababu E, et al. "The protective effects of eugenol on carbon tetrachloride induced hepatotoxicity in rats." *Free Radic Res*. 1995;23(6):617-27.

Naidu KA. "Eugenol—an inhibitor of lipoxygenase-dependent lipid peroxidation." *Prostaglandins Leukot Essent Fatty Acids*. 1995;53(5):381-3.

Nakamoto K, et al. "In vitro effectiveness of mouthrinses against Candida albicans." *Int J Prosthodont*. 1995;8(5):486-9.

Nasel C, et al. "Functional imaging of effects of fragrances on the human brain after prolonged inhalation." *Chemical Senses*. 1994;19(4):359-64

Nenoff P, et al. "Antifungal activity of the essential oil of Melaleuca alternifolia (tea tree oil) against pathogenic fungi in vitro." *Skin Pharmacol*. 1996;9(6):388-94.

Niazi H. *The Egyptian Prescription*. Cairo, Egypt: Elias Modern Press, 1988.

Nikolaevskii VV, et al. "Effect of essential oils on the course of experimental atherosclerosis." *Patol Fiziol Eksp Ter.* 1990; (5):52-3.

Nishijima H, et al. "Mechanisms mediating the vasorelaxing action of eugenol, a pungent oil, on rabbit arterial tissue." *Jpn J Pharmacol*. 1999 Mar;79(3):327-34.

Nordenstrom Bjorn. *Biologically Closed Circuits*. Sweden.

Olson L, et al. "Some toxic effects of lead, other metals and antibacterial agents on the nervous system—animal experiment models." *Acta Neurol Scand Suppl.* 1984;100:77-87.

Panizzi L, et al. "Composition and antimicrobial properties of essential oils of four Mediterranean Lamiaceae." *J Ethnopharmacol.* 1993;39(3):167-70.

Pattnaik S, et al. "Antibacterial and antifungal activity of ten essential oils in vitro." *Microbios.* 1996;86(349):237-46.

Pedersen, M. *Nutritional Herbology, A Reference Guide to Herbs*, Wendell W. Whitman Company, Warsaw, IN (1998)

Pénoël Daniel. *Natural Home Health Care Using Essential Oils.* Salem, UT: Essential Science Publishing, 1998.

Pénoël, MD, Daniel and Pénoël R-M, *Natural Home Health Care Using Essential Oils.* La Drome, France: Editions Osmobiose, 1988.

Pénoël, MD, Daniel and Franchomme Pierre. *L'aromathérapie exactement.* Limoges, France: Jollois, 1990.

Plato. *Chronicles* 156 E.

Pourgholami MH et.al. "Evaluation of the anticonvulsant activity of the essential oil of Eugenia caryophyllata in male mice." *J Ethnopharmacol.* 1999 Feb;64(2):167-71.

Ramadan W, et al. "Oil of bitter orange: new topical antifungal agent." *Int J Dermatol.* 1996 Jun;35(6):448-9.

Recsan Z, et al. "Effect of essential oils on the lipids of the retina in the aging rat: a possible therapeutic use." *J Ess Oil Res* 9, (1997) 53-56.

Reddy AC, et al. "Effect of curcumin and eugenol on iron-induced hepatic toxicity in rats." *Toxicology* 1996;107(1):39-45.

Reddy AC, et al. "Studies on anti-inflammatory activity of spice principles and dietary n-3 polyunsaturated fatty acids on carrageenan-induced inflammation in rats." *Ann Nutr Metab.* 1994;38(6): 349-58.

Restak, MD, Richard. *The Brain.* New York: Random House, 1991.

Rompelberg CJ, et al. "Antimutagenicity of eugenol in the rodent bone marrow micronucleus test." *Mutat Res.* 1995;346(2):69-75.

Rompelberg CJ, et al. "Effect of short-term dietary administration of eugenol in humans" *Hum Exp Toxicol.* 1996;15(2):129-35.

Rompelberg CJ, et al. "Antimutagenicity of eugenol in the rodent bone marrow micronucleus test." *Mutat Res.* 1995 Feb;346(2):69-75.

Rotstein et al. "Effects of aging on the composition and metabolism of docosahexaenoate-containing lipids of retina." *Lipids.* 1987 Apr;22(4):253-60.

Russin et al. "Inhibition of rat mammary carcinogenesis by monoterpenoids." *Carcinogenesis.* 1989 Nov;10(11):2161-4.

Ryman Daniele. Aromatherapy: *The Complete Guide to Plant and Flower Essences for Health and Beauty*. New York: Bantam Books, 1993.

Saeed SA, et al. "Antithrombotic activity of clove oil." *JPMA J Pak Med Assoc*. 1994;44(5):112-5.

Samman MA, et al. "Mint prevents shamma-induced carcinogenesis in hamster cheek pouch." *Carcinogenesis*. 1998;19(10):1795-801.

Schreuder M. Private communication with Brunswick Laboratories, Warcham, MA. March 21, 2001.

Shapiro S, et al. "The antimicrobial activity of essential oils and essential oil components towards oral bacteria." *Oral Microbiol Immunol*. 1994;9(4): 202-8.

Sharma JN, et al. "Suppressive effects of eugenol and ginger oil on arthritic rats." *Pharmacology*. 1994;49(5):314-8.

Shirota S, et al. "Tyrosinase inhibitors from crude drugs." *Biol Pharm Bull*. 1994; 17(2):266-9.

Siurein SA. "Effects of essential oil on lipid peroxidation and lipid metabolism in patients with chronic bronchitis." *Klin Med* (Mosk). 1997;75 (10):43-5.

Skakkebaek NE, Endocrine disrupters and testicular dysgenesis syndrome, Horm Res 2002;57 Suppl 2:43.

Socci DJ, et al. Chronic antioxidant treatment improves the cognitive performance in aged rats." *Brain Research* 693, (1995) 88-94.

Srivastava KC. "Antiplatelet principles from a food spice clove." Prostaglandins Leukot Essent Fatty Acids. 1993;48(5):363-72.

Steinman, David and Epstein Samuel S. *The Safe Shopper's Bible: A Consumer's Guide to Nontoxic Household Products, Cosmetics, and Food,* MacMillan, New York, NY (1995)

Steinmetz et al."Transmission and scanning electronmicroscopy study of the action of sage and rosemary essential oils and eucalyptol on Candida albicans." *Mycoses*. 1988 Jan;31(1):40-51.

Sukumaran K, et al. "Inhibition of tumour promotion in mice by eugenol." *Indian J Physiol Pharmacol*. 1994;38(4):306-8.

Syed TA, et al. "Treatment of toenail onychomycosis with 2% butenafine and 5% Melaleuca alternifolia (tea tree) oil in cream." *Trop Med Int Health*. 1999;4(4):284-7.

Sysoev NP. "The effect of waxes from essential-oil plants on the dehydrogenase activity of the blood neutrophils in mucosal trauma of the mouth." *Stomatologiia* 1991;70(1):12-3.

Takacsova M, et al. "Study of the antioxidative effects of thyme, sage, juniper and oregano." *Nahrung*. 1995;39(3):241-3.

Tantaoui-Elaraki A, et al. "Inhibition of growth and aflatoxin production in Aspergillus parasiticus by essential oils of selected plant materials." *J Environ Pathol Toxicol Oncol*. 1994;13(1):67-72.

The Bible. King James Version. Books of the Old and New Testament.

Tisserand R and Balacs T, *Essential Oil Safety*, Churchill Livingstone, New York, NY (1996).

Tiwari BK, et al. "Evaluation of insecticidal, fumigant and repellent properties of lemongrass oil." *Indian J Exp Biol*. 1966;4(2):128-9.

Tovey ER, et al. "A simple washing procedure with eucalyptus oil for controlling house dust mites and their allergens in clothing and bedding." *J Allergy Clin Immunol*. 1997; 100(4):464-6.

Toyoda M, Morohashi M, "Pathenogenesis of acne," *Med Electron Microse* 2001 Mar;34(1):29-40.

Tyler VE. *Herbs of Choice,* Pharmaceutical Products Press, Binghamton, NY (1994).

Tyler VE. *The Honest Herbal*, Lubrect & Cramer, Ltd., Port Jervis, NY (1995).

Uchida N, et al., "Direct dissolution of gallstones with methyl tert-butyl ether MTBE) via endoscopic transpapillary catheterization in the gallbladder (ETCG)." J Gastroenterol 1994 Aug;29(4):486-94.

Unnikrishnan MC, et al. "Tumour reducing and anticarcinogenic activity of selected spices." *Cancer Lett*. 1990;51(1):85-9.

Valnet Jean. Robert Tisserand, ed. *The Practice of Aromatherapy*. Healing Arts Press, Rochester, VT (1990).

Veal L. "The potential effectiveness of essential oils as a treatment for headlice, Pediculus humanus capitis." *Complement Ther Nurs Midwifery*. 1996 Aug;2(4):97-101.

Vergunst H, et al. "In vitro comparison of different gall stone dissolution solvents." Gut 1991 Feb;32(2):211-4.

Vernet-Maury E, et al. "Basic emotions induced by odorants: a new approach based on autonomic pattern results." *J Auton Nerv Syst*. 1999;75 (2-3): 176-83.

Wagner J, et al. "Beyond benzodiazepines: alternative pharmacologic agents for the treatment of insomnia." *Ann Pharmacother.* 1998;32(6):680-91.

Wahnon R, et al. "Age and membrane fluidity." *Mechanisms of Aging and Development* 50, (1989) 249-255.

Wan J, et al. "The effect of essential oils of basil on the growth of Aeromonas hydrophila and Pseudomonas fluorescens." *J Appl Microbiol*. 1998;84(2):152-8.

Wang, LG, et al. "Determination of DNA topoisomerase II activity from L1210 cells--a target for screening antitumor agents." *Chung Kuo Yao Li Hsueh Pao*. 1991;12(2):108-14.

Wattenberg LW et al. "Inhibitory effects of 5-(2-pyrazinyl)-4-methyl-1,2-dithiol-3-thione (Oltipraz) on carcinogenesis induced by benzo[a]pyrene, diethylnitrosamine and uracil mustard." *Carcinogenesis*. 1986 Aug;7(8):1379-81.

Weyers W, et al. "Skin absorption of volatile oils." Pharmacokinetics. *Pharm Unserer Zeit*. 1989; 18(3):82-6.

Wie MB, et al. "Eugenol protects neuronal cells from excitotoxic and oxidative injury in primary cortical cultures." *Neurosci Lett*. 1997: 4;225(2):93-6.

Yamada K, et al. "Anticonvulsive effects of inhaling lavender oil vapour." *Biol Pharm Bull*. 1994;17(2):359-60.

Yamamoto F, "Direct gallstone dissolution therapy with GS-100." Nippon Rinsho 1993 Jul;51(7):1791-6.

Yamasaki K, et al. "Anti-HIV-1 activity of herbs in Labiatae." *Biol Pharm Bull*. 1998;21(8):829-33.

Yang, KK, et al. "Antiemetic principles of Pogostemon cablin (Blanco) Benth." *Phytomedicine* 1999, 6(2): 89-93.

Yokota H, et al. "Suppressed mutagenicity of benzo[a]pyrene by the liver S9 fraction and microsomes from eugenol-treated rats." *Mutat Res*. 1986 Dec;172(3):231-6.

Youdim KA, Deans SG, et al. "Beneficial effects of thyme oil on age-related changes in the phospholipid C20 and C22 polyunsaturated fatty acid composition of various rat tissues." *Biochim Biophys Acta*. 1999 Apr 19;1438(1):140-6.

Youdim KA, Deans SG, "Dietary supplementation of thyme (Thymus vulgaris L.) essential oil during the lifetime of the rat: its effects on the antioxidant status in liver, kidney and heart tissues." *Mech Aging Dev*. 1999 Sep 8;109(3):163-75.

Youdim KA, et al. "Beneficial effects of thyme oil on age-related changes in the phospholipid C20 and C22 polyunsaturated fatty acid composition of various rat tissues." *Biochim Biophys Acta*. 1999;1438(1): 140-6.

Youdim KA, et al. Effect of thyme oil and thymol dietary supplementation on the antioxidant status and fatty acid composition of the aging rat brain. *Br J Nutr*. 2000 Jan;83(1):87-93.

Young Robert O. *Sick and Tired*. Alpine, UT, 1977.

Yousef RT and Tawil GG. "Antimicrobial activity of volatile oils." *Pharmazie* 1980; 35(11);798-701

Zanker KS, et al. "Evaluation of surfactant-like effects of commonly used remedies for colds." *Respiration*. 1980;39(3):150-7.

Zheng GQ, et al. "Sesquiterpenes from clove (Eugenia caryophyllata) as potential anticarcinogenic agents." *J Nat Prod*. 1992 Jul;55(7):999-1003.

Zhang, et al., Effects of the extracts of pumpkin seeds on the urodynamics of rabbits: an experimental study, J Tongji Med Univ 1994:14(4):235-8.

Appendix A
AFNOR Standards

Roman chamomile

AFNOR/ISO Standards for
Chamaemelum nobile
Gas Chromatograph profile 4.10

CONSTITUENTS	Min%	Max%
Isobutyl angelate + Isoamyl methacrylate	30	45
Isoamyl angelate	12	22
Methyl allyl angelate	6	10
2-methyl butyl angelate	3	7
Isoamyl isobutyrate	3	5
Trans-pino-carveol	2	5
Isobutyl n-butyrate	2	9
Alpha-pinene	1.5	5
Pinocarvone	1.3	4
Isobutyl methacrylate	1	3
2-methyl butyl methacrylate	.51	.5

Lavender

AFNOR/ISO Standards for
Lavandula angustifolia
Gas Chromatograph profile 4.10

CONSTITUENTS	Min%	Max%
Linalol	25	38
Linalyl acetate	25	45
cis-beta-ocimene	4	10
trans-beta-ocimene	1.5	6
terpinen-4-ol	2	6
Lavendulyl acetate	2	—
Lavendulol	.3	—
Beta-phellandrene	traces	.5
Alpha-terpineol	—	1
Octanone-3	traces	2
Camphor	traces	.5
Limonene	—	.5
1,8 cineol	—	1

Eucalyptus globulus

AFNOR/ISO Standards for

Eucalyptus globulus - *Gas Chromatograph profile 4.11*

		Pure Essential Oil		Rectified Essential Oil	
CONSTITUENTS		crushed raw	traditional	70%-75%	80%-85%
1,8 cineol	min %	48	58	70	80
Alpha-Pinene	min % max %	10 20	20 22	traces 20	traces 12
Aromadendrene	min % max %	6 10	1 5	— traces	— traces
Limonene	min % max %	2 4	1 8	2 15	2 15
p-cymene	min % max %	1 3	1 5	1 6	1 10
trans-pinocarveol	min % max %	1 4	1 5	traces 10	traces 6
Globulol	min % max %	.5 2.5	.5 1.5	— traces	— traces

Clary sage

AFNOR/ISO Standards for

Salvia sclarea - *Gas Chromatograph profile 4.10*

CONSTITUENTS		Traditional	Crushed Green
Linalyl acetate	min % max %	62 78	56 70.5
Linalol	min % max %	6.5 13.5	13 24
Sclareol	min % max %	.4 2.6	.4 2.6
D-germacrene	min % max %	1.5 12	1.2 7.5
Alpha-terpineol	min % max %	traces 1.2	1 5

Basil

AFNOR/ISO Standards for

Basilicum ocimum - *Gas Chromatograph profile 4.8*

CONSTITUENTS	Min %	Max %
Methyl chavicol	75	85
1,8 cineol	1	3.5
Trans-beta ocimene	.9	2.8
Linalol	.50	3.0
Methyl eugenol	.3	2.5
Terpinen-4-ol	.20	.60
Camphor	.15	.50

Clove

AFNOR/ISO Standards for

Syzygium aromaticum - *Gas Chromatograph profile 4.8*

CONSTITUENTS	Min %	Max %
Eugenol	80	92
B-caryophyllene	4	17
Eugenyl acetate	.2	4

Cypress

AFNOR/ISO Standards for

Cupressus sempervirens - *Gas Chromatograph profile 4.11*

CONSTITUENTS	Min %	Max %
Alpha-pinene	40	65
Delta-3-carene	12	25
limonene	1.8	5
Alpha-Terpenyl acetate	1	4
Myrcene	1	3.5
Cedrol	.8	7
Beta-pinene	.5	3
D-germacrene	.5	3
Terpinen-4-ol	.2	2

Appendix B

Essential Oils Certified as GRAS or Food Additives by the FDA

CODE:

FA .... FDA-approved food additive
(FL) .... Flavoring agent
GRAS .... Generally regarded as safe

Oil	(FL)	GRAS	FA
Angelica		GRAS	FA
Anise		GRAS	FA
Basil		GRAS	FA
Bergamot		GRAS	FA
Cedarwood			FA
Celery Seed		GRAS	FA
Chamomile, Roman		GRAS	FA
Chamomile, German		GRAS	FA
Cinnamon Bark		GRAS	FA
Cistus			FA
Citronella		GRAS	FA
Citrus rinds (all)		GRAS	FA
Clary Sage		GRAS	FA
Clove		GRAS	FA
Coriander		GRAS	FA
Cumin		GRAS	FA
Dill		GRAS	FA
Eucalyptus glob.	(FL)	GRAS	FA
Elemi			FA
Fennel			FA
Fir			FA
Frankincense	(FL)	GRAS	FA
Galbanum	(FL)	GRAS	FA
Geranium		GRAS	FA
Ginger		GRAS	FA

Oil			
Goldenrod		GRAS	
Grapefruit		GRAS	FA
Helichrysum			FA
Hyssop		GRAS	FA
Jasmine		GRAS	FA
Juniper		GRAS	FA
Laurus nobilis		GRAS	FA
Lavandin		GRAS	FA
Lavender		GRAS	FA
Lemon		GRAS	FA
Lemongrass		GRAS	FA
Lime		GRAS	FA
Mandarin		GRAS	FA
Marjoram		GRAS	FA
Melaleuca alternifolia			FA
Melissa (lemon balm)		GRAS	FA
Myrrh	(FL)	GRAS	FA
Myrtle		GRAS	FA
Neroli		GRAS	FA
Nutmeg		GRAS	FA
Orange		GRAS	FA
Oregano		GRAS	FA
Palmarosa		GRAS	FA
Patchouli	(FL)	GRAS	FA
Pepper		GRAS	FA
Peppermint		GRAS	FA
Petitgrain		GRAS	FA
Pine	(FL)	GRAS	FA
Rosemary cineol		GRAS	FA
Rose		GRAS	FA
Rosewood			FA
Savory		GRAS	FA
Sage		GRAS	FA
Sandalwood	(FL)	GRAS	FA
Spearmint		GRAS	FA
Spikenard			FA
Spruce	(FL)	GRAS	FA
Tarragon	(FL)	GRAS	FA
Tangerine		GRAS	FA
Thyme		GRAS	FA
Valerian	(FL)	GRAS	FA
Vetiver		GRAS	FA
Ylang ylang		GRAS	FA

Appendix C

Bible References

Documenting biblical plants and aromatics is a very inexact science. Not until 1566 did Levinus Lemmens compile the first book on plants. So it is often guesswork to decide what plant of today might be one mentioned in the Bible. Some of the plants of ancient Israel may now be extinct.

Since I have spent so much time in Egypt, Israel, Oman, and Jordan, I have made some suggestions for modern-day essential oils that may be very close, if not the exact same aromatics from millenniums ago.

The oils that I am certain are the same as the varieties known in biblical times are frankincense and myrrh. The hyssop of the Exodus may not be a hyssop we are familiar today. And the composition of onycha is still being debated. Jewish scholar Rashi stated onycha is a kind of root, while others believed it to be a shellfish. I believe it is a resin much like frankincense, called *Styrax benzoin*. Another difficult-to-identify plant is the Rose of Sharon. I suggest it is labdanum or the rockrose we call cistus.

Aloes—Sandalwood *(Santalum album)*

Psalms 45:8—"All thy garments smell of myrrh, and aloes, and cassia, out of the ivory palaces, whereby they have made thee glad."

Proverbs 7:17—"I have perfumed my bed with myrrh, aloes, and cinnamon."

Song of Solomon 4:14—"Spikenard and saffron; calamus and cinnamon, with all trees of frankincense; myrrh and aloes, with all the chief spices:"

John 19:39—"And there came also Nicodemus, which at the first came to Jesus by night, and brought a mixture of myrrh and aloes, about an hundredweight."

Cassia *(Cinnamomum cassia)*

Exodus 30:24—"And of cassia five hundred shekels, after the shekel of the sanctuary,and of oil olive an hin:"

Psalms 45:8—"All thy garments smell of myrrh, and aloes, and cassia, out of the ivory palaces, whereby they have made thee glad."

Ezekiel 27:19—"Dan also and Javan going to and fro occupied in thy fairs: bright iron, cassia, and calamus, were in thy market."

Calamus *(Acorus calamus)*

Exodus 30:23—"Take thou also unto thee principle spices, of pure myrrh five hundred shekels, and of sweet cinnamon half so much, even two hundred and fifty shekels, and of sweet calamus two hundred and fifty shekels,"

Song of Solomon 4:14—"Spikenard and saffron; calamus and cinnamon, with all trees of frankincense; myrrh and aloes, with all the chief spices:"

Ezekiel 27:19—"Dan also and Javan going to and fro occupied in thy fairs: bright iron, cassia, and calamus, were in thy market."

Cedarwood *(Cedrus atlantica)*

Leviticus 14:51—"And he shall take the cedar wood, and the hyssop, and the scarlet, and the living bird, and dip them in the blood of the slain bird, and in the running water, and sprinkle the house seven times:"

Leviticus 14:52—"And he shall cleanse the house with the blood of the bird, and with the running water, and with the living bird, and with the cedar wood, and with the hyssop, and with the scarlet."

Numbers 19:6—"And the priest shall take cedar wood, and hyssop, and scarlet, and cast it into the midst of the burning of the heifer."

Numbers 24:6—"As the valleys are they spread forth, as gardens by the river's side, as the trees of lign aloes which the Lord hath planted, and as cedar trees beside the waters."

2 Samuel 5:11—"And Hiram king of Tyre sent messengers to David, and cedar trees, and carpenters, and masons: and they built David an house."

2 Samuel 7:2—"That the king said unto Nathan the prophet, See now, I dwell in an house of cedar, but the ark of God dwelleth within curtains."

2 Samuel 7:7—"In all the places wherein I have walked with all the children of Israel spake I a word with any of the tribes of Israel, whom I commanded to feed my people Israel, saying, Why build ye not me an house of cedar?"

1 Kings 4:33—"And he spake of trees, from the cedar tree that is in Lebanon even unto the hyssop that springeth out of the wall: he spake also of beasts, and of fowl, and of creeping things, and of fishes."

1 Kings 5:6—"Now therefore command thou that they hew me cedar trees out of Lebanon; and my servants shall be with thy servants: and unto thee will I give hire for thy servants according to all that thou shalt appoint: for thou knowest that there is not among us any that can skill to hew timber like unto the Sidonians."

1 Kings 5:8—"And Hiram sent to Solomon, saying, I have considered the things which thou sentest to me for: and I will do all thy desire concerning timber of cedar, and concerning timber of fir."

1 Kings 5:10—"So Hiram gave Solomon cedar trees and fir trees according to all his desire."

1 Kings 6:9—"So he built the house, and finished it; and covered the house with beams and boards of cedar."

1 Kings 9:11—"(Now Hiram the king of Tyre had furnished Solomon with cedar trees and fir trees, and with gold, according to all his desire,) that then king Solomon gave Hiram twenty cities in the land of Galilee."

2 Kings 19:23—"By thy messengers thou hast reproached the Lord, and hast said, With the multitude of my chariots I am come up to the height of the mountains, to the sides of Lebanon, and will cut down the tall cedar trees thereof, and the choice fir trees thereof: and I will enter into the lodgings of his borders, and into the forest of his Carmel."

1 Chronicles 22:4—"Also cedar trees in abundance: for the Zidonians and they of Tyre brought much cedar wood to David."

2 Chronicles 1:15—"And the king made silver and gold at Jerusalem as plenteous as stones, and cedar trees made he as the sycomore trees that are in the vale for abundance."

2 Chronicles 2:8—"Send me also cedar trees, fir trees, and algum trees, out of Lebanon: for I know that thy servants can skill to cut timber in Lebanon; and, behold, my servants shall be with thy servants,"

2 Chronicles 9:27—"And the king made silver in Jerusalem as stones, and cedar trees made he as the sycomore trees that are in the low plains in abundance."

Ezra 3:7—"They gave money also unto the masons, and to the carpenters; and meat, and drink, and oil, unto them of Zidon, and to them of Tyre, to bring cedar trees from Lebanon to the sea of Joppa, according to the grant that they had of Cyrus king of Persia."

Isaiah 41:19—"I will plant in the wilderness the cedar, the shittah tree, and the myrtle, and the oil tree; I will set in the desert the fir tree, and the pine, and the box tree together:"

Ezekiel 17:3—"And say, Thus saith the Lord God; A great eagle with great wings, longwinged, full of feathers, which had divers colours, came unto Lebanon, and took the highest branch of the cedar:"

Ezekiel 17:22—"Thus saith the Lord God; I will also take of the highest branch of the high cedar, and will set it; I will crop off from the top of his young twigs a tender one, and will plant it upon an high mountain and eminent:"

Ezekiel 17:23—"In the mountain of the height of Israel will I plant it: and it shall bring forth boughs, and bear fruit, and be a goodly cedar: and under it shall dwell all fowl of every wing; in the shadow of the branches thereof shall they dwell."

Zechariah 11:2—"Howl, fir tree; for the cedar is fallen; because the mighty are spoiled: howl, O ye oaks of Bashan; for the forest of the vintage is come down."

Cinnamon *(Cinnamomum verum)*

Exodus 30:23—"Take thou also unto thee principle spices, of pure myrrh five hundred shekels, and of sweet cinnamon half so much, even two hundred and fifty shekels, and of sweet calamus two hundred and fifty shekels,"

Proverbs 7:17—"I have perfumed my bed with myrrh, aloes, and cinnamon."

Song of Solomon 4:14—"Spikenard and saffron; calamus and cinnamon, with all trees of frankincense; myrrh and aloes, with all the chief spices:"

Revelation 18:13—"And cinnamon, and odours, and ointments, and frankincense, and wine, and oil, and fine flour, and wheat, and beasts, and sheep, and horses, and chariots, and slaves, and souls of men."

Cypress *(Cupressus sempervirens)*

Isaiah 44:14—"He heweth him down cedars, and taketh the cypress and the oak, which he strengtheneth for himself among the trees of the forest: he planteth an ash, and the rain doth nourish it."

Fir *(Abies alba)*

1 Kings 6:15—"And he built the walls of the house within with boards of cedar, both the floor of the house, and the walls of the ceiling: and he covered them on the inside with wood, and covered the floor of the house with planks of fir."

1 Kings 6:34—"And the two doors were of fir tree: the two leaves of the one door were folding, and the two leaves of the other door were folding."

1 Kings 9:11—"(Now Hiram the king of Tyre had furnished Solomon with cedar trees and fir trees, and with gold, according to all his desire,) that then king Solomon gave Hiram twenty cities in the land of Galilee."

2 Kings 19:23—"By thy messengers thou hast reproached the Lord, and hast said, With the multitude of my chariots I am come up to the height of the mountains, to the sides of Lebanon, and will cut down the tall cedar trees thereof, and the choice fir trees thereof: and I will enter into the lodgings of his borders, and into the forest of his Carmel."

2 Chronicles 2:8—"Send me also cedar trees, fir trees, and algum trees, out of Lebanon: for I know that thy servants can skill to cut timber in Lebanon; and, behold, my servants shall be with thy servants."

2 Chronicles 3:5—"And the greater house he cieled with fir tree, which he overlaid with fine gold, and set thereon palm trees and chains."

Psalms 104:17—"Where the birds make their nests: as for the stork, the fir trees are her house."

Song Of Solomon 1:17—"The beams of our house are cedar, and our rafters of fir."

Isaiah 14:8—"Yea, the fir trees rejoice at thee, and the cedars of Lebanon, saying, Since thou art laid down, no feller is come up against us."

Isaiah 37:24—"By thy servants hast thou reproached the Lord, and hast said, By the multitude of my chariots am I come up to the height of the mountains, to the sides of Lebanon; and I will cut down the tall cedars thereof, and the choice fir trees thereof: and I will enter into the height of his border, and the forest of his Carmel."

Isaiah 41:19—"I will plant in the wilderness the cedar, the shittah tree, and the myrtle, and the oil tree; I will set in the desert the fir tree, and the pine, and the box tree together:"

Isaiah 55:13—"Instead of the thorn shall come up the fir tree, and instead of the brier shall come up the myrtle tree: and it shall be to the Lord for a name, for an everlasting sign that shall not be cut off."

Isaiah 60:13—"The glory of Lebanon shall come unto thee, the fir tree, the pine tree, and the box together, to beautify the place of my sanctuary; and I will make the place of my feet glorious."

Ezekiel 27:5—"They have made all thy ship boards of fir trees of Senir: they have taken cedars from Lebanon to make masts for thee."

Ezekiel 31:8—"The cedars in the garden of God could not hide him: the fir trees were not like his boughs, and the chestnut trees were not like his branches; nor any tree in the garden of God was like unto him in his beauty."

Hosea 14:8—"Ephraim shall say, What have I to do any more with idols? I have heard him, and observed him: I am like a green fir tree. From me is thy fruit found."

Nahum 2:3—"The shield of his mighty men is made red, the valiant men are in scarlet: the chariots shall be with flaming torches in the day of his preparation, and the fir trees shall be terribly shaken."

Zechariah 11:2—"Howl, fir tree; for the cedar is fallen; because the mighty are spoiled: howl, O ye oaks of Bashan; for the forest of the vintage is come down."

Frankincense *(Boswellia carteri)*

Leviticus 2:15—"And thou shalt put oil upon it, and lay frankincense thereon: it is a meat offering."

Leviticus 2:16—"And the priest shall burn the memorial of it, part of the beaten corn thereof, and part of the oil thereof, with all the frankincense thereof: it is an offering made by fire unto the Lord."

Leviticus 5:11—"But if he be not able to bring two turtledoves, or two young pigeons, then he that sinned shall bring for his offering the tenth part of an ephah of fine flour for a sin offering; he shall put no oil upon it, neither shall he put any frankincense thereon: for it is a sin offering"

Leviticus 6:15—"And he shall take of it his handful, of the flour of the meat offering, and of the oil thereof, and all the frankincense which is upon the meat offering, and shall burn it upon the altar for a sweet savour, even the memorial of it, unto the Lord."

Leviticus 24:7—"And thou shalt put pure frankincense upon each row, that it may be on the bread for a memorial, even an offering made by fire unto the Lord."

Numbers 5:15—"Then shall the man bring his wife unto the priest, and he shall bring her offering for her, the tenth part of an ephah of barley meal; he shall pour no oil upon it, nor put frankincense thereon; for it is an offering of jealousy, an offering of memorial, bringing iniquity to remembrance."

1 Chronicles 9:29—"Some of them also were appointed to oversee the vessels, and all the instruments of the sanctuary, and the fine flour, and the wine, and the oil, and the frankincense, and the spices."

Nehemiah 13:5—"And he had prepared for him a great chamber, where aforetime they laid the meat offerings, the frankincense, and the vessels, and the tithes of the corn, the new wine, and the oil, which was commanded to be given to the Levites, and the singers, and the porters; and the offerings of the priests."

Nehemiah 13:9—"Then I commanded, and they cleansed the chambers: and thither brought I again the vessels of the house of God, with the meat offering and the frankincense."

Song of Solomon 3:6—"Who is this that cometh out of the wilderness like pillars of smoke, perfumed with myrrh and frankincense, with all powders of the merchant?"

Song of Solomon 4:6—"Until the day break, and the shadows flee away, I will get me to the mountain of myrrh, and to the hill of frankincense."

Song of Solomon 4:14—"Spikenard and saffron; calamus and cinnamon, with all trees of frankincense; myrrh and aloes, with all the chief spices:"

Matthew 2:11—"And when they were come into the house, they saw the young child with Mary his mother, and fell down, and worshiped him: and when they had opened their treasures, they presented unto him gifts; gold, and frankincense, and myrrh."

Revelation 18:13—"And cinnamon, and odours, and ointments, and frankincense, and wine, and oil, and fine flour, and wheat, and beasts, and sheep, and horses, and chariots, and slaves, and souls of men."

Galbanum *(Ferula gummosa)*

Exodus 30:34—"And the Lord said unto Moses, Take unto thee sweet spices, stacte, and onycha, and galbanum: these sweet spices with pure frankincense: of each there shall be a like weight."

Hyssop *(Hyssopus officinalis)*

Leviticus 14:49—"And he shall take to cleanse the house two birds, and cedar wood, and scarlet, and hyssop:"

Leviticus 14:51—"And he shall take the cedar wood, and the hyssop, and the scarlet, and the living bird, and dip them in the blood of the slain bird, and in the running water, and sprinkle the house seven times:"

Leviticus 14:52—"And he shall cleanse the house with the blood of the bird, and with the running water, and with the living bird, and with the cedar wood, and with the hyssop, and with the scarlet:"

Numbers 19:6—"And the priest shall take cedar wood, and hyssop, and scarlet, and cast it into the midst of the burning of the heifer."

Numbers 19:18—"And a clean person shall take hyssop, and dip it in the water, and sprinkle it upon the tent, and upon all the vessels, and upon the persons that were there, and upon him that touched a bone, or one slain, or one dead, or a grave:"

1 Kings 4:33—"And he spake of trees, from the cedar tree that is in Lebanon even unto the hyssop that springeth out of the wall: he spake also of beasts, and of fowl, and of creeping things, and of fishes."

Psalms 51:7—"Purge me with hyssop, and I shall be clean: wash me, and I shall be whiter than snow."

John 19:29—"Now there was set a vessel full of vinegar: and they filled a spunge with vinegar, and put it upon hyssop, and put it to his mouth."

Hebrews 9:19—"For when Moses had spoken every precept to all the people according to the law, he took the blood of calves and of goats, with water, and scarlet wool, and hyssop, and sprinkled both the book, and all the people."

Myrrh *(Commiphora myrrha)*

Esther 2:12—"Now when every maid's turn was come to go in to king Ahasuerus, after that she had been twelve months, according to the manner of the women, (for so were the days of their purifications accomplished, to wit, six months with oil of myrrh, and six months with sweet odours, and with other things for the purifying of the women;)"

Psalms 45:8—"All thy garments smell of myrrh, and aloes, and cassia, out of the ivory palaces, whereby they have made thee glad."

Proverbs 7:17—"I have perfumed my bed with myrrh, aloes, and cinnamon."

Song of Solomon 1:13—"A bundle of myrrh is my wellbeloved unto me; he shall lie all night betwixt my breasts."

Song of Solomon 3:6—"Who is this that cometh out of the wilderness like pillars of smoke, perfumed with myrrh and frankincense, with all powders of the merchant?"

Song of Solomon 4:6—"Until the day break, and the shadows flee away, I will get me to the mountain of myrrh, and to the hill of frankincense."

Song of Solomon 4:14—"Spikenard and saffron; calamus and cinnamon, with all trees of frankincense; myrrh and aloes, with all the chief spices:"

Song of Solomon 5:1—"I am come into my garden, my sister, my spouse: I have gathered my myrrh with my spice; I have eaten my honeycomb with my honey; I have drunk my wine with my milk: eat, O friends; drink, yea, drink abundantly, O beloved."

Song of Solomon 5:5—"I rose up to open to my beloved; and my hands dropped with myrrh, and my fingers with sweet smelling myrrh, upon the handles of the lock."

Song of Solomon 5:13—"His cheeks are as a bed of spices, as sweet flowers: his lips like lilies, dropping sweet smelling myrrh."

Matthew 2:11—"And when they were come into the house, they saw the young child with Mary his mother, and fell down, and worshiped him: and when they had opened their treasures, they presented unto him gifts; gold, and frankincense, and myrrh."

Mark 15:23—"And they gave him to drink wine mingled with myrrh: but he received it not."

John 19:39—"And there came also Nicodemus, which at the first came to Jesus by night, and brought a mixture of myrrh and aloes, about an hundred pound weight."

Myrtle *(Myrtus communis)*

Nehemiah 8:15—"Go forth unto the mount, and fetch olive branches, and pine branches, and myrtle branches, and palm branches, and branches of thick trees, to make booths, as it is written."

Zechariah 1:8—"I saw by night, and behold a man riding upon a red horse, and he stood among the myrtle trees that were in the bottom; and behind him were there red horses, speckled, and white."

Zechariah 1:10—"And the man that stood among the myrtle trees answered and said, These are they whom the Lord hath sent to walk to and fro through the earth."

Zechariah 1:11—"And they answered the angel of the Lord that stood among the myrtle trees, and said, We have walked to and fro through the earth, and, behold, all the earth sitteth still, and is at rest."

Onycha *(Styrax benzoin)*

Exodus 30:34—"And the Lord said unto Moses, Take unto thee sweet spices, stacte, and onycha, and galbanum: these sweet spices with pure frankincense: of each there shall be a like weight."

Rose of Sharon—Cistus *(Cistus ladanifer)*

Song of Solomon 2:1—"I am the rose of Sharon, and the lily of the valleys."

Spikenard *(Nardostachys jatamansi)*

Song of Solomon 4:14—"Spikenard and saffron; calamus and cinnamon, with all trees of frankincense, myrrh and aloes, with all chief spices."

Mark 14:3—"And being in Bethany in the house of Simon the leper, as he sat at meat, there came a woman having an alabaster box of ointment of spikenard very precious; and she brake the box, and poured it on his head."

John 12:3—"Then took Mary a pound of ointment of spikenard, very costly, and anointed the feet of Jesus, and wiped his feet with her hair: and the house was filled with the odour of the ointment."

Appendix D

Glossary of Medical Actions

alopecia: baldness, loss of hair

allopathic: refers to conventional contemporary medical approaches using prescription drugs to provide symptom relief in the treatment of illness

amenorrhea: absence of menstruation

anabolism: the creation of body tissue—the opposite of catabolism—usually from other nutrients or components

anesthetic: loss of feeling or sensation; substance which causes such a loss

analgesic: remedy or agent which deadens or relieves pain

anthelmintic: substance unfriendly to worms and parasites; a vermifuge; destroys, expels intestinal worms

anodyne: stills pain and quiets disturbed feelings

antibiotic: prevents the growth of, or destroys bacteria

anticatarrhal: agent which helps remove excess catarrh (excess mucous secreted by inflamed mucous membranes) from the body

anti-emetic: agent which reduces the incidence and severity of nausea or vomiting

antihistamine: counteracts the effects of histamine (which produces capillary dilation and, in larger doses, hemoconcentration)

anti-inflammatory: reduces inflammation

antilithic:	prevents the formation of a calculus or stone
antimicrobial:	agent which resists or destroys pathogenic micro-organisms
antineuralgic:	relieves or reduces nerve pain
antioxidant:	natural or synthetic substances that help inhibit destructive oxygen- and free radical-induced deterioration (oxidation) of substances and tissues in the body.
antipruritic:	relieves or prevents itching.
antipyretic:	reduces fever; see febrifuge
antisclerotic:	prevents the hardening of tissue
antiseptic:	destroys and prevents the development of microbes
antispasmodic:	prevents and eases spasms or convulsions
antitoxic:	antidote or treatment that counteracts the effects of poisons and toxins
antitussive:	relieves coughs
antiviral:	inhibits the growth of virus
aperient:	mild laxative
astringent:	causes contraction of organic tissues
bechic:	anything that relieves or cures coughs; or refers to coughs
calmative:	a sedative
carcinogen:	substance or agent which produces or creates cancer
cardiotonic:	having a stimulating effect on the heart
carminative:	agent which prevents the formation of gas (flatulence) in the intestinal system typically to relieve pain due to colic or cramping.
catabolism:	the breaking down of tissue or material within the body. Digestion is a catabolic process.
cathartic:	purgative, capable of causing a violent purging or catharsis of the body

cellulite: accumulation of toxic matter in the form of fat in the tissue

cholagogue: stimulates the secretion and flow of bile into the duodenum

choleretic: aids excretion of bile by the liver, so there is a greater flow of bile

cicatrisant: agent which promotes healing by the formation of scar tissue

cutaneous: pertaining to the skin

cytophylactic: referring to cytophylaxis: the process of increasing the activity of leucocytes in defense of the body against infection

cytotoxic: toxic to all cells

demulcent: agent which protects mucous membranes and allays irritation

diuretic: aids production of urine, promotes urination, increases flow

edema: a painless swelling caused by fluid retention beneath the skin's surface

emetic: induces vomiting

emmenagogue: induces or assists menstruation

emollient: softens and soothes skin

enteritis: inflammation of the mucous membrane of the intestine

expectorant: promotes the removal of mucous from the respiratory system

febrifuge: combats fever

fungicidal: prevents and combats fungal infection

germicidal: destroys germs or microorganisms such as bacteria

halitosis: offensive breath

hemostatic: arrests bleeding

hepatic: relating to the liver, tones and aids its function

hypertensive: agent which raises blood pressure

hypnotic: causing sleep

hypocholesterolemia: lowering the cholesterol content of the blood

hypotensive: agent which lowers blood pressure

laxative: promotes evacuation of the bowels

lipolytic: causing lipolysis, the chemical disintegration or splitting of fats

microbe: a minute living organism, especially pathogenic bacteria, viruses, etc.

mucolytic: dissolving or breaking down mucous

narcotic: substance which induces sleep; intoxicating or poisonous in large doses

neat: term used for describing the application of essential oil without dilution in a carrier oil

nervine: strengthening and toning to the nervous and nervous system

nephritis: inflammation of the kidneys

neuralgia: a stabbing pain along a nerve pathway

neurasthenia: nervous exhaustion

olfaction: the sense of smell

ophthalmia: inflammation of the eye, a term usually applied to conjunctivitis

otitis: inflammation of the ear

pathogenic: causing or producing disease pruritis: itching

psychosomatic: the manifestation of physical symptoms resulting from a mental state

restorative: agent that helps strengthen and revive the body systems

rhinitis: inflammation of the mucous membrane of the nose

rubefacient: reddening the skin, an agent that reddens the skin by producing hyperemia

soporific: substance which induces sleep

spasmolytic: antispasmodic

stomachic: digestive aid and tonic; improving the appetite

styptic: astringent agent which stops or reduces external bleeding

sudorific: agent which causes sweating

thrombosis: the formation of a blood clot (thrombus)

topical application: refers to applying something directly to the exterior surface of the skin; not internal.

vasoconstrictor: agent which causes narrowing of the blood vessels

vasodilator: agent which causes dilation of the blood vessels

vermifuge: expels intestinal worms

vesicant: causing blistering to the skin

vulnerary: agent which helps heal wounds and sores by external application

Appendix E
Common and Botanical Plant Names

Botanical Name First:

Abies balsamea .Balsam Fir
Abies concolor .White Fir
Achillea millefolium .Yarrow
Acorus calamus .Calamus
Anethum graveolens .Dill
Angelica archangelica .Angelica
Aniba rosaeodora .Rosewood
Apium graveolens .Celery Seed
Artemisia dracunculus .Tarragon
Betula alleghaniensis .Birch
Boswellia carteri .Frankincense
Callitris intratropica .Blue cypress
Cananga odorata .Ylang Ylang
Canarium luzonicum .Elemi
Cedrus atlantica .Cedarwood
Chamaemelum nobile .Chamomile (Roman)
Cinnamomum cassia .Cassia
Cinnamomum verum .Cinnamon Bark
Cistus ladanifer .Cistus
Citrus aurantium .Neroli
Citrus aurantium .Orange
Citrus bergamia .Bergamot
Citrus limon .Lemon
Citrus nobilis .Tangerine
Citrus reticulata .Mandarin
Citrus x paradisi .Grapefruit
Commiphora myrrha .Myrrh
Conyza canadensis .Fleabane
Coriandrum sativum .Coriander
Cuminum cyminum .Cumin
Cupressus sempervirens .Cypress

Cymbopogon flexuosus .... Lemongrass
Cymbopogon nardus .... Citronella
Daucus carota .... Carrot Seed
Elettaria cardamomum .... Cardamom
Eucalyptus citriodora .... Eucalyptus citriodora
Eucalyptus dives .... Eucalyptus dives
Eucalyptus globulus .... Eucalyptus globulus
Eucalyptus polybractea .... Eucalyptus polybractea
Eucalyptus radiata .... Eucalyptus radiata
Ferula gummosa .... Galbanum
Foeniculum vulgare .... Fennel
Gaultheria procumbens .... Wintergreen
Helichrysum italicum .... Helichrysum
Hyssopus officinalis .... Hyssop
Jasminum officinale .... Jasmine
Juniperus communis and *Juniperus osteosperma* .... Juniper
Laurus nobilis .... Bay Laurel
Lavandula angustifolia .... Lavender
Lavandula x hybrida .... Lavandin
Ledum groenlandicum .... Ledum
Leptospormum scoparium .... Manuka
Matricaria recutita .... Chamomile (German)
Melaleuca alternifolia .... Melaleuca alternifolia
Melaleuca ericifolia .... Melaleuca ericifolia
Melaleuca leucadendra .... Cajeput
Melaleuca quinquenervia .... Melaleuca quinquenervia
Melissa officinalis .... Melissa
Mentha spicata .... Spearmint
Mentha piperita .... Peppermint
Myristica fragrans .... Nutmeg
Myrtus communis .... Myrtle
Nardostachys jatamansi .... Spikenard
Ocimum basilicum .... Basil
Origanum compactum .... Oregano
Origanum majorana .... Marjoram
Pelargonium graveolens .... Geranium
Picea mariana .... Spruce
Pimpinella anisum .... Anise
Pinus sylvestris .... Pine
Piper nigrum .... Black Pepper
Pogostemon cablin .... Patchouli
Pseudotsuga menziesii .... Douglas Fir
Ravensara aromatica .... Ravensara
Rosa damascena .... Rose

Rosmarinus CT 1,8 cineol . . . . Rosemary
Rosmarinus CT verbenon . . . . Rosemary Verbenon
Salvia officinalis . . . . Sage
Salvia sclarea . . . . Clary Sage
Santalum album . . . . Sandalwood
Satureja montana . . . . Mountain Savory
Solidago canadensis . . . . Goldenrod
Syzygium aromaticum . . . . Clove
Tanacetum annuum . . . . Blue Tansy
Tanacetum vulgare . . . . Tansy
Thuja plicata . . . . Western Red Cedar
Thymus vulgaris CT linalol . . . . Thyme Linalol
Thymus vulgaris CT thymol . . . . Thyme
Tsuga canadensis . . . . Tsuga
Valeriana officinalis . . . . Valerian
Vetiveria zizanioides . . . . Vetiver
Vitex negundo . . . . Vitex
Zingiber officinale . . . . Ginger

Common Name First:

Angelica . . . . *Angelica archangelica*
Anise . . . . *Pimpinella anisum*
Balsam Fir . . . . *Abies balsamea*
Basil . . . . *Ocimum basilicum*
Bay Laurel . . . . *Laurus nobilis*
Bergamot . . . . *Citrus bergamia*
Birch . . . . *Betula alleghaniensis*
Black Pepper . . . . *Piper nigrum*
Blue cypress . . . . *Callitris intratropica*
Blue Tansy . . . . *Tanacetum annuum*
Cajeput . . . . *Melaleuca leucadendra*
Calamus . . . . *Acorus calamus*
Cardamom . . . . *Elettaria cardamomum*
Carrot Seed . . . . *Daucus carota*
Cassia . . . . *Cinnamomum cassia*
Cedarwood . . . . *Cedrus atlantica*
Celery Seed . . . . *Apium graveolens*
Chamomile (German) . . . . *Matricaria recutita*
Chamomile (Roman) . . . . *Chamaemelum nobile*
Cinnamon Bark . . . . *Cinnamomum verum*
Cistus . . . . *Cistus ladanifer*
Citronella . . . . *Cymbopogon nardus*

Clary Sage .... *Salvia sclarea*
Clove .... *Syzygium aromaticum*
Coriander .... *Coriandrum sativum*
Cumin .... *Cuminum cyminum*
Cypress .... *Cupressus sempervirens*
Dill .... *Anethum graveolens*
Douglas Fir .... *Pseudotsuga menziesii*
Elemi .... *Canarium luzonicum*
Eucalyptus dives .... *Eucalyptus dives*
Eucalyptus citriodora .... *Eucalyptus citriodora*
Eucalyptus globulus .... *Eucalyptus globulus*
Eucalyptus polybractea .... *Eucalyptus polybractea*
Eucalyptus radiata .... *Eucalyptus radiata*
Fennel .... *Foeniculum vulgare*
Fleabane .... *Conyza canadensis*
Frankincense .... *Boswellia carteri*
Galbanum .... *Ferula gummosa*
Geranium .... *Pelargonium graveolens*
Ginger .... *Zingiber officinale*
Goldenrod .... *Solidago canadensis*
Grapefruit .... *Citrus x paradisi*
Helichrysum .... *Helichrysum italicum*
Hyssop .... *Hyssopus officinalis*
Jasmine .... *Jasminum officinale*
Juniper .... *Juniperus communis* and *Juniperus osteosperma*
Bay Laurel .... *Laurus nobilis*
Lavandin .... *Lavandula x hybrida*
Lavender .... *Lavandula angustifolia*
Ledum .... *Ledum groenlandicum*
Lemon .... *Citrus limon*
Lemongrass .... *Cymbopogon flexuosus*
Mandarin .... *Citrus reticulata*
Manuka .... *Leptospormum scoparium*
Marjoram .... *Origanum majorana*
Melaleuca alternifolia .... *Melaleuca alternifolia*
Melaleuca ericifolia .... *Melaleuca ericifolia*
Melaleuca quinquenervia .... *Melaleuca quinquenervia*
Melissa .... *Melissa officinalis*
Mountain Savory .... *Satureja montana*
Myrrh .... *Commiphora myrrha*
Myrtle .... *Myrtus communis*
Neroli .... *Citrus aurantium*
Nutmeg .... *Myristica fragrans*
Orange .... *Citrus aurantium*

Oregano . . . . . . *Origanum compactum*
Peppermint . . . . . . *Mentha piperita*
Pine . . . . . . *Pinus sylvestris*
Patchouli . . . . . . *Pogostemon cablin*
Ravensara . . . . . . *Ravensara aromatica*
Rose . . . . . . *Rosa damascena*
Rosemary . . . . . . *Rosmarinus officinalis CT 1, 8 cineol*
Rosemary Verbenon . . . . . . *Rosmarinus officinalis CT verbenon*
Rosewood . . . . . . *Aniba rosaeodora*
Sage . . . . . . *Salvia officinalis*
Sandalwood . . . . . . *Santalum album*
Spearmint . . . . . . *Mentha spicata*
Spikenard . . . . . . *Nardostachys jatamansi*
Spruce . . . . . . *Picea mariana*
Tangerine . . . . . . *Citrus nobilis*
Tansy . . . . . . *Tanacetum vulgare*
Tarragon . . . . . . *Artemisia dracunculus*
Thyme . . . . . . *Thymus vulgaris CT thymol*
Thyme Linalol . . . . . . *Thymus vulgaris CT linalol*
Tsuga . . . . . . *Tsuga canadensis*
Valerian . . . . . . *Valeriana officinalis*
Vetiver . . . . . . *Vetiveria zizanioides*
Vitex . . . . . . *Vitex negundo*
Western Red Cedar . . . . . . *Thuja plicata*
White Fir . . . . . . *Abies concolor*
Wintergreen . . . . . . *Gaultheria procumbens*
Yarrow . . . . . . *Achillea millefolium*
Ylang Ylang . . . . . . *Cananga odorata*

Appendix F

Essential Oil Application Codes

Application Codes

NEAT = straight, undiluted
Dilution usually NOT required; suitable for all but the most sensitive skin. Safe for children over 2 years old.

50-50 = Dilute 50-50
Dilution recommended at 50-50 (1 part essential oils to 1 part vegetable or massage oil) for topical and internal use, especially when used on sensitive areas — face, neck, genital area, underarms, etc. Keep out of reach of children.

PHOTO = Photosensitizing
Avoid using on skin exposed to direct sunlight or UV rays (i.e. sunlamps, tanning beds, etc.)

20-80 = Dilute 20-80
Always dilute 20-80 (1 part essential oils to 4 parts vegetable or massage oil) before applying to the skin or taking internally. Keep out of reach of children.

Singles

Angelica . . . . .PHOTO 50-50
Basil 50-50
Bergamot . . . . .PHOTO. . . . 50-50
Benzoin .50-50
Cajeput .50-50
Cedar, Western Red 50-50
Cardemom 50-50
Cassia **20-80**
Cedarwood 50-50
Chamomile, German . . . . .NEAT
Chamomile, Roman . . . . .NEAT
Cinnamon Bark **20-80**
Cistus . . . . .NEAT
Citronella 50-50
Clary Sage 50-50
Clove **20-80**
Coriander 50-50
Cumin 50-50
Cypress .50-50
Davana .NEAT
Dill 50-50
Elemi . . . . .NEAT
Eucalyptus dives 50-50
Eucalyptus globulus 50-50
Eucalyptus polybractea 50-50
Eucalyptus radiata 50-50
Fennel . . . . .NEAT
Fir, Douglas 50-50
Fir, Balsam 50-50
Fleabane 50-50
Frankincense 50-50
Galbanum . . . . .NEAT
Geranium 50-50
Ginger 50-50

Goldenrod 50-50
Grapefruit . . . . .PHOTO 50-50
Helichrysum 50-50
Hyssop **20-80**
Jasmine .NEAT
Juniper .50-50
Laurus nobilis 50-50
Lavandin 50-50
Lavender . . . . .NEAT
Ledum .NEAT
Lemon . . . . PHOTO . . .50-50
Lemongrass **20-80**
Mandarin 50-50
Manuka . . . . .NEAT
Marjoram 50-50
Melaleuca alternifolia 50-50
Melaleuca ericifolia 50-50
Melaleuca quinquenervia 50-50
Melissa .NEAT
Mountain Savory 50-50
Myrrh . . . . .NEAT
Myrtle 50-50
Neroli . . . . .NEAT
Nutmeg .50-50
Orange . . . . .PHOTO 50-50
Oregano **20-80**
Palmarosa 50-50
Patchouli . . . . .NEAT
Pepper, Black 50-50
Peppermint 50-50
Petitgrain . . . . .NEAT
Pine 50-50
Ravensara 50-50
Rose . . . . .NEAT
Rosemary CT cineol 50-50
Rosemary CT verbenon 50-50
Rosewood . . . . .NEAT
Sage 50-50
Sandalwood . . . . .NEAT
Spearmint 50-50
Spikenard . . . . .NEAT
Spruce 50-50
Tangerine . . . . .PHOTO 50-50
Tansy 50-50
Tansy, Blue . . . . .NEAT
Tarragon 50-50
Thyme CT thymol **20-80**
Thyme CT linalol 50-50
Tsuga 50-50
Valerian Root . . . . .NEAT
Vetiver .NEAT
Vitex . . . . .NEAT
Wintergreen 50-50
Yarrow .NEAT
Ylang Ylang . . . . .NEAT

Blends

Abuse Relief Blend . . . . .NEAT
Anti-Aging Blend **20-80**
Antibacterial Blend . . . . .NEAT
Antimicrobial **20-80**
Antiseptic Blend 50-50
Antiviral Blend 50-50
Brain Blend . . . . .NEAT
Circulation Blend . . . . .NEAT
Clarity Blend . . . . .NEAT
Digestive Blend . . . . .NEAT
Energy Balance Blend . . . . .NEAT
Emotional Release Blend 50-50
Energy Blend 50-50
Female Blend . . . . .NEAT
Glandular Blend . . . . .NEAT
Headache Blend 50-50
Immune Blend 50-50
Liver Blend 50-50
Male Blend . . . . .NEAT
Mood Lifting Blend . . PHOTO . NEAT
Muscle Relaxing Blend 50-50
Pain Relief Blend 50-50
Respiratory Blend . . . . .NEAT
Romance Blend . . . . .NEAT
Spiritual Blend . . . . .NEAT
Stress Reduction Blend . . . . . . .NEAT
Trauma Blend . . . . .NEAT

Appendix G
Key Scientific Research on Essential Oils

Scientific Research List

1. "Effect of a Diffused Essential Oil Blend on Bacterial Bioaerosols."
2. "Screening for Inhibitory Activity of Essential Oils on Selected Bacteria, Fungi, and Viruses."
3. "Antibacterial Properties of Plant Essential Oils."
4. "Influence of Some Spice Essential Oils on *Aspergillus parasiticus* Growth and Production of Aflatoxins in a Synthetic Medium."
5. "Antioxidant Activity of Some Spice Essential Oils on Linoleic Acid Oxidation in Aqueous Media."
6. "Antimicrobial Activity of Some Egyptian Spice Essential Oils."
7. "Antimicrobial Properties of Spices and Their Essential Oils."
8. "The Antimicrobial Activity of Essential Oils and Essential Oil Components Towards Oral Bacteria."
9. "Anticarcinogenic Effects of the Essential Oils From Cumin, Poppy and Basil."
10. "Effects of Essential Oil on Lipid Peroxidation and Lipid Metabolism in Patients with Chronic Bronchiti."
11. "Effect of Essential Oils on the Course of Experimental Atherosclerosis."
12. "Inhibition of Growth and Aflatoxin Production in *Aspergillus parasiticus* by Essential Oils of Selected Plant Materials."
13. "Odors and Learning."
14. "Weight Reduction through Inhalation of Odorants."
15. "Anti-inflammatory Activity of *Passiflora incarnata* L. in Rats."

ABSTRACTS:

1. Effect of a Diffused Essential Oil Blend on Bacterial Bioaerosols

Author: SC Chao, DGYoung, and CJ Oberg

Journal: *Journal of Essential Oil Research* 10, 517-523 (Sept/Oct 1998)

Location: Weber State University, Ogden, UT

Conclusion: Diffusion of an essential oil blend can significantly reduce the number of aerosol-borne bacteria.

Abstract: A proprietary blend of oils containing cinnamon, rosemary, clove, eucalyptus, and lemon was tested for its antibacterial activity against airborne *Micrococcus luteus*, *Pseudomonas aeruginosa,* and *Staphylococcus aureus*. The bacteria cultures were sprayed in an enclosed area, and this blend was diffused for a given amount of time. There was an 82 percent reduction in *M. luteus* bioaerosol, a 96 percent reduction in the *P. aeruginosa* bioaerosol, and a 44 percent reduction in the *S. aureus* bioaerosol following 10 minutes of exposure.

2. Screening for Inhibitory Activity of Essential Oils on Selected Bacteria, Fungi, and Viruses

Author: SC Chao, DG Young, and CJ Oberg

Journal: *Journal of Essential Oil Research*, Sept./Oct. 2000.

Location: Weber State University, Ogden, UT

Conclusion: Many essential oils were demonstrated to have antimicrobial properties.

Abstract: Forty-five essential oils were tested for their inhibitory effect against bacteria, yeast, molds, and two bacteriophage. Of the oils tested, all oils showed inhibition compared to controls. Cinnamon bark and tea tree essential oils showed an inhibitory effect against all the test organisms and phage. Other oils with broad ranges of inhibition included lemongrass, mountain savory, Roman chamomile, rosewood, and spearmint.

3. Antibacterial properties of plant essential oils

Author: SG Deans, G Ritchie

Journal: *International Journal of Food Microbiology* 5, 165-180 (1987)

Location: Scotland Agricultural College

Conclusion: Many essential oils have antibacterial properties.

Abstract: Fifty plant essential oils were tested in different concentrations for antibacterial activity against 25 genera of bacteria. The ten most antibacterial oils were: angelica, bay, cinnamon, clove, thyme, almond, marjoram, pimento, geranium, and lovage.

4. Influence of Some Spice Essential Oils on Aspergillus parasiticus Growth and Production of Aflatoxins in a Synthetic Medium

Author: RS Farag, ZY Daw, SH Abo-Raya

Journal: *Journal of Food Science*, Vol 54, No. 1, 74-76 (1989)

Location: Cairo University, Giza, Egypt

Conclusion: Essential oils of thyme, cumin, clove, caraway, rosemary, and sage all possess antifungal properties.

Abstract: The essential oils of thyme, cumin, clove, caraway, rosemary, and sage were tested for antifungal properties. The essential oils completely inhibited growth of fungal mycelium and aflatoxin production. The oils from most effective to least effective were: thyme > cumin > clove > caraway > rosemary > sage. The basic components of these oils were determined by gas-liquid chromatography to be: thyme-thymol, cumin-cumin aldehyde, clove-eugenol, caraway-carvone, rosemary-borneol, and sage-thujone.

5. Antioxidant Activity of Some Spice Essential Oils on Linoleic Acid Oxidation in Aqueous Media

Author: RS Farag, AZMA Badei, FM Hewedi, GSA Al-Baroty

Journal: *Journal of the American Oil Chemists Society,* Vol. 66, No. 6 (June 1989)

Location: Cairo University, Giza, Egypt

Conclusion: Essential oils of caraway, clove, cumin, rosemary, sage, thyme possess antioxidant activity on linoleic acid oxidation.

Abstract: Essential oils of caraway, clove, cumin, rosemary, sage and thyme were examined for antioxidant activity in linoleic acid. These oils were all found to have an antioxidant effect which increased when their concentrations were increased. The effectiveness of these essential oils on linoleic acid oxidation was in the following order: caraway, sage, cumin, rosemary, thyme, clove.

6. Antimicrobial Activity of Some Egyptian Spice Essential Oils

Author: RS Farag, ZY Daw, FM Hewedi, GSA Al-Baroty

Journal: *Journal of Food Protection*, Vol. 52 (September 1989)

Location: Cairo University, Giza, Egypt

Conclusion: Essential oils of sage, rosemary, caraway, cumin, clove, and thyme were shown to have antimicrobial properties.

Abstract: Essential oils of sage, rosemary, caraway, cumin, clove, and thyme were studied for their antibacterial effects. The minimum inhibitory concentration for each essential oil was also determined. Various essential oils were inhibitory at extremely low concentrations (0.25-12 mg/ml). Gram-positive bacteria were shown to be more sensitive to the essential oils than were gram-negative. Thyme and cumin oils had stronger antimicrobial activity than the other oils. The chemical structures of compounds in the essential oils were related to the antimicrobial activity.

7. Antimicrobial Properties of Spices and Their Essential Oils

Author: LR Beuchat

Book: *Natural Antimicrobial Systems Food Preservation,* edited by VM Dillon and RG Board, (1994), chapter six, pp. 167-79

Location: University of Georgia, Griffin, Georgia

Conclusion: Many spices and herbs possess antimicrobial properties against various bacteria, yeasts, and molds.

Abstract: Many spices and herbs possess antimicrobial actions. These include plants of the genus *Allium*, such as onions and garlic; spices such as thyme, oregano, savory, sage, cinnamon, clove, vanilla, and others. Microbes inhibited by these herbs and spices include gram-positive and gram-negative bacteria, yeasts, and molds.

8. The Antimicrobial Activity of Essential Oils and Essential Oil Components Towards Oral Bacteria

Author: S Shapiro, A Meier, B Guggenheim

Journal: *Oral Microbiology and Immunology* 1994: 202-208 (Copyright Munksgaard 1994)

Location: University of Zurich, Switzerland

Conclusion: Essential oils of tea tree, peppermint, and sage showed potent antimicrobial action against anaerobic oral activity.

Abstract: Antimicrobial activity of some essential oils on anaerobic oral bacteria was analyzed. The most potent essential oils tested were Australian tea tree oil, peppermint oil, and sage oil. Thymol and eugenol were the most potent oil components.

9. Anticarcinogenic Effects of the Essential Oils From Cumin, Poppy and Basil

Author: K Aruna, VM Sivaramakrishnan

Journal: *Phytotherapy Research*, Vol. 10, 577-580 (1996)

Location: Cancer Institute (W.I.A.) Adyar Madras, India

Conclusion: Essential oils of cumin, poppy, and basil all possess potent anticarcinogenic properties.

Abstract: Essential oils of cumin, poppy, and basil were assessed for anticarcinogenic properties. The activity of glutathione-S-transferase, a carcinogen-detoxifying enzyme, was increased by over 78 percent in the stomach, liver, and esophagus of Swiss mice when they were treated with cumin, poppy, and basil essential oils.

10. Effects of Essential Oil on Lipid Peroxidation and Lipid Metabolism in Patients with Chronic Bronchitis

Author: SA Siurin

Journal: *Klinicheskaia Meditsina*, 75(10):43-5 (1997)

Location: Scientific Group NII of Pulmonology, Monchegorsk, Russia.

Conclusion: Lavender essential oil aids in normalizing lipid levels.

Abstract: Essential oils were tested in 150 patients with chronic bronchitis for their effects on lipid peroxidation and lipid metabolism. Essential oils of rosemary, basil, fir, eucalyptus, and lavender were found to have antioxidant effect and lavender was found to normalize lipid levels.

11. Effect of Essential Oils on the Course of Experimental Atherosclerosis

Author: VV Nikolaevskii, NS Kononova, AI Pertsoviskii, IF Shinkarchuk

Journal: *Patologicheskaia Fiziologiia i Eksperimentalnaia Terapiia* (5):52-3 (Sep-Oct 1990)

Conclusion: Inhalation of lavender and monarda essential oils reduces cholesterol content in the aorta of rabbits, providing an angioprotective effect.

Abstract: Lavender, monarda, and basil essential oils were tested in rabbits for their effect on atherosclerosis. When inhaled, lavender and monarda essential oils did not affect blood cholesterol content, but reduced cholesterol content in the aorta. These oils provide a heart-protective effect.

12. Inhibition of Growth and Aflatoxin Production in Aspergillus parasiticus by Essential Oils of Selected Plant Materials

Author: A Tantaoui-Elaraki, L Beraoud

Journal: *Journal of Environmental Pathology, Toxicology and Oncology*;13(1):67-72 (1994)

Location: Hassan II Institute for Agriculture and Veterinary Medicine, Rabat-Instituts, Morocco

Conclusion: Several essential oils (cinnamon, thyme, oregano, and cumin) were shown to have strong antifungal properties.

Abstract: Essential oils of cinnamon, thyme, oregano, cumin, curcumin, ginger, lemon, and orange were tested on *Aspergillus parasiticus* for antifungal properties. The most inhibitory essential oils were cinnamon, thyme, oregano, and cumin.

13. Odors and Learning

Author: AR Hirsch, MD, LH Johnston, MD

Journal: *Journal of Neurological and Orthopeditc Medical Surgery* 17:119-126 (1996)

Location: Smell & Taste Research Foundation, Chicago, Illinois, USA

Conclusion: Pleasant odors increased performance of individuals on cognitive tasks.

Abstract: This study assessed the effects of hedonically positive odors on performance of cognitive tasks. Results indicate that normally performing subjects completed a cognitive task an average 17 percent faster on subsequent trials when a pleasing odor was present. Further studies are desirable to determine if odors would be useful in general education and education of those with learning disabilities.

14. Weight Reduction through Inhalation of Odorants

Author: AR Hirsch, MD, R Gomez

Journal: *Annals of Clinical and Laboratory Science* (Official Journal of the Association of Clinical Scientists) Volume 24 September-October Number 5

Location: Smell & Taste Research Foundation, Chicago, Illinois, USA

Conclusion: Use of aroma inhalers aided study volunteers in weight loss over a 6-month period.

Abstract: To measure the role of olfaction in weight loss, odorant inhalers were given to 3,193 overweight volunteers. Study participants were instructed to inhale odorants 3 times in each nostril whenever hunger occurred. Average weight loss was 2.1 percent body weight per month. These results suggest inhalation of odorants may induce sustained weight loss over a 6-month period.

15. Anti-inflammatory Activity of Passiflora incarnata L. in Rats

Author: F Borrelli, L Pinto, AA Izzo, N Mascolo, F Capasso, V Mercati, E Toja, G Autore

Journal: *Phytotherapy Research*, Vol. 10, S104-S106 (1996)

Location: University of Naples, Naples, Italy

Conclusion: *Passiflora incarnata* extract was found to have anti-inflammatory activity in rats.

Abstract: Ethanolic extract of *Passiflora incarnata* (passion flower) was tested for anti-inflammatory activity in rats. The extract significantly inhibited swelling and inflammation.

Appendix H
Comparative Antimicrobial Activity of Essential Oils and Antibiotics

The following are test data comparing the antimicrobial ability between essential oils (cinnamon and oregano) and antibiotics (penicillin and ampicillin). The method is disk diffusion and the results are the mean value of three replicates. These preliminary data indicate that essential oils of cinnamon and oregano are comparable with penicillin and ampicillin in inhibitory activity against *E. coli* and *Staphylococcus aureus*.

Material	**Loading amount (µl)***	*Escherichia coli* zone of inhibition (cm)	*Staphylococcus aureus* zone of inhibition (cm)
Penicillin	3	0	3.2
	6	0	3.4
	8	0	3.6
	12	0	3.6
Ampicillin	3	1.9	2.6
	6	2.1	2.6
	8	2.5	2.7
	12	2.6	2.8
Cinnamon	3	2.4	2.4
	6	2.8	2.8
	8	-	3.0
	12	3.0	3.2
Oregano	3	2.6	3.2
	6	3.3	3.6
	8	-	3.6
	12	3.3	3.8

* The concentration of penicillin = 1.76 unit / μl
The concentration of ampicillin = 5 μg / μl

Appendix I
ORAC Research

A brealthrough test developed by USDA researchers at Tufts University in Boston, Massachusetts, is now able to identify the highest known antioxidant foods. Known as ORAC (Oxygen Radical Absorbance Capacity), this test is the first of its kind to measure both time and degree of free-radical inhibition.

ESSENTIAL OILS
ANTIOXIDANT CAPACITY*

Clove	1,078,700
Myrrh	379,800
Citronella	312,000
Coriander	298,300
Fennel	238,400
Clary Sage	221,000
German Chamomile	218,600
Cedarwood	169,000
Rose	160,400
Nutmeg	158,100
Marjoram	139,905
Melissa	134,300
Ylang Ylang	130,000
Rosewood	113,200
Wintergreen	101,800
Geranium	101,000
Ginger	99,300
Bay Laurel	98,900

Continued on next page...

FOODS
ANTIOXIDANT CAPACITY*

Ningxia Wolfberry	25,300
Blueberries	2,400
Kale	1,770
Strawberries	1,540
Spinach	1,260
Raspberries	1,220
Brussels sprouts	980
Plums	949
Broccoli florets	890
Beets	840
Oranges	750
Red Grapes	739
Red Bell Peppers	710
Cherries	670
Yellow corn	400
Eggplant	390
Carrots	210

* Antioxidant Capacity is estimated by Ferric Reducing Power and is expressed as micromole Trolox equivalent (TE) per 100 grams, accurate to plus or minus 5%.

ESSENTIAL OILS ANTIOXIDANT CAPACITY

...Continued from previous page

Eucalyptus citriodora	83,000	Hyssop	20,900
Cumin	82,400	Balsam Fir	20,500
Black Pepper	79,700	Thyme	15,960
Vetiver	74,300	Oregano	15,300
Douglas Fir	69,000	Sage	14,800
Blue Tansy	68,800	Mountain Savory	11,300
Goldenrod	61,900	Cinnamon Bark	10,340
Melaleuca ericifolia	61,100	Valarian	6,200
Spikenard	54,800	Cistus	3,860
Basil	54,000	*Eucalyptus globulus*	2,410
Patchouli	49,400	Orange	1,890
White Fir	47,900	Lemongrass	1,780
Tarragon	37,900	Helichrysum	1,740
Peppermint	37,300	Ravensara	890
Cardamom	36,500	Lemon	660
Dill	35,600	Frankincense	630
Celery Seed	30,300	Spearmint	540
Mandarin	26,500	Lavender	360
Lime	26,200	Rosemary	330
Myrtle	25,400	Juniper	250
Cypress	24,300	Roman chamomille	240
Grapefruit	22,600	Sandalwood	160

Appendix J

Flash Points for Essential Oils

A flash point is the exact temperature at which a substance will ignite. This chart is included for safety reasons. When diffusing essential oils, the mist that floats in the air may appear like water vapor. But you should remember that many oils are flammable and if an open flame is nearby, the diffused oil has the potential to ignite. Use care when diffusing oils, especially those with low flash points.

Oil	Flash Point
Angelica	111°F
Anise	>200°F
Basil	177°F
Bergamot	149°F
Buplevere	108°F
Cajeput	116°F
Calamus	194°F
Canadian red cedar	145°F
Cardamom	154°F
Carrot Seed	144°F
Cedar Leaf	142°F
Cedarwood	>200°F
Chamomile, German	>200°F
Chamomile, mixta	144°F
Chamomile, Roman	150°F
Cinnamon bark	179°F
Cistus	114°F
Citronella	147°F
Clary sage	190°F
Clove	>200°F
Coriander	153°F
Cumin	142°F
Cypress	103°F
Cypress, blue	>200°F
Davana	>200°F
Dill	150°F
Elemi	114°F
Eucalyptus citriodora	176°F
Eucalyptus dives	149°F
Eucalyptus globulus	114°F
Eucalyptus polybractea	112°F
Eucalyptus radiata	130°F
Fennel	168°F
Fir, balsam	107°F
Fir, Douglas	103°F
Fleabane	118°F
Frankincense	102°F
Galbanum	104°F
Geranium	181°F
Ginger	168°F
Goldenrod	118°F
Grapefruit	133°F
Helichrysum	150°F
Hyssop	158°F
Inula	>200°F
Jasmine	>200°F

Oil	Temperature
Juniper	104°F
Laurus nobilis	142°F
Lavandin	168°F
Lavender	157°F
Ledum	147°F
Lemon	109°F
Lemongrass	181°F
Lime	109°F
Mandarin	113°F
Marjoram	149°F
Melaleuca alternifolia	157°F
Melaleuca ericifolia	127°F
Melaleuca niaouli	168°F
Melissa	189°F
Mountain savory	170°F
Mugwort	162°F
Myrrh	>200°F
Nutmeg	110°F
Orange	142°F
Oregano	168°F
Palmarosa	199°F
Patchouli	>200°F
Black pepper	112°F
Peppermint	172°F
Petitgrain	150°F
Pine	103°F
Ravensara	124°F
Rose	156°F
Rosemary	116°F
Rosemary verbenon	103°F
Rosewood	178°F
Sage	146°F
Sage lavender	108°F
Sandalwood	>200°F
Spearmint	149°F
Spikenard	193°F
Spruce	102°F
Tamanu	>200°F
Tangerine	115°F
Tansy, blue	137°F
Tansy	168°F
Tarragon	148°F
Thyme	162°F
Thyme linalol	150°F
Valerian	112°F
Vetiver	>200°F
Wintergreen	191°F
Yarrow	172°F
Ylang ylang	>200°F

Appendix K

Plant Parts Used to Distill Essential Oils

Wood/Bark/Stems
Balsam fir
Blue cypress
Buddah wood
Cedarwood (Himalyan)
Cinnamon
Cypress
Douglas fir
Emerald cypress
Jade cypress
Juniper
Lemon myrtle
Pine
Rosewood
Sandalwood
Spruce
Tsuga
Western red cedar
White fir

Root
Ginger
Patchouli
Valarian
Vetiver

Seed
Anise
Coriander
Fennel
Nutmeg

Leaves/Stems
Basil
Cassia
Cistus
Dill
Elemi
Eucalyptus dives
Eucalyptus globulus
Eucalyptus polybractea
Eucalyptus radiata
Hyssop
Laurus noblis
Ledum
Lemongrass
Manuka
Marjoram
Melaleuca alternifolia
Melaleuca ericifolia
Melissa
Mountain savory
Myrtle
Oregano
Peppermint
Petitgrain
Ravensara
Rosemary
Sage
Spearmint
Spikenard
Tarragon
Thyme
Vitex
Wintergreen

Flowering tops
Clary sage
Geranium
German chamomile
Goldenrod
Helichrysum
Lavender
Roman chamomile
Tansy

Flower
Jasmine *(absolute)*
Neroli *(absolute)*
Rose
Ylang ylang

Gum/Resin
Frankincense
Galbanum
Myrrh
Styrax benzoin

Fruit/Rind
Bergamot
Black pepper
Clove
Grapefruit
Lemon
Mandarin
Orange
Tangerine

Appendix L

Body Systems Chart

Product Type Key:

S Essential Oil Single
B Essential Oil Blend
F Floral Water

Product	Product Type	Nervous System	Cardiovascular System	Respiratory System	Digestive/Elimination	Immune System	Glandular/Hormonal	Emotional Balance	Muscle & Bone	Anti-Aging	Oral Hygiene	Skin and Hair
Abuse Relief Blend	B							●				
Anti-Aging Blend	B									●		
Antibacterial Blend	B				●			●				●
Antimicrobial Blend	B					●				●	●	
Antiviral Blend	B		●	●	●	●					●	
Basil	S		●						●			
Basil Floral Water	F								●			
Bergamot	S				●			●				●
Birch	S								●			
Brain Blend	B	●						●				
Cajeput	S		●	●								
Cardamom	S				●							
Cedar Floral Water	F							●				●
Cedar, Western Red	S											●
Cedarwood	S	●		●								

Product Type Key:

S Essential Oil Single
B Essential Oil Blend
F Floral Water

Product	Product Type	Nervous System	Cardiovascular System	Respiratory System	Digestive/Elimination	Immune System	Glandular/Hormonal	Emotional Balance	Muscle & Bone	Anti-Aging	Oral Hygiene	Skin and Hair
Chamomile, German	**S**	●						●				●
Chamomile, German Floral Water	**F**	●										●
Chamomile, Roman	**S**	●						●				●
Circulation Blend	**B**		●									
Cinnamon Bark	**S**					●						
Cistus	**S**					●				●		
Citronella	**S**								●			●
Clarity Blend	**B**	●						●				
Clary Sage	**S**						●					
Clary Sage Floral Water	**F**						●					●
Clove	**S**		●	●	●	●				●	●	
Coriander	**S**				●		●					
Cumin	**S**				●	●						
Cypress	**S**		●						●			
Digestive Blend	**S**				●							
Dill	**S**				●							
Elemi	**S**											●
Emotional Release Blend	**B**							●				
Energy Balance Blend	**B**	●						●	●			●
Energy Blend	**B**	●						●				
Eucalyptus citriodora	**S**			●								
Eucalyptus Floral Water	**F**			●				●	●			
Eucalyptus globulus	**S**			●					●		●	
Eucalyptus polybrachta	**S**			●								

Product Type Key:

S Essential Oil Single
B Essential Oil Blend
F Floral Water

Product	Product Type	Nervous System	Cardiovascular System	Respiratory System	Digestive/Elimination	Immune System	Glandular/Hormonal	Emotional Balance	Muscle & Bone	Anti-Aging	Oral Hygiene	Skin and Hair
Eucalyptus radiata	**S**			●								●
Female Blend	**B**						●	●				
Fennel	**S**				●		●					
Fir, Douglas	**S**			●					●			
Fir, Balsam	**S**			●				●	●	●		
Fir Floral Water	**F**											●
Fleabane	**S**		●				●					
Frankincense	**S**	●				●		●		●		●
Galbanum	**S**					●						
Ginger	**S**	●			●							
Glandular Blend	**B**						●					
Goldenrod	**S**		●				●					
Grapefruit	**S**		●							●		
Headache Blend	**B**	●										
Helichrysum	**S**		●						●			
Hyssop	**S**	●	●	●								
Immune Blend	**B**					●						
Jasmine	**S**						●	●				
Juniper	**S**				●			●				
Juniper Floral Water	**F**							●	●			●
Liver Blend	**B**				●			●				
Laurus nobilis	**S**			●	●	●						
Lavandin	**S**		●	●					●			
Lavender	**S**	●	●					●				●

Product Type Key:

S Essential Oil Single
B Essential Oil Blend
F Floral Water

Product	Product Type	Nervous System	Cardiovascular System	Respiratory System	Digestive/Elimination	Immune System	Glandular/Hormonal	Emotional Balance	Muscle & Bone	Anti-Aging	Oral Hygiene	Skin and Hair
Lavender Floral Water	F	●										●
Ledum	S				●	●				●		●
Lemon	S			●	●	●				●		
Lemongrass	S					●			●			
Lime	S			●	●	●				●		
Mandarin	S				●					●		●
Marjoram	S		●						●			
Melaleuca alternifolia	S			●		●			●			●
Melaleuca ericifolia	S			●								●
Melaleuca quinquenervia	S			●					●			
Melissa	S							●		●		●
Melissa Floral Water	F	●										●
Antiseptic Blend	B			●								●
Male Blend	B						●					
Mountain savory	S					●						
Muscle Relaxing Blend	B			●					●			
Myrrh	S	●				●	●					●
Myrtle	S			●	●		●		●			
Neroli	S				●							●
Nutmeg	S	●				●	●					
Onycha	S		●					●				
Orange	S				●	●				●		●
Oregano	S			●		●			●	●		
Palmarosa	S		●					●				●

Product Type Key:

S Essential Oil Single
B Essential Oil Blend
F Floral Water

Product	Product Type	Nervous System	Cardiovascular System	Respiratory System	Digestive/Elimination	Immune System	Glandular/Hormonal	Emotional Balance	Muscle & Bone	Anti-Aging	Oral Hygiene	Skin and Hair
Pain Relief Blend	B	●							●			
Patchouli	S											●
Pepper, black	S	●			●							
Peppermint	S	●		●	●				●		●	●
Peppermint Floral Water	F				●				●		●	●
Petitgrain	S							●				
Pine	S			●				●				
Respiratory Blend	B			●								●
Ravensara	S			●		●						
Rose	S							●				●
Rosemary CT cineol	S		●		●				●			
Rosewood	S											●
Sage	S					●	●					
Sandalwood	S	●						●	●			●
Romance Blend	B						●	●				
Spearmint	S				●			●				
Spearmint Floral Water	F										●	●
Spikenard	S							●				●
Spiritual Blend	B							●				
Spruce	S	●		●				●				
Stress Reduction Blend	B	●						●				
Tangerine	S					●		●		●		●
Tansy, blue	S	●										
Tansy	S					●						

Product Type Key:

S Essential Oil Single
B Essential Oil Blend
F Floral Water

Product	Product Type	Nervous System	Cardiovascular System	Respiratory System	Digestive/Elimination	Immune System	Glandular/Hormonal	Emotional Balance	Muscle & Bone	Anti-Aging	Oral Hygiene	Skin and Hair
Tansy Floral Water	F											●
Tarragon	S	●			●							
Thyme	S					●			●	●		
Thyme CT linalol	S			●								●
Thyme Floral Water	F				●						●	●
Trauma Blend	B							●				
Tsuga	S		●	●								
Valerian	S	●										
Vetiver	S	●					●	●				●
Wintergreen	S								●			
Yarrow	S					●	●					●
Ylang Ylang	S		●				●	●				

Appendix M

Five Key Groups of Essential Oil Compounds

Hydrogen
Carbon
Oxygen

Phenylpropanoids – C6 with C3 sidechain (Phenylalanine unit)

Anethole	Eugenol acetate	Cinnamic acid	myristicin
Eugenol	gingerol	Cinnamaldehyde	p-courmaric acid

Monoterpenes – C10 (2 Isoprene units)

borneol	α/β-citronellal	α/β-pinene	linalol
bornyl acetate	cuminaldehyde	sabinene	linalyl acetate
camphene	*p*-cymene	piperitone	d-/l-limonene
camphor	dipentene	terpinene	menthofuran
car-3-ene	fenchone	thujone	menthol
carvacrol	geraniol	thymol	menthone
carvone	nerol	thymyl acetate	menthyl acetate
1,8 cineol (eucalyptol)	geranyl acetate	verbenone	α/β-myrcene
citronellal	geranial/neral (citral)	γ-terpinene	β-ocimene
α/β phellanderene			

Sesquiterpenes – C15 (3 isoprenes units)

α/β-bisabolol	α-curcumene	germacrene B + D	α/β-vetivol
β/δ-cadinene	eudesmol	himachalol	α-ylangene
α/β-caryophyllene	farnesene	himachalene	α-zingiberene
α-copaene	ledol	patchoulol	longifolene
nerolidol	α/β-santalene	α/β-santalol	

Diterpenes – C20 (4 isoprene unite)

Sclareol	carnosol

Triterpenes – C30 (6 Isoprene units)

ginsenoside	glycyrrhizin

Sesquiterpene Content of Selected Essential Oils

Cedarwood	90-95%	Patchouli	65-70%	German Chamomile	45-50%
Vetiver	90-95%	Myrrh	60-65%	Spikenard	45-50%
Sandalwood	85-90%	Ginger	55-60%	Galbanum	10-15%
Black Pepper	70-75%	Vitex	45-50%	Frankincense	7-12%

Index